T0289220

THE THREE BARONS

THE Organizational Chart OF THE Kennedy Assassination

* * * J.W. LATEER JD, CPA * * *

The Three Barons: The Organizational Chart of the JFK assassination
Copyright © 2017 James Lateer

Published by:
Trine Day LLC
PO Box 577
Walterville, OR 97489
1-800-556-2012
www.TrineDay.com
trineday@Icloud.com

Library of Congress Control Number: 2017953909

Lateer , James
–1st ed.
p. cm.

Epub (ISBN-13) 978-1-63424-143-4
Mobi (ISBN-13) 978-1-63424-144-1
Print (ISBN-13) 978-1-63424-142-7
1. Kennedy, John F. -- (John Fitzgerald), -- 1917-1963 -- Assassination. 2. 3. 4.
United States -- Politics and government -- History. 5. Conspiracies -- United
States. 6. Von Braun, Wernher, -- 1912-1977. 7. de Mohrenschildt, George, –
1911-1977. 8. Willoughby, Charles A., – 1982-1972. I. Lateer, James II. Title

First Edition
10 9 8 7 6 5 4 3 2

Printed in the USA
Distribution to the Trade by:
Independent Publishers Group (IPG)
814 North Franklin Street
Chicago, Illinois 60610
312.337.0747
www.ipgbook.com

False face must hide what the false heart doth know.
                                    – Macbeth

DEDICATION

This volume is dedicated to Claudia, Ken and to Herodotus, the father of History

Acknowledgments

In writing *The Three Barons*, I will be forever indebted to a number of people. First, my wife Claudia has given me support and advice on the management of the project. My son Ken designed the impressive cover.

Next, I would like to thank the staff of the Beloit (Wisconsin) Public Library. Cheryl Blake is an expert in inter-library loans and a veteran of 30 plus years in that specialty. Vicki Hahn, also of the Beloit Public Library has arranged training for me and others on the best use of the incredible resources of the Wisconsin Historical Society and its unparalleled collection of history books, one of the best such collections anywhere.

The University of Wisconsin-Madison makes its Library resources available for checkout to the public, which has been an invaluable resource as well. The University clearly doesn't have to bother with amateur researchers such as myself, but true to the UW tradition, they do that anyway and thank goodness.

I would also like to thank Dr. Jeffrey Caulfield, author of the book *General Walker* … for giving me tips on research into original sources and introducing me to the personal papers of James Dombrowski, one of the founders of the modern civil rights movement.

And of course, thanks goes to Mr. Kris Millegan, publisher of Trine-Day who is both a genius and a true American Patriot when we have so few left at this point in our history.

Table of Contents

Introduction

FIVE PEOPLE WITH DOCUMENTED PRIOR KNOWLEDGE OF THE CRIME

Prior to the assassination of President John F. Kennedy, there were five persons with proven advance knowledge that the assassination would occur. We will consider the information about these five in no particular order.

THE PRIOR KNOWLEDGE OF RICHARD CASE NAGELL:

The best book about the assassination of JFK, in the opinion of this author, is *The Man Who Knew Too Much*, by Dick Russell (hereinafter *TMWKTM*).

The book is 824 pages long and deals in depth with all of the issues regarding the assassination. The book is organized, however, around the life of Richard Case Nagell. Dick Russell devoted 17 years of his life to the Nagell case, including interviews with Nagell, friends, relatives of Nagell and reading all the transcripts of the several lawsuits in which Nagell was involved.

Richard Case Nagell was an individual who had been an Army counterintelligence officer in the late 1950's. He had worked for the super-secret Field Operations Intelligence (FOI). This group was so secret that even its existence was not known by anyone on the outside until 20 years after it was founded. The important thing to know about Nagell and the FOI is that the FOI was founded, at the time and in the area of responsibility of General Charles Willoughby. Willoughby is one of our three Barons. He was head of intelligence for General Douglas MacArthur in MacArthur's Far East Command. This included Korea. It was in Korea where Richard Case Nagell began his long relationship with the FOI and Military Intelligence.

According to the book *LBJ: The Mastermind of the JFK Assassination*, by Phillip F. Nelson, Nagell worked closely with Lee Harvey Oswald while Oswald was stationed in Japan. FOI was primarily active in the Far East. The U.S. intelligence activities there had been a continuation of the intelligence administered by General Douglas MacArthur while he was the commanding officer for the entire occupation of Japan. The chief of

MacArthur's intelligence for most of that period was General Charles Willoughby, a noteworthy and mysterious figure both during and after his service there and a right-wing activist in the U.S. after his retirement.

This period of activity along with Oswald was in 1957 and 1958. There, according to Nagell, both he and Oswald participated in an operation having the code name "Hidell,"

According to Nagell, the alias Hidell would alert intelligence agents that an officer of military intelligence was using it. The alias A. J. Hidell was one which Oswald would continue to use as an alias all the way up to the events in Dallas.

On July 15, 1958, Nagell returned from the Far East with his Japanese bride. Leaving the Army, Nagell soon took a job as an investigator for the California Department of Alcoholic Beverage Control. There Nagell was shot in the leg because he was somehow involved with the investigation of organized crime.

A quote from *TMWKTM* reads as follows:

> At the same time, extremist elements of the right wing were forging the new Anti-Communist Liaison. The network of Charles Willoughby extended to several other ex-MacArthur military leaders and all the way to West Germany. Instrumental were Dallas's H.L. Hunt oil family, Oklahoma preacher Billy James Hargis, and intelligence agent-turned-journalist Edward Hunter, who coined the term "brainwashing." A paramilitary arm was established in Southern California under retired colonel William P. Gale.

In 1962, Nagell traveled to Mexico City. He went to a place called Hotel Luma where the manager named Warren Broglie was active in various foreign intrigue activities.

His bartender was named Franz Waehauf.

Broglie was acquainted with the CIA chief in Mexico City, Win Scott. He was also friends with an ex-FBI agent who in 1962 was the CIA's leading surveillance man in Mexico City, responsible for the electronic bugging of the Soviet and Cuban embassies.

Since Nagell was a veteran intelligence agent, he was never very specific about the events in Mexico City, but the takeaway from Nagell was that the bartender Waehauf recruited him into some kind of intelligence assignment. Following this event, Nagell said that he had a CIA contact whose name was "Bob."

Nagell was instructed to take the bait offered by "a foreign government." (Author's note: this is an example of "code speaking," referring only ambiguously to facts, yet conveying at least some meaning). As a result of these events, Nagell claimed that he became a double agent for the CIA and the Soviets.

In *TMWKTM* is the following quote:

> Nagell says that the CIA "double agent" mission he was about to embark on involved his participation in a 'disinformation' project directed against the Soviet Embassy at Mexico City in 1962 at the onset of the so-called Cuban Missile Crisis.

Nagell was apparently assigned the task of monitoring Oswald after Oswald returned from his defection to the Soviet Union. Remember that the FBI was also overtly monitoring both LHO and his wife. According to author Russell, Nagell made a cross-country trip at one point, and stopped off to visit Oswald. Despite their close relationship, Nagell never would disclose to Russell exactly who ordered the visit to check up on Oswald

Nagell became aware that Oswald was involved with two Cuban exiles. They were named "Angel and Leopoldo." These two, were in turn involved with a CIA-backed group of violent Cuban exile extremists called Alpha 66.

"Angel and Leopoldo" supposedly accompanied Oswald to a particular apartment in Dallas which was occupied by a woman named Silvia Odio. Author David Kaiser has written an impeccably foot-noted book called *The Road To Dallas*, published by the Harvard University Press. In that book, Kaiser refers to this supposed incident involving Sylvia Odio as the most important evidence regarding the assassination.

The reader should observe, even at this early point in the Nagell story, something about the entire universe of assassination evidence. This point is that a particular purported fact (like the "Angel and Leopoldo" information) has led to an unbelievably long, fruitless, intensely examined wild goose chase. The Silvia Odio information may well have been something, but it came to nothing.

That is not to say, however, that Nagell was not a CIA or more likely, a military intelligence agent. After all, it is *certain* that he had at two months advance warning of the JFK assassination.

In both *TMWKTM* by Russell and *LBJ: Mastermind*, by Nelson, there is an account of various interviews with an ex-CIA operative named Colonel William "Bill" Bishop. By including statements by Bishop, both authors believe to a certain degree in the credibility of Bishop. (Bishop, incidentally, was suffering from terminal cancer at the time of the interviews.) Bishop clearly supports the involvement of Richard Case Nagell in various activities involving Oswald along with the activities of various other JFK conspirators including those in New Orleans and other places.

Let's go right to the bottom line with Nagell. It turns out that Nagell claimed that the Soviets had advance knowledge of the JFK assassination.

Because of this fact, Nagell claimed that he was ordered by the Soviets to murder Oswald because the Soviets were against the assassination.

Nagell refused to kill Oswald. Then, rather than take the risk of being caught up in an investigation of the murder of a President, Nagell entered a bank in El Paso, Texas on September 21, 1963 and staged a fake holdup. As a result, he was jailed in El Paso. Nagell had an entire past history of getting himself admitted to various hospitals (or similar schemes) when he need an alibi. Nagell had carefully picked the crime he would commit, because the robbery of a federally insured bank would immediately involve the FBI. The Court records in El Paso contain any number of statements by Nagell which represented an obvious attempt by him to alert the FBI and other authorities of the impending assassination.

As a result of this whistle-blowing by Nagell, he was sent to the Springfield, Missouri military medical (and mental) facility. This facility was a favorite place used by the military to confine whistle-blowers like Nagell and Abraham Bolden. Bolden was the very first African-American Secret Service Agent as well as a JFK assassination whistle-blower after the fact. In fact, Bolden and Nagell were in cells opposite one another at the Springfield, Missouri facility.

And at the very end of the almost endless struggles of Nagell following the assassination, he was offered a full-salary military medical disability settlement based upon a plane crash which he survived in the 1950's. This effectively closed down any further information which he might have provided to investigators after that.

The Prior Knowledge of Eugene B. Dinkin

The most important thing to know about Eugene B. Dinkin is that when he found out about the assassination, he was an NSA staff person assigned to Army Intelligence and was stationed in Metz, France. Metz is a 2½ hour drive from Bonn, Germany. It sits on the German border and was an obvious listening-post for spying on Germany. Metz was actually the terminus of a cross-country communications zone operated by the U.S. Army in France and was not a NATO place. Metz was entirely controlled by the U.S. outside of any NATO command. It was on the German border, but German authorities could not arrest any U.S. spies there because it was inside France. Thus, the Army did not have to worry about interference from local authorities. This is always a concern in the intelligence field.

Eugene B. Dinkin was a young NSA cryptologist assigned to the U.S. Army, stationed in Metz in the months before the Kennedy Assassination. Like Richard Case Nagell, Dinkin was a military intelligence whistle-blower prior to the assassination.

Somehow, apparently in the course of his work, Dinkin encountered information which led him to believe that there was a plot afoot to assassinate President Kennedy. (We will discuss further how exactly Dinkin found out). But in September, 1963, Eugene B. Dinkin became desperate to do whatever he could to foil the assassination. He told his friends about the situation, then traveled to various press rooms, United Nations offices and U.S. Embassies both in nearby Switzerland and Luxembourg to blow the whistle to various authorities.

In making this effort around Europe to blow the whistle, Dinkin had gone AWOL from his post. After a few weeks, he feared not only that he would be charged with being AWOL (which he clearly was) but that the situation would turn into one of desertion which, of course, could result in a prison term or even the death penalty. The most important issue relating to Dinkin was the question of how he found out about the assassination in advance.

Dinkin received his education at the highly regarded program in Psychology at the University of Illinois in September, 1960. This was a program which emphasized behaviorism and conditioned response. From this program, Dinkin would have specialized knowledge about how propaganda works and what are its principles. (This author earned the same degree from the same program only ten years later).

Dinkin was a cryptographer. Since he knew of the assassination in advance, the likely explanation was that he learned about it because information pointing to the plot was included in encrypted military communication. Dinkin, however, claimed he had found out in advance about the assassination because he was analyzing newspapers to spot any trend or significant information that was being published. Dinkin claimed he was using a technique called "psychological sets." This is, in fact, an established psychological theory often used by Madison Avenue advertising agencies.

If Dinkin had been reading the Ukrainian anti-Communist Press with such publications as the ABN Correspondence, the Ukrainian Bulletin, or the Ukrainian Quarterly, then he could have been following the Stashynsky Case. Even Bogdan Stashynsky himself thought that there was something much bigger in the works than the murder of Stepan Bandera. If Dinkin was any good at his job, he could easily have connected the dots regarding the unwarranted publicity about the alleged Soviet Assassination Department.

This claim by Dinkin seems impossible on its face. However, as a graduate of the University of Illinois psychology program, it is not impossible that Dinkin had found out about the assassination just as he claimed, i.e. from newspapers. As a graduate of a program that specialized in the modification of behavior using psychology, Mr. Dinkin could easily have been recruited by the NSA for study of such things as propaganda. Studying the flow of information in the European press and similar research programs could have also have been part of his work.

But the most useful information to be derived from the case of Mr. Dinkin is that he precisely identifies the perpetrators of the JFK assassination as "certain members of the military along with some right-wing economic interests." (Note he doesn't say to which country the military or the economic interests belonged. Both could have been German, British or French for that matter). This assessment lines up precisely with the various facts which we have encountered at this point, or will encounter in later chapters. It is unlikely that Dinkin could have known specifically about "right-wing economic interests" being involved in the assassination without some kind of leak. There could well have been rumors or even facts about the assassination plot rampant around military intelligence headquarters in Metz.

Mr. Dinkin came from an ordinary background. He was a graduate of Hyde Park High School in Chicago. Not very much is known about his life aside from the events that related to his role as a Kennedy assassination military whistle-blower. He was recently alive and living in Van Nuys, California, which happens to be the location of Hughes Aerospace, part of the empire of the late Howard Hughes. He was retired and died around 2010. Where he was living in his last years may be totally unrelated to the Dinkin case, but maybe not. It is not certain in which occupation Mr. Dinkin worked for the last 50 years. It should be mentioned that in 1992, Dick Russell in his monumental book *TMWKTM* listed Mr. Dinkin as *the one most important witness* who could be interviewed as of 1992, should an opportunity occur.

The conventional wisdom is, of course, that if there were a conspiracy to kill Kennedy, somebody would have talked. Well somebody did talk! All of this is even more intriguing because of the recent famous situation of NSA officer Eric Snowden. Like Dinkin, Snowden was an NSA whistle-blower motivated by his own concept of patriotism. Apparently some of the moral dilemmas in the espionage business never change.

As you read his story, it should be noted that Dinkin sent a whistle-blowing letter, not to JFK, not to J. Edgar Hoover, but to Robert Kennedy at the Justice Department. Of course, it goes without saying that as a cryptographer and codebreaker for the NSA, Dinkin would have had access to the very highest levels of top secret communications for the government and the U.S. Military. If he specifically knew the actual date of the assassination in advance, which he did, he undoubtedly would know about the relationships between JFK, Hoover, Robert Kennedy, the military command and all the rest. On top of that, add the fact that Mr. Dinkin was a very intelligent and idealistic individual.

Background on all of the information in this section can be found at two excellent websites: www.educationforum.ipbhost.com/index.php?-showtopic=7078 and www.history-matters.com/archive/jfk/cia/russho lmes//104-10438/104-10438-10154/html/104-10438-10154_0001a.htm).

There are a few more details found in government documents which add still more to the amazing story which we will quote as follows:

EUGENE B. DINKIN In December, 1963, it was reported that Beth Cox, who was residing in France with an American schoolmate, had a boyfriend named Howard C. Cowen stationed in Metz, France, with the United States Army.

Beth Cox was informed that one of Howard C. Cowen's acquaintances "translated or decoded the G.I. paper's headlines to read 'Kennedy will be assassinated Thanksgiving Day,' and that this acquaintance later changed the date to November 22, 1963, the very date of the assassination, all in advance.

On March 4, 1964, Lieutenant Colonel W. L. Adams, Jr., Assistant Chief of Staff, G-2, furnished the following...: Captain Howard C. Cowen, assigned to the United States Army Depot at Metz, France, advised on February 18, 1964, that during the evening of November 22, 1963, he (Cowan) conversed with an acquaintance named Dennis De Witt. During the conversation, De Witt said that a friend of his, Eugene Dinkin, had predicted President Kennedy's assassination for November 22, 1963.

According to De Witt, Dinkin had first predicted that the assassination would take place on November 28, 1963, but later reportedly changed the date to November 22, 1963. Captain Cowen reported the above conversation to officials of the 766th Army Intelligence Corps Detachment at Metz.

A short time later, Captain Cowen also related his conversation to a girl friend named Beth Cox. ... Colonel Adams stated that Eugene B. Dinkin was the subject of a closed investigation by the Office of the Assistant Chief of Staff, G-2, United States Army Communications Zone, Europe. (There are also allegations that Dinkin was NSA, detailed to the Army in Europe.)

He advised further that according to local Army records at Metz, France, on February 18, 1964, PFC Eugene B. Dinkin, RA 16710292, was reassigned to Walter Reed Hospital, Washington D.C., as a patient on December 3, 1963. [note the lack of symptoms or diagnosis].

On April 1, 1964, Mr. Eugene B. Dinkin, ... advised Agents of the Federal Bureau of Investigation that he had been recently discharged from the United States Army after having been in detention for four months while undergoing psychiatric tests. Dinkin advised that while stationed in Europe with the United States Army in 1963, he had begun a review of several newspapers including the *Stars and Stripes* as an exercise in "psychological sets." He explained that he had taken courses in psychology at college and was extremely interested in this subject matter. He advised that "psychological sets" was a term referring to a series of events, articles, et cetera which, when coupled together, set up or induce a certain frame of mind on the part of a person being exposed to this series.

He stated that this method of implanting an idea was much in use by the "Madison Avenue" advertising people who attempted to influence one who was exposed to these "psychological sets" to "buy" the product being advertised, whether this product was physical or an idea.

Dinkin stated that while so reviewing the newspapers for "psychological sets," he discovered that *Stars and Stripes*, as well as certain unidentified Hearst newspapers, were carrying a series of "psychological sets" which he believed were deliberately maneuvered to set up a subconscious belief on the part of one reading these papers to the effect that President John F. Kennedy was "soft on communism" or "perhaps a communist sympathizer."

Further study of these newspapers and the "psychological sets" contained therein made it evident to Mr. Dinkin that a conspiracy was in the making by the "military" of the United Stated, perhaps combined with an "ultra-right economic group," to make the people of the United States believe that President Kennedy was, in fact, a communist sympathizer and further, that this same group planned to assassinate the President and thus was preparing these "psychological sets" to pave the way for this assassination to the point where the average citizen might well feel that "President Kennedy was sympathetic to communism and should have been killed."

In addition, Dinkin believed the "psychological sets" were adjusted to present a subliminal predisposition to the effect that a "communist" would assassinate President Kennedy. Dinkin advised that he discussed his theories with certain individuals stationed with him in the Army, but had declined to furnish this information to persons of authority in the United States Army since he believed that the plot against President Kennedy was being set in motion by high ranking members of the military. He said that in October, 1963, his research into the "psychological sets" appearing in *Stars and Stripes* had led him to the conclusion that the assassination of President Kennedy would occur on or about November 28, 1963.

He stated that his research had not, in fact, reflected a certain date, but that he believed the assassination would take place on or about a religious or semi-religious occasion which he felt would be picked by the group behind this plot in order that the murder itself would become even more reprehensible to the average citizen because of the religious connotations.

Since he believed that the plot consisted in part of throwing blame for the assassination onto "radical left-wing" or "communist" suspects, he stated that the religious tie-in would lead the average citizen to accept more readily the theory that a "communist" committed the crime since "they were an atheist group anyway."

As a result of his opposition to [compulsory purchases of Savings Bonds by the Military] ... according to Dinkin, he was removed from his position in the code section and transferred to an Army Depot at Metz, France.

October 25, 1963, Dinkin went to the United States Embassy at Luxembourg where, he stated, he attempted for several hours to see a Mr. Cunningham, the Charge d'Affaires at the Embassy. He stated that he sent word to Mr. Cunningham by phone. He said that Cunningham refused to see him in person or to review the newspapers and research papers which Dinkin said were evidence proving his theory of the impending assassination.

Dinkin advised that he spent approximately two hours with the United States Marine Corps guard at the Luxembourg Embassy and had generally set forth his theories to this individual, whose name he did not know.

Following this incident, Dinkin was notified by his superiors that he was to undergo psychiatric evaluation on November 5, 1963. Due to this pending development, Dinkin said he went absent without leave to Geneva, Switzerland where he attempted to present his theory to the editor of the *Geneva Diplomat,* a newspaper published in Geneva, Switzerland. In addition to this editor, Dinkin spoke to a Mr. Dewhirst, a *Newsweek* reporter based at Geneva. Dewhirst would not listen to Dinkin's theories.

While in Switzerland, Dinkin attempted to contact officials of "Time-Life" publication and succeeded in speaking to the secretary, name unknown, of this organization in Zurich. According to Dinkin, all of his efforts in Luxembourg and Switzerland were made to present to appropriate officials his warning of the impending assassination of President Kennedy.

When he was unable to accomplish his purpose in Switzerland, Dinkin advised that he then returned to Germany where he gave himself up to the custody of the military authorities. Dinkin advised that he first became aware of this "plot" to assassinate President Kennedy in September, 1963.

At first, he did not have enough facts, as taken from the newspapers, to support his theory, but as of October 16, 1963, he felt that his research into the "psychological sets" had substantiated his theory.

As of October 16, 1963, he wrote a registered letter to Attorney General Robert F. Kennedy in which letter he set forth his theory that President Kennedy would be assassinated, adding that he believed that this assassination would occur on or about November 28, 1963. He stated that he signed this letter with his own name and requested that he be interviewed by a representative of the Justice Department.

He stated that he never received any answer to this letter, nor was he ever contacted by any representative of the Justice Department prior to this interview with Agents of the Federal Bureau of Investigation.

Dinkin advised that the following individuals would have knowledge of his theory and predictions, having been informed of these predictions by Dinkin prior to November 22, 1963:

PFC Dennis De Witt
United States Army

PFC Larry Pullen
United States Army Headquarters Company

Sergeant Walter Reynolds
Headquarters Company, WSAGD

Also listed were Dr. Afar (phonetic), a civilian psychology teacher employed by the United States Army at Metz, France and R. Thomas … Switzerland. Thomas was an Indian student attending the University at Fribourg with whom Dinkin discussed his theories immediately prior to his return from Switzerland to France.

Dinkin advised that on his return to the custody of the United States Army in November 1963, he was held in detention. While in detention, he stated he was contacted by a white male who identified himself verbally as a representative of the Defense Department. This individual asked Dinkin for the location of the newspapers which Dinkin had compiled as proof of the theory of the assassination of President Kennedy. This individual stated that he desired to obtain these proofs and would furnish Dinkin a receipt for the papers. Dinkin advised that he instructed this individual as to where the papers were located at the base, at which point this man left. Dinkin advised that on his release from detention, he discovered that all of his papers and notes were missing and presumed that the individual mentioned above had taken them.

He never received any receipt for his papers.

Mr. Dinkin advised that he had undergone numerous psychiatric tests at Walter Reed Army Hospital in Washington, D.C. He stated that he was aware that the Army psychiatrist had declared him to be "psychotic" and a "paranotic." He said that several of the tests given him were familiar to him from his studies in psychology at the University of Chicago. [actually it was the University of Illinois].

Because of his familiarity with these tests, and his background knowledge as to what the test answers should be, he believed it impossible that the results of these tests could have shown him to be "psychotic" and "paranotic." He stated that if he had desired, he could have faked the answer to prove he was sane even if he were, in fact, mentally disturbed.

Mr. Dinkin stated he believed that the psychiatric evaluation given him by the Army psychiatrist was, in fact, an attempt on their part to cover up the military plot which he had attempted to expose.

Dinkin advised that during his detention at Walter Reed Army Hospital, arrangements had been made through his family for him to be given a psychiatric test by a private psychiatrist chosen by his family.

He stated when these arrangements were finally made, he had declined the services of this private physician. Dinkin explained that he had reached a point where his only desire was to be released from custody and discharged from the Army. He stated that in order to do this, he had felt it necessary to "go along" with the examining Army psychiatrist and pretend that he had, in fact, been suffering from delusions but was now cured. He was afraid that should an outside psychiatrist examine him and be told by Dinkin the facts as set forth herein, that this psychiatrist would probably believe Dinkin to be mentally disturbed, and this would result in further detention for Dinkin.

Mr. Dinkin stated that he was well aware that his theory and the facts surrounding his attempts to bring this theory to the proper authorities was extremely "wild" and could be construed by a person untrained in psychology to be "crazy."

Despite this, Mr. Dinkin advised he was still of the belief that there had been, in fact, a plot perpetrated by a "military group" in the United States and aided and abetted by newspaper personnel working with this military group, which plot had to do with the assassination of President John F. Kennedy.

After enduring this incredible situation and more or less landing on his feet Eugene B. Dinkin was not through. In 1975 he filed a civil rights lawsuit against the United States government on the grounds that his civil rights had been violated. While testifying in that lawsuit, additional information came out. Dinkin stated that "blame would then be placed upon a Communist or Negro, who would be designated as the assassin; and believing that the conspiracy was being engineered by elements of the military, I did speculate that a military coup might ensue…"

No one will ever know what happened to the letter that Dinkin sent to Robert Kennedy. Keep in mind that, if the letter was sent October 16, 1963, it would have taken at least a week to reach Washington. By November 2, 1963, the Chicago Plot had taken place so that the White House would have known that there were serious problems at that point.

One last fact relating to the Dinkin story is this: according to some information relating to Dinkin and the Jim Garrison investigation, there was some theory to the effect that Dinkin's duties in Metz, France included the monitoring of the telephone traffic of the French OAS. The details surrounding the French OAS can be found in the book *Target De Gaulle: the True Story of the 31 Attempts on the Life of the French President* (1975) by Pierre Demaret and Christian Plum.

The French OAS was only a tiny shadow of the force portrayed in the JFK literature. The French OAS was not a strong, solid, sinister, well-established and powerful organization. This is the image portrayed in the JFK research community. In fact, the French OAS, at least the ones involved in the de Gaulle assassination attempts, was a small group and constantly changing. For each assassination attempt, the leader Jean Bastien-Thiery was being paid by unknown benefactors to kill de Gaulle. Bastien-Thiery could barely scrape together 3 or 4 plotters in each of the three major attempts on de Gaulle. Bastien-Thiery himself was considered to be outside the OAS organization, operating as a lone-wolf. The make-up of the plotters' group seemed to experience a 100% turnover after each attempt. The attempts against de Gaulle only occurred during the brief time when the status of French Algeria was up in the air. That was in 1961 and 1962. Once the independence of Algeria was established the French OAS basically disappeared.

There was only one associate of the French OAS who had any generally known international connections. That man was named Jacque Soustelle who was an asset of British Intelligence. He was not responsible for any known event regarding the OAS plots.

While it is true that the CIA tried to make a secret deal with the OAS behind the back of President Kennedy, it was a proposal to arm 1,000,000 Algerian-based Frenchmen to take over Algeria. It was totally fantastic and was quickly squelched by JFK as soon as he heard of it.

If Eugene B. Dinkin learned of the assassination from anyone, it was the U.S. military and not the French OAS.

The Prior Knowledge of Melba Christine Marcades a/k/a Rose Cheramie

Possibly the most colorful character in the Kennedy assassination story is Rose Cheramie, irreverently referred to by some writers as Ramblin' Rose.

What is most important about the case of Rose Cheramie was that she was traveling to Dallas to (in her own words) "to kill President Kennedy" and then move on to Galveston, Texas. She was traveling in the company of Sergio Arcacha-Smith. Sergio was one of the top three or four members of the anti-Castro Cuban community in New Orleans. Sergio was an associate of Carlos Bringuier who had been arrested after a fight with Lee Harvey Oswald in New Orleans. Bringuier's office was in the same building as Guy Banister, a consensus member of the JFK assassination plot. If Sergio Arcacha-Smith were traveling to Dallas that night, he could have been on some kind of errand in relationship to the assassination. Rose Cheramie, likely a prostitute, was in his company. This implicates Arcacha-Smith in, among other things, human-trafficking.

Just two days before the JFK assassination, the hospital in Eunice, Louisiana placed a call to Lt. Francis Fruge. Fruge was an officer of the Louisiana State Police. He was told that an accident victim had just been brought in and that she was not badly injured, but that she was on heavy drugs.

The victim told Fruge that her name was Rose Cheramie. That name turned out later to be only one of the many names she used.

Fruge placed her in jail at the City of Eunice, Louisiana. Fruge then got an emergency call and was told that Rose had started to experience extreme withdrawal symptoms and that she needed medical care. Fruge then made arrangements for Rose to be transported from Eunice to Jackson, Louisiana, to the Jackson State Mental Hospital.

Fruge testified to all of the following details as a witness before the House Select Committee On Assassinations (HSCA) in 1978.

Rose Cheramie had become much more calm as the result of a sedative administered to her in Eunice. So as Fruge was driving her to Jackson, she began to share a fantastic story.

She said she had been traveling with two men she described as Latins, and they were en route to Dallas from Miami. Their goal in Dallas was threefold: 1) pick up Rose's child, 2) kill President John F. Kennedy and 3) proceed on to Galveston, Texas to meet an incoming ship. On the incoming ship would be a load of heroin being delivered to them by a particular seaman.

Rose was the courier for the money to pay for the drugs. Since there was no mention of Rose being in possession of any large sum of money, she must have been intending to get the money for the drugs in Dallas. Once in their possession, the drugs would be taken into Mexico. Although the intention of the plan was for the two men to accompany Rose all the way to Mexico, something went badly wrong with the plan in a nearby brothel called the Silver Slipper Lounge.

The two men traveling with Rose met a third man at the nearby brothel. There, according to Lt. Fruge, the little gang broke up because Rose became unruly. Both men, together with Mac Manual, the manager of the place, just tossed Rose out.

Rose started hitchhiking but she was soon impacted by a car on State Route 190. The driver of that car was the one who took her to the local hospital as described above.

As Fruge later testified before the HSCA: "She said she was going to, number one, pick up some money, number two, pick up her baby, and, finally, to kill Kennedy."

After arriving at the Jackson State Hospital, strange things began to happen. Rose had informed the nurses at the hospital that the JFK assassination was going to take place. Then as she and some nurses were watching the television she described the assassination in real time just before it occurred. She actually said "this is when it's going to happen" before it actually took place. The nurses, in turn, told the Doctors and others about Cheramie's prediction."

Although the assassination was not reported in real time on the local TV stations, they must have been reporting in general on the president's visit before and during the time when it happened.

Even more amazing things would follow: according to a psychiatrist named Dr. Victor Weiss, after Jack Ruby killed Lee Harvey Oswald on the morning of November 24th, Rose told either he or her prior psychiatrist that day that she knew both Ruby and Oswald. She said she had seen them sitting together on occasions at Ruby's club. In fact, Fruge later confirmed the fact that she had worked as a stripper for Ruby.

After he had discounted, naturally, the talk of killing Kennedy, Lt. Fruge later stated as follows: "When she came out with the Kennedy business, I just said, wait a minute, wait a minute, something wrong here somewhere." He further described her in this manner: "Now, bear in mind that she talked: she'd talk for awhile, looks like the shots would have effect on her again and she'd go in, you know, she'd just get numb, and after awhile she'd just start talking again."

By the time the assassination took place, Rose Cheramie had come completely to her senses and the heroin was out of her system. The whole story was corroborated years later by a doctor who had been an intern there at the Jackson State Hospital. This doctor was interviewed by the *Madison Capital Times* in Madison, Wisconsin where he was working as a doctor. He stated that he and the other interns were told of the warning of the plot in advance of the assassination.

Rose Cheramie also revealed to Dr. Weiss her role as a worker at Jack Ruby's night club and that she had been forced to make the trip to Miami to pick up the drugs, which was the thing that triggered off the whole situation.

Lt. Fruge then called the Jackson State Hospital. He said he told them: "no way in the world to turn her loose until I could get my hands on her." So on November 25th, Fruge went up to Jackson again to talk to Cheramie.

Lt. Fruge then really got down to business. He found that the two men with whom Rose had been traveling seemed to be part of the conspiracy. After the assassination took place (there was no evidence that these men were to actually be shooters), the men were to pick up $8000 from a home in Dallas. Then they would go to Houston, then to Galveston, where the sailor was to transfer the shipment of heroin to them.

Fruge investigated and corroborated the entire story, including the facts about the ship coming into Galveston, the name of the sailor with the heroin, the name of an underworld character the trio was dealing with, and the possession by Rose of clothes for her baby.

Another important fact was that, when Rose and Fruge were traveling together, after her release from the hospital as part of the investigation, she saw a newspaper which said:"investigators or something had not been able to establish a relationship between Jack Ruby and Lee Harvey Oswald."

When Cheramie read this headline, she said, "Them two queer sons-of-a-bitches. They've been shacking up for years." She added that she knew this to be true from her experience of working for Ruby. Next, Lt. Fruge had his own boss, Colonel Morgan, call up Captain Will Fritz of the Dallas Police, assuming they would be very interested in all the above events, but when Colonel Morgan hung up, he turned around and told us: "They don't want her. They're not interested."

When asked by Fruge, Rose declined to share her story with the FBI. Fruge, however did go back to the Silver Slipper brothel and interview the manager, Mac Manual. Through the use of mug shots, Manual identified one of Rose's companions as Sergio Arcacha Smith. That name is important as will be shown below.

On September 4, 1965, Rose Cheramie was allegedly run over by a car. This time her skull was crushed and she was killed, near Big Sandy, Texas. This can be found in a well-respected website. (Maryferrel.org).

A recent book entitled *HIT LIST: An In-Depth Investigation Into The Mysterious Deaths of Witnesses to the JFK Assassination* by Richard Belzer & David Wayne contains a short passage provided to the authors by Walt Brown.

This passage on page 51 states information that the second "accident" by which Rose Cheramie died occurred on the property of either Jerome Ragsdale or Paul Rothermel.

Paul Rothermel was the Security Chief for H. L. Hunt, the oil billionaire who was connected in some rather odd ways to the JFK assassination. Also, despite the fact that the death of Rose Cheramie was handled as an accidental death, the coroner's report showed a "stellate" wound on her forehead. The stellate wound can only be caused by one thing: a gunshot. That is because when a gun is placed right on the forehead, for example, the exploding gases from the gun barrel have to have a place to escape so they rip the skin in a star-shaped pattern, hence the descriptive word "stellate" means star.

In the opinion of the author, the most significant part of the Rose Cheramie evidence is the implication of Sergio Arcacha Smith. Smith was one of the two or three most important Cuban exile leaders in New Orleans and was an associate of Carlos Bringuier. Bringuier was, of course, the Cuban who set up Oswald in the FPCC fracas in New Orleans. Bringuier was also the one who phoned in information to authorities about Oswald the very moment when Oswald was apprehended.

THE PRIOR KNOWLEDGE OF JOSEPH MILTEER

In his monumental book, *General Walker and the Murder of President Kennedy,* Author Dr. Jeffrey Caulfield devotes more attention to Joseph Milteer that almost anybody else, including General Walker himself.

What is most important to know about Joseph Milteer is that, not only did he have detailed advance knowledge of the assassination, but he was in Dallas watching it. Probably the best theory about the role of Joseph Milteer in the assassination is that he was a backup patsy if Lee Harvey Oswald somehow botched his crucial role as patsy. Milteer knew that the Secret Service was complicit. The Secret Service was micro-managing the paperwork as to the whereabouts of Milteer. One minute he was officially in Dallas on 11-22-63, the next minute he was in Quitman or Valdosta, Georgia. Then he was officially back in Dallas. The Secret Service couldn't seem to make up their minds about the location of Milteer. This could well have been because he would have been somehow blamed for the assassination if the need occurred.

In *TMWKTM*, Joseph Adams Milteer in 1963 was described as a 61 year-old wealthy individual who lived in Quitman, Georgia.

Milteer was active in ultra-right causes. He was regional director of the Constitution Party which was backing Strom Thurmond to run for president of the United States.

Also in the Constitution Party was William P. Gale, formerly with General MacArthur in the Philippines and active in 1963 in the Minuteman movement. Gale was friends with General Edwin Walker of Dallas and had stayed as a guest at Walker's home in July, 1963. Milteer was active in the National State's Rights Party which was involved in dynamiting an Atlanta synagogue.

According to Russell, Milteer traveled constantly. At a New Orleans gathering, Milteer ran into an old friend his age named Willie Somersett, a union organizer from Miami and a member of the Ku Klux Klan. What Milteer did not know was that Somersett had been acting as an FBI informant for nearly a decade. In February, 1962, Somersett also became an informant for the Miami police. After meeting with Joseph Milteer, Somerset would present testimony to a judge, where he described Joseph Milteer as "the most violent man I know."

In June, 1963, Milteer was in Dallas. He would meet there with a widely read right-wing journalist, Dan Smoot, author of the *Dan Smoot Report*.

Willie Somersett ran into Milteer again in early October, 1963, at a meeting in Vero Beach, Florida. According to Somersett, Milteer helped formulate "plans to put an end to the Kennedy, King, Khrushchev dictatorship over our nation."

In mid-October, 1963, Judge Gelber of Miami suggested that Willie Somersett secretly tape recorded his next meeting with Milteer.

The following transcript, [which has been heavily edited by your author], reveals some very disturbing information relative to the events of November 1963 in Dallas.

This is a transcript of a tape-recorded conversation on 9 Nov 1963 by Miami Police informant William Somersett, with right-wing extremist Joseph Milteer. The transcript is taken from Harold Weisberg's essay "The Milteer Documents" in the book *The Assassinations: Dallas and Beyond*.

(In this version, INFORMANT has been replaced with SOMERSETT, and SUBJECT with MILTEER).

MILTEER: Just like me at home there folks want to know, "Joe, where do you get all of your information?" "Well, I get it, that is all you are interested in." That is the way you have got to operate.

SOMERSETT: Well, that is what I say, if you are going to take Brown in, and Brown is going to be one of the head men, the man behind you, then you have got to talk to Brown a little bit, and tell him, you know, "You have got to be a little more conscientious, especially on these bombings, and killings," after all he comes right out with it.

MILTEER: We have got to let him understand, that, that is his operation, and not ours.

SOMERSETT: Yeah, that is true. We don't care, if he wants to go to Birmingham and blow up a church, let him. That is right. Hell, he didn't say these things in any way to try to get us into trouble, because the only one who could be in trouble would be him, he was confessing on his damn self, he wasn't confessing on us, because we hadn't done a damn thing.

MILTEER: I have a man who is the head of his underground of his own up there in Delaware, and since I worked on the Supreme Court

SOMERSETT: You worked on the Supreme Court.

MILTEER: Yeah, three and a half years.

SOMERSETT: Well, that is why he wanted you to go, then, well, them things have got to be done, but outside the Party, we have got to be mighty careful who the hell we let know anything. Now, here is one thing you have got to realize, transporting dynamite across the state line is a federal offense, well you better let them know that.

SOMERSETT: I don't know, I think Kennedy is coming here on the 18th, or something like that to make some kind of speech, I don't know what it is, but I imagine it will be on the TV, and you can be on the look for that, I think it is the 18th that he is supposed to be here. I don't know what it is supposed to be about.

MILTEER: You can bet your bottom dollar he is going to have a lot to say about the Cubans, there are so many of them here.

SOMERSETT: Yeah, well he will have a thousand bodyguards, don't worry about that.

MILTEER: The more bodyguards he has, the easier it is to get him.

SOMERSETT: What?

MILTEER: The more bodyguards he has the more easier it is to get him.

SOMERSETT: Well how in the hell do you figure would be the best way to get him?

MILTEER: From an office building with a high-powered rifle, how many people [room noise--tape not legible] does he have going around who look just like him? Do you know about that?

SOMERSETT: No, I never heard that he had anybody.

MILTEER: He has got them.

SOMERSETT: He has?

MILTEER: He has about fifteen. Whenever he goes any place they [not legible] he knows he is a marked man.

SOMERSETT: You think he knows he is a marked man?

MILTEER: Sure he does.

SOMERSETT: They are really going to try to kill him?

MILTEER: Oh, yeah, it is in the working, Brown himself, Brown is just as likely to get him as anybody. He hasn't said so, but he tried to get Martin Luther King.

SOMERSETT: He did ?

MILTEER: Oh yes, he followed him for miles and miles, and couldn't get close enough to him.

SOMERSETT: You know exactly where he is in Atlanta don't you.

MILTEER: Martin Luther King, yeah.

SOMERSETT: Bustus Street [phonetic].

MILTEER: Yeah 530.

SOMERSETT: Oh Brown tried to get him huh?

MILTEER: Yeah.

SOMERSETT: That is right. They are individual operators, we don't want that within the party. Hitting this Kennedy is going to be a hard proposition, I tell you, I believe, you may have figured out a way to get him, you may have figured out the office building, and all that. I don't know how them Secret Service agents cover all them office buildings, or anywhere he is going, do you know whether they do that or not?

MILTEER: Well, if they have any suspicion they do that of course. But without suspicion chances are that they wouldn't. You take there in Washington, of course it is the wrong time of the year, but you take pleasant weather, he comes out on the veranda, and somebody could be in a hotel room across the way there, and pick him off just like [fades out].

SOMERSETT: Is that right?

MILTEER: Sure, disassemble a gun, you don't have to take a gun up there, you can take it up in pieces, all those guns come knock down, you can take them apart.

SOMERSETT: Boy, if that Kennedy gets shot, we have got to know where we are at. Because you know that will be a real shake, if they do that.

MILTEER: They wouldn't leave any stone unturned there no way. They will pick up somebody within hours afterwards, if anything like that would happen just to throw the public off.

SOMERSETT: Oh, somebody is going to have to go to jail, if he gets killed.

MILTEER: Just like that Bruno Hauptmann in the Lindbergh case you know [Dials telephone].

On the afternoon after the assassination, Somersett met Milteer again in a train station in Jacksonville, Florida. They then drove together to Columbia, South Carolina, where Milteer had a session planned with some Klan members. During the journey, Somersett later told the Miami police, "he [Milteer] told me that he was connected with an international underground. He said there would be a propaganda campaign too on how to prove to the Christian people of the world that the Jews ... had murdered Kennedy. He was very happy over it and said "well, I told you so. It happened like I told you, didn't it? It happened from a window with a high-powered rifle."

On November 27, 1963, the FBI went to see Milteer, who "emphatically denies ever making threats to assassinate President KENNEDY or participating in any such assassination. He stated he has never heard anyone make such threats."

One of the "suspicious deaths" cited by Jim Marrs in the Kennedy case was that of Joseph Milteer, director of the Dixie Klan of Georgia. Marrs corroberates that information that Milteer was secretly tape-recorded thirteen days before the assassination telling Miami police informant William Somersett that the murder of Kennedy was "in the working." Milteer died in 1974 when a heater exploded in his house.

The House Select Committee on Assassinations reported in 1979 that Milteer's information on the threat to the President "was furnished [to] the agents making the advance arrangements before the visit of the President" to Miami, but that "the Milteer threat was ignored by Secret Service personnel in planning the trip to Dallas." Robert Bouck, Special Agent-in-Charge of the Secret Service's Protective Research Section, "... testified to the committee that threat information was transmitted from one region of the country to another if there was specific evidence it was relevant to the receiving region."

The specificity of the Milteer information speaks for itself. For a broader perspective on the relationship between Southern Segregationists and right-wing paramilitary groups such as the Minutemen, one can refer to the book *Where Rebels Roost: Mississippi Civil Rights Revisited* (2005) by Susan Klopfer. This book is the definitive work on the history of Mississippi civil rights battles in the 1950's and 1960's.

According to the portrayals set forth by Klopfer, the White Citizen's Councils were organized rather quickly in direct response to the school integration movement. They included middle class white citizens. In contrast the Ku Klux Klan was made up of poorer whites and was thus more violent than the Citizen's Councils.

During the insurrection which occurred at the University of Mississippi in 1962 when James Meredith tried to enroll, the Ole Miss students combined with outside militants and the KKK to carry out a true armed insurrection on American soil. In addition, General Edwin Walker was present there as more or less a cheerleader to the riots and nothing more. However, this insurrection was spontaneous and involved outsiders with no real connection to local Mississippi segregationists.

Aside from the riots at Ole Miss, the local segregationists, (at least in Mississippi where the worst racial terror occured) were not regularly involved with outsiders or paramilitary groups.

Against this background, Milteer was apparently connected to the Minuteman-type paramilitary extremists who were bombing churches and involved in similar acts which we would now label as terrorist. There was apparently no real plan for these activities outside of the depraved personalities of those involved. There is no indication that the actual Minutemen, led by Robert DePugh, were even close to being well organized enough to plan and carry out the Kennedy assassination. They couldn't even be counted on to keep up the security needed to conceal such a plot. The reckless talk of Milteer is a prime example of this problem.

The prior knowledge of Milteer has to be attributed to very specific rumors arising from the bragging of disorganized elements around the South. Or he could have found out from Secret Service sources. This was not anywhere near to being considered proof of Milteer's direct involvement in the assassination plot as a perpetrator. It could be said that the "lunatic fringe" as they were called in the 1960's were virtual vacuum cleaners in scrounging around in the underworld that existed in the South which included the KKK, the Cuban exiles, the oil billionaires, FBI and CIA informants and even the Russian Tsarists and Neo-Nazis.

We know that Jack Ruby, after the assassination, was in mortal fear of anti-semitic groups. It is very likely that part of the attraction of the plotters to Ruby, and the involvement of Ruby was in part to blame Jewry in the assassination. After all, there were billboards in Dallas which were prominently signed by a local right-wing Jew. It was these billboards that put Ruby on the defense on this issue.

It's also well known that the New Orleans FBI office, just days before the assassination, received a warning from the Director [Hoover] that stated that a right-wing extremist group was possibly planning an assassination in Dallas. This somewhat sounds like the Minutemen or a similar violent group.

Dr. Jeffrey Caulfield in *General Walker* reports that Milteer claimed to be part of the "international underground." *International*. Who would think of the Southern Segregationist movement as international? Also, Milteer stated that there was a lot of "Catholic money" involved in the assassination. Caulfield interprets this as Catholic money from Catholic New Orleans. This could have been the case. But then there were the prominent Catholic activists such as Konrad Adenauer and Heinrich von Bentano of Germany. And also, we must include Senator Thomas J. Dodd, House Speaker John W. McCormack, former Congressman Charles Kersten and Mayor Richard J. Daley of Chicago. There were many possible Catholic individuals and groups involved in the assassination.

But from examining the above information, it does not seem that the information proves that Joseph Milteer was in any way a participant in the JFK assassination, nor that any right-wing paramilitary group were involved or were the perpetrators. Milteer could merely have heard a rather detailed rumor and was trying to look like a big shot to his friend or friends. However, the information which Milteer had definitely qualifies him having prior knowledge of the assassination.

THE PRIOR KNOWLEDGE OF SANTOS TRAFFICANTE

By far the weakest and most insignificant case for prior knowledge of the Kennedy assassination is the apparent statement of the mob boss of Tampa, Santos Trafficante, in September, 1962. He mentioned to an informant that Kennedy would be "hit" before the next election.

The most significant fact regarding this information is that it qualifies as the earliest mention on record by anyone regarding a possible assassination.

The fact that it is alleged to have happened in September, 1962, lines up very well with many early rumors about Soviet missiles in Cuba and JFK's response or late response to the Cuban Missile Crisis which reached a climax in October, 1962.

Santos Trafficante, Jr. is described on page 37 of *TMWKTM* as a Tampa-based Mob boss, involved in CIA plots against Fidel Castro. The most important facts relating to Trafficante as the information has played out in very recent years, is that Trafficante had interests, probably drug running, in Cuba under Batista.

When Castro took over, Trafficante was jailed by Castro in Cuba. His quarters in jail were apparently fairly luxurious. According to reports, Trafficante shared a cell there with the paramilitary soldier-of-fortune Loren Hall and he was visited in jail by, among others, Jack Ruby while he was in custody. Trafficante was supposedly ransomed (by persons unknown) and returned to Florida.

Trafficante was involved in some way with CIA plots to assassinate Castro, but these plots never came to anything. The plots were apparently supervised by Robert Kennedy and they went by the code-name Operation Mongoose.

It has more recently been suggested that after Batista fell and Castro took over, Trafficante may well have continued running drugs, this time working with Castro himself. That would make Trafficante, in effect, a double agent.

If the above were true and he was a double agent, that could explain how he found out so early about the impending assassination of Kennedy. Castro had an excellent intelligence service, best described in the book *Brothers in Arms: The Kennedys, the Castros and the Politics of Murder*, by Guss Russo.

The following paragraph is excerpted from the Anthony Summers website:

> "Mark my word," Trafficante is reported to have said to a close associate in September 1962, "this man Kennedy is in trouble, and he will get what is coming to him.... He's not going to make it to the election. He is going to be hit."

There is very little credibility, in the opinion of your author, to the theory that the Mafia killed Kennedy. It is a theory that seems to be useful to those who want a "cover" because they hesitate, for whatever reason, to postulate more realistic possibilities. As we know, as of this writing, the official position of the media and most of the government, despite the findings of the HSCA, is that Oswald was the lone gunman and that only Oswald bears responsibility.

Notes:

LBJ: The Mastermind of the JFK Assassination Paperback (2013) by Phillip F. Nelson.

Websites which provide information on Dinkin include: www.educationforum.ipbhost.com/index.php?showtopic=7078.

The original military documents can be found at (www.history-matters.com/archive/jfk/cia/russholmes//104-10438/104-10438-10154/html/104-10438-10154_0001a.htm). [The above information as extracted from the government files was contributed by Lee Forman in the Education Forum 12/2/05].

You can find material which supports the following information about Rose Cheramie in: Jim DiEugenios, *The Assassinations*, Phillip Nelson, *LBJ: Mastermind*, and Dick Russell, *TMWKTM*.

The facts relating to Rose's role as a stripper are: (Reported in a memo of Frank Meloche to Louis Ivon as part of the Jim Garrison investigation, 5/22/67) (3/13/67) In fact, Fruge later confirmed the fact that she had worked as a stripper for Ruby. (Louisiana State Police report of 4/4/67).

Regarding what Rose told Dr. Weiss, see: (Memo of Frank Meloche to Jim Garrison, 2/23/67) as part of the Garrison conspiracy investigation to take place in New Orleans.

About Fruge's phone call to the Jackson State Hospital, see: Fruge's HSCA deposition, p. 12.

Regarding Fruge's conversation with Rose about the relationship between LHO and Ruby, see: (Fruge's HSCA deposition p. 19).

The Mary Ferrell website mentioned in the text can be found with the following link: [(https://www.maryferrell.org/wiki/index.php/Rose_Cherami).

As cited in the text, see: *Hit List: An In-Depth Investigation into the Mysterious Deaths of Witnesses to the JFK Assassination* (2016) by Richard Belzer and David Wayne.

Regarding the location of Rose's fatal pedestrian accident, *Hit List* authors cite: (footnote # 186--Walt Brown, Ph.d., 26 Oct 2012, email to author).

The transcript of the Milteer can be found at: [http://www.maryferrell.org/wiki/index.php/Transcript_of_Milteer_Somersett_Tape] Note: The "transcript" mentioned in the text is specifically a transcript of a tape recorded on 9 Nov 1963 by Miami Police informant William Somersett, recording a conversion with right-wing extremist Joseph Milteer. The transcript is taken from Harold Weisberg's essay The Milteer Documents in the book The Assassinations: Dallas and Beyond (in this version, INFORMANT has been replaced with SOMERSETT, and SUBJECT with MILTEER). Portions referring to Kennedy are in bold.

Regarding the matter mention as stated by Jim Marrs, see: from[en.wikepedia.org/wiki/John_F._ Kennedy_assassination_conspiracy_theories].

Where Rebels Roost … Mississippi Civil Rights Revisited 2nd Edition by Susan Klopfer, MBA, Fred Klopfer, PhD and Barry Klopfer, Esq.

The following is one of the best JFK assassination references: *Brothers in Arms: The Kennedys, the Castros, and the Politics of Murder* (2008) by Gus Russo and Stephen Molton.

The following paragraph is excerpted from the Anthony Summers website as mentioned in the text: [http://anthonysummersandrobbynswan.wordpress.com/2013/11/23/the-claims-that-mafia-bosses-trafficante-and-marcello-admitted-involvement-in-assassinating-president-kennedy/].

Chapter 1

INTRODUCTION TO THE THREE BARONS AND THE JFK ORGANIZATIONAL CHART

T hanks to the Internet and the passage of time, it is now possible to put together the plot of the JFK assassination. It is also now possible to know a great deal about the perpetrators and why they did it.

My research efforts began on the 50th anniversary of the assassination. There was week-long coverage on C-Span. Since that time, I have read 145 books on the events surrounding the assassination.

It is hard to know where to begin. So we will start with just a sample of the newest (and previously unknown) evidence surrounding the JFK assassination.

In reading and analyzing the 145 books, I have been able to gain an understanding of the plot down to small details. Along the way, I have assembled a database of 1500 names. These were names that were most frequently cited in the 30 best books I could find on the assassination. These are books which I believe are objective. They represent evidence which I feel presents a new diverse viewpoints and theories. Near the end of this book, I will present the results of my application of statistical factor analysis applied to this database. This factor analysis in itself has produced some startling information.

But we will start with evidence which is new in the world of JFK assassination research. Let's look at our first example:

Senator Thomas J Dodd was brought up on ethics charges in the Senate in 1966. In the hearings before the Senate Ethics Committee former Congressman Charles Kersten of Wisconsin was questioned about three mysterious letters. These letters were sent to the three Kennedy brothers on November 7, 1963. This was just two weeks before the assassination:[1] Quoting from the transcript of the hearings:

> **Mr. Sonnett** [attorney for the Committee]: Would you read that letter into the record?
>
> (Mr. Kersten reads the letter):

Mr. Kersten: "Dear Senator Kennedy [referring to Sen Edward Kennedy] Believing that it may be difficult for a letter of mine to be seen by the President, I am taking the liberty of enclosing a copy which I respectfully request you call to his attention. Sincerely, Charles Kersten.

Mr. Sonnett: Now, will you refer to the letter [by you to] President Kennedy of November 7, 1963, next to that document, and read that into the record?

Mr. Kersten: Dear Mr. President: The Senate Internal Security Subcommittee has been contemplating a hearing in Munich about the murder of the Ukrainian underground leader, Stepan Bandera by former Soviet agent Bogdan Stashynsky.... He was tried for murder in the German High Court at Karlsruhe in October-November 1962. I [Kersten] participated in the trial as counsel for Mrs. Bandera, the victim's wife.... The facts of the case are unique. Stashynsky received intensive training as a KGB killer of anti-communist leaders in the Free World...

Former Congressman Kersten was giving a strong warning to JFK. And it wasn't just a warning sent to JFK. He also warned both Robert F. Kennedy and "Theodore Kennedy" [Edward M. Kennedy]. Kersten warned that Soviet agents, trained for assassination, were out to get the leaders of the free world. And all this happened just two weeks before the assassination of JFK.

So, does this raise any red flags in the mind of the reader? In fact, this was literally a "red flag," a real Communist red flag. And it was being waved in the face of the President and his brothers just 15 days before JFK was murdered. Was this just a coincidence?

And who was former Congressman Charles Kersten? Few Americans have ever heard the name Charles Kersten. Why was he bringing up the topic of Soviet assassination just two weeks prior to the JFK assassination? We will also find out about the strange case mentioned by Congressman Kersten; the case of defector Bogdan Stashynsky. Why did the case of Stashynsky (who was an alleged Soviet-trained assassin), follow such a precise and suspicious timetable?

There was a bizarre chain of events which began in 1959 with the death of Ukrainian hero Stepan Bandera. Next came a trial of Stashynsky for the alleged murder before the Supreme Court of Germany. After the trial, Senator Thomas J Dodd traveled back and forth to Germany. Was Dodd trying to call attention to this fictional Soviet murder plan? In 1967, Senator Dodd was censured by the Senate. In the censure hearings, a disturbing fact came to light. Dodd has a close relationship with certain ex-Nazi's in Germany. He was making a desperate attempt to meet with them just prior to the death of JFK.

Now, let's take another prime bit of very suggestive evidence.

In 1968, journalist Eric Norden obtained a unique interview with the leader of the Minutemen, which was a home-grown American terrorist organization. The name of the leader was Robert DePugh. The interview by Eric Norden was published by *Playboy* magazine. It also appeared in the *Twentieth Anniversary Playboy Reader* (1969):

> Quoting DePugh: "I've often thought of writing a book called *1001 Ways to Kill a Man Without Using Firearms* – dedicated to Senator Dodd, of course."

Why did DePugh make that veiled reference to Senator Dodd? Did DePugh know all about Dodd and the Stashynsky case? We know that as leader of the Minutemen, DePugh was connected to many members of the extreme right. The title of the article in *Playboy* was "The Paramilitary Right."

Some people may argue that the activities of Senator Dodd regarding the Stashynsky case were only for the purpose of creating a general fear of the alleged Soviet murder program. Maybe Dodd didn't know who the victim would be. Legally Dodd, by his actions, could have been convicted of being an accessory to murder. In the legal definition of accessory to a crime, it includes anyone who participates in a cover up before the act, but not necessarily in a cover up after the fact. It would be naïve to think that Dodd didn't know the details. My verdict: *at least suspicious and very possibly guilty!*

In his monumental 780 page book *General Walker: And The Murder Of President Kennedy*, Dr. Jeffrey Caulfield makes a very persuasive case about Lee Harvey Oswald. Caulfield wrote that during his time in New Orleans, Oswald was acting according to a plan. That plan was carefully designed by Senator James O. Eastland of Mississippi. It was a cynical plan designed to brand dozens of civil-rights groups in the South as Communist. This plan could have destroyed these groups before the courts. How was Eastland intending to prove these groups were Communist? Eastland was going to prove that all of these groups were associated with a young Communist named Lee Harvey Oswald.

Senator Eastland was not just a minor figure. Eastland was a formidable power in the Senate: he was Majority Leader and Chairman of the powerful Senate Judiciary Committee. Eastland was also the official chairman of the Senate Internal Security Subcommittee. And Senator Thomas Dodd was the permanent *Acting* Chairman of that same subcommittee. Eastland and Dodd were, to all appearances, partners in crime.

The personal papers of Senator Eastland were donated upon his death to the Law School at the University of Mississippi. The papers were locked in a room. No researcher or historian was allowed to see them for 50 years. When they were finally revealed, they had been severely "sanitized."

This is just some of the evidence. There is much more.

Author Joan Mellen recently published a book entitled *Farewell to Justice*. This book is a study of the Jim Garrison investigation into the JFK assassination. The climax of the Garrison investigation was the prosecution of Clay Shaw (a New Orleans businessman) for participating in the murder of John F. Kennedy.

Shaw was acquitted. However, the information developed by Garrison served to prove that there was a conspiracy to murder JFK. One of the major revelations published by Jim Garrison in his book *On The Trail Of The Assassins* was information about a shadowy organization called Permindex. Permindex was a front organization which had a mysterious subsidiary known as Centro Mondiale Commerciale. "Centro" was first located in Rome. Then it was banished to Switzerland. Eventually it moved on to South Africa under the protection of the South African apartheid government.

In her book, Joan Mellen states that Centro was a CIA front. Mellen reports that "in the ranks of Permindex were actual Nazi's and Neo Nazis." In the Garrison investigation, Guy Banister was one of three major suspects. Mellen quotes (Banister operative) Tommy Baumler who said "those who killed John F. Kennedy were those who wanted to kill [Charles] de Gaulle."

Remember also the Kersten threats? Kersten wrote of Soviet plans to murder leaders of the free world. There were, in fact, three major assassination attempts against the French President starting in late 1961 and ending in September 1963. They were funded by an anonymous group known only as "The Old General Staff" and the money was passed through one single person. The true source of this money is, to this day, unproven.

There is another book which is a "must read" for any student of the Kennedy assassination and American history. The name of the book is *The New Germany and the Old Nazis,* and the author is T. H. Tetens. Tetens was a veteran scholar who specialized in the geopolitics of Germany. Author Tetens lists three things that our State Department wanted us to believe about Germany:

(1) the decision to make defeated Germany into an ally was a good decision

(2) the Germans had changed profoundly and had developed a truly democratic society and,

(3) Dr. Konrad Adenauer [was] a leader whose counsel was sought throughout the world.

Tetens believed that none of these things were true. He was one of the leading experts and scholars on German geopolitics. He was a veteran of 30 year's research and had worked on the War Crimes Commission from 1946-1948.

Tetens also had something to say about "Centro." According to Tetens, in the 1950's and the 1960's there was an organization of ex-[military] officers, high government officials, jurists, educators, industrialists and church leaders from Germany It was called the "Committee for Justice and Trade." Tetens states "According to [a] report in the *Deutsche Soldaten Zeitung*, this group was closely affiliated with a propaganda center in Switzerland, the Centro Europa…" Tetens describes "Centro" as a relief organization for former Nazi war criminals around the world.

Add to the mix the following: the same Nazi *Deutsche Soldaten Zeitung* (a/k/a *National Zeitung*) which was mentioned by Tetens, was also mentioned by assassination author Dr. Caulfield in his book *General Walker*.

Writes Caulfield, "while Walker was in Shreveport, [11-23-63], miraculously, an obscure Nazi-oriented German Newspaper, *The National Zeitung*, located him [Walker] and interviewed him…" The newspaper even had Walker's hotel room number and Walker hadn't given it to them.

We have already seen a very tangled web. Senator Dodd and former Congressman Charles Kersten were closely involved with certain people in Germany. These people were dealing with assassinations and in particular, the possible assassinations of free world leaders. This list of free world leaders would probably include Charles de Gaulle or John F. Kennedy. And added to this, the leader of the Minutemen, Robert DePugh, seemed to link Senator Dodd to the subject of assassinations. What did DePugh know about Senator Dodd and how did he find out? Did DePugh read the record of the censure hearings against Dodd? Why would he do that? Or did DePugh know all the true details about the role of Dodd in the JFK murder from some other source?

In later chapters, we will explore all these clues and leads in depth. We will for the first time, explain the actions of the two JFK whistleblowers who worked for military intelligence. These two tried to blow the whistle and to foil the assassination. We will also hope to explain for the first time what motivated Jack Ruby to murder Oswald. As we untangle this web of intrigue, we will explain the unexplained. And most important of all, we will (for the first time after more than 50 years) show the reader an organizational chart of the JFK assassination.

IGNORANCE IS BLISS

This exhaustive research has satisfied a desire on the part of this author which began in 1963. It was then when the earthshaking news of the assassination was announced on a high school public address system. This desire was given impetus by the book *Crossfire* by Jim Marrs and also the Oliver Stone movie *JFK* which came out in 1992.

But what is the fundamental challenge in JFK assassination research? This fundamental problem is the primary reason which explains why the JFK assassination has never been adequately explained in any previously published book. This question has to be answered before research can go further. This question is, how much do we really *want* to know about who killed JFK? How much is our country ready to handle?

Many authors who have written about the JFK assassination have not been sincerely interested in solving the JFK mystery, although some have made outstanding contributions.

In my opinion, the best approach is to treat the JFK case as what it really is: a murder. To make a case against a murderer, one has to weigh all the facts and establish a theory of the case. There are written complaints and briefs which are created to support the theory of the case. Too many JFK authors have adopted an approach of "throwing in the kitchen sink."

With the singular exception of New Orleans District Attorney Jim Garrison, no researcher, investigator or anyone else has had in his job description the assignment of finding out who murdered JFK. The mission statement of the Warren Commission was "to evaluate evidence presented to it by the FBI." The task of the author of assassination books is, after all, to sell books. In defense of such outstanding authors such as Dr. Jeffrey Caulfield, Dick Russell and Michael Collins Piper, some have decided primarily to mine the information and generate as much evidence as possible for posterity. Despite reams of evidence, the JFK case has obviously never been solved either legally or in the minds of Americans.

In my opinion, patriotic Americans should consider it priority one to analyze and discover who murdered JFK and how. If the reader does not share this type of commitment or perspective, he should read no further.

This type of case can't be put on the back of a lone "nut." This case can't be solved by only examining forensics. To understand this case, the reader must be willing to take as broad a perspective as necessary to reach understanding. If that requires familiarity with the price of beans in China, then so be it. If it requires a complete understanding of the politics in the U.S. from 1935 to 1963, then that's just what it takes.

Every closed door must be opened. That means that reading one single sentence or one paragraph won't suffice. For example, to decide on the guilt or innocence of Baron George de Mohrenschildt, his entire life story must be researched in some detail.

As in most classical murder cases, the JFK case could turn on one single strand of hair, or one single drop of blood. There would never be any murder trials at all if conviction required a mountain of probative evidence. In the famous case against star athlete O.J. Simpson for the murder of his wife, the case turned on the barking of a single dog. If the dog had barked only ten minutes earlier, Simpson would have been convicted. And this was after the presentation of months of evidence. But for the barking dog, none of it had been decisive.

Notes:

A key citation throughout this work relevant to Senator Thomas J. Dodd are the Senate hearings referenced as Investigation of Senator Thomas J. Dodd. : Hearings, Eighty-ninth Congress, second session ... pursuant to S. Res. 338, 88th Congress. PT. 1-2 by United States. Congress. Senate. Select Committee on Standards and Conduct. Published 1966.

A Farewell to Justice: Jim Garrison, JFK's Assassination, And the Case That Should Have Changed History (2007) by Joan Mellen see page 136.

The New Germany And The Old Nazis by Tete Harens (T.H.) Tetens (1961) at p. 203.

Target de Gaulle : the thirty-one attempts to assassinate the General by Christian Plume and Pierre Demaret (1974).

Chapter 2

THE ORGANIZATIONAL CHART OF THE DE GAULLE PLOT WITH BACKGROUND AND EXPLANATION

One of the best assassination books to start with is entitled *Target de Gaulle: The True Story Of The 31 Attempts On The Life Of The French President* by Christian Plume and Pierre Demaret. This book provides some unique information. As was mentioned in the prior chapter, an associate of Jim Garrison believed the same people who murdered JFK also tried three times (or maybe more) to kill de Gaulle.

At a fundamental level, the book by Plume and Demaret provides a very good model of what a plot to kill a president looks like. Of the 31 attempts claimed, there were actually only three that rise to the level of out-and-out serious attempts. One was called Pont-Sur-Seine, another Petit-Clamart and the last Ecole Militaire.

Most people assume that the assassination attempts on President Charles de Gaulle were the work of the French OAS. The French colony of Algeria was fiercely demanding independence in 1960. People in France who opposed Algerian independence lost faith in the French military to prevent this from happening. For this reason, a civilian organization was formed outside the French government called the organization de l'armée secrete, or OAS (a French acronym) which was made up of former military officers and personnel. A former French general named Raoul Salan was named as its leader. Salan had been commander of the French military in Algeria, but resigned in 1958 and moved to Spain.

In a bizarre episode, there was a meeting between General Salan and the top CIA official in France. In a letter dated December 12, 1961 which traveled all the way to the desk of President Kennedy, General Salan asked Kennedy to intervene in the war in Algeria. The pretext was to keep Algeria out of the hands of Communists. It is incredible that, following this request, the CIA agreed to arm 1 million men in Algeria for this purpose. When JFK found out about this, he countermanded this absurd CIA proposal.

According to Plume and Demaret, there were three groups which wished to "eliminate" de Gaulle.

1). The Old General Staff, inaccurately described as "of the Army."

2). The French Army itself which was, in fact, divided on the issue and

3). Supporters of French Algeria who were organizing completely in secret.

The following is important for the JFK reader to know. In January 1961, certain "mysterious" forces in France, drawn from the worlds of finance, politics, the Army, and the French government, had been at work undercover. On a certain date in 1961, these forces decided to start taking major risks. Per Plume and Demaret:

> The group which made a special impact on 5th January was closely connected with world Catholicism; its composition alone is proof; most of them were ultra-nationalist Catholics. This group was known, somewhat misleadingly, as the "Old General Staff." It was a group which was behind the two major assassination attempts at Pont-sur-Seine and Petit-Clamart. Both attempts were directed by Lieutenant-Colonel Bastien-Thiry; in conversation with his associates, he continually referred to certain mysterious superiors.

Various JFK researchers claim that the de Gaulle attacks were sponsored by the FBI, U.S. Military Intelligence or by NATO itself. Superficially, this would seem to be confirmed by the fact that, at some point after the several assassination attempts, de Gaulle ordered NATO troops off French soil. At the time, de Gaulle claimed that the presence of the NATO command center on French soil actually compromised French sovereignty. The line commanders of NATO at that time were, in turn, General Lauris Norstad and General Lyman Lemnitzer. Interestingly, in the LBJ phone calls during the week following the assassination, General Norstad was being forcefully promoted as a candidate to sit on the Warren Commission. Supposedly, according to some authors, French Intelligence traced the money for the de Gaulle assassination attempts back through the NATO headquarters. In this period, the NATO Secretary General, Dirk Stikker was a close personal friend of German Chancellor Konrad Adenauer. Further, the top ranking military person in NATO (who was the Permanent Chairman of the Military Committee), was General Adolf Heusinger who had been the right-hand man to Hitler on the Russian front.

The authority of authors Plume and Demaret seems superior to that of the assassination researchers who make claims regarding the role of the French OAS. Of course the group of Catholic activists, financiers, and related private interests mentioned by Plume and Demaret could have very loosely fit the description of the JFK plotters. The plotters were at least allies of world Catholicism, though not necessarily Catholic and some were even anti-Catholic (like the Southern segregationists and extreme Nazi's).

Unfortunately, Plume and Demaret are not helpful enough to name names of these Catholic activists. However, Plume and Demaret do compare them to the Catholic "Cagoule" movement from 1935-1937. To get some names, we must refer to the book *The Action Francaise: Die-Hard Reactionaries in Twentieth Century France*, by Eugen Weber. To quote Weber (writing in 1962) at page 283:

> The most dangerous force on the Extreme Right in France since the mid-1950's has been a secret organization that closely resembles the prewar Cagoule. Its leaders are difficult to identify, but they have apparently infiltrated the highest level of the civil service and the military hierarchy, even to the point of being able to remove compromising evidence about themselves from the files of the security police...
>
> Among the suspects arrested in connection with the attempted assassination of de Gaulle in September, 1961 there were petty noblemen with names like Martial de Villemandy [civilian], Cabanne de la Prade [civilian], Barbier de Blingnieres [military] and Boucher de Crevecoeur [civilian].

This is an organizational chart of the plot at the time of the Petit-Clamart attack:

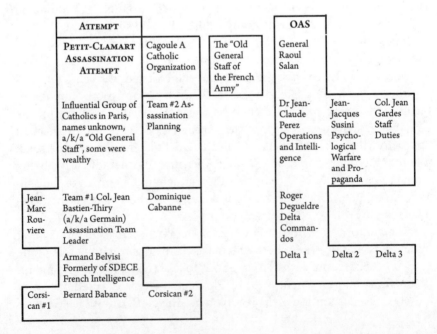

ATTEMPT			OAS		
PETIT-CLAMART ASSASSINATION ATTEMPT	Cagoule A Catholic Organization	The "Old General Staff of the French Army"	General Raoul Salan		
Influential Group of Catholics in Paris, names unknown, a/k/a "Old General Staff", some were wealthy	Team #2 Assassination Planning		Dr Jean-Claude Perez Operations and Intelligence	Jean-Jacques Susini Psychological Warfare and Propaganda	Col. Jean Gardes Staff Duties
Jean-Marc Rouviere	Team #1 Col. Jean Bastien-Thiry (a/k/a Germain) Assassination Team Leader	Dominique Cabanne	Roger Degueldre Delta Commandos		
	Armand Belvisi Formerly of SDECE French Intelligence		Delta 1	Delta 2	Delta 3
Corsican #1	Bernard Babance	Corsican #2			

The first and last attacks employed IED's or roadside bombs. However, the biggest attack was at Petit-Clamart and it was a military-style sniping and crossfire attempt using machine guns. Over 100 rounds actually hit the Citroen sedan in which President de Gaulle and his wife were riding. One bullet pierced the hem of the dress of Mdm. de Gaulle. The President himself was unscathed. And that was thanks mostly to his driver who sped away immediately despite having to drive on 4 flattened tires.

We might ask why experts label this type of attack a military-style attack? The first reason is that it requires discipline; discipline is the specialty of the military. Second, there is an excellent chance to get away.

When you add the element of a crossfire, you greatly increase the possibility of success. With a crossfire, there is no one direction by which the victim can escape. Multiple points of the compass are covered. Obviously the very use of a military-style attack points to the military (or at least experienced mercenaries or the paramilitary).

Another type of assassination attack is the walk-up shooter. This has been the mode of three out of the four U.S. Presidential assassinations. It is easy to accomplish the walk-up attack by use of the "lone nut." Of course such a "lone nut" can be acting on behalf of just about anybody. There are innumerable examples of this type of plan: e.g. Presidents Garfield and McKinley and Governor George Wallace in 1972. It also includes failed attempts on Gerald Ford in 1975 and Ronald Reagan in 1981. Another was Robert Kennedy in 1968. The downside of this plot is that the shooter will get caught and usually executed unless he kills himself first. If you believe that Lee Harvey Oswald was the lone shooter, he would be placed in this category. If Lee Harvey Oswald were actually willing to sacrifice himself, (as would the average lone nut), he would have more likely been a walk-up shooter rather than a sniper from a window.

A third method is the IED or the roadside bomb. This has been used many times, often in the most sensational cases. Examples are the Pont-Sur-Seine and Ecole Militaire attempts on de Gaulle. Also, many people don't realize that a bomb was part of the overall plot for the successful assassination attempt on Archduke Franz Ferdinand of Austria. Ferdinand was actually killed by a walk-up shooter. This famous case triggered off World War I. Again, most people don't realize that the killing of Franz Ferdinand is now thought to have involved Serbian military intelligence. Another very famous assassination using a bomb was that against Czar Alexander II of Russia in 1881.

A fourth style is the Mafia hit. It is similar to the walk-up shooter only because it involves one person individually shooting another. But that's where the similarity ends. The Mafia may pick a very public place such as when the victim is eating in a restaurant or even having his hair cut in a barber's chair. The latter was used in the murder of Albert Anastasia in 1957. That murder along with the famed St. Valentine's Day massacre in Chicago, were bold, terrifying attacks that send a message to virtually everybody in the U.S. including the police, the rival gangs, the citizenry, and even the politicians. An alternative to the dramatic public execution often used by the Mafia is the more common Mafia "hit." This involves isolating someone in a dark alley, then to walk up to or drive up and shoot them without warning. Then, ideally, the killers take the body and dump it in the nearest river. This usually includes providing the corpse with a pair of "concrete shoes." This type of hit is the proverbial "gangland slaying." The message to the police is clear. It is a plainly a gangland slaying. It has been done by professional killers. In these killings, the perpetrators are never caught. So if you are the police, you should not waste your time investigating.

The final type of assassination is by poisoning. This is very rare these days. It was used in the ancient world, most famously involving King Mithradates who lived in the ancient Middle East. According to legend, Mithridates ingested a small amount of arsenic every day. This immunized him when his enemies tried to use arsenic to kill him. More recently and in the same spirit of mythology, the CIA had tried to poison Fidel Castro, either by ordinary poison, a poisoned cigar, a poisoned seashell, a poisoned diving suit or even injecting him with cancer, (the last method according to author Judyth Vary Baker).

Another example of alleged poisoning is the case of alleged Soviet agent Bogdan Stashynsky which will be discussed in depth in later chapters. Supposedly, Stashynsky used a cyanide spray gun to kill Ukrainian hero Stepan Bandera. The facts surrounding this case and this method are very shaky as we shall see.

The drawback to poisoning is that it may fail because it is hard to deliver the poison. It involves a great deal of luck. Also, with the advent of modern science, there is more access to treatment and antidotes. With the advent of modern forensics, there is a greater chance of tracing the poison back to the killer.

So the takeaway from all of the above is this: if there were multiple snipers in Dallas, and they used a cross-fire, this fact would point to a military (or paramilitary) group as being responsible for the act of shooting John F. Kennedy.

Notes:

Target de Gaulle, by Plume and Demaret is cited at p 79.

Chapter 3

WHY HAS THE JFK CASE NEVER BEFORE BEEN SOLVED?

THE MOUNT EVEREST-SIZED PILE OF ASSASSINATION EVIDENCE.
There are many reasons why the murder of JFK remains officially unsolved.

First, there have only been roughly 100 serious books in which the authors try to explain the assassination. While some of these authors have spent almost an entire lifetime with their research, many have spent a lot less. The longest periods of research have been on the part of authors like Mark Lane, Jim Marrs, Dick Russell and Dr. Jeffrey Caulfield. Amazingly, Mark Lane started out as the lawyer for Oswald's family the weekend of the assassination. Lane published his most recent book in 2012, so that's 50 years of research. Dr. Caulfield started his research in 1992 and published in 2015. Russell spent 17 years with his research before publication.

But arrayed against these authors have been tens of thousands or maybe hundreds of thousands of CIA employees, military intelligence staff, FBI, Secret Service and other government workers. No one will ever know exactly how many government employees have worked on the JFK cover-up.

We do know one thing, however. The cover-up did not have to be organized or co-ordinated. Take for example the locking-up of the James O. Eastland records at Ole Miss. The Dean of the University law school did not have to know who killed JFK. All he needed was to have one researcher approach him and ask to see the records and tell him he was working on the JFK case. The minute the Dean heard that, the door was locked. *Instantly.*

There were at least three Federal Judges who appear to have helped in the cover-up, apparently out of concern for national security. They didn't know who killed JFK. It is very likely that all they knew was that they got a call from Washington asking them to dismiss a case, or possibly make a ruling. They would have done it, no questions asked. That's just how governments work. And that's the problem that the 100-odd researchers have been up against since 1963.

And then there are the lone gunmen theorists. Some of these authors have a background in law enforcement or as prosecutors, such as Vincent Bugliosi. Bugliosi wrote a book with 1648 pages trying to prove the lone gunman theory. One can only ask, does Bugliosi think life is too long, so he gladly wasted all that major part of his life to perpetrate a lie? And Vince was a former prosecutor. We can hope he did better by the many defendants he prosecuted.

Let's face it. The brave researchers such as Jim Marrs and Dick Russell were self-selected. They were not hired with a top-flight background in criminal investigation. If one wants to read a book by a top-flight criminal investigator, read *A Simple Act of Murder: November 22, 1963* by Mark Fuhrman and Stephen Weeks. As many readers might know, Fuhrman was the detective with the top reputation for investigation in the Los Angeles Police Department. He gained fame by his work in the crime of the decade, the O. J. Simpson murder case in 1994-1995. Displaying his talents, Fuhrman takes the "magic bullet" theory and rips it to shreds. But he then turns around and displays his loyalty to law enforcement and to the government. He dismisses the cover-up as only a matter of wounded pride and vanity. He blames embarrassment on the part of investigators who were trying to sweep their shoddy investigation under the rug.

Next in importance is the sheer volume of evidence and potential evidence in the case. When the evidence in each book is counted based on the average evidence per page times the number of pages, it is possible to estimate it. It comes out to around 1000 items of evidence per book. Of the 1000 items, about half is new or unique to the particular book. With 100 major books, that makes 50,000 items of evidence. Our definition of "evidence" here includes even a small fact such as "John Doe was in New Orleans on September 15, 1963." Another example would be "it was 73 degrees in Dallas when JFK was shot." And so on. Even though these facts are minute, the important thing is this: a serious researcher has to pick his way through all 50,000 facts! There is no shortcut.

Another analysis put together by this author is a 1500-name database. This database was assembled by counting the top 80 to 120 names cited most often in the index of 31 unique, non-repetitive books. (Lone gunman books were excluded!) Of the 1500 names, only about 350 were cited a sufficient amount of times in more than one book. In a later chapter, the results of some statistical analysis of these names and these books will be presented.

The important point here is that out of 1500 names, any one of the names could theoretically be a JFK murderer. There is no shortcut to avoid sifting through all 1500 names.

It is possible be bitten by the JFK assassination bug and it lasts quite a while. For people like author Mark Lane, it lasts a lifetime.

LOGICAL RULES OR PRINCIPLES USEFUL IN EVALUATION OF THE ASSASSINATION

There are 10 principles which should be followed in the evaluation of the JFK evidence. They could be called the "Ten Commandments of Assassination Research."

Some logical rules, which your author has developed or selected, are: as follows:

1: Motive, means and opportunity.

2: When you have eliminated the impossible, you have the answer.

3: If you are judging a theory which offers an explanation for otherwise unexplained facts, you should believe it.

4: Some of the first information to come out can sometimes be the best information.

5: When a key witness makes a statement that sounds totally unbelievable, it almost always turns out to be true in the end.

6 There are no impossible coincidences.

7: If a career, salaried member of the espionage community makes a statement, he is very possibly lying. (That's his talent and his job).

8: There may be some evidence which is covered up by law enforcement out of sheer embarrassment and nothing more.

9: *Cui Bono?* This is Latin for "Who Benefits."

10: Follow the money.

A SUGGESTED LIST OF THE 10 BEST ASSASSINATION BOOKS,
ALPHABETICAL BY AUTHOR

Me & Lee, by Judyth Vary Baker

Above The Law, by James Boyd

General Walker and The Murder Of President Kennedy, by Jeffrey Caulfield, MD

The Ordeal of Otto Otepka, by William J. Gill

Dope, Inc.: The Book That Drove Henry Kissinger Crazy, by David Goldman and Jeffrey Steinberg

Farewell, America, by James Hepburn

JFK: The CIA, Vietnam and the Plot to Assassinate John F Kennedy, by Fletcher Prouty

The Man Who Knew Too Much, by Dick Russell

Brothers in Arms: The Kennedys, the Castros, and the Politics of Murder, by Gus Russo and Stephen Molton

The New Germany and the Old Nazis, by T H Tetens

For further reading, the "Hearings on the Censure of Thomas Dodd" (1966) published by the U.S. Senate are must reading and available for free on hathitrust.org.

The Dog-Whistle Books

One category of books, about which you won't read anywhere else but here, are the dog-whistle books.

What in the world are the dog-whistle books, you might ask? These will be so-called because there were people back in 1964-1969 who knew who murdered JFK. There were more than a few. The problem for these people was naked fear. As graphically illustrated in the book *Hit List*, there were over 100 witnesses in the JFK case who were murdered, most of them with impunity in broad daylight.

The most famous of these was investigative journalist Dorothy Kilgallen. Dorothy's name was a household work back in the 50's and 60's. She was as well-known to TV viewers as Oprah Winfrey or Judge Judy are today. Dorothy was the only person lucky enough (or unlucky enough) to be allowed to interview Jack Ruby in total privacy. But Dorothy spoke out of school a little too loudly. When she did that, she was dead by sundown and her notes were stolen. And notes that she had given to a friend were also stolen.

Having been witness to the Kilgallen tragedy, other authors or journalists were loath to publish what they knew or found out about the assassination. But then a facet of human nature began to emerge.

Many people on the fringes of the assassination information were, by definition, narcissistic. If you're close to people who would perpetrate or condone the murder of an elected President, your character might be in question. But these narcissistic people realized that they knew something that could make their name famous in a small way, down through the ages. So the dog-whistle book was invented.

Authors like William J. Gill or James Boyd who wrote on the subject of Otto Otepka and Thomas J. Dodd, respectively, figured out that they could write all the facts they knew about the assassination without actually mentioning it. The only way anyone would know what they were doing so, was when the facts eventually came out. Then they would be credited (and be famous). Another way a dog-whistle book is discovered is when a researcher discovers that the author had to know about the assassination in order to write his book.

Here is a partial list of the dog-whistle books familiar to this author.

Washington Through a Purple Veil, by Lindy Boggs

Above The Law, by James Boyd

The Ordeal of Otto Otepka, by William J. Gill

The Case Against Congress, by Drew Pearson and Jack Anderson

Despoilers of Democracy, by Clark Mollenhoff

Self-Destruct: Dismantling America's Internal Security, by Robert Morris

Note:

Hit List: An In-Depth Investigation into the Mysterious Deaths of Witnesses to the JFK Assassination (2016) by Richard Belzer and David Wayne

Chapter 4

A Statement Of The Facts In Dealey Plaza 11-22-63

THE IMPORTANCE OF THE BASIC FACTS

This is the first step in looking at the JFK case. It should be said at the outset that mention of military intelligence is not intended to impugn the honor of the loyal military officers present in Dealey Plaza. There could be many explanations for their activities, none of which would necessarily point to their individual guilt in the murder.

DALLAS, NOVEMBER 1963:

On November 22, 1963, President John F. Kennedy and his wife Jackie Kennedy visited Dallas. The primary purpose of the trip was to travel in an open car in a motorcade through the City of Dallas so that thousands of people would come out to see the President. If successful, this would enhance his standing with the voters of Dallas.

The motorcade would pass through an open area known as Dealey Plaza. A small map of the motorcade route appeared on the cover of the *Dallas Morning News* before the assassination. There is a question as to whether that map actually showed Houston and Elm Streets where the shooting occurred. However, a contention by prosecutor Jim Garrison that the route was changed at the last minute, does not appear to be supported by evidence.

From Dealey Plaza, the motorcade would continue on to the Dallas Trade Mart where Kennedy was scheduled to speak to an assembled audience. Riding in the middle jump-seat directly in front of President Kennedy was Texas Governor John Connally. Vice-President Lyndon Johnson had argued forcefully for Texas Senator Ralph Yarbrough to take that position but he was overruled by the President. Vice-President Lyndon Johnson was in an open car several cars behind Kennedy. LBJ's car was, however, close to the Texas Schoolbook Depository when the shots were fired.

The proposed motorcade route had been driven ahead of time on November 14 by Secret Service Agents Winston Lawson and Forrest Sorrels. After doing that, they met regarding security with Chief of Police Jesse E.

Curry, Assistant Chief Charles Batchelor, Deputy Chief N. T. Fisher and several other officers.

Deputy Chief George L. Lumpkin also contributed in planning the security arrangements. The major security issues were; first, what area of Dallas would be brought under security and what would be the levels, and which agency would be providing the security in the various locations. A sub-category of the security plan would be whether the windows of the tall buildings along the motorcade would be watched. This would include making sure all windows were closed and that there were no guns protruding from a window.

There were two particularly dangerous issues regarding the security plan. First, any sort of warehouse-type building is considered a special threat to a motorcade, because there would likely be no workers in any one place at any particular moment.

The second major issue is that of the "dog-leg" turn. The Secret Service Manual specifically forbade a motorcade turn in the road greater than 90 degrees. This is because a very sharp angle would require the limousines to slow to a crawl, thus making the occupants sitting targets.

The motorcade passed in front of a warehouse-type building, the Texas School Book Depository. And the turn from Houston Street onto Elm Street directly in front of the TSBD was 120 degrees.

When the motorcade departed the airport, the order was as follows: 1) the pilot car, 2) the lead car, 3) the Presidential car, 4) the Presidential follow-up car, 5) the Vice Presidential car, 6) the Vice Presidential follow-up car 7) other cars—press, dignitaries, buses and others.

Other anomalies in the security plan were such items as the formation of the motorcycles surrounding the Presidential car. Normally, the motorcycle escort would surround the Presidential limo. Instead, the motorcycle officers formed completely behind the Presidential limo. The press-pool car was normally very near the front of Presidential motorcades to facilitate pictures. In Dallas, the press-pool car was six cars behind the Presidential limousine.

There were more anomalies such as the question as to which agencies would be providing what coverage and where? The Dallas Police and the Secret Service were providing the coverage. The Dallas Police area of coverage ended at the intersection just before the motorcade entered Dealey Plaza. Other than the Secret Service agents riding in the motorcade, there were no agents in Dealey Plaza nor was any agency officially providing security in Dealey Plaza.

The Dallas Sheriff's Department building was located overlooking Dealey Plaza. In fact, the prisoners in the County Sheriff's building were able to watch the motorcade from the jail windows. However, the Sheriff's department was strictly instructed *not* to provide security for the

President of any kind. Immediately following the shooting, though, they went into action confiscating film and cameras, and identifying and even detaining witnesses.

There is a conflict in the facts regarding the role of Military Intelligence and security. Whenever there is a Presidential visit within the area covered by a Military Intelligence post, the members of the unit report to the location of the visit to augment the resources of the Secret Service.

In his book *JFK: The CIA, Vietnam, and the plot to Assassinate John F. Kennedy,* Col. Fletcher Prouty states that the 112th Military Intelligence unit at Fort Sam Houston in San Antonio were ordered to stand down and not to participate in the security. (There is not corroboration of this, however).

The sequence of the cars in the motorcade was as follows:

Pilot Car	Dallas Police Homicide Detective Billy L. Senkel
	Dallas Police Homicide Detective F.M. Turner
	Deputy Chief George L. Lumpkin, driver
	Lieutenant Colonel George Whitmeyer
Lead Car	Dallas police Chief Jesse Curry, driver
	SS Agent Forrest Sorrels
	SS Agent Winston Lawson
	Dallas County Sheriff J.E. Decker
Presidential Limousine S.S.	S.S. Agent William Greer, driver
	Agent Roy Kellerman
	Governor and Mrs. John Connally
	President and Mrs. John Kennedy
Presidential Protection	Special Agent Kinney
	Asst. Special Agent A. Roberts
	Asst. Special Agent McIntyre
	Asst. Special Agent Ready
	Asst. Special Agent Landis
	S.S. Agent Clint Hill
	Presidential Aide Kenny O'Donnell
	Presidential Aide Dave Powers

In Peter Dale Scott's, *Deep Politics and the Death of JFK,* at page 257, Scott describes a meeting between three members of related Federal Agencies on the morning of November 22, 1963. The parties present were Frank Ellsworth(ATF), Agent, James Hosty (FBI) and Ed Coyle, an Army Intelligence agent. Scott speculates, and this author would agree, that this meeting was somehow related to the suppressed context of certain events relating to the Oswald firearms.

James Hosty was Ellsworth's regular FBI contact for Ellsworth's duties in the ATF. Hosty was also the FBI agent who was monitoring Lee and Marina Oswald up until the assassination. The meeting lasted until 45 minutes prior to 12:30 P.M., the time of the shooting.

In addition, Deputy Police Chief George Lumpkin and Ed Coyle both worked at least as reservists with military intelligence. The third such member of Military Intelligence was James W. Powell.

Powell and Ellsworth were both inside the TSBD after it was quickly sealed following the shooting.

When the motorcade traveled through most of downtown Dallas before entering Dealey Plaza, many of the employees of the TSBD went out on their lunch hour to watch the President pass by.

After turning onto Houston Street and then turning onto Elm, and after a few hundred feet, there were at least three shots, (many said four). The timing of the alleged fourth shot would have been in between the other three. There was a first shot, a possible second shot and then the last two shots. Most witnesses said the last two shots were very close together. Six witnesses saw a person or persons in the right-most sixth floor window, several also saw a protruding rifle. About half of the witnesses in Dealey Plaza looked or ran toward the TSBD. The remainder ran toward a rising park-like location, henceforth known as the "Grassy Knoll."

The first shot hit President Kennedy in the throat. Another shot struck him in the back. A third struck Governor Connally, passing through his chest from the rear and then wounding him in the wrist.

The final shot that hit President Kennedy was the devastating head shot, which apparently hit him from the front, knocking him backwards into the lap of his wife. The head shot took out a significant portion of his brain. The brain matter was scattered in a sort of mist that covered much of the area to the rear of the limousine.

There was a witness who was a combat veteran standing near the motorcade. On hearing the noise made by the rifle or rifles, he immediately fell to the ground. He knew the sound was that of a high-powered rifle. Governor Connally, a hunter, said later that he recognized the noise as that of a rifle. Every Secret Service agent riding in the motorcade, though, stated that he thought the sound to be that of firecrackers.

In rounding the corner on to Elm Street, the motorcade slowed to an estimated eleven m.p.h. Although the Presidential limousine was equipped with a powerful engine and although the Secret Service driver is trained to gun the powerful engine upon hearing shots, the reaction to the sounds of the gunfire produced the opposite result. The Presidential limousine, if anything, slowed down. And the driver, S.S. Agent William Greer turned, after the first shot, to look at Kennedy. Then after the later shots, he turned again to observe Kennedy.

According to some observations, at the time of the fatal head shot, the brake lights of the limousine were on.

On a decorative concrete pedestal not thirty feet from the limousine, amateur photographer Abraham Zapruder was taking an 8 mm movie of the entire assassination using his new Bell and Howell camera. The entire sequence of the movie lasted about twenty seconds. Wikipedia says 26.6 seconds.

The order of the shots described above may not be accurately known. An apparent fourth shot hit a curb to the left of the limousine. Since that curb shot went 20 or 30 feet away from the limousine, missing the entire street, it probably could not have come from either the TSBD or the Grassy Knoll. If you stretch a line back from where that shot hit the curb, past the point where the President's head would have been, and continue that path in a straight line, that line leads to the second floor of a building facing Dealey Plaza called the Dal-Tex building. Police quickly arrested a person in the lobby of that building. The person in question, known as Eugene Hale Brading (a/k/a Braden) had ties to organized crime and other assassination-related people. The actual participation of Brading, however is not supported by direct evidence.

In a Military Intelligence memo to M.I. headquarters in San Antonio, dated 11-27-63, an M.I. agent named Lt. Colonel Robert Jones reported certain facts to San Antonio. Jones had learned these facts from an unnamed M.I. source in Dallas. The source had gotten these facts through the Dallas Police.

"On November 20 last, the Dallas Police sighted two unknown men sighting in a rifle near scene where President was assassinated. Rifle being sighted in at two silhouette targets. Old model car seen in vicinity of men. Police circled to contact men and they disappeared."

The memo was from SAC San Antonio, addressed to the FBI Director and the FBI Special Agent in Charge in Dallas. This memo in its original can be viewed at the following website, viewed on March 18, 2015 at the maryferrell.org website.

The maryferrell site document is headed "FBI 62-109060 JFK HQ File, Section 12" which is the key to the location of the file in the actual archive.

The above detailed citation is provided to the reader because of the fact that this document seems to decide the issue of the "grassy knoll" and whether there were shooters there.

It would be an understatement to say this memo is of great significance and it raises the following issues:

1. Virtually all police reports concerning a crime include at least some type of description of the suspects, such as "white males," "dressed in tee shirts," etc.

2. Why would the *two* men be sighting one rifle at *two* silhouette targets, if they intended to kill just one person, i.e. the President? One of them could have been merely an assistant. Were they out to kill not one person, but two?

3. This memo argues against the commonly held theory that assassins slipped into the country and then afterward slipped immediately out.

4. The memo also belies the theory that the Oswald accomplices were professional killers. Professional killers wouldn't foolishly expose themselves to capture in this way unless the complicity of the Dallas police was so widespread that they had no fear of arrest.

5. Why would either the Dallas Police or Military Intelligence pass along this story? Either (a) they had no inkling yet that the lone gunman theory was to be mandatory or (b) they were trying to distance themselves from any accusations of complicity. The fact that the report went from Dallas Police to Military Intelligence suggests that lower-ranking policemen were trying to bypass their superiors with this information.

6. If the story were merely an invention, why did any of the authorities want to raise the issue of two possible intended victims?

7. Is it normal, to"sight" a rifle, in this way? Does one have to go to the scene of a future shooting for sighting? Do hunters have to go out into the woods where the deer live in order to sight a rifle to shoot them? Your author has no knowledge which would resolve this question.

8. Where were these alleged cardboard targets placed? Was it in the middle of the street where Kennedy's limo would be driven? Wouldn't this activity draw more attention than just the Dallas Police? Wouldn't there be any number of drivers who would have seen men doing this by the roadside, and be likely to recall this event after the assassination?

9. If the Dallas Police had detained anyone on the grassy knoll sighting rifles wouldn't there be witnesses to this who would come forward after the assassination?

This story of the sighting of the rifles could have been created as a false narrative to further the assassination plan. It could be an invention of either military intelligence or the Dallas Police. This could be an effort in disinformation, not unlike the apparent phony Oswald sightings and impersonations prior to November 22. But on balance, this report seems more likely to be true and accurately reported.

At the moment of the assassination, the Dallas Police immediately sealed off the TSBD within only 90 seconds of the shooting. There was a story started or invented by someone, to the effect that Mr. Roy Truly, the manager at the TSBD, lined up all the employees. So the story went, there was only one employee missing. That employee was Lee Harvey Oswald. This story is false. As mentioned above, there were at least 20 to 30 employees who were outside the building when it was sealed off. They never returned to work according to interviews with these employees themselves. Further, the TSBD contained not only the business of the book distribution, but several offices of book publishers with employees who did not work for Mr. Truly in the distribution of textbooks.

Since the President had been killed in front of their eyes, most people would conclude that there would probably not be much work done that afternoon. One employee, however, did leave the TSBD in a different direction and that was Lee Harvey Oswald.

According to a later reconstruction, it is theorized that Oswald traveled from the TSBD to the rooming house where he lived on foot, then by hiring a cab, then by a public bus. Stopping at the rooming house to pick up a revolver, he then headed for the Texas Theater. On the way, it was alleged that Oswald shot and killed a Dallas policeman named J.D. Tippit.

After Oswald sneaked into the theater without paying and sat down to watch the movie, the police entered the theater and apprehended him after a scuffle.

The movements of Oswald can be explained as follows: LHO knew that after the assassination, he would likely be killed "resisting arrest" even if he did not actually resist. For this reason, he picked up his revolver to protect himself from such a fate. Next, he went to the Texas Theater because, if he were apprehended there, the Police would have so many witnesses that foul play on their part would be impossible.

Lee Harvey Oswald had been an employee of the TSBD for only a few weeks. The morning of the assassination, he rode to work with a friend and co-worker named Buell Wesley Frazier. In the car that morning, Oswald carried a package which he stated were curtain rods. The authorities speculated that this package contained Oswald's disassembled rifle.

When one traces the hypothetical movement of Oswald from the sixth floor window, down the stairs and into the lunchroom where he was placed by various employees, it is questionable whether Oswald could have moved that fast.

The first policeman into the TSBD entered about 90 seconds after the shooting. His name was Marrion L. Baker. The following information was taken from his testimony before the Warren Commission.

Officer Baker quickly met up with Roy Truly, the building manager, to search the building. The two men immediately encountered Oswald in the second floor lunchroom drinking a bottle of pop from a vending machine in the lunch room. Truly informed Officer Baker that Oswald was an employee, so the two resumed their search. The Officer apparently assumed that the shooter would not have been an employee.

Baker and Truly continued on up the stairway for an unknown number of floors. Then they entered an elevator and took it up as far as it would go which has been described as being the fifth floor. Then they walked up some more stairs and onto the roof. Apparently Officer Baker was thinking that the shooting would most likely have come from the rooftop.

However, in this initial ascension of the stairs and elevator, somehow the 6th floor was skipped entirely. The progress was from the 5th to the roof which was the 7th.

The 6th floor was the floor from which the shots were fired.

In some manner or other, the sixth floor was allegedly later searched and the authorities found a "sniper's nest" there. This nest was a semi-circle of 50 pound book boxes, stacked several layers high, thus obstructing a view of the suspect window from elsewhere on the floor. The extreme difficulty of stacking these boxes in a short time was demonstrated as part of a private research investigation. Further, there was no time for Oswald to do the stacking. And finally, there would have been no purpose, since Oswald was allegedly alone when the shooting took place. If he weren't, he would surely have encountered the other persons on the floor with him.

The next problem is the rifle.

The rifle, and indeed both of Oswald's purported weapons are key to the solution of the assassination events. There is no agreement in the evidence of exactly where and when the Oswald rifle was discovered. The best information has it being found on the 4th floor. Oswald would not have had time to make a separate stop on the 4th floor.

The rifle was initially identified as a German 7.65 Mauser. This identification was made by the law enforcement officers, considered to be their best experts. The actual brand of the alleged murder weapon, according to the Warren Commission was a 6.5 Mannlicher-Carcano Italian-made war surplus weapon.

The Mannlicher-Carcano was a bolt action rifle, but it accepted a clip of 4 bullets. Oswald was alleged to have attempted the assassination with only four bullets in his possession. The last of the 4 bullets was found still in the firing chamber. But it was claimed that the rifle still had the clip *attached* when it was discovered.

The problem is that with this Mannlicher-Carcano, after the final bullet enters the chamber, the clip is automatically ejected. But no empty clip was ever reported to be found.

There is a photograph which shows an officer holding up the rifle and it has no clip. However, there is another photo which shows the clip still attached. Apparently, the rifle as preserved in the evidence archives today has no clip.

Another problem with the story of the rifle is the assembly and dis-assembly process. The breaking down of the rifle required tools. No tools were found. At some point it was stated the Oswald used a dime for a screwdriver. There has never been any proof of whether this is even possible, or how long it would take to accomplish. We will leave the major questions relating to the purchase of Oswald's weapons to a later chapter.

Some of the remaining facts of importance include the shooting of Officer Tippit. The type of revolver allegedly used by Oswald to kill the policeman has an enlarged barrel. This type of barrel makes it impossible to match the bullets which killed Tippit to the gun of Oswald. All the witnesses except one failed to identify Oswald as the killer of Tippit. That one witness had changed her story from her original version. One witness saw two men flee the scene. There were four bullets found at the scene of the shooting of Tippit. Two of the four were of one brand, the other two of another brand. And the shell casings were three of one brand and one of another.

Notes:

The book by Col. Prouty which will be cited many times is referenced as: *JFK: The CIA, Vietnam, and the plot to Assassinate John F. Kennedy*, Col. Fletcher Prouty.

The following book by Scott is referenced in Chapter 4. It is cited as *Deep Politics and the Death of JFK*, by Peter Dale Scott at page 257. Scott is perhaps the leading author when it comes to exploring the true facts of such events as the JFK Assassination, the 9-11 attacks and similar subjects.

Since the reader may have difficulty in even believing that this intelligence memo actually exists, the following citation information can be used by the reader to confirm the information therein: In a Military Intelligence memo to M.I. headquartes in San Antonio, dated 11-27-63, [xxwww.mary-ferrell.org/mffweb/archive/viewer/showDoc.do?docId=62262&relPageId=83] FBI 62-109060 JFK HQ File, Section 12."

Chapter 5

THE FACTS SURROUNDING THE PRISONER OSWALD

THE SITUATION IMMEDIATELY AFTER THE SHOOTING

After the shooting, President Kennedy was driven to Parkland Hospital where, after attempted futile treatment, he was pronounced dead at 1:00 P.M. His body was placed in a casket. There was a disagreement between the Secret Service and the Dallas Police as to where the autopsy would be conducted. By Texas law, the autopsy of any homicide victim must be done by the Coroner in Dallas.

The Secret Service, however, acting under orders from the new President and other federal officials, took the body to the airport. The body was placed aboard Air Force One and flown back to Washington along with President Johnson and the widow, Mrs. Kennedy.

The autopsy was conducted at Bethesda Naval Hospital by military doctors. There were discrepancies regarding the autopsy. First, there was a break in the chain of custody of the body. This resulted in uncertainty about the whereabouts of the body from the time of unloading from Air Force One to the time when the autopsy began. The caskets had been changed.

The description of the wounds differed between those observed by the doctors in Parkland Hospital in Dallas and those observed by the autopsy doctors. Although it is a universal practice with gunshot victims to trace the trajectory of the bullets through the body, this was not done. There was a dispute within the military team as to who was ordering particular steps in the autopsy due to rank and position. Finally, there was inconsistency between the autopsy photos and the diagrams and notes included in the evidence. If the autopsy was faked in any way, many believe this would have been done out of a concern for national security. There may have even been a plan for such a fake autopsy if circumstances required it due to a national emergency.

OSWALD ARRESTED.

Following his arrest, Oswald was taken to the Dallas Police department for processing and held in the jail for interrogation. The case was under the supervision of Detective Will Fritz of the Dallas Police.

As reported at "www.archives.gov/research/jfk/warren-commission-report/chapter-5.html#interrogation," the following took place:

During the period between 2:30 P.M. Friday (11-22-63) and 11:15 P.M. Sunday morning (11-24-63), Oswald was interrogated for a total of approximately 12 hours, 30 minutes. That broke down to seven hours on Friday, three hours on Saturday during three interrogation sessions and on Sunday less than two hours. All took place in the office of Captain Will Fritz.

Those present included Dallas detectives, investigators from the FBI and Secret Service and occasionally other officials, particularly a post office inspector and a U.S. Marshall.

In all more than 25 different persons participated in or were present at some time during the interrogations. There was no tape recording, although there was a room next door entirely outfitted with tape recording equipment used to interrogate suspects. The was no stenographer or court reporter. The only records are the notes kept by the participants.

During 8 hours on Friday and up to 8 hours on Saturday, Oswald was being stalked inside the crowded corridors of the 3rd floor where he was being held and interrogated. Jack Ruby, a local strip club operator was there during those periods. He was carrying a gun and was twice in the same room as Oswald. Once he even tried to force his way into Fritz's office where Oswald was being interrogated.

On Sunday morning, 11-24-63, Oswald was brought to the basement parking garage in the police station where a car was waiting to transfer him to the County Jail. Although the time of the transfer was first announced as 10:00 A.M., it was delayed until 11:20 A.M. At exactly 11:20, Jack Ruby walked into the parking garage, approached Oswald who was manacled, and shot him in the abdomen. It appears that the transport of Oswald was delayed from 10:00 A.M. to 11:20 A.M. because the police were coordinating with Ruby. Oswald was held until Ruby was present at 11:20 A.M. to kill him.

The FBI, the Dallas Sheriff's Department as well as the Dallas Police all received anonymous telephone calls prior to the transport warning that Oswald would be killed that day.

Chapter 6

Baron George DeMohrenschildt, The Parasite Pretender

Next to Lee Oswald, Baron George de Mohrenschildt is the most widely acknowledged obvious participant in the plot to assassination John F. Kennedy.

Most of the basic facts about de Mohrenschildt are widely known, in part because of the intense interest in him raised by the Warren Commission and the House Select Committee on Assassinations.

Background on George de Mohrenschildt

There have been at least three serious books on George de Mohrenschildt just in the past two or three years. One is de Mohrenschildt's own brief autobiography edited by Michael Rinella. Rinella is one the nation's leading experts on de Mohrenschildt. Another is a detailed biography by Nancy Wertz Weiford which is 786 pages full of details on de Mohrenschildt. Both books display impeccable scholarship on this very crucial subject. A third biography of George de Mohrenschildt is by author Joan Mellen who, as has been mentioned, has also written about the Jim Garrison investigation.

Most dedicated assassination buffs could almost recite the biography of George de Mohrenschildt off the top of their heads. One could say that there has been overkill on the subject of de Mohrenschildt. Yet he pops up in these pages as one of our three Barons.

De Mohrenschildt sometimes called himself a Baron, but technically, in the world of Baronies, only the eldest brother inherits the right to the title. (This whole topic sounds outdated, but for our purposes, it must be taken seriously). George was not the eldest brother. Therefore he was not a Baron. Case closed.

But it takes some patience to analyze this. For many people walking this planet, even at the late date of this writing, this stuff matters (and God knows why). For JFK, these theories of Barons, Counts, Princesses and all the rest produced a fatal result. One could easily argue that JFK literally got his brains blown out based on outdated theories that belong in *Grimm Fairy Tales*.

George de Mohrenschildt was born on April 17, 1911 in Mozyr, which is near Minsk; both cities today lie in the nation of Belarus. The de Mohrenschildt family had a hodge-podge of ethnicities. His father was of German, Swedish and Russian descent. His mother was of Polish, Russian and Hungarian descent. Of course, then, as now, the boundaries of all those countries were in a state of flux, depending on the vagaries of wars and treaties. Back in Europe, prior to his immigration to the U.S., George and the rest of his family were known as von Mohrenschildt, not de Mohrenschildt. When George arrived in the U.S. in 1938, he made the change from "von" to the French "de." Per biographer Weiford, it was the case that, technically, only George's older brother Dimitri could use the prefix "von" because that signified Baron. But what did the others in the family use? Nothing? This does not seem clear and there are many, many people in the U.S. and elsewhere whose names include "von" and they can't all be Barons. So what are the real facts on this question? To this writer, it is still an unknown and probably irrelevant. We will next sharpen our perspective on George de Mohrenschildt by applying the scissors of analysis to the de Mohrenschildt biography, *Faux Baron* by Nancy Wertz Weiford.

There has always been deception when experts discuss George de Mohrenschildt. There is deception regarding his politics. There is deception regarding his alleged connection to the CIA. There is deception about the reasons for his famed "walking tour" through Mexico and Central America. There is deception about his role in Haiti.

Author Weiford begins her explanation of the politics of de Mohrenschildt by describing the politics of his wealthy father, Sergius de Mohrenschildt. At the time of the last Czars of Russia, the de Mohrenschildt family was in St. Petersburg Russia where George's uncle Petro Ludwig von Mohrenschildt was appointed Charge' d'affairs for the eastern one-quarter of the city of St. Petersburg. This was a lofty position which was granted under the reign of Czar Nicholas II.

George's father Sergius was made Governor of the Province of Minsk under a commission also granted by Czar Nicholas II. In his position as Governor, Sergius also served as an elected representative of landholders of the region. Author Weiford writes: "[Sergius] von Mohrenschildt was torn between the desires for personal freedoms [of the peasants] and the benefit of being a part of the court hierarchy."

This seems to be a questionable statement. Even in the U.S., when voting was done by landowners as such, the voting is typically weighted by acreage, not *per capita*. Real estate taxes are levied by the value of the holdings, not *per capita*. Even if Sergius were elected, it is unlikely that the large landowners and the small landowners had an equal vote. The picture painted by Weiford is of George's father leading a mob of peasants with pitchforks, demanding their rights from the Czar. Not!

George's father Sergius came into possession of a very large estate of about 6000 acres in Poliese which is now in Belarus. This estate had been both in Poland at times, and in Belarus at other times, depending on the results of war and treaties. But even before the Communists took charge, the 6000-acre estate had been divided up among landless peasants. The central quest for the de Mohrenschildt family, for the rest of the lives of Sergius and George, was to try and reacquire that 6000-acre estate. And, failing that, to have day dreams about it when they should have been working at a regular job.

The importance of this quest to the JFK case can't be overemphasized. If you own such an estate, and it is farmed by hundreds of serfs or peasants: *You don"t have to work. The peasants do the work.* The landowners can just go to parties, collect artwork, and eat bon-bons.

To American sensibilities, this concept is the very picture of a degenerate, parasitic lifestyle. In the U.S. (in the antebellum South), there were the plantations and slaveholders. But the slaveholders had to work hard. It is not easy to spend your days whipping slaves, I'm sure. And then sometimes, you have to chop off their foot so they can't run away. That's work, too. But for the de Mohrenschildt family, as estate holders, this author understands the situation of the de Mohrenschildt estate as being somewhat different for them when compared to Southern slave-owners on their plantations in the U.S.

The first difference was that all the European landowners had titles. George de Mohrenschildt considered himself a Baron, even though technically he was not. Even if he lost the estate, which he did, that title of Baron was like a little card in his pocket which he could carry with him. This portable card entitled him to either get back his estate, or a similar estate or some other equivalent special perk should the Czar or Kaiser or some similar regime ever be re-established in his homeland.

If one wishes to understand the JFK assassination, one *cannot* spend too much time on grasping this reality. This system of titled nobility was thankfully destroyed in the U.S. in 1776. But in Dallas, Texas, in 1963, it was alive and well in the minds of parasites like de Mohrenschildt and other "White Russians" who had settled there. According to the theory of the divine right of kings, God picked the Czar and the Czar picked the de Mohrenschildts. Simple as that. God really liked the Czar and he also, obviously, liked the de Mohrenschildt's because the Czar liked them. As for the rest of us, not so much. To us, God was indifferent.

For the White Russians of Dallas, beloved by God and the Czar, these theories and this lust for the idle, parasitic lifestyle justified complicity in the murder of a President. After all, John F. Kennedy was elected by the American people, but he wasn't picked by God. Only the Czar, Kaiser Wilhelm and the others were picked by God. So believed both Baron Charles A. Willoughby and Baron George de Mohrenschildt. As for Baron Wernher von Braun, he was too busy working and sending the first man to the moon to think about it.

Dimitri, the older brother of George de Mohrenschildt, immigrated to the U.S. in 1922, having landed first in Vancouver, British Columbia. Upon arriving in American, Dimitri for some unknown reason was able to rocket to the top of U.S. society. In the same year he arrived, 1922, he was able to enter Yale as a freshman. He was then able to join the Yale Elizabethan Club and the Yale Literary Magazine. This was pretty incredible for a young man who just gotten off the boat. He had no family in the U.S. who would have been able to make an arrangement like this which allowed him to waltz into Yale. Again, this is a hint of the sinister, under-the-table network at play for these Czarist pretenders in the U.S. Apparently, Dimitri went straight to Skull and Bones, (did not pass go, did not pay $200).

Both George and his father Sergius, because they had lived in Poland for the necessary ten years, had become Polish citizens. George had become part of the Polish Cavalry to fulfill his duty of military service as a citizen of Poland. His father Sergius had been jailed by the Bolsheviks (bad luck for a liberal like him). George attended school in Poland, graduating from the Gymnasium in 1929 and the Polish Cavalry academy in 1931.

George went on to get a degree from the University of Liege in Belgium, writing a thesis on the influence of the U.S. in Latin America. Conceivably, he could have studied this subject anticipating entry to the U.S. as a spy. As things turned out, from the 1940's to the 1960's, he bounced between the U.S. and Latin America. Many people believe he did this in the role of a spy, working for German interests, Nazis or their close associates.

After completing his studies, he traveled around Europe. While traveling, he filed journalistic pieces about, among other things, the Spanish Civil War (which lasted from 1936 to 1939). According to Weiford, he had contacts for those stories who were fighting on the side of Franco. Franco was the eventual winner of the Spanish Civil War. He was a fascist dictator and a close ally of Hitler and Mussolini during that time.

George arrived in the U.S. in May 1938. British Intelligence informed the U.S. authorities that George was working for German (Nazi) Intelligence. To summarize these allegations of spying, one only needs to know that he was repeatedly stopped, searched, investigated many times by the FBI, the INS and other assorted law enforcement agencies during the wartime period. Every single person in every agency came to the same conclusion: George was, at best, a Nazi sympathizer, or more likely a German spy.

Author Weiford attempts to blame this fact on the idea that J. Edgar Hoover was a prejudiced person, and he was persecuting George because of his German-sounding accent. A suggested reading for anyone interested in this question would be two books on the subject of the FBI during

World War II by former FBI agent Raymond J. Batvinis: *Hoover's Secret War Against Axis Spies: FBI Counterespionage During World War II* and *The Origins of FBI Counterintelligence*. These scholarly books, published by the University Press of Kansas, leave no doubt whatever that J. Edgar Hoover was an excellent law enforcement official, conscientious to a fault, at least during this period. It is unclear why Weiford would want to cover for George by dismissing an opinion voiced by J. Edgar Hoover without justification. Personally, it seems obvious to your author that George was a German spy at some level or other.

A lot of biographical details about George de Mohrenschildt can be skipped because almost all of them are a distraction from the basic issues. Those basic issues are: first, George's personality; second, his loyalties and third, his motivations. If those are discovered, all the rest falls right into place.

It is well known by JFK buffs that George and his brother Dimitri were connected to the Bouvier family, JFK's in-laws. Jackie Bouvier Kennedy Onassis knew George de Mohrenschildt as "Uncle George" while she was still a grade-school girl. Also, Dimitri de Mohrenschildt had a roommate relationship with a connection to George H.W. Bush. Dimitri also married into an indirect relationship to the Rockefeller family through in-law relatives called the Hookers.

THE NAZI CONNECTION AND GEORGE DE MOHRENSCHILDT

In late 1940, George attended a showing of a "daring" documentary shown at the Ritz-Carlton in New York. It was a film produced by his supposed cousin named Berend Rudoph Konstantin Maydell or Count Maydell. Although Maydell is classified as a fifth cousin according to some, author Mellen writes that Maydell was of no relation at all to the de Mohrenschildts.

The film was called "Spain in Arms" and it glorified the Spanish Civil War, sympathizing with the Franco victory. This film was produced by a company called Film Facts, Inc. The film had a musical score, sound effects and narration and had been showing in cities across the U.S. Sounds expensive. According to JFK researcher John Bevilaqua, Count Konstantin was a spy who was working for a Nazi German Intelligence Chief, General Reinhard Gehlen, who himself was a high officer in the Nazi Abwehr or spy community. Interestingly, Gehlen, throughout the War, served on the Eastern Front.

The connection between de Mohrenschildt and this film raises more questions than it answers. First, why was George viewing a pro-fascist propaganda film in the first place? Did he have pro-fascist friends who invited him? The film was being shown at the Ritz-Carlton, so this implies that there were wealthy pro-fascists who arranged for this showing.

Author Mellen writes that the Film Facts company was organized by Pierpont Morgan Hamilton, a grandson of J. Pierpont Morgan. This raises an explosion of contradictions. In her description, Mellen describes Film Facts, Inc. as struggling financially and thus suggests that Pierpont Morgan Hamilton was a financial fly-by-night like de Mohrenschildt. Actually, per Wikipedia, Pierpont Morgan Hamilton was a well regarded WW I pilot for the Army Air Service. He was described as the scion of the Alexander Hamilton-descended family as well as the J.P. Morgan family.

Between the Wars he was an international banker, presumably either with J.P. Morgan or with Morgan contacts. J.P. Morgan was considered the exclusive international bank for Great Britain. It is extremely unlikely that Pierpont Morgan Hamilton would have deliberately affiliated himself with a Nazi spy like Maydell. In fact, early in 1942, Hamilton went back into active duty with the U.S. Army Air Corps. His immediate assignment was in Air Corps Intelligence as liaison with the Royal Air Force.

If Hamilton had worked with Nazi spy Maydell through Film Facts, Inc. then Film Facts, Inc. could very well have been a front corporation for the British SOE under Sir William Stephenson. The British would have been trying to ensnare Nazi spy Maydell, in which they apparently succeeded.

But let's look at the role in this of George de Mohrenschildt. De Mohrenschildt was in the U.S. as a Polish citizen with a resident visa as a Pole. His biographers report that, after seeing the film by Maydell, he wanted to do the same sort of thing. So he contacted the Polish consulate. At that time, Poland-proper was soon under occupation by Hitler. So the Polish consulate he contacted would have been the Polish Government-in-Exile, located in London, and must have been financed by the British. If there were money to be spent on propaganda films, it would have been British money.

The reporting by the biographers on the subject of the timing of this period is confusing. In the narrative about George's Polish citizenship, the fact is that at this time, Poland was being overrun by Hitler and partitioned between Germany and Russia. There is no information whatsoever as to how this affected de Mohrenschildt, either philosophically or in terms of his legal status and papers.

Biographer Mellen reports that the success of George's proposed film called "Poland Forever" was dependent on receiving footage of the actual fighting from Germany. If Poland were occupied by Hitler, then the footage must have been found somehow in occupied Poland, either the German occupied part or the part occupied by Russia. These facts involving de Mohrenschildt and the film must have happened after Poland was occupied. Otherwise, there would have been no film of the fighting involving Poland.

De Mohrenschildt's father was still living in Nazi Germany. There are some claims that his father, after the war, was recruited by post-war German intelligence. We know that post-war German intelligence was being run by either the CIA, the British SOE, General Reinhard Gehlen or a combination of these. It looks like his father may have been his contact to supply the film footage from Nazi Germany.

The film footage destined for George de Mohrenschildt from Germany was seized by British Intelligence before it arrived in the U.S. All of this makes it look like British Intelligence considered de Mohrenschildt to be in the same category as Maydell; i.e.; a Nazi spy whom they were trying to ensnare or entrap and hand over to U.S. authorities. Quoting biographer Weiford, George contacted the Polish Consulate and convinced them to finance the studio and production costs at Cine-Laboratory for a short 45 minute film to be called "Poland in Arms." Supposedly, George did all the film cutting, production, and editing for this film. Later in life, he would list this as one of the major things he had accomplished in life that could be verified and proven.

Baron von Maydell

George de Mohrenschildt told the Warren Commission that he thought that Maydell was a White Russian who thought he could get the return of his Russian estate with the help of the Germans. This sounds more like the life story of George de Mohrenschildt.

In 1942, de Mohrenschildt went traveling in the South with a woman named Lilia Larin. He stopped in Corpus Christi, Texas where he got in contact with Baron George Edward Farenthold, a local businessman. The two got together in a bar in Corpus Christi, where George was noticed loudly voicing pro-German sentiments.

From there, George traveled to Mexico with Lilia Larin. After arriving in Mexico City, he was ordered to leave Mexico by a high Mexican official. Biographer Weiford tends to blame all these security-related government actions taken against de Mohrenschildt on either romantic rivalries over a woman or the ethnic prejudices of the FBI. But where there's smoke, there's fire when it comes to the involvement of de Mohrenschildt and these allegations of Nazi spying.

After receiving his orders to leave Mexico, George was confronted by an FBI "hold" order forbidding him to re-enter the U.S. The grounds for this were that George was "a Nazi sympathizer or possibly an agent." Weiford presents this as groundless. When he finally re-entered the U.S. at Laredo, Texas, he was interviewed by Captain Mellick of the U.S. Military Intelligence Division.

J. Edgar Hoover responded to a request for information by Assistant Secretary of State Adolf Berle, Jr. about whether de Mohrenschildt should be allowed entry to the United States. This meant that the case of de Mohrenschildt had reached the very top level of the State Department. In mid-September, 1942, the Office of Military Intelligence issued a report on de Mohrenschildt which listed his associations with Carmen Barnes and Bertram Wolff, who were on security watch lists. A "refusal" or "lookout" was put on his passport file, based on a suspicion he was a Nazi agent.

George then went back to New York and re-connected with a friend by the name of Pierre Freyss who was reportedly working in the oil business and at the same time working for French Intelligence. Again, the relationship between Freyss, France and the German defeat and occupation of France is treated by biographer Weiford as if it never happened. Just as the question of the occupation of Poland is never discussed regarding George's supposed Polish citizenship, the question of whether Freyss continued with French Intelligence when France became Vichy France is never even brought up. So the issue of a French Intelligence connection on the part of de Mohrenschildt is problematic. His connection with Nazi Count Maydell is, however, quite solid.

The State Department, the FBI and the INS all conferred and they all agreed that if de Mohrenschildt ever left the U.S., he should never be allowed to return. Biographer Weiford makes the assumption that these professionals simply didn't know what they were doing and they didn't like George's German-sounding accent.

Upon returning to New York, de Mohrenschildt tried to join the OSS, but was refused, again, upon the conclusion of the investigators that he was either a Nazi sympathizer or a Nazi spy. He moved into a rooming house. Also living at the rooming house was a friend of Grace Buchanan Dineen. Grace was later convicted of espionage for Germany and sentenced to twelve years in prison. The name of this friend of Dineen was Patricia Deuel. At this time, De Mohrenschildt was again reported to the FBI by a man named Clifford Pinchot and another by the name of Pierre Haas as being a likely Nazi agent.

Returning to New York City from a temporary stay in Venezuela, he learned that his friend Baron Konstantin Maydell had been released from Ellis Island Prison by a Federal Judge after serving only four years.

In 1944, George decided he needed more schooling. The de Mohrenschildt family knew both Alexis Wirren who had started the Russian Student Fund and Alexandra Tolstoy, daughter of Leo Tolstoy, who had started the Tolstoy Foundation in 1939 to help assimilate Russians into American society. With a small stipend from these sources, George was able to enroll at the University of Texas in Austin and he then earned his master's degree in petroleum geology.

George de Mohrenschildt had petitioned to become a U.S. citizen in 1943 but his petition was only granted in 1949. After WWII he had moved to Venezuela where he worked for Pantepec Oil, a company owned by the family of William F. Buckley. It was revealed years later that Buckley was a sometime CIA agent after graduating from Yale. In 1950, George launched an oil investment firm with his step-nephew Edward Hooker (the cousin of the Rockefellers) with offices in New York City, Denver and Abilene, Texas. The Hooker connection to the Rockefellers was through George's brother Dimitri.

In May, 1946, George and his brother Dimitri attended the wedding of his Rockefeller-related nephew Edward Gordon Hooker. One of the ushers at the wedding was future U.S. President George H.W. Bush. Bush had been a close friend of Dimitri since rooming with Edward Hooker at Andover prep school.

In August, 1946, George made a move to Rangely, Colorado where he was to have the only job in his life where he achieved any degree of success and stability. Rangely was a rough, western, frontier-type of place where the oilfields were for the first time being explored and exploited. George work as a Field Engineer. In Rangely, he met William Charles "Ted" Savage who would prove to be his true (possibly best) friend for the next 30 years. Over the years, there were a large number of people that George described as close friends. But the difference between friendship and financial and other dependency, in the case of George de Mohrenschildt, is hazy.

As previously mentioned, in early 1950, George contacted Edward G. Hooker and they started an oil promotion partnership and drilled wells in the Southwest and Midwest. Also at this time he met Sam Ballen, owner of High Plains Natural Gas, who became along with Savage, an enduring long-term friend of George over the following years.

GEORGE DE MOHRENSCHILDT MOVES TO DALLAS

The next information reported by author Nancy Wertz Weiford is some of the most significant information in the entire JFK assassination literature. It has been neglected and unreported by all other researchers. She explains that in Dallas there were two Eastern Orthodox churches. The St. Nicholas Church in Dallas had been formed through a man known as Metropolitan Anastasy. Anastasy had authority over all Russians of his religion who lived outside of Russia. Its membership was limited to those Russians who were, or were descended from, escapees from the Bolsheviks. These were defined as "White Russians." The leader of this church was the well-known JFK assassination figure Paul Ragiorodsky who was probably, based on overwhelming evidence, a player in the JFK assassination.

The second church was St. Seraphim, which was formed through the Metropolitan Leonty which represented the Russian Orthodox Greek

Catholic Church in North America. The leader of this church in Dallas was George Alexandrovich Bouhe who was born in St. Petersburg, Russia in 1904. Bouhe fled Russia in 1924, becoming a U.S. citizen in 1939. Bouhe's profession was that of an accountant in Dallas.

George de Mohrenschildt was introduced into Dallas society through both Ragiorodsky and Bouhe. Author Weiford really whets the appetite of the JFK reader when she throws out this intriguing bit of information about the two Eastern Rites and the two Churches.

If the St. Nicholas Church in Dallas was made up only of "victims" of the Bolsheviks, one wonders how many people were in that Church? The church is still in existence. According to the St. Nicholas website, the church was founded in the early 1900's and "died out in the 1960's." According to researcher Jim DiEugenio, the Russian Orthodox Church was a recipient of CIA funds. Author Alan Allen reports that there were 25 families who made up the membership of St. Nicholas in Dallas. All of these families were "victims" of the Bolsheviks, (i.e. they had lost their cushy lifestyle with servants and peasants waiting on them hand and foot). So what were the sermons about each week? Probably the same topic: Joe Stalin.

So we have to add a third nest of politico-religious extremists to the list of JFK suspects. JFK researchers already know about the right-wing Protestant Evangelical extremists like Billy James Hargis and Gerald L.K. Smith who flooded the airwaves in Texas and elsewhere with religious paranoia. They were sometimes called "The Christian Fright-Peddlers." Then we also have the militant Catholic fanatics which include Joe McCarthy, Pat McCarran, Congressman Charles J. Kersten, Cardinal Spellman, the FBI-connected Father John Francis Cronin and finally, Thomas J. Dodd.

Now we can add the congregation of St. Nicholas.

In 1952, de Mohrenschildt settled in Dallas where he took a job with oilman Clint Murchison. In Dallas, he joined the Petroleum Club, joined the Dallas Council of World Affairs and taught at a local college. George's associates in Dallas included oilmen Paul Ragiorodsky, George Bouhe and Lawrence Orlov. Ragiorodsky hired George for an oil industry consulting job for a brief time, but he reportedly had a low opinion of George according to those who knew both of them.

In 1959, George married Jeanne Le Gon, who was his fourth wife. The prior three wives had not worked out well, but Jeanne Le Gon was the perfect wife for George and they stayed married for many years. From 1960 to 1961, George and Jeanne claimed to have walked 5000 miles from the Mexican Border to the Panama Canal.

What is seldom mentioned by JFK researchers is that the background of Jeanne was the heritage of the Russians from Harbin, China. In his book *The Russian Fascists*, author John J. Stephan reveals the story of An-astase Vonsiatsky of Connecticut, easily the most open and notorious White-Russian gangster ever to operate in the U.S. Vonsiatsky was from Harbin, China and author Stephan equates Russian fascism with those who came from Harbin. Why did George and Jeanne have such a won-derful relationship despite George's terrible track record as a husband? It would be fertile ground to explore, whether de Mohrenschildt's wife Jeanne had her own connection to political intrigue, independent of her marriage. This is another door which, to the knowledge of this writer, has never been opened.

In the de Mohrenschildt biographical manuscript edited by Michael Rinella, it is clear that George was only one of a succession of Oswald babysitters. He first visited Lee Harvey Oswald in the company of Col. Lawrence Orlov, a person of Russian or Polish ancestry with even closer ties to CIA agent J. Walton Moore than George and Jeanne.

We will later examine the question of whether Orlov, who had a Jew-ish wife and a Jewish father was actually deliberately involved with LHO by George in order to implicate a person of the Jewish faith, as was done in the case of Jack Ruby. Oswald had numerous babysitters in the Dal-las White Russian community (and even outside that community) in the persons of Ruth Paine and Michael Paine. J. Walton Moore was the full-time CIA representative in Dallas. Moore is a major suspect in many books on the JFK assassination, but there has never been a smoking gun discovered regarding Moore and the assassination. Over a four-year peri-od, George and his wife Jeanne had exchanged dinner engagements with Moore in each other's homes.

The rest of the story of George de Mohrenschildt is well known to JFK readers and need not be repeated here. Suffice it to say that George de Mohrenschildt scandalized people in Dallas by greeting his Jewish acquain-tances with "Heil Hitler." He once gave a speech which glorified the history of Hitler's Vlasov Army. This created a major disturbance among George's social circle in Dallas. Given his history and background, it seems beyond doubt that de Mohrenschildt was a Nazi sympathizer and certainly had some connection to Nazi Germany, either through his own connections or through his father who lived there from the 1930's until he died.

There were multiple situations involving George de Mohrenschildt that suggest he might have been on a CIA mission. One was the walk-ing tour through Mexico and Central America. George and Jeanne just happened to be in Guatemala where the CIA-funded Cuban Exiles were training for the Bay of Pigs invasion. When he returned from the walk-ing tour, he wrote up a 600-page book including information on social conditions in Central America. He tried to sell this book to the U.S. State Department.

In 1963, when JFK was looking for a plan to remove the Haitian dictator Francois Duvalier, George de Mohrenschildt was in Washington, driving around in a convertible with Clemard Charles, a Haitian who was being proposed by some as a replacement for Duvalier. Were all of these very unusual situations just co-incidences?

In the Spring of 1963, George was involved with the "backyard photos" showing Oswald with the rifle. He also was involved with the reported role of Oswald in the alleged shooting incident involving General Edwin Walker. Since there is conflicting information about whether Oswald ever even had that rifle in his possession or as to the time when he acquired it, it is possible that George was requested to lie to the authorities to some extent about the photos and the rifle.

So how do we wrap up the story of George de Mohrenschildt, as it relates to our theory of the JFK assassination?

1. An Oswald babysitting operation was run through the "White Russian," Anti-Bolshevik Bloc of Nations (ABN) or a similar connection, not directly through the FBI or the CIA. Since the St. Nicholas Church had a ready-made group of militant anti-Soviet and politically motivated people all under one roof, that may have been the connection.

2. Paul Ragiorodsky, leader of St. Nicholas is high on the list of JFK suspects and he may have been the point-man for the Oswald babysitting because of his gravitas within the oil industry, inside Dallas and with the White Russian Community there.

3. When Oswald moved from the White Russians to living with the Paines, he switched from being supervised by the White Russians to the true international Nazis through Walter Dornberger (possibly in concert with Dornberger's friend Wernher von Braun). Dornberger was the supervisor of Michael Paine at Bell Aerospace. This setup was probably masterminded by West German Intelligence Chief Reinhard Gehlen who was high up in the true Nazi network worldwide and in their role in the assassination plot. Gehlen may have masterminded the entire scheme of the assassination, at least from the European and Nazi side. Or it could have been masterminded by other Nazi cohorts, possibly in cooperation with ex-CIA Director Allen Dulles.

4. The supervision of Oswald in his alleged ordering of weapons was supervised through Senator Dodd and his SISS/Juvenile Delinquency Committee in partnership with their friends in the ATF. Alternatively, Oswald could have been acting under instructions from Roy Frankhouser/Dan Burros/National Security Council channels. Both of these would have fit a very similar pattern with the weapons

possession issue as the pretext for the contact and interactions with Oswald. Treasury Secretary C. Douglas Dillon was in charge of both the ATF and the Secret Service.

5. When Oswald was in New Orleans, he was supervised by Clay Shaw and David Ferrie, through the Catholic activist/European Permindex/Dr. Alton Ochsner connections. Alternatively, when in New Orleans, Oswald could have been acting as an agent and reporting to the SISS committee chaired jointly by Senator James O. Eastland and the Nazi-connected Senator Thomas J. Dodd. Or very likely, both could have been true at the same time.

6. All of the above connections were compartmentalized and kept totally separate from the actual shooters. The Oswald babysitters likely never knew that LHO would be a patsy or that the assassination was even in the works, excepting Ragiorodsky.

7. George de Mohrenschildt was a "temp." That means he was always on the hunt for an opportunity to profit financially by working on projects for the Nazis during World War II and for the CIA, German interests, White Russians or ex-Nazis in the 1950's and 1960's. Like Oswald, he was too unstable and financially-motivated to be a long-term CIA agent like J. Walton Moore. His babysitting of Oswald was only at the request of and under instructions from his "big oil" and White Russian friends. He was probably not privy to advance information about the pending assassination or the precise role of Lee Harvey Oswald in it. However, when he fled the U.S. and went to Haiti in mid-1963, he probably had figured it out, at least generally.

8. George de Mohrenschildt's finances may have been subsidized in a major way by these one-at-a-time intelligence assignments. He didn't seem to have a large enough source of income based on the sparse jobs which he officially held to maintain the lifestyle he was leading.

To summarize, George de Mohrenschildt is on the JFK organizational chart because he did certain acts necessary to the assassination under orders from the organizers of the plot. At minimum, he was an Oswald babysitter. He could also have had a role in the Oswald weapons situation and information gathering and reporting certain things to the plot organizers when asked for specific information.

Notes:

See Wikipedia "George de Mohrenschildt," retrieved 10-9-2016, last modified 10-5-2016 for general information about the life of George de Mohrenschildt.

Rinella's editing work on de Mohrnschildt is called *Lee Harvey Oswald as I Knew Him* by George de Mohrenschildt, author, Michael A. Rinella, editor (2014).

The Faux Baron: George de Mohrenschildt, by Nancy Wertz Weiford is cited frequently and is an outstanding JFK assassination resource.

Author Joan Mellen's book in George de Mohrenschildt is:*Our Man in Haiti: George de Mohrenschildt and the CIA in the Nightmare Republic* by Joan Mellen.

Two excellent books which portray the role of J. Edgar Hoover and his role in counter-intelligence during WWII are *The Origins of FBI Counterintelligence,* by Raymond J. Batvinis (2007), *Hoover's Secret War against Axis Spies: FBI Counterespionage during World War II* by Raymond J. Batvinis (2014) These two books are published by the University Press of Kansas.

A good discussion on Count Konstantin von Maydell can be found at https://deeppoliticsforum. com/forums/archive/index.php/t-2763.html, John Bevilqua article on Konstantin von Maydell and his status as an agent of the Nazi Abwehr of General Reinhard Gehlen.

For a broader picture of Pierpont Morgan Hamilton who was an associate of George de Mohrenschildt, see Wikipedia "Pierpont Morgan Hamilton," retrieved 10-10-16, last updated 6-11-16.

For information supporting the claim in this chapter which involve the CIA and the Russsian Orthodox Church see *Destiny Betrayed: JFK, Cuba, and the Garrison Case* Second Edition Edition by James DiEugenio, p194.

The Russian Fascists: Tragedy and Farce in Exile, 1925-1945 by John J Stephan (1978) is valuable reading about the Russian fascists in the U.S., the most prominent of which was Anastas Vonsiatsky of Connecticut. Some JFK researchers assign a significant role in the assassination to Vonsiatsky although there isn't a great deal of convincing evidence available to support the specifics of this claim.

Chapter 7

Baron Tscheppe-Weidenbach
a/k/a
Gen. Charles A. Willoughby

Charles Willoughby Immigrates to the U.S.

Our second Baron who was very likely directly involved in the JFK assassination was General Charles Willoughby. To assassination researchers, the most significant fact about Willoughby is a claim made by an anonymous and totally unidentified source. This is virtually the only alleged fact in all of the assassination literature that was and remains totally unattributed. Yet it carries such a ring of truth that the two top JFK authors, Caulfield and Russell, both give it a prominent place in their stories.

This was a claim from a source in Canada that Willoughby was the top person in the JFK assassination plot. This unknown source suggested that this had been determined by computer. The recipient of this tip, Dick Russell, featured it in his book *The Man Who Knew Too Much* (TMWKTM) which is the best and most comprehensive books ever written on the assassination. The most famous line from the anonymous letter was:

> YOUR CANADIAN COMPUTERS RESEARCHING THE AS-
> SASSINATION OF JOHN KENNEDY DEVELOPED LEADS
> TO A MAN NAMED TSCHEPPE-WEIDENBACH BORN IN
> HEIDELBERG, GERMANY AS HAVING MASTERMINDED
> THE ASSASSINATION..."

Charles Andrew Willoughby, according to his own reporting, was indeed born in Heidelberg, Germany but his name was, according to him, Adolph Karl Weidenbach. He claimed to be the son of Baron T. Tscheppe-Weidenbach whose wife's name was Emma Willoughby Tscheppe-Weidenbach and she was said to be from Baltimore, Maryland. A reporter from the *New York Journal* tried to verify these facts in 1952, but came up with questions. His birth name and lineage is still in dispute to this day.

What is certain is that Willoughby emigrated from Germany to the U.S. in 1910, and in October, 1910, he enlisted in the U.S. Army. He rose from private to sergeant and was honorably discharged in 1913. It is claimed that Willoughby gained admittance as a senior to Gettysburg College in Gettysburg, Pennsylvania because he had studied both at the University of Heidelberg and the Sorbonne. He graduated from Gettysburg College with a B.A. in 1914. Since Universities routinely maintain records of their attendees one would think that Willoughby's attendance at those institutions could be verified, but it has not.

Upon his graduation in 1914, he again went into the military, this time with a commission as a second lieutenant in a Reserve Corp. He spent that time teaching German and military studies at some prep schools while a Reserve Officer. But with World War I in the offing, he went into the regular army under the name of Adoph Charles Weidenbach and became a captain in the American Expeditionary Force.

Suspiciously, he changed his name from Adolph Charles Weidenbach, Tscheppe-Weidenbach or whatever it had been, to Charles Andrew Willoughby. As a young man, he could speak fluent English, Spanish, German, and French while later in life he added Japanese.

The military career of Willoughby was meteoric. He became a Second Lieutenant and then a First Lieutenant all in the same day, then Captain before that same month of June was out. He was then trained as a pilot by the French Military. Suspicion surrounded him because of his involvement with a female French spy who was later shot. Then he was called back to Washington and investigated by U.S. Army intelligence for being a pro-German sympathizer, or implicitly, a spy.

In the book *The Secret War Against the United States in 1915*, by Heribert von Feilitzsch, the author describes in great detail the intricate German spy network in the U.S. beginning in the 1890's and continuing on without interruption (likely to this very day). German spies were paid through Bayer Company and Hamburg-American Cruise Lines. After describing the situation of Willoughby 1910 to 1918, in a personal e-mail to this author, von Feilitzsch gave a "clear yes" to the question of whether Willoughby would likely have been a German spy at that time. And it does not seem to demand rocket science, according to von Feilitzsch, to figure that out.

In the book by von Feilitzsch, it is made clear that at least two major German spies in 1915 were essentially double agents and this seemed to please the U.S. side quite well. Frederico Stallforth and Felix Sommerfeld were both known to be running the German spy ring, yet they were not touched by wiretapping or prosecution. Stallforth even went on to join the OSS in World War II.

In the early 1920's, Willoughby became involved in American military intelligence while stationed in San Juan, Puerto Rico. Willoughby served as attache in Ecuador, Columbia and Venezuela, then in the 1920's was decorated for some reason by Mussolini. Around this same time he was toasted in Madrid by General Franco and his Falangist Party, Franco being a general whom Willoughby admired second only to his mentor, General Douglas MacArthur. Willoughby then went on to teach at the Army General Staff College in Fort Leavenworth, Kansas.

The most noteworthy of the postings of Willoughby was when he became Chief of Intelligence for General MacArthur in World War II. He achieved the rank of Major General on April 12, 1945. He remained Chief of Intelligence in Japan under the American Occupation which was commanded by General MacArthur.

So only a few chapters into our story, we have two of the Three Barons, Willoughby and de Mohrenschildt, having been formally investigated for being suspected German spies. And the third, Wernher von Braun, was an acknowledged member of the SS under Hitler. Does anyone see a pattern here?

Author Dick Russell got the goods on General Willoughby very early in his virtual bible of assassation research, TMWKTM. On page 124, he relates some valuable information about General Charles Willoughby.

Erich Franz Theodor Tülff von Tschepe und Weidenbach
(28.01.1854 - 01.02.1934)
place of birth:
Königreich Preußen XG, General der Infanterie

German General of Infantry Tülff von Tschepe und Weidenbach commanded the VIII. Army Corps during the First World War. Following a two-year period of inactive reserve status, he was appointed military governor of the Wallachia region in southern Romania, where he served until War's end.

WILLOUGHBY BECOMES INTELLIGENCE CHIEF UNDER MACARTHUR

It is not stretching the point, writes Russell, to say that Charles Willoughby was a racist, anti-Semite, that MacArthur referred to him as "my little Fascist" and that he was an "odd, clever and little-known man." MacArthur's reference to "my little Fascist" is all the more intriguing since Willoughby stood 6' 3" and weighed 220 pounds. (Apparently MacArthur looked at the world through distorted goggles).

Another personal note is that the notorious right-wing eccentric Clare Boothe Luce and Willoughby had an affair when she was in the Far East, (a claim that can easily be found by a search on both their names on the web).

McArthur and Willoughby kept the wartime OSS (predecessor of the CIA) out of the territory of MacArthur's command while the War was in progress. This was because MacArthur thought there were too many leftists in the CIA. Following the War, when MacArthur was in charge of the occupation of Japan, the two Generals often put CIA personnel under surveillance around the CIA base at Atsugi, Japan near Tokyo.

A Japanese national named Kushiro Hattori had been the private secretary to Japanese General Tojo, who was hanged as a war criminal in 1946. Willoughby was head of MacArthur's intelligence in the occupation. Despite his connection to Tojo, Willoughby allowed Hattori to set up his own post-war spy agency in Japan, affiliated with the U.S. Army G-2 intel command.

Mentioned by Dick Russell, was the fact that a son of this same Hattori had visited Lee Harvey Oswald when Oswald was stationed in El Toro Marine base in California in 1959. Willoughby also allowed a man named Jack Canon to start up a group called the Zed group in the late 1940's. This group has been linked by a Soviet author named Mikhail Lebedev to CIA hits, an international fascist movement, and even to the JFK assassination, although this is not supported by any other source.

The commander of the well-documented department of military intelligence called the "FOI" claimed that Willoughby was the one who started it. As is discussed in another chapter, military intelligence agent Richard Case Nagell was affiliated with the FOI. Since Lee Harvey Oswald was in the Far East, serving in Japan around the early days of the FOI and doing some spying there, some have speculated that Oswald was also affiliated with the FOI at some point. This has never been proven.

The FOI began as a joint venture between Willoughby's Far East intelligence operation and the CIA. But when President Harry S. Truman famously fired General Douglas MacArthur for insubordination in April, 1951, Willoughby was also terminated.

In the Spring of 1950, however, Willoughby had information about a Soviet spy ring called the Sorge organization. He turned over this information to the stongly anti-Communist Richard M. Nixon.

After his firing in 1951, Willoughby began his career as a private sector, right-wing, self-appointed operative whose activities began to span the globe. In April, 1952, Willoughby accompanied an American military mission to Franco's Spain. At that time, there was thought of placing American bases in Spain. But after the mission ended, Willoughby stayed there for another three months. Coincidentally, at the same time ex-Nazi Otto Skorzeny came to Spain to set up his international Nazi network or ratline. Skorzeny had been an SS colonel under Hitler.

Per Dick Russell, the Odessa Organization which was made up of reprobate Nazis, included three branches. Odessa had been set up in 1943 by Nazi Martin Bormann, who realized the Nazis would lose the War. One branch of Odessa was the spy ring of General Reinhard Gehlen which became part of the CIA. Next was the system of "ratlines" or escape networks for Nazis around the world. It operated in countries such as Paraguay, South Africa, Egypt, Mexico, Brazil, Argentina and Indonesia.

The third branch of Odessa was a system for moving Nazi money. Otto Skorzeny was the son-in-law of Nazi financial genius Hjalmar Horace Greeley Schacht. Schacht was Hitler's brilliant banker and all-purpose financial manager and deal maker. As all criminal financial enterprises are prone to do, Schacht set up a maze of front companies to disguise the nature of his purpose. It was just such a front company known as Permindex in Switzerland, funded with Nazi money, which provided and/or laundered the money for the JFK assassination.

Author Russell provides the rawest of raw meat regarding Baron Charles Tscheppe-Weidenbach Willoughby: in a letter dated March 17, 1955 to CIA director Allen Dulles, Willoughby made an astounding proposal.

In this letter, which Russell discovered at the Douglas MacArthur Memorial Archives in Norfolk, Virginia, Willoughby reveals the smoking gun regarding his role in the JFK assassination. Willoughby starts by bragging about his connections with Fascist Dictator Francisco Franco in Spain. Then he says he can develop the same sort of fascist connections in Germany.

"My father's family (though a divorce took place), is unimpeachable in Wilhelminian society. I am in touch with very high level people."

This single sentence was the proverbial mouthful. It shows the following:

1. Willoughby was very likely the son of Erich Franz Theodor Tülff von Tschepe und Weidenbach, who was a very high-ranking Prussian general in World War I and the only known Tscheppe-Weidenbach who could qualify as unimpeachably Wilhelminian.

2. This heightens the likelihood that Willoughby came over from Germany as a "Wilhelminian" spy for Kaiser Bill himself and that he maintained divided loyalties his entire life. He must have been torn between the German way of life, America, and a love of authoritarian anti-democratic politics of whatever variety, in whatever country.

3. Willoughby longed to bring back the glory days of Prussian nobility, which was part and parcel of White Russianism, European Monarchism and all the rest. He apparently shared this desire with Baron George de Mohrenschildt, though not necessarily with von Braun. After all, von Braun actually wanted to work for a living and accomplish something, unlike the would-be European pretenders to "nobility."

4. Hitler's regime was, in actuality, transparent to these Wilhelminians. Hitler was merely an annoyance. The Nazi's were laid low, but

to Willoughby, the Wilhelminians were back in the saddle and operating in the same way that they always had done. In the 1950's, per this letter, they apparently outranked even the most successful "ex"-Nazis who were in power in West Germany at the time. This would include former Nazis such as Hans Globke, Ludwig Erhard and Foreign Minister Heinrich von Bentano.

5. Willoughby's Wilhelminian friends happened to be the social superiors even of Dr. Konrad Adenauer who despised the Protestant Prussians. Willoughby was suggesting, in effect, to go over the head of Adenauer and set up a fascist Wilhelminian group, ostensibly even more fascist than the fascist Nazi's. The message was, "Why waste time with reprobate Nazis (who were working with their friend Allen Dulles) when the Wilhelminians were available?"

6. The top man among Wilhelminians, perhaps world-wide, would be Dr. Wernher von Braun, his father being a Prussian noble and very powerful in German Government even before Hitler. Von Braun was the ultimate unimpeachable, indispensible (and invulnerable) Wilhelminian, and Willoughby could very well have gained his support. And ditto for von Braun's best friend Walter Dornberger.

7. John J. McCloy, who bossed the Warren Commission, began his career with the Wilhelminians before the days of Hitler. Willoughby underscores the power of these Prussian figures, dating back to the days of the Teutonic Knights in the 1200's and before. Apparently, they weren't going away anytime soon. Per Vladimir Lenin, "he who controls Germany, controls Europe, controls the world."

This is a lot of dynamite loaded into one simple letter. And when Willoughby's suggestion to Allen Dulles went nowhere, he followed up with another suggestion, almost as nefarious as the first one. On October 30, 1955, Willoughby offered to set up social club connections between American GI's and German soldiers at the level of privates and corporals throughout Germany. Keep in mind that West Germany, at the time, was being run either by ex-Nazis or "Wilhelminians" (take your choice). So our American GI's could become infected with Nazi fascism or worse. Real nice guy, this Willoughby!

After being rejected by Dulles and revealing an intense case of sour grapes, he wrote again to Allen Dulles on December 3, 1955 deploring the fact that the CIA would not accept his offers. He blamed that fact on the old feud between the intelligence community and MacArthur dating from WWII.

But author Russell has an even more disturbing story to relate. As of October, 1957, the spy network of Nazi General and former CIA employee Reinhard Gehlen extended its influence into the Far East. In October,

1957, there was a far-reaching and ominous conference in Asia which involved Chaing Kai-shek of Nationalist China (i.e. Taiwan), Syngman Rhee of South Korea, Ngo Dinh Diem of South Vietnam and Gehlen's spy organization. Also present was a German named Fritz Cramer who was a former German intelligence officer. Cramer was at that time the head of a right-wing vigilante group that hunted leftists at the bidding of private industrialists, presumably in Germany. The ominous addition to this fascist cabal was the American Security Council. Per author Russell, the ASC was a partner to the Fritz Cramer group. The American Security Council and the Anti-Bolshevik Bloc of Nations Organization were the two private organizations (among those which included prominent Americans) most heavily involved in the JFK assassination, in the opinion of this writer. (These groups would have provided face-to-face background support to the plotters, although not necessarily participating in the actual Dallas operation).

In his definitive work on the assassination, *General Walker*, Dr. Jeffrey Caulfield presents some information on Fritz Cramer. At page 319 Caulfield writes: "On May 20, 1961, Major Archibald Roberts, working at the U.S. Army Information Office in New York, wrote General Willoughby in Washington, D.C. and told him 'it would be very helpful to our campaign to enlist German professionals on the post to assist in the expose of *Overseas Weekly*.' Roberts told him that Fritz Cramer in Bonn, Germany – who published an anti-Communist newspaper – could help their cause and secure files on the publishers of *Overseas Weekly* and 'help tie in the Commie technique of the operation.' Roberts asked Willoughby, 'can we impose on your prestige to establish contact with this man, General?' Roberts concluded the letter saying 'all we're after is evidence that will enable us to destroy Marion Respach [an editor of the newspaper], smash *Overseas Weekly*, and expose the International Communist Conspiracy.' On May 25, 1961, [General Edwin] Walker wrote Roberts and thanked him for his great work. He told him 'I am worried about nothing.'"

Joseph W. Bendersky has written extensively about military intelligence, especially between the World Wars. He has included Charles Willoughby in his well-regarded analyses. According to Bendersky, in post-WWII America, Willoughby's right-wing allies and associates included General Albert Wedemeyer, Senator Arthur Vandenberg (R.MI), and most importantly, the powerful publisher of the *Chicago Tribune,* Robert McCormick. Per Bendersky, American Catholic anti-Communists especially liked Willoughby, with such people as Monsignor Fulton J. Sheen writing him long letters and publicly claiming to having prayed often for Willoughby.

Bendersky characterized Willoughby's philosophy as pitting the "white race" which had special talents against "the teeming millions of the Orient and Tropics." This was stated by Willoughby, having served in the past as the U.S. attache in Venezuela, Colombia and Ecuador. Willoughby considered the Russians not to be real white people, but part of "Mongoloid-Panslavism." It is obvious that Willoughby was not skilled in anthropology. He saw a battle between Saxon and Cossack. As mentioned previously, it is apparent that when Willoughby immigrated to the U.S., he retained his German racial-type nationalism which transcended Nazism and had roots, actually, in the dim world of pre-history.

Colonel Robert McCormick wrote to Willoughby on the subject of the Spanish dictator General Francisco Franco. He felt that Jews in the U.S. had prevented the diplomatic recognition of Franco's government as revenge for the Spanish Inquisition.

During the Korean War, Willoughby had worked with Generals George E. Stratemeyer and Edward M. Almond, two of MacArthur's top generals. These men, along with Willoughby were sought after by Congressional committees for their advice on political-military matters. Stratemeyer, in particular, had testified on the Korean War before the Senate Internal Security Subcommittee (SISS). Conservative political views, especially on racial matters, dominated the thinking of these right-wing retired generals and the Congressional Committees were apparently applauding their thinking. Stratemeyer in particular endorsed the thinking of former Army Intelligence officer John Beatty, who wrote a book portraying Nazi Germany as a country "strangled" economically, politically and militarily and forced into war against its will. Beatty's book touched off a prolonged firestorm of controversy because of its anti-Semitic and pro-Nazi content.

Bendersky describes "the old wartime clique" of military generals as persisting and showing a great deal of continuity well into the 1950's and even beyond. He names General Bonner Fellers, Major General Ralph C. Smith, Col. Truman Smith (a reputed Nazi-sympathizer before WWII), Stratemeyer, Wedemeyer, General Robert E. Wood (CEO of Sears, Roebuck) and General Charles Willoughby as members of this clique. Willoughby, for his part, was working with the John Birch Society in order to publish a new edition of his book, *MacArthur.*

According to Bendersky, following World War II, the vicissitudes of the Cold War generated a "renewed admiration for German culture." Two of these right-wing retired military figures, Col. Truman Smith and General Albert Wedemeyer renewed the relationships they had with German officers before the war. The most prominent Nazi General involved was, per Bendersky, General Hans Speidel. Despite being an "ardent" Nazi and serving as Rommel's chief of staff, Hans Speidel had been made commander of NATO ground forces. This fact was also noted by author T.H. Tetens in his book on Nazi resurgence.

Charles Willoughby advocated a restored Germany. He wanted all the Eastern Territories forfeited by Germany after the war to be returned. Willoughby was on record opposing the war crimes trial of the Krupps whom he described as martyrs.

WILLOUGHBY AND DR. WALTER BECHER

Both, Bendersky and Tetens specifically detail the unsavory relationship maintained between Charles Willoughby and Dr. Walter Becher. Becher had been a Nazi Party editor when the Germans occupied Czechoslovakia. After World War II, he not only belonged to Neo-Nazi parties, he organized something called the Witiko-Bund and became the spokesman for millions of Germans who were expelled from the Eastern Territories and had become refugees inside of West Germany. In the early 1950's Becher set up a very effective German lobby in Washington, D.C.

Becher had to have been part of the Bundesnachtrendiest, the BND, which was the West German Intelligence agency run by former Nazi General Reinhard Gehlen. This can be deduced from the fact that he died in Pullach, Bavaria. Pullach was a small town in which the only industry was the main headquarters of the Gehlen spy agency. This headquarters had been set up by Gehlen back when he worked for Allen Dulles as a CIA employee. The headquarters in Pullach was maintained thereafter.

The reader should focus on Becher and Gehlen, because Gehlen was likely a facilitator of the JFK assassination and Becher was his representative in the U.S. Bendersky informs us that Becher had a close relationship with various senators and congressmen. One of Becher's close confidants was George Brada. Brada was the author of a 1953 book on Free Czechoslovakia. Brada wrote about an "Asiatic race" which was subverting the entire planet by means of "intrigue." This left no doubt that Brada was promoting the idea that Communism and Jews were the same and that they must be eliminated even more thoroughly than they had been by Hitler.

According to Bendersky, Charles Willoughby maintained close contact with Becher and Brada for the next twenty years, presumably between 1945 or 1950 well into the 1960's or 1970's. Willoughby was involved with conferences of the German expellees from the forfeited Eastern Germany well into the 1960's. Brada claimed in conversation with Willoughby that American politicians with whom his friend Walter Becher spoke privately, always complained about Jews. Becher and Brada were still trying to gain acceptance by the U.S. government even under Richard Nixon as late as 1969.

In *General Walker*, assassination expert Dr. Jeffrey Caulfield provides additional information on Walter Becher. At page 550, he states that Walter Becher attended the 1964 Republican convention and wrote a glowing article on Goldwater in the *Deutsch National-Zeitung*. Dr. Caulfield further states that Becher made frequent trips to visit American political leaders on the far right in the 1950's, including Senator Joseph McCarthy and William Jenner, and was reportedly the liason between neo-Nazi groups in West Germany and the U.S.

Charles Willoughby was also the military editor of a prominent right-wing, anti-Semitic magazine called *American Mercury*, and also a frequent contributor. When anti-Semitism went totally out of fashion in the U.S. post-WWII, Willoughby became embroiled in a feud with conservative publisher William F. Buckley over the merits of *American Mercury*. Despite this anti-Semitic connection, Willoughby tried to "make nice" with the powerful American Jewish Committee and lauded the State of Israel.

From 1957 to 1967, Willoughby maintained close relations with German spy Walter Becher and his friend George Brada. Becher considered Willoughby their most important political contact in the U.S. Willoughby also served as a consultant on matters of military intelligence in the 1950's, working with both U.S. G-2 executive officer Colonel Frederick D. Sharp as well as Army Chief of Staff General Maxwell D. Taylor. As late as 1958, Willoughby was an expert witness for the Senate Foreign Relations Committee on the Cold War.

This chapter cannot be complete without a recitation of the disturbing facts about Walter Becher brought to light by German expert T.H. Tetens in *The New Germany and the Old Nazis*. Becher joined the Nazi party as early as 1931, although he rejoined in 1938. Because he wanted to boost his brand back in Germany, Becher decided to first build an influential organization or network of connections in the U.S. This, he theorized, would translate into influence back in the old country.

Walter Becher's main Congressional contacts became Senators William Jenner (R.IN) and Joseph McCarthy (R.WI) and House members Francis E. Walter, B. Carroll Reece, Albert H. Bosch and Walter E. Judd. Writing in 1961, Tetens states that while Becher was at that date chairman of the All-German Bloc in the Bavarian Landtag and Secretary of the Sudeten-Deutsche Association, his main power came from Washington. In the minds of Germans, their only hope for the return of the Eastern Territories lay in the political influence of Walter Becher in America, chiefly in the State Department and Congress.

In 1961, of the 53 million people in West Germany, 10 million (20%) had come from the Eastern Territories lost to Germany due to the War. These people still carried a heavy grudge against the appeasers of Stalin at Yalta and Potsdam. In 1961, the position of the Adenauer Government both in speeches in the Bundestag and elsewhere was that Germany would never accept the Oder-Niese eastern boundary line. Tetens, a top expert on German geopolitics, says that expelling the Sudeten Germans from their homes and their exile in West Germany was just payback for their role in helping the SS murder several hundred thousand people in Czechoslovakia and elsewhere during the war.

Despite this theory propounded by Tetens, the fact is that Britain and, to a lesser extent, France and Russia would do anything possible to weaken Germany. Britain had always pursued a policy of preventing 1) the unity of all Germans under one government and 2) German self-sufficiency in food because of the British desire to blackmail Germany by use of a naval blockade. Since France and Russia were always in fear of Germany, the British were the only ones with enough military might and favorable geography to be able to continually, time after time, dismember Germany.

Obviously the Germans expelled from the Sudetenland were just plain expelled. There was no due process to find out if they, as individuals, had aided the Nazis. Very likely most of them had never harmed anybody. Clearly this act by the U.S. and Britian was every bit as evil as mass eviction has always been dating back to the Cherokee Trail of Tears in the U.S. or the Babylonian Captivity of the Old Testament. This is true whether done by Stalin, Hitler, Churchill, Roosevelt or whoever.

That said, Walter Becher was riding the crest of a wave of hatred by Germans against the U.S. and Britain over this issue. It is easy to see why the Sudeten Germans would consider the murder of a U.S. President just a small down payment in payback for their plight. In March, 1959, General Charles de Gaulle stated at a press conference that the Oder-Neisse line was Germany's definite eastern border and should not be changed. In response, Bonn said "the German borders are still those of December 30, 1937."

For our analysis of the JFK assassination, we should note that John Foster Dulles felt that the unstable Oder-Niesse line could lead to an atomic holocaust. But when Tetens was writing in 1961, there was no diplomatic solution on the table. The Sudeten expellees still looked to the activities of Becher in the U.S. as their only hope. Small wonder that Becher held them in the palm of his hand.

In 1957, influential Congressman Usher L. Burdick inserted a Walter Becher article in the *Congressional Record*. In 1959, German newspapers reported more successes of Becher with the U.S. Congress. Becher was traveling the U.S. for weeks at a time working on this issue. Per Tetens, he had access to 71 newspapers and 32 million listeners on the Mutual Broadcasting Network. Becher claimed the support of 150 Congressmen. The German newspaper *Volksbot* published letters and telegrams on the refugee issue from Herbert Hoover, Generals Charles Willoughby, Pedro del Valle, Albert Wedemeyer as well as various politicians.

Tetens reports the names of members of Congress who sent letters of support. He lists about 50 names. For our purposes, the names that stand out are James O. Eastland, Thomas J. Dodd, Prescott Bush, Strom Thurmond, Speaker John W. McCormack and Charles J. Kersten. Some of these like Bush and Kersten were no longer in office. But Dodd, Eastland and McCormack were most likely directly involved in the JFK assassination as we shall see later in later chapters.

While author Bendersky lists Walter Becher's ally as George Brada, Tetens mentions Dr. Richard Sallet. He says that in Washington, Dr. Sallet conducted a campaign of pity for the Volksdeutsche and threatened that they would make trouble in Europe if their homelands were not returned to them. It was through the efforts of Sallet, says Tetens, that Congress and the State Department responded with some degree of sympathy. Like George Brada, Sallet had written on the subject of German-related historical issues.

Our standard for including a person on the JFK organizational chart is that the person must have made a material contribution to the plot, beyond just moral support or giving an anonymous donation of funds. So what is the case against Charles Willoughby?

> 1. There is the anonymous letter sent to author Dick Russell which unequivocally names Willoughby as the "mastermind" of the assassination. This letter was considered credible enough to be included in the two most thorough and credible JFK assassination books: TMWKTM by Dick Russell and *General Walker* ... by Dr. Jeffrey Caulfield.

> 2. JFK was murdered by an alliance of the worldwide Nazi/fascist network in partnership with the Southern Segregationist leadership. Of the Americans with connections to the worldwide fascist networks, Willoughby probably had the most due to Λ) his career in military intelligence and B) his high level participation with insiders in right-wing circles like the American Security Council, H.L. Hunt, Billy James Hargis and others.

> 3. Willoughby had been head of intelligence for the entire nation of Japan for the five years of the U.S. occupation. No other military or civilian intel figure could come close to that level of country-wide responsibility. Only General Reinhard Gehlen, head of West German intelligence, and/or General Charles Willoughby had the German loyalty and skills to co-ordinate a German-U.S. based plot like the JFK conspiracy.

> 4. Uniquely, Willoughby saw himself as the prototypical "Wilhelminian," which is a loyalty to the Prussian tradition of German history. This attitude blended perfectly with that of the other two Barons: De Mohrenschildt and von Braun, both of whom have also been implicated in the plot by some excellent sources.

On the other side of the ledger are the following arguments against including Charles Willoughby:

1. He was living in Washington at the time of the assassination. Almost all of the known, proven plotters were in Dallas or New Orleans, either residing, or there on the day of the assassination. The members of Congress such as Eastland and Dodd were not, but they were frantically traveling to either New Orleans or Germany immediately before the assassination in their respective roles.

2. Willoughby did not have an organization reporting to him as did Reinhard Gehlen, the Senate Committee Chairmen, the Dallas Police, the National Security Council and others. The "chief" of an assassination plot has to have "Indians" to do the work. Who were Willoughby's Indians? Did certain people in the National Security Council, military intelligence and German intelligence turn to Willoughby purely for his intelligence organization experience, knowledge and skills?

For our purposes, Willoughby is in the plot, primarily, because of his Wilhelminian philosophy which he shared with kingpins John J. McCloy and the two other Barons. Birds of a feather…

Notes:

The first and most important citation in this chapter is from *The Man Who Knew Too Much*, by Dick Russell, p. 691. This book will be cited as TMWKTM in future chapters.

Some very good general information about Charles Willoughby is on Wikipedia "Charles A. Willoughby," retrieved 10-6-2016, last modified 5-30-2016.

The following book by von Feilitzsch provides new insight into German espionage in the U.S. starting in the 1890's and continuing through World War I as described in the book by von Feilitzsch. The title is *The Secret War on the United States in 1915: A Tale of Sabotage, Labor Unrest, and Border Troubles*, by Heribert von Feilitzsch.

In *TMWKTM*, as cited in the text Russell, at p. 124. relates information about Willoughby's right-wing background. At p. 131, Russell presents the story of the Far Eastern connection of Willoughby and ex-Nazi General Reinhard Gehlen.

The Jewish Threat: Anti-Semitic Politics Of The U.S. Army by Joseph W. Bendersky, is one of the two most valuable resources for in information on General Willoughby. At p. 397, Pendersky describes the connection between Willoughby and Col. Robert McCormack of the *Chicago Tribune* and other right-wing activists associated with the two. At page 398, he discusses the immigration to the U.S. of General Willoughby. At page 402, Bendersky relates Willoughby's attitude of approval toward the fascist Franco Regime. Then at page 411, it is Willoughby's connection to the John Birch Society.
  Starting at page 416, Bendersky portrays the close relationship between Willoughby and Walter Becher, a West German politician and possibly a German spy. Finally, at page 420, Pendersky describes the fued between Willoughby and conservative journalist William F. Buckley.

Another source of information about Willoughby is *The New Germany and the Old Nazis* by T. H. Tetens. At page 106 of his book, Tetens describes the role of ex-Nazi General Hans Spiedel to all of these events involving Willoughby. Then at page 122, Tetens relates disturbing facts about the above named Walter Becher. At page 123, Tetens connects Becher to Senator Joseph McCarthy, Senator Walter Judd and other conservative U.S. politicians. Finally, at page 135 Tetens describes the position of Becher on the issue of German boundaries. This was the issue upon which the career of Becher was built and it played an important role in U.S.-German relations.

Two other authors who were connected to Willoughby and Becher and who had credibility in the U.S. based on their publications were: George Brada who wrote *History of the Council of Free Czechoslovakia* and of the Personnel of Radio Free Europe and Richard Sallet who wrote *Russian-German Settlements in the United States*, published by the North Dakota Institute for Regional Studies, 1974.

Chapter 8

CONGRESSMAN CHARLES KERSTEN

We have seen in a prior chapter that former Congressman Charles Kersten sent letters to all three Kennedy brothers on November 7, 1963 warning of a Soviet murder apparatus which was allegedly designed to murder Western leaders and other people. This act by Kersten betrays two facts: first, that Kersten had advance knowledge of the assassination and second, Kersten was a person with very poor judgment, despite having a passion for anti-Communism, especially in Eastern Europe.

Charles Joseph Kersten was born in Chicago on May 26, 1902. He was the son of Charles Herman Kersten and Nora A. Gillespie. He was a resident of Milwaukee, Wisconsin as early as 1923. He was married to Mary Edith McKinnon around 1930 and the first of his six children, Edmund, was born on July 28, 1932. As of 1940, Kersten was a resident of Whitefish Bay, a pleasant and well-to-do suburb just to the north of Milwaukee on the shore of Lake Michigan.

Kersten attended Marquette University and was treasurer of the Marquette Glee Club for 1922-1923. He graduated from Marquette with an LLB in 1925. In 1925 and 1926 he did some postgraduate study in Washington, D.C. and spent a year of travel in Europe. In World War II, he was a member of the Coast Guard Reserve. For a period of 7 years, he was a deputy district attorney in Milwaukee.

KERSTEN AND SENATOR JOSEPH MCCARTHY

In 1943, Joseph McCarthy began his political career starting a campaign for the U.S. Senate. McCarthy's campaign committee in Milwaukee was led by attorney Arlo McKinnon and his law partner, Charles Kersten. McCarthy was on the ballot in 1946 but lost in the Senate primary to Alexander Wiley, who was the senior Senator in Wisconsin from 1939 to 1963. Wiley left the Senate in 1963 as the senior Republican member.

In the 1946 race for the Senate, there was a significant amount of scandal surrounding Joseph McCarthy's activities as a judge in Appleton, Wisconsin, 100 miles north of Milwaukee. It was alleged by McCarthy's opponents that he arranged for the transfer of divorce cases from Milwaukee to Appleton so that he could grant "quickie" divorces to clients of the McKinnon & Kersten law firm. Arlo McKinnon, Kersten's law partner, was also Kersten's brother-in-law. McKinnon was the brother of Kersten's wife, Mary Edith. One case, Kordos v. Kordos had dragged on for months and months, but when transferred to Appleton, McCarthy granted the divorce to the plaintiff in two days. This practice is especially cynical since both McCarthy and Kersten made careers as Catholic activists and the Catholic Church has always had a fierce and well-known opposition to divorce.

In 1946, Charles Kersten ran for Congress in Milwaukee's Fifth Congressional district.

There were various Republican candidates running for office in Wisconsin at that time who emphasized anti-Communism. Kersten's opponent in the Republican primary, incumbent Frank Keefe, stressed the alleged Communist infiltration of the U.S. Charles Kersten, who would be known for his entire career as a radical anti-Communist, asked voters to "put Kersten in and keep the Communists out." Kersten won election to Congress in 1946 from a district that was normally Democratic, so his hold on his Congressional seat was never secure.

The spectacular story of Kersten's Congressional career began immediately upon his reaching Washington D.C. in 1947. Apparently, Kersten had made some important contacts when he did his "post-graduate" work in Washington in 1925-1926. Or perhaps his connections as a graduate of Marquette, an outstanding Catholic University, came to the fore.

KERSTEN, NIXON AND JFK

For some reason which is not clear, Kersten became immediate best friends with both Congressman John F. Kennedy and Congressman Richard M. Nixon. Both of them were newly elected. The 80th Congress was the first to be controlled by Republicans since the 1920's. As the new Congress was sworn in on January 3, 1947, John W. McCormack, the former Democratic majority leader, was replaced as leader and became minority whip. Former Speaker of the House Sam Rayburn became minority leader. Both Kennedy and Nixon were assigned to the Education and Labor Committee. At that time, the number of investigative committees and subcommittees in the Congress had reached an incredible thirty-nine.

John W. McCormack had chaired the Dies committee starting in 1934. The Dies Committee was the predecessor of both the House Un-American Affairs Committee (HUAC) and the McCarthy Committees in the Senate. The second of the two committees allowed to the freshman Kennedy was the District of Columbia Committee. For Nixon, his second committee was HUAC. Within days of joining his first committee, Nixon asked his freshman classmate Charles Kersten to find someone who could instruct him all about Communism. It's not clear why Nixon would be making such a request of

Kersten. It's likely, just by circumstances, that anti-Communist activists and McCormack were pressuring Nixon in this regard and pointing Nixon in the direction that this would soon take. It should be noted that according to author Matthews, JFK displayed disdain regarding McCormack.

When asked by Nixon, Kersten mentioned anti-Communist Father John F. Cronin. Cronin had also tutored Kennedy on Communism at Cape Cod at some time prior to that. Incredibly, *Nixon and Kennedy together* began making trips to the home city of Father Cronin, Baltimore. Father Cronin had been the author of a publication "The Problem of American Communism." One person specifically mentioned in the writing of Cronin was the now infamous Alger Hiss.

Father John Cronin was born in 1911, attended parochial schools in New York, then studied at Holy Cross College from 1923 to 1925. Two years later, he transferred to Catholic University of America, earning a PhD in 1935. His ordination as a priest took place on May 19, 1932. In 1933 or 1934, Cronin became a professor of economics at St. Mary's Seminary in Baltimore. During the period 1940-1941, an FBI agent approached Cronin to meet and exchange information and he agreed.

The young Congressman Richard Nixon got an opportunity to discuss foreign policy with President Harry S. Truman. Congressman Edward Devitt of Minnesota arranged a meeting with Truman on July 2, 1947 which lasted 15 minutes. The meeting included Nixon, Caleb Boggs of Delaware and Congressman Charles Kersten. The topics discussed were Russian intentions, European relief, German rehabilitation, Manchuria, the Balkans and the Dutch East Indies.

Richard Nixon spoke regularly to a radio audience on a program in California. In one segment, he invited his friend Charles Kersten to join him on the program as his guest. The two discussed foreign policy. Kersten described the takeover of Czechoslovakia by infiltration. Kersten spoke harshly about Franklin Roosevelt, saying that he had been fooled at both the Yalta and the Tehran conferences.

Kersten and Nixon had both visited seven Eastern European bloc embassies, accompanied by a reporter from the Associated Press. All of the Eastern bloc U.S. ambassadors attacked U.S. policy and refused to criticize the Soviet Union. Nixon and Kersten also partnered on a House resolution which would have required the U.S. to form alliances in Western Europe.

Nixon became involved in investigations involving Communist turncoat Whittaker Chambers. Chambers had made a secret statement regarding the Communist background of State Department figure Alger Hiss. Kersten advised Nixon to give the transcript of Chambers' statement to John Foster Dulles to read. Nixon and Charles Kersten rode the train together to New York to present the transcript to Dulles. Both John Foster Dulles and his brother Allen Dulles were at that meeting.

Kersten, Nixon and JFK all sat together on the Education and Labor Committee. Kersten had a special cause in the area of labor, since a strike in his home district in Milwaukee had shut down a plant producing war materials in 1941.

In the Education and Labor Committee, JFK had attacked certain labor leaders in Milwaukee for being Communists. Kersten compared JFK's attack to the opening shots of the Minutemen at Lexington and Concord. This happened in the context of a hearing on May 1, 1947. Witnesses, called to the hearing by Kersten, included two Communist labor leaders from Milwaukee named Harold Christoffel and Robert Buse.

JFK pointedly asked Buse "Would you consider Russia a democracy?" Buse: "I would not know. I do not think so." But one of the next witnesses was a famous turn-coat Communist named Louis Budenz. Budenz testified that the Milwaukee strike was part of a Communist plan led from Moscow by Stalin. JFK moved the committee to cite Christoffel for perjury. As a result, Christoffel was indicted, convicted and sentenced to five years in prison for perjury but the conviction was overturned by the U.S. Supreme Court.

Kersten and JFK traveled together on a junket in Europe in the summer of 1947. On the trip, JFK was visiting his ancestral home in Ireland but fell seriously ill. This was when he was first diagnosed with Addison's disease. On the return trip from Europe, traveling on the Queen Elizabeth, JFK was actually given the Catholic last rites due to the serious nature of his illness. Nixon was also embarking for Europe, on the Queen Mary. JFK left a note for Nixon with the addresses of his sister and other women he could look up in Paris. Per Nixon's secretary, Nixon reacted only with embarrassment to this message and never followed up.

While Charles Kersten's travels and anti-Communist indoctrination were taking place in Washington, Kersten was also deeply involved with partisan politics back in Wisconsin. Kersten was a friend and early supporter of Senator Joseph McCarthy of Wisconsin. Kersten was elected in 1946, lost in 1948, then won again in 1950 and 1952. He lost his final election in 1954.

There are some political roles which Kersten played in Wisconsin which shed light on his character. Some of his issues also involved national politics, chiefly the epic confrontation between his friend Joe McCarthy and the 1952 Republican candidate, Dwight D. Eisenhower.

There were only a few candidates in Wisconsin who were unabashed McCarthyites, and one of the most adamant was Charles Kersten. In 1952, seeking election after a gap of two years, Kersten boasted of his friendship with McCarthy. In his largely Democratic district, however, Kersten won by only a small margin in 1952. According to the *Milwaukee Journal*, Kersten won in 1946 but was defeated in 1948 because the State Department of Taxation revealed that he paid no taxes over a period of three years.

As the McCarthy-Eisenhower relationship unfolded in the 1952 election, a major Republican convention took place in Milwaukee. At this convention Senator McCarthy spoke of "tragic blunders and high treason in the nation's foreign policy." For his part, Charles Kersten claimed that there was bitterness and disagreement in Russia identical to the split in the Republican Party. Kersten claimed that without this disagreement, the people of Russia would eagerly throw the Communists and the Stalin regime out.

Veteran progressive Republican Senator Alexander Wiley refused to attend this convention and he was criticized by the McCarthyites for praising Truman's Secretary of State Dean Acheson.

It was at this juncture that Charles Kersten made probably his most important contribution to national partisan politics. At the 1952 Republican convention, John Foster Dulles drafted the platform plank on foreign policy. But the most controversial passage in that plank came from Congressman Charles Kersten. The Kersten language spoke of the importance of giving hope and encouragement to the "captive" peoples of Eastern Europe. It committed the United States to taking some sort of action to liberate all of Eastern Europe or, failing that, to liberate at least some portion. This part of the Party plank was widely known to have come directly from Kersten and it was considered a concession on the part of the Eisenhower forces in favor of the McCarthyites. As would happen more than once, Kersten's addition to the Republican Party platform in 1952 would prove to be by far the most controversial item in the entire platform. Kersten was not a person who did things half-way.

In a pro-Ike speech in 1952, Charles Kersten lambasted Arthur Schlesinger, Jr. who was an advisor to Ike's opponent Adlai Stevenson and was also a Harvard professor. At the convention, Kersten and the McCarthyites attacked Secretary of State George C. Marshall. Ike quickly had to speak up in defense of his friend and fellow general. On September 3, 1952, McCarthy made his first appearance in Wisconsin. In his speech there he railed against Alger Hiss and related topics. In Peoria Illinois, Ike and Joe McCarthy spent half an hour in Ike's hotel room hammering out some of their differences. According to some who were there, Ike spoke to McCarthy "with white-hot anger;" however, Ike then went directly to Milwaukee and delivered a pro-McCarthy speech.

In 1956, Charles Kersten attempted to gain the Republican nomination for the U.S. Senate. In the eyes of some, Kersten disgraced himself by alleging a "miserable plot" by a GOP party faction against another faction. Kersten named the state GOP chairman as part of this plot. In the 1956 primary campaign, a pamphlet published by Kersten attacked sitting Republican incumbent Senator Alexander Wiley as a "one-worlder and an internationalist." It also said the GOP had been taken over by "pro-Communists."

Another major role of Congressman Kersten was his chairmanship of the House Select Committee to Investigate Communist Aggression and its various hearings which were targeted toward specific countries in turn, such as the Baltic States, Poland and others.

When one reads and examines the exhibits in Kersten's Committee Report on the Baltic States, it is the outstanding document, in the opinion of this author, for the justification not only for McCarthy's crusade, but indeed for the entire Cold War following World War II. The report features page after page of photographs of priests, murdered and martyred. Then there are photographs of the butchered corpses of the murdered priests piled up like logs or sides of beef.

This publicity, which was provided to the public is on a higher level than any other such relevant information known to this author. And the intensity of feeling, indeed the abject horror shown provides a hint as to the true stakes in the bitter feud between certain Catholic factions surrounding the issue of Communism. This unfortunate feud led to the perhaps unintended consequence of the murder of the first Catholic President, John F. Kennedy.

The CIA was established under the National Security Act of 1947. In 1950, the fourth director of the CIA, General Walter Bedell Smith listed its duties as 1) psychological warfare 2) paramilitary operations 3) denial of strategic materials 4) stockpiling for war preparation 5) organizing sabotage teams for resistance operations and 6) planning stay-behind networks in case of invasion or military occupation of an area.

In 1951, Congress publicly authorized $100 million for covert actions which in 2016 dollars would be $926 million or almost one billion dollars. In 1939, the U.S. had no intelligence department except for solitary military attaches at some foreign embassies which numbered only, at most, 100 persons worldwide. But in less than ten years, the U.S. had authorized almost $1 billion *on just covert actions*, which were in addition to other more conventional intelligence funds.

Various members of Congress proposed specific covert actions such as "stirring up trouble in China" or "stirring up guerrilla activity in China." The CIA had revealed a list of 50 covert actions that were going on at that time. CIA Director Walter Bedell Smith often expressed worries to subordinates that covert operations would, in terms of attention and funding, overshadow all other types of intelligence gathering, which were really more fundamental and important.

At this point in history, Congressman Charles Kersten enters the intelligence stage. In August, 1951, Congress approved the Kersten Amendment. This amendment authorized $100 million for covert action against the Soviet Union.

Charles Kersten hated the Truman Administration strategy of containment. After Kersten was first sworn into office in 1947, he chaired a House Subcommittee which wanted to examine education and labor in the Soviet Union. Unfortunately, the USSR denied Kersten and his investigators the required visas to do this. In response, Charles Kersten requested that Secretary of State George Marshall *expel all Russian nationals from the U.S.* This request was also refused.

Paul Linebarger, who had experience in military intelligence in World War II, wrote an article which was placed in the *Congressional Record.* The article demanded the beginning of covert operations against the Soviet Union. By way of rebuttal, Secretary of State Dean Acheson said in a speech "we do not propose to subvert the Soviet Union." Charles Kersten was horrified by this. Per author David M. Barrett in his work on the CIA and Congress, Kersten was working closely with the exiled Russian academics at Washington's Catholic Georgetown University School of Foreign Service, the same faculty that had motivated Joseph McCarthy to begin his anti-Communist crusade.

Kersten began to introduce resolution after resolution advocating support for dissidents and exiles behind the Iron Curtain who wished to overthrow the governments there. Kersten found his chance when he introduced an amendment to a foreign aid package called the Mutual Security Act. The Kersten Amendment, generated untold controversy. It passed overwhelmingly in the Congress. It called explicitly for "armies of exiles" to be formed in Europe to either overtly or covertly invade and defeat the Soviet Union. It provided $100 million for this purpose.

The international reaction was immediate. The Soviet Foreign Minister, speaking at the U.N., said the Kersten Amendment "pays traitors and war criminals," which implies that Kersten was possibly in league with former Nazis. In a *New York Times* article, it was suggested that Kersten himself was concerned that the United Nations would itself label his amendment "terrorism." In Kersten's reaction to this, he seemed to be a defender of terrorism. He was quoted saying, "One of the main objectives of real liberation movements is to strike terror into the hearts of communist tyrants." This statement was read into the House of Representatives record. Per author Barrett, this language referring to terror made some Washington insiders wary of Kersten.

One month after the Kersten Amendment passed, Allen Dulles (Deputy Director of the CIA) felt he had to meet with Kersten and tell him that the CIA had plenty of secret funds available and that publicly voting funds for covert operations was counter-productive. Two members of the House, Mike Mansfield and John Vorys, were attending a United Nations committee meeting when asked about the Kersten Amendment. In that setting, they were forced to lie, telling the General Assembly "there are in this law no aggressive acts or aggressive threats contemplated against the Soviet Union or against any of the countries it dominates." The real purpose of this Act, they said, was defense of the North Atlantic area.

As soon as Ike became President, he informed Kersten that Congress should not pass laws or resolutions about covert operations. Kersten's committee planned hearings in Europe some time in 1954. Radio Prague denounced Kersten as "the American organizer of espionage and murder."

In part because of pressure from Kersten and his allies, Senator Lyndon Johnson (now a party leader) took action supporting U.S. covert activity to overthrow the leftist Arbenz government in Guatemala. House Minority Leader John W. McCormack spoke in favor of LBJ on this issue.

In 1954, Charles Kersten, chairman of the House of the Select Committee on Communist Aggression, was defeated in his election. According to Barrett, after the election, Walter Pforzheimer (a long-time CIA icon) who was Legislative Counsel for the CIA, advised Lyman Kilpatrick, Inspector General of the CIA, to alert Allen Dulles about the availability of Kersten to work in intelligence. Kersten wound up, according to Barrett, working as a "consultant" to the White House on "psychological warfare." Wikipedia reports that Kersten worked for Ike "under Nelson Rockefeller" in that role, but that arrangement is not mentioned in other sources.

After working for the Eisenhower administration in 1955 and 1956, Kersten returned to Milwaukee to practice law.

The next fact known about Charles Kersten is that he served as the lawyer for the family of Ukrainian nationalist Stepan Bandera in the murder trial of Bogdan Stashynsky. From 1956 to at least 1966, Kersten practiced law in Milwaukee.

He apparently ran a general practice in partnership with his brother-in-law Arlo McKinnon. He later brought his son into his law practice. Although his practice was a general one, he represented a Hungarian woman in Ohio who was accused of throwing objects at Soviet Ambassador Andrei Gromyko. He also got involved in vocal opposition to the Committee to Abolish HUAC at a campus rally at the University of Wisconsin-Milwaukee. Another such situation was Kersten's participation in an effort to brand an article in the University of Wisconsin's student newspaper *The Daily Cardinal* as being Communist in nature.

But as the pictures in this chapter show, he was far from finished in his role as an activist when it came to issues of politics in Eastern Europe.

In his book TMWKTM, author Dick Russell states that Charles Kersten was America's chief member of The World Anti-Communist Steering Committee.

This appearance shown in the following photograph, by Congressman Charles Kersten in Toronto received little or no mention in the U.S. press. However, one can easily discern the "ABN" in the background which is the acronym of the Anti-Bolshevik Bloc of Nations organization. This

Vice President Nixon Receives a "Freedom Award" Plaque from Americans of Ukrainian Descent in Chicago

Vice President Richard M. Nixon met in Washington, September 19, 1960, on the day when Premier Khrushchev arrived at the U.N., with 202 nationality leaders at an all day conference which the groups held in the Capital. The groups also attended a White House conference at which President Eisenhower. spoke. Among the representatives of 25 groups attending from 19 states were, shown here left to right: Charles Kersten, Milwaukee, Wisconsin; Vice President Nixon; and John Duzansky, Chicago, Illinois.

TWO U.S. ATTORNEYS CHARGE KHRUSHCHEV WITH MURDER OF UKRAINIAN LEADERS

THE HON. CHARLES J. KERSTEN   DR. JAROSLAW PADOCH

KALRSRUHE, Germany, October 16, (UPI).—Two American attorneys plan to accuse Soviet Premier Khrushchev of murder before an international tribunal.

Former U. S. Congressman Charles J. Kersten of Milwaukee, and Dr. Jaroslaw Padoch of New York, addressed the West German Supreme Court today at the conclusion of the espionage-murder trial of Bogdan N. Stashynsky, a confessed Soviet political assassin.

Kersten said he and Padoch have taken steps to accuse Khrushchev and Soviet Minister of State Security General Alexander Shelepin as responsible for the murders committed by Stashynsky.

Stashynsky admitted being an agent of the Soviet State Security Ministry (KGB) and confessed using a special cyanide spray gun to kill Ukrainian nationalist leaders Lev Rebet and Stepan Bandera in separate assaults in Munich in 1957 and 1959.

The Americans represent Bandera's widow. They did not say where they hoped to lodge their accusation. Ukrainian nationalist sources said there are plans to accuse Khrushchev and Shelepin before the UN Human Rights Commission.

Stashynsky defected to the West in August 1961 and made a full confession.

Hon. Charles J. Kersten (USA) addressing the Rally, Toronto, Canada, on June 23rd, 1963

group is featured prominently in the discussion of right-wing groups in the book *General Walker and the Murder of President Kennedy* by Dr. Jeffrey Caulfield. If any right-wing groups had any role in the assassination, the Anti-Bolshevik group would be high on the list of suspected involvement.

And of course, as stated elsewhere in other chapters, on November 7, 1963, just two weeks before the JFK assassination, Charles Kersten sent letters to the three Kennedy brothers warning of the danger of Soviet-sponsored murder. Kersten testified before Congress that he, in fact, had sent these letters (so this apparently happened).

Notes:

For proof that Congressman Charles Kersten sent assassination-related letters to the Kennedy brothers on November 7, 1963, see Investigation of Senator Thomas J. Dodd: Hearings, Eighty-ninth Congress, second session ... pursuant to S. Res. 338, 88th Congress. PT. 1-2 by United States. Congress. Senate. Select Committee on Standards and Conduct. Published 1966, p.313.

For the amazingly close relationship between JFK and Nixon which shaped the Cold War, see *Kennedy and Nixon: The Rivalry That Shaped Postwar America*, by Christopher Matthews. The relationship of both to Congressman Kersten is described at page 46. Also, at page 52, the dismissive attitude by JFK toward Congressman McCormack is reported.

Information on the Dies Committee and Congressman John W. McCormack, see *The Committee: The Extraordinary Career of the House Committee on Un-American Activities* by Walter Goodman at p. 10.

The Contender: Richard Nixon, The Congress Years (1946-1952), by Irving F. Geilman, describes Father Cronin at p. 99 and at p. 124 the author discusses Kersten, Nixon and JFK.

Milwaukee Journal, November 9, 1950. This is the date of the article referred to in the text.

Distinguished Service: The Life of Wisconsin Governor Walter J. Kohler, by Thomas C. Reeves, talks about Kersten and Wisconsin politics at p. 218 and about Kersten's Senate run in 1956 at page 359.

As mentioned in the text, this report is the most powerful document which justifies the Cold War of any writing known to this author in all writings on that subject. It is cited as Investigation of Communist Takeover and Occupation of Poland, Lithuania, and Slovakia, Sixth Interim Report: hearings before the United States House Select Committee To Investigate Communist Aggression and the Forced Incorporation of the Baltic States into the Soviet Union, Subcommittee on Poland, Lithuania, and Slovakia, Eighty-Third Congress, second session, on Sept. 30, Oct. 1, 21, 22, 1954. by United States. Congress. House. Select Committee on Communist Aggression. Published 1954 Congressman Kersten deserves complete credit for producing this heart-wrenching expose.

The CIA & Congress: The Untold Story From Truman To Kennedy, by David M. Barrett tells the entire story of Congressman Kersten and his unhelpful actions which impacted the CIA. Especially relevant pages of the work by Barrett regarding Kersten can be found at pps. 95, 103-4,107 and 205.

In *The Man Who Knew Too Much,* by Dick Russell (*TMWKTM*), Kersten's role in the trial of Bogdan Stashynsky is discussed in Russell quotes from Kersten's summation at the trial of Stashynsky. Kersten, of course, was counsel for the family and this is discussed at p. 596 of *TMWKTM* by Russell.

Chapter 9

THE TWO FOILED PLOTS IN NOVEMBER, 1963

THE CHICAGO PLOT

In the book *Ultimate Sacrifice, John and Robert Kennedy, the Plan for a Coup in Cuba, and the Murder of JFK*, by Lamar Waldron, with Thom Hartmann, the reader will find the best presentation of the evidence available about the Chicago Plot.

One of the most important sources for Waldron was former Senate Investigator (and researcher), Bernard "Bud" Fensterwald. Fensterwald was one of the most aggressive early assassination researchers and the author of the book *The Assassination of JFK: By Coincidence or Conspiracy*. Fensterwald was also at one time a Senate Investigator for the Senate Subcommittee for Privileges and Elections, a subcommittee of the Senate Foreign Relations Committee under the powerful Chairman J. William Fulbright. The Senate Foreign Relations Committee was related to a committee known as the Gillette Committee. The Gillette Committee investigated Senator Joe McCarthy. In the opinion of this author, since Fensterwald was involved (in real time) with the events spanning the period from the McCarthy era all the way to Watergate, he should be considered a source with a possible vested interest or point of view.

Oswald's trip to Chicago, which occurred in the weeks after his well-publicized New Orleans incident and prior to the Chicago attempt is something of which most historians are unaware.

Oswald's trip to Chicago included a brief stop in Atlanta. In the late summer of 1963, JFK had originally planned to visit Atlanta and give a major speech, but local Democrats had urged him to cancel or scale back the appearance because of concerns about JFK's stance on civil rights. Apparently, plans had already been made for Oswald to visit Atlanta en route to Chicago, and his trip plans remained in place. The author of an investigation into the Ku Klux Klan writes that "one of her sources told her that Oswald, in the summer of 1963, had called on [Klan] Imperial Wizard James Venable in his office in Atlanta seeking the names of right-wing associates."

Oswald apparently continued on to Chicago, but first stopped at the University of Illinois at Urbana. An FBI memo says Oswald reportedly inquired at the office of the Assistant Dean of Students about Cuban student organizations, and asked the secretary "if...she had ever seen him on TV in New Orleans." The FBI memo says Oswald "expressed interest in any campus organization advocating humanist views" to the secretary.

Someone wanted to leave a trail connecting Oswald to Chicago, prior to the attempt to assassinate JFK there.

According to Abraham Bolden, (a Secret Service officer whose situation is to be discussed in depth in this chapter) [HSCA 180-10070-10273 interview with Abraham Bolden 1-19-78, declassified 1-5-96], "on or around October 30, 1963...the FBI sent `a teletype message to the Chicago Secret Service office stating that an attempt to assassinate the President would be made on November 2, 1963, by a four-man team using high-powered rifles."

At some point in 1963, the Secret Service was tipped off about a possible assassination plot against a Kennedy motorcade in Chicago (crediting a Secret Service memo).

"In addition, Secret Service agents were shown four photos of the men alleged to be involved in the plot" There may have been names attached; but Abraham Bolden remembers the names Gonzales and Rodriguez.

The names Gonzales and Rodriguez would also appear regarding the Tampa plot and the Tampa Fair Play for Cuba committee (FPCC) discussed below.

The Secret Service found the four men mentioned above staying at a rooming house in Chicago, which because of the transient nature of most rooming houses, is another indication that at least some of the men were not local.

An unconfirmed source from the Cuban community claimed that the men had Montreal connections. Also, according to Bolden, the Secret Service blew the surveillance of the four subjects. Apparently, for some reason, the Chicago Police had not wished to be involved or in any way to supplement the surveillance.

The HSCA report also states that "on October 30, 1963, the Secret Service learned that an individual named Thomas Arthur Vallee, a Chicago resident who was outspokenly opposed to President Kennedy's foreign policy, was in possession of several weapons." Secret Service agents interviewed Vallee and found him to have M-1 rifles and ammunition. According to Edwin Black, Vallee's place of employment looked "out over the Jackson Street exit ramp where Kennedy's limousine would have been" traveling during the motorcade. There were numerous sources that confirmed that Vallee worked in a location where he would have had a straight shot at the President's slowing motorcade.

Thomas Arthur Vallee, according to Edwin Black of the *Chicago Daily News*, was an ex-marine, had returned to Chicago in August 1963 and had been involved, like Oswald, in training anti-Castro Cubans.

According to a Warren Commission document Vallee was discharged honorably by the Marines as being a paranoid schizophrenic with homosexual features, yet was allowed to re-enlist only 1½ years later. [This sounds, very much like the mysterious, almost random type of paperwork gyrations within the military records of Lee Harvey Oswald]. This only adds credence to the theory that Oswald was only one of many possible similar agents being run by military intelligence at the time. Since Vallee was a supposed John Birch Society type, he could have been an ideal candidate to be of use in infiltrating right wing groups in that period.

In Waldron's book *Ultimate Sacrifice*, at page 630, he attributes information to researcher Vince Palamara which says, "Mr. Vallee claimed he was framed by someone with special knowledge about him, such as his 'CIA assignment to train exiles to assassinate Castro.'"

On or about Thursday, October 31, 1963, just one day after the Chicago agents' pretext interview of Vallee "Vallee's landlady called the [Secret] Service office and said that Vallee was not going to work on Saturday," according to the testimony of Agent Edward Tucker to Congressional investigators. The agent testified that because Saturday was "the day of JFK's visit to Chicago," this information "resulted in the [Secret] Service having the Chicago Police Department surveil Vallee."

Author Waldron questions why the Secret Service wouldn't have asked for surveillance if the landlady hadn't called ... [because Vallee] "would have been at his job with a clear shot at JFK's motorcade. ... Secret Service agents kept watch on two members of the four-man assassin team. But ... the surveillance ... was blown."[27][HSCA 180-10070-0273 interview with Abraham Bolden 1-19-78, declassified 1-5-96].

[*Ultimate Sacrifice*, p. 633] With their surreptitious surveillance blown, the Secret Service felt it had no choice but to go ahead and detain the men. Black writes that "the two men were taken into custody (but not actually arrested or *booked*) in the very early Friday hours and brought to the Secret Service headquarters. There are no records that any weapons were found in their possession or back at the rooming house.[Black, op. sit.]

[*Ultimate Sacrifice*, p. 646] Although the Warren Commission was aware of both Vallee and the rumors of the four-man threat, they never bothered to interview Vallee, and neither did the HSCA or any other government committee investigating the JFK assassination.... Even today, dozens of Secret Service files on Vallee have not been released (more than a decade after his death) and they are deemed so sensitive that they can't even be released in heavily censored versions, as many documents have been.

[*Ultimate Sacrifice*, p. 648] Yet even with all Vallee's weapons, and the reported threats against JFK, Vallee was only convicted a month and a half after JFK's death of "Unlawful use of a weapon and in addition was imposed a $5 suspended fine on a traffic violation."

Abraham Bolden, the first black Secret Service officer, went public with his knowledge of certain facts related to the JFK assassination. His revelations got him into severe trouble with authorities who were apparently motivated by a desire to cover up the truth about the assassination. As a result, Bolden was framed for a crime and sent to prison.

On December 5, 1967 while Bolden was serving his sentence at the United States Medical Center for Federal Prisoners in Springfield, Missouri, attorneys John Hosmer (Bolden's Lawyers), Mark Lane (author of *Rush to Judgment*), and Richard V. Burnes (assistant to Jim Garrison) held a new conference in which they stated they had received information from Bolden that the Secret Service was aware of a prior assassination attempt on Kennedy in Chicago. According to the attorneys, the Secret Service had been informed that an attempt on the President would be made in Chicago which resulted in the cancellation of his visit due to safety concerns. They stated that Bolden said he and other agents had shadowed a suspect due to this report.

On March 21, 1970, Sherman Skolnick appeared on an FM radio program with Ted Weber of WTMX and stated that Bolden was falsely imprisoned to prevent him from revealing that there was a plot to kill Kennedy in Chicago. The *Chicago Sun-Times* reported that they attempted to contact Bolden regarding the allegations, but he refused to comment.

The following month on April 6, Skolnick filed suit with the United States District Court in Chicago against the National Archives and Records Service stating that the agency had illegally suppressed documents that pointed to what he claimed was a plot to assassinate Kennedy at the Army-Air Force game in Chicago on November 2, 1963. His suit demanded that the Warren Commission – that stated Lee Harvey Oswald acted alone in killing Kennedy – be declared "null and void."

Three of the eleven documents attached to the suit, (documents which Skolnick said were sent to him by an undisclosed person), were FBI reports pertaining to the assassination of Kennedy. The plaintiff also claimed that they had recently been declassified and that they related to the arrest of Thomas Arthur Vallee. According to Skolnick's suit, Vallee was an Oswald look-alike and one of four or five people who conspired to assassinate Kennedy in Chicago, but that the attempt was aborted following a traffic stop in which Vallee was found to have a concealed rifle in his possession. Possession of a concealed rifle was likely to have been a crime in Chicago by itself.

The suit stated that the assassination attempt was rescheduled for three weeks later in Dallas. Skolnick said that the Warren Commission forwarded materials to the Archives that connected Vallee to Oswald by way of the rifle and a 1962 Ford Falcon. In response, the United States Department of Justice was reported to have "no comment" and National Archivist Marion Johnson said he had seen nothing in the Archives that connected Vallee to an assassination attempt.

Time magazine reported that "a former Secret Service agent" was among those mentioned by Skolnick. Skolnick later told Kenn Thomas of *Steamshovel Press* that a "mysterious courier" gave him a "pile of documents about the Chicago plot against Kennedy" that had been compiled by Bolden. In that interview, Skolnick claimed that the "secret documents" had been stolen from the National Archives. In June 1970, Skolnick petitioned Judge Huber Will of the United States District Court for the Northern District of Illinois for a stay of the proceedings. Skolnick said that he could not receive a fair hearing and would resume the case "when the time best suits the occasion." On Monday, June 22, Judge Will ordered the stay.

In 1975, the allegation of a "Chicago plot" was reiterated in an issue of *Chicago Independent*. The author Black was reported to have drawn upon Skolnick's research and first hand information provided in part by Bolden and in part by those "people with information about the alleged plot" who sought out Skolnick.

THE TAMPA PLOT

Following the foiled attempt in Chicago, a second plot unfolded in Tampa, Florida.

Four days before he was killed in Dallas, President Kennedy visited Tampa. There he addressed the Steelworkers Union and then later in Miami the Inter-American Press Association (IAPA). To the latter group, Kennedy delivered a major speech on Cuba, part of which was said to have been designed to be a signal which would confirm his support for certain persons who might be involved in a possible coup in Cuba.

In the course of this trip, (which included a long motorcade that began and ended at MacDill AFB in Tampa), Kennedy met privately with the commander of MacDill, a base where a quick-strike unit was prepared to intervene in Cuba if called upon. As author Peter Dale Scott has pointed out, MacDill AFB was the recipient of the special message from a Dallas Police Department officer named Stringfellow, informing the Quick-Strike unit that the accused assassin was a Cuban Communist, a possible attempt to instigate a mobilization for an invasion of Cuba.

Also in the course of the visit to Tampa, the Secret Service and local authorities investigated a plot to shoot the President with a high powered rifle while he rode in the motorcade. The plan also had a patsy, Gilberto Lopez. Lopez was a Cuban affiliated with the FPCC, with whom Oswald was also associated. Lopez was allegedly trying to get back into Cuba, and eventually did so, via the same route Oswald allegedly tried to take, via Texas and on to Mexico City.

News of the Tampa plot was confined to a single newspaper report, and picked up by the UPI, but Lamar Waldron and Thom Hartmann explore this plot further and in some detail in their books.

The Tampa attempt featured even more parallels to Dallas than the Chicago Plot: They include a long presidential motorcade in an open limo, a hard left turn to slow JFK's limo down in front of a red brick building which, like the TSBD in Dallas, had many unsecured windows. There was to be a gunman with a high-powered rifle planning to shoot from a building, and there were reports to officials of organized crime involvement. A key suspect in Tampa named Gilberto Lopez was a young white male of slender build, a government asset, and a former defector who had a Russian connection in his background. Like Oswald, Lopez was seen as apolitical or anti-Castro by some, yet had gotten into a fight over seemingly pro-Castro statements. Lopez was also linked to Oswald prior to the Tampa attempt.

But, prior to the Tampa attempt, there are reports that Oswald was in Tampa, meeting with members of the Fair Play for Cuba Committee, people whom the FBI would certainly call "subversives." The alleged Oswald trip to Tampa can't be dated precisely, but most reports place it somewhere in the few weeks leading up to the day of the November Tampa attempt.

One of the two surviving small articles mentions "a memo from the White House Secret Service dated Nov. 8 [that] reported: "Subject made statement that he will use a gun.... Subject is described as white, male, 20, slender build, etc." That memo, cited in a November 23, 1963 article in the *Tampa Tribune* may no longer exist in Secret Service files. The suspect's description in the memo matches either Gilberto Lopez described by the FBI "age 23, 5'7", 125 lbs ... fair complexion") or Lee Harvey Oswald far better than the initial description that would be issued in Dallas four days later, after JFK was shot. The Oswald description in Dallas caused a lookout to be issued for a thirty-five-year-old man. The article in the *Tampa Tribune* also quoted Tampa Police Chief J.P. Mullins as saying that there were two people involved in the threat, and "he did not know if the other two persons may have followed" JFK "to Dallas." At a time near the JFK assassination, the FBI had obtained some information through an informant about a possible assassination attempt. The information came from right-wing Minuteman operative named Joseph Milteer.

In his first interview about the subject since 1963, former Tampa Police Chief J.P. Mullins confirmed the existence of the plot to authors Waldron and Hartmann in 1996. He indicated that the threat in question was not part of a far right threat that was based on the Joseph Milteer information. Mullins didn't recall that the Milteer threat had been shared with the Tampa police. Chief Mullins also said that they [the Tampa Police] had not been told about the recent Chicago plot to kill JFK. However, when given the full names of the two men linked to Gilberto Lopez whose last names were Rodriguez and Gonzales, Mullins thought they sounded familiar. He couldn't say for sure. He recalled that no suspects were arrested that day, but said that if a suspect wasn't taken "into custody on some legal pretext, they'd keep them under surveillance," which was similar to what happened with Vallee and the other suspects in Chicago. He said that "the Secret Service gave us names to watch for, and our own Intelligence Unit had names to watch for," but Oswald's name "wasn't on any [watch] list."

Regarding the Tampa motorcade, Mullins said a "Secret Service agent told him it was the President's longest exposure in the U.S. – the only one longer was in Berlin." JFK's motorcade was scheduled to go from MacDill Air Force Base to Al Lopez Field, then to downtown Tampa and the National guard Armory. It would then travel to the International Inn, and finally back to MacDill Air Force Base. According to an article about the motorcade, "the Tampa police alone supplied 200 of the department's approximately 270 uniformed force." In addition, "four hundred men from federal law enforcement agencies such as the U.S. Air Force also saw duty, "including law enforcement officers from the state, six counties, and the cities of St. Petersburg and Clearwater," With a total of six hundred trained professionals guarding JFK, it's clear how serious the security concerns were.

An anonymous Tampa official told ... [Waldron and Hartmann] that one of the three places that especially concerned the Secret Service was a bridge, though he didn't understand why at the time. Once we informed him that Chicago newsmen had told a former Senate investigator that the Chicago plot involved a "planned assassination attempt from one of the overpasses," the official said he finally understood the Secret Service's concern about the bridge. The other two places the Secret Service was concerned about were 1) "a place where gangsters hung out" and 2) the Floridian Hotel (sometimes referred to as the Grand Floridian).

The high Florida law enforcement official identified the full name of a man linked to Gilberto Lopez and the Fair Play for Cuba Committee. This man "was watched closely in conjunction with JFK's visit." The man's last name was "Rodriguez." The official was aware of Gilberto Lopez, whom he called "Gilbert" and "thought he was an informant" for some agency. However, he didn't connect Lopez at the time to the JFK threat; that would come later, after JFK's death, when the FBI and others began investigating Lopez.

The Florida official confirmed that "JFK had been briefed he was in danger."

One of the few Secret Service documents which have survived relating to the Tampa motorcade, because it was provided to Congressional investigators, says that "underpasses [were] controlled by police and military units, [while the] Sheriff's office secured the roofs of major buildings in the downtown and suburban areas."

In fact, the Minuteman extremist Joseph Milteer himself commented on the aborted hit when he spoke to covert Miami police informant William Somersett, after JFK's death. Somersett, the informant, told investigators that Milteer "said that Kennedy could have been killed" on his trip to Florida, "but somebody called the FBI and gave the thing away, and of course, he was well guarded and everything went "pluey," and "everybody kept quiet and waited for Texas."

Notes:

See *Ultimate Sacrifice, John and Robert Kennedy, the Plan for a Coup in Cuba, and the Murder of JFK,* by Lamar Waldron, with Thom Hartmann, which provides the best presentation of the two other assassination attempts on JFK in October-November 1963.

The Assassination of JFK: By Coincidence or Conspiracy, by Bernard Fensterwald (1977).

Dr. Jerry D Rose Stoner; *An Introduction, The Fourth Decade,* November 1995. This article documents the visit by Lee Harvey Oswald to the Imperial Wizard of the KKK James Venable in Atlanta.

HSCA 180-10070-10273 interview with Abraham Bolden 1-19-78, declassified 1-5-96 documents the teletype sent to the Chicago Secret Service by the FBI on 10-31-1963.

HSCA 180-10105-10393, Secret Service memo 3029-63, declassified in 1992 documents tipoff to Service about attempts against JFK other than in Dallas, i.e. Chicago and Tampa.

In *Ultimate Sacrifice* at p. 625, the alleged Montreal Connections of the suspects is mentioned.

HSCA report supra, p. 231 is referenced in the text with regard to Vallee.

.HSCA report supra, P 231: This citation documents the reference in the text about Vallee.

Chicago Daily News, 12-3-63 articles by writer Edwin Black document the information attributed in the text to the *Chicago Daily News.*

Refer to the Warren Commission Document 117 which can be found in the Mary Ferrell Foundation website describes the alleged paranoid schizophrenic condition of Vallee.

Author of *Survivor's Guilt: The Secret Service and the Failure to Protect President Kennedy,* by Vince Palamara at p. 72 documents the allegation of Vallee's CIA-connected history.

HSCA 180-10071-10276, 1-19-78 interview summary of Edward Tucker as described in text.

https://en.wikipedia.org/wiki/Abraham_Bolden,HSCA 180-10070-0273 interview with Abraham Bolden 1-19-78, declassified 1-5-96. This source is important because it reveals some details of the two plots known to Abraham Bolden.

"The Tampa Plot in Retrospect" –(A Newspaper Article By William Kelly) This newspaper article is the slender thread which preserves proof that the Tampa plot actually took place as described in this chapter.

In *Ultimate Sacrifice* at p. 653, the fact is presented that neither the Warren Commission nor the House Select Committee on Assassinations bothered to investigate or gather facts about the Chicago or Tampa plots.

As referenced in the text, see Ch 54 in *Ultimate Sacrifice*, note 6 Rory O'Connor, "Oswald Visited Tampa," Tampa Tribune 6-24-76; phone interview with confidential high Florida law enforcement source 12-10-96; Skip Johnson and Tony Durr, "Ex-Tampan in JFK plot?," *Tampa Tribune* 9-5-76.

In *Ultimate Sacrifice*, p. 685 the Mullin interview is documented. See Ch.56, note 8, Phone interview with J.P. Mullins 12-10-96.

Ch 56, In *Ultimate Sacrifice* by Waldron and Hartmann, note 13 the phone interview with confidential high Florida law-enforcement source 12-10-96 is described.

See Ch 56 of *Ultimate Sacrifice*, note 17 RIF 154-10002-10423 also cited by Vince Palmera discussing the surveillance of rooftops and buildings along the Tampa motorcade route.

Chapter 10

McCarthyism: Joe McCarthy and the Kennedy Family

In the period from 1949 to 1963, the political base was built which provided the background for the assassination of John F. Kennedy. Of course no one knew that this tide would lead to the death of a sitting President. But the important question is not which brand of bullets killed JFK. The question is who in the U.S. Government and in Western Europe provided the political base for the act and for the cover-up. As you will see as you read on, once you figure out the above concept, then all the forensic and other details fall into place like magic!

There are a number of reasons why an explanation of the JFK assassination begins with the story of Senator Joseph McCarthy:

1. Working for Joe McCarthy, his committee and its successor, was the only job Robert Kennedy ever held from 1953 to 1961, when he became Attorney General, except for two or three months during that period.

2. McCarthy was a militant Catholic anti-Communist activist as were both Kennedy's prior to 1959. Both Kennedy's were involved in the McCarthy Committee in one or both of its two forms.

3. While militant Catholic anti-Communism was not the prime factor in the assassination, it was a necessary precedent and a major contributing factor.

4. The change from militant Catholic anti-Communism to a tolerant attitude toward former Communists like Alger Hiss by both Kennedys in 1959 was intolerable to the power brokers in the Senate and was considered a major betrayal by those brokers.

5. McCarthy was the pioneer of the 1950's Red-baiting type of committee chairman. A parallel committee to the McCarthy Committee, the SISS committee, can be shown to be the political hub of the assassination plot. The methods and philosophy of the McCarthy Committee and the Senate SISS Committee were nearly identical and cannot be separated when seeking an understanding of the JFK assassination.

6. Congressman Charles Kersten of Wisconsin was a close political partner to McCarthy in Wisconsin. As we have described, Kersten later became involved in working for Eisenhower in psychological warfare and Kersten almost certainly betrayed a knowledge of the assassination before it occurred.

7. McCarthy was one of three militant Catholic senators from the North who managed the Catholic side of the anti-Communist alliance with Southern segregationists. The other two were Senator Pat McCarran and Senator Thomas J. Dodd. Their backgrounds and careers followed the same path and can best be understood together.

The fear of Communism began as soon as the West received news of the Russian Revolution in 1917. But this fear lay mostly in abeyance until 1945 and the victory of the Soviet Union over Hitler.

The Spanish Civil War occurred from 1936 to 1939. This war pitted Communists against Fascists in a bitter struggle to the death. But in this war, most Americans who fought battled side by side with the Communists. In the first 30 years of the history of Soviet Communism, a great many people thought of it as a well-intentioned experiment. They assumed that it would meet the fate of all similar experiments in the past. Communism, they thought, would sooner or later collapse under the sheer weight of human greed. It took a long time, but that is, of course, what eventually happened.

But as for the Catholic Church, they did not have the luxury of waiting. Communism was feeding primarily on their flocks. As the forces of Stalin rolled over Eastern Europe, they encountered mostly Catholic countries such as Ukraine, Poland and Lithuania. And in these Eastern countries, there were appalling atrocities committed against Catholic clergy, since the Communists could seemingly not co-exist with Catholicism.

Against this backdrop arose the virulent anti-Communist, Senator Joseph McCarthy. Although almost every American has heard many times over about the nature of McCarthyism, most never knew that the prime motivation of McCarthy was his faithfulness to his religion. McCarthy received his first encouragement and advice from Catholic experts in international relations at the Georgetown University School of Foreign Service in Washington. It is for this reason that we will examine the background of McCarthyism and how McCarthy laid the foundation of a movement that was, ironically, a major factor in the assassination of the first Catholic President, John F. Kennedy.

The first fact that jumps out about McCarthy is that he was almost an honorary member of the Kennedy family. When Robert F. Kennedy graduated from law school at the University of Virginia, the only job he wanted was to be head counsel for the Permanent Subcommittee on Investigations, the McCarthy Committee.

RFK was hired by McCarthy and was to remain as either an assistant counsel or counsel for that committee or its later modified form until September 1959, with only a few months' hiatus during that period. RFK served the McCarthy Committee until it merged with the Labor Committee. It was renamed the Senate Rackets Committee – or the McClellan Committee – as it was referred to in the press. Since Senator John F. Kennedy was a member of the Labor Committee before the merger, the Kennedy brothers served together on behalf of the Committee as it investigated mobsters and labor racketeers.

What most people are never told, is that the stated purpose of the McClellan Committee was to investigate Communists in the Labor movement. Barry Goldwater was a major force on the McClellan Committee in that cause. The transformation of the McCarthy Committee from an anti-Communist to a "Labor" committee mirrored the conversion of the Kennedy brothers from militant Catholic anti-Communist activists to, some would say, apologists for known Communists.

This conversion did not sit well with the international Catholic clergy.

SEN. JOSEPH McCARTHY

Joseph McCarthy was born and reared in a rural area near the towns of Grand Chute and Appleton, Wisconsin. Joe's community was mostly German. His father Tim was an Irish Catholic and fathered ten children. The children were taken to church in Appleton. Around this time, Appleton became one of the larger cities in the region.

McCarthy earned his high school diploma in only one year, at age 20. In the years prior, he had earned a significant amount of money by starting his own business raising chickens.

The Fox Valley of Wisconsin was also heavily Catholic. Appleton was 40% Catholic; nearby Green Bay was 73% Catholic. So, not only was the community in which Joe McCarthy grew up mostly Catholic, but when he left the Fox Valley, he was to spend the following five years at Marquette University in Milwaukee, a Jesuit institution. There he presumably earned his bachelors degree in some form, since he also graduated with a degree in law which normally follows the undergraduate baccalaureate. In addition to earning both his degrees there, Joe also participated as an amateur boxer.

Like the unique Fox Valley of Wisconsin, Milwaukee would be somewhat atypical when compared to other large cities in the Midwest. It featured many residents of German heritage who lived on the north side and many of Polish heritage who lived on the south side. Milwaukee was more old-world in its outlook than a typical American city. Being settled by Germans and Poles, some undoubtedly may have brought such attitudes as anti-semitism and other prejudices from the Europe of the 1800's.

Wisconsin was the birthplace of the Progressive movement led by Senator and Governor "Fighting Bob" La Follete. Wisconsin had the first income tax and introduced unemployment insurance to the U.S. The anti-slavery Republican Party began in the tiny Wisconsin community of Ripon. Despite this fundamentally liberal tradition, Wisconsin gave the country Senator Joe McCarthy. Unfortunately for his state, his name in the form "McCarthyism," became an unpleasant addition to Webster's dictionary.

McCarthy had an almost uncanny talent when it came to the art of character assassination. There is no school which offers a major in character assassination. There is no academy of libel, no college of slander. So how did McCarthy gain this almost unique skill in this very nasty art? And why did someone like Joseph McCarthy become so involved with the Kennedy family and why did he turn out to be a close friend of Robert F. Kennedy right up until his death in 1957? Let's dig a little deeper.

After graduation from law school Joe quickly, on his own, opened a private law office. As a small town attorney with many competitors, the office of judge was a quick way to get financial security. To achieve this office, Joe ran a political campaign against a much older incumbent judge. Joe may have been a born politician. At age 30, Joe became the youngest person ever to be elected as Circuit Judge in the history of Wisconsin. To understand the character of Joe McCarthy, one can look at the reason for these very rapid achievements.

At first glance it would seem that finishing high school in just one year might indicate that a person was a young prodigy. In the case of Joe McCarthy, though, the case is quite different. McCarthy was often quick across the finish line, as when he became a judge at a record young age.

But McCarthy would always be like a runner cutting across the infield to the finish line. He never had patience to achieve goals methodically. It was this trait which caused him to grab onto anti-Communism. It was a quick way for him to be at the center of attention.

If not for his rabid anti-Communism, Joe would have had to patiently develop a reputation as a leader and a successful Senator. He would have to develop contacts, friendships, accomplishments and newspaper endorsements. For McCarthy, Red-baiting was a short-cut to instant attention and, albeit negative, notoriety.

In his habit of cutting across the infield on his way to the finish line, one could ask who was cheated along the way? The sad answer is: McCarthy's desire for notoriety didn't require him to climb the slopes of seniority to wait his turn. He realized he could get instant fame and notoriety by slandering and defaming people. Under the law of Senatorial immunity, he couldn't be sued libel and slander.

Joe got enough experience as a judge at such a young age that he learned how to exercise authority in his courtroom. The power possessed by a judge is something rarely experienced by someone 30 years old. This position immediately taught Joe how to exploit the power of the law. Joe would also learn how to find a middle ground between the arguments of opposing counsel. And he would learn how to make quick decisions to resolve the countless issues that come up in trials, hearings and other proceedings. Finally, he obviously learned quickly which types of arguments succeed and which arguments are doomed to fail.

Soon after Joe's accession to the bench, World War II broke out. He enlisted in the Marines at the age of 33. He received a direct commission as an officer. During the War, he saw combat duty as an aviator and served in the South Pacific on bombing runs.

After the war, he returned to Wisconsin and soon ran for the Senate. The Wisconsin constitution made it illegal for a person to hold public office in addition to his position as judge. The Wisconsin statutes enforced this law by making this practice a felony. But one of Joe's political friends got the penalty of felony repealed for Joe. So it was merely illegal and unconstitutional, but not a felony for him to hold these two offices. He was elected to the Senate and remained on the payroll as a judge. His excuse for doing this was that everyone is entitled to maintain their source of income and the position of judge was his source of income. Although it was illegal, McCarthy didn't stand on formalities.

McCarthy's personal qualities included extroversion, the habitual borrowing of money from friends, gambling, drinking (which would eventually cause his early death), playing the stock market and generally leading a fast-paced, helter-skelter lifestyle.

Some of those who knew him claimed that he enjoyed the company of many women and that women flocked around him. Others pointed to a lack of any steady female companionship and that he "was not the marrying kind." There isn't any evidence that Joe even had more than one date with any female up until his marriage in his 40's. There were no signs of Joe settling down into an ordinary everyday relationship, which might have been of benefit to him and his career. There was clandestine information passed between journalists of possible gay behavior, though never proved.

His marriage just before his death at age 45 was less about romantic attachment and more about an employer-employee relationship with his eventual wife and staffer Jean Fraser Kerr. All this probably makes sense. Joe would have made a terrible husband by any standard. When Joe finally married at age 45, he was well on his way to serious health problems stemming from his alcoholism.

THE MALMEDY MASSACRE

After being elected to the Senate, Joe's early legislative interests included just two issues: 1) public housing and 2) investigating the Malmedy massacre.

McCarthy, for no logical reason, took an intense interest in the Malmedy Massacre. The key to this part of the McCarthy story is that upon becoming Senator, he was immediately taken over to Europe and involved in a case involving Nazis.

This pattern was also followed by one of McCarthy's successors, Senator Thomas Dodd. Dodd had been assistant prosecutor at the Nuremberg Trials. The third McCarthyite Senator, Pat McCarran of Nevada was also involved in Europe: in his case it was face-to-face involvement with Hitler ally Francisco Franco, dictator of Spain.

The Malmedy massacre occurred during the Battle of the Bulge, when a German SS division captured a group of American soldiers, and then proceeded to machine gun 83 of them to death in cold blood. In the immediate vicinity of this atrocity, up to 500 people were killed by these German soldiers.

Some American military personnel responded in kind by allegedly torturing or otherwise mistreating the Germans who had committed these acts. Various Quaker and several other Church groups got involved in this issue. The Malmedy massacre wound up in a Senate investigation. The Special Investigations Subcommittee was involved in the investigation and McCarthy was a member.

Joe became emotionally involved in the Malmedy massacre situation. This was especially true when it was alleged that a Communist over in Europe had stirred the whole issue up just to give America some bad publicity.

In the Malmedy case, the position taken by Joe was opposite to that taken by the U.S. military. This anti-military attitude would surface again in when he investigated the military for allegedly harboring Communists.

After the Malmedy Massacre, Joe found other issues with which to be involved. He introduced an amendment to the European Recovery Act. This amendment was approved by Arthur Vandenberg, a prominent moderate Republican. It required the return of all prisoners of war as a precondition for any economic aid for any country.

Joe, however, went even further. He called for the repudiation of certain portions of the Yalta and Potsdam agreements relating to the theory that prisoners of war could somehow be considered war reparations. Joe labeled this concept of reparations as foreign to American principles. For some reason, Joe considered himself so important that he could reverse the outcome of a major event like the Yalta or Potsdam conferences. This was a sign of McCarthy's grandiosity. Somehow he believed that he could second-guess the work of such world figures as Stalin, Churchill, Roosevelt, or Truman. His proposal was also a typical cheap shot and an empty exercise. Repudiation of Yalta or Potsdam would obviously never happen.

DINNER AT THE COLONY CLUB

It was not long after that when Joe McCarthy jumped directly into the business of hunting and bashing Communists. There is some debate about how and why this happened. Historians tend to agree on one point: that this all began over a famous "dinner at the Colony Club."

On January 7, 1950, McCarthy met with three people at a dinner at the Colony restaurant in Washington, DC. The three were Charles Kraus, William A. Roberts (the attorney for investigative journalist Drew Pearson) and Father Edmund A. Walsh, 63, founder of the Georgetown School of Foreign Service.

Drew Pearson, along with his partner, Jack Anderson, were journalists who "poked their nose" into the affairs of the U.S. Government, often behind the scenes. They did so to an extreme which has no parallel in post-2000 journalism. Father Walsh, also at the table, was founder of the Foreign Service School at Catholic Georgetown University. This university had achieved preeminence in Washington higher education, especially when it came to foreign policy. If any issues of national importance were discussed over that dinner they would likely be foreign policy. This was a time of great international uncertainty and upheaval. Most historians date the beginning of McCarthy's anti-Communist crusade to that dinner in 1950. It should also be mentioned that Joe claimed to be initially motivated in his anti-Communist crusade by James Forrestal, the first Secretary of Defense.

But there is still a third theory. In his 1968 book, Roy Cohn, a close associate of McCarthy, claimed that a military intelligence officer at the Pentagon distributed a 100-page FBI report to four Senators. According to Cohn, this officer hoped that at least one of the four Senators would take up the anti-Communist crusade. According to this story, three of the Senators refused – but Joe agreed.

As a factual matter, there were two other people who prompted Joe McCarthy to launch his unbridled, mostly single-handed attack on worldwide Communism. The first of the two was Joseph P. Kennedy, patriarch of the Massachusetts Kennedy clan. Kennedy was a Catholic activist and leading spokesman and personal friends with Eugenio Pacelli, who ruled as Pope Pius XII from 1938 to 1958. Kennedy invited McCarthy to his Hyannis Port compound as a guest starting in the late 1940's. He apparently also encouraged one or more of the Kennedy daughters to date McCarthy, which, fortunately for them, never went anywhere.

Let's take a closer look at that situation. McCarthy was an alcoholic with no real kind of life going for him. The idea that Joseph P. Kennedy would push McCarthy on his daughters is just another example of the character of Joseph P. Kennedy. He would not hesitate to use his own family as props in his wide-ranging plan for America.

One can add to this the fact that McCarthy hired Robert Kennedy as counsel for his Permanent Subcommittee on Investigations. Joseph P. Kennedy had landed this job for RFK. According to the story, Kennedy, Sr. was promised that RFK would soon be made chief counsel. Of course, this never happened. RFK then resigned from the staff of the Committee. It is hard to see how this kind of job, with the questionable reputation which the Committee soon developed, would be of interest to a person just beginning his career in the law and had a world of opportunities.

The second high-level instigator for Joe McCarthy's career was J. Edgar Hoover. McCarthy and J. Edgar Hoover dined at a local restaurant in Washington on a regular basis. McCarthy was the only elected official who made use of Hoover's box seats at a local racetrack when Hoover was absent. Just for the record, Hoover was not a Catholic activist, he was a Presbyterian so McCarthyism spread quickly beyond the world of Catholic activism.

It would be a mistake to ignore the obvious role of the above mentioned Catholic priests in getting McCarthy's anti-Communist crusade off the ground. And importantly, there was also Joseph P. Kennedy himself. For two decades, Kennedy had been considered by many, including Franklin Roosevelt, to be the preeminent Catholic in the United States.

We have mentioned the devastating civil war in Spain where the Communist-supported democratically elected Republic had been forced from power. This victory had been achieved by General Francisco Franco. Franco had characterized his counter-revolution in Spain as a crusade on behalf of the Catholic Church. Anti-clerical forces in Spain had set fire to convents. The Republicans had been democratically elected, but they were secular in outlook. Their only real ally was Joseph Stalin.

Another example where the Church was pitted against Communism was Italy. In 1958, the CIA had run its largest operation of the decade. The intelligence agency had spent over $10 million on the country's moderate political parties trying to avert an expected electoral victory by the Communists. In hindsight, it seems impossible to imagine how there could have been a Communist threat in Italy, since Italy has always been 99% Catholic and was home to the Vatican. It was called, after all, the *Roman* Catholic Church. Hard to imagine a Roman Catholic Church centered in a Rome which was Communist.

In France during World War II, the French resistance had been spearheaded by the Communists. The Communists in France were almost the only force ruthless enough to stand up to the Nazis. In France, these same Communists ex-partisans were still around after World War II, and thus were considered as part of the threat of Communism.

And as if all the above issues were not enough, the Soviet military had occupied all of Eastern Europe and probably had the military capability to overrun the entirety of Europe if they so chose. Communism reigned in Yugoslavia which bordered on Italy. In this nightmare scenario, one could imagine St. Peter's Church being turned into a museum of Communism. One could envision statues of Lenin and Stalin decorating St. Peter's Basilica. In the worst case scenario, the Catholic Church could have been relegated to survive only in Ireland and the poor countries of Latin America. History would have changed beyond imagination.

And on top of all of this was the galloping threat of worldwide Communism. It was not just a threat in Eastern Europe, but all around the globe. In the U.S. there soon arose an even more pressing situation, the "loss of China" to the Communists. This China situation was very traumatic to American conservatives. Still another hot spot was Korea. On top of that, there was the defeat of the French by Vietnamese Communists at Dien Bien Phu in 1954 and there was impoverished and vulnerable Latin America. And finally there was the imminent collapse of the great colonial empires of Britain, France, the Netherlands, Belgium and Portugal.

Onto this chaotic scene rode Joe McCarthy.

As has already been seen with the Malmedy investigation, Joe was prone to plunge headlong, suspiciously and with great emotion into his favorite controversies. Because of U.S. democratic principles, the Communist Party was allowed to appear on election ballots everywhere in the U.S. This status was upheld and enforced by the courts. According to democratic principles, if Communism was a bad idea, that should be the decision of the American people and not a decision made by an invisible minority with vested interests. McCarthy did not see things that way.

The problem soon arose, however that parties like the Communists advocated the violent overthrow of the government. With the horrors of the 1930's and World War II still fresh in the minds of Americans, it seemed suicidal to allow such parties to threaten the government, regardless of how feeble they were in terms of numbers. In national elections, the Communists generally received about 100,000 votes out of tens of millions.

But despite the small following of the official Communist Party, there was a far more serious problem: Soviet spies. Hiding behind the Constitution, Communist spies and sympathizers had infiltrated the American government, political parties and other assorted organizations.

The McCarthy Committee Is Born

The Congress already had experience with two committees that were set up to investigate Communists. One committee was run by Congressman Hamilton Fish, Jr. a notorious isolationist whose activities bordered on the criminal and later went down in disgrace. Another committee was that of a rabid Texas anti-Communist named Martin Dies. That Committee was known first as the Dies Committee and later as the House Un-American Affairs Committee, or HUAC. Martin Dies, like Fish, ultimately went down in disgrace.

These anti-Communist Congressmen were like watchdogs who went down because they had bitten a few too many people. Americans wanted watchdogs. They didn't want constant political mayhem.

When one studies the history of these anti-Communist committees, it seems like the elected Presidential administrations such as that of Franklin Roosevelt and Harry Truman secretly encouraged them. The Presidents found it convenient for these committees to do their dirty work for them, while they hypocritically expressed disdain for them. There were [during the 1950's and 1960's] from 530 to 535 members of Congress. 534 of these claimed they were largely unaware of and helpless in the face of an out-of-control individual like McCarthy. So one could say that the dirty work of the U.S. Government (against real or imagined Communists) was put on the back of the lone-wolf McCarthy at the height of his influence. It all depended on how one looked at things in the 1950's and the days of the Red Scare.

By the acts and rules of Congress, Joseph McCarthy eventually became Chairman of a committee called the Permanent Subcommittee on Investigations. This Committee had a number of staff including lawyers and investigators. It was this Committee for which Robert F. Kennedy served as assistant counsel and later as counsel for the Democratic minority.

Following next in line after the Fish committee, the Dies committee (HUAC) and McCarthy's PSI committee, came the Senate Internal Security Subcommittee or SISS. SISS will be discussed in a later chapter of its own. So we see that there was a whole array of committees engaged in the hunt of the pro-Communists in the U.S.

On February 9, 1950, Joe McCarthy gave his landmark speech delivered at Wheeling, West Virginia. It was then when he began his unsubstantiated charges, the most famous of which was a claim that there were 205 Communists in the State Department. This figure was examined over and over in various settings. It never came close to being substantiated.

The fiction is usually presented that Democrats such as Adlai Stephenson, and even moderate Republicans like Dwight Eisenhower were under attack by McCarthy but were helpless to do anything about it. Looking back now we can see that the alleged helplessness of the moderates was a major misrepresentation. In fact, it was the right-wing members of both parties (the Democrat-Republican conservative coalition) which supported McCarthy in his excesses. We will now expand on how this devious McCarthy-driven system really worked.

As a first step in this bi-partisan, anti-Communist campaign ,the Democrats picked a fairly conservative, non-Southern, *Catholic* Democrat named Pat McCarran (from Nevada) to head up the SISS committee. The SISS committee soon became known to many as the McCarran Committee. Next, they picked another fairly conservative, non-Southern, *Catholic* Republican named Joe McCarthy to lead the Permanent Subcommittee on Investigations.

All of this anti-Communist activity in the Senate was on top of and in addition to the actions of the House Un-American Activities Committee. This whole superstructure of anti-Communist Congressional committees landed directly in the backyard of the Kennedy Administration. We will expand on this topic in later chapters.

This strategy bordered on the diabolical. In picking a conservative, non-Southern Democrat or Republican as America's designated anti-Communist, the Democrats could avoid appearing as if they were adopting reactionary Republican tactics. They would not stand accused of following the same policies as arch-conservative Southern Democrats. The Northerners wanted to avoid this because these Southerners were tainted by such things as segregation, lynching and the KKK.

The key thing to understanding the anti-Communist system is to note that the membership of all these hand-picked committees *only included ultra-conservatives* drawn from both parties. Further, the northeastern "progressive" or "liberal" Democrats were usually led by big-city ethnic Catholic machine politicians aligned with Mayor Richard J. Daley of Chicago and other Northern machine bosses. These Northern Democrats would tend to unite around Catholic-backed anti-communists. We tend to forget that most of the Democratic voters of that era were ethnic Italians, Poles and Irishmen. Their respective voters were either consciously or indirectly in sympathy with worldwide Catholic anti-Communism. Communism was, of course, almost everywhere atheistic and aggressively anti-religious.

The HUAC committee in the House included only staunch anti-communists. For a short period, HUAC was identified with the well-known anti-Communist Congressman Richard M. Nixon. But because the House was much larger and more diffuse, there was no one person on HUAC who was set up as a "bad guy" like McCarran, McCarthy (or as Dodd was later) in the Senate. The Senate was much better suited to this scapegoating strategy because there were only a handful of powerful Senators who ran the Senate. This limited group could operate easily, speedily, informally, clandestinely and confidentially.

Philosophically, the Congress did not at first wish to openly outlaw the Communist Party. The Supreme Court might not even have allowed that to happen because of the guarantee of freedom of association in the Constitution. So sometimes, rather than calling Communism what it actually was, the Congress invented code-words like "Un-American Activities." This particular phrase was mocked by the Supreme Court in at least one opinion. The Court asked "How could you make 'un-American activities' a crime? How could you possibly define it?"

Another legalism which became a code-word for Communism was "loyalty." This word was used in combination with "security." The dictionary defines "security" as a stock or bond. Or, alternatively, "the freedom from being threatened." People can be threatened by many things. How does the word "security" directly point to Communism? And then there is loyalty. How do you define loyalty to the country and in its laws? What qualifies as disloyalty? Can someone be loyal to America and Communism at the same time? If not, why not?

THE STATE DEPARTMENT BECOMES ENEMY #1

When in 1948 and 1949 McCarthy began his attack against Communism in the U.S., the battlefield was almost exclusively the U.S. State Department. The U.S. State Department was the only battlefield for one reason and that was, that one-third of the globe in 1950 was Communist. Further, another one-third (including countries like India or Indonesia) was "neutralist." Those neutralist countries became so out of fear of the Communist countries, mainly China. That statistic looked ominous to many Americans.

Therefore two-thirds of the State Department around the globe would be either living in, or involved with countries that were not anti-Communist. And as President Kennedy said at one point, the White House does not, by itself, have the resources to create foreign policy. To do that, you need a bevy of experts and lots of resources. Only the State Department had those resources.

This worldwide situation was immensely frustrating to the American right-wing. Sending an ultra-conservative ambassador to the Soviet Union to dispense virulent anti-Communistic material and beliefs simply would not work. Almost by definition, anyone who had spent a career studying Russia or China could not walk away from his lifetime commitment just because his country of interest adopted Communism or fascism or any other such system. Expertise on a foreign country necessarily has to be transparent to the type of political system of that country. Otherwise, an expert, say a professor, would be out of work when a country like Russia or China either went Communist, or kicked out the Communists. A country such as China or Russia remains on the map even if parties and governments change hands. This is just reality in the world of career diplomacy and international affairs.

Let's focus for a moment on McCarthy's Permanent Subcommittee on Investigations, which will hereinafter be called the PSI. One of the first employees of his committee, as was mentioned earlier, was Robert Kennedy.

On November 9, 1949, McCarthy sent a 3000 word statement to Wisconsin newspapers which made reference to a HUAC list of subversives. This list resulted in unfair accusations against many on the list and damaged their reputations.

McCarthy's biographer Thomas C. Reeves in *The Life and Times of Joe McCarthy: A Biography*, places the date on which McCarthy went rabidly anti-Communist as some time in late 1949. This date was a month before the supposed contact with the military intelligence agents.

In mid-October 1949, McCarthy inserted an article in the Congressional Record, accusing some of those involved with U.S. Far Eastern policy as being sympathetic to Communism. That included veteran Foreign Service officer John Stewart Service, who was a regular target of right-wing abuse. We will see the name of John Stewart Service show up in the climactic investigation of State Department employee Otto Otepka, which occured in conjunction with the JFK assassination.

Within a week of this article McCarthy hired a speech writer named Charles H. Kraus who had been working with Father Edmund Walsh at Georgetown University.

For some perspective on the alleged Communist problem, one can cite the vote received by the Communist presidential candidate in 1932. He received only 103,000 votes out of tens of millions. There was a more serious problem in the labor union movement. The Congress of Industrial Organizations, the CIO, was considered by most observers to be infiltrated by Communists to some degree.

In 1930 the Fish committee, mentioned previously, recommended that the CPUSA (Communist Party) be outlawed. In 1938, the House had created HUAC which compiled a file of 1 million cards containing information on the "loyalty" of those listed. HUAC was the very first permanent standing committee ever created by the House. All other committees had to be approved by vote every year. In 1945 and 1946, HUAC was dominated by John Rankin (D. Miss) and in 1947 and 1948, by J. Parnell Thomas,(R. NJ).

On March 13, 1948, Truman issued his Directive #9835 on Executive Privilege. This executive order was a prelude to a confrontation between the executive branch and Congress over foreign policy. This battle centered on policy regarding Communism and how to fight it. This battle was a major force among several factors which led to the assassination of JFK.

Executive order #9835 forbade any employee of the Executive Branch from delivering classified information to a committee of Congress. On August 3, 1948, appearing before HUAC, Whittaker Chambers (a Communist turncoat) charged that State Department employee Alger Hiss was a subversive. Hiss had begun to work at the State Department in 1936. On December 15, 1948, he was indicted on perjury charges. Hiss would have been charged with sedition, but the statute of limitations had run out.

During the 1940's, the issue of China flared up in the Far East. China triggered the first Red Scare. Senator Pat McCarran (from Nevada and tied to gambling interests) became involved in the "China Lobby" debate. Soon after this came McCarthy's Wheeling speech on February 9, 1950, which blasted the State Department.

As of July 26, 1946, James F. Byrnes was Secretary of State. Byrnes was a conservative Republican who had been appointed by the Democratic administration. Also at that time, there was a mass transfer of New Deal employees from discontinued welfare programs to the State Department. The anti-Communists hated the New Deal and at the same time, they hated the State Department, so 285 of these New Deal employees at state were soon banned from employment. They were allegedly suspected of subversion or homosexual practices. 79 of them had been fired after beginning work. The war against the State Department went into high gear.

In March 1948 Secretary of State Dean Acheson refused to turn over files of 57 alleged spies under Truman's Order 9835. McCarthy attacked this as "sealing loyalty files."

From the outset, there was a division in Congress between the Foreign Relations Committee and the conservative anti-Communist committees such as SISS and HUAC. Democratic party leaders met on February 21, 1950 with Tom Connally of Texas, Chairman of the Senate Foreign Relations Committee. They decided that McCarthy's charges against the State Department should be investigated by the Senate Foreign Relations Committee.

THE TIDINGS COMMITTEE FIGHTS BACK AGAINST McCARTHY

Senate Majority Leader Scott Lucas turned the McCarthy probe over to a Subcommittee with Sen Millard E. Tydings of Maryland, soon to be called the Tydings Committee. Chief Counsel was Edward P. Morgan, 36, a professional anti-Communist. Assistant Counsel was Robert Morris, N.Y. with close connections to the far right. Judge Robert Morris in 1963 was to be part of the JFK conspiracy.

J. Edgar Hoover was furious with McCarthy over the Wheeling speech. Hoover thought McCarthy's speech was reckless. Hoover also supplied an investigator to the Tydings Committee. His name was Donald Surine. Surine had been with the FBI for 10 years, but had been fired for involvement with a prostitute. For the next several years, an informal group of three persons, (McCarthy, Surine, and an FBI man) met with J. Edgar Hoover every week regarding issues of Communism and subversion.

The Tydings Committee began in earnest to investigate the issues regarding Communist infiltration raised by Joseph McCarthy. Seth W.

Richardson, chairman of the Civil Service Loyalty Review Board (for the entire Federal Government) testified and explained their procedures. At the Tydings Committee hearings, Owen Lattimore appeared. In a memo in August, 1949, foreign policy expert Lattimore had recommended that the U.S. stop support for Chiang Kai-shek and withdraw from entanglements in Korea.

On May 3, 1950, Truman allowed the Tydings Committee members to examine employee loyalty files without notes or copying. Truman complained that four committees of the 80th Congress had already examined them. (On June 21, 1950 John Stewart Service appeared before the Tydings Committee. As previously mentioned, John Stewart Service would be a name which would be debated in the fateful investigation of Otto Otepka which climaxed just a week before the assassination.

The Tydings Committee Report was pro-Democrat and ripped Henry Cabot Lodge and Senator Hickenlooper for failing to study the loyalty files. Henry Cabot Lodge and Hickenlooper refused to sign the Tydings Report. The Senate Foreign Relations Committee voted 11-0 to end the Tydings investigation. The full Senate voted to accept the Tydings Report 45-37 on strict party lines. It was said "the debate was the most rancorous since Reconstruction."

Don Surine, the investigator and close associate of McCarthy, dealt with General Charles Willoughby and General Douglas MacArthur. Willoughby (who was thoroughly discussed in his own previous chapter) was an extreme conservative and was influential in right wing circles well into the 1960's. Like Judge Robert Morris, Willoughby would be a member of the JFK conspiracy in 1963. McCarthy and his staff received classified documents from the FBI, CIA and Army Intelligence. Money and tips on Communists poured in, as much as $125,000. McCarthy gambled some of the money at the racetrack.

Several wealthy Protestant Texans started to take an interest in McCarthy. Among them were Clint Murchison, H.R. Cullen and H.L. Hunt, names well known to Kennedy assassination researchers. At or near the same time, John Stewart Service was rehired by Dean Acheson and put on a personnel board. Walter Winchell, the widely read investigative journalist, Fulton Lewis and Paul Harvey, both conservative radio broadcasters were all pro-McCarthy.

THE MCCARRAN COMMITTEE JOINS THE ACTION AGAINST ALLEGED COMMUNISTS

The McCarran Act passed on September 23, 1950 over Truman's veto. The Senate Internal Security Subcommittee (a.k.a SISS, or the McCarran Committee) was created on December 21, 1950 to help enforce the McCarran Act. We will devote an entire chapter later in this book to SISS and its almost certain involvement in the JFK assassination. The activities of SISS had a significant influence on the activities of the McCarthy Committee.

Senate Majority Leader Scott Lucas of Illinois, a Democrat, was challenged in 1950 for his Senate seat by Republican Everett Dirksen, a former Congressman. At this early stage in his career, Dirksen tended toward the extreme end of the conservative spectrum. In 1950, the Republicans gained 5 Senators and 25 new House members including Senator Dirksen. But the Republicans failed to gain control of either body. Dirksen would be the Republican Senator closest to the JFK plot, although he was never proven to be overtly involved as would be certain other powerful Senators.

John F. Kennedy once jokingly described his father, Joseph P. Kennedy as a "Taft Democrat." This, or course, was a humorous contradiction in terms. The senior Kennedy termed American foreign policy to be "suicidal" and called for a withdrawal from Korea and Western Europe. For this stance, Joseph P. Kennedy was applauded by Republican Senator Robert Taft, the Hearst newspapers and former President Herbert Hoover.

As an illustration of how high were the tensions in Washington surrounding the Red Scare, McCarthy himself, at a party, became involved in a physical brawl with journalist Drew Pearson in which he pinned back Drew Peason's arms, kneed him twice in the groin and took a swing at him. It took Richard Nixon to break up the fight. (The reader can recall that Joseph McCarthy was a former amateur boxer). McCarthy was the ranking member of the Executive Expenditures Committee under which the Permanent Investigations Subcommittee was formed.

This relationship between the budgeting of expenditures and investigations of Communists was a prime example how a committee (or in this case a subcommittee) can start secret investigation of a topic which is totally unrelated to the mission of its parent committee. We will see in the following pages how Robert F. Kennedy was addicted to this rogue committee process. The atmosphere of the rogue committee played right into the high-handed (one might say sneaky) methods of the political Kennedy family members.

In January, 1951, the Republican Committee on Committees decided to name Joe to both the Permanent Subcommittee on Investigations and the Senate Subcommittee on Appropriations. The latter Subcommittee had jurisdiction on *State Department funds*. So McCarthy gained the power of the purse over the State Department.

Notes:

The information about Senator Joseph McCarthy presented in this chapter and the following chapter is derived mainly from the definitive biography on McCarthy by University of Wisconsin-Parkside Professor Thomas C. Reeves. It is cited as follows: *The Life and Times of Joe McCarthy: A Biography* (1997) by Thomas C. Reeves.

More information of the same type about McCarthy and Wisconsin politics can also be found in a similar, almost a companion volume. This biography of Governer Kohler contains much information about the guerilla war which supposedly was waged between McCarthy and Eisenhower, some important aspects of which occurred in Wisconsin. The latter work is cited as follows: *Distinguished Service: The Life of Wisconsin Governor Walter J. Kohler, Jr.* (2006) by Thomas C. Reeves.

The personal papers of McCarthy have been either entirely withheld (for about 50 years) or culled, edited or otherwise sanitized by the family with the help of the Archives at Marquette University where the papers have resided since his death. Just as the behavior of McCarthy brought shame on himself and many others, the furtive manner with which his personal papers have been dealt allowed him to continue bringing a shadow over his associates even from the grave. Some say sunlight is the best disinfectant. But those who harbor darkness such as would (by inference) be found in his papers, are a testament to what should be avoided at all costs by scholars. When people having something to hide, that speaks for itself. If McCarthy were merely an honorable foe of Communism, then his papers should have been a shining beacon for like-minded idealists. Apparently not so much.

The books by Reeves were largely put together based on the exhaustive newspaper coverage, mainly by Wisconsin newspapers like the *Milwaukee Journal Sentinel* and the *Wisconsin State Journal* and *Capitol Times*. These newspaper knew McCarthy best. Since the material in Reeves' books is mostly from public newspapers, none of his information is particularly controversial and thus needs no special citations due to doubt or controversy over its nature. Between the two books, Reeves leaves out no details. These are model products of the scholarly enterprise.

The books by Reeves are not in any way biased against McCarthy, in the judgment of this author. However, there are two other works which paint a positive picture of McCarthy and whose authors felt McCarthy's measures were necessary and justified. These can be cited as: *God, Church, and Flag: Senator Joseph R. McCarthy and the Catholic Church, 1950-1957* (2011) by Donald Crosby and *Blacklisted by History: The Untold Story of Senator Joe McCarthy and His Fight Against America's Enemies* (2009) by M. Stanton Evans.

Chapter 11

High Drama Engulfs The McCarthy Committee

There was a theoretical balance of both parties on the anti-Communist committees. But the lopsided allocation between liberals and conservatives from both parties was a crucial act which enabled the assassination of JFK. In fact, one could point to the stacking of these committees as *the most critical* act of any that contributed to JFK's demise.

We have to consider that the McCarran Act (which was the basis for the activities of the Senate Internal Security Subcommittee) passed by a two-thirds vote of a Democratic-controlled Congress despite the fact it was vetoed by Democratic President, Harry S. Truman. This arrangement seemed to signal the seizure of control of the U.S. government by a coalition of Southern Democrats, big city eastern ethnic Catholic anti-Communist bosses and Republicans who were very conservative. In the Senate as of that date, there were 22 Senators from the former Confederate southern states. 19 of them were strong conservatives. When combined with the 37 Republicans most of whom were also conservative, that yielded a total of as many as 57 conservative votes. With such a nearly two-thirds majority of conservatives at hand, and an extreme right-wing group at that, you could wonder why this faction didn't just impeach Truman and remove him from the picture. They clearly had the numbers.

This process eventually led to a literally fatal confrontation between the executive and legislative branches. The conservatives viewed this divide as no less than one between capitalism and those who were enablers of Communism. The executive branch by its very nature must make practical decisions based on fact and not on hysteria. If strict anti-Communism were the only priority, then President Roosevelt could not have allied our country with Stalin's Russia. We could have wound up fighting Hitler, Mussolini, Stalin and Japan all at once. Or we, the U.S., could have sided with the strongly anti-Communist Hitler. Either way, the U.S. could have lost badly and our way of life could have been irretrievably lost for a very long time. Our government couldn't function at all if pure anti-Communism were the only priority.

Some people like Joseph P. Kennedy, urged the U. S. Government to simply ignore Communism. These people felt that Communism would eventually collapse under its own weight. In hindsight, we know that this is exactly what happened almost 30 years later.

In hindsight, we now know that the American people wound up with the best of both worlds in the 1950's as a result of the battle between Capitalism and Communism. Following the tradition of anti-colonialism begun in the American Revolution, the U.S. applauded the demise of the British Empire. Ironically, this end to British domination of other countries only happened under the threat of Soviet power and the faithfulness on the part of FDR to the ideals of Washington and Jefferson.

One could suggest that, from the grave, the ideals of Washington and Lenin *teamed up* to bring freedom to billions of subject people. And further, because of the threat of Communism, FDR was able to pass the Social Security program, unemployment insurance, workman's compensation and many other progressive programs of the New Deal. Some would call the New Deal a bribe to persuade the American people to reject the economic security offered by Communism. Yet Americans did not have to live *even one day* under Soviet Communism to enjoy these benefits. There were no American Gulags. There was no American Berlin Wall.

So who lost badly under the dominance of Senator Joseph McCarthy and his extremism? Maybe it was the blacklisted people in Hollywood. Or perhaps it was the 50,000 soldiers killed in both Korea and Vietnam. Or then it might have been the weakened executives, Truman and Eisenhower. But the main victim was Kennedy; most especially Kennedy.

There was at the time a second Senatorial anti-Communist committee. It was known as the McCarran Committee or SISS for short. On it sat Pat McCarran, James Eastland of Mississippi, William Jenner of Indiana, and Homer Ferguson of Michigan. All three were militant ultra-conservatives. Then came Herbert O'Connor of Maryland, Willis Smith of North Carolina and Arthur Watkins of Utah. They were also conservatives but were not fanatics.

Almost every member of the SISS committee had gone on record to claim that there were a great many traitors in the State Deparment. This committee was essentially a verbal hit squad taking aim at both the President and the makers of foreign policy, the State Department and the Senate Foreign Relations Committee in particular. This conflict continued and was not resolved until JFK was killed on November 22, 1963 in Dallas.

At first, Joe McCarthy had a great deal of influence over the SISS committee. He named his friend and employee, Robert Morris as Chief Counsel. Let the reader make sure to remember the name Robert Morris. We will follow the activities of Morris from this early beginning in the 1950's right up almost to the day of the assassination. Morris was soon joined as a staff worker on SISS byBenjamen Mandel, hand-picked by McCarthy as

Director of Research, a post Mandel had held at HUAC. McCarthy also designated Don Surine (one of his allies) for the staff of SISS as an investigator. After this, though, Surine still remained identified with McCarthy. At least for a brief time, (during the period of the Red Scares), there was a right-wing counter-revolution of sorts led in the U.S. by just one man, Joe McCarthy. No one, not even the President, dared stand in his way.

On February 10, 1951, SISS seized the documents of the Institute of Pacific Relations from a farm in Massachusetts where they were stored. Although the FBI had examined these IPR files, the FBI had kept the contents secret even from McCarthy and McCarran. As will be discussed in a later chapter, the attitude of the Institute of Pacific Relations with regard to Communism is an enigma. Even at this writing, there is a dearth of information about the IPR. SISS staffer Don Surine smuggled the IPR files from the farm to the Hearst Newspaper Office. HUAC was also involved with these actions.

SISS began intensive hearings on IPR from July 25, 1951 to June 20, 1952. During that same time, SISS also held hearings on the following:

1. Subversive aliens in the United States;

2. Communist tactics in youth organizations.

3. Subversive infiltration of radio, TV and entertainment.

4. Subversive control of the Distributive, Processing and Office Workers' Union.

5. Subversive infiltration of the telegraph industry.

6. Subversive influence in the Dining Car and Railroad Food Workers' Union.

7. Unauthorized travel behind the Iron Curtain.

8. Subversive control of the United Publishing Workers of America and

9. Espionage of attachés at embassies.

Headlines inspired by these investigations led to a Second Red Scare. In an attempt to fight back against the McCarthy-induced paranoia, Truman proposed a President's Commission on Internal Security and Individual Rights. This Commission would hopefully provide objective information on the issues inflamed by McCarthy. Truman tried to placate the fanatics. He had named Republican Seth Richardson to the Subversive Activities Control Board. This Board was yet another, fourth anti-Communist body. Also, Truman appointed Herbert Hoover's conservative friend Hiram Bingham as Richardson's cohort on the State Department Loyalty Review Board. This Loyalty Review Board worked full time just on "loyalty" issues with State Department employees.

The Chairman of Truman's Security Commission was Admiral Chester Nimitz. It soon became known as the Nimitz Commission. This would soon be derailed as the Democratic Chairman of the Judiciary Committee was able to use legislative means to sabotage the Nimitz Commission, and it was soon dissolved. It is to be noted that McCarran, a Democrat was eager to inflict this kind of damage on a Democratic presidency, which was especially ironic since Truman himself was a fairly conservative former Southern Democratic Senator. But Truman was not nearly as fanatically conservative on the issue of Communism as were the "Irish radical" twins, McCarran and McCarthy.

Truman's PCIC commission was able to change the State Department rules regarding the Loyalty Review Board. The old standard for "convicting" an employee by the Board was changed from "reasonable *grounds* exist for belief that the person involved is disloyal," to "a reasonable *doubt* as to the loyalty of the person involved." This was Executive Order 10241 and, among other things, it relieved the board of having to show that the employee was disloyal at the *present time. Past associations* with anything smacking of leftist political beliefs, even long ago, could be grounds for firing from the State Department.

Under the aggressive leadership of Hiram Bingham, a self-proclaimed "old-fashioned conservative," the Loyalty Review Board went quickly into action. By March of 1952, it had reopened the cases of 2756 employees who had previously been reviewed. This was out of a total of 9300 employees. One can only imagine the disruption this caused to State Department workers trying to do their jobs. Using legally privileged libel and slander tactics, these McCarthyite fanatics struck terror into the State Department.

We will see certain names crop up at this point. These same names will still be in play ten years later, up to the month of October, 1963, just three weeks before the assassination. In June, 1951, "China hand" John Paton Davies was suspended by the State Department. Employee O. Edmund Chubb was also suspended following action by HUAC. Chubb was then cleared by Secretary of State Dean Acheson and he was finally demoted to the Division of Historical Research. In December 1951, John Stewart Service, a perennial whipping boy of the extreme right, was fired by the State Department.

A woman named Anna Rosenberg, who was up for nomination for Assistant Secretary of Defense, was investigated by the Senate. Senators Richard Russell and Lyndon Johnson were given erroneous information about her. As it turned out, McCarthy was proven wrong because hers was a case of mistaken identity and Ms. Rosenberg was confirmed.

The following story, which hit the newspapers on February 12, 1951, should be of the *utmost interest* to JFK assassination researchers. This was the case of Charles Davis. Davis was a young African-American who was born in Dallas in 1927. He had become a Communist before he was twenty years old. The case of Charles Davis is an obvious precedent to the story of Lee Harvey Oswald. The Davis case was an example which shows it is possible to grow up in a conservative state and community, and then after becoming a Communist, enlist in the U.S. Military for purposes of infiltration.

Charles Davis was dishonorably discharged from the U.S. Navy after only one year on grounds of homosexuality. Davis then returned from the Navy to California and began working as a Communist journalist there. After joining a left-wing organization called the California Labor School, that organization sent Davis to Europe, with the purpose of participating in Communist activities there.

Shortly after arriving in LeHavre, France, Davis approached the U.S. Embassy in Paris wanting money. He also attended meetings and was even asked to make some speeches. Unfortunately for him, he stole an overcoat and was arrested. In November, 1949, Davis went to the American consulate in Geneva, Switzerland, offering to begin spying for the United States against the local Communists.

The Vice-Consul of the U.S. Embassy in Geneva, S.R. Tyler, took Davis seriously enough to suggest that he report on his continuing Communist relationships and activities to the U.S. Embassy on a periodic basis. Davis, in his new role as a would-be spy, followed up with Tyler on these instructions, but Tyler was not able to pay Davis for these services.

According to testimony given later by Davis, the Vice-Consul suggested to Davis that he *contact Senator Joe McCarthy* because, he said, McCarthy may have money available to pay for Davis' anti-Communist information. On June 5, 1950, Davis wrote to Senator McCarthy and described his repudiation of Communism and willingness to spy on Communists in Europe.

Davis' letter apparently was first routed to McCarthy's investigator Don Surine who showed it to McCarthy. McCarthy decided to send SISS committee counsel Robert J. Morris to meet Davis in Paris where he was living. There's that name Robert Morris popping up again. Morris suggested that instead of himself (Morris) traveling to Europe, that contact with Davis could instead be made by John E. Farrand, a thirty-two year old attorney living in Paris with whom Morris was acquainted.

McCarthy wrote Davis a letter in which he cautiously expressed interest in whatever documents Davis could provide concerning "certain persons" in Europe. Coincidentally with Davis contacting McCarthy, the American Embassy in Paris suddenly had a small amount of money to pay to Davis, encouraging him to continue his espionage activities. The person who gave Davis this money was Jack West, a legal attaché at the Embassy who was later determined to be an FBI agent.

Although McCarthy should have realized by this time that Davis was not going to be helpful, he sent a letter to Davis telling him that he would be contacted by Attorney John Farrand, the acquaintance of Counsel Morris. Farrand told Davis that what he wanted most was information on John Carter Vincent and John Stewart Service. Farrand gave Davis between $200 and $250 which McCarthy had sent him by wire transfer. Farrand met Davis three more times in the next two months.

Apparently on his own initiative, the Oswald-like Davis concocted a plan to incriminate John Carter Vincent. Davis sent a telegram to Vincent signed "Emile Stamphi." Stamphi was a well known Swiss Communist. The telegram instructed Vincent to send information on Alex Jordan. Jordan was a young left-wing black American. Davis made a transatlantic phone call to McCarthy, reaching him at his home, then sent a copy of the fake telegram which ostensibly incriminated Vincent.

McCathy's investigator Don Surine sent the bogus telegram to the FBI. McCarthy called it to the attention of the CIA. Soon, Davis was arrested by the Swiss political police. He was convicted of espionage by the Swiss, sentenced to eight months in jail, and then ordered out of the country. McCarthy and Surine immediately backtracked, creating a false story claiming that they knew almost nothing about Davis. Davis went on to file a $100,000 lawsuit against McCarthy alleging that McCarthy broke a contract between McCarthy and himself. The alleged contract was described by Davis as being for the purpose of spying on the State Department. The lawsuit was dismissed and the case disappeared from the news columns.

For the JFK researcher, the Davis case could have much wider implications. Some have suggested that Lee Harvey Oswald may have been acting as an agent of SISS in 1963. This case proves that, at least in 1951, a Senate committee was willing to employ its own spies in Europe. Further, in the Davis case, SISS and McCarthy showed interest in Davis because he was believed to be a Communist and therefore was particularly useful to them. Also, in working through attorney Farrand, SISS and McCarthy showed they would gladly conspire with private right-wing extremists and apparently use their money to fund their spy operations. In the opinion of McCarthy biographer Thomas Reeves, this activity amounted to subversion of the U.S. Government. The story of Charles Davis is found at page 365 of the Reeves biography.

Lee Harvey Oswald was involved with the U.S. State Department in his defection. He received funds from the State Department to finance his return from the Soviet Union. The case of Charles Davis looked like a clear precedent for this type of activity.

In April 1951, President Truman fired General Douglas MacArthur. The Republican Policy Committee unanimously approved a declaration asking "whether the Truman-Acheson-Marshall triumvirate was preparing for a 'super-Munich' in Asia." The Committee consultant who made this assertion was Julius Klein. The name of Julius Klein keeps popping up in many of the important books about the Kennedy assassination. Later on, we will devote an entire chapter discussing General Klein. He was involved with Senator Thomas Dodd in the 1960s. His name was tied to the Kennedy assassination conspirators in a magazine called the *Executive Intelligence Review*. There is testimony by Klein before the Senate Ethics Committee which corroborates this connection.

Senator William Burnett Benton, a Rhodes Scholar, was an outspoken enemy of McCarthy. He had served in the State Department as Assistant Secretary for Public Affairs before being appointed to the Senate. Benton filed charges with the Subcommittee on Privileges and Elections. This became known as the Gillette Committee and this committee investigated McCarthy. The Gillette Committee eventually filed a report known as the Hennings report finding McCarthy guilty of several (mostly insignificant) infractions.

In a Massachusetts Senatorial election contest between Republican Henry Cabot Lodge and John F. Kennedy, McCarthy Committee Council Roy Cohn reported to sources that Joseph P. Kennedy asked Joe McCarthy to steer clear of Massachusetts. Despite the fact that Joe McCarthy was in many ways a creation of Joseph P. Kennedy, Kennedy felt that since McCarthy would be campaigning for the Republican Henry Cabot Lodge, that the presence of McCarthy and his activities would hurt, not help, his son JFK in Massachusetts. This proves how convoluted the McCarthy anti-Communist crusade had become. It overlapped party lines and wound up pitting Republican McCarthy against his mentor Joseph P. Kennedy who had himself helped launch McCarthyism.

At the beginning, JFK was a very strong anti-Communist. In January, 1949, more than a month before the February Wheeling speech by McCarthy, Congressman Kennedy had lashed out, attacking the policies of "the Lattimores and the [China expert John King] Fairbanks" of the State Department. JFK blasted the Yalta accords and Secretary of State General George C. Marshall. At that time, JFK strongly supported the McCarran Committee. JFK was clearly on the side of McCarthy at that time.

In Mid December, 1952, a panel of the Civil Service Loyalty Review Board recommended the dismissal of China expert John Carter Vincent (a 25-year veteran of the Foreign Service), despite Vincent's having been cleared four times by the State Department's Loyalty-Security Board.

Eisenhower Becomes President And The Eisenhower-McCarthy Feud Begins

Following the Republican victory in the Senate in 1952, in late November of that year, McCarthy announced he would chair the Permanent Subcommittee on Investigations, a/k/a the McCarthy Subcommittee. Republicans on the Subcommittee would be McCarthy, Karl Mundt, Everett Dirksen, and Charles Potter. Democratic floor leader Lyndon B. Johnson appointed three freshmen Democrats: W. Stewart Symington, Henry M. Jackson and John L. McClellan.

John Foster Dulles became the new Secretary of State under the incoming Eisenhower Administration. One of the first acts of Dulles was to dissolve a State Department Committee which had cleared John Carter Vincent on the loyalty question. But then Republican appointee Dulles personally cleared Vincent of all charges. As Secretary of State, John Foster Dulles had to confront the realities facing his State Department employees. He did not have the luxury (which the McCarthyites had) of wallowing in the anti-Communist mud.

Dulles was warned by right-wing millionaire Alfred Kohlberg about John Carter Vincent. Kohlberg was the financial backer of a right-wing publication called *Plain Talk*. Three days after the 1954 elections, Dulles fired another State Department employee by the name of John Paton Davies, Jr. The grounds cited were a "lack of judgment, discretion and reliability."

The first bill passed by the new Eisenhower Administration was from the Foreign Relations Committee. This bill created a new post at the State Department. The title was Under Secretary of State for Administration and Operations. Designed, in part, to guard against subversive infiltration of the Foreign Service, this post went to Donald B. Lourie, President of Quaker Oats Corporation. The post of Chief Security Officer went to McCarthy's friend, Scott McLeod. McLeod was a former FBI agent and former Senate staff member in the office of Senator Styles Bridges (R.NH)). McLeod became the anti-Communist enforcer at the State Department.

In the McCarthy Subcommittee, McCarthy appointed his friend Robert J. Morris as Chief Counsel. There was already a General Counsel by the name of Francis Flanagan (a former FBI agent), so the Committee would have *two* head lawyers (which was apparently acceptable to McCarthy).

Joseph P. Kennedy asked that Robert F. Kennedy become Chief Counsel of the McCarthy Committee. Instead of working for the McCarthy committee, Morris decided to remain with the SISS committee. However, McCarthy then hired attorney Roy Cohn as the Chief Counsel of his committee instead of Robert Kennedy. RFK became Assistant Counsel. Joseph P. Kennedy was promised that RFK would soon become Chief Counsel. This never happened.

When he was attending the University of Virginia Law School and serving as the President of the Legal Forum there, Robert F. Kennedy had invited McCarthy to be a speaker. Politically, RFK could easily qualify as a McCarthyite. The University of Virginia still possesses a paper he wrote while at law school attacking Roosevelt's "sellout" at Yalta. Robert Kennedy also had a strong personal fondness for McCarthy that would continue for many years. Cohn brought in a whole new atmosphere to the committee. He was friends with Richard Nixon, J. Edgar Hoover, Walter Winchell and George Sokolsky (a Hearst columnist). At that time, these four men were the most influential contacts possible for a person to have in Washington.

Don Surine was named Assistant Counsel on the McCarthy Committee. He was joined on the McCarthy staff by Daniel G. Buckley, ex-Communist Howard Rushmore (a Hearst reporter), and the Cohn-hired "unpaid Chief Consultant" G. David Schine. McCarthy began to battle with the rival McCarran Committee over jurisdiction in the war against Communism. McCarthy at first proposed three "Sub-Sub" Committees (which never came to pass). He then made a partnership with the McCarran Committee for sharing information. This agreement also included a third committee, HUAC.

By mid-April, 1953, there were 8 probes in progress. McCarthy wanted access to IRS and classified FCC files. McCarthy began opposing the nomination of James B. Conant, former President of Harvard University as High-Commissioner of Germany. John F. Kennedy announced that he would vote in favor of Conant. William F. Buckley began writing speeches for McCarthy. Buckley was both a CIA asset and would also become the nation's leading conservative journalist/publisher.

As an example of the dysfunction created by McCarthy and his activities, McCarthy opposed the nomination of Chip Bohlen as ambassador to the Soviet Union. When Stalin died on March 5, 1953, there was no U.S. Ambassador in Moscow to deal with the serious events which soon followed. As we have noted before, injury to the State Department in situations like this would likely cause harm to America.

John Foster Dulles approved Chip Bohlen personally as a candidate after reviewing his FBI files. The Foreign Relations Committee approved Bohlen unanimously. On the Senate floor, McCarthy charged that Dulles had cleared Bohlen over the objections of Scott McLeod, the State Department's Security Officer. Scott McLeod would become the lightning rod of the State Department war that may have ultimately contributed heavily to the assassination of JFK. This will be explained in the chapters dealing with the case of Otto Otepka, an employee of the State Department.

As the Eisenhower Administration was becoming more and more frequently pitted against McCarthy and McCarran, Vice President Richard Nixon began to act as Eisenhower's liaison with the radical right. The opposition to Bohlen was based in part on the fact that Bohlen had been present at the Yalta conference with Roosevelt, Stalin and Churchill. Everett Dirksen famously told reporters "I reject Yalta and I reject Yalta men." Though later in his career Dirksen would be promoted as a moderate, the wise old man type, at this stage Dirksen was as radically right-wing as McCarthy and his allies. As we shall see, Dirksen was the Republican closest to the actual assassination plot itself.

In the Senate, voting against Bohlen were McCarthy, Bridges, Bricker, Dirksen, Dworshak, Welker, Goldwater, Hickenlooper, Malone, Mundt, and Schoepel, joined by the two Democrats, McCarran and Edwin Johnson. These names represented the sinister extremist opposition to the Eisenhower Administration. This group seemed to oppose virtually every act of the executive branch (of either party) right up into the administration of LBJ and even beyond. Apparently the purpose of these Senators in voting against Bohlen was to require the appointment of a right-wing candidate to each and every important State Department position around the world. We will see how this irresponsible pattern of confrontation would ultimately end in tragedy and disaster for the country.

When the Republicans gained control of the Senate in 1953, Senator William Jenner (R. IN) became Chairman of SISS. SISS traveled to N.Y. to probe U.N. employees, then to Washington and Boston to probe private schools. HUAC began to probe for Communists in New York education and Hollywood. They summoned Methodist Bishop G. Bromley Oxnam and grilled him for 10 hours. In early February 1953, the McCarthy Subcommittee began hearings on State Department files.

In mid-summer of 1953, Joe McCarthy reached the height of his political career. In that period, he got an endorsement from Francis Cardinal Spellman. In 1953, there emerged into the spotlight a large-scale data analyst named Joseph Brown Matthews. Matthews started as a Methodist minister, switched to being a Communist and then back to being an ultra-right wing McCarthyite. He was, however, an expert on Communism, having worked for the Dies Committee and was the creator of the huge filing system of the House Un-American Affairs Committee. Matthews had written an outrageous article to the effect that the greatest number of Communists in the U.S. were to be found amongst the Protestant clergy.

Shortly after Matthews was hired the word got out to the public and the Protestant clergy began to protest from the pulpit and otherwise. At this time, many historians feel that McCarthy was at the absolute apex of his popularity. Dr. A. Powell Davis, minister of All Souls Church in Washington, D.C. finally voiced the opinion that McCarthy was, "to a great extent," the de facto ruler of the United States. It is hard for the reader 70 years later to evaluate the degree to which McCarthy was in fact running the country. It is significant, however, that the first person to come out and make that claim would be a Protestant religious leader, which indicates that McCarthy was unpopular among a spectrum of American citizens.

Who was motivating McCarthy besides McCarthy himself? At this stage around 1953, McCarthyism had spread from its beginning with Mc-Carthy and the three Catholic activists. Its base in Congress now includ-ed right-wing conservative Republicans like Sen. Everett Dirksen (R.IL), and Sen. Karl Mundt (R.SD) and former Congressman, Senator and now Vice President Richard M. Nixon. Southern Segregationists were also in-cluded; Senators like Strom Thurmond.

In May 1953 came Eisenhower's Executive Order 10450 which elimi-nated the distinction between "loyalty" and "security." The effect of this or-der was to blur the difference between firing someone for subversion on the one hand, and for something like homosexuality on the other. This allowed McCarthy to claim that there were a large number of subversives being un-covered because this definition conflated communism, alcoholism, homo-sexuality and any other type of behavior perceived to be dangerous.

THE CENSURE AND DEATH OF SENATOR JOSEPH MCCARTHY

McCarthy spoke out against Allen Dulles for refusing to allow CIA agents to testify before his committee. McCarthy and his staff were planning to investigate the CIA. That would have been ugly. On July 10, 1953, the three Democrats on the McCarthy Committee resigned in protest. Arthur Eisen-hower, brother of Dwight Eisenhower, publicly equated Joe with Hitler.

The armistice with North Korea was announced on July 27, 1953. In June of 1953, McCarthy formed plans to investigate the U.S. Army, an ill-fated decision as we shall soon see. "Moderate" Everett Dirksen intro-duced legislation barring government employment to anyone taking the 5th Amendment.

Joe McCarthy married Jean Kerr on September 29, 1953. Some thought that this was a way to combat rumors that McCarthy, 45, was gay. Pope Pius XII sent "paternal and apostolic" blessing to the new couple. And then (per committee counsel Roy Cohn), there came new informa-tion on Communists in the Military.

Joe tried to accuse the highly respected General Maxwell Taylor and diplomat John J. McCloy of being involved in a reported plot. This sup-posed plot was designed to place 125 German Communists in the Office of the High Commissioner of Germany. Joe had gone out further and fur-ther on a precarious limb. At this time, the McCarthy committee staff had grown to include 11 investigators.

McCarthy granted the minority Democrats the right to choose their own counsel. They chose Robert F. Kennedy. When the Democrats took over the Senate, Robert F. Kennedy would become the Chief Counsel of the McCarthy Subcommittee in 1955. The Committee continued the investigation into espionage at Fort Monmouth, N.J. Then, under the direction of Kennedy and Senator McClellan, it merged with a Senate labor-related subcommittee to allow a change of direction and to delve into the issue of organized crime and labor racketeering. When the McCarthy Committee merged with the Labor Committee to form the McClellan Committee, the stated mission of the newly merged committee was to investigate Communists in the labor movement. Both JFK and RFK were involved in this new mission. Barry Goldwater was also a member.

The two Kennedy's hijacked the new McClellan Committee and took it off the tracks it had previously followed. It was supposed to investigate Communists in the labor movement. Instead, it became focused on labor issues, financial corruption and mainly on labor leader Jimmy Hoffa. Although they didn't know it at the time, the two Kennedys were playing with fire. The McCarthy Committee was the nerve center of the world-wide battle against Communism. To run that committee into the ditch was unforgivable according to the special-interest adversaries of Communism.

Toward the end of 1953, McCarthy had vacationed in the mountains of Mexico with actor Ward Bond and Clint Murchison. Murchison was very close to J. Edgar Hoover. He paid for Hoover's annual vacation to his California race track. Perhaps significantly, Murchison was also a Texas oil millionaire. According to an LBJ mistress named Madeleine Brown in her book *Texas In The Morning*, Murchison hosted a party for the Kennedy assassination conspirators at his home the night before the assassination.

On February 24, 1953, Everett Dirksen was called to the White House and told by Ike to 1) get Roy Cohn fired, 2) end the practice of one-man committee hearings and 3) strip McCarthy of his power to unilaterally issue subpoenas.

Ike and his counselors had decided to force a change. Ike had concluded that the attacks on the Army by McCarthy were caused by Roy Cohn's gay relationship with G. David Schine. Cohn had tried to force special treatment of Schine by the U.S. Army where Schine was a private serving on active duty.

The Army had appointed attorney Joseph Welsh as its counsel in the hearings. McCarthy had tried to smear a young law firm colleague of Welsh as being involved somehow in pro-Communist activities. In defense of his young colleague, Welsh uttered the famous words "Let us not assassinate this lad further, Senator. You have done enough. Have you no sense of decency, sir, at long last? Have you no sense of decency?"

After the hearings, Cohn and minority counsel Robert F Kennedy almost came to blows over Cohn's threat to "get" the junior Senator from Washington, Henry Jackson. Cohn claimed that Jackson had written something that was pro-Communist. McCarthy sensed trouble. He swiftly transferred one of his favorites, Don Surine, away from SISS and back to his personal staff for protection.

LBJ Favors The Censure Of McCarthy

Favored by minority leader Lyndon Johnson, a special committee of 3 Republicans and 3 Democrats was picked to decide on a censure of McCarthy. The members were picked by majority leader William Knowland and Lyndon Johnson, who was thought to be much smarter than Knowland and was thus able to put his own allies on the Committee. The members were:

> R-Arthur Watkins (Utah)
> D-Edward C. Johnson (Colo)
> R-Frank Carlson (Ks)
> D-John C. Stennis (Miss)
> R- Francis Case (SD)
> D-Samuel Ervin (NC)

Because congressional moderates were still intimidated by McCarthy, on August 24, 1954 the Congress passed the Communist Control Act. It determined that "The Communist Party is the agent of a hostile foreign power" and that it "should be outlawed." This was a major new step toward anti-Communism.

The six-man bipartisan Watkins Committee unanimously voted to censure Joseph McCarthy on two grounds 1) his treatment of Senator Robert C. Hendrickson on the Gillette Committee and 2) his denunciation of General Ralph W. Zwicker, who had testified before his committee. They came close to adding a third count based on the violation of executive privilege over classified documents. In the elections of 1954, Democrats regained control of the Senate and the House.

At the annual Catholic War Veterans meeting Msgr. Edward R Martin, as a representative of Cardinal Spellman supported McCarthy in Brooklyn and formed a group called "Save McCarthy." He [McCarthy] likened himself to Martin Dies. Dies was a Red-hunter driven from public life by Roosevelt and the Democrats. Senator Barry Goldwater spoke out, saying "censure would be a victory for Communism." Senator John Stennis, noted for his basic fairness and integrity, strongly urged censure. Senator Stennis, serving as chairman of the Senate Ethics Committee, later presided over the next censure of a rabid anti-Communist Catholic activist and northern state Senator, Thomas Dodd, in 1967.

On *Meet The Press*, Senator Sam Ervin spoke against McCarthy. Ervin called for actual expulsion of McCarthy from the Senate. Senators

Dirksen and Goldwater were among McCarthy's supporters. In the final wording, the motion against McCarthy was to "condemn" him, rather than "censure" him, for abuse of the Gillette Committee and the Watkins Committee, was only the third in Senate history.

In the summer of 1956, in Appleton, McCarthy was experiencing delirium tremens as a result of his alcoholism. In January, 1957, with the help of Cardinal Spellman, the McCarthy's adopted a child. On May 2, 1957, Joe McCarthy died at age 48 of hepatic failure. At a requiem mass held for him, there were 72 priests, monsignors and bishops.

Notes:

The information in Chapter 11 on Senator Joseph McCarthy can be found almost entirely in the definitive and very objective classic biography of McCarthy called *The Life and Times of Joe Mc-Carthy: A Biography*, by Thomas C. Reeves. This book is completely objective and relies on information largely gathered from Wisconsin and other newspapers. The personal papers of Joseph McCarthy have never been easily available to historians, having been only partially released almost 50 years after his death.

Other relevant information on the subjects covered in Chapter 11 can be found in *The Ordeal of Otto Otepka* by William J. Gill. Another, more general, but incisive source is the book *Diplomat Among Warriors* by Robert D. Murphy.

Chapter 12

JUDGE ROBERT J. MORRIS

I f JFK assassination research is like walking through a haunted house at Halloween, then Robert J. Morris is the skeleton that seems to pop up everywhere.

We first met Judge Robert Morris when he was at a meeting in New York in 1954. Also at the meeting were Princess Alexandra Tolstoy, Metropolitan Anastsy of the Russian Orthodox Church and retired General Charles Willoughby (one of the Three Barons). All three of these people were either part of the JFK plot or very close to the center of it.

Judge Robert J. Morris was a virulent anti-Communist in the period from the 1940's to the 1990's. He served as a lawyer for various legislative and Congressional Committees from the 1940's on. His most important Congressional Committee role was as lawyer for the Senate Internal Security Subcommittee chaired at times by Senators James O. Eastland and Thomas J. Dodd.

Morris was President of the University of Dallas at the time of the assassination. He was privy to confidential information surrounding the Otto Otepka case in October, 1963. Given his long-time relationship with the Senate Internal Security Subcommittee (which was in the vortex of the assassination plot) and his presence in Dallas on November 22, 1963, Morris was very likely involved with the assassination. At the very least, his biography tracks closely the movement which culminated in the assassination and provides a clear road-map of the forces that resulted in the JFK murder.

EARLY LIFE

M orris was born in Jersey City, New Jersey on September 30, 1914. He was raised in New Jersey and was a graduate of St. Peter's College a Catholic Jesuit College, (now a university) located in Englewood Cliffs, New Jersey. After his bachelor's degree, he graduated from Fordham University School of Law. In a book which he wrote called *Disarmament, Weapon of Conquest,* he sets forth his resumé at page 148 as follows:

> Counsel and Chief Counsel, U.S. Senate Internal Security Subcommittee 1951-1958. [In the text of his book, Morris states that he was Counsel or Chief Counsel from 1950 to 1953, and again from 1956 to 1958.]

Counsel U.S. Senate Foreign Relations Committee 1950 (Tydings Committee).

Advisor U.S. Senate Rules Committee 1954.

Officer-in-Charge Advance Psychological Warfare Section of CIN-PAC on Guam 1945.

Officer-in-Charge Soviet Counterintelligence Third Naval District 1941-1943; Officer-in-Charge Counterintelligence Third Naval District 1945. Morris reached the rank of Commander in the Navy.

Justice Municipal Court New York City 1953-1956.

President of University of Dallas 1960-1962.

Presently (1979) columnist and civil libertarian.

Like the head of the American Nazi Party, George Lincoln Rockwell, Morris had risen to the rank of Commander in the Navy. This is probably an unfair comparison except that it illustrates that the military was not picky when it came to the extreme politics of its higher ranking officers. Another prime example would be General Edwin Walker.

After being chosen to serve as president of the University of Dallas in 1960, Morris got into conflict within the university because of his extreme right-wing anti-Communist beliefs. He left that position in 1962. Also in 1962, he served as attorney for General Walker, who was arrested and charged with inciting a riot during the insurrection at the University of Mississippi in September, 1962. Morris convinced a grand jury not to indict Walker.

ROBERT MORRIS AND JOSEPH MCCARTHY

When the Tydings Committee investigated Senator McCarthy, the Republican minority members insisted that New York lawyer Robert Morris be hired as their counsel. Morris worked diligently to defend McCarthy and afterward was hired on to McCarthy's staff.

When ex-Communist Louis Budenz appeared before the McCarthy Committee in 1950 to accuse an assortment of people of being Communist, he admitted that he had discussed the case of alleged Communist Owen Lattimore with four extreme anti-Communists: Arthur Kohlberg, Charles Kersten, Robert Morris and J.B. Matthews. Notice that Kersten and Morris, both Catholic activists were working closely with the McCarthy Committee. J. B. Matthews was the nation's leading expert on the statistics and the technical aspects of organized Communism in the U.S. and had been employed for that purpose by the House Un-American Affairs Committee. Arthur Kohlberg had been the leader of the China Lobby which supported the regime of Chaing Kai-shek. (Chaing Kai-shek was a Methodist).

In late December, 1950, the Senate authorized another Congressional investigation into internal security matters and the Senate Judiciary named Pat McCarran, who was Chairman of Judiciary, to chair the new Senate Internal Security Subcommittee (SISS) Privately, Joe McCarthy had McCarran name his friend and staff member Robert Morris as Chief Counsel of SISS with sole right to hire the assistants of his choice. One he picked was research director Benjamin Mandel, who would go on to serve many years in that position. Mandel had held that same job title for HUAC. Also assigned to the new Committee was Don Surine, an investigator who was technically still a staff member of McCarthy's office.

In January, 1951, Robert Morris was involved in a seizure of documents from a farm in Maine. The documents were "dead files" from an organization called the Institute of Pacific Relations (IPR). The IPR was founded in 1925 and was funded by the Rockefeller Foundation. Its purpose was to analyze and discuss issues related to countries of the Pacific rim. Arthur Kohlberg, who was previously mentioned as an associate of Robert Morris, was a dissident member of IPR. When the documents were seized, that action triggered a multi-year investigation of the IPR by SISS and other investigators. The charge against the IPR was that it was riddled with Communists and that it had been responsible for the loss of China to Communism.

One of the most thorough and valuable books about the JFK assassination is *General Walker and the Murder of President Kennedy* by Dr. Jeffrey Caulfield. This book has nearly 800 pages of text. It represents research begun in 1992 and lasting through the book's publication in 2015. The central thesis of *General Walker* is to put the blame for the JFK assassination, not so much on General Walker, but rather on the Senate Internal Security Subcommittee of which Robert Morris was the chief counsel. In *General Walker*, Robert Morris is cited on more than 50 pages based on the book's index.

Dr. Caulfield studies SISS when it changed from only investigating Communism to also investigating civil rights activists and furthering the segregationist agenda of its official chairman, Senator James O. Eastland of Mississippi. According to Caulfield, Robert Morris was a close friend of General Walker. As mentioned, Morris served as Walker's attorney at Ole Miss during the 1962 insurrection there.

In 1956, Guy Banister and Hubert Badeaux of the intelligence unit of the New Orleans Police Department were both assisting Senator Eastland in his investigation of Communists in the civil rights movement. At this time, Robert Morris was Chief Counsel of SISS. In 1957, Badeaux, Banister and Louisiana "Godfather" Leander Perez testified to the Louisiana legislature on the subject of "subversion and racial unrest." Also involved in these activities in Louisiana at the time was Kent Courtney. Morris and Courtney both wrote brief books on the subject of nuclear disarmament in 1963. The books were, in some respects, almost clones of one another in length and subject.

Dr. Caulfield has gathered some interesting information about Robert Morris. According to Caulfield at page 546, Morris told the press that on the day of the assassination, he had observed the JFK motorcade from the window of his Main Street office in Dallas, which was five blocks away from the assassination.

Robert Morris was a member of the American Security Council.

The American Security Council (ASC) was an organization established in 1955. One of the founders was General Robert Wood who at the time was chairman and president of Sears, Roebuck & Company headquartered in Chicago. The other was Col. Robert McCormick, the extreme right-wing publisher of the *Chicago Tribune*. Their immediate purpose was to combat Communist subversion in the U.S. Government. Some of the members they first recruited were Douglas MacArthur, Sam Rayburn, Ray S. Cline, Thomas J. Dodd, W. Averell Harriman, Nelson A. Rockefeller, Eugene V. Rostow, John G. Tower, Lyman Lemnitzer, John K. Singlaub, Lawrence P. McDonald and Patrick J. Frawley.

The ASC found strong support among companies in the defense industry. Some even described the ASC as a front organization for the military-industrial complex. Companies which funded the ASC included General Dynamics, General Electric, Lockheed, Boeing, Motorola, and McDonnell-Douglas.

Even today, the American Security Council is controversial. It is one of those conservative groups or individuals which have no Wikipedia articles. This is because right-wing extremists will take down the article as soon as it is posted. Like other such groups, we have to look to the Spartacus Educational website for a description.

Of the above members, the following have some connection to the assassination of JFK: Thomas J. Dodd, Eugene V. Rostow and General Lyman Lemnitzer. Robert Morris mentions the American Security Council approvingly several times in his book *Self-Destruct*. He describes it as a "civilian group which can't be gagged."

In *General Walker*, at page 105, Dr. Caulfield writes that Robert Morris and Herbert Philbrick were collaborating on a book about the JFK assassination. Philbrick was a spy upon whose life the TV show "I Led Three Lives" was based. In using factor analysis to analyze the JFK data, Philbrick's name comes up very near the top of the list of suspects (but the reason for this cannot be determined). Caulfield reports that in Dallas in 1963, Robert Morris was in charge of screening members of the Dallas Minutemen, whose leader was General Edwin Walker.

Another discovery by Caulfield was a connection between Robert Morris and Larrie Schmidt, a young man directly involved in the events in Dallas.

Schmidt was the one who placed the ads which greeted JFK in Dallas on 11-22-63. The ads were bordered in black and accused JFK of treason. Dick Russell, a JFK assassination author, relates a rumored story in Dallas that Larrie Schmidt and his brother Robert drove Lee Harvey Oswald to the home of General Edwin Walker in April, 1963, when LHO allegedly took a rifle shot at Walker. Larrie's brother Bob was a chauffeur for Walker.

Larrie and Bob Schmidt were enlisted men from the Army who arrived in Dallas just a few months before the assassination. Robert Morris had possibly arranged a job for Larrie at an ad agency with which he had worked. He invited Schmidt to deliver a speech to a group gathered at the Morris home.

Caulfield writes [Charles] "Willoughby was a close associate of Benjamin Mandel, research director for Senator Eastland's ...[SISS] Willoughby was also close to Robert Morris, a former counsel of Eastland's SISS, and contributed money to Morris' failed 1958 Senate campaign."

We read in the *Ordeal of Otto Otepka* by William J. Gill, that when Otepka was fired in October, 1963 as a result of a fierce battle in SISS, the first person to announce it was Judge Robert Morris in Dallas.

In writing his book *Suite 3505* about the Goldwater campaign, author William J. Gill reports that Robert Morris was on the initial 25 person committee to promote the candidacy of Barry Goldwater in the 1964 election. Gill also states that Morris was the member most often consulted on issues by Goldwater's campaign manager early in the Goldwater campaign.

We could go on and on about the ubiquitous Judge Morris, but we will end with an overview of the issues covered in his book *Self-Destruct* (1979):

1. China runs an intelligence operation in the U.S.

2. Enforcement of internal security laws and procedures is being lost.

3. Washington planners rejected a moderate anti-Batista movement which could have prevented Castro from coming to power.

4. The Soviets overthrew the Afghan president in 1978 and replaced him with a former U.S. State Dept. employee who was a Communist.

5. The KGB controls the Russian Orthodox Church.

6. The FBI can't do the work of SISS and HUAC because the FBI has to follow the law.

7. General MacArthur had always warned against a U.S. war on mainland Asia.

8. Since 1967, the ACLU has openly welcomed Communist members.

9. After J. Edgar Hoover died, the FBI was wrecked by its opponents.

10. The old imperial colonial system was mostly a constructive force.

11. In the JFK administration, the U.S. agreed to a U.N. world government and the transfer of the U.S. military to a Soviet-controlled U.N. directorate.

12. During the 8-year tenure of Robert S. McNamara, no new weapons were approved.

13. Presidents Nixon & Ford were indifferent about outing Communists.

14. Morris re-hashes the Owen Lattimore case from the McCarthy era.

15. Alger Hiss was an advisor to the Institute of Pacific Relations.

16. As counsel for SISS, Morris was the official liaison to MacArthur.

17. In 1950, the CIA put a "Bay of Pigs-style" exile force into Albania and, like the Bay of Pigs, it was massacred.

18. Lee Harvey Oswald was involved with Japanese Communists while serving in Japan in the late 1950's.

19. Terrorism was, as of 1979, the major enemy of the U.S.

20. The U.S. should not have returned people to the U.S.S.R. who had been caught fighting alongside Hitler and wore German uniforms.

21. The United Nations is a threat to our sovereignty and we should remove sanctions from Rhodesia and apartheid South Africa.

We shall leave the subject of Judge Robert Morris by repeating the rationale for the JFK assassination which was parroted both by Morris, William J. Gill in *The Ordeal of Otto Otepka*, and elsewhere. Morris recounts at page 54 of *Self-Destruct*:

> ...John Foster Dulles died in 1959. Then, one by one, those Senators who had been most courageous in supporting the work of internal security died or retired and they were seldom replaced by men of comparable determination. Sensing this, the Communist forces within the United States moved in for a campaign to destroy the entire national security system.

This theory was the pretext for the JFK assassination. It said that following the election of 1958 when liberals got control of the Senate and the death of John Foster Dulles occurred in 1959, things started going downhill in the fight against internal Communism. JFK switched from being a Catholic activist and anti-Communist to being soft on Communism. With a directive called "Bulletin 7277," JFK agreed to turn the U.S. military over to the United Nations. In another symbolic act, the Senate failed to confirm Eisenhower's science advisor and conservative voice Lewis Strauss to Ike's cabinet.

The last straw came when the Senate approved the Nuclear Test Ban Treaty sponsored by the Kennedy Administration. The belief was that the U.S. was going to be vulnerable to a Soviet nuclear first-strike. Therefore, due to this treachery on the part of JFK, he had to be assassinated to save the nation.

More than any other individual, Judge Robert Morris was at the center of the action which led step-by-step to the JFK assassination.

Morris ran for the Republican nomination for the U.S. Senate from New Jersey in 1958 when he was still Chief Counsel for SISS. Then in 1964 and 1970, Morris ran for the Republican nomination for Senate from Texas. His opponent both times was George Herbert Walker Bush.

In 1976, Morris ran for the conservative American Independent Party presidential nomination against a Louisiana conservative named John Rarick and former Governor of Georgia, Lester Maddox.

Then in 1982, Morris entered the Republican Senatorial primary in New Jersey, but dropped out early. In this latter race, Morris stated that his major issue was Soviet expansionism. Then again in 1984, he entered the New Jersey Republican Senate primary.

The description of the career of Robert J. Morris is presented above both 1) because he was probably involved in the JFK assassination and 2) his fanaticism illustrates the type of individuals who perpetrated the assassination.

Notes:

Information in this chapter from and about Robert Morris comes mainly from his books *Disarmament, Weapon of Conquest* and *Self-Destruct: Dismantling America's Internal Security*.

Information provided by Dr. Jeffrey H. Caulfield can be found in his iconic work *General Walker and the Murder of President Kennedy: The Extensive New Evidence of a Radical-Right Conspiracy*.

Chapter 13

THE NATIONAL SECURITY COUNCIL

When we discuss the National Security Council (NSC) in the context of the assassination, we must begin with one of the most blatant of the claims and accusations that exist anywhere in the assassination literature. The claim was made by federal informant Roy Frankhouser and is reported in the book *Final Judgment* by Michael Collins Piper, at page 319:

> In a series of exclusive interviews [with a little-known publication]…former National Security Council operative Roy Frankhouser has provided information which conclusively demonstrates that the National Security Council planned and co-ordinated the November, 1963 assassination of President John F. Kennedy.

Based on circumstances, it is virtually impossible that any other part of the government besides the NSC could have been responsible for co-ordinating or at least giving final approval to the assassination. This fact is based on 1) the history of the National Security Council (which was created for the very purpose of limiting presidential powers) and 2) the NSC consisted of members decided by federal statute, not by the President and which in 1963 included the Vice President, the Secretaries of Defense and State, the Chairman of the Joint Chiefs as advisor, and, usually by invitation, the Secretary of the Treasury.

Very few people in the U.S. knew at that time or know even now about the National Security Council, what it is, when it was started or why it exists. When one begins to read and research the history of the National Security Council, the material almost reads like science fiction.

Those readers who remember the Iran-Contra scandal during the Reagan Administration in the 1980's at least know something about the National Security Council. Lieutenant Colonel Oliver North was a rogue National Security Council employee and as a result, he ended up being convicted of a felony. What the reader should know about the rogue NSC of the Reagan years is that certain CIA employees were temporarily *attached* to the NSC, so these Iran-Contra covert actions were considered to be NSC activities although they involved CIA agents.

The purpose of this strategy is that the NSC is not subject to oversight by Congress. The only oversight of the NSC is by the President himself.

And this presents a problem when the activity of the NSC happens to be plotting the murder of the President.

In the year 1947, several institutions were created which are now famous (if not infamous): the Department of Defense (DOD), the National Security Council (NSC), the National Security Agency (NSA), the CIA and the Joint Chiefs of Staff (JCS). This is quite a list. And, unbelievably, all this was officially invented by an international banker (significantly with Jewish ancestry and connections, though not Jewish) named Ferdinand Eberstadt.

According to the biographers of Ferdinand Eberstadt – Robert Perez and Edward Willett – Eberstadt created this list of (mostly spy) agencies by following the model of the Congress of Vienna, which took place in 1815.

So why was our Federal Government re-invented in 1947 according to the plan of the Congress of Vienna? The Congress of Vienna took place following the defeat of Napoleon at Waterloo. It was a plan to attempt to reverse the effects of the French Revolution and to re-impose Monarchism in Europe under the leadership of the Czar of Russia and the British throne.

And so, in 1947, 150 years later, we have the National Security Act of 1947, which could be viewed as a counter-revolution in itself. In creating the NSC, the DOD, the CIA and the NSA, the idea was to bury the New Deal and avoid a repeat of the FDR regime. After all, at Yalta and Potsdam, FDR, Stalin and de Gaulle represented the tradition of the three revolutions, the American, the French and the Russian.

The odd men out at Yalta and Postdam were 1) the British Monarchy (and the British Empire), 2) assorted pretenders to the thrones of Italy, Russia (the Czarist White Russians) and other smaller countries, 3) the remnants of the French colonies (which had not been part of the French Revolution) and 4) any number of surviving Nazis and Ukrainian, Vichy-French and Eastern European Nazi-collaborators. And we should also mention, the pro-Monarchist Vatican, which still clung to the ancient "divine right of kings."

It is this counter-attack by European Monarchists against the U.S. Government (and the Soviet Government and de Gaulle) which is personified in the persons of the Three Barons – Baron Tscheppe-Weidenbach, Baron George de Mohrenschildt and Baron Wernher von Braun.

In the U.S., these reactionary, counter-revolutionary Europeans were represented by international bankers such as the Dillon, Read partners led by Clarence Dillon, the Kuhn, Loeb bank represented by Robert Strauss, the Rockefellers, Joseph P. Kennedy, and former President Herbert Hoover. For some unknown reason, Harry S. Truman (a highschool graduate and woefully inept), turned the keys to the U.S. Government over to this group. And so we had banker Ferdinand Eberstadt (a so-called expert in government – not!) designing a new version of the

U.S. Government, at the head of which was to be the newly created National Security Council.

At one point, Eberstadt and his allies proposed that the President of the U.S. would serve on a committee that included four cabinet members and himself. And on this five member Committee, the President *would only have one vote!* That absurd proposal is the whole story of the National Security Council in a nutshell.

This list of NSC members included the four most powerful people in the government aside from the President. For some reason which is not entirely clear, the Attorney General has been excluded from the National Security Council from the beginning, both by statute and by practice. The absence of the Attorney General was icing on the cake for the NSC should they ever desire to eliminate the President. It is also an implicit admission that the NSC would be involved in activities which by their nature would be illegal. Why else would the Attorney General be excluded? Excluded in this manner were both the Department of Justice and the FBI.

To fully understand the problems with the NSC in the JFK administration one must realize that John F. Kennedy believed that it was better at times *that he absent himself from NSC meetings* in order to not unduly influence their decisions and not to inhibit open discussion. This was another good example of how JFK made unwise decisions which jeopardized his personal safety and abdicated the priceless authority he possessed as the President.

This is a chart of the National Security Council during the Eisenhower Administration:

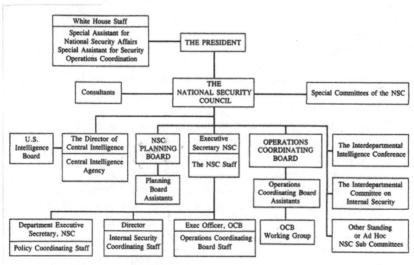

The Eisenhower NSC, 1953–1961 (organization as of 1959)

SOURCE: U.S. Congress. Senate. Organizing for National Security. Selected Materials. Prepared for the Committee on Government Operations and its Subcommittee on National Policy Machinery (Pursuant to S. Res. 248, 86th Congress). Washington, U.S. Govt. Print. Off., 1960, p. 8.

The following is quoted from a study prepared by the Congressional Research Service:

The Kennedy NSC, 1961-1963

President John Kennedy, who did not share Eisenhower's preference for formal staff procedures, accepted may of the recommendations of the Jackson Committee and proceeded to dismantle much of the NSC structure, reducing it to its statutory base. Staff work was carried out mainly by the various departments and agencies, and personal contacts and ad hoc task forces became the main vehicles for policy discussion and formulation. The NSC was now one among many sources of advice.

Kennedy's National Security Adviser, McGeorge Bundy, played an important policy role directly under the President. The nature of this position was no longer that of a "neutral keeper of the machinery"; for the first time the Adviser emerged in an active policymaking role, in part because of the absence of any definite NSC process that might preoccupy him.

Kennedy met regularly with the statutory NSC members and the DCI, but not in formal NSC sessions. Studies and coordination were assigned to specific Cabinet officers or subordinates in a system that placed great emphasis on individual responsibility, initiative and action. The Secretary of State, Dean Rusk, was initially seen as the second most important national security official in the President's plans, and Kennedy indicated that he did not want any other organizations interposed between him and Rusk. However, Kennedy came to be disappointed by the State Department's inability or unwillingness to fill this role as the leading agency in national security policy.

At the beginning of the Kennedy Administration, the NSC was reportedly cut from seventy-one to forty-eight and "in place of weighty policy papers produced at regular intervals, Bundy's staff would produce crisp and timely National Security Action Memoranda (NSAMs). The new name signified the premium that would be placed on 'action' over 'planning. With an emphasis on current operations and crisis management, special ad hoc bodies came into use. The outstanding example of this was the Executive Committee (ExCom) formed in October 1962 during the Cuban Missile Crisis, which orchestrated the U.S. response to Soviet moves to introduce missiles in Cuba.

Organizational Changes: Kennedy added the Director of the Office of Emergency Planning to the NSC, replacing the Director of the Office of Civil and Defense Mobilization. It was planned that the new appointee would fill the role originally envisioned for the National Security Resources Board in coordinating emergency management of resources.

The Planning Board and the Operations Control Board were both abolished (by Executive Order 10920) in order to avoid the Eisenhower Administration's distinction between planning and operations. The NSC staff was reduced, and outside policy experts were brought in. Bundy noted that they were all staff officers:

"...If his Cabinet officers are to be free to do their own work, the President's work must be done—to the extent that he cannot do it himself—by staff officers under his direct oversight. But this is, I repeat, something entirely different from the interposition of such a staff between the President and his Cabinet officers.

Evaluation: Some critics attacked the informality of the system under Kennedy, arguing that it lacked form an direction, as well as coordination and control, and that it emphasized current developments at the expense of planning. As noted, Kennedy himself was disappointed by the State Department, on which he had hoped to rely. In retrospect, Kennedy's system was designed to serve his approach to the presidency and depended upon the President's active interest and continuous involvement. Some critics, both at the time and subsequently, have suggested that the informal methods that the Kennedy Administration adopted contributed to the Bay of Pigs debacle and the confusion that surrounded U.S. policy in the coup against President Diem of South Vietnam in 1963.

For purposes of illustration, presented below is a chart of the Nixon NSC structure.

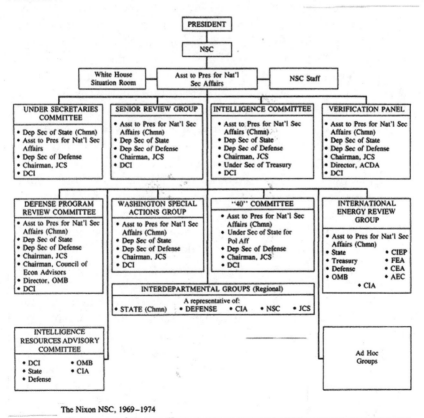

The Nixon NSC, 1969–1974

SOURCE: Prepared by the Congressional Research Service, Library of Congress

MCGEORGE BUNDY

As can be seen from the charts, the President's National Security Advisor is in charge of the staff of the National Security Council. This could well mean he was in practical control of the activities of the Council since the staff reported to him.

In his widely read and acclaimed book *JFK: The CIA, Vietnam, and the Plot to Assassinate John F. Kennedy*, author Col. L. Fletcher Prouty provides evidence at page 280 that McGeorge Bundy was involved in a situation that indicated advance knowledge of the assassination.

Prouty focuses on a meeting of JFK's cabinet held in Honolulu, Hawaii on November 20, 1963. According to the Pentagon Papers, the cabinet meeting in Hawaii was dominated by discussions about issues set out in National Security Memorandum #273, published November 26, 1963. NSAM #273 recommended an escalation of the U.S. commitment to Vietnam. But this proposed escalation was diametrically opposed to the JFK policy of a pullout, which he had announced in NSAM #263, published on October 11, 1963.

McGeorge Bundy prepared and signed the cover letter for NSAM #263. This Bundy cover letter avoided any mention or endorsement of the pullout from Vietnam which Kennedy had ordered in the memo. Bundy was apparently involved in planning the agenda for the Honolulu meeting on November 20, 1963, at least to the extent that the agenda was governed by or included in certain national security memoranda.

Prouty's point is this: how could the cabinet be discussing escalation of the Vietnam War on November 20, 1963, two days before JFK was killed? JFK had ordered a pullout, not an escalation. And further, the Cabinet was conveniently out of the continental U.S. at the time, and thus isolated. Prouty concludes that the debate prior to the assassination could only have occurred based on advance knowledge of someone, most likely Bundy, that the President was not going to be around after November 22, 1963.

So to analyze the possible involvement of the National Security Council in the assassination, we must look deeper into the beliefs, attitudes and political affiliations of McGeorge Bundy.

McGeorge "Mac" Bundy was born on March 30, 1919 and raised in Boston, Massachusetts. He was the third child in an old Republican family. His two older brothers were named Harvey and William. William would later become famous along with Bundy himself. Bundy's father, born in Grand Rapids, Michigan, had served as a law clerk for Justice Oliver Wendell Holmes and then became a prominent Boston attorney. His father was a close associate of Henry L. Stimson, who served Herbert Hoover as Secretary of State and Franklin D. Roosevelt as Secretary of War. Bundy's mother was even higher on the Massachusetts social register. She was related to the Cabots, the Lowells and the Lawrences and her uncle was a president of Harvard University.

Bundy attended the private Dexter Lower School in Brookline, Massachusetts and then the top prep school in the U.S., the Groton School, where he placed first in his class. He was admitted to Yale College where his older brother William was a sophomore. Bundy majored in mathematics and was tapped as a member of the "Skull and Bones" fraternity.

When World War II broke out, McGeorge Bundy entered the military in 1941 and served as an intelligence officer. He entered as a private, but within one year he had made captain. He served in the U.S. Army during World War II as an aide to Admiral Alan Kirk, who was in naval intelligence.. In that capacity he assisted with the planning for the invasions of Sicily and France (In 1951, Admiral Kirk would become a major figure in peacetime intelligence groups, working for, among others, the National Security Council).

The Bundys met and befriended Colonel Henry L. Stimson at some point in time. As Secretary of State under Herbert Hoover, in 1931 Stimson appointed McGeorge's father Harvey Bundy as his Assistant Secretary of State. Later, Bundy's father served again under Secretary of War Stimson.

Under Stimson, the elder Bundy's title was Special Assistant on Atomic Matters. Part of his duty was to serve as liaison between Stimson and the director of the Office of Scientific Research and Development, Vannevar Bush. William and McGeorge grew up knowing Stimson as a family friend and colleague of their father. The senior Bundy also helped implement the Marshall Plan.

Immediately after he left the armed forces in 1946, Bundy was given the chance to work with Secretary Stimson on the latter's autobiography, which was to be published under the title *On Active Service* in 1948.

After World War II, and with high-level experience in Military Intelligence on his resumé, Bundy was selected for the Council on Foreign Relations in 1949. He worked with a study team on implementation of the Marshall Plan. After that, Bundy signed on to the staff of Thomas A. Dewey, the 1948 Republican presidential candidate, as a consultant on foreign policy issues.

Although Bundy lacked an advanced degree, he was next appointed as a professor of government at Harvard University. In 1953 he was the youngest dean ever to serve Harvard's Faculty of Arts and Sciences, where it was said that he worked to develop Harvard as a merit-based university. This theory of "merit-based" was apparently propounded despite the obvious fact that Bundy had achieved nothing academically to merit working for the prestigious Harvard University. The reader is left to conclude that Bundy's definition of "merit" was "highly meritorious social or intelligence agency connections." Bundy became a full professor at Harvard within five years in 1954.

In 1961 he joined Kennedy's administration.

So why did JFK choose McGeorge Bundy as National Security Advisor? Paul Nitze was a person of significant influence on the transition team for JFK in 1960. Nitze wrote in his autobiography regarding the issue of JFK's transition from the Eisenhower administration. As a starting point, Nitze recounts that Bundy possibly had exerted some influence in putting together the 1952 Republican Platform with respect to the plank on foreign policy. If that were true, that would put Bundy together on that 1952 project with John Foster Dulles and Congressman Charles Kersten. That 1952 platform plank was particularly controversial because it demanded freedom for the people behind the Iron Curtain.

Since Eisenhower would be the person to change the Republican Party from isolationist to globalist, this platform plank would have been a major piece in that transition. Nitze writes that the plank represented a vicious attack on prior Truman administration foreign policy (i.e. globalism). Nitze claims that he, Nitze, switched from Republican to Democrat because of Ike's embrace of this plank which Nitze took as too radical for his taste. Adding up all of the above, this could indicate that Bundy had made an impression as a radical globalist/anti-Communist with beliefs similar to those of John Foster Dulles and possibly Congressman Kersten.

Although Bundy considered himself a Republican, for some reason he supported John F. Kennedy when JFK ran against Richard Nixon in 1960. As a result, he became acceptable to Kennedy and the latter appointed him as Special Assistant to the President for National Security. This position headed up the National Security Council. As the reader learns more and more about the secret National Security Council, it becomes obvious that, as head of the NSC, it could be said that Bundy became in some respects the boss of the President, although even the very bright JFK apparently didn't realize this prior to assuming office. (If he did, he would never have appointed a Republican and a former Thomas A. Dewey staffer to such a powerful position in his administration).

But let us look at the bigger picture of how JFK went about picking his cabinet. If, as we are contending here, JFK's cabinet was involved in his own murder, then there was an obvious problem in the way he picked it!

The discussion of JFK's method in picking his cabinet must include, primarily, the way he picked Dean Rusk, his Secretary of State, Robert S. McNamara, his Secretary of Defense and C. Douglas Dillon, his Treasury Secretary. These were the most important cabinet positions.

In his book *Kennedy*, historian Theodore Sorensen offers an explanation: "...Kennedy had no political or even personal tie with either Rusk (who had supported Stevenson for the nomination) or Republican McNamara and [he] knew Dillon had supported Nixon." Per Sorensen, Pentagon Research Director Herbert York claimed that he was the earliest

Kennedy supporter in the top ranks of the new Defense Department: all the others had favored Rockefeller, Symington, Johnson or Stevenson.

It is very important that historian Theodore Sorensen takes care to relate in a footnote an "allegation" that Joseph P. Kennedy was responsible for the nominations of Rusk and McNamara. This "allegation" carries the ring of truth. But why does Sorensen characterize this possibility as an allegation? The dictionary defines allegation as "a claim or assertion that someone has done something illegal or wrong..." In this one footnote, Sorensen betrays what he undoubtedly suspects: that Joseph P. Kennedy decided to fill his son's administration with people who would carry out the agenda of JPK, even though these people might actually be mortal enemies of his son. That ugly fact is a fact that every historian realizes: that Kennedy senior would eagerly treat his own children and family as sacrificial lambs, sometimes with a barbarity which can only be paralleled in the dark recesses of human history. JPK was the pig that eats the piglets.

Even granting that J. P. Kennedy picked people at the top cabinet level, there were still at least 50 candidates which were hand-picked by JFK himself for lesser positions. In this process of selection, there were several persons or groups which were important. One was the Brookings Institute, a think tank. Another was Washington attorney and Democratic influence-peddler Clark Clifford. A third was Richard Neustadt, a top national expert on the subject of Public Administration and who had helped to create the National Security Council and the National Security State itself.

In this transition, there was a potential trap. Ike's people might try to involve the incoming Kennedy people in things which would be, in reality, Republican programs or policies. According to historian Arthur Schlesinger, Jr. , outgoing Treasury Secretary Robert B. Anderson tried to persuade a Kennedy person to go to Germany to discuss the issue of the U.S. gold supply. This idea was not accepted by JFK, who put Paul Nitze on that project instead. (We will see later that Robert Anderson was prominent in the LBJ phone calls in the week after the assassination and was a close associate of Judge Robert Morris).

With regard to a similar issue in the lame-duck period, however, Ike took action which Kennedy might not have taken himself: Ike terminated diplomatic relations with Cuba and thus beat JFK to that switch.

In describing the Ike-Kennedy transition, historian Schlesinger raises the specter of bankers, industrialists, lawyers, generals and foundation presidents, among whom JFK had few, if any, acquaintances. This is a prime example of why Schlesinger is regarded as a poor, if not dishonest historian. Rusk and McNamara were not "acquaintances" of JFK, but he picked both of them. JFK had been in Congress since 1946. He honeymooned with Jackie at Montego Bay in Jamaica in a resort which was a mecca for the rich and famous. To say he didn't know any bankers, industrialists and generals is ridiculous. JFK had to know the big Wall Street bankers. He had to know who the top generals like Eisenhower, MacArthur, Omar Bradley, Lucius Clay, James Gavin and others.

No, the circumstances of the cabinet choices of JFK all point to the theory that his cabinet was foisted upon him in one way or another. And the theme seemed to be that Joseph P. Kennedy and his type wanted to put the wealthy class like the Rockefellers, the Dillons and the J. P. Morgan's back in charge of the government, a position they hadn't enjoyed since the administration of Herbert Hoover.

This force was christened "The Establishment" by a writer in 1955. Schlesinger specifically lists the Rockefeller, Ford and Carnegie Foundations and the Council on Foreign Relations as the front organizations of these establishment special interest groups.

Although it is just another wild, nonsensical claim, it should at least be mentioned that Schlesinger made a claim about the "Establishment." He wrote "…it had not recovered from a 1957 [JFK] speech attacking French policy in Algeria which had shocked it to its core and even created the myth that Kennedy was anti-NATO, a cardinal Establishment sin." To translate this comment for the reader, what Schlesinger is really saying here is that JFK's policy on Algeria (in or around 1962) played a major role in his assassination. The issue of Algeria was not even on the radar in 1957 when compared to issues like Berlin and the gold outflow; and the issue of Algeria had absolutely no bearing on whether JFK was pro or anti-NATO. NATO was conceived as a defense against the Soviet Union, after all, not as a vehicle to influence the war in Algeria. This is just more Arthur Schlesinger, Jr. nonsense. Kennedy is quoted by Schlesinger as saying that he didn't care how a potential appointee voted (i.e. Republican or Democrat)! If true, this was to become (literally) a suicidal policy.

Schlesinger names Robert A. Lovett and John J. McCloy as the two leaders of the Establishment at the time of the JFK transition. Lovett would have a deciding role in JFK's cabinet-level picks. Having refused any appointment for himself, Lovett recommended Robert S. McNamara for Secretary of Defense. Paul Nitze, a long-time Washington foreign policy insider, had chaired a task force on national security, so his voice was also heard in these discussions.

As mentioned above, Richard Neustadt was one of the nation's leading experts on both the subject of Public Administration and also on the National Security State. He had been involved during the Truman Administration on questions involving the National Security State. Because of the "security" expertise of Richard Neustadt, the following question must be asked: did Neustadt (or McCloy, Nitze or others) consider the control of the Secret Service by the Department of the Treasury a factor in choosing an appropriate Secretary of the Treasury? Was there any concern on the part of an expert like Neustadt regarding the issue of whether the Secret Service would be well managed or adequately funded under one Treasury candidate versus another? The issue of the appropriate supervision of the Secret Service was discussed (belatedly) in detail before the Warren Commission after JFK was dead: too late by then!

Since there had not been a Presidential assassination since William McKinley, such an issue would not have been automatically in the forefront. But would an expert in national security such as Neustadt be aware of that aspect of security, that is, the physical security of the President and "the loyalty of the Palace Guard?" If Neustadt was not thinking of this issue, he surely should have been.

Returning to the topic of McGeorge Bundy, we find that he was appointed as National Security Advisor in 1961. He was considered one of Kennedy's "wise men." Bundy played a crucial role in all of the major foreign policy and defense decisions of the Kennedy administration and was retained by Lyndon B. Johnson for part of his tenure. Bundy was involved in the Bay of Pigs Invasion, the Cuban Missile Crisis, and the Vietnam War. From 1964 under Johnson, he was also Chairman of the 303 Committee, responsible for coordinating government covert operations. Bundy was a strong proponent of the Vietnam War during his tenure, believing it essential to contain Communism. He supported escalating United States involvement, including commitment of hundreds of thousands of ground troops and the sustained bombing of North Vietnam in 1965. Studies of the memoranda and policy papers since those years have revealed that Bundy and other advisors well understood the risk but proceeded with these actions largely because of domestic politics, rather than believing that the U.S. had a realistic chance of victory in this war.

He left government in 1966 to serve as president of the Ford Foundation, serving in this position until 1979.

From 1979 to 1989, Bundy served as a professor of history at New York University. He helped found the group known as the "Gang of Four," whose other members were Robert McNamara, George F. Kennan and Herbert Scoville; together they spoke and wrote about American nuclear policies. They published an influential article in *Foreign Affairs* in 1983, which proposed ending the U.S. policy of "first use of nuclear weapons to stop a Soviet invasion of Europe." During this period, Bundy wrote *Danger and Survival: Choices About the Bomb in the First Fifty Years* (1988). Their work has been credited with contributing to the SALT II treaty a decade later.

After serving at the Ford Foundation, in 1979 he returned to academia as professor of history at New York University, and later as scholar in residence at the Carnegie Corporation. Bundy was with the Carnegie Corporation from 1990 to 1996.

He died in 1996 of a heart attack.

WALT WHITMAN ROSTOW

A lthough W.W. Rostow was not a member of the National Security Council at the moment of the assassination, he has to be included in a discussion of this topic for two reasons.

First, Rostow was the most influential advisor to both JFK and LBJ on the issue of foreign policy.

Second, the selection of Rostow as Deputy National Security Advisor under McGeorge Bundy was of great import in the saga of Otto Otepka. Since Rostow had served as an important fixture in the National Security Council, it is likely that he retained a great deal of influence in the NSC after he left to work for the State Department. Indeed, Otepka biographer William J. Gill implies (or his remarks could be interpreted) that Dean Rusk and W.W. Rostow were the kingpins in the assassination plot within the administration.

Walt Whitman Rostow (also known as Walt Rostow or W.W. Rostow) was born on October 7, 1916. He was an economist and a political theorist who served as Special Assistant for National Security Affairs to U.S. President Lyndon B. Johnson, 1966-69.

Prominent for his role in the shaping of U.S. foreign policy in Southeast Asia during the 1960s, he was a staunch anti-communist, noted for a belief in the efficacy of capitalism and free enterprise, strongly supporting U.S. involvement in the Vietnam War. Rostow is known for his book *The Stages of Economic Growth: A Non-Communist Manifesto* (1960), which was used in several fields of social science.

His older brother Eugene Rostow also held a number of high government foreign policy posts.

Rostow was born in New York City to a Russian Jewish immigrant family. His parents Victor and Lillian Rostow, were active socialists, and named Walt after Walt Whitman. His brother Eugene, named for Eugene V. Debs, became a legal scholar, and his brother Ralph, after Ralph Waldo Emerson, a department store manager.

Rostow entered Yale University at age 15 on a full scholarship, graduated at 19, and completed his Ph.D. there in 1940. He also won a Rhodes Scholarship to study at Balliol College, Oxford, where he completed a B.Litt. degree. In 1936, during the Edward VIII abdication crisis, he assisted broadcaster Alistair Cooke, who reported on the events for the NBC radio network. After completing his education, he started teaching economics at Columbia University.

During World War II, Rostow served in the wartime U.S. spy agency known as the OSS under William J. Donovan, known as "Wild Bill" Donovan to his friends. Among other tasks, he participated in selecting targets for U.S. bombing in Europe. Nicholas Katzenbach (who would become the Attorney General of the U.S.) at one time joked: "I finally understand the difference between Walt and me [...] I was the navigator who was shot down and spent two years in a German prison camp, and Walt was the guy picking my targets."

In 1945, immediately after the war, Rostow became assistant chief of the German-Austrian Economic Division in the Department of State in Washington, D.C.. In 1946-1947, he returned to Oxford University in England as a professor of American History. In 1947, he became the assistant to the Executive Secretary of the Economic Commission for Europe, and was involved in the development of the Marshall Plan.

Rostow went on to spend a year at Cambridge University in England as a professor in the field of American Studies. He was professor of economic history at the Massachusetts Institute of Technology from 1950 to 1961, and a staff member of the Center for International Studies at MIT from 1951 to 1961. In 1954, he advised President Dwight Eisenhower on economic and foreign policy, and in 1958 he became a speechwriter for Ike. In August 1954, Rostow and fellow CIA-connected MIT economics professor Max F. Millikan convinced Eisenhower to massively increase U.S. foreign aid for development as part of a policy of spreading American-style capitalist economic growth in Asia and elsewhere, backed by the military.

While working as national security advisor, Rostow became involved in setting the United States' posture towards Israel. Although he supported military and economic assistance to Israel, Rostow believed that increased public alignment between the two states could run counter to U.S. diplomatic and oil interests in the region. After reviewing the May 1967 report from the Atomic Energy Commission team that had inspected the Israeli nuclear facilities at Dimona along with other intelligence, Rostow informed President Johnson that, though the team found no evidence of a nuclear weapons program, "there are enough unanswered questions to make us want to avoid getting locked in too closely with Israel."

In 1960, Rostow published *The Stages of Economic Growth: A Non-Communist Manifesto*, one of the major historical models of economic growth, which argues that economic modernization occurs in five basic stages of varying length: traditional society, preconditions for take-off, take-off, drive to maturity, and high mass consumption. This level of complex thinking was typical of Rostow. That's why Rostow became such an iconic figure in U.S. planning in many areas. This became one of the important concepts in the theory of modernization in social evolutionism. Though complex, many dismissed this thesis because it would not realistically apply in places like Latin America or Africa south of the Sahara.

This theoretical work impressed presidential candidate John F. Kennedy, who appointed Rostow as one of his political advisers, and sought his advice. When Kennedy became president in 1961, he appointed Rostow as deputy to his national security assistant McGeorge Bundy. Later that year,

Rostow became chairman of the U.S. Department of State's policy planning council. After Kennedy's assassination, Lyndon B. Johnson promoted Rostow to Bundy's job after Rostow wrote Johnson's first State of the Union speech. As national security adviser, Rostow was responsible for developing the government's policy in Vietnam, and was convinced that the war could be won. He became Johnson's main war hawk and played an important role in bringing Johnson's presidency to an unhappy end.

When Richard Nixon became president, Rostow left office, and over the next thirty years taught economics at the Lyndon B. Johnson School of Public Affairs at the University of Texas at Austin with his wife Elspeth Rostow, who later became dean of the school. He wrote extensively in defense of free enterprise economics, particularly in developing nations.

Because Rostow possessed such an overwhelming intellect, he could not have remained in the JFK administration and been unaware of the assassination plot. Indeed, just hours after the assassination, his brother Eugene Rostow called LBJ with a complete plan for a Warren Commission strategy. Some say that Eugene Rostow, in so doing, was working with a group who had put together the Warren Commission concept (implicitly in advance of the assassination). Otepka biographer William J. Gill writes darkly about Rostow's character.

DEAN RUSK

On the issue of the National Security Council, the person next in importance after McGeorge Bundy was Secretary of State Dean Rusk.

David Dean Rusk was born February 9, 1909. He was the Secretary of State from 1961 to 1969. His term began under the Kennedy Administration and ended with the presidency of Lyndon Johnson. He was among the top three longest-serving Secretaries of State.

Dean Rusk was born in Cherokee County, Georgia. His parents were Robert Hugh Rusk and Frances Elizabeth Clotfelder. He was educated in Atlanta public schools and worked in a law office for two years before deciding to attend Davidson College, a Presbyterian school where he worked his way through for all four years and also played football, graduating in 1931 (Traditionally, everyone at Davidson could join the football squad as a freshman, at least in later years). Rusk married Virginia Foisie on June 9, 1937. The Rusks had three children.

Rusk became a cadet in ROTC and commanded a battalion of ROTC reserve cadets. Rusk was a very successful scholar. He graduated Phi Beta Kappa and earned a Rhodes Scholarship to study in England. While in the Rhodes Scholar program, he earned a BS and MA degree from St. John's College in Oxford University. For his excellent scholarship, he received the Cecil Prize, a prestigious honor, in 1933. Rusk then went on to study at the University of Berlin and earned a law degree from the University of California-Berkely in 1940. This would be his fourth college degree, having studied in four renowned colleges and universities by the time he was 31. All this while also having played college football and commanded a ROTC battalion.

When WW II broke out, he joined the infantry as a Captain in the reserves. He served as a staff officer in the China-Burma-India theater. At the end of the war he was a colonel. He won both the Legion of Merit and the Oak Leaf Cluster military awards.

Rusk began his State Department career in 1946 as assistant chief of the Division of International Security Affairs. He was Deputy Under-Secretary of State in 1949. He then served in a number of positions which led to his appointment as Assistant Secretary of State for Far Eastern Affairs in 1950. As head of Far Eastern Affairs, he played a major role in the U.S. decision to enter the Korean Conflict in 1950. Rusk was known as a cautious diplomat and always sought international support.

Upon returning to the U.S. in 1945, Rusk went to work for the War Department, soon to be merged into the Department of Defense. His job was with United Nations Affairs. It was Rusk's idea to split the Korea's along the 38th parallel. He began his career with the State Department in 1946 as assistant chief of the Division of International Security Affairs. Next he became Deputy Undersecretary of State in 1949, and was put in charge of Far Eastern Affairs in 1950.

From 1950 to 1961, Rusk was President of the Rockefeller Foundation.

On December 12, 1960, Rusk was selected by the newly elected John F. Kennedy as his Secretary of State.

Rusk was sworn in on January 21st, 1961. Rusk was an advocate of the use of military force in the battle against Communism. In an example of this philosophy, Rusk remained totally non-committal in the debate which preceded the disastrous Bay of Pigs operation. An expert named Sheldon Stern has reviewed the tape recordings of the deliberations at the height of the Cuban Missile Crisis in the meetings of EXCOMM committee of the National Security Council. Stern claims that it was the contributions of Rusk to the discussion that averted nuclear war. This would be a viewpoint not supported elsewhere in the reporting of the Cuban Missile Crisis debates and probably exaggerates the role of Rusk. The credit for avoiding nuclear war at that point is generally given to JFK himself and no one else. Rusk was, as mentioned in the previous paragraphs, generally a military hawk – as was demonstrated over and over again in the Vietnam War.

After the assassination and well into the period of the Johnson Administration, Rusk became a target of anti-war protests, all because of his never-ending support for the Vietnam war. Rusk met with diplomat Llewellyn Thompson and Soviet Foreign Minister Andrei Gromyko during the important 1967 Glassboro Summit Conference.

In his autobiography entitled *As I Saw It*, Rusk admitted that he did not have a good relationship with President Kennedy. That is a considerable understatement considering that he was perhaps one of the perpetrators of the President's assassination. The role of Rusk in the assassination might be suggested due to two factors: 1) his powerful connection to the Rockefeller clique which would at least have made him aware in advance of the assassination and 2) by the dark portrayal of Rusk by Otepka biographer William J. Gill. As we shall see, Gill almost certainly had some inside informantion about the assassination after the fact. Kennedy was generally unsatisfied with the State Department as an institution. Some historians view Kennedy's attitude as a desire to be his own Secretary of State. This is an incredibly simplistic, even a nonsensical analysis. Author Theodore Sorensen has claimed that Kennedy disliked the tendency of Rusk to be non-committal in meetings. More likely, Kennedy's dissatisfaction with Rusk, if it did exist, was that the fact the Rusk lacked loyalty to the United States, pure and simple. For reasons that we will next analyze, Rusk was more worried about following the philosophies of the British, the Rockefeller family and other special interests. Kennedy, being a very astute person, would have figured that out.

There were rumors of JFK's possible dismissal of Rusk prior to his assassination, but Rusk might have hypothetically helped solve that problem for himself by assisting in Kennedy's murder.

Rusk offered his resignation to the new President, Lyndon B. Johnson, but that would have been perfunctory. Considering the circumstances and confusion after the assassination, the next President would likely not have been eager to cross Rusk or others who may have been among the plotters. When Johnson died in 1973, Rusk praised the former president.

During the Johnson Administration, Rusk was caught in the middle of President Charles de Gaulle's withdrawal from NATO and Johnson's resulting anger. Johnson asked Rusk to communicate his resentment against de Gaulle over the situation.

As previously mentioned, Rusk went on to be a major hawk in the divisive struggle to support the Vietnam War against growing disapproval and rancorous public protests.

After he left the State Department, Rusk became a professor of international law at the University of Georgia beginning in 1970 and held that position until his retirement in 1984.

Rusk died of heart failure at the age of 85 on December 20, 1994. A building at the University of Georgia was named Dean Rusk Hall in his honor.

ROBERT S. MCNAMARA

When discussing Robert S. McNamara and the National Security Council, it must be stated at the outset that McNamara was the one member of the NSC who was probably not involved in the assassination and who, if he knew about it (which he probably did not) would not have participated or approved based on his background, his record and his personality.

This conclusion is based on two facts. First, during the first week of tape recorded LBJ phone calls, LBJ rudely hung up the phone on McNamara when the latter tried to call him. He treated the call as if it were a wrong number. This response from LBJ was unique. Out of 120 phone calls, only McNamara got this rude treatment by LBJ. Hanging up would not be a way for LBJ to express his thanks for becoming the President if LBJ thought Mc-Namara had a part in the plot.

Second, McNamara, like Kennedy, was a secular Catholic. He grew up in California, a secular melting-pot and not a state with ethnic ghettos of Italians, Poles and Irishmen like Massachusetts and the states of the Northeast. He attended the University of California, while virtually the entire inner circle of the JFK administration and indeed, Washington D.C. itself, was part of the Yale-Harvard and Rockefeller-type Northeastern clique.

McNamara never attended any Catholic schools to the knowledge of this author. When JFK was pitted against extreme Catholic activism in the person of Senator Thomas J. Dodd, former Congressman Charles Kersten, Judge Robert Morris and others, McNamara would have most likely allied himself with the liberal JFK. Of course, the Vietnam War was a huge issue when it came to the Catholic Church and the Diem brothers. Every Catholic, staunch or otherwise, would have to have held an opinion on that issue.

Robert Strange McNamara was an American professor, business executive and the eighth Secretary of Defense, serving from 1961 to 1968 under presidents John F. Kennedy and Lyndon B. Johnson. McNamara remains the Defense Secretary with the longest service in U.S. history.

McNamara was born in San Francisco, California on June 19, 1916. His father was a shoe wholesaler and his mother was Clara "Nell" Strange McNamara. His family was of Irish descent, coming to Massachusetts in 1850 and then went west to California. As previously mentioned, although a Catholic, McNamara apparently did not attend Catholic schools, though this is not completely clear in the historical record. He attended the University of California at Berkeley and graduated in 1937 with a degree in Economics. He then attended Harvard Business School and earned an MBA in 1939.

McNamara married Margaret Craig, his high-school sweetheart on August 13th, 1940. After one year at the accounting firm of Price, Waterhouse, he went back to Harvard as a professor of accounting. In 1943, he entered the USAF as a captain and served in World War II in the Office of Statistical Control. His main responsibility was the analysis of the efficiency and effectiveness of the B-29 bomber, especially in the raids carried out by controversial Air Force General Curtis LeMay over Japan. When he left the service in 1946, he had earned the rank of Lieutenant Colonel.

In 1946 Charles "Tex" Thornton, a colonel under whom McNamara had served, started a management group. Thornton would later be a business contact of George de Mohrenschildt, when Thornton was head of a Dallas Bank. Thornton had seen Ford Motors as a company in need of serious reform. Henry Ford II (a WWII Navy veteran) hired Thornton's group which became know as the "Whiz Kids."

McNamara pushed for the design of the Ford Falcon, a very small car for its day, which was introduced in the Autumn of 1959. On November 9, 1960 McNamara became the first president of Ford Motor Company who was not a Ford family member. He was only in that job for a month. In 1960, President-elect John F. Kennedy offered McNamara the job of Secretary of Defense, which after much discussion, he accepted.

According to Ted Sorensen, a Kennedy advisor, JFK regarded McNamara as the star of his team. He relied on McNamara not just for military advice, but in economics as well. McNamara was one of the few who socialized with Kennedy. At the funeral of Robert Kennedy in 1968, McNamara was one of the pallbearers. McNamara used his statistical and accounting knowledge to analyze logistical and related issues in Vietnam such as the effectiveness of defoliants and the success of bombing there.

Beginning in 1961, Kennedy along with McNamara decided to switch the overall military strategy of the U.S. from the "massive retaliation" favored by Eisenhower to the "flexible response" which relied much more on conventional forces. To the European allies, this new strategy could mean the sacrifice of Western Europe to the Soviets, who had overwhelming superiority in conventional forces. On the issue of "flexible response" alone, McNamara would not have been a friend of the JFK plotters with their anti-Communist fervor and West German connections.

Kennedy wanted a greater ability to counter Communist led "wars of liberation." In reality, this strategy implied a type of "Vietnamization," whereby local forces would be enlisted to fight their own battles.

In the midst of the October 1962 Cuban Missile Crisis, McNamara served as a member of EXCOMM, a committee at large of the National Security Council along with related individuals. McNamara was a strong proponent of the strategy of blockade which eventually prevailed.

McNamara increased the size of conventional forces and increased air and sea-lift capability. He provided more funds for space research and development. Importantly to the topic of the assassination, he combined the intelligence functions of the service branches into one Defense Intelligence Agency. This new agency was therefore under the control of the Defense Department and the Secretary of Defense.

If each service had exclusive control of their intelligence agencies, it only stands to reason that it would be impossible to get all four agencies to agree on an issue like a Presidential assassination. When the Defense Department itself was created, little thought was given to the evil side of basic human nature. The priority was placed only upon financial efficiency. This got both Kennedy and McNamara in trouble in the short term, although as we shall see, according to author H.H. Nieburg, McNamara's efficiency theories reaped great benefits in the longer term.

None of McNamara's procurement policies were popular with the military and their allies in Congress. Some critics such as Col. L. Fletcher Prouty have claimed that his policies were an attempt to put military pork-barrel dollars under the control of the White House rather than Congress.

McNamara directed the Air Force to adopt the Navy's F-4 Phantom and A-7 Corsair combat aircraft, a consolidation that was quite successful. Conversely, his actions in mandating a premature across-the-board adoption of the untested M16 rifle proved catastrophic when the weapons began to fail in combat. McNamara tried to extend his success by merging development programs as well, resulting in the TFX dual service F-111 project. This was the fighter called the General Dynamics F-111B. It was intended to combine Navy requirements for a Fleet Air Defense (FAD) aircraft and Air Force requirements for a tactical bomber. His experience in the corporate world led him to believe that adopting a single type for different missions and service would save money. He insisted on the General Dynamics entry over the DOD's preference for Boeing because of commonality issues. Though heralded as a fighter that could do everything (fast supersonic dash, slow carrier and short airfield landings, tactical strike, and even close air support), in the end it involved too many compromises to succeed at any of them. The Navy version was drastically overweight and difficult to land, and eventually canceled after a Grumman study showed it was incapable of matching the abilities of the newly revealed Soviet MiG-23 and MiG-25 aircraft. The F-111 would eventually find its niche as a tactical bomber and electronic warfare aircraft with the Air Force.

McNamara's tendency to take military advice less into account than had previous secretaries and to override military opinions contributed to his unpopularity with service leaders. It was also generally thought that one of his favorite ideas, "Systems Analysis," rather than being objective, was tailored by civilians like himself to support decisions they had already made for other reasons. In practice, the data produced by the analysis was so large and so complex that (while it was available to all interested parties), none of them could challenge their conclusions.

Among the management tools developed to implement PPBS were the Five Year Defense Plan (FYDP), the Draft Presidential Memorandum (DPM), the Readiness, Information and Control Tables, and the Development Concept Paper (DCP). In a book called *In The Name of Science*, H.L. Nieberg wrote that these methods allowed McNamara to tame the military-industrial complex.

McNamara traveled around Vietnam many times to study the situation directly and he was always more reluctant to approve force increases than were the military commanders.

McNamara believed that the "Domino Theory" was the prime cause for entering the Vietnam War. In an interview he announced, "prior to his death, President Kennedy did not speak of a withdrawal from Vietnam, but McNamara believed JFK would have withdrawn had he lived." This, of course was untrue or inaccurate because Kennedy had, in fact, signed an order of withdrawal just a week before the assassination.

McNamara often noted his close personal friendship with Jackie Kennedy, and claimed she asked for a stop to the killing in Vietnam.

As the controversy over the Vietnam War continued to heat up in the mid and late 1960's, McNamara became an ever more controversial figure. Rumors circulated that he would leave office. In early 1967, McNamara wrote a memo for LBJ suggesting that the fighting be turned over to the Vietnamese, which Johnson rejected. In November 1967, Johnson announced that McNamara would leave the Pentagon to become President of the World Bank.

McNamara left office on February 29, 1968. The President awarded him the Medal of Freedom and the Distinguished Service Medal.

Robert McNamara served the World Bank from April 1968 as head to June 1981, when he retired at age 65.

In later years, McNamara acknowledged that the firebombing of Tokyo by General LeMay would have been rightfully regarded as a war crime had the United States not won the war.

McNamara kept up his participation in politics in later years and made statements critical of the invasion of Iraq by the Bush Administration. McNamara and the other living Secretaries of Defense met with President Bush at the White House briefly to discuss the war.

McNamara died in his sleep, at his house in Washington, D. C. in 2009 at the age of 93. He was buried in Arlington National Cemetery.

Lyndon B. Johnson

Suffice it to be said that as of 1958, the Vice-President was a statutory member of the National Security Council. His biographical information and the manner in which JFK placed him in power is too well known to merit special treatment in the discussion of the National Security Council. There are no issues in the analysis of the role of the NSC in the assassination which point in any way to LBJ in particular.

What can be stated regarding LBJ is 1) he was very active in the space race and the committees in Congress which had oversight in that area and 2) his statutory membership on the NSC does not automatically implicate him in an NSC plot against JFK. We must remember that JFK himself was a statutory member of the NSC. What good did that do him? Another key thing to remember is that during the heyday of HUAC, SISS and the McCarthy Committee, LBJ showed no interest at all in being part of rogue investigative committees. LBJ did all his work out in the open and on the table for everybody to see. Also, as Vice-President, LBJ had no army of staff to carry out any part of the assassination as did McGeorge Bundy, C. Douglas Dillon and the Joint Chiefs of Staff and the Congressional Committees. JFK plotter Thomas J. Dodd claimed to be "an LBJ man" but there is no evidence that LBJ and Dodd colluded on much of anything. LBJ undoubtedly knew about the plot in advance as did his friend J. Edgar Hoover. But since others were going to pull off the murder, he had no reason to implicate himself. What if JFK had lived? Why put your neck in the noose if you were LBJ? There could always be a Jim Garrison or many Jim Garrison's. Why take the risk?

C. DOUGLAS DILLON

As Treasury Secretary, C. Douglas Dillon was not a statutory member of the National Security Council. But according to a consensus of the information about the Council, the Secretary of the Treasury was the one office whose occupant was most often included in Council meetings by invitation.

Clarence Douglas Dillon who was born on August 21, 1909. He was an American diplomat and politician who served as U.S. Ambassador to France (1953-1957) and as the 57th Secretary of the Treasury (1961-1965). He was also a member of the Executive Committee of the National Security Council (ExComm) during the Cuban Missile Crisis.

Dillon was born in Geneva, Switzerland, the son of American parents, Anne McEldin (Douglass) and financier Clarence Dillon. Although Dillon grew up as a patrician, his paternal grandfather, Samuel Lapowski, was a poor Jewish immigrant from Poland. After leaving Poland, his grandfather settled in Texas after the American Civil War and married Dillon's Swedish-American grandmother. Dillon's father later changed his family name to Dillon, his grandmother's maiden name. Dillon's mother was descended from Grahams Lairds of Tamrawer Castle at Kilsyth, Stirling, Scotland.

Dillon began his education at Pine Lodge School in Lakehurst, Ocean County, New Jersey which he attended at the same time as the three Rockefeller brothers Nelson, Laurance, and John. He continued at the Groton School in Massachusetts, then at Harvard University, A.B. magna cum laude 1931 in American history and literature.

In 1938 be became Vice-President and Director of Dillon, Read & Co., a firm that bore his father's name. After his World War II service on Guam, Saipan, and in the Philippines, he left the United States Navy as Lieutenant Commander decorated with the Legion of Merit and Air Medal. In 1946 he became chairman of Dillon, Read; by 1952 he had doubled the firm's investments.

Dillon had been active in Republican politics since 1934. He worked for John Foster Dulles in Thomas E. Dewey's 1948 presidential campaign. In 1951 he organized the New Jersey effort to secure the 1952 Republican nomination for Dwight D. Eisenhower. He was also a major contributor to Eisenhower's general election campaign in 1952.

President Eisenhower appointed him United States Ambassador to France in 1953. Following that appointment he became Under Secretary of State for Economic Affairs in 1958 before becoming Under Secretary of State For Polical Affairs the following year.

In 1961, John F. Kennedy, a Democrat, appointed the Republican Dillon to be Treasury Secretary, despite Dillon's support for Nixon in 1960.

Although it was said by some that JFK chose Dillon because he wanted a "sound money" man at Treasury, Dillon was obviously not the only sound money man who could have been chosen.

JFK first met Dillon in 1956 at Harvard, when Dillon was grand marshall of a Harvard event and JFK was receiving an honorary degree at the same event. After the ceremony, the two went to a club called the "Spee Club" where both were members and then, following that, they were sometimes golfing companions. Per authors Perez and Willett, Dillon was the wealthiest Secretary of the Treasury since Andrew Mellon in 1928. Dillon remained Treasury Secretary under President Lyndon B. Johnson until 1965.

Dillon proposed the fifth round of tariff negotiations under the General Agreement on Tariffs and Trade (GATT), conducted in Geneva 1960-1962; it came to be called the "Dillon Round" and led to substantial tariff reduction. Dillon was important in securing presidential power for reciprocal tariff reductions under the Trade Expansion Act of 1962. He also played a role in crafting the Revenue Act of 1962, which established a 7 percent investment credit to spur industrial growth. He supervised revision of depreciation rules to benefit corporate investment. A close friend of John D. Rockefeller III, he was chairman of the Rockefeller Foundation from 1972 to 1975. He also served alongside John Rockefeller on the 1973 Commission on Private Philanthropy and Public Needs, and under Nelson Rockefeller in the Rockefeller Commission to investigate CIA activities (along with Ronald Reagan). He had been president of Harvard

Board of Overseers, chairman of the Brookings Institute, and vice chairman of the Council on Foreign Relations.

With his first wife, Dillon collected impressionist art. He was a long-time trustee of the Metropolitan Museum, serving as its President (1970-1977) and then chairman. He built up its Chinese galleries and served as a member of the Museum's Centennial committee. He personally donated $20 million to the museum and led a fundraising campaign, which raised an additional $100 million.

The best and almost the only source of information on C. Douglas Dillon is to be found in the biography of his father called *Clarence Dillon: Wall Street Enigma* by Perez and Willett. Like General Lyman Lemnitzer, as a youth C. Douglas Dillon engaged in drastically anti-social behavior. He was expelled from school for throwing the teacher's books out the window onto trolley tracks. He once deliberately tossed a match into a pail of gasoline for kicks, which touched off a major fire.

As Treasury Secretary, C. Douglas Dillon was in charge of the ATF and the Secret Service. Since the latter was almost certainly complicit in the assassination, that puts C. Douglas Dillon squarely in the center of the plot. As a Republican activist and the boyhood friend of all three Rockefeller brothers, Dillon had the connections to tie together the entire plan. Further, his business partners Ferdinand Eberstadt, James Forrestal, William Draper and Paul Nitze had almost dictated and written the crucial, formative part of U.S. history from 1935 at least up to and past 1963. When he testified before the Warren Commission, Allen Dulles called him "Doug" in the official transcripts and testimony. That pretty much says it all.

C. Douglas Dillon received the Medal of Freedom in 1989 and was also a member of the Society of Colonial Wars.

Dillon died of natural causes at the New York-Presbyterian Hospital in New York City at the age of 93.

THE JOINT CHIEFS OF STAFF

The Joint Chiefs of Staff do not figure prominently in the discussion of the National Security Council, or indeed in the entire discussion of the assassination. This is explained by the following facts:

First, before 1958, the Joint Chiefs were merely "advisors" to the NSC. After 1958, the Chairman of the Joint Chiefs was made a member of the NSC. But also in 1958, the Joint Chiefs were deprived of actual command of any troops or subordinates, save the direct staff of the Joint Chiefs.

Most people assume that the Joints Chiefs included the top commanders of the Army, Navy, Air Force and Marine Corps. That was true before 1958. But the Joint Chiefs were divorced from their commands in the respective services. For this reason, in his book *Countdown for Deci-*

sion, recently retired General John B. Medaris of the Army described the Joints Chiefs as "a debating society."

Second, when JFK established the Defense Intelligence Agency, all of the intelligence agencies of the branches were placed under the central control of the Defense Department, hence under the control of the Secretary of Defense, not under the control of the Joint Chiefs. This further removed the Joint Chiefs from having a central role in the assassination. It should be noted that JFK's new Defense Intelligence Agency was weak, disorganized and he did not have a very good, quality relationship with other departments.

On October 1, 1962, JFK elevated General Maxwell Taylor to the chairmanship of the Joint Chiefs of Staff, replacing General Lyman Lemnitzer. In a book recently written and published by the Joint Chief of Staff itself, the poor relationship between JFK and the JCS is described:

> By the time the Cuban missile crisis ended, relations between the Kennedy administration and the Joint Chiefs of Staff (Taylor excepted) were at an all-time low. In contrast, Kennedy's public stature and esteem had never been higher. Lauded by his admirers and critics alike for showing exemplary statesmanship, fortitude, and wisdom in steering the country through the most dangerous confrontation in history, the President emerged with his credibility and prestige measurably enhanced. But to end the crisis he made compromises and concessions that his military advisors considered in many ways unnecessary and excessive.

Since JFK's close confidant General Maxwell Taylor was the Chairman of the Joint Chiefs at the time of the assassination, their active participation in the plot was unlikely. Further, none of the individuals on the JSC on 11/22/1963 has any known connection to any of the facts and issues surrounding the plot itself. That is not to say, however, that some in the military or certain parts of military intellingence were not involved. They probably were, especially regarding the security in Dealey Plaza and the JFK autopsy. Also, as we shall see, the presence of a former Hitler associate as head of the NATO Defense Committee with offices in the Pentagon in 1963 throws additional dark shadows over the military in regard to the assassination.

GENERAL LYMAN LEMNITZER

The discussion of the Joint Chiefs of Staff and the JFK assassination most properly relates to General Lyman Lemnitzer. Ironically, Lemnitzer was not a member of the Joint Chiefs at the time of the assassination. However, he is the only member of the JFK Joint Chiefs whose name is usually mentioned regarding the assassination. Fortunately, for JFK researchers, there is a very objective biography of Lemnitzer available, written by L. James Binder who was a former editor-in-chief of *Army* magazine.

It should be mentioned that in a closing chapter, there will be discussion of factor analysis and the assassination. However, just to tantalize the reader, it can be stated that out of 191 people analyzed in the factor analysis process, General Lyman Lemnitzer came out number 1 in being statistically associated with the assassination plot. This happens by virtue of Lemnitzer being associated quite often with the plot by many assassination authors and also because at the time of the assassination, he was head of NATO. In this position he could be described as an international leader. According to the statistics, this places Lemnitzer in dead-center of the international forces which caused the assassination to occur as well as being on the list of suspects.

In the interest of balance, we will begin the analysis of Lemnitzer (known almost universally as "Lem"), with the high opinion of Lemnitzer held by Col. Fletcher Prouty. We have already relied on information from author Prouty to get to the truth about the role of McGeorge Bundy in the assassination plot.

Prouty served either directly under (or closely with) Lemnitzer for an extended period. Prouty writes:

> I was the first chief of the Office of Special Operations and continued in that office until 1964, while General Lyman Lemnitzer and, later, Gen. Maxwell Taylor were the chairmen of the Joint Chiefs of Staff (p.364,n.11)

> Lemnitzer and his close friend Gen. David M. Shoup [Commandant] of the U.S. Marine Corps were traditional soldiers. They had never been "Cold Warriors" or Cold War enthusiasts…

Our analysis will be somewhat at odds with the high opinion expressed by Prouty, a circumstance of which you, the reader, will have to resolve for yourself. We will just attempt to present relevant facts. But one must also attempt to evaluate the character of Lemnitzer in order to decide whether he was involved in the plot. His visibility in the events surrounding the assassination is just too great to do otherwise.

It was a combination of circumstances which vaulted General Lemnitzer to the top of the list *in re* the assassination. On November, 1962 Lemnitzer was appointed as commander of NATO, effective on January 1, 1963.

To the JFK researcher, the salient points regarding Lemnitzer could be described as "rich in subtle controversy." In the world of historical analysis of national leaders, Lemnitzer cuts a boring, but at the same time confusing, figure. This was because of his unorthodox career priorities and experiences. If you understand the confusing situation of Lemnitzer, then you can better understand the entire relationship of the military to JFK, to NATO and to the assassination.

To begin with, Lemnitzer's biographer treats Lemnitzer (as in a phrase attributed to the sharp tongue of Alexander Pope) by "damning him with faint praise." As a military author, biographer Binder minimizes outright criticism of Lemnitzer. But at the same time, there is the obvious omission of anything praiseworthy that might be expected from a military writer. The best that can be said is that Binder considered Lemnitzer harmless.

The reader can be offered the overall impression that biographer Binder presents of General Lemnitzer. He portrays Lem as a man, above all else, concerned with playing golf. He was very involved in affairs in his small town home of Honesdale, Pennsylvania and rarely expanded his scope of civic responsibilities beyond Honesdale. His main preoccupation was to fight to have dams or parks around Honesdale named after himself, as he believed was befitting his service. He was a man who fit best into a local Masonic Lodge (of which he was a devoted member).

Lemnitzer was born on August 29, 1899. He was raised a strict (presumably German) Lutheran. His ancestors had come to the U.S. from the province of Saxony in Germany. They came in 1860 and his grandfather immediately became embroiled in the Civil War raging in his new adoptive country. The story of Lemnitzer's father is all too typical of the furtive atmosphere that surrounds Lemnitzer and his life story.

The family was always told that his father served time at the Confederate POW camp known as Libby Prison, in Richmond. After that, he was supposedly transfered to Andersonville Prison in Georgia. But when modern researchers discovered the truth, they found that his father was actually imprisoned in a Union stockade for 1 ½ years for desertion.

Like JFK's Treasury Secretary, C. Douglas Dillon, Lemnitzer apparently had some antisocial tendencies as a youth. He and a friend built a pipe bomb a foot long and four inches in diameter and set it off near the downtown in Honesdale. Not surprisingly, the bomb brought down trees and hurled rocks into the air. This event (and the anger of the townspeople) was widely reported in the local newspaper. According to sources, Lemnitzer always considered this bomb as an achievement. He would continue this unfortunate attitude throughout his life and career. He tended to consider things to be achievements when they were in most respects embarrassments.

Lem served during peacetime at the key Far Eastern fortress of Corregidor. He became a protégé of General Stanley Embick. Embick, like Lem, was from rural Pennsylvania and was a successful but extremely eccentric military administrator and strategist. Embick's unique, stubborn and persistent dislike of the British is treated as humorous by most writers and was as well by his contemporaries. Unlike most military men, Embick actively supported peace demonstrators in the streets. For Lem, Embick wrote the word "outstanding" where other evaluators wrote "mediocre." Importantly, Lem was consistently rated as outstanding on only one quality: his ability to relate to civilians. Although his biographer does not comment on this sad fact, this ability is not what you would pick for a genuine military commander or hero, much less for the top military man in the country. Amazingly, being the top military man is where Lem eventually wound up.

At the time that Lem made a career of the Army, officers had to choose a track on which they would stay for the duration of their careers. Lem made the short-sighted choice of the (boring) coastal artillery. This branch would end up being abolished during his tenure there.

In World War II, Lem became chief of the Plans Division of the Army Ground Forces under Gen. Leslie McNair who, in turn, had Gen. Mark Clark as his boss as Chief of Staff. In 1942, Lem became a full Colonel. Two weeks later, he was a Brigadier General. He had risen from Major to General in 7 months. General Mark Clark was a favorite of Ike and Lem was a favorite of Clark.

In 1942, Clark and Lem were aboard a British submarine attempting to carry out Operation Kingpin. This operation involved a secret meeting with a Vichy-French General named Giraud who was then covertly transported by sub to meet with General Eisenhower at Gibralter. The bottom line of the mission was this: the fascist Vichy-French Admiral Francois Darlan remained in charge in French North Africa and Ike, Clark and Lem made a deal with him to support him in this role. This was despite the fact that he was an open ally of Hitler. FDR was furious about this and this mistake of judgment nearly got Eisenhower fired as commander in North Africa. In the eyes of some historians, this put a cloud over Ike for being neutral or insensitive on the issue of fascism. Yet for the rest of his life, Lem considered his minor participation in Kingpin as his greatest military achievement.

Lem was part of the problem-ridden capture of French North Africa. But for most of the remainder of the war, he was assigned to the command of British General Sir Harold Alexander. Lem and Alexander became friends for life.

Lem is given credit for being the chief planner for the landing at Anzio during the Italian Campaign. Again, in another example of a disaster masquerading as a success, Lem and Air Force General Lauris Norstad were the planners for the pointless and immoral destruction of the 1500-year-old historic landmark, the Abbey at Monte Cassino. Ironically, the names of Lemnitzer and Norstad are the two military names which are the most outstanding in the writings of assassination researchers. Norstad preceded Lem as Supreme Commander of NATO. And Nortstad came very close to being a member of the Warren Commission.

In his first openly shady operation, Lemnitzer and Allen Dulles were in Bern, Switzerland (in 1945) negotiating with German Nazi General Karl Wolff for the surrender of German forces in Italy. As we shall see over and over, the uncanny ability of Dulles to always wind up dealing with Nazis can be attributed to only one thing – essentially, he was one!

During Operation Sunrise, when Nazi General Wolff offered to surrender German forces in Italy, Lem's biographer L. James Binder suggests that this information was kept from FDR. Allen Dulles and Lemnitzer may have been responsible for withholding the information, which, if true, would have been Lem's first experience with committing treason.

It's probably no accident that Lem found himself in the company of an unsavory person like Allen Dulles, stabbing his elected commander-in-chief in the back. Lemnitzer was apparently one of those people we have all encountered in the workplace. They get ahead, not on ability, but their willingness to do illegal or unethical things without asking questions. Apparently, that description fit the up-and-coming General Lyman Lemnitzer.

The negotiations over the surrender of Northern Italy by the Nazi's involved one major issue. That was the question about how to prevent Stalin from having a hand in taking any Italian territory. The worry was that Stalin might get his hands on Vatican City. To a large extent, the possible Communist control of the Vatican would be the predominant worry in Europe from 1945 to 1963 and even into the 1970's. The horror story headline would be "Commies take over Vatican City?" If not Armageddon, this would be at least a large down payment.

Lemnitzer's probable role in betraying FDR happened because FDR considered good relations with Stalin to be necessary in order to finalize the war and to maintain order in Europe. Even Eisenhower believed that co-operating with Stalin had allowed the war to be won and was well worth it.

Think about it. Co-operating with Stalin enabled the defeat of fascism. All of the U.S. Generals in Europe assumed that such co-operation on some level would continue to yield benefits well after the war. But we know that even before WWII, there were some Americans who were secretly rooting for Hitler. This might even have included (in their heart-of-hearts) Herbert Hoover or General Douglas MacArthur. (In fairness to MacArthur, he apparently sincerely believed in imposing American, not fascist, values on the Japanese when he was in charge of the occupation).

The reality is that the pro-fascists never really changed their stripes because they thought, deep down, that the first priority should have been defeating Communism rather than tangling with Hitler. After the War, the anti-Communist, pro-fascists made a comeback. They launched the Red Scares and McCarthyism. Fortunately, there were Generals in the military like Eisenhower and George Marshall whose top priority was democracy. Like FDR, they had no use for fascism, though Marshall admired Chiang

Kai-shek to the very end and Ike was all too willing to wink at McCarthyism and follow the misguided advice of Allen Dulles.

Following WWII, Lem's commander in the war, General Alexander, became governor-general of Canada for 6 years. The two would remain lifelong friends. After the War, Lem succeeded his mentor General Stanley Embick as the Army representative on the four-person Joint Strategic Survey Committee (JSSC) which had overall charge of strategic planning for the military.

In 1948, Lem was called to the Office of James Forrestal, the first Secretary of Defense. He was named to the Military Committee of the Five Powers (the Brussels Pact) with the U.K., France, Belgium, Netherlands and Luxemborg. He was chosen because of his experience working under British General Alexander in World War II.

This Committee of the Five Powers soon developed into NATO. As we will see later, this opportunity to be there at the birth of NATO probably caused Lem to have more loyalty to NATO than to America when he was forced to chose in 1963. That's probable, but not necessarily proven by evidence.

The manager of the Office of Military Affairs at the Pentagon was Najeeb E. Halaby. He was a friend and close associate of Lem's at the Pentagon. Lem's biographer describes the resignation (and soon after), the death of Secretary of Defense James Forrestal. Binder calls it "an assumed suicide," a tragedy which occurred around this same time.

Lem's associate Najeeb E. Halaby, had what could be called a shadowy career. He was a graduate of Stanford and Yale Law School. At the time he was working with Lem, he had been advisor to King Ibn Saud of Saudia Arabia. He then helped Paul Nitze write NSC 68, which set in motion the Cold War, the Hydrogen bomb and other such sinister forces. In 1953, Halaby became affiliated with the Rockefeller family.

When Ike became president, he put Lem on a committee which decided whether the U.S. strategic policy should be 1) containment 2) roll-back or 3) drawing a line in the sand to justify a nuclear attack. The committee was headed by George F. Kennan and it decided on the option of containment. Ike started the "new look" which opted for the alternative of massive retaliation over conventional war-making. This was less expensive and allowed for major cuts to conventional forces. As a strategy, massive retaliation was also highly favored by West German Chancellor Konrad Adenauer.

In 1955, Lem got his 4th star and was put in charge of the Far East Command. On October 4, 1957, he was named Vice-Chief of Staff for the Army and second in command to General Maxwell Taylor. (Taylor would become a long-term rival of Lemnitzer). Lem was soon involved with the Redstone missile facility involving Wernher von Braun and General John B. Medaris, followed by the launching of Sputnik. He was next put in charge of the transfer of the missile scientists to NASA. Eisenhower once made the statement "Lem is a lot smarter than Max [General Maxwell Taylor]." This idle assessment and comment portended much for the future of the two and ultimately for JFK.

The Defense Reorganization Act of 1958 ended the JCS committee system and took away the actual command of the military branches from the JCS. General Medaris thought this turned the JCS into a "debating society." It gave the President much more control over the Army and the Defense Department. At this time, General Lauris Norstad as commander of NATO advocated the use of military force to open a road to Berlin but Eisenhower refused.

Around 1958, three top generals, Maxwell Taylor, James Gavin and Matthew Ridgeway, all left the Army over differences about policy. General John B. Medaris, (head of the Redstone Arsenal) also resigned in protest in order to write a very critical book on policy. In his book, Medaris wrote that Eisenhower was actually a below-average military mind and was making some bad military decisions. On July 1, 1959, Eisenhower appointed Lem as Chief of Staff for the Army.

Lemnitzer's biographer L. James Binder wrote that Lemnitzer was non-partisan "to a fault" and that even his immediate family did not know how he voted. After the political conventions of 1960 were over, Ike named Lemnitzer as Chairman of the Joint Chiefs of Staff. In this role, he was the leader of the JCS in advising the National Security Council. In March 1960, Ike started a paramilitary campaign against Castro under the "Special Group" (also called the 5412 Committee) which included the State and Defense Departments, the CIA and the National Security Office. When the abortive Bay of Pigs was attempted and then failed, Lem ordered the JCS to remain silent and not to respond to criticism from any quarter.

When JFK assumed the office of President, Lemnitzer met with the new cabinet. He offered seven alternatives to deal with the threat of Castro: 1) non-military pressure, 2) fomenting an internal uprising 3) a "Cuban" (covert) invasion force 4) employment of U.S.-supported guerrilla forces 5) an invasion of "volunteers" with overt U.S. military support 6) a U.S. military invasion accompanied by Latin American "volunteers" and 7) a unilateral U.S. military invasion. Five days later, the JCS sent McNamara a recommendation for forceful action. The following day, JFK met with LBJ, Rusk, McNamara, Bundy, Lemnitzer, Dulles and Paul Nitze (Assistant Secretary of Defense for International Security Affairs). Most of the CIA and the military estimated that the chance of success for the Bay of Pigs invasion was from 15% to 20%. Ordinarily, this would have meant cancellation of the mission.

Following the failure at the Bay of Pigs, there was a closed hearing on it before the Senate Foreign Relations Committee. Although Senators Wayne Morse and Homer Capehart supported Lemnitzer, Albert Gore and Russell Long called for him to be fired. In the wake of the Bay of Pigs, Allen Dulles, Richard Bissell and General Charles P. Cabell were fired from the CIA. All of the Joint Chiefs of Staff kept their jobs. In addition, around this time General Lauris Norstad was forced out as Supreme Commander of NATO by JFK and McNamara.

In his new administration, JFK tended to use ad hoc committees instead of existing committees and structures. Lem knew the Joint Chiefs were being bypassed by JFK. Because of his strong feelings about such things, JFK appointed General Maxwell Taylor as his military advisor in the White House. Thus, he interposed General Taylor between himself and the Joint Chiefs.

At a July 20, 1961 meeting of the National Security Council, General Thomas Francis Hickey, chairman of the Net Evaluation Subcommittee of the Joint Chiefs of Staff was in the midst of presenting a plan for a surprise nuclear attack on the Soviet Union. Incredibly, this attack was planned for 1963, two years later. According to the plan, it would be preceded by a "period of heightened tensions." The main proponents of this plan, according to a military aide to Vice-President Johnson, were the two old cronies Lyman Lemnitzer and Allen Dulles.

LBJ was not present at the meeting. As they had done in World War II, Lem and Dulles were working as a team on this and as usual, the cynical Dulles was apparently using the suggestible Lemnitzer as the military front man (and fall-guy) for this absurd proposal. JFK asked 1) how many Russians would be killed and 2) how long would Americans have to wait underground in fallout shelters to survive? According to an oral history recorded by Deputy Secretary of Defense Roswell Gilpatric, when Kennedy heard the answers and realized how disgusting the discussion was, he stood up and abruptly walked out of the meeting.

On March 13, 1962, the JCS proposed the infamous Operations Northwoods to JFK. The documents which revealed this plan were not declassified until November 18, 1997. This incredible plan would have involved the Joint Chiefs of Staff in planning and carrying out real bombings and similar events on U.S. streets. It would have killed innocent Americans in order to blame Castro and justify a U.S. invasion of Cuba. Lemnitzer's biography was published in 1997 and Binder didn't mention Operation Northwoods. The information on Northwoods apparently wasn't available to him.

Per Binder, McGeorge Bundy, JFK's National Security Advisor was unhappy with the arrangement where Maxwell Taylor became JFK's military advisor. Taylor's decisions dealt with intelligence, Berlin and Southeast Asia.

Lemnitzer was not a proponent of the Vietnam War. He voiced hesitancy about prospects for success in Southeast Asia and felt a war there would drain crucial resources from NATO. When he did voice his opinion on the issue, he advocated a direct military attack against North Vietnam.

It became clear to Lemnitzer that he would not be reappointed to a second term as Chairman of the Joint Chiefs of Staff. In the Spring of 1962, Lemnitzer was invited to the home of his WWII commander, Field Marshall Earl Alexander near Windsor Castle in England. Alexander asked him whether he would like to become head of NATO. When he got back to Washington, he received a visit from a military attaché from the West German Embassy. This man told Lemnitzer he was acting on behalf of Chancellor Konrad Adenauer. The attaché made the same proposal to Lem as had Alexander.

Despite the fact that the next man in line for the NATO post was General Earle Wheeler, JFK gave in to pressure from Prime Minister Harold MacMillan and German Chancellor Konrad Adenauer and appointed Lemnitzer. It was technically illegal for Lemitzer to assume the post, since by law it had to be held by a person on active duty. The law did not include a retired officer as being on active duty, even if recalled into that status.

Lemnitzer served well as NATO commander in all respects, being especially attentive to the errant President of France Charles de Gaulle. De Gaulle had a special interview with Lem prior to his being appointed NATO commander. Oddly, Lemnitzer happened to be appearing with de Gaulle at a public ceremony when the 3rd major assassination attempt against de Gaulle occurred. (Some say it was actually the 7th). This was the "flower pot bomb." It was organized by Jean-Jacques Susini, a co-founder of the OAS and the second-in-command to Jacques Soustelle, who was a long-time asset of British Intelligence and like Susini, was also living at the time under the protection of Italian intelligence.

This assassination attempt is known as the attempt at the Toulon Memorial. The attempt failed because the bomb in the flower pot had become rain-soaked and burned rather than exploded. No one will ever know if the presence of Lemnitzer at this attempt to kill de Gaulle was coincidental or if there was a more sinister connection. (In JFK research, it usually turns out that there are no really honest coincidences).

Lemnitzer died on November 12, 1988 in Washington, D. C.

To summarize, the examination of the life and career of Lyman Lemnitzer yields the following issues and conclusion for the JFK researcher:

> 1. Lemnitzer had a history of co-operation with Allen Dulles in dealing with Nazis and had been part of the Darlan affair and boasted about it, which could indicate an indifference about the issue of fascism.

> 2. While Lemnitzer was not a political partisan or McCarthyite like Generals Willoughby, MacArthur and Wedemeyer, he was attuned to civilian politics and well informed about issues current in the Congress.

> 3. He was "hired" as head of NATO by Chancellor Konrad Adenauer and the British, and not selected by JFK.

> 4. He had been insulted by JFK over the disastrous Bay of Pigs and for the plan for a pre-emptive nuclear strike against Russia scheduled

for 1963. Finally, he was not reappointed for Chairman of the JCS because of the criminal Operation Northwoods plan with which he had been involved. There was probably no love lost between Lem and JFK.

5. There was evidence that the money for the plots to kill de Gaulle had run through NATO headquarters, before or possibly during Lemnitzer's tenure there. There was at least one attempt on de Gaulle when Lem was commander of NATO.

6. As NATO commander, Lemnitzer would probably have placed his responsibility to NATO above his responsibility to JFK. This would be because Lemnitzer had been involved in the founding of NATO. His predecessor at NATO (and Lem's long-time associate) General Lauris Norstad had refused to answer the question of whether he would prioritize NATO over the U.S. should he have to choose.

7. He was neutral when it came to his opinion of General Charles de Gaulle. De Gaulle was heartily disliked by the fascists who murdered JFK.

8. In part because of the endorsement of Lemnitzer by author Col Fletcher Prouty and because of his generally non-conspiratorial and non-partisan history, it is difficult to clearly determine whether Lemnitzer was part of the plot to murder JFK. However, if he found himself in a bad position on that issue, he wouldn't have been a hero, either. The bottom line is that Lemnitzer was a go-along guy. Given his pivotal position in NATO, he has to be considered a part of the plot nevertheless. This is backed up by the statistical analysis which will be presented in a closing chapter.

Notes:

Final Judgment: The Missing Link in the JFK Assassination Conspiracy by Michael Collins Piper p 319.

The National Security Council: An Organizational Assessment, by Richard A. Best, Jr. December 28, 2011, www.crs.gov, RL30840.

Notes McGeorge Bundy

The information in this chapter about McGeorge Bundy can be found in Wikipedia under McGeorge Bundy, recovered on 10-12-16:

Another source of the information in this chapter is the biography of the Bundy brothers by Kai Bird called *The Color of Truth: McGeorge Bundy and William Bundy: Brothers in Arms.*

The quotations from Arthur Schlesinger, Jr. can be found in *A Thousand Days: John F. Kennedy In The White House* (1965).

The material from author Col L. Fletcher Prouty is from *JFK: The CIA, Vietnam and the Plot to Assassinate John F. Kennedy.*

Notes Walt Whitman Rostow

The information in this chapter on Walt W. Rostow is widely available and can be found on several internet sites which present general information on major figures such as Rostow; specifically, one such source is http:/wilsoncenter.org.

Notes Dean Rusk

Some of the general information on Rusk is found at page 425 of Congressional Directory, 89th Congress, Second Session, January 1966.

On the internet, by far the best source on Rusk is his brief biography to be found at Anonymous. "Biography of Dean Rusk." Davidson College. Retrieved 2008-02-03. https://www.davidson.edu/offices/international-studies-program/about-dean-rusk-31.

Another internet source is "Famed Fraternity Members." Kappa Alpha Order. Retrieved 2008-02-03.

Also consult "Parks Rusk Collection of Dean Rusk Papers." Richard B. Russell Library for Political Research and Studies. University of Georgia. pp. Biographical Note. Archived from the original on May 17, 2008. Retrieved 2008-02-04.

Finally, there are the memoirs of Rusk called *As I Saw It*, by Dean Rusk and Tom Rusk.

Notes Robert S McNamara

As we have seen in previous chapters, much of the best and most concise analysis about the policy problems involved in the JFK assassination can be found in *JFK: The CIA, Vietnam, and the Plot to Assassinate John F. Kennedy* by Col. L. Fletcher Prouty. His book is cited again in this section.

For information on McNamara, including that which is presented in this chapter, refer to *Counselor: A Life At The Edge Of History* by Theodore Sorensen.

Another obvious reference is *In Restrospect: The Tragedy and Lessons of Vietnam* by Robert S. McNamara.

A book which is specifically referenced in the above section is *In The Name Of Science* by H. L. Neiburg. This book is a classic which describes in detail the issues of technology and weaponry in the Eisenhower and JFK administrations.

There was a film called *The Fog Of War: Lessons From The Life Of Robert S. McNamara* for which a transcript is available for reference related to McNamara.

Notes C Douglas Dillon

As mentioned in the chapter, the best source of information about Dillon is found in the book *Clarence Dillon: Wall Street Enigma* by Robert C. Perez and Edward F. Willett beginning on page 136.

There is also a brief biography called "C. Douglas Dillon" at the John F. Kennedy Presidential Library.

Chapter 14

ROY FRANKHOUSER
AND DAN BURROS

As mentioned in the prior chapter dealing with the National Security Council and the assassination, Roy Frankhouser claimed in an interview that he worked on the JFK assassination as an agent of the National Security Council. This sensational claim merits both further discussion and an examination of the activities of Frankhouser in the years before and after the assassination.

Roy Everett Frankhouser, Jr. (often misspelled as "Frankhauser"), was born on November 4, 1939. His father was Roy E. Frankhouser, Sr. and his mother was Dorothy Butler Frankhouser. His most noteworthy office which was publicly known was as Grand Dragon of the Ku Klux Klan in Pennsylvania. He also had numerous other connections. Two of these were with the American Nazi Party and as a security consultant to Lyndon LaRouche and the LaRouche organization. Frankhouser was reported by federal officials to have been arrested at least 142 times, according to the *New York Times*. He was convicted of federal crimes in at least three cases, including dealing in stolen explosives and obstruction of justice. Irwin Suall, of the Anti-Defamation League, called Frankhouser "a thread that runs through the history of American hate groups." No one person described in JFK assassination research can match the diversity and ingenuity of Frankhouser in his clandestine career as an infiltrator and as an informant. Not even Lee Harvey Oswald.

Frankhouser was born in Reading, Pennsylvania. He attended Northwest Junior High School through the tenth grade, and became active in racist causes. As a teenager, he collected Nazi paraphernalia and uniforms. He joined the Ku Klux Klan at age 14. He joined the U.S. Army on November 6, 1956 on his 17th birthday, which was the first day he could legally enlist. He served one year as a paratrooper before receiving an honorable discharge on November 18, 1957. He joined the American Nazi Party in 1960.

What kind of a person was Roy Frankhouser? In an article published in *Playboy* magazine in June 1969, author Eric Norden interviewed both the leader of the Minutemen named Robert DePugh and his associate Roy Frankhouser. This article also appeared in the *Twentieth Annual Play-*

boy Reader. Norden gives a graphic description of Frankhouser at page 241 of the *Reader*:

> He was a slight young man of 29 with close-cropped black hair, a pencil-thin moustache and one good eye. Articulate and sophisticated, he was a type more likely to be found debating Marcuse in campus New Left salons than regaling red-necks in the satin sheets of a KKK grand dragon.

Soon after leaving the Army, Frankhouser joined the American Nazi Party, led by George Lincoln Rockwell. He was later described as a protégé of Rockwell's. At about the same time, he also joined J. B. Stoner's National States Rights Party. His first recorded arrest occurred at age 22 when he kicked a policeman in the shins during a 1961 protest in Atlanta. He was often a violent counter-demonstrator in civil rights protests around this time.

By the early 1960's, he had become active in Robert Shelton's United Klans of America. Frankhouser became the Grand Dragon for Pennsylvania in 1965, according to author Dennis King. At roughly the same time, Frankhouser also became active in the Minutemen organization led by Robert Boliver DePugh which had headquarters in the tiny community of Norborne, Missouri.

He participated in Nazi party rallies and Klan demonstrations, being arrested often for disorderly conduct. Fellow Klansmen nicknamed him "Riot Roy" as reported by author Patsy Sims in her book on the Klan. According to Frankhouser, he lost his eye in an attack by pipe-wielding Jews in 1965. In another version, he lost it during a fight with blacks in a Reading bar. A third story is that he lost it during the Bay of Pigs invasion.

There is an excellent biography of Dan Burros called *One More Victim* by Gelb and Rosenthal. Since Lee Harvey Oswald had Burros' name and address in his notebook, it is important to understand who Burros was and what the activities were in which he was engaged.

Briefly, Burros was raised a Jew but became a Nazi. He was born in 1937 and thus was two years older than Frankhouser. Like Frankhouser, Burros enlisted in the Army at age 17 or 18 and served under General Edwin Walker in the military action in Little Rock, Arkansas in integrating Central High School. There is no direct evidence that Burros had any interaction with General Walker, though he was in proximity to Walker during this action. He left the Army after three years in 1958.

Burros was sent to a neuropsychiatric department because of three feigned suicides. Moving back to New York, Burros began to collect Nazi paraphernalia. He left a job after 1½ years in January, 1960. His reputation as a Nazi had spread to the New York Police Department. He began corresponding with lone-wolf Nazis around the U.S. and the world. He had received a letter from Nazi Colonel Hans-Ulrich Rudel who had fled to Argentina and possibly on to Egypt after World War II. As will be explained in later chapters, Hans-Ulrich Rudel was a major figure among expatriate ex-Nazis. Rudel had close associations with the most conspiratorial of the reprobate ex-Nazis scattered around the globe including Col. Otto Skorzeny and Werner Naumann. Burros joined his first Fascist party, the British National Party in early 1960. Soon after, he moved to Arlington, Virginia to join the American Nazi Party.

In 1960, Burros took part in an action where 17 persons were arrested and Rockwell was committed to a mental hospital. In 1961, Burros met Roy Frankhouser. Frankhouser had visited Nazi headquarters on an "inspection" trip as an officer of the Citizen's Council of America. Frankhouser found Burros to be an especially "fun" person.

In March of 1961, an English Fascist named Michael Slatter who headed a small Nazi "cell" in New Orleans, told Rockwell he could raise money for a Nazi expedition to New Orleans. Burros took part in the expedition, which is famously known to historians as the "Hate Bus." Rockwell was arrested in New Orleans on this expedition.

Since Lee Harvey Oswald had the name of Dan Burros in his notebook, this Hate Bus expedition would have put Dan Burros in New Orleans near the time when Oswald lived there, although Oswald would have still been in the Soviet Union at the specific time that the Hate Bus arrived. Oswald returned to the U.S. in June, 1962. This Fascist New Orleans group was known as the National States Rights Party and Rockwell soon washed his hands of them. Author Dr. Jeffrey Caulfield in his book *General Walker* presents reams of information on these right-wing organizations and their role in the JFK assassination, such as it was.

On November 5, 1961, Dan Burros deserted the American Nazi Party and moved back to New York with fellow Nazi John Patler. The two started a magazine. The first issue was July, 1962 and it featured a noose with the words "Impeach the Traitor John F. Kennedy." It was Burros' address in New York in particular that Lee Harvey Oswald had in his notebook, which would fit time-wise with the time Burros was there and with the date when Oswald returned to the U.S.

The new party which Burros and Patler started in New York was called the American National Party and they lived in a neighborhood of New York which was almost entirely German-American. The bars there were frequented by former German soldiers.

Burros was associating with Roy Frankhouser at this time. Burros also was in contact by mail with racists in the U.S., U.K., South Africa and West Germany. It was also in 1961 that General Edwin Walker was forced to resign his command in West Germany by President John F. Kennedy for distributing radical right-wing propaganda to his troops. Recall that Burros served under Walker at Little Rock.

Burros was also an associate of James H. Madole. Madole founded and led the National Renaissance Party from 1948 to 1981. This party was a full-fledged Nazi Party of the Hitlerite variety. On July 24, 1964, Burros and others were sent to New York's Sing Sing Prison but Burros stayed only two weeks because of an appeal bond posted by his mother's uncle.

In 1965, Burros and Roy Frankhouser resumed their friendship from American Nazi Party days. Frankhouser tried to interest Burros in KKK activities. Almost immediately, Burros became the Grand Dragon of the KKK in New York. At virtually the same time, Burros was apparently being set up for disgrace as being both a Nazi and a KKK leader who was actually Jewish. The *New York Times* featured this story on the front page. Burros, upon finding this out, took up a carbine and shot himself both in the heart and in the head a total of three times.

Was this set up as just a convenient way to eliminate someone whose name and address was known to Lee Harvey Oswald? Since Roy Frankhouser was a confirmed agent of the National Security Council and claimed to have worked on the JFK assassination for the NSC, there was clearly a confluence of events here. Let's list them out.

At times during the period when he was friends with Roy Frankhouser, Dan Burros could have been acting as an intelligence "cut-out" for purposes of relaying mail between overseas Nazis, Frankhouser and the NSC, New Orleans right-wing people and Lee Harvey Oswald himself. This could explain why Oswald had the current address of Burros in his notebook.

This defamation of Burros in the *New York Times* coincides with the desire of the European-based Nazis to defame and disgrace Jews in the eyes of the American people. This is clearly an "old-world," European concept which was (and is) alien to the thinking of people in the U.S. We will also see this in their attempt to defame Jack Ruby and Bernard Weissman of the U.S. Army in Dallas at the time of the assassination.

In 1962, Oswald returned from the USSR. In 1961-62, Gen. Edwin Walker came back to the U.S. from West Germany. He was Burros' former commander in Little Rock. He came back after being fired by JFK. At the same time, Burros was corresponding with persons in West Germany and associating with former German soldiers in a German neighborhood in New York City. Burros was an associate of veteran U.S. Nazi cult figure James Madole. And Frankhouser began his association with Burros in New York at the same time.

Burros had ridden the Hate Bus to New Orleans and met up with New Orleans Nazi's just months before Oswald returned from Russia. The hate bus riders met with members of the National States Rights Party. Oswald was soon to live and operate as an agent in New Orleans himself. And Oswald had Burros' New York street address in his notebook when arrested. And Burros published a magazine threatening JFK.

The biographers of Dan Burros, Gelb and Rosenthal, did not believe there was evidence that Frankhouser murdered Burros, in part because there was a suicide note written by Burros, who had a medical history of threatening suicide. But was he deliberately driven to suicide by those who had access to the front page of the *New York Times*, just months after the Warren Commission had published their findings? Keep in mind that Roy Frankhouser was involved with Burros off and on from 1961 to when he died in 1965. Frankhouser at various times was a proven National Security Council operative, although he "officially" began in that role in 1972. There is no doubt, however, that Frankhouser was a government informant at the time he was a associating with Burros. Burros himself was an informant for the NYPD.

In 1966, Frankhouser appeared before the House Un-American Activities Committee as part of its investigation of the Ku Klux Klan. He reportedly pleaded the Fifth Amendment more than 30 times rather than answer their questions, according to the *Washington Post*.

Many of the questions from the Committee involved the suicide of Klan member Dan Burros. Dan Burros, a prominent member of the American Nazi Party as well as the Klan, committed suicide in Frankhouser's apartment in 1965.

It is significant that Frankhouser was one of the few defendants at the HUAC hearings who was not sentenced to prison for contempt of Congress. Shortly after this, Frankhouser became an informant for the FBI. He was almost certainly an informant or government operative of some kind before this.

His role as an FBI informant lasted until 1971. Frankhouser had a close working relationship with another Klan figure, Robert Miles, who lived in the Detroit area. Miles was also an FBI informant who bombed school buses in Pontiac, Michigan in 1971. At the trial of Robert Miles, the relationship of Roy Frankhouser to the FBI became public and his cover was lost.

In the Robert Miles case, Frankhouser was charged with stealing dynamite for Miles. He pled guilty to this offense and received two five-year terms but only on probation. When this happened, Robert Shelton of the Klan dismissed Frankhouser from the United Klans of America.

In 1972, he marched down Fifth Avenue in Manhattan wearing a black storm trooper's uniform to defy a city ban on wearing Nazi outfits in public. That same year, Frankhouser approached the FBI about working as an informant, offering information on groups such as black militants, the Jewish Defense League, the Irish Republican Army and Black September.

The National Security Council approved a mission in which he was sent to Canada to infiltrate Black September, but he was unsuccessful. To the knowledge of this author, this agency of Frankhouser with the NSC is the only reported instance of an NSC agent in all of the JFK literature. That's how private and secretive the covert activities of the NSC were and, of course, the NSC was not subject to Congressional oversight or any accountability to anyone except the President himself.

Frankhouser was also an organizer of the Minutemen and a member of the National States' Rights Party, the National Renaissance Party, the Liberty Lobby, and the White Citizens Council.

Frankhouser was convicted of conspiring to sell 240 pounds of stolen dynamite in 1975. The charges included selling explosives which were used in the bombing of a school bus in Pontiac, Michigan that killed one man. During the trial he revealed he was a government informant, saying he was acting on behalf of the ATF. The government denied his assertion. Though he faced up to fifty-one years in prison, he was sentenced to two concurrent five-year probation terms as part of a plea agreement. Lyndon LaRouche initiated a legal defense on behalf of Frankhouser. When the LaRouche movement learned that Frankhouser was an informant, it saw that as evidence of the "FBI-CIA-Rockefeller-Buckley" control of the extreme Right, and an example of how government connections could immunize criminal behavior.

Frankhouser became a security consultant for Lyndon LaRouche in 1979. We will examine the LaRouche organization in a separate chapter, including the role of Frankhouser in that organization.

As a result of his relationship with the LaRouche organization, Frankhouser was found guilty on December 10, 1987 of obstruction of a federal investigation into credit-card fraud committed by LaRouche and his followers. He was sentenced by US District Judge Robert E. Keeton to three years and a $50,000 fine. After his conviction, he was granted immunity against further prosecution and compelled to testify against LaRouche. Frankhouser appealed his conviction on April 3, 1989, arguing that his case should not have been severed from the main case, that his counsel had inadequate time to prepare, and that he was not provided with allegedly exculpatory evidence. The appeal was rejected in July.

Frankhouser's next notoriety came in the 1980s when he appeared regularly on Berks County, Pennsylvania public-access television with his own white supremacist shows called "Race and Reason" and "White Forum."

Then in April, 1993, Frankhousr was arrested for stabbing a KKK guard at a KKK event He was acquitted of that crime on the grounds of self-defense.

Next, in 1995 Frankhouser was convicted in Boston for helping to destroy evidence relating to desecration of synagogues and attacks on blacks. Frankhouser had been sought by the FBI for nine months. At the time, Frankhouser was allegedly the leader of the Pale Riders faction of the KKK. He was sentenced at that time to 25 months in prison. He won a partial victory on appeal.

In 1997 Frankhouser, then Grand Dragon of the United Klans of America in Pennsylvania was accused of harassing a woman named Bonnie Jouhari and her daughter. She worked at the Reading-Berks Human Relations Council on issues of discrimination. After failing to get redress from government agencies, Jouhari convinced the Southern Poverty Law Center to take her case. Frankhouser eventually settled this case with terms set by the Judge. He had to complete 1000 hours of community service and make public apologies to Jouhari and her daughter on his white-oriented TV show and through local newspapers. But further, Frankhouser had to pay the two 10% of his income for a decade, and undergo "sensitivity training." This settlement was supported by HUD Secretary Andrew Cuomo and Reverend Jesse Jackson and by the President of the NAACP.

But some experts on civil liberties such as David Bernstein[43] use this case as an example of unfair curtailment of free speech.

Next for Frankhouser was a role as pastor of the Mountain Church of Jesus Christ which was a branch of a movement led by Frankhouser's friend Robert E. Miles. Frankhouser held services in his home and tried to qualify for a tax exemption for his residence. The house apparently had a tiny room for worship with a small altar. Along with this were Klan flags, Hitler pictures and pictures of crosses burning. However, as of 1998 County tax officials refused to recognize it as a church because Frankhouser was not an actual ordained minister.

Still actively engaged in his lifetime of illicit protests and anti-social activities, Frankhouser fought for freedom for the KKK to demonstrate in Lancaster, Pennsylvania in 2001. He labeled himself a spokesman for the American Knights of the Ku Klux Klan although the group did not recognize any role for him in their organization.

Frankhouser died of a heart attack in West Reading, Pennsylvania in 2009, where he had lived since 2006. He left no known spouse, children, heirs or other descendants.

Notes:

The following references are the main sources for the information in this chapter. There are many sources too numerous to mention for the various and sundry facts regarding the amazing career of Roy Frankhouser.

Information provided by Dr. Jeffrey H. Caulfield can be found in his iconic work *General Walker and the Murder of President Kennedy: The Extensive New Evidence of a Radical-Right Conspiracy.*

Mentioned in the above text is *One More Victim: The Life and Death of an American-Jewish Nazi* by

A. M. Rosenthal and Arthur Gelb.

Information on Frankouser and LaRouche is found in *Dennis King, Lyndon LaRouche and the New American Fascism*, Doubleday. ISBN 978-0-385-23880-9 (1989).

Also cited in the above text is *The Klan* by Patsy Sims, University Press of Kentucky. p. 63. ISBN 978-0-8131-0887-2.(1996).

Another source is John Mintz, (December 18, 1987). "Defense Calls LaRouche, Followers 'Most Annoying'; Trial Begins for Leesburg Group Accused of Obstructing Probe Into Its Fund-Raising." *Washington Post*. p. A18.

And last, on the issue of Roy Frankhouser and free speech, see David Bernstein. *You Can't Say That! The Growing Threat to Civil Liberties from Antidiscrimination Laws*. Cato Institute, 2003. page 74.

Chapter 15

THE TORBITT DOCUMENT: "THE NOMENCLATURE OF THE ASSASSINATION CABAL"

The Torbitt Document, subtitled "Nomenclature of an Assassination Cabal" is considered by some to be the foundation stone of accurate research on the JFK assassination. It appeared in the decade of the 1960's and was published under the pseudonym William Torbitt in 1970. This document was covertly circulated, since it was not officially published by any publishing company, and it was attributed to a pseudonym. No one knows for sure, since the source of the Torbitt Document has never been proved although various theories have been proposed.

It may be misleading to attribute an air of infallibility to this document. It was published again in 1996 by Adventures Unlimited Press under the title *NASA, Nazis & JFK: The Torbitt Document & the Kennedy Assassination,* with an introduction by Kenn Thomas and a forward by David Hatcher Childress. Some of the same information, with variations, is to be found in an article in a magazine called the *Executive Intelligence Review* entitled "Permindex: Britain's International Assassination Bureau," by Jeffrey Steinberg and David Goldman, hereinafter *EIR,* which was published in 1981.

It is possible to quantify the similarities and differences between the Torbitt Document and the well-known article in the *EIR.* If one takes a list of names cited in each document and records the number of times the names are cited in each, the result shows a 50% correlation between the two. A list of names cited only by the *EIR* article and not by Torbitt are as follows:

Churchill, Winston
Eisenhower, Dwight
Gatlin, Jerry Brooks
Klein, Julius
Mantello, Georgio
Portanova, Enrico
Rosenbaum, Tibor

Sarnoff, Robert
Seligman, Hans
Soustelle, Jacques
Vesco, Robert

Names cited by Torbitt but not by the *EIR* are as follows:

Arcacha-Smith, Sergio
Baker, Bobby
Bowen, John
Connally, John
Daletz, Morris
Gatlin, Maurice
Hunt, H L
Jenkins, Walter
Johnson, Lyndon B
Jones, Clifford
Korth, Fred
Levinson, Ed
McKeown, Robert
McWillie, Lewis
Murchison, Clint
Soccaras, Carlos Prio

Something that one might notice first is that probably three of the twelve *EIR* names would likely be Jewish and also that *EIR* features international conspiratorial-type names like Georgio Mantello, Portanova and French OAS collaborator Jacques Soustelle. On the other hand, ten out of the sixteen which are only mentioned by Torbitt but not by *EIR* are Texans or Texas-connected: Baker, Connally, Hunt, Jenkins, Johnson, Jones, Korth, Levinson, McWillie and Murchison.

Another metric is to compare the correlations of both Torbitt and *EIR* to both of the books by Jim Garrison. There is a 60% correlation of Torbitt with both Garrison books, *Heritage of Stone* (1970) and *On The Trail Of The Assassins* (1988). But *EIR* correlates only 20% to the 1970 Garrison book and 40% to his 1988 book. Since the correlation increased by 20% from 1970 to 1988, one could hypothesize that Garrison picked up 20% of the information in his later book directly or indirectly from the EIR magazine article. The name Permindex does not appear in the first Garrison book but is cited five times in the second. It is the Permindex information which is most important in the *EIR* article. The Torbitt Document was released in 1970, just after Jim Garrison wrote his first book, *Heritage of Stone*.

There are two theories as to the real source of the Torbitt information. The first theory holds that it was written by the attorney for researcher and author Penn Jones who lived in Waco, Texas, whose name was David Copeland. The second theory was that someone, perhaps Copeland or Jones, had sources that included someone in the FBI or some foreign intelligence agents.

One has to keep in mind that, (according to the authors of the book *Hit List*), there have been over 100 witnesses or journalists murdered since the assassination in order to guarantee their silence. It is reasonable to assume that, although the Torbitt information has never been disproved, it is also likely that it is not complete. If it were, the perpetrators or the U.S. government would have found a way to suppress it one way or another, even by committing murder if necessary. Therefore, the most likely conclusion is that both the *EIR* and the Torbitt Document represent disinformation. In the classic manner of disinformation, half of it has to be true in order to cause its acceptance, but the other half must be withheld or else it would not be disinformation. It would be the truth.

We will now summarize the Torbitt information chapter by chapter. In later chapters, we will present more details about the EIR information and how it relates to Roy Frankhouser, who was a National Security Council agent and a CIA and FBI informant.

It is important to note that not one word of the Torbitt Document has proved false since it was published in 1970. We will now discuss only the subjects of the individual chapters in a very brief manner for the purpose of weaving the information into our overall presentation.

The first chapter deals with the entity known as Permindex. As will be discussed in later chapters, the Permindex organization was possibly started by and for ex-Nazis from WWII, with only a secondary purpose of promoting fascism generally. But leaving that aside, we will start by analyzing the information as presented in the document itself. This organization was apparently given its basic form by one of several persons. It might have been Clay Shaw, the defendant in the Garrison prosecution. It also could have been L.M. Bloomfield, a British-Canadian-FBI-Zionist figure whose personal papers have never been released by the courts to this date. Another person involved was General Julius Klein, a nefarious Zionist public relations operative whose name pops up in key places in various investigations.

The Torbitt Document lists five subsidiaries of Permindex. They are as follows:

1) The Solidarists (neo-Nazi's, White Russians and monarchists),
2) The ACCC (a Protestant church and British Monarchy group).
3) The Free Cuba Committee of Carlos Prio Socarras (a friend of Richard Nixon's).
4) The Joe Bonanno mafia family and their syndicate and

5) NASA (Security Division) which was, (according to Torbitt), headed by Wernher von Braun, which included DISC, (Defense Industrial Security Command) and FBI Div. 5, all under J.Edgar Hoover who was head of U.S. counter-intelligence (excluding CIA).

This last point (that von Braun headed NASA) is factually incorrect: NASA was headed by James Webb. Von Braun was head of the division of missile development at the Redstone Arsenal in Alabama, (one of 4 divisions of NASA). Later on, we will discuss in great detail the possibility of the involvement of Wernher von Braun in the assassination.

What is known is that Permindex first became active in Rome, Italy in 1958 but was very quickly expelled from there for trying to re-establish the Italian monarchy. Permindex then relocated to South Africa. Its members included a large group of conspiratorial types mainly from Europe and generally fascist in outlook. Permindex has also been accused of the several attempts on the life on Charles de Gaulle in addition to plotting and carrying out the JFK assassination.

The second chapter brings in the names of J. Edgar Hoover and Ferenc Nagy. Interestingly, in the book *The American Pope: The Life and Times of Francis Cardinal Spellman*, by John Cooney, Ferenc Nagy was mentioned as the former prime minister of Hungary and he was entrusted with the crown of St. Stephen, which could be used to reestablish the monarchy in Hungary. Clay Shaw (tried for the murder of JFK) and Bloomfield are also mentioned by Torbitt. Another claim, in the *EIR* article related to the Torbitt document, is that of General John Bruce Medaris (an anti-Semite and Nazi sympathizer) who was head of the Defense Industrial Security Command during the mid 1950's. In a December 1957 Senate hearing, Medaris and his assistant, Wernher von Braun, denounced President Eisenhower before the Senators. They demanded that the U.S. space and missile effort be placed entirely under DISC. Ike caved in to this for a year, then switched and handed these programs over to a new civilian agency, NASA. According to authors Steinberg and Goldman, Ike also simultaneously attempted a breakup of RCA and United Fruit. According to Steinberg and Goldman, these two companies (with vast influence on U.S. foreign policy), were proprietaries of the clandestine, super-secret British S.O.E., the Special Operations Executive branch of British MI6 Intelligence. All information about the British S.O.E. post-1945 is still classified. There is no available information about the S.O.E. since then.

According to Steinberg and Goldman, the scope of the above intrigue triggered Ike's infamous warning of the "military-industrial complex." Many feel this warning stemmed from Ike's physical fear of these interests.

In the third chapter, there are added the names of Roy Cohn and General John Medaris. Roy Cohn was the sometimes-hated Chief Counsel for the Senate Permanent Subcommittee on Investigations, chaired by the also sometimes-hated Senator Joe McCarthy. Medaris was a General in charge of the Army Ballistic Missile Agency and the patron of Wernher von Braun in the missile industry. Torbitt also claims that Medaris actually plotted a military takeover of the U.S. Government under Eisenhower.

The fourth chapter deals with the attempts on de Gaulle.

The fifth chapter treats the allegation that the Defense Intelligence Agency supported a rebellion of the dissident French Generals, known as the OAS, under de Gaulle. In his book on the subject cited in a previous chapter, Christian Plume supports this claim in general by reporting an offer by the CIA to provide arms for a million persons in French Algeria. Plume reproduces the text of a letter written by Kennedy which quickly reversed this offer.

The sixth chapter describes the activities of Permindex and the company Double-Chek from Miami, Florida which was used as a front by the CIA for activities in the U.S. These activities are the same ones generally repeated by researchers involving Clay Shaw, David W. Ferrie and other JFK conspirators.

The seventh chapter deals with Albert Osborne, a leader of the ACCC, which stands for American Council of Christian Churches. This organization was apparently real. Osborne was analyzed by the Warren Commission as accompanying Oswald on a trip to Mexico City.

The west coast division leader of ACCC named E.E. Bradley was indicted by Jim Garrison in New Orleans in the JFK case. The claim made about ACCC is 1) it was an organ of the British monarchy and 2) it maintained a bevy or "school" for 25 assassins in the town of Puebla, Mexico.

The eighth chapter cites Gordon Novel and Jean de Menil. This is red-hot information. First, de Menil was a "White Russian" (losers in the Russian Revolution and Russian Civil War). The White Russians in Dallas were involved up to their eyeballs in the conspiracy both before and after the assassination. Second, de Menil and his family were the owners of Schlumberger oil services company. A warehouse owned by this company in Houma, Louisiana was used by the CIA to store illicit weapons for use against Castro. More importantly, Judy Vary Baker, the author and mistress of Oswald, reports in her book *Me & Lee*, that Oswald was flown on the Schlumberger corporate airplane on one leg of his critical and controversial trip to Mexico City weeks before the assassination. Gordon Novel, a lesser figure, was a known bag man for assassination money around the world, specifically regarding the attempts on de Gaulle.

The ninth chapter discusses Ferenc Nagy, mentioned above and also Wernher von Braun.

The tenth chapter deals with accusations of nefarious international activities centering around such major entities as the Marshall Plan, the

German Munitions Cartels, the Tryall Compound and so forth. There is a lot of smoke there but, personally, your author does not see much fire.

The eleventh chapter deals with a man named William Seymour and the agency known as the Defense Industrial Security Command (DISC). First, Seymour was an alleged Oswald double. The Oswald doubles issue leads quickly into the arena of space alien autopsies and bigfoot. There were clearly some Oswald impersonations, but the claim is made that Oswald and Seymour were indistinguishable. Not possible … unless they were identical twins separated at birth. Second, however is the issue of DISC. What most people don't know is how fundamental defense plant security was to the FBI and British Intelligence in World War II. It would be even more so in the atomic and the missile era. However, the public and this author know absolutely nothing about how this paramount problem is handled and who handles it. So this DISC entity probably existed and operated in such a secret cocoon that we know nothing about it and will probably never know anything about it. Could DISC have organized the assassination?

So, that is a thumbnail sketch of the Torbitt File. It is apparently 100% accurate, and it is as superficially unbelievable as it is interesting.

Notes:

There are four main sources for this chapter. Their significance has been made clear in the text:

NASA, Nazis & JFK: The Torbitt Document & the Kennedy Assassination, with an introduction by Kenn Thomas and a forward by David Hatcher Childress.

The Executive Intelligence Review article entitled "Permindex: Britain's International Assassination Bureau", by Jeffrey Steinberg and David Goldman which we will refer to most often as *EIR*.

Hit List: An In-Depth Investigation into the Mysterious Deaths of Witnesses to the JFK Assassination 1st Edition, by Richard Belzer and David Wayne.

The American Pope: The Life and Times of Francis Cardinal Spellman, by John Cooney.

Chapter 16

LYNDON LaROUCHE AND THE EXECUTIVE INTELLIGENCE REVIEW

Correlations	HERI-TAGE	TOR-BITT	EIR
TRAILASS	0.72	0.61	0.40
HERITAGE	1.00	0.60	0.20
TORBITT	0.60	1.00	0.50
EIR	0.20	0.50	1.00

One of the most intriguing studies in the investigation of the JFK assassination is the role played by Lyndon LaRouche in (at least) the cover-up in the aftermath of the assassination. Having refined one's skills by analyzing covert activities of all types which surround the assassination, it becomes fascinating to see how Lyndon LaRouche and Roy Frankhouser partnered in their very creative covert activities. For our purposes, the most significant of these LaRouche activities was the publication of a weekly newsmagazine by the LaRouche organization entitled "Executive Intelligence Review."

Lyndon LaRouche was supposedly a right-wing extremist in the 1970s and 1980s. The operative word is "supposedly." That word is appropriate because the public image created about LaRouche had nothing at all to do with his actual activities. We will explain how this deception worked and why it occurred.

Lyndon LaRouche was born September 8, 1922 in Rochester, New Hampshire. His family soon moved to Lynn, Massachusetts where young Lyndon was raised. His father, Lyndon, Sr., was born a Catholic but converted to the Quaker faith while in his teens. Being of military age when World War II broke out, Lyndon LaRouche, Jr. became a conscientious objector, owing to his Quaker background. Later, he enlisted in the Army in 1944 and served in the Burma theater.

As a youth, LaRouche was involved with ideas and theories about a variety of issues. He was obsessed with trying to analyze things and figure things out. A psychologist might look at this and suggest some sort of thought disorder. This is characterized by neologisms (inventing one's own words), flight of ideas, illogical thinking or wandering from the topic and never returning to it. Though he was never officially medically diagnosed with this problem, he made a career of profiting from just this type of nonsensical speech and thinking.

In 1948, LaRouche applied to become a member of the Socialist Worker's Party. The SWP, was later made famous by an even more notorious would-be member, namely Lee Harvey Oswald.

In 1954, LaRouche moved to New York and was married. He remained a member of the SWP from 1949 to 1966. LaRouche later claimed that he became an FBI informant after the 1950's. The date when LaRouche began his relationship with the U.S. government has never been precisely determined. Estimates range from as early as 1967 to as late as 1975.

The specialty of LaRouche was ideology. As a member of the SWP, he taught classes using a three-volume edition of *Das Kapital* by Karl Marx. LaRouche then migrated from the SWP to the Students for a Democratic Society, more commonly known as the SDS. The SDS became famous mostly during the protests against the Vietnam War in the late 1960's. LaRouche led a spin-off from the SDS known as the National Caucus of Labor Committees (NCLC). The NCLC became his main group for the next two decades. During that time, there were various sub-groups branching off from the NCLC for particular purposes such as running for elections and publishing books and periodicals.

At this same time, another spin-off of the SDS was an even more radical group called the Weathermen. The FBI and other law enforcement groups were involved in a virtual war against the Weathermen in the 1960s and 1970s. The Weathermen actually carried out bombings and terrorism in a campaign which became a full-fledged danger to the country.

By the early 1970's, Lyndon LaRouche began to change his focus and he started to criticize the Rockefellers and the CIA. He used his influence in the NCLC to convert it from Communist to Fascist, which would have been a nearly impossible feat. In fact, such a conversion is prima facie ridiculous.

Since it is agreed by historians that LaRouche was in full cooperation with the FBI and the CIA by 1975, it becomes more and more obvious that in this period, the NCLC actually became a private intelligence organization run by LaRouche. It represented nothing less than a partial outsourcing of much of U.S. government intelligence. LaRouche and his group began to function in large part for the purposes of the intelligence community.

In 1975, members of the NCLC began what would be an 11-year alliance with Roy Frankhouser. Frankhouser's activities first involved working with Dan Burros (and possibly indirectly Oswald) in New York from

1961 to 1965. Then from 1965 to 1971, he was infiltrating the KKK and the Minutemen. He gave his famous *Playboy* interview to Eric Norden in January, 1968. In 1972, he was ordered by the National Security Council to go to Canada and infiltrate a group of terrorists called Black September.

So, in 1975, Frankhouser told LaRouche, his followers and the NCLC that he had a pipeline to the CIA (or some special source inside). He called this imaginary source "Mr. Ed" after the TV show by that name which featured a talking horse. Of course, in 1974 two *Washington Post* reporters, Woodward and Bernstein, turned up with a mysterious source in the FBI called "Deep Throat," which led to the resignation of Richard Nixon. So this sort of thing must have been in the wind in 1974-1975.

Roy Frankhouser was hired by LaRouche as a security staff member. The most prominent authors who write about LaRouche claim that Frankhouser spent the next 14 years inventing the information he claimed came from "Mr. Ed" and feeding it to the LaRouche organization. This seems a ridiculous assumption. Despite his faulty thinking, Lyndon LaRouche was nevertheless an extremely intelligent person. He would have known the difference between information coming from the CIA compared to things invented by Frankhouser, especially over a 14-year period.

The followers of LaRouche who populated the NCLC were always described in the mainstream media as cult members. They were portrayed as being similar to the Hari Krishna group which was quasi-religious or the followers of the Reverend Sun Young Moon, a deviant religious sect.

To understand why this happened, one must realize that by the mid-1970's the liberal wing of the Democratic Party had succeeded in wresting power away from the Republican/Southern Democratic coalition for the first time since the New Deal. This was manifested in the investigation of the CIA by the Church Committee of the Senate in 1975 and the creation of the House Select Committee on Assassinations in 1976. Next came the election of the truly liberal (and honest) Jimmy Carter.

For the intelligence agencies, the perfect solution to avoid investigations and embarrassments like the Church Committee was to delegate a significant part of its function to LaRouche and his group. In this regard, the most important feature of the LaRouche NCLC was the publication of a weekly newsmagazine called "Executive Intelligence Review." This magazine was, as its title suggests, full of intelligence related information.

As mentioned above, Lyndon LaRouche had a unique way of thinking and theorizing. One way to describe it is "stream of consciousness" *a la* James Joyce or William Falkner. Another way to describe it is somewhat like Soviet propaganda. Soviet propaganda was presumably used to brainwash political dissidents in the U.S.S.R. and so LaRouche used his rambling and disconnected theories to brainwash the members of his group, the NCLC.

An example of "LaRouche-speak" would be "Adolph Hitler was a friend of the Jews. He did them a favor by expelling them from Germany before they could be exploited by the capitalists. Henry Kissinger is a tool of the capitalists, therefore Henry Kissinger is the main enemy of the Jews and Hitler was their friend but they didn't realize it." And so on. Although the ideology of LaRouche was reported in the press as fascist, when it is examined objectively, it was mere gibberish. Another claim by LaRouche was that the CIA created the ghetto culture of blacks in America and that jazz music is a form of brainwashing directed at blacks. LaRouche became anti-Semitic but he used the name of Henry Kissinger as a code-word for his anti-Semitism. Similarly, he blamed countless things of which he disapproved on the "British." He wasn't really either anti-Semitic or anti-British. He merely talked in these nonsensical code words to create a facade of having a dogma. Really, his only dogma was his likely acceptance of funding from the intelligence community.

In 1977-1978, 25% of the NCLC were Jewish. The two most important "security" workers for LaRouche were Jeffrey Steinberg and Paul Goldstein. Goldstein had problems with LaRouche's anti-Semitism but was brainwashed to accept it again.

LaRouche's biographer Dennis King claims that LaRouche was some sort of genius when it came to the subject of fascism. Per King, LaRouche was the first thinker to deal with the following together (a) the state (b) the economy (c) culture (d) race and (e) the military. But in all likelihood, this would be because in his speech and in his writings, he threw together totally unrelated things with no rhyme or reason. LaRouche was likely being funded by the intelligence agencies, possibly the CIA, so whatever ideology which he may have had in his mind likely made no difference at all in his actions on behalf of these agencies.

Of interest to the JFK assassination researcher is the fact that LaRouche recruited ex-Nazi scientists like Hermann Oberth, the German inventor of the rocket. The LaRouche magazine *EIR* published an article by retired General John B. Medaris, who is associated by some with the JFK assassination. In this article, Medaris defended Nazi scientist Arthur Rudolph who was deported back to Germany in 1989 as a war criminal. Brigadier General Paul-Albert Scherer, former chief of West German military counter-intelligence, joined the bandwagon of support for LaRouche.

In the 1980's, LaRouche began to push the idea of an anti-missile system, usually called an ABM system or in the 1980's, "Star Wars." In doing so, LaRouche's people became a front for the same old military-industrial complex that had always sought military weapons boondoggles.

It is truly amazing when the entire stretch of intelligence policy is examined starting in 1918 through the LaRouche era. As reported in his book *The Jewish Threat* by Bendersky, between the World Wars, military intelligence was concerned with 1) the Jewish influence on our government coming from Jewish international banks, and 2) the influence of British intelligence figures like Sir William Wiseman (who was also a partner in the Jewish bank, Kuhn, Loeb). After World War II, the OSS and the CIA recruited Nazi spies like Reinhard Gehlen and Nazi scientists like Wernher von Braun. One of the main reasons that the CIA was established was so the U.S. would not have to be dependent on British intelligence as it was in most of World War II.

In focusing on the British and Jews and linking up with former Nazi's around the world, LaRouche and his organization merely continued the themes that U.S. intelligence had followed ever since World War I. This was not ideology, it was plain vanilla U.S. intel policy.

So now we come to the point of this chapter. On November 14, 1981, the *EIR* of LaRouche published an iconic article naming 144 names and claimed to have the truth regarding the JFK assassination. In 1978, the *EIR* published the book entitled *Dope, Inc.*, which contained mostly the same information.

In the biography of LaRouche, author King describes the tactics of LaRouche. King says that LaRouche tended to cast blame for various evils on such Jewish people as the Bronfman family, philanthropist Max Fisher or banker Felix Rohatyn. But if non-Jews were partners or compatriots of the alleged sinister Jews, LaRouche would conveniently omit any mention of them.

There are two things that are very likely. First, the information about the Kennedy assassination published in *EIR* in November, 1981 was probably fed to LaRouche by Frankhouser, who had inside knowledge and CIA sources regarding the assassination. Second, the *EIR* information follows the LaRouche pattern. If one eliminates the Jews mentioned in the EIR article such as Tibor Rosenbaum and Hans Seligman, and also the British names such as Sir William Stephenson and Winston Churchill, then the EIR article is largely accurate regarding the information on the JFK assassination and likewise the information in the book *Dope, Inc.*

The information is incomplete. But eliminating Jewish and British names, it is accurate as far as it goes. And because of the Roy Frankhouser connection to LaRouche, the EIR article has to be considered CIA disinformation of the highest quality. Discussing the Permindex organization, the article calls it "an international band of protected killers, drawn from the ranks of the Nazi and fascist gestapos of World War II ..." But then the article proceeds to bring in the British SOE and alleged assassins in the pay of the British crown along with many Israeli banks and bankers who had nothing at all to do with the assassination.

The article could have stopped with "Nazi and fascist gestapos" and quit while it was ahead.

Notes:

Most of the information in this chapter is available in the single best book on the subject of Lyndon LaRouche. That book is *Lyndon Larouche and the New American Fascism* by Dennis King.

Also referred to in this chapter is a well-known JFK assassination resource in a periodical called the *Executive Intelligence Review* in an article published in November 14, 1981 entitled "Permindex: Britain's International Assassination Bureau," by Jeffrey Steinberg and David Goldman.

Much of the same information presented by Steinberg and Goldman in the *EIR* article cited above can also be found in a book called *Dope, Inc.: The Book That Drove Henry Kissinger Crazy*, by Executive Intelligence Review.

Chapter 17

THE ARMY, THE AIR FORCE AND THE ASSASSINATION

On November 26, 1963, James Webb, the NASA administrator called LBJ and said, "We have "a real problem with the military." He said this problem was that the military, specifically the Air Force, wanted approval of a manned military space program. Of all the phone calls involving 92 persons in the week following the assassination, there were only four contentious issues discussed. Two were the tax bill and the Civil Rights Bill. Another was additional secret service protection for Jackie Kennedy. The only issue that was discussed in this period which was "coming out of left field" was this issue of militarization of space.

In less than three weeks after the assassination, on December 12, 1963, Robert McNamara approved the creation of a manned military space station. This space station would consist of a Gemini capsule with a cylindrical space station attached. The military personnel on board would have a 90-inch telescope with which to spy on the Soviets. This concept was sometimes called "Blue Gemini." This program lasted on paper until the late 1960's but as far as it is known, no actual military space station was ever created. The concept became obsolete as unmanned reconnaissance satellites greatly improved and served the same function of the Blue Gemini program.

JFK had managed to achieve three major agreements which worked to stop the militarization of space. One was "open space" which was a tacit agreement with the Soviets whereby reconnaissance satellites were allowed. The second was the Nuclear Test Ban Treaty which would eliminate testing of nukes in space. A third was a Soviet-U.S.-U.N. agreement banning WMD in space. John J. McCloy was JFK's arms control negotiator. McCloy wound up running the Warren Commission.

Immediately after the assassination, LBJ stopped any efforts to de-militarize space. This held true throughout his presidency. His only achievement was a treaty in 1967, which only formalized the tacit agreement which JFK had already reached with the Soviets.

The major issue on space weaponization was reconnaissance. For this purpose, the National Reconnaissance Office was set up. This was a very large organization which no one in the U.S. outside of the military even knew about. It was set up in 1961 and the first time any information about it came out in the press was 1973. It goes without saying that this type of Pentagon/CIA absolute secrecy would provide the ideal environment to discuss or plan for a role in an assassination plot with little fear of reprisal.

The only military figure named in the Torbitt document as either a first or second-level JFK conspirator was Major General John B . Medaris. Medaris was head of the Army Ballistic Missile program at Redstone Arsenal and Mussel Shoals, Alabama. Medaris was the supervisor of this program until he resigned after NASA was created in order to, among other things, write a book about military/missile issues. Medaris had supervised Wernher von Braun and his rocket team for four years. Von Braun was also named by the Torbitt file as a JFK conspirator. Von Braun had made a statement to the effect that space was the high ground and that whoever controlled space militarily, would control the world. Von Braun conceived the idea of a military space station with a giant telescope with which to spy on the Soviets.

The JFK assassination author who was in the best position to have accurate information about the assassination was Colonel L Fletcher Prouty. Prouty had served as the CIA-Pentagon liaison at the time of the assassination and was in charge, at one point, of briefing Secretary of Defense Robert McNamara on defense issues. In his book *JFK: The CIA, Vietnam and the Plot to Assassinate John F. Kennedy* Prouty blames the "military-industrial complex" i.e. defense contractors, for the assassination.

In his own book *Countdown for Decision*, General Medaris demonstrates unique understanding of the dynamics of the military hierarchy, the federal bureaucracy, and the science of the missile program. Medaris was intellectually brilliant as would be expected of someone who was head of the U.S. missile program and supervisor of Wernher von Braun. Medaris emphasized that, while the Army had arsenals, such as the Redstone Arsenal which he commanded, the Air Force by contrast had no research infrastructure. As a result, Air Force missile and space programs were entirely held captive by, and were dependent on the defense contractors with whom the Air Force dealt.

Among the small number of major defense contractors working on the main Air Force contracts in the late 1950's and early 1960's was RCA. RCA was run by General David Sarnoff. Sarnoff was one of the 92 persons LJB talked to in the week following the assassination. Both Sarnoff and RCA were reputedly connected with British Intelligence and by that connection also to the JFK assassination according to the Executive Intelligence Review. In their iconic article on the assassination, according to the EIR, General Medaris together with RCA and von Braun actually put President Eisenhower in a state of fear and under a threat because of the creation of NASA. Apparently, the military and contractors wanted the space program to be under military command, not civilian control as with NASA. According to EIR, it was this fear of RCA, Medaris and von Braun which prompted the infamous "military-industrial complex" warning in Ike's farewell address.

One of the other largest Air Force missile contractors was Bell Aircraft. The head of development for Bell was Dr. Walter Dornberger, lifelong best friend of Wernher von Braun and a brilliant scientist/engineer in his own right. Dornberger was also the supervisor of Michael Paine at whose house Lee Harvey Oswald slept the night before the assassination.

Many authors now believe that the Senate Internal Security Subcommittee was heavily involved with Lee Harvey Oswald as well as the assassination. The long-time acting chairman of SISS, Senator Thomas Dodd, was censured by the Senate. In the hearings regarding his censure, it was discovered that Dodd was intimately involved both politically and financially with General Julius Klein. Klein was, according to an article in the leading German newsmagazine, *Der Spiegel* published on 10-04-1963, the West German "Shadow Ambassador" to the U.S. In his testimony, Klein made specific reference to his business relationship with the retired General John Medaris. Klein was also the public relations representative of Lionel Corporation. Lionel was also a minor defense contractor and was owned by JFK conspiracy suspects Roy Cohn and Joseph Bonanno.

William J. Gill was biographer for State Department employee Otto Otepka. Otepka was, like General Klein, heavily involved with the Senate Internal Security Subcommittee. In writing the Otepka biography, which is titled *The Ordeal of Otto Otepka*, Gill reveals an intimate knowledge of the events surrounding the assassination. Gill was well-connected to William F. Buckley, Richard Mellon-Scaife, the Barry Goldwater campaign manager and other right-wing interests. It should be mentioned that assassination author Joan Mellen in her book *Farewell to Justice*, connects Otto Otepka to the assassination.

Among other pertinent facts, Otepka had been investigating Lee Harvey Oswald. Otepka felt his firing from the State Department was because of his Oswald investigation. The important issue in connecting the Otepka case to the space weaponization issue is the Nuclear Test Ban Treaty of 1963. Biographer Gill cites the Nuclear Test Ban Treaty negotiated by JFK as the straw which broke the camel's back between JFK and the military. Gill reports that General Thomas Power, commander of the Strategic Air Command, was the only active-duty military figure to speak out against the Nuclear Test Ban Treaty.

To summarize, it is the opinion of this author that all of the major special interest groups in 1963 got their payoff by, at least, agreeing to turn their backs on the assassination. The Civil Rights groups got the Civil Rights Act. The foreign interests like the British and West Germans got rid of a President who had a very "independent" foreign policy agenda which went against the reunification of Germany and dealt in a friendly manner with the Soviets.

The military got a new President, LBJ, who froze arms control and pandered to the military contractors such as Bell Helicopter and escalated Vietnam, which the military thought was a necessity.

Finally, although it can't be said that weaponization of space was the cause or the issue which alone brought about the assassination, if was probably true that space weaponization was the litmus test which made LBJ much more "military friendly" than his predecessor, JFK.

Chapter 18

THE INTERNATIONAL BANKERS

CLARENCE DILLON

In the opinion of this author, the most important international banker in the story of the JFK murder is a person of whom few have ever heard. His name was Clarence Dillon. He was the father of C. Douglas Dillon, Treasury Secretary under JFK: and C. Douglas Dillon was in charge of the Secret Service in Dallas on November 22, 1963.

The most outstanding fact about Clarence Dillon is that his life story ran in an uncanny parallel to the life of Joseph P. Kennedy, father of JFK. Both were considered financial geniuses in the 1920s with reputations for aggressive financial deals. Both foresaw the Crash of 1929 and got their money comfortably out of the market before the crash.

During the 1930s both realized that the glory days of big money control of government died with the crash. Then they both focused their energies to begin influencing the government where they thought the new financial power lay. But the big similarity between the two was the use of surrogates to control the government. Joseph P. Kennedy operated through his numerous children. Clarence Dillon operated through his younger partners and protégés.

Clarence Dillon was the owner of Dillon, Read & Co. DR had the outward appearance of a partnership like the other investment company partnerships of the time such as J. P. Morgan and Kuhn, Loeb. The difference was that DR was really a legal corporation and Clarence Dillon controlled more than 51% of the stock. Thus, instead of having to cooperate with partners, Dillon entirely controlled the financial situation of his "partners." He could set their salaries at whatever level he wished. Likewise, he could decide their commissions and their annual percentage of the profits. But most importantly, he could decide their share of ownership, if any, of the firm and its assets. He could arbitrarily cut a "partner" entirely out of the firm and leave him destitute.

A famous writer and economist of the time, Eliot Janeway, described Clarence Dillon thus: "Dillon was a mean, miserable bastard; there was not a generous bone in his body." According to another associate, Hugh Bullock, Dillon was "a mean, tight-fisted bastard." According to a famous partner of DR by the name of Dean Mathey, "he [Clarence Dillon] was probably the meanest man who ever lived, at least according to his part-ners."

Dillon married into a prominent Milwaukee family and his wife was related to the Dun's as in Dun and Bradstreet, the financial research com-pany. During World War I, Dillon was connected to the War Industries Board. Leading financiers including Kuhn, Loeb giant Jacob Schiff rec-ommended Dillon to the head of that board, the powerful financier Ber-nard Baruch. Dillon became deputy to Baruch.

Dillon entered the investment banking field and took over the firm William A. Read & Co. which had been on Wall Street since the early 1800's. After numerous power struggles within the company, Dillon took full control and changed the name to Dillon, Read & Co. In 1925, Dillon, Read had 1000 employees and Clarence Dillon got 40% of the profits.

In the 1920's one of Dillon's most profitable relationships was with banker Ferdinand Eberstadt. But in 1928, the two parted company due to a dispute over their shares of the partnership profits. Eberstadt was unique, because he had the intelligence and strong will not to allow him-self to be trapped into the one-sided financial arrangements which typ-ified the dealings of Dillon. Eberstadt formed his own separate partner-ship and was very successful at it.

In the early 1920's another star began to rise at Dillon, Read. His name was James Forrestal. Forrestal had been named "most likely to succeed" by his entire graduating class at Princeton, where he had been editor of the important student newspaper, the *Daily Princetonian*, a breeding ground for successful future journalists. In 1930, Forrestal was given entire man-agement authority over Dillon, Read and Clarence Dillon then "retired," supposedly devoting full time to the more idle lifestyle of the wealthy. At that time, Clarence Dillon was only 48 years old.

Between the Wars, Dillon, Read became involved in the floating of international sovereign debt for foreign governments. DR was more asso-ciated with German deals while J.P. Morgan was more closely identified with the U.K. Dillon opened a DR office in Paris (which remained open until 1939). In January, 1925, DR floated a loan for the Thyssen com-pany, a giant in German industry. As will be discussed elsewhere, as of 1928, German tycoon Fritz Thyssen is now thought to have been the only source of funds for Hitler's fledgling Nazi Party. (After World War II, the Thyssen family became neighbors in the Brazilian jungle with Nazi exile Martin Bormann). The most important German deal for DR was the cre-ation of United Steel Works, a German version of U.S. Steel in America.

Another famous protégé of Clarence Dillon was Paul Nitze. In a con-versation quoted by Dillon's biographers Perez and Willett, Dillon told Nitze that the wealthy held political power only rarely in history. One such period was 1865 to 1929. This conversation between Dillon and Nitze took place before the Great Depression. Dillon predicted that there would be a very long depression and because of that, Washington would take back control from the wealthy. This was basically the "mission statement" by which Dillon operated. From the end of the depression until his death in 1979, Dillon worked non-stop to reverse this situation and help the wealthy to regain the control they had lost in 1929.

In one of Dillon's trips to France in the 1930's, he visited the Paris Rothschilds. On their suggestion, he bought the Chateau Haut-Brion. This was one of the five top wine-growing vineyards or estates in France. When Dillon left the active business of investment banking, he did so in order to pursue an even more avid love affair; that was the desire to climb as far up socially in the world as he could. The purchase of the Chateau Haut-Brion was part of that obsession.

When Hitler overran France in 1940, Dillon's status in France, both in occupied France and in Vichy France became problematic. Chateau Haut-Brion was in occupied France, and the Germans used it as a base. The famous Condor bombers were based there. These were Focke-Wulf FW 200 airliners which were converted to long range bombers. They sank hundreds of allied ships. Dillon's biographers stand behind the Dillon claim that the Germans couldn't find the wine cellar there so none of the wine was seized or lost. Personally, it seems that the Germans (who invented the V-2 and the jet airplane) would be capable of finding the wine cellar in a winery. The argument by Perez and Willett seems a camouflage for possible tacit cooperation between Dillon and the Germans.

Per Perez and Willett, in the early 1930's, Dillon "turned his attention to solving global problems." It would seem more accurate to say that Dillon turned to helping foment global problems. Apparently, Dillon was a lifelong Republican, although he was not noted to be openly partisan regarding electoral politics. In 1932, Dillon offered his services to FDR (who declined them) and in 1936, Dillon met privately with FDR in the Oval Office to offer FDR suggestions, especially regarding matters of taxation.

Dillon vacationed at a family resort estate at Dark Harbour, Maine. He had friends there who included the Winthrop Aldriches, the Marshall Fields and Charlie Auchincloss. One of his best friends at Dark Harbor was the famous artist Charles Dana Gibson, brother-in-law of Nancy Lady Astor. Dillon, Read partner Paul Nitze speculated on some possible extra-marital activities involved in Dillon's frequent trips to Europe which included visits to the Astors. Another British person with whom Dillon spent time was Philip Kerr, the British Ambassador to the U.S. who was also a friend of Lady Astor's.

At this point, the description of Dillon's political activities by his biographers goes off the tracks. Their claim was that Dillon sought out famous persons just to meet them out of a sense of curiosity. According to them, Dillon only wanted to share thoughts with these associates. The trouble with this theory is that almost all of these associates were Nazi sympathizers or Nazi collaborators. Especially prominent in this circle were Philippe Petain, who was tried and convicted of treason by the French after the war. Another was Pierre Laval, who was executed by the French as a Nazi collaborator. In his defense, Dillon also was acquainted with Daladier and Reynaud, who opposed the Germans.

But perhaps the most telling relationship was a three-way conversation reported in his biography involving Dillon, Edward VIII (the Duke of Windsor) and Pierre Laval. Dillon reported that when alone with the Duke of Windsor, the Duke expressed pro-Nazi sympathies and "talked like a child." Of course the Duke was dethroned by the Royal Family because of his Nazi sympathies and Laval was later executed by the French for the same reason. It's not clear why Dillon would be involved in a three-way conversation with these two. We do know, however, that Dillon kept open his office in Paris until 1939, continued to own and run Chateau Haut-Brion in occupied France and after the war, continued his banking business in France.

Since he had intimate conversations with Vichy France officials like Petain and Laval, the only reasonable conclusion is that he had "one foot in" Vichy France. Like George de Mohrenschildt, who allegedly worked for French intelligence around this same period, the relationship with the Vichy government is never explicitly dealt with, but the omission speaks loudly enough on its own.

We should briefly summarize the many tentacles which Clarence Dillon had inside the American government:

First, his long-time former associate Ferdinand Eberstadt had been put in charge of single-handedly writing up and creating the U.S. National Security State including the National Security Council, the CIA, the NSA and the Department of Defense.

Second, James Forrestal, Dillon's long time manager of Dillon Read, became the last Secretary of the Navy and the first Secretary of Defense, only to die mysteriously in a presumed suicide after a falling-out with the U.S. government.

Third, his partner Paul Nitze worked for Nelson Rockefeller during World War II in a private spying operation in Latin America. Under Truman, he became Director of Policy Planning at the State Department. After serving in a crucial role in picking the Cabinet for JFK, Kennedy appointed him Assistant Secretary of Defense for International Security Affairs. In 1963, he became Secretary of the Navy and served until 1967.

Fourth, Dillon's son C. Douglas Dillon served as 1) Ambassador to France, 2) Under-Secretary of State for Economic Affairs, 3) Under-Secretary of State in another capacity and finally 4) Secretary of the Treasury for JFK.

Fifth, Dillon, Read partner William H. Draper II describes his own role in the U.S. Government (in an oral history at the Truman Library) as follows:

> I went to Germany, going to France first, while the war was still on, with General [Lucius] Clay, preliminary to the occupation which he was expecting to take over in Germany under General [Dwight D.] Eisenhower. I was asked by General Clay to take on the responsibility for the economic side of the occupation. Then General Eisenhower left for the United States where he became Chief of Staff of the Army. General Clay eventually became Commander in Chief for the European Theater in addition to handling occupied Germany.
>
> After about two years in Berlin dealing with the German economy – in July of '47 I returned to the United States.... While there, Secretary of War [Robert] Patterson resigned; General Kenneth Royall was made Secretary and he asked me to become Under Secretary, which after consulting General Clay for obvious reasons, I accepted.
>
> My duties for the next two years were primarily supervision of the three occupations: Germany, Japan and Austria, although I became Acting Secretary when Mr. Royall was away from Washington.

Immediately after the War, Draper returned to Dillon, Read. Historians treat Draper as "the eyes and ears" of those who had a vested interest in how the ex-Nazis, especially the industrialists like the Krupps, the Flicks and the Thyssens, were treated during and after the occupation of Germany.

Except for Eberstadt who ran his own firm, Clarence Dillon entirely controlled the financial situation of Nitze, Draper, Forrestal and his son C. Douglas Dillon, basically holding them financial hostages.

A more candid source of information about Clarence Dillon is a book by Haruo Iguchi about Japan around the period of World War II. On July 3, 1940, the head of Nissan, Ayukawa Toshisuke set up a meeting between his confidante, Miho Mikitaro and Clarence Dillon. In this book, Iguchi describes how Clarence Dillon "thought the China issue [Japanese occupation of China] as far as it concerned the U.S., the U.K. and Vichy France could be resolved if the U.S. and Japan took the same position on the European war." In contrast to the way his biographers portrayed Dillon, author Iguchi describes in detail how Dillon was intimately involved in trying to avert war with Japan in return for the U.S. to allow Dillon,

Read to sponsor massive trade deals with Japan and Japanese-occupied Manchuria.

When Dillon was negotiating with the Japanese and the U.S. Government, Iguchi mentions his involvement not only on behalf of the U.S. and the U.K. but he also was advocating for the Hitler-dominated puppet government of Vichy France. At the very least, Clarence Dillon was indifferent to fascism and he was probably just as comfortable with Nazi Germany as with any other foreign government. This was especially true if he could benefit financially by doing deals for Dillon, Read. In these international efforts, Clarence Dillon was often working together with ex-President Herbert Hoover. Author Iguchi clearly believes that Clarence Dillon was the last best hope of avoiding war between the U.S. and Japan in 1941.

After World War II, the strongest lobbying for prioritizing economics over political reform in Japan came from three people. They were Herbert Hoover, James Forrestal and William Draper. This gives an inkling of the behind-the-scenes power wielded by Clarence Dillon in U.S. foreign policy. Iguchi also demonstrates that Dillon was using his massive influence in the U.S. government and U.S. foreign policy to benefit Dillon, Read (and thus himself) financially by gaining priority in business deals.

Last, but not least, among the likely connections of Clarence Dillon to the JFK assassination was his choice of a vacation retreat. On January 1, 1956, Dillon completed a luxury vacation home on Montego Bay, Jamaica. This home was called "High Rock." It was located only a mile away from the Tryall Compound of Sir William Stephenson. As most JFK assassination researchers know, *The Torbitt File* by William Torbitt claims that the JFK assassination was planned at the Tryall Compound in Jamaica.

This area of Jamaica overlooking Montego Bay was frequented by the wealthy. The British royal family had a retreat there. That retreat was gifted by the royal family to Sir Winston Churchill in gratitude for his role in winning World War II. Sir William Stephenson developed the Tryall Compound on Montego Bay, which some have described as a Fort Knox for spies. It consisted of separate condominiums to which various conspirators could be invited for the planning of covert operations.

During the Suez Crisis in 1956, British Prime Minister Sir Anthony Eden moved the official seat of government to Montego Bay. As part of the World War II lend-lease program, the U.S. military had constructed an airfield there. Many of the world's largest airlines had direct flights to Montego Bay. Perhaps the most famous resident was Ian Fleming, who wrote the James Bond novels at Montego Bay. Fleming owned a vacation home there beginning after World War II. Fleming was an employee of British Intelligence as well as a journalist. Some experts have theorized that the James Bond novels themselves were part of a propaganda campaign. This campaign popularized the concept of SMERSH and the supposed Soviet assassination program (which was blamed by some for the JFK murder).

So, the prior paragraphs establish the motive, means and opportunity of Clarence Dillon to have a major involvement in the JFK assassination. The major opportunity lay in the fact that his son and banking partner C. Douglas Dillon, as Secretary of the Treasury under JFK, controlled the Secret Service. And Clarence Dillon controlled C. Douglas Dillon, so this is not such a stretch as it might at first seem.

Also, as Treasury Secretary, C. Douglas Dillon controlled the function of the ATF, which was a major presence in Dallas and was in the middle of the Oswald weapons controversy. The ATF worked through its agent Frank Ellsworth who was involved in the Lee Harvey Oswald weapons scenario.

KUHN, LOEB

The investment bank which had the most sinister reputation between the Wars was Kuhn, Loeb. This began with Kuhn, Loeb partner Jacob Schiff who financed the Russo-Japanese War. Partner Paul Warburg invented the Federal Reserve System. According to author Ron Chernow in *The Warburgs*, Paul Warburg sat down in a comfortable easy chair one day with a pencil and paper and wrote out the Federal Reserve Act off the top of his head.

Between the wars, international investment banks were divided into Jewish banks like Kuhn, Loeb and M.M. Warburg of Hamburg, Germany, and Protestant banks like J. P. Morgan. Kuhn, Loeb was perhaps the most financially successful of all the international investment banks on Wall Street. Kuhn, Loeb successfully resisted all attempts of writers to publish information about it. The best source for information on Kuhn, Loeb is the aforementioned book by Ron Chernow *The Warburgs*.

Another prominent partner of Kuhn, Loeb was Sir William Wiseman. Like Clarence Dillon, Wiseman owned a villa at Montego Bay. Wiseman was the man who ran the British intelligence which was successful in bringing the U.S. into World War I on the side of the British.

Another famous Kuhn, Loeb partner was Lewis Strauss. Strauss was a right-wing figure who was prominent from the World War I period up to the time of the Kennedy administration. He began as a colleague of financier Bernard Baruch in World War I, who was an advisor to the U.S. government. Strauss had worked on financing certain technological projects. Through this avenue, he was passed off as an expert on science. During the Eisenhower Administration, he was the chief scientific advisor to Ike despite the fact that he lacked even a college degree in any subject.

During the Eisenhower administration, Strauss became embroiled in a feud with physicist Robert Oppenheimer, the father of the hydrogen bomb. This feud smacked of the familiar theme in many Western movies, where Washington wasn't big enough for both Strauss and Oppenheimer and one of them had to go.

Strauss was successful in branding Oppenheimer a Communist and because of that he was denied a security clearance and fired from his job. In 1959, in the waning days of the Eisenhower administration, the newly elected 86th Congress, infused with Liberal Democrats, refused to confirm Strauss as Secretary of Commerce when he was nominated by Eisenhower. This confrontation which had erupted between conservative Republicans and Liberal Northern Democrats lasted right up until November 22, 1963.

After being accused of being a Communist and resigning in disgrace, Robert J. Oppenheimer was nominated during the Kennedy Adminstration for the Enrico Fermi award, which was viewed as an attempt by JFK to rehabilitate the reputation of Oppenheimer. This award was granted by LBJ in the week after the assassination. There is no evidence, however, that Strauss or any other Kuhn, Loeb partners (except perhaps Sir William Wiseman circumstantially) had any role in the death of JFK.

THE WARBURGS

The Warburgs were not a bank, but they were the preeminent family in international banking between the wars. The New York branch of the Warburgs was led by Felix Warburg who was a partner of Kuhn, Loeb. The European (German) branch was led by Max Warburg, the brother of Felix. Despite being Jewish, the Warburgs considered themselves German and were very patriotic when it came to supporting Germany. Because of their transatlantic family connections, the Warburgs were able to play both sides against the middle when it came political issues such as German reparations from World War I.

The German Warburgs owned M.M. Warburg which was the largest bank in Hamburg and one of the two largest banks in Germany. During the rise of Hitler, their bank was "aryanized," which meant that a non-Jew was put in charge and the Warburgs were cheated out of their financial interest in the bank by the Nazis.

In 1940, Jimmie Warburg (a son of Felix) joined an informal group called the Century Group which included John McCloy, Allen Dulles, Dean Acheson and Frank Polk (a mentor of Dulles).

Eddie Warburg was a son of Max Warburg. Max had come to the U.S. at an early date. Eddie became an American and was appointed to U.S. Air Force Intelligence. However, he declined to participate in the Nuremberg Trials. He thought the Germans should judge themselves. He also declined an offer from John J. McCloy to participate in the Control Commission, preferring to remain a neutral observer.

The Warburgs fled Germany. Max went to the U.S. and Siegmund Warburg, the son of Max set up a bank in London. Siegmund became the most successful Warburg outside Germany and had financial dealings in England, France and the U.S. Like Kuhn, Loeb there is no evidence connecting the Warburgs to the JFK assassination

FERDINAND EBERSTADT

Perhaps the most unbelievable role of an international banker in the background of the JFK assassination was that of Ferdinand Eberstadt. Eberstadt began his career with an important connection. During World War I he had a close working relationship with financial wizard Bernard Baruch, who made a major contribution because of his expertise in helping to finance the war.

Eberstadt attended Princeton where he made a lifelong friend in James Forrestal.

Eberstadt was not Jewish, but his aunt had married a partner in Kuhn, Loeb so he was considered to be well-connected to Jewish banks. His grandmother was related to the Paris Rothschilds. Although raised Catholic, his mother converted to the Lutheran church. Eberstadt was considered the leading U.S. expert on finance involving Germany in the 1920's.

As mentioned above, Ferdinand Eberstadt began his banking career affiliated with Clarence Dillon. This duo separated because of a dispute over profits.

During World War II, Eberstadt worked on economic issues for the U.S. Government. He invented the controlled materials plan (CMP). This became a key to unsnarling bottlenecks in allocating steel, copper and aluminum. In 1946, he was asked by James Forrestal, then the Secretary of the Navy, to create a plan for possible unification of the military under a Department of Defense. Forrestal went on to become the first Secretary of Defense but resigned under pressure and died in 1949. His death was ruled a suicide but it could have been an assassination. He supposedly jumped from the 9th floor of Bethesda Naval Hospital where he was an inpatient being treated for depression (though the depression ward was on the first floor).

In 1947, Ferdinand Eberstadt was named Chairman of the Hoover Commission. This Commission created the National Security State, inventing the National Security Council, the CIA, the NSA, the Defense Department and other brand new organs of government. The impetus for this massive reorganization was the desire of the Republican and Southern Democratic Coalition to avoid a repeat of the New Deal under a powerful President such as FDR. Also, at this time, the political career of General Dwight Eisenhower was looming. This was another reason for conservatives and people in the Congress to fear a powerful presidency.

Although Eberstadt had an incredibly powerful and inexplicable role in the invention of the National Security State, there is no particular evidence linking him to the JFK assassination. Eberstadt's position at that time was much like that of Lewis Strauss or Herbert Hoover. These men were, in general, behind-the-scenes leaders of the conservative wing of the Republican Party. But unlike the extreme anti-Communist Republicans like Nixon or McCarthy, they did not lead a lifestyle of conspiracy and they did not actively advocate covert operations against the Soviet Union or in Eastern Europe. Eberstadt and Herbert Hoover were more interested in pro-business policies rather than the militant anti-Communism or fascist sympathy which would be the cause of the murder of John F. Kennedy.

CHASE MANHATTAN AND THE ROCKEFELLER BROTHERS

The power and influence of the Rockefeller family need not be rehashed in this space. Such Rockefeller followers as Dean Rusk, C. Douglas Dillon and John J. McCloy were selected by JFK for high positions in his administration. Before his scandalous divorce, Nelson Rockefeller was seen as the likely nominee of the Republicans to oppose JFK in 1964.

Despite all of this, the Chase Manhattan Bank, which was owned by the Rockefellers, was not identified with specific foreign countries and the liberal Rockefeller family was disliked, if not despised, by the Southern Democratic segregationists and the Taft-Hoover old-line Republicans. The fact that JFK appointed so many Rockefeller associates to his administration was a plus, not a minus for the Rockefellers regarding JFK. They would have less influence among the LBJ Texas crowd. Further, it's unlikely that the Rockefellers would have needed to murder Kennedy, since they had all the influence on the U.S. and its policies that they could possible want. They would have had little to gain by being associated with a murder of any kind and for any reason.

Although Nelson Rockefeller operated a spy ring in Latin America during World War II, he was on the side of Brazil, which he persuaded to declare war on Hitler. He and Brazil were opposed by Argentina, which was pro-German.

THE ROTHSCHILDS

No list of international bankers would be complete without mention of the Rothschilds. The Rothschilds were the preeminent international bankers in the period between the wars. There is no evidence at all that ties the Rothschilds to the JFK assassination save for their position at the very top of international banking. International bankers tended to work in a coordinated way to manage the vagaries of international finance. If one or two international bankers decided to support the JFK assassination, then they all would likely have known about it in advance, though not necessarily be participants or even supportive.

In the world of "Jewish" banking, the Rothschilds dominated Britain, France and Austria. However, the Warburgs dominated Germany through M.M. Warburg of Hamburg and through their prominent role in Kuhn, Loeb in America. The links to the JFK assassination have much more connection to America and Germany than to France, England and Austria.

However, there is one important link between the French Rothschilds and an assassination suspect, Clarence Dillon. Clarence Dillon withdrew from active management of his fantastically successful investment bank of Dillon, Read in 1930. He then went to Europe where he operated a branch office of Dillon, Read in Paris. At this time, Clarence Dillon became obsessed with trying to climb the Old World social ladder in Europe, from where his family had originated in the 1800's.

Acting on the advice of the French Rothschilds, Dillon purchased the Chateau Haut-Brion. The Chateau Haut-Brion was one of the five most prestigious French wineries. When the Germans invaded France in 1940, Dillon closed his French office, but he retained the Chateau Haut-Brion. During the War, the Nazis used the Chateau as a base to launch their very successful Condor bomber program. This involved converting Condor commercial airliners into bombers. These planes then attacked Allied shipping. Supposedly, the Nazis never discovered the wine cellar at the Chateau. More likely, the Nazis left the wine intact as a courtesy to Dillon. The role of Dillon during the Vichy period in France remains a murky subject.

Since the Rothschilds were based in England and France, they escaped the "aryanization" program that was sweeping Germany, Poland and the rest of occupied Eastern Europe. However, the Rothschilds fared worse in Austria, where their estates were seized. After the war, they recovered their estates.

Clarence Dillon clearly had fascist-leaning friends in France before the war and presumably during the war as well. These could have included Pierre Laval, the President of Vichy France who was hanged for treason by the French after the war. However, there is no ostensible connection between the Rothschilds, the Nazis or Vichy France, so it is likely that the Jewish Rothschilds would not have been happy to see ex-Nazis launch an assassination plot against the U.S. President.

Notes:

Clarence Dillon: A Wall Street Enigma by Robert C. Perez and Edward F. Willett. At page xiii, a Dillon, Read banker and famous tennis star named Dean Mathey labeled Clarence Dillon "a mean bastard."

In the Perez and Willett biography at p. 123, the authors reported that in 1930, Clarence Dillon turned his attention from Wall Street to the task of solving global problems.

The oral history of William Draper, cited in the text can be found at the website of the Truman Library: https://www.trumanlibrary.org/oralhist/draperw.htm

Available information on Clarence Dillon is limited when his vast influence over the government of the U.S. through his Dillon, Read employees is considered. One objective and unbiased reference is the book *Unfinished Business: Ayukawa Yoshisuke and U.S.-Japan Relations, 1937-1953* by Haruo Iguchi. This book provides information about an issue that many probably suspected: the connection between Dillon's vast political influence and profiteering from his web of political connections.

For information on both the Warburgs and the firm of Kuhn, Loeb, virtually the only resource is *The Warburgs: The Twentieth-Century Odyssey of a Remarkable Jewish Family* (2016) by Ron Chernow. This book by Chernow is an astounding book. Chernow has an encyclopedic knowledge of virtually every Warburg and every relative of the Warburgs. Further, since the firm of Kuhn, Loeb apparently went to great lengths to restrict the availability of information about itself, Chernow's book The Warburgs is also the definitive source for information about Kuhn, Loeb. Add to this his insightful description of the personality of diplomat and banker John J. McCloy and his rendition of the on-the-scene front-line events during the Holocaust. Every true history buff should read this book carefully.

The Will to Win: A Biography of Ferdinand Eberstadt: (Contributions in Economics and Economic History) by Robert C. Perez and Edward F. Willett (1989) provides complete background information on Ferdinand Eberstadt who was (for some bizarre reason) the creator of the U.S. national-security state which is, unfortunately, still with us in the form invented by Eberstadt as of this writing.

Another excellent work about Eberstadt is *Eberstadt and Forrestal: A National Security Partnership, 1909-1949* (Williams-Ford Texas A&M University Military History Series) (1991) by Jeffery M. Dorwart.

Chapter 19

THE SOLIDARISTS AND WHITE RUSSIANS OF DALLAS

There are certain characters that were involved in the assassination as residents of Dallas who came from a Russian or Eastern European background. This small community was preyed upon by the intelligence community to become intelligence assets because of their vulnerable situation. They had old-world values, old-world pretensions and vanities. Many had experienced fascism as very ordinary. Some had experienced the horrors of war, flight from their homeland, hideous choices surrounding such issues as torture, genocide, displacement from kith and kin. We will try to share the basic story of these individuals. They were involved in the assassination before-the-fact by "babysitting" Lee Harvey Oswald. They were involved after-the-fact by arranging for careful translators for Marina Oswald while she was being interrogated about the assassination and in some cases they testified before the Warren Commission and elsewhere as witnesses and spoke to the media.

COLONEL LAWRENCE ORLOV

Colonel Lawrence Orlov was a resident of Dallas who became acquainted with Lee and Marina Oswald following their return from the Soviet Union in June, 1962.

Orlov was born in Massachusetts in 1899. He was the son of Samuel Lippa Orlovsky, who was born in Russia on February 15, 1851. Samuel Orlovsky was Jewish and was naturalized on April 12, 1893 as an American citizen in Boston. Lawrence Orlov attended the prestigious Boston Latin School. While there, he was a star on the track team and set a record for the 45-yard hurdles which stood for several years. After that, he was educated at Harvard University. All of his siblings were salesmen or dress manufacturers or worked in similar vocations. None were military or intelligence-related and none were still maintaining their overseas loyalty to Russia as were the White Russians who came to the U.S. around the same time.

Lawrence Orlov served in World War I as a field clerk at the Northeastern Department Army Headquarters. His discharge was delayed because his services as a support person of some kind were needed. For this reason, he was transferred in 1919 to work with the debarkation force at

Newport News, Virginia. This duty involved helping to bring back the remaining U.S. soldiers from Europe.

Later, following his graduation from the University, he moved to the Texas-Louisiana area. In 1927, he set up a company with a partner by the name of Sam Weiner called Westerly Supply Company. This was in Winkler County near the New Mexico state border with Texas. This fact is reported by authors Hollace Ava Weiner and Kenneth Roseman in *The Lone Stars of David: The Jews of Texas*. In 1934 he was living in Tyler, Texas. In Tyler, he listed his occupation as an oil operator. In the 1940 census, he was living in Alexandria, Louisiana in the home of his mother-in-law. Her name was Flora Nachman. At that date, he was married to Amelia "Ame" Nachman. Ame was Jewish. They he had a four-year-old son, William Samuel. His occupation was listed as an oil promoter. During the period of World War II, the Orlovs lived in the Alexandria-Pineville community in Louisiana. In 1947, Lawrence Orlov moved from Alexandria, Louisiana to San Antonio according to the Alexandria city directory.

An article in *The San Antonio Light*, published in 1946 corroborates the fact that Orlov was a veteran of World War I. In the Second World War, in 1942, he entered the military at age 43 and served until 1945. In 1948, he was living in San Antonio. In the article in the *San Antonio Light* on October 13, 1946 the writer specifically mentioned Lawrence Orlov. It was written that he he was a veteran of both World Wars and had served during World War II at San Antonio's Kelly Field. The article went on to state that Orlov was being hired by a new company that used tons of aluminum secured from the War Assets Administration to produce aluminum awnings for use in homes and stores in Southwest Texas.

This was apparently the Aluminum Products Co., which Orlov listed as an address in the City Directory of San Antonio in 1948. In the article about Aluminum Products Co., it stated that the company was hiring only veterans but the only veteran mentioned in the article was Lawrence Orlov. At that time, he also listed a business address of Ackman Sales Co. at 408 Water St. in San Antonio.

It is not clear where Orlov lived from 1948 to 1961. The entries in the city directories in the Baton Rouge, Louisiana area in the 1950's list only his wife Ame and his son William Samuel Orlov. That could simply be due to a different manner of gathering information for that particular city directory, perhaps going door-to-door during business hours. From the record, it is possible that he and his wife were divorced or separated some time between 1948 and 1961. However, both Lawrence and Ame had been associated in various records with the city of Carlisle, Pennsylvania. This began after 1978. So if they were not living together from 1948 to 1961, they were back together as of the late 1970's. It is unlikely they were ever separated. Any confusion about this comes from the fact that Lawrence left no paper trail from 1948 to 1961.

Ame drew a Social Security benefit in Carlisle and Lawrence was buried at the nearby Indiantown Gap National Cemetery, which was about 50 miles west of Carlisle. Ame died on October 8, 1980 at Alexandria, Rapides Parish, Louisiana and was buried there in a Jewish cemetery. Lawrence lived until September 20, 1989 and his last residence was listed as Carlisle, Pennsylvania.

The earliest record of him as a Dallas resident is 1961. He was still a resident as late as 1977. In the Dallas city directory, Orlov not only listed his residence in 1961 and 1962, but in 1964, he listed a new business address that belonged to BFC Oil & Gas Co., which was a subsidiary of Newpark Resources, Inc. Newpark was founded in 1964. This company was in business for several decades and may be still. Newpark Resources, Inc. showed up in published legal case reports since it was involved in several fairly ordinary legal disputes. Those disputes appear to be fairly typical for that sort of oil business, involving contracts, patents, real estate titles and similar issues. In 1967, his business address was 511 North Akard [Building] Suite 931 and in 1970, it was 1030 Fidelity Union Life Building, still in Dallas. Soon after that he was listed as retired in the city directories. At that time he would have reached 71 years of age.

Orlov was a regular handball partner with the Special Agent in Charge of the Dallas CIA office, J. Walton Moore. Since Orlov had once held a State record for the 45-yard hurdles, he may have been playing handball merely because of an interest in athletic pursuits. It was erroneously believed by some that it was Orlov who first introduced the Oswalds to George de Mohrenschildt. Orlov was not a native of Russia and did not speak Russian. There is no indication that Orlov would have been a practicing member of an Eastern Orthodox church of any sort, as were Paul Ragiorodsky and his associate George Bouhe. Author Nancy Wertz Weiford in *Faux Baron* did not list Orlov as a member of the Russian Orthodox Church in Dallas. Since Orlov had been living in various smaller communities in Louisiana and Texas since the 1920's, it would have been unlikely that he would have found Eastern Orthodox congregations there over the years. Orlov's father was also Jewish and buried in a Jewish Cemetery in Massachusetts. It should be noted that in his obituary, his religion was "Unitarian." Unitarian, in the opinion of this author, can sometimes be used as a cover on the issue of religious affiliation since it can be very generic and "low maintenance."

Lawrence and Ame had a son William Samuel who was born in 1936. Ame was listed in the 1940 census as a field welfare worker for the State of Louisiana. She had also listed herself as a worker for her Parish government in the welfare field in another year during that period. Their son William Samuel Orlov was shown in the Louisiana State University yearbook in 1955 and was majoring in commerce. In 1957, William Samuel listed his occupation as an auditor for the State of Louisiana Department

THE THREE BARONS AND THE JFK ORGANIZATIONAL CHART

of Revenue. William Samuel apparently enlisted in the military after earning an MBA at LSU and served from 1957 to at least 1970 in the Army or the Army Reserves. He was an impressively decorated veteran in Vietnam, gaining several bronze star awards in air action.

One could ask the question as to whether Orlov had some connection to Military Intelligence. He served at Kelly Field in San Antonio during World War II. Since he enlisted in the Army at age 43 with a wife and child and attained the rank of Colonel in only 3 years, that could indicate service in intelligence or at least his possessing some type of skill that was of special use to the military. He could have gotten a start in Military Intelligence during World War I when he worked as a Field Clerk at the headquarters of the Northeastern Department Army Headquarters. According to one book on the subject, the Northeastern Department headquarters in Boston, along with the other 5 Department Headquarters in other large cities, was very involved with Military Intelligence matters. Riots in major cities, including Boston, were a very real possibility at this time.

As previously mentioned, in Baton Rouge and Alexandria, Louisiana, Ame's name along with William Samuel appeared in the city directories in the late 1950's and up to 1960. Lawrence was not listed. However, beginning in 1961, Lawrence's name began to be listed in the Dallas city directory, but with no mention of Ame or William Samuel.

Considering he was educated at Harvard, Lawrence's professional life seemed rather barren. He was listed as working for BFC Oil & Gas Co while living in Dallas, but the office seemed to move around. At one point, his business address was Suite 931 in the Five Eleven North Akard Building in Dallas. One account in a JFK assassination book describes that building as containing at least one seedy "broom closet" type of office with a JFK witness, an attorney named Jarnigan, in that office. Jarnigan had reported seeing Oswald and Ruby together at Ruby's club, but had later clammed up. If he worked in the same building as Orlov, the conversations in the parking lot might have been very interesting.

Like George de Mohrenschildt, the oil business activities of Lawrence Orlov were apparently very basic and attracted no particular notice. This could mean he was getting financial support for some hidden Army Reserve intelligence function or as an informant, especially since he was a regular handball companion of the Agent in Charge of the Dallas CIA Office. There is absolutely no evidence regarding this point and since Lawrence never testified to the Warren Commission or any other investigation, we don't know anything more than what is in the public record. Due to the fact that the government investigations avoided Orlov like the plague, our theory of his usefulness to the Nazi plotters because of his Jewish background remains very plausible.

When he died, he was buried at Indiantown Gap National Cemetery in Indiantown, Pennsylvania. The nearby Fort Indiantown Gap was the headquarters of the 4th Psychological Operations Battalion and the 6th Psychological Operations Battalion at various times. This post was used both in the resettlement of Vietnamese refugees in the mid 1970's and Cuban refugees in the 1980's. During World War II, troops were sent from Fort Indiantown to the Island of Fiji for deployment in the Pacific. The Fort's primary purpose is described as a training facility for the Pennsylvania National Guard but it is also described as being fairly far removed from ordinary Army activities due to its remote location. It is possible that Lawrence and Ame moved to Carlisle to be closer to their son William Samuel, who could have been stationed at Fort Indiantown Gap. Or they could have moved there to be closer to friends and service members they knew during World War II if Lawrence had served at Fort Indiantown Gap where he was buried. They had no known connection to Pennsylvania prior to their move there and there is no hint of why they moved from Texas to Pennsylvania.

Lawrence Orlov's last residence listed in his Social Security record was Carlisle, Pennsylvania, 43 miles from Fort Indiantown Gap. The Social Security records of Orlov's wife Ame show that her last Social Security benefit was received in Carlisle, Pennsylvania. However, she only obtained her Social Security card in 1962. Ame died in 1980. Lawrence died in 1989.

We must consider the fact that Lawrence Orlov was called "Colonel Orlov," but there is only very general information as to the nature of his military service or where he served. All we know is that he served at Kelly Field in San Antonio in World War II and also in Guam. Further, the Warren Commission, the Garrison Investigation and the House Select Committee on Assassinations completely avoided Colonel Lawrence Orlov. No one interviewed or called him to testify. This was in spite of his key role in welcoming Oswald back from the USSR. The other White Russian Oswald "babysitters" were interviewed and most testified in depth.

To add all of this information up, it seems remotely possible that there was a "false defector" program and that Oswald was part of that program. That explains why Colonel Lawrence Orlov would be greeting the Oswalds upon their return, especially since Orlov was not a White Russian and did not speak Russian. Orlov could conceivably have been on the receiving side of the false defector program, helping in resettlement and utilization of the returning defectors as intelligence assets. But it was George de Mohrenschildt, not Lawrence Orlov, who took the initiative in seeking out the Oswalds.

However, Orlov was friends with the head of the Dallas CIA office, J. Walton Moore. Since Moore was likely monitoring Oswald because of involvement with the FBI counter-intelligence function, he could have suggested that Orlov help him out and find a way for the Oswalds to be resettled. This could have purely been a charitable motive. Another theory as to why Orlov was handball partners with J. Walton Moore was that he had a pipeline into the Dallas Jewish community which would undoubtedly be a rich source of information for a CIA agent. There is no information that Orlov and Jack Ruby, who, like Orlov, either was Jewish or had a Jewish extended family in Dallas, had any known relationship with each other.

When one-time (probable) Nazi agent George de Mohrenschildt first met Lee Harvey Oswald and his wife, Marina, he was in the company of Col. Lawrence Orlov. In a manuscript written by de Mohrenschildt which is appended to the House Select Committee on Assassinations report, de Mohrenschildt mentions Col. Lawrence Orlov. According to de Mohrenschildt, he and Orlov were in Fort Worth on business when they both decided to visit Lee Harvey Oswald and his wife for the first time. De Mohrenschildt mentions that Orlov thought that Marina was beautiful, but that he was not in agreement with Orlov on this point. De Mohrenschildt fails to mention whose idea it was to make the visit. Thus, he leaves the impression that it was the idea of Orlov.

But de Mohrenschildt also stated at another time that he and Orlov were at the offices of attorney Max Clark on business. Again, it is not stated that the subject of Oswald came up at that meeting, but since Max Clark was married to Princess Scherbatoff, a/k/a Gali Clark, the effect of this story is to associate Orlov together with Gali Clark and de Mohrenschildt in the minds of investigators and later generations of researchers. When de Mohrenschildt quickly follows up the meeting with Orlov and Oswald with a phone call to CIA Agent J. Walton Moore, Orlov is then further embroiled in these relationships.

George de Mohrenschildt seems to have deliberately tried to incriminate Orlov on the basis of wanting to visit Oswald and his wife Marina. Keep in mind that de Mohrenschildt was likely a Nazi spy at some point and was considered by many officials to be a Nazi sympathizer.

The big question, of course, is this: George de Mohrenschildt was very likely a Nazi spy and was known to give his Jewish friends a "Hitler Sieg Heil Salute" according to author Nancy Wertz Weiford. He even gave a speech lauding the Vlasov Army, a group of Nazi collaborators. Why would Orlov, who was apparently Jewish and/or was married to a Jewish wife, be involved in pawning off Oswald to de Mohrenschildt, a Nazi spy and known Nazi apologist? The most obvious answer would be that the Nazis who planned the assassination wanted to taint Orlov, who had a Jewish heritage and wife, with the murder of Kennedy as they tried to taint Jack Ruby.

If the Warren Commission or other investigators interviewed Orlov, Orlov might have popped off with ramblings about "anti-Semites" like Jack Ruby did during his Warren Commission testimony. And on a more sinister note, if Jewish groups or even the Israeli Mossad got wind of, and were monitoring the assassination plot, then Orlov could have been in there gathering information for the protective Jewish parties watching from afar. This could explain why Orlov was a regular handball player with the Agent in Charge of the Dallas CIA office, J. Walton Moore. This fact could have come out during testimony by Orlov before the Warren Commission.

The next generation of Orlovs seemed to remain in Carlisle until the 1990's. Orlov's son was apparently married and lived a very stable life. As mentioned, William Samuel became a Vietnam War hero and apparently lived an All-American life, despite having the Oswald monkey on the family's back. At the date of this writing, William Samuel is apparently living somewhere in the Midwest at age 81. In living down this unwanted connection to the Oswalds, one could count him and the Orlov family as minor American heroes in their own right.

The biggest unsolved issue is where did Colonel Lawrence Orlov live and work from 1948 to 1961? Since Orlov's wife Ame lived in Baton Rouge as well as Alexandria, it is likely that Orlov lived there also. Two things about Baton Rouge should be mentioned whereby Lawrence Orlov could have become involved with the JFK assassination while living in Louisiana.

First, segregationists like Leander Perez, DeLesseps Morrison, Guy Banister, James O. Eastland and David W. Ferrie would have been very active with their racist activities in Alexandria and Baton Rouge in the mid and late 1950's. Since Ame Orlov and Samuel Orlov both found work with the State Government of Louisiana, this could have been due to some connection with the right-wing politics of the Louisiana State Government. Since the Louisiana Sovereignty Commission, the Louisiana Un-American Affairs Committee and the White Citizen's Councils were rising up around this time, any State employee would be aware of this. The problem is that the Orlovs were of Jewish heritage. It is unlikely that they would have been allowed to join forces with the militant segregationists, much less conspire with them to murder JFK.

Second, both I G Farben and Standard Oil had giant facilities in Baton Rouge at various times around and after World War II and probably into the 1950's. As we will discuss in another chapter, IG Farben and Standard Oil both had financial interests which could have been at play in relation to the JFK assassination. Since we don't know for which oil business Lawrence Orlov worked in Baton Rouge or Alexandria, he could have become an amateur-type operative for one of the powerful oil interests which played a role in the assassination. But there is absolutely no evidence which would suggest this.

Perhaps more research could reveal whether Colonel Orlov could have been a reservist active in psychological operations for the Army when he was one of the first persons to welcome Lee Harvey Oswald and Marina Oswald back from Russia in 1962. It would be helpful to know the nature of his service in World War I. But there is no real evidence to support any hypothetical relationship to intelligence work one way or the other. For all appearances, Orlov was just caught up in the maelstrom of events with only the best of intentions.

JEAN DE MENIL

Jean De Menil, or John de Menil, to which his birth name was changed, was a European who is featured prominently in JFK assassination research. He was born Baron Jean Marie Joseph Menu du Menil in Paris in 1904. In 1931 he married the French heiress Dominique Schlumberger whose family controlled a world-wide oil service corporate empire. Menil was a banker in Paris, but later moved to Houston, Texas and became President of Schlumberger Overseas and Schlumberger Surenco. Schlumberger remains to this day one of the two largest oilfield services companies in the U.S. and probably in the world. Schlumberger provides infrastructure for the production of oil.

The Torbitt File, published as a book entitled *NASA, Nazis & JFK* by Adventures Unlimited Press in 1996, makes extensive references to de Menil. It states that de Menil escaped from Russia at some time between 1917 and 1923. This would make him a White Russian. The accuracy of this is unclear.

The de Menil's were not White Russian and they lived in Houston, so they were not a part of the Dallas White Russian Community. Further, de Menil and his wife were French Catholics. The reason that they are connected by some researchers to the JFK assassination is twofold.

First, the Schlumberger company owned a warehouse in Houma, Louisiana. This warehouse was used by the CIA as a weapons depot for the various Cuban Exile covert operations against Castro around the time of the assassination. Some witnesses placed Lee Harvey Oswald in the midst of these operations in 1962 or 1963. The Torbitt file, analyzed in a separate chapter prior to this one and mentioned previously, specifically names de Menil as involved in the plot.

Second, in her book *Me & Lee*, Judyth Vary Baker, alleges that Lee Harvey Oswald traveled on the Schlumberger private aircraft when he traveled from New Orleans, to Texas and finally by bus to Mexico City in September, 1963.

The de Menils and Schlumberger were among the most influential oil people in Texas. Further, Jean de Menil was born a Baron and his ancestor had been made a Baron by Napoleon in 1813. This connection to France and presumably at least an acquaintance with prominent French Catholic fascists would seem to outweigh in significance any connection to White Russians.

Considering that de Menil was in the midst of wealthy European fascists and equally wealthy Houston oilmen, there are surprisingly few probative details pointing to him as involved in the JFK plot. However, based on the issue of the Houma warehouse and the claim about the use of the Schlumberger aircraft to transport Oswald, de Menil must be included in the organizational chart of the assassination.

Paul Raigorodsky

It has been mentioned in our discussion of Baron George de Mohren-schildt, that Paul Raigorodsky was the lay leader of the St. Nicholas Russian Orthodox Church in Dallas. There is an excellent description of the history of this faith in Dallas in a Wikipedia article viewed on December 10, 2016, the link to which is reproduced in the notes to this chapter.

Raigorodsky was on oilman like George de Mohrenschildt. He testified as a witness and provided information to the Warren Commission. He died in the same month as his friend George de Mohrenschildt and thus couldn't testify to the House Select Committee on Assassinations. Author Jim Marrs considers this a "mysterious death" although it was regarded by all as a death from natural causes at the time.

In an article cited later in this chapter, the author Stig states that Raigorodsky and Governor John Connally were investors in the Tryall Compound Resort near Montego Bay, Jamaica. This resort is believed to be a staging or planning area for the assassination in the minds of some JFK authors and researchers. For our purposes, we will only suggest that there was probably a lot of informal and social contact between many of the principals who surrounded the assassination plan, mostly from a distance. We know that the father of JFK's Treasury Secretary, C. Douglas Dillon whose name was Clarence Dillon had a resort home nearby called "High Rock." Of course, C. Douglas Dillon commanded the Secret Service so this nexus cannot be entirely discounted.

The White Russians had two main functions in the assassination plot: First, they served as the welcoming committee for Lee and Marina Oswald upon their return from Russian in 1962. They allowed the Oswalds to reside in their homes periodically.

Second, they provided confidential translators when the FBI and other agencies interviewed Marina Oswald following the assassination. This allowed the FBI to avoid using their own Russian translators. Such an FBI translator would have been a witness to the many inconsistencies and evasiveness of Marina Oswald. Indeed, Marina's testimony was fixed and rigged. She wound up with $250,000 cash in the bank, supposedly from the many small-time fans she had around the country who sympathized with her. Actually, she was seen secretly entering the offices of oilman H.L. Hunt just a few days after the assassination. So Marina was amply paid with hush money. She spoke only Russian. So Paul Raigorodsky and his friends were crucial in smoothing over the Lee/Marina situation in Dallas.

Princess Scherbatoff a/k/a Gali Clark

One of the charming figures in this scenario is Princess Scherbatoff, a Russian Princess married to Texas attorney Max Clark.

When Lee Harvey Oswald returned from the Soviet Union in June, 1962, he applied for work at the Texas Employment Commission. Virginia Hale, a lady who worked there and whose husband was with the Security Division of General Dynamics in Fort Worth, took an interest in helping Oswald. She gave Oswald the phone number of Max Clark, knowing he was married to Gali Clark who was from Russia and spoke Russian. She apparently had heard that Marina Oswald spoke only Russian or had some similar reason for making this referral to Clark and his wife. These facts can be found on the following website, viewed 12-10-2016 called www.reopenkennedy-case.net.

According to Stig, the author of the article on the above mentioned site, Gali Clark was not called to testify to the Warren Commission, nor did she provide any affidavits or other evidence. In Warren Commission testimony, Paul Raigorodsky states that Gali is a sister to Prince Sherbatoff who lives in both New York and Jamaica. We have mentioned above the connection of Jamaica and Montego Bay to the assassination in the minds of many researchers.

Another cousin of the Princess was Alexis Scherbatow who worked for the Tolstoy Foundation. We will see in a later chapter that Alexandra Tolstoy, who founded the Tolstoy Foundation, was on a committee to investigate Soviet kidnapings along with at least two individuals who were deeply involved with the assassination plot. These were Baron Charles A. Willoughby and Judge Robert Morris. This committee was active in the mid-1950's.

Gali Hughes Clark was the heiress to a massive industrial empire in Russia which was lost when the Bolsheviks took over in 1917. Her family's industries had employed, among others, a young Nikita Khrushchev. The people who had owned properties and estates in Russia prior to the Revolution had definitely not given up the hope of getting their wealth eventually returned to them. Your author can affirm the fact that as late as the early 1980's, Czarist bonds were being carried on the books of the largest Trust Company in Wisconsin as legitimate securities (though their value was obviously very hard to estimate or price).

So the presence of a bona fide Russian Princess in the Dallas-Fort Worth area was not an insignificant fact. And as we have seen and will see throughout this writing, the backbone and the motivation of the JFK assassination plot came from Europe. And specifically, it has to be appreciated that these White Russian pretenders were not just believers in Old World fairy tales. They were willing, at the least, to murder anyone including a U.S. President in their attempt to satisfy their greed and their desire to regain the cushy lifestyle to which they felt entitled.

FERENC NAGY

A nother name which is often mentioned in relationship to the White Russians is that of Ferenc Nagy. Nagy was the former Premier of Hungary and the top leader in Hungary until he was forced to flee to Switzerland by the Soviets.

Assassination researchers are very fortunate because Nagy left a brilliantly written memoir entitled *The Struggle Behind the Iron Curtain*, published in 1948. This memoir brings home to the reader just how impossible it was for members of our American government to cope with individuals like Nagy who had been through the bath of fire in pre-World War II and post-War World War II Europe. They had learned all the cunning, the evil and the dirty tricks from Hitler and Stalin. Our leaders just weren't up to snuff by comparison to Nagy, the White Russians or the ex-Nazis.

Nagy was very vain about his political gifts. When he found his country in trouble and essentially "up for grabs" after the fall of Nazi Germany, Nagy instinctively knew what to do. He had two trusted political advisors, one of whom was a Catholic priest from the background of the monastery. Nagy, acting with the assistance of these advisors, made a valiant attempt to avoid the inevitable. The Soviets had Hungary surrounded and they eventually imposed Communism on the hapless country.

Nagy was generally flexible and open minded. He had to be in order to stay in the saddle of leadership in Hungary during this turmoil. He had to improvise principles of government "on the fly" as events swirled around him. He represented the Peasant Party, which included roughly half the people of Hungary. But despite representing the peasants, in his memoirs, Nagy often let his regressive, conservative prejudices show through. He was outraged at the idea that workers would be included in judicial panels to judge people accused of economic crimes. Management would be fine. But not workers. This despite the fact that Nagy led the Peasant Party.

For the JFK researcher, the take-away is that Nagy was not either Catholic or Eastern Orthodox, but rather he was a Presbyterian. He was not deprived of any vast estates or wealth by the Communists. In fact, some believe that when the Communists forced him finally to flee to Switzerland for the sake of security for his family, he took with him some of the wealth of Hungary.

Nagy came to the U.S. following this chaotic downfall as Hungarian leader. During the Hungarian uprising of 1956, the Soviet press claimed that U.S. intelligence had made use of Nagy and his influence to help stoke the rebellion. Without even researching this point, one could conclude that this had to be true. With the unparalleled political acumen of Ferenc Nagy, keeping him away from the Hungarian revolt would be like tethering the proverbial fire dog when he smelled the fire.

There have been published claims that Nagy came to Dallas four or five weeks before the assassination. Some claim that Nagy was the infamous "umbrella man" who used his umbrella to signal when the shooting of JFK should begin.

Based on the persona of Nagy as revealed in his memoirs, it seems highly unlikely that he had any involvement in the JFK assassination. Because he was not a White Russian, nor was he a Nazi, a Catholic, a fascist, nor a political extremist, he would have no motive to participate in the murder of an elected leader like JFK. While still the leader of Hungary, he used his wits to fight hard for his version of democracy. His democracy was somewhat rigged, but he wanted the people to feel in control of their government and have the right to vote. Also, unlike Germany and Russia, Hungary did not have a whole network of ex-Nazis and displaced aristocracy waiting in the wings for the fall of Communism. According to a Pew Research study published in 2009, Hungarians who lived under both Communism and, more recently, capitalism, responded in favor of Communism by a factor of 10 to 1.

As stated previously, in the biography of Francis Cardinal Spellman, Nagy was given possession of "the crown of Saint Stephen" which could be used for reinstatement of a monarchy in Hungary. Or then again, Nagy could have disposed of it for profit. Who knows?

It would seem like the Hungarian situation and thus the situation of Nagy was totally unlike the German, Ukrainian and Russian situations and therefore Nagy would not fit in very well at all with the killers of JFK.

Notes:

https://en.wikipedia.org/wiki/Saint_Seraphim_(Orthodox)_Cathedral, updated 11-21-2016, viewed 12-10-16. This is cited in text in section for Paul Ragiorodsky.

On information related to Jarnigan and the officing of Lawrence Orlov, see *The Girl on the Stairs: My Search for a Missing Witness to the Assassination* ...By Barry Ernest, p. 74.

Negative Intelligence: The Army and the American Left, 1917-1941By Roy Talbert, Jr. for information about Orlov's experience in World War I.

Chapter 20

THE THREE GOVERNMENTAL INVESTIGATIONS OF THE KENNEDY ASSASSINATION

I t is the intent here only to summarize (and critique) the three major investigations into the assassination of John F. Kennedy. Most Americans know what these investigations were about, what they achieved and what are the opinions as to their credibility. One website chosen (at random) cites the figure that 70 percent of Americans believe in a conspiracy in the JFK assassination. This same rough percentage was also mentioned in a recent documentary on the History Channel. This has been true since the release of the Oliver Stone movie *JFK* in 1991.

It is probably not possible to analyze the faith which the public has in each of the investigations as compared to the others. These include the Warren Commission, the Garrison investigation and the HSCA. But it can easily be seen that the vast majority of the public believes in a conspiracy. This would imply more faith in the credibility of the HSCA and Garrison in comparison to the Warren Commission.

THE WARREN COMMISSION

T o state what almost ever researcher has concluded, the Warren Commission was basically an effort to calm the public and carry out the elaborate cover-up in the aftermath of the assassination.

When viewed in this manner, it is easy to see, first, why the Warren Commission was necessary. Your author tries to show in these pages that SISS may have overseen the assassination plan. Therefore only a nearly identical entity could effectively carry out the cover-up. Further, the makeup of the Warren Commission was hand-tailored to fit the design as a commission for legal and political purposes.

One could argue that if the Warren Commission were truly designed to investigate the crime of the JFK assassination, then it should have been made up of forensic experts, noted big-city homicide investigators, military investigators, retired Federal judges and experienced FBI experts. But there was another, more important agenda for the Warren Commission as was put in writing by Assistant Attorney General Nicholas Katzenbach, J.

Edgar Hoover and the military, among others. That agenda was to execute a pre-planned cover up.

It is a very simple idea. Who would LBJ ask to operate the cover-up? Who were the individuals most capable of operating an effective cover-up? The perpetrators! Who else could truly anticipate what facts were lurking at the bottom of that nasty barrel? To ask it another way: in the United States, when murders are committed, then covered up, what percentage are covered up by the perpetrators? 98%? – 99%? – just pick a number.

The majority of the Warren Commission consisted of members of Congress, including Hale Boggs, (D. LA), John Sherman Cooper (R. KY), Gerald Ford (R. MI) and Richard Russell (D. GA). These were all conservatives, three of whom were from the South. It should be noted that, as will be presented in a later chapter, Rep. Hale Boggs was involved in the cover-up even when Oswald had not yet been killed.

Although the Warren Commission Report blamed Lee Harvey Oswald for the assassination, the Commission hedged its wording to say only that they had *discovered no evidence* except that which implicated Lee Harvey Oswald. So they did not state unequivocally that there was not a conspiracy in their official opinion, only that they had received no evidence of it.

EARL WARREN

Because of his infamous tenure as Chief Justice of the Supreme Court, most people who were of age in the 1960's and 1970's were all too familiar with the name Earl Warren. Warren had been the Republican Governor of California. He was named to be the Chief Justice by President Eisenhower. Ike later supposedly claimed the this was "the worst damn mistake I ever made." Actually, this was probably disingenuous as were many statements of a similar nature made by Ike on similar subjects, especially about McCarthyism.

It is well-known that the name Earl Warren became a byword for extreme liberalism, especially when it came to racial issues or Communism. Warren supposedly cried when he was asked to agree to serve on the Warren Commission. He was also famous for saying that the truth could not be revealed about the assassination, "not in our lifetimes." So much for the fair, impartial jurist Earl Warren.

JOHN J. MCCLOY

We should begin with the most harsh quote we have about John J. McCloy. The brilliant author and expert on German affairs, T. H Tetens quotes the leading German periodical *Der Spiegel*, saying that *Der Spiegel* had once described McCloy as having an "almost pathological love for Germany." Tetens is by far the most insightful author in the opinion of your author on post-war German history. Apparently Tetens and *Der Spiegel* were in agreement on this point when it came to John J. McCloy.

Some of the best information about John J. McCloy comes not from his biographer, Kai Bird, but from the matchless author Ron Chernow, the biographer of the Warburgs. Chernow describes McCloy as "a short, balding affable man … who enjoyed hobnobbing with the rich and powerful, and his career had long been intertwined with the Warburgs. His mother, a hairdresser, used to do Frieda's [Frieda Warburg] hair during summers at Bar Harbor." When McCloy joined the prestigious Cravath law firm in 1924, he did legal work for Freddie and Felix Warburg, who were partners at Kuhn, Loeb.

There is John J. McCloy in a nutshell. McCloy had begun his career working for nine years as a lawyer on the Black Tom explosion, a gigantic act of German sabotage during World War I. During this time, he actually shared box seats with Hitler cronies Himmler and Goering in Hitler's personal section of seating during the 1936 Berlin Olympics.

As Assistant Secretary of War, McCloy had opposed the bombing of the rail lines leading to Auschwitz. He had also been in personal charge of the internment of the Japanese citizens in the West during World War II. From 1947 to 1949 he had been chairman of the World Bank. From 1949 to 1952, he was High Commissioner in the U.S. sector of Occupied Germany. Then he became Chairman of the Chase Manhattan Bank from 1953 to 1960. Chase was owned by the Rockefeller family. From 1954 to 1970, he was Chairman of the Council on Foreign Relations. The CFR had been founded by the Rockefellers.

As High Commissioner of Germany, he had commuted the sentences of Friedrich Flick and Alfred Krupp, the two worst corporate Hitler collaborators. Acting on the advice of German-Jewish banker Eric Warburg, McCloy reversed the policy whereby German industry was being dismantled as a hedge against German militarism. When McCloy was in the midst of deciding which Nazi war criminals to [essentially] pardon, he and his wife invited to their home Princess Helene von Isenburg, who was nicknamed the "mother of Red-Jackets" [Nazi War Criminals]. Mrs. McCloy sent the Princess a check to financially aid the imprisoned Nazi's. McCloy's wife, born Ellen Zinsser, was a third cousin of the wife of Konrad Adenauer, Auguste "Gussie" Zinsser.

ALLEN DULLES

So much has been written about Allen Dulles that little space will be devoted here to him and his career. But when one reads exhaustively about the characters involved or suspected of involvement in the JFK assassination, one comes across some prize tidbits which tend to throw a spotlight on an otherwise murky subject.

This is the case with Allen Dulles. Dulles had joined the State Department during the period of World War I. Even at that early date he was specializing in intelligence. One of his earliest postings was at Constantinople. Author Joseph W. Bendersky wrote a very important work on anti-Semitism in military intelligence. He states that anti-Semitism was rampant in the diplomatic service at that time. He says that prominent Jew Felix Frankfurter was referred to as Hot Dog. He quotes Allen Dulles, writing from the American Embassy in Constantinople, repeating a remedy he had heard from a friend for "Jewish troubles," namely a 'ham bone amulet' to keep off the evil eye of some of our h___ nosed friends." Later, in a letter which minimized the seriousness of problems which Jews were encountering in Poland, Dulles wrote that a report on the subject "is a typical bit of Jewish propaganda."

Uki Goni was the author of the book *The Real Odessa*. At page 10 of that book Goni quotes a "bone-chilling" statement made by Dulles in his WWII negotiations with the Nazis. Goni found the statement in U.S. files: "He [Dulles] was fed up with listening all the time to outdated politicians, emigrés, and prejudiced Jews. In his view a peace had to be made in Europe ... while he had scant sympathy for Soviet Russia, he did not reject National Socialism in its basic ideas and deeds ... he added that it would be unbearable for any decent European to think that the Jews might return someday"

HALE BOGGS

Both Jim Garrison and the HSCA investigated a man named Raymond Broshears who was a friend of David W. Ferrie. As reported by Dr. Caulfield in *General Walker*, Raymond Broshears said that his friend David Ferrie had told him that Hale Boggs was one of the "names in relationship to the assassination of President Kennedy." Dr. Caulfield adds a disclaimer that the meaning of this is unclear to him.

Following the assassination, a right-wing group called INCA in its publication *Victory* contains the following quotes.

Remarks by Rep. Boggs, on "Oswald Speaks":

> Just a few hours after President Kennedy's death, I sat with Ed Butler in my office in the Capitol and listened to this recording. What I heard was one of the things which prompted me to suggest and support the formation of a bipartisan Presidential Commission to investigate the assassination. I later served on that Commission. I believe this recording is a most significant historical document.

Remarks by Sen. Dodd, on "Oswald Speaks":

> I asked Ed Butler to come to Washington to testify before the Senate Internal Security Subcommittee a few hours after President

Kennedy's assassination, at a time when Oswald was still alive. Ed Butler brought this recording with him. What we heard convinced us that Oswald's commitment to Communism, and the pathological hatred of his own country fostered this commitment, had played an important part in making him into an assassin. This important and historical record completely demolishes the widespread notion that Oswald was a simple crackpot who acted without any understandable motivation.

One can draw the conclusion from the timing of events as described above that Sen. Thomas Dodd and Rep. Hale Boggs were both involved in the frame-up of Oswald. Sadly, or should we say boldly, Dodd and Boggs were not even subtle with their ridiculous "in-your-face" claims.

Hale Boggs was a Congressman from New Orleans. There has been no biography written about Boggs, but the best source for information was the memoir written by his widow Corinne "Lindy" Boggs who also succeeded Boggs in his Congressional seat from Louisiana. The vanity of Mrs. Boggs overcame her. She couldn't resist writing what could be called a "dog-whistle book." This is a book which seems innocuous, but is designed to give a perverted sort of credit after the true facts about the JFK assassination are eventually revealed. In this manner, people like Mrs. Boggs can be remembered by history as having played a role in this historic event, while not revealing such during their lifetime. There are several similar examples of such books discussed elsewhere in this volume.

Boggs' brother Robert was a Jesuit priest and Dean of Students at Loyola University in New Orleans. Boggs graduated from Tulane University in New Orleans in 1934. As a student he was generally a progressive. He and his wife claimed to be part of the "reform" movement in Louisiana Democratic politics. There is no mention, however, of any reforms instituted by this group, which included the cousin of Mrs. Boggs, Mayor De-Lesseps Morrison of New Orleans. In this case "reform" was a code-word which related to the battle between Catholic Democrats in New Orleans and the KKK-minded anti-Catholic Democrats in upstate Louisiana.

The only arguable "reform" was the assassination of Governor Huey Long. Cynically, Corinne "Lindy" Boggs seemed to justify both the murder of Huey Long and JFK as necessary because they had created political tensions that had to be released. That in itself tells you volumes about both Boggs and his wife. As mentioned elsewhere, JFK counted the Boggs' as personal friends. As early as 1946, when Mrs. Boggs was in the hospital with hepatitis, Boggs would bring JFK, who had himself suffered from hepatitis, to the hospital to offer her encouragement.

Per Mrs. Boggs, "Congress worked gingerly with President Kennedy." She recounted a conversation with a priest, where she admitted that she was campaigning for two relatives at the same time when they were running for office against one another. "You should have been a Jesuit," as she reported cynically the reaction of the priest. And this typified her attitude about life and presumably reflected also that of her husband with whom she was very close. She portrayed herself as a "Southern belle," looking at life through a royal purple veil. Unfortunately, this role of Southern Belle included, at least in spirit, the plantation wife who supervised the whipping of slaves, the chopping off of feet, the lynchings, etc. which are portrayed in movies about the antebellum South.

Boggs got his daughter Barbara a job working in the JFK White House to set up a volunteer corps. Mrs. Boggs reports that "some groups got uncontrollably angry" at JFK over Civil Rights. They became murderers of the President. They just couldn't help it! Mrs. Boggs arranged for a last minute visit to the White House in November, 1963 so she could show off her "connections" to the President for her mother and her mother-in-law. She had to hurry, because her husband was very likely going to help murder the President at any time now. You know, it was "uncontrollable."

Boggs became Majority Whip and then Majority Leader of the House. Speaker Carl Albert was to retire in 1978 and Boggs was slated to succeed him. But on October 16, 1972, the light plane carrying Boggs back from a trip to Alaska vanished without a trace in the rugged mountains southeast of Anchorage. Although the largest search party in Alaska history was mounted, no trace was ever found, although various other previously unknown crash sites of small aircraft were discovered.

It has been reported in some sources that the person who drove Boggs to the airport was actually a young William Jefferson Clinton. Dating back to at least the mid-1960's, Hale Boggs had become a serious alcoholic. Some historians or researchers have speculated that because of his worsening alcoholism, the FBI worried that Boggs would "talk out of school" about his role in the assassination, perhaps while under the influence.

The daughter of Hale and Corinne "Lindy" Boggs, Barbara Boggs, was quoted by her mother as saying "when I want to do something directly, she thought of her father, but when she wanted to do something 'indirectly,' I thought of my mother." Mrs. Boggs and her cynicism gives her the medal in the eyes of this author as the most reprehensible "leader" involved in the the assassination. Mrs. Boggs and David Rockefeller were longtime friends. Toward the end of her career, Mrs. Boggs was instrumental in starting the Democratic Leadership Council, which led to the eventual election of Bill Clinton as President.

To the knowledge of this author, there were only three leaders who spoke or wrote with any degree of approval about the JFK assassination. Those three were Mrs. Hale Boggs, Senator Thomas Dodd and Herbert Hoover through his son Allan Hoover.

Apparently, for Hale Boggs or at least for Mr. and Mrs. Boggs, duplicity was a virtue, hiding behind the "purple veil" was the way to go through life. For the cadre of people in New Orleans who had the blood of both Huey Long and JFK on their hands, one can only shake one's head in discouragement.

John Sherman Cooper

One of the least well-known members of the Warren Commission was Senator John Sherman Cooper, Republican from Kentucky. But Senator Cooper was far from unimportant in both American history and with regard to the Warren Commission.

Fortunately, there is a very well written biography about Cooper called *John Sherman Cooper: The Global Kentuckian*, written by Robert Shulman. Much of the following information can be verified in that excellent volume.

John Sherman Cooper was born in Somerset, Kentucky in 1901. His father was reputed to be the wealthiest man in Somerset. Cooper was tutored by a neighbor until he was in the sixth grade. In High School, he delivered the commencement address. His topic was "The German Spy System." After High School, he started out at Centre College in Danville, Kentucky and then transferred to Yale. At Yale, he was voted the most likely to succeed in his class. At Yale, he became a member of Skull and Bones, the secret society often associated with conspiracy theories and alleged covert activities. After Yale, he attended Harvard Law School for two years. He had to drop out for financial reasons, but at Harvard he acquired the polish he would later use in holding important positions in government.

In the 1920's, he spent 8 years as a county judge. Cooper's father had graduated from the University of Kentucky Law School and had been a Collector of Internal Revenue under Theodore Roosevelt.

In 1942, after rejecting the offer of an officer's commission, Cooper enlisted in the U.S. Army as a private. He was then sent to Officer's Candidate School and graduated second in his class. After fighting under George Patton, in July, 1944, Cooper became a courier for the military police and then was trained to be an expert in the U.S. Military Government of Germany, charged with the task of helping rebuild the Judicial System in Bavaria. At the end of 1945, Cooper was the legal advisor in repatriating 300,000 former slave laborers used by the Nazi's back to their proper countries.

But there is more information on Cooper which is very important to our story of the assassination. While working on the repatriation of the slave laborers, Cooper worked with such groups as the World Council of Churches, the Papal Emissary and the Jewish Agencies. There were some complaints against Cooper by these groups. They claimed that he personally picked 239 new Judges for Bavaria. He was supposedly charged with weeding out Nazis. Most historians agree that the Judiciary was one profession where Nazis were deliberately allowed to remain in post-War Germany. History has suggested that the weeding out of Nazis from the German State Governments like Hesse and Bavaria, was not very effective. We know that General Patton himself, who was in charge at one point in Bavaria, was believed to be soft or too sympathetic toward the Nazis.

Most importantly, Cooper placed Ludwig Erhardt into the economics ministry and Erhard remembered him for this. As we will explore in the chapter on the LBJ phone calls, Ludwig Erhard was the new Chancellor of Germany, in office less than four weeks when Kennedy was shot. Erhard was given priority over all other foreign leaders following the assassination and was a special guest of LBJ at his Texas Ranch.

Author T.H. Tetens, a leading expert on the Nazi's, is quoted frequently in these pages. Tetens quotes *New York Times* correspondent Delbert Clark who reported that as Minister of Economics Erhard was in full cooperation with the Nazi regime, was advisor to Nazi Gauleiter [mayor] Buerckel in the Saar region of Germany and also the chief of the Hitlerite Institute for Industrial Research.

John Sherman Cooper was a "one-worlder" and won appointment to an open Senate seat in 1946. He believed that nations should be free to choose Communism but that the Marshall Plan would discourage this. After losing his Senate seat, he was appointed the U.S. delegate to the U.N. replacing John Foster Dulles.

Cooper had seven key State Department assignments.

> United Nations.
> Special Assistant to Dean Acheson to help form NATO.
> Ambassador-at-large to assist Acheson with building the Atlantic Pact.
> Ambassador to India.
> Secret emissary of JFK to Moscow.
> Delegate to the U.N. for the Legal Committee to define "aggression."
> Ambassador to East Germany.

While on a European fact-finding mission for Secretary of State Dean Acheson, the U.S. High Commissioner John J. McCloy invited Cooper to have dinner with Chancellor Konrad Adenauer and himself.

The domestic life of John Sherman Cooper is a story in itself. He was first married to an Army nurse but was divorced. He then married socialite Lorraine Rowan McAdoo. She was formerly married to Robert McAdoo, son of Woodrow Wilson's Treasury Secretary. Then she married a

"Palm Beach Playboy" named Tom Shevlin, Jr. but was again divorced. Following that, Secretary of State John Foster Dulles asked John Sherman Cooper to marry Ms. McAdoo Shevlin. He was then named Ambassador to India, complete with a socially accomplished wife at his side.

In his first non-appointed Senate service, President Eisenhower had asked Cooper to run for a Senate seat. He won in 1956 and was immediately placed on the Foreign Relations Committee.

As one of the great ironies of the JFK assassination, John F. Kennedy counted Cooper as one of his personal friends along with such other members of Congress like Rep. Hale Boggs and Senator George Smathers. The Cooper-JFK relationship began while both served on the Senate Labor Committee. The Kennedy's and the Coopers were dinner guests at each others' homes beginning in 1957. While on the Warren Commission, Cooper eagerly helped to whitewash the murder of his "friend" JFK. Brutus or Judas, take your choice.

Cooper was considered a "German hand" because of his service in Bavaria during World War II and he was named the first U.S. Ambassador to East Germany for that reason. Like Allen Dulles and John J. McCloy, John Sherman Cooper had a face-to-face history with German Nazis. This was his special qualification to serve on the Warren Commission. As we shall see in a later chapter, this background was the subject of a special mention in the post-assassination phone calls when the subject of the Warren Commission was discussed.

RICHARD RUSSELL

Senator Richard Russell was a famous figure in Senate history. A Senate Office Building was named for him due to his lengthy and influential service. Russell had served as Governor of Georgia before being elected to the Senate. Russell was a segregationist. However, he was considered a "law and order guy" as were fellow segregationists Strom Thurmond and John Stennis. That meant that Russell believed in above board and "on the table" restriction of voting rights for blacks through such means as poll-taxes and literacy tests. He simply felt that whites in Georgia should not and would not submit to black county governments in the one-third of Georgia counties where blacks were in the majority. This may sound evil and of course it was. But Russell wasn't a believer in terrorism against blacks and lynchings and often pointed out that lynchings had been substantially decreased during his term as Governor.

Russell was a proponent of the liberal economic policies of the New Deal. He was especially strong when it came to liberal agricultural price supports for cotton. He also was Chairman of the Armed Services Committee from 1951 to 1969 and also Chairman of the Committee that oversaw the CIA.

Russell was considered by many to be the Senator with the most influence over his colleagues, more influential than even Senator Lyndon B. Johnson. Russell became discouraged when liberal Democrats scored their important victory in 1958 which gave them control of the Senate and put them ahead of the Republican-Southern Democrat coalition. After this happened, Senator William Fulbright began his reign as Chairman of the Senate Foreign Relations Committee, with liberal Senator Frank Church as his right-hand man. Both were disliked by conservatives and staunch ant-Communists of both parties.

When LBJ called Russell to ask him to serve on the Warren Commission, there ensued the most rancorous phone call that LBJ probably ever made. LBJ apparently knew that he had to have the support of Russell in the cover-up of the assassination. Russell was not in favor of the cover-up. We know this by the position he took in the LBJ phone call. Russell later made derogatory comments and statements about the "lone gunman" theory. He also attempted to boycott the signing of the final report of the Warren Commission, although the Commission ignored him on that point.

To summarize, both Richard Russell and fellow Southern Democrat John Stennis apparently wanted the truth to be told about the assassination. Russell even pressured LBJ to have Stennis included in the Warren Commission. Unfortunately, despite good intentions, both of them failed.

GERALD FORD

Since Gerald R. Ford was our 38th President, he is well-known and little needs to be said about him. He was picked for the Warren Commission because he was a member of the House of Representatives and he was a Republican. This served to balance out the Warren Commission, which was legally and in reality a joint committee of the Congress except in name. LBJ needed a Republican from the House on the Warren Commission because the Republicans together with the Southern Democrats in the Congress had just helped conspire to murder JFK. It is as simple as that.

Ford had been an All-America football player at the University of Michigan. He married the once-divorced Betty Ford who became famous for founding the Betty Ford Institute for treatment of substance abuse which was a pioneering effort. Unfortunately, his marriage to Betty Ford worked out less and less well in their golden years. Ford was criticized by some for abandoning his hometown in Michigan for his retirement, choosing instead to become a virtual hometown citizen in Palm Springs, one of the two or three wealthiest cities in California.

More importantly, as the nation soon learned after Ford became President, he had no ideology, no particular ideas and stood for absolutely nothing. There are very few Americans who were of age during his Presidency who can name a single thing he stood for. The exception of course, was his pardon of Nixon. As a member of the Warren Commission, he also helped pardon the murderers of JFK. I guess his name should have been Gerald Pardon Ford.

The only two outstanding facts about Gerald R. Ford are these: first, he was working as a retail clerk as a very young man when a customer came in the store and said "Hi, I'm your father." Ford had been raised in ignorance of the fact that he was adopted by his step-father and had to learn the truth in this brutal manner. Second, after he was being considered for the Warren Commission he began to get invites to such events as Bilderberg meetings and the like. So Ford was a late comer to the "inside Washington" events like the making of the National Security State, the flirtation with ex-Nazi's and fascists and the JFK assassination. But he was amply rewarded by being appointed President without even having to stand for election. All must agree that this was not an insignificant payback. Washington rewards its own.

THE JIM GARRISON INVESTIGATION

JIM GARRISON

The second official investigation of the Kennedy assassination was the Jim Garrison investigation in New Orleans. This investigation was dramatized in the 1991 film *JFK* directed by Oliver Stone and starring Kevin Costner. This investigation was also discussed in depth by Garrison himself in his famous book *On The Trail of the Assassins*.

Garrison was the elected District Attorney of Orleans Parish (county) at the time of the assassination. The reason he started his investigation of the JFK assassination was because at least three of the main players (David W. Ferrie, Clay Shaw and Guy Banister) lived in and operated out of New Orleans. The precipitating cause for Garrison starting his investigation was the "bug" put in his ear by Senator Russell Long of Louisiana, who secretly mentioned off the record to Garrison that he had serious questions about the true story of the assassination.

The father of Russell Long, Huey Long had been assassinated while Russell was only a teen-ager. That assassination involved the same interest groups and possibly one or two of the same people who murdered JFK.

Garrison was a graduate of Tulane Law School, but his family had Iowa roots. In the personal opinion of your author, Iowa is a very squeaky-clean place when it comes to strict compliance to laws and procedures. Garrison himself emphasized his Iowa roots in his book.

Let's face it, Louisiana (although a very pleasant and interesting state), has a reputation for political corruption along with Illinois and New Jersey. But Garrison was apparently a totally honest official motivated by patriotism who wanted to do right by his country. Garrison tried to start his investigation in secrecy, but the word leaked out and the press began intense publicity about the investigation. Garrison's resources were limited, so he accepted volunteers to help him along.

Some of these volunteers turned out to be CIA operatives.

The Garrison investigation lasted from 1966 to 1969. Garrison was portrayed in the national press as a buffoon, a lunatic, and an unscrupulous politician obsessed with political gains and publicity at any cost. He went nationwide, appearing on the Johnny Carson show and writing an article in *Playboy* magazine.

CLAY SHAW

Garrison had three main suspects as the plotters of the assassination: David W. Ferrie (a CIA-connected pilot and adventurer), Guy Banister (an ex-FBI and CIA plotter extraordinaire), and Clay Shaw (a lifelong spy and a professional international conspirator). All three of these suspects had been openly connected to Lee Harvey Oswald, and in the case of David W. Ferrie, since LHO was a teenager.

Unfortunately for Garrison, Guy Banister had already died of a heart attack before the investigation began. And worse, after he arrested David W. Ferrie, Ferrie died violently hours after he was released on bail. This untimely death came only hours after Ferrie had described himself as "a walking deadman" because of his fear of retribution from the JFK conspiracy plotters.

The only good news for Garrison was regarding Clay Shaw. As fifty years of evidence has shown, Shaw was possibly the "hinge," or served the central function in the plot. According to Judyth Vary Baker, Shaw was a payroll agent for the assassination as well as the related plot to weaponize cancer to be discussed in greater detail in a later chapter. Shaw was possibly a main player in, or even the founder of the Permindex organization. The Permindex assassination organization will also be discussed in detail in a later chapter.

Clay Shaw was born on March 17, 1913 in Kentwood, Louisiana, the son of a United States Marshall. At age 5 he moved with his family to New Orleans. *In A Farewell to Justice*, author Joan Mellen discusses both Shaw and Permindex. Mellen classifies the Permindex organization as run by the CIA and known to have financed the French OAS. She describes how Shaw dropped out of Warren Easton High School in New Orleans in the 11th grade. In November, 1942, he enlisted in the U.S. Army. Mellen states that Shaw was put both in Officer's Candidate School (OCS) and the medical corps.

Then, Mellen says, Shaw was "discovered" by military intelligence and was made an aide to General Charles O. Thrasher. In that role, he rose to the rank of major. At that time, Thrasher was in charge of transferring

German POWs to the French. Shaw worked in the Army Counter-Intelligence Corp. (CIC) and was decorated by the Government of France with a Croix de Guerre and Legion of Merit, and with a similar decoration by the Government of Belgium.

In a World War II history book, it was reported that General Thrasher was involved in the Battle of the Bulge. If that were the case and if Clay Shaw was his aide-de-camp, then that would explain why Shaw could have been awarded the French Croix de Guerre which would normally have been associated with heroism, not covert intelligence operations.

The following appears on a blog regarding the military career of Clay Shaw. Although it was not posted by a recognized author or historian, it does on its face seem to offer useful details about Shaw's military service. It was posted by Thomas H. Purvis on May 1, 2007. Purvis was, among other things, the Commanding Officer, Special Forces Schools Advanced Airborne Committee and held numerous other combat positions in the military. The military service of Thomas H. Purvis can easily be verified on websites which contain such background military and other information.

"Although I can not immediately quote the exact source, Clay Shaw became assigned to the OSS, working in the 'Recovery' section. This section of the OSS was assigned responsibility for attempting to track down and recover the stolen monies; gold; silver; art; art objects; antiquities; etc; etc; etc; which Hitler had looted from the countries which he over ran, as well as what was confiscated from the German Jews."

In that regard, Clay Shaw was assigned to and worked with that section which had responsibility for recovery of stolen art works. Somewhere, boxed away, I have much of this information as well as the source data.

However, in one Government file, information relative to Clay Shaw was found in the same box as the records which dealt with the I. G. Farben case.

It is suspected, though certainly not confirmed, that Clay Shaw still performed "contract" work for the CIA, relative to the continuation of the search for stolen items. If accurate, then this information explains Clay Shaw's interests in South American countries, and especially those which considerable numbers of German Nazi's fled to after the fall of Germany. It should also be noted that JFK was "pushing hard" for the recovery and return to the rightful owners of many millions of dollars of this stolen property, much of which was known to be stashed away in Swiss Banks.

The above information from the posting by Thomas H. Purvis is a lesson in itself. Purvis came across information linking Clay Shaw to the General Aniline and Film case. Virtually no one, probably including Purvis, could imagine that Shaw was somehow involved with the recovery of German property and few people even knew what the GAF case was about. But this bit of information drives the dagger right to the heart of the assassination conspiracy. It supports the tried and true theory of "follow the money." The largest amount of money directly at stake in the JFK assassination was clearly the settlement of the IG Farben-GAF case. This is seemingly just an offhand comment on a blog by Purvis but it suggests a direct line existed between the IG Farben corporation and Clay Shaw.

Author Joseph P. Farrell describes the beginning of the relationship of Major Clay Shaw with the Nazis by writing:

> Worse yet, when the Nazi rocket scientists led by Von Braun surrendered themselves to the American armies overrunning their country, it was then that Von Braun and his associates encountered another player in the drama, Clay Shaw. 'Von Braun first met Clay Shaw in 1945 when he, Walter Dornberger and about 150 other Nazi rocket scientists abandoned Peenemunde and traveled south to join the American forces in Germany close to the French border. The Nazis were brought to the Deputy Chief of Staff's headquarters where Major Clay Shaw was aide-de-camp to General Charles O. Thrasher.

Author Mellen states that when Shaw returned from Europe after the War, he began employment with the Mississippi Shipping Company, which was a CIA front organization.

If, as stated by author and German expert T H Tetens, it was true that Permindex was basically a fund set up by and for the benefit of ex-WWII Nazis, then this puts an entirely different cast on the image of Clay Shaw. This totally undermines the image of Clay Shaw as an eccentric, gay New Orleans socialite who cavorted with right-wingers exclusively in New Orleans.

We have found that the Reinhard Gehlen Nazi spy network was in total charge of CIA spying in Europe at that time. This was, in effect, a merger of the Gehlen network and the CIA as far as Europe was concerned. Clay Shaw apparently ran a branch operation of this merged entity in New Orleans which did the bidding of German industrialists as well as German, French and Italian Fascists and the CIA. From this connection, we can see that the U.S. never really defeated Germany and the Nazis, but rather, the Nazis went right on undermining the U.S. Government at least from 1945 up to the mid-1970s.

Shaw was then seen by witnesses passing money to Lee Harvey Oswald in the nether-world of Louisiana swamp conspiracy, somewhere north of Lake Ponchartrain. In 1967, Senator Russell Long suggested to Jim Garrison that he, Garrison, should investigate the assassination. Garrison began an investigation which charged Clay Shaw with homicide in the murder of JFK. Although many on the jury believed that Shaw was involved, Garrison could never prove a motive.

Although Garrison promoted the theory that Shaw was motivated by his role as a CIA operative, proving such a connection became impossible. So Clay Shaw went free. Shaw died on August 15, 1974 of lung cancer at age 61.

DAVID FERRIE

Ferrie is one of the most storied figures in the assassination literature. Yet not much of a connection has ever been demonstrated between Ferrie and the overall JFK conspiracy.

David W. Ferrie was born in 1918 in Cleveland, Ohio. He studied for the Catholic priesthood in the early 1940's but failed in that attempt, possibly because of emotional problems. He became a trained pilot and flew airliners for Eastern Airlines. But Ferrie was also a pedophile. He was very involved with the Civil Air Patrol, an organization of youthful pilots. One member of his squadron of Civil Air Patrol Youth was Lee Harvey Oswald. This connection was around 1955 when LHO would have been 16.

The political beliefs and motives of David W. Ferrie were confusing. He was at first a supporter of the overthrow of Cuban dictator Batista, but changed his mind and began to work closely with the anti-Castro Cubans in New Orleans after 1959.

According to Oswald girlfriend Judyth Vary Baker in her memoir *Me & Lee*, David Ferrie was involved in the plan to weaponize cancer which was the brainchild of the sinister Dr. Alton Ochsner, a known right-wing fanatic.

Garrison's suspects are generally believed to have been Clay Shaw, David Ferrie and Guy Banister. Unfortunately, Ferrie and Banister died prematurely after Garrison began to focus on them. Ferrie died February 22, 1967, just a day after he was released from protective custody by Jim Garrison. Because of the quick timing of his death in this manner, most researchers believe Ferrie was murdered just as Ferrie himself had predicted he would be.

Probably the most direct theory in which to connect Ferrie to the assassination would be his ongoing fanaticism regarding his Catholic religion. After being rejected in his pursuit of the role of priest, Ferrie became involved in some official capacity with an offshoot of the Catholic Church called the Old Roman Catholic Church of North America. If Ferrie had such a burning desire to be a priest, one would have to conclude that he was active in some Catholic circles in his practice of his religion. New Orleans was thick with such types of activists.

When Lee Harvey Oswald was arrested, there were very strong rumors or actual reports that LHO carried the library card of David W. Ferrie in his wallet. Author Judyth Vary Baker offers the best explanation of this. Ferrie was involved along with Oswald in the operation to find a form of cancer that could be used as a biological weapon.

Anyone who knows anything about medical schools knows that not just anyone can use a medical school library. Apparently David Ferrie had "jumped through the hoops" to become eligible to use the Tulane University Medical School Library, but Lee Harvey Oswald hadn't. So when LHO was sent to the library to fetch medical books for Dr. Ochsner, Dr. Mary Sherman or for someone else, he had to use the library card which belonged to Ferrie.

GUY BANISTER

In addition to the film *JFK* and Garrison's book, there is a third source of information about the Garrison investigation. It is the book *A Farewell To Justice: Jim Garrison, JFK's Assassination, and the Case That Should Have Changed History*, by Joan Mellen. This book was published in 2013 and hence is up-to-date with the latest evidence regarding the assassination.

The third suspect of Jim Garrison in the JFK murder investigation was Guy Banister. Since Banister died on June 6, 1964, he was not available during the full term of the Warren Commission nor to the investigators of Jim Garrison.

What is known for certain is that Banister had all the connections possible to the people and, more importantly, the type of people who perpetrated the assassination. Banister was born on March 7, 1901 in Monroe, Louisiana. He joined the FBI in 1934. He was present when John Dillinger was gunned down on the streets of Chicago. While in the FBI, Banister worked on investigating Communists and his work was admired by J. Edgar Hoover. He rose to the level of Special Agent In Charge in Chicago. Banister left the FBI and retired at age 53. His early retirement was thought by some to have been due to emotional issues.

Upon retirement, Banister moved to New Orleans and went to work with the New Orleans Police Department. His duties included running a string of informants who were investigating left-wing activities at Tulane and LSU as well as other places in Louisiana. But after he was dismissed from the NOPD, Banister founded his own private detective agency in New Orleans.

It was around that time, 1956, when Banister began cooperating with Senator James O. Eastland. Eastland was Chairman of the powerful Judiciary Committee and also Chairman of the Senate Internal Security Subcommittee (SISS) which was charged with investigating Communists. In his investigation, Garrison found records linking Banister to many members of European "titled nobility" and international jet-set types.

Eastland brought his hearings to Louisiana and interrogated Civil Rights leaders of the time like James Dombrowski. All of this activity is documented in detail in the iconic book, *General Walker* by Dr. Jeffrey Caulfield.

WALTER SHERIDAN

The largest single influencing factor in this investigation was the intervention of a man named Walter Sheridan. Walter Sheridan was an ex-FBI man who became seen as the right-hand-man of Robert Kennedy. Sheridan was dispatched to New Orleans to foil the Garrison investigation, presumably by RFK himself, or with the blessing of RFK.

In any event, Sheridan used both interference in the operation of the investigation and also his employment by NBC News to create false publicity that went nationwide. With that kind of millstone around his neck, Garrison made a brave but futile attempt to break the case and convict the guilty parties.

Another impediment to the Garrison investigation was the fact that he could not extradite witnesses from other states. Conservative Republican Governor John Rhodes of Ohio refused to extradite Gordon Novel. Governor John Connally of Texas refused to extradite Sergio Arcacha Smith, a man with proven advance knowledge of the assassination. This was true even though Connally himself had been shot during the assassination. Even Conservative Governor Ronald Reagan got into the act by refusing to extradite Mr. E. E. Bradley. This was the first time in the history of California that a governor had refused to extradite a person under indictment for murder.

One small item of evidence mentioned by Garrison in his book has loomed large in more recent years. In his book, Garrison describes how he tried to summon five employees of the Reily Coffee Company (who had worked with Oswald) to testify. All of these employees, within a day or two, were given new, higher paying jobs with NASA. NASA had a large facility in New Orleans which manufactured the Saturn moon rocket but was actually owned by Boeing. One of these five employees was hired *at Cape Canaveral* in Florida! Immediately following their hire, NASA forbade them to talk to Garrison.

Garrison concluded that NASA was involved, at least in the cover-up. Of course we now know that Judyth Vary Baker worked with Oswald at Reily Coffee. Reily Coffee was functioning, in part, as the front for the weaponized cancer project in co-operation with some intelligence agency or agencies. The other Reily employees were irate because even though Lee Harvey Oswald was being paid, he usually disappeared and was not doing any work, or so it appeared.

NASA was implicated by Garrison and was also accused as a suspect in the *Torbitt Document*. Finally, NASA appeared again in the person of General Walter Dornberger, best friend of Wernher von Braun. As will be discussed in a later chapter, Michael Paine, who was subordinate to Dornberger at Bell Aerospace, gave up his own bedroom to Oswald and his family for two months preceding the assassination.

The final outcome of the Garrison investigation was a verdict of not guilty in the prosecution of Clay Shaw. A follow-up prosecution of Clay Shaw for perjury was dismissed contrary to statute by a Federal Court.

As stated above, Garrison was ex-military, ex-FBI and an elected official. Because of these connections, Garrison was simply not going to point the finger at the military, the FBI or any other elected official. This is simply reality. It is the way things work in government. Further, since the Mafia was active in New Orleans and Garrison had to "work around" the Mafia as a prosecutor, the Mafia was not blamed either.

That left Garrison with only the CIA to blame, which he did openly and it *has* been proved that Clay Shaw, Ferrie and Banister had CIA connections. Garrison was unable to *prove* this CIA connection and hence he had no motive for murder which he could prove in his court case.

THE HOUSE SELECT COMMITTEE ON ASSASSINATIONS

The House Select Committee on Assassinations, hereinafter HSCA, was organized in September 1976 to investigate the assassinations of JFK, RFK and MLK. The first chairman Thomas N. Downing of Virginia retired in January, 1977 and was replaced by Rep. Henry Gonzales of Texas.

Presidential advisor Cliff Carter had given the bloody clothes worn by John Connally when he was shot along with JFK to Congressman Henry Gonzalez the day of the assassination to preserve as evidence. So Gonzalez was literally the only elected official in the country who was attempting to solve the assassination from the very beginning. This, of course, is hard to explain or even comprehend, but it happened.

The first counsel to the HSCA was an attorney named Richard A. Sprague. The real reason for the creation of the committee, at least in the opinion of Sprague, was that President Jimmy Carter was the only truly honest recent President either before the assassination or since. Therefore, Carter allowed the investigation to move forward. This could also probably be said about the beginning of the Church Committee which investigated the CIA. That never happened before Carter and hasn't happened since.

Sprague too was too honest, intending to forcefully investigate the case with heavy use of lie detectors and other aggressive investigative techniques. It soon became apparent that the Congress, although desiring the investigation, didn't want any surprises, so they replaced Richard A. Sprague with G. Robert Blakey as counsel. Since the forte of Blakey was investigating the Mafia, it was apparently pre-arranged at least informally that the blame would be placed on the Mafia. This was done in private speeches and other revelations personally made by Blakey but not in the committee report.

The second major feature of the HSCA is that it precipitated an horrendous series of murders of witnesses. In the book *Hit List: An In-Depth Investigation into the Mysterious Deaths of Witnesses to the JFK Assassination,* by Richard Belzer published very recently in 2013, the author details almost 100 witnesses in the assassination who were murdered. It is fair to say that the greatest number of deaths and the most flagrant and obvious murders of witnesses occurred in connection to the HSCA investigation.

Belzer claims that there were six FBI agents and officials alone who were murdered within a period of six months prior to their expected testimony to the HSCA.

Mobsters Johnny Roselli and Sam Giancana were known to have been murdered to prevent their testimony. The very top potential witness, George de Mohrenschildt, died violently hours before his interview. De Mohrenschildt was the best friend and "baby sitter" for Oswald just months before the assassination. He also had life-long ties to intelligence activities. It was claimed he committed suicide but (for some odd reason), the relatives with whom he was staying on the day before his scheduled testimony just happened to have a loaded shotgun propped against the wall beside his bed!

The HSCA investigation has been blessed with a book written by the chief investigator named Gaeton Fonzi. It is called *The Last Investigation: A Former Federal Investigator Reveals the Man Behind the Conspiracy to Kill JFK* and was first published in 1993.

It should be said that Fonzi did not, in fact, reveal any such man. The takeaway from the book by Fonzi is that Claire Booth Luce, a hyper-notorious right wing "dragon lady" of the period, along with a Cuban named Antonio Veciana, succeeded in wasting the time of the investigators so the Committee got almost nowhere in their investigative efforts.

The record of the HSCA was better when it looked at forensic evidence and forensic experts. Through the efforts of the cover-up community since the days of the HSCA, the results and conclusions of forensics and forensic experts have been obscured. Suffice it to say that the conclusions published by the HSCA did not necessarily agree with the actual results of the forensic analysis.

The HSCA held that there was a conspiracy to kill JFK. However, it used the most evasive and imaginative way possible to make this finding and then immediately close the book on the assassination before the cover-up artists could work their destruction. HSCA was able to say in their report that there was a conspiracy, but get off the hook (due to lack of time) from having to track down the conspirators.

This happened because of an audio dictabelt recording made by a motorcycle radio located near the limo when the shots were fired. Since the cover-up people would immediately deny and dispute any and all evidence, no matter what is was, the HSCA found this evidence on the last day of the investigation. They then promptly closed the case before the cover-up people had a chance to find dishonest experts who would dispute the dictabelt evidence. Such dishonest experts were quickly found, but not before the HSCA case had been closed.

The acoustic experts (the best in the country) analyzed the sounds on the dictabelt and graphed or mapped the sound waves into four "peaks" which were identical to those obtained by test firing guns in Dealey Plaza. Then they looked again at the Zapruder film and marked down the timing of the visual evidence of the shots hitting the victims. The timing was identical between the audio and visual evidence.

Although the cover-up experts came forth with claims that these results were mistaken, the die had been cast. The dictabelt recording proved four shots had occurred, which could not have all been made by Lee Harvey Oswald in the time available to him.

To show how ridiculous all of the above arguments really are, we only have to look at the evidence published by the Warren Commission. In that evidence is a receipt signed by the FBI for a bullet removed from the body of JFK, received from Dr. Humes who performed the autopsy. According to the lone gunman theory, both of the two known bullets hitting JFK passed through the body of the President. There would be no bullets in his body. This proof, like so much of the other evidence, was hiding in plain sight.

To summarize and reconcile the three investigations, everyone agreed to disagree.

Notes:

John J. McCloy

The New Germany and the Old Nazis (1961) by T.H. Tetens where Tetens is tough on McCloy.

The Chairman: John J. McCloy & the Making of the American Establishment (1992) by Kai Bird. This is the definitive biography of McCloy.

The Warburgs: The Twentieth-Century Odyssey of a Remarkable Jewish Family (1994) by Ron Chernow which gives a brief summary of the relationship between McCloy and the Warburg family.

Allen Dulles

The "Jewish Threat": Anti-Semitic Politics of the U.S. Army, by Joseph W. Bendersky p. 96 and p.99 which relates the blatantly anti-Semitic quotes attributed to Dulles by credible people.

Hale Boggs

Washington Through a Purple Veil: Memoirs of a Southern Woman (1994) by Lindy Boggs. Since Hale Boggs never wrote any memoirs, nor is there a biography on him, this autobiography by his wife serves very well as a source for information about Boggs. Mrs. Boggs is candid and sometimes shocking in her candor.

John Sherman Cooper

John Sherman Cooper: The Global Kentuckian (2004) by Robert Schulman. We are fortunate that there is a good biography on Cooper since few ever suspected his connection to ex-Nazis like Chancellor Ludwig Erhard and his relationship to East Germany.

Richard Russell

There is a good biography available on Russell called *Richard B. Russell, Jr., Senator From Georgia* (Fred W. Morrison Series in Southern Studies) (2002), by Gilbert C. Fite. This is a balanced and credible book and shows that Russell, like all Southern Segrationists of his day, were not always cut from the same mold when it came to following the law.

Jim Garrison

On The Trail of the Assassins (1991) by Jim Garrison.

A Farewell to Justice: Jim Garrison, JFK's Assassination, And the Case That Should Have Changed History (2007) by Joan Mellen.

Clay Shaw

A Farewell to Justice by Joan Mellen, p. 389 describing Shaw and Permindex.

Battle of the Bulge: Hitler's Ardennes Offensive, 1944-1945 By Danny Parker, p. 153 where the possible roles of both Thrasher and Shaw were suggested in the Battle of the Bulge.

Unfortunately, this extremely valuable information posted on the internet by Thomas H. Purvis has not been picked up by assassination authors. It does seem, however, to be very credible and according to resources available to the author, Purvis was a person who existed, perhaps is alive at the date of this writing and did serve in the military as he reports in the following citation. http://educationforum.ipbhost.com/index.php?/topic/4085-thomas-h-purvis/

Purvis bio: Former Captain, United States Army, Combat Veteran of Vietnam. Tours of duty with: a. 82nd Airborne Division, b. 173rd Airborne Brigade, c. 3rd Special Forces Group, d. 5th Special Forces Group, e. 6th Special Forces Group, f. Commanding Officer, Special Forces Schools Underwater Operations Committee, g. Commanding Officer, Special Forces Schools Advanced Airborne Committee, h. HALO Instructor, Halo Committee, Special Forces Schools.

Awards and qualifications: a. Meritorouse Service Medal, b. Bronze Star Medal (2nd), c. Armed Forces Expeditionary Force Medal, d. Master Parachutist rating, e. Military Free Fall Parachutist rating, f. Military Diver's badge & rating, g. Special Forces Officer qualification, h. Nuclear Weapons Employment Officer qualification, i. Special Forces Instructor Rating. Other: a. Special Forces Narrator, Strike Command Demonstration BRASS STRIKE V and BRASS STRIKE VI., b. Co-participant in film for President's Council on Physical Fitness with Apollo XIII, Astronaut James Lovell, c. USPA Class "C" Sport Parachutists & Jumpmaster ratings, d. Professional Association of Diving Instructors, Instructor Rating, e. Original applicant for Son Tay Prison Raid Team (deleted due to orders to return to VN), f. Original participant in group which set HALO/FF altitude record at Ft. Bragg, NC by exiting at 29,700 feet height.

http://educationforum.ipbhost.com/index.php?/topic/9885-clay-shaws-military-careerim-trying-to-find-outi/ – The Internet posting discusses the connections to the CIA and that JFK was aggressive about returning property looted by the Germans and others from deceased Jews in World War II.

In LBJ and the Conspiracy to Kill Kennedy: A Coalescence of Interests by Joseph P. Farrell one can find a discussion of Clay Shaw and his connection to ex-Nazi scientists, some of whom came to work for the U.S. after World War II.

The House Select Committee on Assassinations

Hit List: An In-Depth Investigation into the Mysterious Deaths of Witnesses to the JFK Assassination, by Richard Belzer published in 2013, is a top source for information about the plethora of witnesses who were apparently murdered prior to their possible testimony before the HSCA.

The Last Investigation: A Former Federal Investigator Reveals the Man Behind the Conspiracy to Kill JFK by Gaeton Fonzi, first published in 1993. This book gives inside, personal history about the frustrations encountered by the HSCA in trying to reopen the JFK case. Fonzi was a lead investigator in that effort and also a good writer as proven by the quality of this book.

Chapter 21

U.S. ANTI-COMMUNISM IN THE 1950S AND 1960S

The most important question to be answered about the Kennedy assassination is this: which individuals were at the top of the organizational chart of the assassination plot? In other words, how high up the chain of command was the leader of the plot in either the U.S. Government or in any other local or international group which might have authorized the assassination?

First, we have to examine the history of anti-Communism inside the U.S., both in the Government and elsewhere. Second, we have to look at the details of the structure of the all-powerful U.S. Congress to show what would be the motive, means and opportunity for persons in the Congress to carry out the assassination.

Most people think of Communism as it was known in the 20th century as having begun with Karl Marx. We have all probably heard the story of Marx. Marx was unemployed and with time on his hands, wrote the very famous book *Das Kapital*, or "the capital." To begin with, *Das Kapital* is basically unreadable. Try to read it sometime. It really doesn't make much sense and when I tried to read it years ago, I quickly put it back on the shelf.

But the spirit of Communism was around long before the birth of Karl Marx. To find the roots of Communism, you probably have to go back to the middle ages. It was at that time that certain religious orders began to live a communal sort of lifestyle. In fact, a few convents or monasteries in the Mediterranean area have been around almost since the time of Christ.

The ancestors of the modern corporation, for example, were both municipalities and also monastical orders.

In the U.S., there were various sects, not all celibate, who established communal societies in the United States. The most famous was New Harmony, Indiana, which was an experiment in a small scale form of communism. Likewise, Tank Town, which formed the beginning of Green Bay, Wisconsin, was a communal group of Moravians from Europe whose settlement in Green Bay was sponsored by a wealthy Norwegian idealist named Nils Otto Tank.

In fact, it is amazing how many states of the U.S. actually began with the establishment of communal types of towns and communities. In Iowa, it was the Amish and the Amana Colonies.

As mentioned, in Wisconsin it was Tank Town and also the Mormons who settled in Burlington, Wisconsin in the 1840's. And there was the Swiss Colony in New Glarus, Wisconsin, also a religious group which came there at a very early date in Wisconsin history. And there were the Mormons, who first lived in Missouri, then in Illinois, then moved out to the Salt Lake area in Utah. And finally the Amish, who were and still are spread over an amazingly large number of states in the U.S.

This is not to say that the Mormons or the Amish were Communists. However, all of the above groups were motivated to establish communities based on commitment to an ideal, usually religious, upon which their community was organized. This is to be distinguished from the later towns and cities which were based on the individual homesteader or early real estate developers who were motivated by financial interest.

It is important to look at American attitudes toward these early collectivist experiments in order to understand the attitude of people in general toward Communism when it took its modern form under Karl Marx. Based on the experience with these early groups, Communism was considered by most to be a "noble experiment." People thought it would be great if it worked, but everyone knew that none of these experimental communities lasted very long.

A more militant form of Communism had come into existence, however in certain countries. In the French Revolution for example, the Jacobins who incited the French Revolution were collectivists. However, the French Revolution form of Communism was not peaceable. It featured the use of the guillotine and the slaughter of thousands of the aristocracy. If the Communist experiment was attempted anywer except in the wilderness, violence soon followed.

The Mormons were always able to flee from angry mobs in their early history. That was because there were always empty spaces to which they could flee. But the later Communists such as in France and other places had to resort to violence and revolution to defend their programs.

So after the French Revolution, there was the Paris Commune of 1870. In Winnipeg, Canada at the same time as the Paris Commune, the radical Louis Reil led a rebellion and declared a Communist state in Manitoba, just a few hundred miles from Minneapolis, Minnesota. It took an invasion of Canadian troops to quell that situation.

And eventually this militant form of Communism led to the Russian Revolution of 1917 in which Communism was implemented on a violent and massive scale. Communism took control of the largest country on earth geographically. This government became the Soviet Union.

But the key thing is this: most people at this stage, even granting the actual reality of the Soviet Union, continued to view Communism as an idealistic experiment. People assumed that Soviet Communism would sooner or later fall apart like all the previous attempts to establish communal societies. So the attitude toward Soviet Communism on the part of many people was benign. Aside from the military threat of the Soviet Union, many felt that whether a country had a Communist government or not, was simply the business of the people of that country. Communism was viewed as just another foreign, totalitarian type of government. It was anti-democratic, but so was monarchism, fascism, oligarchies, theocracy, apartheid, and feudalism. Across the world, anti-democratic governments abounded.

Another serious problem with the treatment and reaction to Soviet Communism was that the USSR was a closed society and it was very difficult to get information about what was actually going on. News traveled slowly in those days, especially in a county as vast as the Soviet Union.

The earliest negative experience in the U.S. with actual modern Communism was with the cousin of the Communist, the anarchist. It was an anarchist who assassinated President William McKinley. There were bombings carried out by anarchists in the U.S. and in Europe. So at the time of the Russian Revolution in 1917, there was no real official policy or concern about the Communist activity happening in Russia.

This situation persisted even between the World Wars. In Spain in 1937, a popularly elected government called the Republic sank into the Spanish Civil War in which the Republic was supported only by the Communist Soviet Union. There were many Americans who went to Spain to fight in the Spanish Civil War. The fact was, however, all of these American volunteers in the Spanish Civil War fought on the same side as the Soviet Communists. These American volunteers were famously known as the Abraham Lincoln Brigade.

Although the Republicans in Spain were a democratically elected government, the western democracies refused to lend any support. The elected leaders in Spain were opposed by fascists under General Francisco Franco. Franco was aided by the German fascist dictator Adolph Hitler and the Italian dictator Benito Mussolini.

General Franco, the victor in this war, claimed that he had fought a crusade for the Catholic Church. By 1937, the Communists were opposed chiefly by the religious clergy, mainly (though not exclusively) in the Roman Catholic Church. As we will discuss in other chapters, the Eastern Orthodox religions also played a major role in opposing Communism.

In the U.S., England, Germany and other countries of Northwest Europe, there was never much fear of Communism taking over the government. That was because all of these countries were legitimate democracies. It would have been impossible for Soviet-style communists to ever win a majority of the votes in the U.S., England, France or Germany. In the U.S. in the 1930's, Communists were on the ballot, but they never won more than 100,000 votes out of the tens of millions cast.

The next major influence on the opinions of Americans toward Communism was the alliance between the U.S., Britain and the Communist government of Joseph Stalin. Because of geography, Stalin's Soviet Union was destined to be the ally of the U.S. and Britain. And Stalin made an excellent ally. In all the various conferences such as Tehran, Yalta and Potsdam, whatever Stalin promised, Stalin delivered. This stood in sharp contrast to the often perfidious behavior of Churchill.

And most importantly, the Soviet Union bore the brunt of the battle against Hitler. The Soviets lost ten percent of their population in World War II. Despite these huge losses, Stalin kept his pledge to enter the war against Japan on the side of the U.S.

So against this background of cooperation with Stalin and a benign view of Communism held by most Americans, enters Senator Joseph McCarthy.

The U.S. Congress had a history of investigating Communism. There was a committee of the House of Representatives called the Dies Committee. It operated from 1938 to 1944. The fact was that the Dies Committee and several earlier versions of the Dies Committee were intended to investigate not only Communism, but also fascism and anarchism and even as some suggested, the KKK.

When Senator Joseph McCarthy began his crusade against Communism, the prior enemies of democracy such as fascism and anarchism had been defeated and almost totally eradicated. So McCarthy had a wide-open field and was able to focus his efforts exclusively on Communism.

For the reader of this book, the most important thing to know is this: Anti-Communism in the U.S. was almost entirely the work of special interests. If you look at the major figures involved in the anti-Communist crusade of the late 1940's and later, you will find representatives of groups which suffered particular damage due to Communism in foreign countries.

When the Communists took over in China under Mao Tse-tung, there were people in the U.S. who backed Chiang Kai-shek. Unknown to most people, Chiang Kai-shek was a Methodist. Can you imagine how history would have been different if China were run by a Methodist regime? There were many Americans who had personal knowledge of China due to their work as missionaries there. The actual John Birch for whom the John Birch Society was named, was a Protestant missionary (and also part of the U.S. Military there) prior to the takeover of the Communists.

One can easily divide the rabid anti-Communists of the 40s and 50s between 1) the China Lobby (who lost out to Mao), 2) the Catholic Church (which was threatened by Communism in southern Europe, Latin America and Vietnam), 3) the White Russians and their eastern European and Tsarist friends (who were ousted by the Soviet Bolsheviks) and 4) the thousands of anti-Castro Cubans who had been dispossessed by Castro. It is no accident that the White Russians and the anti-Castro

Cubans have most frequently been accused of complicity in the Kennedy assassination by the majority of authors. The other two were different. The China Lobby had become defunct by 1963 because China was obviously lost to the Communists without any hope of redemption. The final group, the Catholic Church has never explicitly been accused by any authors on the assassination. That apparently is because its role was limited to a background one, with the only actual Catholic activist conspirators being Senator Thomas J. Dodd, and possibly William F. Buckley and his close friend E. Howard Hunt of the CIA.

By far the most politically powerful group of those I have mentioned was the Catholic Church. And the person generally considered to be the most prominent Catholic in the U.S. was Ambassador Joseph P. Kennedy.

There is no separating Senator Joseph McCarthy and the Kennedy patriarch,. Kennedy entertained McCarthy at the Kennedy compound on Cape Cod. McCarthy dated Kennedy's daughters. Joseph P. Kennedy arranged for Robert F. Kennedy to be hired as assistant counsel on McCarthy's committee. It has been claimed by some historians that Robert F. Kennedy working for McCarthy's committee was a temporary fluke. It is claimed that RFK quickly learned how bad McCarthy was.

The truth is entirely different. Although RFK resigned from McCarthy's committee after six months, he was quickly hired back as counsel to the minority Democrats. RFK was only absent from McCarthy's committee for a few months during the period of 1952 to 1959. The fact that RFK was the counsel for the *minority Democrats* isn't all that significant. As we shall see, McCarthy's committee (as well as the related Senate Internal Security Subcommittee) was stacked with right-wing rabid anti-Communist Democrats.

Near the time of McCarthy's death, McCarthy's committee morphed into the McClellan committee. The McClellan committee focused on corruption in labor unions. What most people don't know is that the rabid anti-Communists on the McCarthy-McClellan Committee were mostly interested in investigating Communists in labor unions.

So as McCarthy's anti-Communist slander campaigns began and raged on, the Kennedy family was involved up to their ears in the entire situation. And it is a straight line, repeat, *a straight line* from McCarthyism to the JFK assassination.

Chapter 22

JFK and the Rogue Committees of Congress

To understand the JFK assassination, one must have a working understanding of the way committees of Congress operate. As mentioned before, the committee system of Congress was operating as if *on steroids* from 1946 until 1964.

For almost as long as there has been a Congress, there have been committees of Congress. When the first Congress came into session, Committees were used to study and recommend legislation. At first there were *ad hoc* committees. These were the most functional of the various types of committees in carrying out the overall program of the Congress as a whole.

These ad hoc committees avoided the problem of the committees of Congress becoming miniature legislatures unto themselves. This situation soon changed. Because of the need of particular expertise in legislating, standing committees soon became necessary.

Well before the 1950's, there had been a succession of Congressional Committees investigating Communism and other unpopular political causes.

In 1918-19, there was the Overman Committee which was a subcommittee of the Senate Judiciary Committee. It started by investigating possible sedition by German sympathizers in World War I, and then moved to investigating Communist elements in the U.S. The activities of this committee contributed to a very early scare surrounding Communism in 1919.

In 1930, the Fish Committee was expressly devoted to investigating Communists and Communist groups in the U.S. In this cause, the Committee investigated the ACLU and Communist presidential candidate William Z. Foster.

Next came the McCormack-Dickstein Committee, which lasted from 1934 to 1937. This was a House Committee which began by focusing on foreign propaganda. They investigated a famous rumored plot to overthrow the U.S. Government by a fascist cabal.

Though never completely substantiated, according to a book by Allen Weinstein et. al. called *The Haunted Wood*, Congressman Samuel Dickstein was receiving $1250 per month from the Soviet NKVD (spy agency) which wanted more information about fascist and anti-Communist groups from the Committee.

After this came the Dies Committee which operated from 1938 to 1944. The Dies [rhymes with lice] Committee was chaired by conservative Texas Congressman Martin Dies. Its mission was to investigate disloyalty and subversive activities of citizens and government employees, either Communist or fascist. One party investigated by the Dies Committee was the Soviet inspired American Youth Congress, an affiliate of the Commintern from Russia. The Dies Committee was noteworthy for two facts. First, it pioneered the practice of, basically, libeling and slandering people to intimidate and suppress individuals or opinions which they considered subversive. Second, this committee began to collect huge amounts of information on many thousands of people. It filled 600 file cabinets with cards. These cards were used to investigate people who applied for employment or for other purposes.

HUAC, the House Committee on Un-American Activities replaced the Dies Committee from 1938 to 1975. It is HUAC with which most Americans are familiar.

It was before the HUAC committee that freshman Congressman Richard M. Nixon made his name by attacking State Department official Alger Hiss for being a Communist. Hiss had been one of FDR's top advisors at the conference with Stalin at Yalta, where many accused FDR of handing over Eastern Europe to the Soviets. Because of this, Hiss was forbidden to ever work again for the State Department.

Hiss was also prosecuted and found guilty of perjury. The Hiss case was still heavily used by conservatives as of 1963 when they were emphasizing the threat of Communism. We will see the Hiss case pop up again just before the JFK assassination in the case of Otto Otepka. There was a rumored threat making the rounds in Washington during the Kennedy Administration that there would be an attempt to actually bring Alger Hiss back to the State Department. This threat may have pushed some conservatives over the edge regarding their reaction to the JFK assassination and their attitude about the cover-up.

One of the big HUAC controversies was with regard to Jack Ruby. In an FBI document dated November 24, 1947, it was disclosed that Jack Ruby was working around that time as an informant for Congressman Nixon. Because of this relationship, Nixon requested that Ruby not be required to testify before HUAC. History doesn't record the exact nature of Ruby's activities on behalf of Nixon. But this connection seems to disprove the argument that Ruby was just a sentimental strip-club owner who wore his heart on his sleeve, etc.

In analyzing the JFK assassination one of the most important question in the judgment of your writer is why all the members of Congress remained silent about the JFK assassination. It wasn't until the House formed the House Select Committee on Assassinations in 1977 that Congress openly showed any interest as to who killed Kennedy. Millions of Americans probably wondered why Congress was indifferent, even though they, as elected officials would not be immune to assassination. This silence and cover-up seems potentially suicidal on the part of any elected official who might have enemies, which every member of the Congress would have.

To address this question of Congressional silence, the reader should try to understand the hostility between Congress and the Executive in the period from 1945 to 1963.

Starting in 1945, their was a push to limit the powers of the presidents. And one of the members of Congress who worked the hardest to expand the powers of Congressional Committees was Congressman Everett Dirksen of Illinois. Everett Dirksen was a member of the Senate Internal Security Subcommittee (SISS) on the very day of the JFK assassination. And we will show that SISS had complicity in the JFK assassination, or at the very least, was active in the cover-up – even before the fact.

According to Neil MacNeil, in *Dirksen: Portrait of a Public Man*, Dirksen, in 1943 wanted to expand the powers of Congressional Committees. He worked to establish a Committee on Congressional Reorganization. His motive was to curtail the inroads made by the Presidency against the powers of Congress. Again, citing MacNeill at page 72, Dirksen wanted Congressional Committees to have on staff those who had worked in the various departments. The idea was that the Congressional staff person would be something of an informant to the Congress, who would betray bureaucratic secrets or motives of the leadership of their former executive department.

One could argue, of course, that departments of the executive branch should not have anything to hide from the Congress in the first place. But as we shall see in later chapters, especially in the case of Otto Otepka of the State Department, the Congressional Committees used these "informants" to try and set the priorities and agenda of the executive departments whenever they disagreed with that department. Senator Joe McCarthy, to cite an extreme example, openly invited each and every employee in the executive branch who had differences with their bosses to contact him, and he would step in.

Dirksen biographer MacNeil, at p. 116, stated "within himself he harbored an inherent animosity toward the executive branch of government as such ... he had [felt] like many Senators, that somehow their election by the people gave them an automatic superiority to all members of the executive branch, save only the President, who was elected too."

It is difficult to separate the rise of the Congressional Committees and the global spread of Communism. In 1946, not only did the Congress grant its committees the ability to hire professional staff, but the Legislative Reorganization Act of 1946 also stated that the records of the committees became the property of the committee so they could more easily hide their activities from the public.

It seems apparent today, that the entire gearing up of Congressional Committees was because of the perceived threat of Communism. But in 1946 and 1947, two other important things took place. One was the creation of the CIA in 1947. The other was the merger of the Secretaries of War and the Navy into one cabinet position, Secretary of Defense. We will see over the next pages how all three of these decisions led inexorably toward the assassination of President Kennedy.

What most people never consider is that the Warren Commission was nothing more or less than the fourth Congressional Committee in the line of SISS, HUAC and Joe McCarthy's Permanent Subcommittee on Investigations or PSI.

In their book *Committees in Congress*, by Christopher J. Deering and Steven S. Smith, published by *Congressional Quarterly*, the authors deal with two very interesting facts. First, at page 26 they list seven different eras or periods in the history of Congressional committees, beginning in 1789. The fourth such period is called, according to the authors, the period of "Committee Government." This period lasted from 1947 to 1965 and followed the enactment of the Legislative Reorganization Act of 1946.

For our purposes there are two noteworthy items which appear in this 1946 Act. First, committees were for the first time allowed to hire professional staff. They were allowed 4 such staff. Second it is specified that the records of each committee are the property of the Congress and of the committee. This is contrary to the normal policy of, for instance, state government, where all public records are generally available to the public and the press, with only specific exceptions. Deering and Smith also state that this 1946 Act "consolidated Congress' oversight powers within the respective committees."

Why do political science scholars label this period "Committee Government?" It is apparently because they feel Congressional Committees of that era were in charge of the Government. One thing is certain. The power of Congressional Committees has never been anywhere near what it was in this 18-year period.

Going further in the analysis of Deering and Smith, the general principle is that structure of committees and their procedures is determined by the political environment in the U.S. as it existed at the time. For instance, when Liberal Democrats where predominant in the 1970's, the Democratic Party as an entity had much more influence with lawmaking than the heretofore powerful committee chairmen in Congress.

Conversely, when Republican Speaker Newt Gingrich had his day in the mid-1990's, major adjustments and reforms were put in place to please the more conservative mood of the electorate, especially with regard to budgeting and Federal deficit spending. Deficits were anathema to the Republicans of that decade.

It is very tempting to put a puzzle in place surrounding the ascendancy of the elderly Southern "mossback" committee chairman of that 18-year period. With the U.S. squaring off against the Soviet Union in the Cold War, "invulnerable" Southern conservative chairmen were handed the keys to the government because our country felt it needed hatchet men to fight off Communism.

According to this theory, true fighters of Communism simply would not be found among ordinary elected officials. Leaders like Adlai Stevenson and Eleanor Roosevelt just couldn't be allowed to have much power if the Soviets were to be contained or hopefully defeated.

The reader will see, as we move forward, that the employment of unelected professional staff for the first time in the Congressional committees had a direct effect on the power of the "safe" Southern committee chairmen such as Richard Russell of Georgia and James O. Eastland of Mississippi. In fact, one could go as far as to say that the almost unlimited access men like Joe McCarthy had to professional staff and investigators was a deliberate purpose of the 1946 Legislative Reorganization Act. It made possible both the Joe McCarthy and the House Un-American Activities committees, just to name two.

But the most important fact revealed in the book by Deering and Smith, is that various types of Congressional committees (including many out-of-the-ordinary committees) are still considered by political scientists as being Congressional committees. These committee types include ad hoc committees, congressional subcommittees, conference committees, task forces, joint committees, select committees, special committees, summit committees and commissions.

Summit committees are defined as including members from the executive branch. Commissions, an example of which was the Warren Commission, are defined as more formal bodies created by statute or executive order. Unlike other committees, commissions can include persons from outside the government, or as in the case of the Warren Commission, a member of the judiciary. Implicitly, to qualify as a committee of Congress, Senators and Congressmen would still be in the majority which they were, of course, in the Warren Commission.

The majority of SISS in 1963 consisted of Thomas Dodd (D. CT), James Eastland (D. MS), Olin Johnson (D. SC), Sam Ervin (D. NC), John McClellan (D. AR) Everett Dirksen (R. IL), and Roman Hruska (R. NE). All seven of those men were conservatives. There was a majority of five from the South.

There was not one Liberal Democrat. There were only two moderates, both Republicans: Kenneth Keating (R. NY) and Hugh Scott (R. PA). The above was true even though, according to Gilbert C. Fite, the biographer of Richard Russell, there had been a tidal wave of liberal Democratic Senators that swept into office in the 86th Congress in 1958. In 1958 when Thomas Dodd was first elected to the Senate, the Democrats were blessed with a 65-35 majority in the Senate. Yet there were only eleven former Confederate states, which would provide only 22 Senators, not all of whom were conservative Democrats. In these states there were a few southern liberals like Ralph Yarbrough of Texas, a Democrat and William Fulbright of Arkansas. And even many Republicans were considered liberal back at that time.

So what was the situation with SISS and the Warren Commission, regarding their support in Congress as a whole? To ask this in another way, what was the size of the right-wing conservative element in the Congress?

For comparison, let's use a similar example of a comparable issue. This would be the vote by conservatives against the Nuclear Test Ban Treaty. The sentiment towards this treaty in some ways tracked the attitudes which SISS held towards JFK. And looking back to the specific time in question, some considered the Test Ban Treaty to be a litmus test on a politician's tolerance toward Communism and the Soviet Union. Some writers also imply that the issue of the Nuclear Test Ban Treaty precipitated the fatal dislike of some in the Congress for JFK.

The vote against the treaty featured only 19 negative votes. Even the arch anti-Communist Senator Thomas J. Dodd switched sides and voted in favor. The last die-hard opponents of the Treaty included right-wing ideologues like Barry Goldwater and Strom Thurmond. So why was there so much support for SISS and the Warren Commission with a mostly Liberal Congress? In the opinion of this author, it was because the ultra-right faction of the Congress was deliberately empowered to operate as the hatchet-men in their opposition to and hopefully destruction of the Red Menace. Their mission, no matter how distasteful, was accepted as a necessary evil by the liberals of the day.

Endnote:

On the subject of the flood of liberals resulting from the elections of 1958, see *Richard B. Russell, Jr. Senator From Georgia* (Fred W. Morrison Series in Southern Studies) (2002) by Gilbert C. Fite.

Chapter 23

SENATOR PAT MCCARRAN AND THE SENATE INTERNAL SECURITY SUBCOMMITTEE

SENATOR PAT MCCARRAN BEGINS THE SISS COMMITTEE

Despite being somewhat obscure, this committee nevertheless played a crucial role in the assassination of the President.

In this chapter, we will discuss the numerous issues and cases which involved this committee in the years before and including 1963.

Most people in middle age or older have heard of Senator Joe McCarthy. Few have heard of Senator Pat McCarran. Those who have studied McCarthyism, however, recognize that Senator Pat McCarran was almost the equal of Joe McCarthy in fomenting the Red Scare atmosphere of the late 1940's and early 1950's.

McCarran was a Senator from Nevada, first elected to the Senate in 1932. McCarran grew up on a ranch in that state. His parents were immigrants from Ireland. McCarran's father was an Irish nationalist, displaying the flag of Sinn Fein at his ranch. Sinn Fein was the infamous Irish terrorist organization which worked for Irish independence during that period.

McCarran was 30 years older than Senator Joe McCarthy, but the similarities between the two were striking. Both men went through their early school years four grades behind their classmates. McCarran graduated from high school at age 21. Both men were forced by circumstances to spend their adolescence raising livestock by themselves. McCarthy raised chickens, McCarran raised sheep.

Adolescence is the time when a young person builds connections to his peer group. Almost everyone went through this experience in their early teens. McCarthy and McCarran were deprived of a normal adolescence. Being four years older than their classmates would likely cause them some degree of ostracism. This could well explain why both men became senators who totally disregarded the peer pressure of the Senate. Both McCarthy and McCarran seemed to enjoy being the odd man out.

Senator Pat McCarran was a Democrat, but he sided with conservative Republicans on most issues, particularly in foreign policy. Although McCarran grew up on a ranch far from any city, he was a devout Catholic. It is not clear how often he was even able to attend church. Nevertheless, his parents trained him well when it came to supporting his Catholic religion.

McCarran had five children. Two of them were nuns. It was undoubtedly true that McCarran's opinions on foreign policy were dictated by the hierarchy of his church.

McCarran was generally supportive of worker's rights. Most people would not identify Nevada as a place where worker's issues and unions would be particularly important. It was, however, just the opposite. The mining industry in Nevada was the largest employer and labor strife was rampant. McCarran was a defense lawyer and largely supportive of the underdog. He was not a particularly strong critic of Roosevelt's New Deal. He had, however, one issue in his mind which dominated all others. That issue was his rabid opposition to Communism.

Students of the anti-Communist movement of the 1940's and 1950's (usually called McCarthyism) realize that anti-Communism was led by people who had a special stake in the international battle against Communism.

First there was the China Lobby. This was a group who had a special interest in China. The most ardent proponent of the China Lobby was Arthur Kohlberg. He at one time had a business that imported Chinese textiles, which was threatened by the Chinese Communists. Others in the China Lobby were sympathetic to Protestant missionaries who were very active in Nationalist China.

In Europe, however, it was a different story. In 1936, the Spanish Civil War broke out. Although that war pitted a democratically elected government against the anti-democratic fascist Francisco Franco, President Roosevelt failed to support democracy in Spain out of fear of the political power of the Catholic Church in the U.S.

After the Soviet occupation of Eastern Europe, Communism and Catholicism squared off in a fierce confrontation. The Soviet policy was to suppress Christianity in any form. Even in countries outside the iron curtain such as Italy and Spain, Communism was strong. Many worried that Communists would be elected in Italy following the war.

It was against this background that Pat McCarran (along with Joe McCarthy) began their crusade against Communism. Although they both claimed that their mission was to eliminate Communists from employment in the U.S. Government, their real target was the U.S. State Department. The wanted to dictate U.S. foreign policy as it related to Communism.

There were obvious situations where U.S.interests coincided with the interests of Communists abroad. The most important was the U.S. alliance with the Soviet Union of Joseph Stalin for the purpose of defeating Hitler. It is to the everlasting credit of Franklin Roosevelt that he recognized Fascism as the greatest danger to American freedom. There was little chance that the U.S. would ever go Communist. The power and influence of Fascism in the U.S. was another story.

While Joe McCarthy used a vicious form of libel and slander against his perceived enemies, Pat McCarran used an entirely different strategy. McCarthy and McCarran actually did not get along very well as personalities and had a somewhat conflictive relationship as Senators. McCarran, for his part, was able (because of seniority) to gain the chairmanship of the powerful Senate Judiciary Committee.

Forty percent of bills in Congress went through the Senate Judiciary Committee. It was responsible for processing appointments of all Federal judges including the Supreme Court.

McCarran used two vehicles to reach his anti-Communist goals. One was the Internal Security Act of 1950, usually called the McCarran Act. The other was the Senate Internal Security Subcommittee which was a subcommittee of the parent Senate Judiciary Committee.

The Senate Internal Security Subcommittee was created on December 21, 1950 by a Senate resolution. Its purpose was to study and investigate 1) the administration, operation and enforcement of the Internal Security Act of 1950, 2) to study and investigate the extent, nature and effects of subversive activities in the United States. This included not only espionage and sabotage. It also included infiltration into the government of persons under the domination of the organization controlling the world Communist movement. Beyond that, it also covered any movement which sought to overthrow the Government of the United States by force or violence. This subcommittee was given the power to subpoena witnesses and documents.

The chairmen of the Senate Internal Security Subcommittee (SISS), were Patrick McCarran (D, Nevada 1950-1053), William Jenner (R, Indiana 1953-1955) and James O. Eastland (D, Mississippi 1956-1977). For some as yet unknown reason, Eastland appointed Senator Thomas J. Dodd as acting chairman and Dodd ran the Committee during the Kennedy Administration.

The initial composition of SISS was extremely significant. Pat McCarran, as Chairman of the Senate Judiciary Committee, appointed himself as the first chairman. He then picked the three most conservative Democrats James O. Eastland (D. MS), Herbert O'Connor (D. MD) and Willis Smith (D. NC). For the Republicans there was Homer Ferguson (R. MI), William Jenner (R. IN), and Arthur Watkins (R. UT).

The overview of the power of Committees of Congress in the period 1947-1965 has been presented in the chapter which dealt with the Warren Commission. That prior explanation of committees in general also precisely applies to the establishment of SISS.

One important fact should be mentioned, however. After the takeover of the Judiciary Committee by the Republicans because of the election of

1952 and then the death of Pat McCarran in 1954, James O. Eastland became the Chairman of the Senate Judiciary Committee. This gave him the power to appoint the members of SISS. Eastland was arguably the most conservative member of the entire Senate, with the possible exception of Sen. Strom Thurmond of South Carolina.

In his memoir *True Compass*, Sen. Edward Kennedy described how Eastland (in 1963) personally appointed him to the Judiciary Committee and to all of the other committees on which he, Kennedy, served. To find out his committee assignments, Kennedy had to make a pilgrimage to the office of Senator James O. Eastland.

There was, however a personal-preference factor to Senate appointments. Senators had to have some interest in serving on the committee to which they were appointed and so there was some degree of self-selection. Kennedy wrote that Eastland happened to appoint him to exactly the committees which he already desired.

The Internal Security Act of 1950 established the Subversive Activities Control Board to investigate a limited, though important, number of subjects. One was subversive activities and another was the promotion of the idea of a totalitarian dictatorship in the U.S. In theory, this included a dictatorship of either a Fascist or Communist nature. However, the aim was clearly at the Communist threat. Persons engaged in these activities could be detained and jailed if engaged in espionage or sabotage. An example of the tenor of this Act, made picketing a Federal Courthouse a felony if intended to influence jurors or trials.

SISS was very much like both the House Un-American Activities Committee (HUAC) and the Permanent Subcommittee on Investigations (PSI), usually known as the McCarthy Committee. One can see by the appointment of these multiple redundant committees that anti-Communism was "big business" in the Congress at that time.

Earlier, the Legislative Reorganization Act of 1946 had substantially strengthened the power of Congressonal committees. Prior to this Act, Congressional Committees had only limited clerical staff and no professional staff or experts.

Under the Act, the Committee was allowed four professional staff members and six clerical staff members. Because of the new allocation of professional staff, SISS was able to hire multiple experts as attorneys, researchers and investigators.

From the very beginning of SISS, attorney Jay Sourwine served as the counsel for SISS. Sourwine was from Nevada and was a protégé of Senator Pat McCarran. Research director Ben Mandel also began working for SISS from its inception. Not only did SISS have its own professional staff, it had its own office. And for all practical purposes, a subcommittee like

SISS was entirely the creature of the Chairman of the parent Judiciary Committee. This was a setup for potential disaster.

SISS could operate entirely in secret if McCarren so chose. It could investigate anything without limitation. It could call anyone as a witness and swear them in under oath. And most of its minutes and records were not available to the public, and have still never been, after more than 50 years at the time of this writing!

There was perhaps an even more extreme practice. The necessary quorum for a committee meeting was one. Thus McCarran or anyone designated chairman could travel around the country by himself operating as a one-man SISS committee (which happened often).

Under the Legislative Reform act of 1946, a House member was limited to one committee (not necessarily one subcommittee) and a Senator was limited to two committees, with certain exceptions for both bodies. An interesting quote found in the casebook *Cases and Materials on Legislation, 4th Edition 1969* by Nutting, Elliot and Dickerson at p. 78 is as follows:

> Abuse of power by the invisible power-wielders … is a natural hazard of the staff system. There are at least 250 separate committees, subcommittees, special committees, select committees and joint committees in Congress today [1963]. The total fluctuates, usually upward, as new subcommittees are named. Each of these panels has a chairman and each chairman has a staff which is wholly responsible to him-except for a scattering of staff men named by the minority party. The staff of the Judiciary Committee and its 14 subcommittees in the Senate, for example, numbers about 180-patent experts; immigration experts; internal-security experts; experts on "charters, holidays and celebrations," on juvenile delinquency, on refugees and what-have-you.

It is interesting that this was written in 1963. This passage was quoted from an article by Roland Evans, Jr. in the *Saturday Evening Post*, June 8, 1963 titled "The Invisible Men Who Run Congress." The *Saturday Evening Post* was the journal of author William J. Gill who will be discussed in depth in a later chapter. This article was written 6 months before the JFK assassination. Note that the article happened to mention the Senate Judiciary Committee. And it highlights the topic of juvenile delinquency. As we shall see, the Subcommittee on Juvenile Delinquency was chaired at that very time by Senator Thomas J. Dodd who is a major focus of our research and of this book.

What kind of investigations did SISS engage in? They could be listed in part (as examples) as follows:

1.) The loss of China to the Communists.

2.) The Institute of Pacific Relations.

3.) Suspected Soviet activity in the United States.

4.) Infiltration of the Federal Government, especially the State Department.

5.) Immigration.

6.) The United Nations and Americans employed by the U.N.

7.) Youth organizations.

8.) Television, radio and the entertainment industry.

9.) The defense industry.

10.) Labor unions.

11.) Schools, Colleges and Universities.

In the 1960's the scope was expanded to include:

1.) Civil rights and racial issues.

2.) Campus disorders.

3.) Drug trafficking.

The current estimate of the amount of microfilm in the U.S. Government or Senate Archives which captures the records of SISS is 547 feet. That statistic dwarfs that of, for instance, the Subcommittee on Patents and Trademarks. The latter committee has 34 feet of film over a similar period. To your author, it is a horrible commentary on our system of government if a secret committee could be engaged in this many activities, yet virtually no one in the U.S. had ever heard of them.

After the fall of Senator McCarthy and his Personal Subcommittee on Investigations, SISS was working almost single-handedly in the arena of rabid anti-Communism in the Senate. We can look at some of the covert activities that SISS began in this period.

The most exteme claim against SISS is probably the following quote from the book *Where Rebels Roost* by Susan Klopfer at p. 205. She writes:

> Over the years, rumors have raged about the ability of SISS to form concentration camps for "emergency" situations ... and having its own SISS secret commandos who at the time made raids on alleged Communist organizations fully equipped with silenced machine guns and grenades. [Wikipedia]

Following the death of McCarran and the downfall of Joe McCarthy which began in March, 1954, the committee activity in the Senate relating to the extreme anti-Communist cause became relatively dormant. The work of the House Un-American Affairs Committee (HUAC) continued. HUAC had become well known in the 1940's in the heyday of Richard Nixon and his "pumpkin papers" revelations. But by the mid-1950's, HUAC had not made any new or sensational headlines. It is interesting to note that HUAC was well known and is well known to this day. But by contrast, the Senate Internal Security Subcommittee was and has always been basically invisible to students of U.S. history.

Another false legend is that RFK turned the committee toward investigating organized crime instead of Communists. Actually, the McCarthy Committee was merged with the Labor Committee so that both RFK and JFK were working together on what then became known as the McClellan Committee, named after Chairman John L. McClellan (D. AR).

The reason for the merger was that the Republicans were told the committee would investigate Communists in the Labor movement, of which there were many. What followed was what some would call a "Kennedy double-cross." After a cursory probe of Walter Reuther and the CIO (which was limited to financial issues), RFK took the investigation off-track to investigate Jimmy Hoffa. And that was because Hoffa was considered to be a Republican labor leader.

Senator Joseph McCarthy was and continued to be a close personal friend of RFK right up to McCarthy's death in 1957. And the rest of the story is that the Kennedy brothers and their father all agreed that both open and clandestine Congressional investigations were a perfectly good way to run the U.S. Government and that Congressional investigations were "where the action is."

With the takeover of Cuba by Castro and the activity of the Pathet Lao Communists in Laos and nearby Vietnam, the menace of Communism flared up anew. These events along with the liberal trend of the 1958 Congressional elections, caused McCarthy-type anti-Communist hysteria to re-emerge in the Senate. This new higher priority of the fight against Communism began during the years from 1959 to 1963 and continued at a higher level after that. This period came at the end of the Eisenhower administration. It carried over into the beginning of the administration of JFK.

The role of "special interests" in the fight against Communism should never be overlooked. In Vietnam, there were the French colonialists. In Cuba, there were any number of special interests ranging from the Mafia, to millionaire American property owners to the Catholic Church itself. In both Vietnam and Cuba, Communism threatened entrenched Catholic and colonial interests. Therefore, this led to the involvement of influential Catholics in the Senate such as Thomas Dodd and, indirectly, other influential Catholic party leaders such as Joseph P. Kennedy. This type of liberal politician was especially powerful in the Democratic northeast where they often controlled powerful Democratic party machines and city governments.

Although President Dwight Eisenhower had only just begun to plan covert operations to remove Castro, it was John F. Kennedy who became President at the actual time when Castro made his sharp turn to the left and towards Communism. Following this worrisome and potentially dangerous takeover of Cuba by Fidel Castro, SISS also emerged with an assortment of covert and other activities aimed at destroying the Communist regime of the Castro brothers.

This menu of covert activites would eventually include the bizarre plan to weaponize cancer as described by authors Judyth Vary Baker and Ed Haslem. Judyth Vary Baker, for those who don't know, was the girlfriend of Lee Harvey Oswald during the months prior to the assassination.

The main actors in the weaponized cancer plan were activists like the very famous Dr. Alton Ochsner of New Orleans. Dr. Ochsner had a relationship with SISS, at least in the week after the JFK assassination when Oswald was being framed. But in addition to the cancer plan, there were other such covert operations. Some of these activities came close to the type of plans that were supervised by Robert Kennedy. These Robert Kennedy plans had the code name Mongoose.

We should at this point explain several new and important facts. James O. Eastland of Mississippi, a Democratic arch-segregationist and conservate had (as of 1962) 12 years' experience as a member and then chairman of SISS. His Republican ally, Everett Dirksen, had also been with him on the committee since the beginning of SISS. Jay Sourwine, chief counsel of SISS and Ben Mandel, research director, had also been the staff people in charge of SISS since its beginning.

Senator Thomas Dodd had been elected to the Senate in 1958 and by 1960 was placed in charge of SISS by James Eastland. Eastland was the official chairman, but he allowed Assistant Chairman Dodd to run SISS. This arrangement was either because of limitations due to seniority rules or limits on the number of committee chairmanships allowed to each Senator. Looking at the bigger picture, the Eastland-Dodd arrangement reflected the behind-the-scenes alliance between Southern conservatives, Republicans and the few militant Democratic Catholic anti-Communists from the Northeast who were serving in the Senate at the time.

The list of militant Catholic Democratic Senators and staff included Joe McCarthy, Pat McCarran, Robert and John F. Kennedy. Joseph P. Kennedy had been active behind the scenes. Now the list included Senator Thomas Dodd.

Picking up on the activities of SISS when JFK became president, we can find revealing information about this updated role of SISS at a well known website which is referred to in the notes.

To begin this story, we have to introduce a man named Nathaniel Weyl. Weyl was a mysterious individual who we know testified before SISS as early as February 19, 1952. In that testimony, he said he had been a member of the same Communist "cell" as Alger Hiss.

The testimony of Nathanial Weyl was "the only outside support [Whittaker] Chambers' testimony [denouncing Hiss] ever received." By the time he testified in 1952, Weyl, a freelance writer, had written several books about treason and espionage. Also at this time in 1952, Hiss was in jail and public support was building for a new Hiss trial. Even If there were a new trial for Alger Hiss, because the new trial could vindicate Hiss, this would be a blow to the political career of then Vice President Richard Nixon. By this time, Weyl had become a strong anti-Communist.

Following the premature deaths of both Sen. McCarthy and Sen. McCarran, the issue of rabid anti-Communism basically went on the back burner in the Senate. McCarthy's committee, the Permanent Subcommittee on Investigations was converted, as we have explained earlier, into the McClellan Committee under the leadership of chief counsel Robert Kennedy.

Looking at the relationship of SISS and the new administration of JFK, possibly the most important sutiuation was the war for control of the State Department which involved SISS and Otto Otepka. However, SISS and another Dodd committee, (the Senate Committee on Juvenile Delinquency), were both involved in a labyrinth of plots, investigations, covert operations and other activities during the brief administration of JFK. We can pick up, for illustration, another story involving JFK and SISS during 1962. This involved another scenario which is well known to researchers in the field of the JFK assassination. That is, the Bayo-Pauley raid on Cuba.

THE BAYO-PAULEY RAID

The reader should be reminded of our premise that anti-Communist activities were generally promoted *most insistently* by people or "special interests" who had a particular dog in the furious fight against Communism.

The Cuban issue escalated following the Bay of Pigs in 1961 and the Cuban Missile Crisis in 1962. In late 1962 and into early 1963, JFK was working to open up a special line of communication with Castro. As always, JFK was interested in defusing explosive confrontations such as the hideously dangerous Missile Crisis where the possible destruction of the *earth itself* hung in the balance.

Involved in this complicated plan were Nathaniel Weyl, (who was at that time a right-wing anti-Communist writer), John Martino (an "ex"

CIA operative) and William Pawley, (a right-wing millionaire). This new, secret line of communication was an attempt by JFK to bypass the CIA in order to get unfiltered information about Castro and Cuba.

As part of the cast of characters involved in the anti-Communist crusade were expatriate Cuban exiles along with a few soldiers of fortune, mercenaries who had traded their para-military training and skills for fame and fortune.

Like JFK, some anti-Castro leaders did not trust the CIA either. These names would include millionaire Pawley, Agent Martino and mercenary Gerry Patrick Hemming. William Pawley was a very wealth man who had owned the street railway in Havana before Castro took over. Following the pattern of the China Lobby, Pawley was one of those people who had lost property to Communists and wanted to get it back should Castro be either assassinated or otherwise deposed. The anti-Castroite Cubans and mercenaries such as Hemming were setting up meetings to solicit money from Florida conservative leaders to back a mission against Castro.

Although there were numerous missions against Castro on the drawing board during that time, this particular one was designed to smuggle two Soviet Army colonels out of Cuba. Supposedly, these Russians knew something about nuclear missiles still being kept by the Soviets in Cuba. If true, this would be a large black eye for JFK. In reality, this story of the Soviet Colonels was probably made up for the purpose of getting money from wealthy anti-Castroites like William Pawley.

Gerry Patrick Hemming made a trip, well known to JFK researchers, to visit California in 1963. He was accompanied by his friend and fellow mercenary Loren Hall. They picked up an expensive rifle in California and then traveled to Dallas where they picked up a trailer full of military-style weapons. In Dallas, this weapons trailer was, for a time, parked in the driveway of the assistant to oilman H.L. Hunt, another wealthy anti-Castroite (and the richest man in the world at the time). The reader should be alert to any issues of trafficking in weapons because of the presence of the ATF, in Dallas in particular. As we will see, the ATF figures into theories about the plot to murder JFK.

From Dallas, Hemming and Hall traveled to southern Florida where a famous raid would be launched known to historians as the Bayo-Pawley raid. It was Hemming's right-hand man Howard Davis who had gotten word to Kennedy about the Russian colonels through a New York financier by the name of Theodore Racoosin.

As a result of a meeting with various anti-Castroites, powerful Senator James O. Eastland, chairman of the Senate Judiciary Committee and the Senate Internal Security Subcommittee (SISS) became involved in the situation. Eastland urged Pawley to help Martino arrange the secret mission. It was code-named Operation Red Cross.

Life magazine's Dick Billings accompanied several men on the Bayo-Pawley mission. These included Pawley, Martino, William "Rip" Robertson, and a number of Cuban exile guerrillas, led by Cuban operative Eddie Bayo. (Billings would soon be stationed at *Life's* temporary bureau at the Adolphus Hotel in Dallas covering the Kennedy assassination. There he would aid Richard B. Stolley and C.D. Jackson of *Life* in the negotiations to buy the Zapruder film.

One of the raiders, "Rip" Robertson, was a former World War II Marine frogman from Texas. Robertson had helped the CIA overthrow Guatemalan Dictator Jacobo Arbenz for the benefit of United Fruit Company. He was also the commander of the boat named "Barbara J" used in the Bay of Pigs landing and was one of the first two men ashore.

Hemming and his fellow mercenary Loren Hall dropped off the weapons from Dallas, which were still in the above-described trailer, to a location on the beach in Florida from which the Bayo-Pawley raid was launched. Hemming then traveled to Washington to meet with either James Eastland personally, or Eastland and SISS.

This case clearly illustrates how personally involved Eastland and the SISS were in the covert operations against Castro. The next important information about the secretive activities of SISS and its relationship to the murder of JFK began to surface later in 1963 immediately after the JFK assassination.

Lee Harvey Oswald famously tried to start a chapter of the Fair Play for Cuba Committee (FPCC) in New Orleans in the summer of 1963. SISS had investigated the FPCC on December 2, 1961 and again in April, May, June and October of 1962. Near the end of this book, we will wind up with an entire chapter which summarizes the work of Dr. Jeffrey Caulfield as recorded in *General Walker and the Murder of President Kennedy: The Extensive New Evidence of a Radical-Right Conspiracy.*

This work, which was published in 2015, represents virtually the life's work of Dr. Caulfield as far as historical research is concerned. From 1992 to 2015, Dr. Caulfield left no stone unturned regarding the role of the radical right in the assassination. Importantly, he essentially blames the entire assassination on James O. Eastland and the SISS, although he nominally blames General Edwin Walker.

Your author arrived at the same conclusion as Dr. Caulfield without the benefit of any of the information uncovered by Dr. Caulfield regarding Eastland and his activities in New Orleans in the summer and fall of 1963.

It hardly needs to be said that if one can conclude that SISS was largely to blame for the assassination both by examining the activities of Senator Thomas J. Dodd and the case of Ottepka and also independently from the actions of Eastland in New Orleans, then it is pretty much "case closed" regarding the guilt of Eastland, Dodd and the SISS.

Dr. Caulfield never comes out and accuses Lee Harvey Oswald of being an, official agent for or staff member of the SISS. On page 742 of *General Walker*, Dr. Caulfield essentially says as much when he says that Oswald was working on tainting SCEF through the FPCC. Unless Oswald was working for an agency of the State of Louisiana for which there is absolutely no evidence, then the only official agency which was trying to taint the Southern Conference Educational Fund (SCEF) was SISS under the direction of Senator James O. Eastland. In a later chapter, we will independently prove that Oswald was an agent of SISS from the moment he returned from Russia. This can be done purely by analyzing the actions of State Department employee Otto Otepka, who was himself an agent of SISS.

OTHER SUSPICIOUS ACTIVITIES OF SISS RELATED TO THE HIT

As of 1963, SISS employed an investigator named Al Tarabochia. He was formerly with the Miami Police Intelligence Department. At the moment of the arrest of Oswald, Tarabochia was contacted by Carlos Bringuier, the Cuban who helped frame Oswald in the Oswald debates.

It is apparent that in the months before the assassination, there was almost endless intrigue surrounding the anti-Castro movement. It seems that for each and every anti-Castro Cuban living in the U.S., there was a plot or plan to rid Cuba of Castro. JFK was apparently trying to get the truth about these activities, or at least to be kept updated on what was going on. Both Kennedy brothers were walking a fine line.

The Kennedy brothers wished to be rid of Castro, that's clear. But they also wanted to avoid another embarrassing incident like the Bay of Pigs. And further, they wanted to avoid the danger of armed Cubans complete with bazookas, grenades, dynamite and whatever, meeting and prowling around the southeastern U.S. subject to irrational action with possibly disastrous consequences. And then there were the jokers in the deck, groups like the Minutemen and individuals like General Edwin Walker who had launched a full-blown armed insurrection already at Ole Miss in September, 1962.

We can see from declassified records that SISS was also very involved on a day-to-day basis with these covert operations against Castro. At the same time, SISS and the Juvenile Delinquency Subcommittee were busy investigating other fringe groups like the Fair Play for Cuba Committee (FPCC) and the Socialist Worker's Party (SWP). It is difficult to believe that SISS was totally surprised by the assassination of JFK. In the judgment of this author SISS may have played at least a minor, active role in the assassination plot and SISS was *definitely* heavily involved in the cover-up.

SISS however, would not be able to have direct supervision over the shooters and the operatives on the ground in the assassination. To suggest that would be going too far. But it seems certain to this author that the Dodd committees at least provided significant political cover for the assassination cabal members, whoever they were.

In Warren Commission Document #3084 headed FAIR PLAY FOR CUBA COMMITTEE, there is a paragraph which quotes the "New York Times" edition of January 11, 1961 that "at a hearing before the United States Senate Internal Security Subcommittee on January 10, 1961, Dr. Charles A. Santos-Buch identified himself and Robert Tabor as organizers of the FPCC. He also testified that he and Taber obtained funds from the Cuban Government which were applied toward the cost of the afore-mentioned advertisement. [in the *New York Times*]." This document also mentions the Socialist Worker's Party (SWP). Of course, Lee Harvey Oswald had made a virtual temporary career in 1963 based on his putative involvement with the FPCC and the SWP.

In his book *Act of Treason*, author Mark North has the following quotation under the heading "7/3/63 WEDNESDAY: The Senate internal security subcommittee released today testimony by Robert Taber, former executive secretary of the Fair Play For Cuba Committee, at closed hearings held in April 1962, quoting the *New York Times* of that date.

We know that Jack Ruby on the night of the assassination, famously corrected the Dallas District Attorney Henry Wade in the 11:00 P.M. press conference in the Dallas City Jail. With Lee Harvey Oswald present, Ruby reminded Wade that Oswald was involved with the FPCC, not another group which was mentioned. *How did Jack Ruby know that?* And why did SISS just happen to be investigating the SWP and the FPCC the same week that Oswald was being framed using these groups to connect LHO to Communism.

So we see that the Senate Internal Security Subcommittee had a continuing relationship with a witness who was an organizer of Oswald's Fair Play for Cuba Committee. SISS was dealing with the topic of the FPCC off-and-on at least from the period January 10, 1961 until July 3, 1963. For some reason, SISS under chairman Senator Thomas Dodd chose to release 15 month-old testimony regarding SISS within a couple of weeks of the time that Lee Harvey Oswald was arrested in New Orleans.

On Feb. 20, 1967, Sen. Dodd introduced the transcript of "Oswald Self-Portrait in Red" into the record. (Cong. Rec. pp. S2262-2266) He also made the following remarks:

> ...Mr. Butler, who was known to me prior to the assassination, called my office immediately after it to inform me of his debate with Oswald. At my request he came to Washington to testify before the Senate Internal Security Subcommittee, and he did so on

Sunday, November 24, 1963 ... I intend to speak at some length on this general subject soon, and I hope to make public the testimony of Mr. Butler before the Senate Internal Security Subcommittee on November 24, 1963.

Quoting from the above-cited website, "In response to a letter which cited part of these remarks by Sen. Dodd, J.G. Sourwine, Chief Counsel of SISS, advised in a letter dated October 10, 1967 as follows: "No testimony of the nature described in your inquiry of October 5, 1967 as been released by the Internal Security Subcommittee."

It should also be added that, in addition to Mr. Ed Butler, Dr. Alton Ochsner (the MD working with Judyth Vary Baker and David Ferrie on weaponized cancer) testified to SISS at the same time as Ed Butler. The testimony of Ed Butler has never been released, as of this writing in 2016.

One can only draw a single conclusion from the timing of events as described above. Sen. Thomas Dodd and Rep. Hale Boggs were both involved in the frame-up of Oswald. Sadly, or should we say boldly, Dodd and Boggs were not even subtle in their ridiculous in-your-face claims.

How could all this travel, information and testimony before SISS happen within the hour when Kennedy was shot?

Senator Dodd, as we will see in a later chapter, had been a professional prosecutor. He was the assistant prosecutor for the U.S. Government at the Nuremberg War Crimes Trials after World War II.

At a time before Oswald was killed, why would any prosecutor be taking official testimony from a potential witness in a murder case at the very time the suspect had been caught. And remember, it would be almost two days later when Oswald was killed. Dodd, as a veteran prosecutor would have to assume that, when caught, Oswald was presumably going to be tried for Kennedy's murder.

Senator Dodd even boldly admits that he knew Ed Butler prior to the assassination. Why would Butler be testifying to SISS so close to the moment when Oswald was killed?

In a separate document which is part of the assassination evidence, there is a statement that says Mr. Carlos Bringuier called Al Tarabochia, the investigator for SISS at the moment when Oswald was arrested. Bringuier, along with Butler, were the ones who went the farthest toward framing Oswald as a Communist. This was before the assassination, in the summer of 1963.

Why were these operatives calling Boggs, Dodd and Tarabochia instead of the Dallas Police or the FBI? Why would Carlos Bringuier, a militant Cuban exile (independently) call SISS investigator Al Tarabochia? The President had just been murdered.

Did Boggs, Dodd or Tarabochia ever get around to calling the FBI or the Dallas Police? We don't know. And if it was so important, why has

Ed Butler's testimony not been released after 50 years? Butler, in his testimony to SISS, either said something to incriminate himself, others, or he must have given away the most sensitive secret in American history. Maybe some day his testimony will be released to the public and we will know the answer.

None of the above makes any sense at all, unless you assume that Boggs, Dodd and SISS had at least some involvement in the assassination plot, either before (as seems likely) or at least after the fact.

And then Boggs was appointed to the Warren Commission. Folks, to this author, the question of a high-level assassination conspiracy just isn't a mystery anymore.

There is one final issue that comes out of the theory whereby the leaders of the Senate were somehow involved in the JFK assassination. That issue is this: if the Senate were implicated, wouldn't this point toward LBJ, since LBJ was the "master of the Senate?" This is a very serious point. This question about the possible complicity of LBJ will be analyzed in depth in other chapters.

The next important information about the secretive activities of SISS and its relationship to began to surface later in 1963 immediately after the JFK assassination.

It is important to remember that officially, SISS was temporarily chaired by Senator Thomas Dodd. As we will examine in our chapter on Senator Dodd, it was Dodd's other committee, the Senate Subcommittee on Juvenile Delinquency which was engaged in an investigation of mail-order weapons sales.

The main two vendors of mail-order weapons which Dodd was investigating in the Spring of 1963 were Seaport Trading of Los Angeles and Klein's Sporting Goods of Chicago. Lee Harvey Oswald allegedly bought his pistol from Seaport Trading and his Mannlicher-Carcano rifle from Klein's Sporting goods. It is completely documented that Dodd had requested both of these weapon vendors to supply his Subcommittee with all their records about mail-order sales for that period.

Also, one of the major groups which Dodd was accusing of buying these mail-order weapons was the American Nazi Party. The name of that group was found, for no known reason, in the notebook of Lee Harvey Oswald.

As we have discussed in our statement of facts about the assassination, the ATF agent in Dallas named Frank Ellsworth was in a special meeting in Dallas between himself, FBI agent James Hosty and Army Intelligence officer Ed Coyle. The purpose of that meeting has never been discovered. It is also believed that Ellsworth was one of those officials who was allowed to interrogate Oswald while he was in the Dallas jail.

There are many irreconcilable facts surrounding Oswald's weapons purchases. The first questionable fact would be the violation of postal regulations. Oswald rented the post office box in the name of Lee Oswald. However, Oswald allegedly purchased the gun using the alias "A.J.Hidell." It was against post office rules for someone other than the P.O. box owner to receive mail in their box. We can see the wisdom of this. It avoids arguments about lost items and likewise avoids a loss of revenue to the post office due to people doubling up on P.O. boxes.

There is absolutely no evidence of Oswald having purchased ammunition for either weapon. The evidence about the shooting of Officer Tippit shows that there were four shots fired at Tippit and that there were two bullets from one manufacturer and two from another. So the lack of proof as to Oswald purchasing his ammo is even more questionable since he would have somehow purchased ammo for the revolver *made by two different manufacturers.*

Next there is the question of why Oswald would buy through the mail and not anonymously for a lower price from Dallas gun sellers? There were a number of outlets selling the Mannlicher-Carcano rifle in Dallas which were readily accessible to him. Oswald apparently had to buy his ammunition in Dallas. Probably the most important question is why did Oswald try to advertise among his friends his ownership of his rifle by way of the backyard photos and especially posing with both his rifle and issues of Communist newspapers?

The last Oswald rifle issue is one dear to the heart of this author, having been a bank officer.

The money order that Oswald allegedly used to pay for the mail order rifle was put in evidence. However, missing from the money order were the "tracks" or the endorsement stamps on the back. These endorsement stamps are absolutely necessary if one claims that the money order was used for a purchase. This is just the type of detail which would have been overlooked by someone forging evidence.

These apparent co-incidences are not really co-incidences. The only logical theory about Oswald and his weapons is that Oswald was led to believe that he was working on a large weapons sting. This sting was ostensibly aimed at fly-by-night mail-order weapons outlets. That's why Oswald had no clips, no ammunition in his possession, no cleaning equipment for the rifle, no tools necessary to assemble and disassemble the rifle, and no paraffin evidence of every firing a rifle on November 22, 1963. But this ATF weapons-sting theory can explain all of his activities regarding the rifle.

Most important, however, is the fact that the weapons-sting theory explains the connection between Oswald and both of the Senate Sub-committees chaired by Senator Thomas J. Dodd.

So at this point in our narrative, you have SISS (and/or Dodd's other committee, the Juvenile Delinquency Subcommittee) involved in a weapons sting involving Oswald. Further, SISS was involved in investigating the Fair Play for Cuba (FPPC) in the same month as Oswald was pretending for no known reason to infiltrate the FPCC (even though Oswald was the only member in New Orleans.).

Then, within minutes of the arrest of Oswald, SISS was contacted by Carlos Bringuier, the framer of Oswald. And before Oswald was dead, SISS was taking testimony from Oswald-framer Ed Butler. Butler's testimony has never been declassified. The same day Oswald was killed, on a Sunday morning, Ed Butler and Dr. Alton Ochsner were already in Washington giving testimony to SISS about Oswald. Then you have Dr. Ochsner and Oswald both involved in the egregious weaponized cancer plan.

And you find Jack Ruby publically correcting the Dallas District Attorney in a press conference as to the fact that Oswald was involved in the FPCC.

Regarding the events of November 22, 1963, SISS would not have been able to have direct supervision over the shooters and the operatives on the ground. They would have most likely worked through the ATF, the Secret Service, the military, military intelligence or, less likely, through a collection of right-wing international paramilitary operatives who would have enjoyed the protection provided by SISS in Congress.

The most current of information tends to incriminate the worldwide network of ex-Nazis from World War II who would have been working together with Southern racists and White Russians in Dallas as well as Senator Dodd and SISS.

To summarize, it seems clear that the hub of political authority which supported the JFK assassination lay in the workings of SISS. Through Senator Thomas Dodd, SISS was linked to Europe, ex-Nazis and a worldwide network of fascist-minded players who were both anti-Communist and haters of JFK.

Notes:

The following book is cited by name in the text:
Cases and Materials on Legislation, 4th Edition 1969 by Nutting, Elliot and Dickerson at p. 78

Another source cited by name in the text is an article by Roland Evans, Jr. in the *Saturday Evening Post*, June 8, 1963 titled "The Invisible Men Who Run Congress."

As mentioned by name in the text, see: *True Compass: A Memoir* (2009) by Edward M. Kennedy.

For one of the only (even summary) biographies of Senator James O. Easland, see *Gothic Politics in the Deep South*, by Robert Sherrill, at p. 198.

The following is cited in the paragraph beginning "picking up on the activities of SISS" and is described as a "well-known website" in the text: [http://xxxwww.acorn.net/jfkplace/09/fp.back_issues/17th_Issue/rambler3.html

See *Alger Hiss: The True Story* (1976) by John Chabot Smith at page p. 143 n.for support regarding the buildup of public demand for a second trial for Alger Hiss in 1952.

For a description of the presence of Billings, Martino, Robertson and others on the Bayo-Pawley raid, see *The Fish Is Red: The Story of the Secret War Against Castro* (1981) by Warren Hinckle William W. Turner at page 172.

For a description of the role of Dick Billings in the purchase of the Zapruder Film, see *The World of Time Inc.*, (1986) by Curtis Prendergast with Geoffrey Colvin,, p. 125; and Richard B. Stolley, "Four Days in Dallas: 25 Years Later," *Columbia* [University] magazine, Oct. 1988, p. 58.

Mentioned by name in the text is the iconic book *Where Rebels Roost... Mississippi Civil Rights Revisited* (2005) by MBA Susan Klopfer, Ph. D. Fred Klopfer, and Barry Klopfer, Esq.

Act of Treason: The Role of J. Edgar Hoover in the Assassination of President Kennedy, by Mark North quoting *NY Times* 7-3-63; refer to page 286 on the issue of the belated release of the testimony of Robert Taber by SISS.

The following is a citation for the INCA publication Victory as mentioned by name in the text: jfk.hood.edu/Collection/Weisberg%20Subject%20Index%20Files/B%20Disk/Butler%20Edward%20Scannell/Item%2036.pdf read from the internet by your author on 5-14-2015.

A citation for another INCA fact is: INCA [phonograph] records "Oswald Self-Portrait in Red" and "Oswald Speaks," and the December 11, 1963 (Vol. 1,#1) edition of "Victory," the official INCA publication, excerpts available at jfk.hood.edu website, see note 8. This citation also relates to the introduction into the Congressional Record of information about Ed Butler and Lee Harvey Oswald by Senator Thomas Dodd.

One of the most important paragraphs in the entire assassination literature is Chapter 17, footnote 64 in *The Man Who Knew Too Much*, by Dick Russell. This lengthy note supports the fact that only an hour or two after the assassination, the New Orleans Cuban exile activists by the name of Carlos Bringuier called Al Taraboccia, investigator for SISS in Washington with detailed biographical information about Lee Harvey Oswald.

Chapter 24

SPEAKER JOHN W. MCCORMACK AND THE PLOT TO KILL LBJ

DID LBJ MASTERMIND THE JFK ASSASSINATION?

In the opinion of your author, the guilt of Eastland and Dodd would not necessarily point to the guilt of LBJ. There are, however, several major factors which *could* implicate LBJ. First of all, Senator Dodd loudly claimed to be "an LBJ man." That is curious, since Dodd represented Connecticut, which is totally removed from the South and Texas in particular. Why would Dodd claim to be an especially strong follower of LBJ?

Dodd's main motivation in choosing his role in the Senate was his own anti-Communist orientation. LBJ was never seen as a particularly rabid anti-Communist or a Red-Baiter. LBJ was a New Deal Democrat. He had been a strong supporter of Franklin Roosevelt. Most of the rabid anti-Communists like Richard Nixon, Herbert Hoover, Sen. Everett Dirksen and Sen. James O. Eastland were generally opposed to any liberal ideas. On the other hand, Catholic anti-Communists like Sen. Joe McCarthy, Sen. Pat McCarran and Joseph P. Kennedy stood apart from southerners when it came to labor and social issues.

It has been said by some authors that Joe McCarthy never enjoyed much support in the South. When Senator Richard Russell was Governor of Georgia, he nearly lost his office because he appointed just one Catholic to a minor Board of Trustees in his state. That is an example of the strong anti-Catholic sentiment among average people in the South. Many KKK types considered blacks, Jews and Catholics to be enemies of the Southern lifestyle.

Why would Dodd, in the immediate aftermath of the assassination, be so enthusiastic about the accession of LBJ to the presidency? Kennedy's family, at least, had been in part the creators of McCarthyism by their friendship with and support of McCarthy. Joseph P. Kennedy was a close ally of Francis Cardinal Spellman, the most powerful Catholic clergyman in the U.S. at the time.

It doesn't seem that Dodd had an ambitious legislative program or agenda which LBJ could have helped him to enact, based on LBJ's Senatorial power. Dodd's modus operandi seemed to be the use of the secret investigative committee, not the enactment of important legislation. In this he had much in common with Robert Kennedy and McCarthy. LBJ on the other hand was interested in moving legislation, not clandestine investigation. LBJ operated out in the open. Although friends with J. Edgar Hoover, LBJ never seemed to relish the trampling of privacy rights or the suppression of certain ideologies.

Let's face it, when LBJ became president, he immediately launched into the Great Society. The Great Society was a rehash of the New Deal of Roosevelt, the Fair Deal of Truman and the New Frontier of JFK. This was not a conservative program. And LBJ was never a proponent of the more sinister principles of the segregationist Senators like Eastland and Richard Russell. Both of these Senators held to a Mississippi Sovereignty Commission-type attitude and felt great sympathy for the KKK and were indifferent to terrorism against blacks and lynchings. LBJ had pointedly refused to sign the infamous Southern Manifesto written in 1956 by Senators Strom Thurmond and Richard Russell. This manifesto was the litmus test to be considered a Southern segregationist. LBJ refused to sign.

And finally, LBJ was no longer in the Senate. As Vice-President, he was at least acting formally as a member of the Executive Branch. There is no suggestion that LBJ was secretly feeding information to Congressional Committees or getting involved in the assault of the Congress on the State Department. There was a battle of JFK, RFK, Walt W. Rostow and Walter Sheridan on one side and Dodd, Eastland and Dirksen on the other. LBJ was not in that picture.

The personal papers of James O. Eastland were sealed off in a manner which was indefinite and intended to be permanent following the assassination. The Kennedy family helped hide the autopsy photos from the public and encouraged the slipshod autopsy at the very hour of the assassination. There is not a hint of any comparable secretive behavior or issue with regard to LBJ. His tapes, which reveal his conversations with many people immediately after the assassination, have not been hidden or edited to hide anything with only a few, very minor exceptions.

Author Mark North, in his examination of the involvement of J. Edgar Hoover, was not able to find any actual incriminating evidence against Hoover. The role and involvement of LBJ, a close friend of Hoover, seems to be the same as Hoover's. LBJ found himself in the middle of the situation. Both Hoover and LBJ had a basically constructive attitude toward their role in the government. Neither LBJ nor Hoover allowed personal greed or their affinity to their particular religion or ideology to trump their fidelity to the Constitution.

And neither Hoover nor LBJ had a special axe to grind with Communism. Communism just wasn't going to take over the U.S. and Communism *especially* was not going to take over the South. Of all the things the South had to fear, for instance racial integration or labor unions, Communism wasn't high on the list. Except for Miami with the Cuban issue, anti-Communism wasn't a special focus with Southern leaders such as Richard Russell or Strom Thurmond.

One exception was James O. Eastland. Eastland was partners with Senator Pat McCarran and his obsession with "Internal Security" from the very beginning. Another exception was oilman H.L. Hunt of Dallas. Hunt was financially supporting neo-Nazis in Eastern Europe, especially in Ukraine, which no one in the South ever heard of. The common denominator there could have been oil. As revealed in the memoirs of Edward Kennedy, Eastland had a strong focus on oil dealings as obviously did H.L. Hunt. And oil was an international commodity.

So, in the opinion of the author, complicity of the Senate did not mean complicity of LBJ.

SPEAKER JOHN W. McCORMACK AND THE PLOT TO KILL BOTH JFK AND LBJ

A case can be made that the true plan of the fascists involved in the JFK assassination was to kill both JFK and LBJ and install Speaker John W. McCormack as President. As Speaker of the House, McCormack would be next in line for the Presidency. Let's just list the issues and factors which point in this direction.

THE SHOOTERS DETAINED ON THE GRASSY KNOLL

As reported in our chapter on "The Facts in Dealey Plaza," it was reported in a military intelligence memo dated 11-27-63 "On November 20 last, the Dallas Police sighted two unknown men sighting in a rifle near scene where President was assassinated. Rifle being sighted in at two sillhouette targets" If these men were sighting at two silhouette targets, the two targets would necessarily be some distance away from one another. On its face, this suggests two shooting victims were targeted.

LBJ APPEARING WITH JFK IN PUBLIC AND AGAINST SECRET SECURITY RULES

Many assassination authors have noted that it was against Secret Service policy to allow both the President and Vice-President to appear together in public. The reason for that should be obvious. Yet in Dallas on 11-22-63, both JFK and LBJ were riding in open cars underneath the windows of the Dallas School Book Depository. In fact, LBJ's car was two cars behind the car of JFK. When the fatal head shot was fired at JFK from the grassy knoll, LBJ's car would have been right under the window where Lee Harvey Oswald was perched.

If JFK was being "set up" by the whole well-planned scenario in Dallas, then it looks like LBJ was "set up" and "wide open" in the same way.

LBJ DUCKS BEHIND THE FRONT SEAT BEFORE THE SHOOTING STARTS

The classic book about the possible complicity of LBJ is *LBJ: The Mastermind of the JFK Assassination*, by Phillip F. Nelson. Nelson's book is probably the best-written account of the assassination as far as professional writing is concerned. On page 403, he quotes Mary Mitchell, who was standing under the window of the Book Depository when the shooting began. In her testimony to the Warren Commission, she describes seeing the car "in which Senator Yarborough was riding." Nelson infers from her statement that she should have said "the car in which Lyndon Johnson was riding," but that LBJ was not visible. Nelson says that LBJ was not visible because he had already begun to duck down behind the front seat of the limo, suggesting he knew in advance that shooting would be starting at that point in time.

Nelson says:

> Given the situation in the motorcade, there was no rational explanation for Johnson's actions throughout the motorcade...that required him to practically lie on the floor of the car just before reaching Elm Street. This is, no reason other than the one which should be obvious: he was afraid the shooters might fire off a volley at him instead of shooting only at Kennedy, as they had been ordered to do, by him.

Though author Nelson is near the top of the list of logical assassination analists, his conclusion in the previous paragraph is not, in fact, logical. If LBJ were ducking down before the shots began, he must have feared and/or known the assassins were out to get him as well. Why would you hire assassins to kill your boss and be afraid they would kill you, too? The facts scream out only one conclusion. The JFK assassination plot was a partnership between European ex-Nazis and certain evil Southern segregationists. The intent of the European fascists who were working through Senator Thomas Dodd was to kill both JFK and LBJ so they could have a rabid Catholic Northern Democratic President who was cut from the same cloth as were they. That man would be Speaker of the House John W. McCormack.

The problem encountered by the European fascists was that the other partner in league with Senator Dodd, the sinister James O. Eastland of Mississippi, had other ideas. The last thing Eastland would want was another Catholic President with a liberal social agenda when he could instead have a fellow Southerner and former Senate ally as President in the person of Lyndon Johnson.

So Eastland tipped LBJ off ahead of the assassination. Of course LBJ had to go through all the paces and not interfere. Kennedy was being stalked. There had been the Chicago assassination attempt and another in Tampa, within just days. LBJ knew the murderers were powerful, organized, worldwide and unstoppable. To them, LBJ was a dead man walking. But if he could survive Dealey Plaza, then he would be President and would be in a safer (though still not completely safe) position.

THE PHONE CALL BETWEEN LBJ, MAYOR DALEY AND JOHN W. MCCORMACK

On December 3, 1963, there was a phone call between the powerful Richard J. Daley of Chicago, Speaker of the House John W. McCormack and President Lyndon Johnson. The tone of the call was confrontational. Mayor Daley was berating McCormack and LBJ because the Congress was busy passing the "Cotton Bill" when Daley was demanding action on the Civil Rights Bill and the Tax Bill. Daley refered to LBJ as "that fellow from the South." McCormack was defending the importance of the Cotton Bill, but he was clearly the mediator in this confrontation.

Mayor Daley was undoubtedly complicit in the JFK assassination. The so-called "Chicago Plot" had taken place on November 2, 1963. The Chicago Police turned the investigation over to the Secret Service and walked away from the case. This decision, where four snipers had been found laying in wait for JFK, could not have been made by the Chicago Police without the knowledge and consent of Mayor Daley. One could go further and suggest that the Chicago Plot itself was pre-arranged by Daley and the plotters, which seems the more likely scenario.

The significance of the Daley-LBJ-McCormack phone call is to be found in the context of that call. Also, one must look at the political dynamic. Senator Thomas Dodd was a Northern Catholic activist. Mayor Richard J. Daley was almost as Catholic as the Pope himself. Speaker McCormack was also apparently a militant Catholic anti-Communist activist. LBJ must have been aware that he was in a phone conversation with two militant Catholic leaders, when militant Catholic anti-Communists in Europe along with Senator Dodd had just succeeded in murdering his boss in partnership with Eastland and friends. But the European forces were clearly predominant in the plot. So they could easily target LBJ next. LBJ must have been only too aware of that.

THE SCARCITY OF INFORMATION ABOUT SPEAKER JOHN W. MCCORMACK

One of the obvious giveaways in JFK assassination research is when the personal papers are unreasonably restricted. Another one is if Wikipedia articles are very brief, cursory, devoid of important information and seem to be often taken down or changed. Still another is when there is no biography written about someone who was very famous and would normally have a published biography available.

There are many examples of famous people in the JFK assassination literature who fall into this category. The Canadian, Major Louis Bloomfield, had his papers sealed by the courts even when this sealing was contrary to statutes and laws. Senator James O. Eastland donated his papers to the University of Mississippi Law School and access was refused for many decades. Much was eventually found missing. There is no biography of Eastland.

Others are General David Sarnoff of RCA, Rep. Hale Boggs, Senator John Stennis, Senator Joseph McCarthy (whose papers were sequestered), the investment bank of Kuhn, Loeb and the Senate Internal Security Subcommittee (SISS). Another in the same category is Speaker of the House John W. McCormack.

There have been biographies of people of much less renown. In fact, there is a biography of an Irish Tenor named John McCormack. There is a biography of Representative Carl Albert who was majority leader under McCormack. There is a biography of Tip O'Neill, another famous Boston Speaker of the House. But there is not a biography about the most noteworthy Speaker of the House in the 20th Century.

According to a website that contains information about personal papers, Boston University has 66 feet of microfilm of McCormack's personal papers. So there is not a lack of available information about McCormack.

In these modern times, another way to judge information about a person is their page on Wikipedia. The Wikipedia article on McCormack is fraught with blatant problems. It is like it was "written by a fan" says Wikipedia. "It is like a reflection or opinion essay," says Wikipedia. Also, there are not sufficient citations.

What we do know for sure about McCormack is that he was born in 1891 and that he had little education. He managed to pass the Massachusetts Bar Exam despite having no high school or college education. He must have been of above average intelligence to do that.

McCormack was elected to Congress in 1928. He was to be reelected 20 times. He became Majority Leader of the Democrats in 1940 and served in that capacity until 1961 when he became Speaker of the House upon the death of Sam Rayburn. In 1934, he became chairman of the Dies Committee. The Dies Committee was a predecessor to the House Un-American Affairs Committee (HUAC). Martin Dies was a radical anti-subversive individual who liked to grandstand and enjoyed the attention that came with sensationalizing security issues.

McCormack was actually a co-chairman of the Dies Committee because the man in line for the chairmanship, Samuel Dickstein, felt uncomfortable investigating Nazis. Dickstein was Jewish.

After chairing the Dies Committee for a year, McCormack filed a committee report that recommended 1) registration of agents of foreign governments, 2) subpoena powers running across the entire U.S. for Congressional Committees. Both of these suggestions went on to become law. When he was chairing the committee hearings, McCormack was regarded as courteous to the witnesses and not trying to draw attention to himself, as did co-chair Samuel Dickstein. The report also denounced both Fascism and Communism in various contexts. So McCormack was a hunter of Communists as a Congressman when Senator Joe McCarthy was only 26 years old.

But what is lacking is any information about what legislation McCormack sponsored, introduced and favored.

Senator Thomas Dodd and Representatives Charles Kersten and John W. McCormack seemed to have similar political priorities. Dodd and Kersten could fairly be called Catholic partisans. The following chart shows the frequency in which the names of all three men were cited in Ukrainian nationalist periodicals from World War II up until the mid-1960's. The Anti-Bolshevik Nations Correspondence would be the best indicator. These Ukrainian types of publications are only available to the knowledge of this author at the academic website Hathitrust. Although other such publications are there dating from the 1940's or early 1950's, the ABN Correspondence is only there beginning with issues dated 1961 and after, (even though ABN had existed for more than a decade as of 1961):

		Thomas Dodd	Charles Kersten	John W. McCormack
Abn Correspondence				
1961-1962		3	7	0
1963		3	8	0
1964		7	6	2
Ukrainian Bulletin				
1952		0	3	0
1956-1959		22	14	15
1960		3	2	3
1961-1962		8	5	3
1963		6	4	1
1964-1966		20	4	10
Ukrainian Quarterly				
1946-1948		0	0	0
1949-1950		0	0	0
1951-1952		0	15	0
1953-1954		0	3	0
1955-1956		5	21	1
1957-1958		0	7	0

1959-1960		14	4	2
1961		1	4	1
1962		0	5	0
1963		1	8	0
1964		2	2	1
1956-1966		4	3	0
1967		1	0	0

As can be seen from the above data, Speaker of the House John W. McCormack was cited in a pattern that was similar to Senator Dodd and Congressman Kersten. Senator Dodd was an insider in the assassination plot. Congressman Kersten, though not necessarily an insider, apparently had advance knowledge of the plot and was involved before the fact with the Europeans who were planning to blame the assassination on the Soviets. From all appearances and until more detailed information or a biography of. McCormack becomes available, it is a strong possibility that the plotters would have been ecstatic if he were to become the President.

LBJ was set up in an open limo just two cars away from JFK, within the shadow of the Texas School Book Depository with Lee Harvey Oswald (or someone) peering from a window, possibly with rifle in hand. And LBJ ducked.

There is one available book which deals with Speaker John W. McCormack. That book is *The Austin/Boston Connection* by Anthony Champagne and others. In that book, McCormack is revealed to be a bald-faced liar. He claimed his father had died when he was 13 and that his father was Irish. He said his three older siblings had died in infancy. None of those three things were true.

On page 128 of the Champagne book, it is stated that "McCormack's core support came from 20 to 25 members of the House who came from Catholic urban constituencies and which members were themselves Catholic."

Champagne explains that the Texas and Massachusetts delegations ran the House of Representatives because, uniquely among Democrats, neither Texas nor Massachusetts had many African-Americans. This gave their delegations freedom to maneuver on the hot-button issue of civil rights. Arch-conservative South Carolina Congressman L. Mendel Rivers called McCormack "the most anti-Communist man in the country." (Champagne, p. 131).

If Speaker of the House McCormack had become President under such circumstances, one could be sure that Martial Law would have been declared. It would have had to have been. What other choice would there be? And the conservative Admirals and Generals on the Joint Chiefs of

Staff and in other major commands would have (unfortunately) made Martial Law permanent, or at least until the situation stabilized and the question of catching the perpetrators was resolved.

The would have been the scenario which the World War II Nazis still surviving would have considered their World War III.

Notes:

Cited in the text is *LBJ: Mastermind of the JFK Assassination*, by Phillip F.Nelson, p. 474.

To hear the phone call between LBJ, McCormack and Mayor Richard J. Daley, see: http://web2.millercenter.org/lbj/audiovisual/whrecordings/telephone/conversations/1963/lbj_k6312_02_14_daley_mccormack.wav

For information about McCormack and the Dies Committee, see: *The Committee: The Extraordinary Career of the House Committee on Un-American Activities*, by Walter Goodman, p. 10.

As cited and quoted in the text, see *The Austin-Boston Connection: Five Decades of House Democratic Leadership, 1937-1989* by Anthony Champagne, Douglas B. Harris, James W. Riddlesperger, Jr, and Garrison Nelson (2009).

Chapter 25

COMMENTARY ON THE LBJ PHONE CALLS

MAJOR POINTS AND ISSUES

The LBJ phone calls represent one of the most obvious and homogeneous groups of original sources available to provide background and information on the assassination. There has been a book written specifically on this subject by author Max Holland, which was published in 2004 and is referenced in the notes following this chapter. The book by Holland covers calls from November 22, 1963 all the way until 1967. Since most of the calls speak for themselves, presenting the analysis of other authors here would be redundant and does not fit the purpose of this chapter.

The calls which will be analyzed here run from November 22, 1963 until November 30, 1963 with one exception which occurred December 3, 1963. The calls are conveniently accessible at maryferrell.org.

In our analysis here, an attempt will be made, not to take the calls as individual calls, but rather as a group and look for common characteristics and themes. This general impression can then be placed side by side with the general conclusions we have reached from evidence from of the other sources. The two sets of conclusions should match up. The calls have to mirror, or at least allow for our overall theory of the assassination.

The following are the issues that emerge from the phone calls in declining order of importance:

1. In his phone call about the Warren Commission with James O. Eastland, LBJ mentions two names as having "international" experience. The names were John Sherman Cooper and John McCloy. LBJ tries to blame the "Russian thing" but the only international experience that Cooper and McCloy were known for was with Germany, and specifically Nazi's. LBJ seems to know this, but tries to camouflage it with respect to Cooper. This is the biggest smoking gun in the phone calls.

2. LBJ tells McGeorge Bundy he will meet with, among others, the new German Chancellor Ludwig Erhard and British Prime Minis-

ter Alec Douglas-Hume but that he intends to snub French President Charles de Gaulle.

3. He informs advisor Jesse Kellam that he intends to invite German Chancellor Ludwig Erhard to his ranch. LBJ wants to get in good with Erhard, since Erhard and his henchmen have likely just murdered JFK, and LBJ could be next. This is major supporting evidence of the "German connection."

4. The Civil Rights bill was demanded by civil rights leaders in order for them to play ball and not ask for more investigations. JFK was murdered by a combination of the very worst enemies of African Americans; ironically the assassination was not targeted directly at their immediate situation. For them the Civil Rights Bill was a nice bonus from a bad situation.

5. Virtually all of the 98 persons who were on the phone calls had an official or logical reason to be talking with LBJ. Everyone had an official title, was or had been an advisor to LBJ, or had some special expertise to offer the new President. Many were regional political leaders such as state governors.

6. What was the role of LBJ in these calls? He was functioning as a funeral director more than anything else, channeling everyone's feelings as well as ideas about where to go from here.

7. The proportion of Republicans to Democrats on the calls among Senators was 12-6 in favor of Democrats.

8. The likely conspirators with whom LBJ spoke were Eastland, Dodd, Boggs, Bundy, Dulles and Richard J. Daley of Chicago. We should put a question mark on that issue beside the name of Speaker John W. McCormack.

9. There were no calls with C. Douglas Dillon. When talking to Ted Sorensen, LBJ said "I just got Doug Dillon out of here" and quickly added "that was on the budget" To quote Shakespeare , LBJ "answereth where none doth inquire." LBJ seemed to feel a need to explain why he was meeting with Dillon even though nobody asked. He may have been hesitant to say he and Dillon were discussing security or Secret Service. LBJ and Dillon may also have been discussing Secret Service information about Oswald or similar sensitive information. LBJ wanted to emphasize "it was about the budget." He offered no other such explanation about any meetings he had with anyone or what they talked about in any other conference where he had been in this period. Or LBJ may have been feeling guilty or worried about meeting with someone he felt to be a JFK assassination plotter.

10. The most amazing thing about the calls was the proportion of people who were "happy campers." This is not to mean that these people were happy that JFK had been killed, but rather they were happy with the way the aftermath was being handled. Not one person expressed an overall sense of worry or an attitude of pessimism about anything.

11. The most *unhappy* camper was Senator Russell Long, whose own father, Huey Long had been assassinated. His father Huey Long had possibly been assassinated by the same political faction in Louisiana who were deeply involved in the JFK assassination. That would not make your day. Judge Leander Perez had actually been standing beside Huey Long when he was shot. Perez played a very large role in the segregationist movement in Louisiana in 1963. LBJ treated Senator Russell Long very coldly and distantly, very rare for LBJ.

12. Robert S. McNamara seemed essentially unhappy and his call was treated as a wrong number. Apparently LBJ pretty much hung up the phone on McNamara.

13. Senator Richard Russell was hot! He wanted an honest investigation and, incredibly, he was the only one who did. His call seemed to last forever and was the longest of any of the calls, running to 8 pages of transcript.

14. Out of 98 persons who were on the phone in the week after the assassination, 18 discussed the Warren Commission. The WC is usually the only thing mentioned in regard to the phone calls., We can tell from the calls that the people who were selected for the WC were pre-ordained by the particular array of interest groups who were stakeholders. Only one person seemed to have a pre-arranged plan for the Warren Commission. The only pre-arranged plan was suggested by Yale Law School Dean Eugene Rostow and his suggestions were not followed in any respect. The lines of power and the facts of the case led straight to the result as to membership and authority with no real disagreement. As stated elsewhere, since the majority of the Warren Commission were members of Congress, the WC would legally have been considered a Committee of Congress if such an issue were raised in a court.

15. By their reactions, the Republicans proved (1) that they knew *a priori* about the assassination, at least generally, and (2) they were crude, rude and insensitive in "rubbing it in" in a way which was shocking. Ex-President Herbert Hoover (as related by his son Allen) came out and said he wasn't sad about the murder. Minority Leader Charles Halleck said that, to him, going hunting was more important than worrying about approving Secret Service protection for Jackie.

16. As Committee Chairmen, the Southern Democrats were analogous to pilots (they numbered 19). The Republicans were analogous to the infantry (they numbered 37). This is a metaphor which aptly describes the relationship between the two in-groups in providing political support for the assassination and cover up.

17. Ike's former Treasury Secretary Robert B. Anderson was the only person who seemed to have had a bigger and louder voice than was either justified or appropriate. Of all the callers who were only private citizens, he was by far the most likely to have been privy to the details of the plot. This was because of his relationship with assassination suspects like General Charles Willoughby and Judge Robert Morris. Anderson was also known for having poor judgment. This poor judgment might have been in play because Anderson, a near-plotter, was trying to gloat or throw his weight around in the aftermath of the assassination.

18. There was no evidence of LBJ masterminding the assassination. He was handling matters that were within his purview, i.e. placating Senators and getting a rough idea of the evidence and the case against Oswald from J. Edgar Hoover.

19. In his phone call with Senator Dodd, LBJ said, "well you're my man on that Committee. You know I put you on it cause … I put you on there and damned if you haven't done more there…" Dodd answered "I'm a Johnson man…" Obviously, since Dodd was the acting Chairman of the SISS subcommittee and the subcommittee had been in the middle of the assassination plot, LBJ was referring to SISS. Dodd was also a member of the parent committee of SISS, the Judiciary Committee. But LBJ would not refer to the Judiciary Committee as "that committee." Dodd was also on the Subcommittee on Juvenile Delinquency, but LBJ was more likely referring to SISS. This was LBJ's way of claiming he had supported the SISS involvement in the assassination. But when LBJ appointed Dodd to SISS in 1959, the assassination had not even been dreamed of by anyone.

20. Don Cook, President of American Electric Power, was calling LBJ to set up a meeting within the week with an unnamed group of men. Cook was apparently calling to confirm LBJ's willingness to proceed with the sale of General Aniline and Film Company (GAF). GAF had been seized from the German Company IG Farben under the Trading With The Enemy Act during World War II. GAF had been owned by the U.S. Government Alien Property Trustee since World War II. JFK had not yet agreed to sell, since the sale of GAF was approved in December, 1963. This case of General Aniline and Film was probably a very large factor contributing to the assassination.

The following are highlights of the 120 phone calls with 98 parties during the period previously outlined"

SENATORS

MIKE MANSFIELD-D. MT-Secret Service for Jackie .

SPESSARD HOLLAND, D. FL-Naming of Cape Kennedy.

CLINTON ANDERSON-D. NM, Oppenheimer, Strauss, Space, Tax Bill-LBJ-"the President had made an award to Oppenheimer... I don't think we should cancel that..."

HUBERT HUMPHREY-D. MN-tax bill, civil rights bill, Walter Reuther met with Scandinavians, Willi Brandt.

BOURKE HICKENLOOPER-D. IA WC McCone, Russell.

THOMAS J DODD-D. CT-Will announce WC, study "this assassination thing", "you're my man on that committee..." TD: "I'm a Johnson man, you know that.." TD-"I'll do anything you want.."

J W FULBRIGHT-D. AR- LBJ: You can sit with Russell on CIA cmte, I want you to know all the CIA tells you...

JOHN SHERMAN COOPER-R. KY-LBJ-"I want you on WC-"JSC replies "What?-I'll do it of course."

RUSSELL LONG-D. LA-RL "what do you know about McKeithen?" LBJ-"not a thing" [no cordiality].

HUGH SCOTT-R. PA-LBJ "On a panel with Saltonstall & Pastore, you were very partial to me.."

LEVERETT SALTONSTALL-R. MA-LBJ "You were on a panel talking nice..." "I'm a prisoner..."

EDWARD M KENNEDY-D. MA-EMK called LBJ: EMK "my mother and my family appreciate you." LBJ-"You're in my prayers..."

RALPH YARBROUGH-D. TX-LBJ "we must close ranks, especially with Connally being injured..."

RICHARD RUSSELL-D. GA-RR "Only Hickenlooper & Fulbright will sit on my CIA cmte"-RR "Can RFK nominate someone to the WC?" LBJ "no."

GEORGE SMATHERS-D. FL-LBJ-"we've got to keep the JFK aura till the election..." Tax Bill, Civil Rights Bill,Budget.

EVERETT DIRKSEN-R. IL-WC,LBJ "we will wrap up the 3 divisions of government..." EMD-" I've talked to Eastland,McClellan."

JAMES O EASTLAND-D. MS-WC-LBJ-"this Dallas thing...Cooper has international experience... McCloy will help with the international a little bit..." JOE- "Russell is irked."

GEORGE AIKEN-R. VT-1st call is erased; LBJ "I want your Gov. of Vermont to go to Zanzibar." (Zanzibar had recently gone Communist).

THOMAS KUCHEL-R. CA-WC-LBJ-"We could kill 39 million people:[with the A-bomb] the Chairman is a patriot... I supported Ike when I was a Senator..."

WARREN MAGNUSON-D. WA- WM-has words of encouragement for LBJ.

CONGRESSMEN

JOE KILGORE-D,TX-"Come up to the little house [LBJ says of White House]", mentions PM of Denmark, Prince of Cambodia.

LES ARENDS- R,IL--WC-LBJ-" I want a defense man, CIA, For. Rel., a Hoover man ..."-JS Cooper is discussed.

CARL ALBERT-D,OK-LBJ "don't want things going on in House and Senate ..." WC.. CA on WC "no thanks!"

JACK BROOKS-D,TX-Chmn House Judiciary Cmte-Chmn House Cmte Gov Operations, Nat. Sec. Sub- committee [on Air Force One 1 11-22-63].JB-"I've done a little work with some of these brothers."

CHARLES HALLECK-R,IN-WC- LBJ says, "I'll appoint a commission ... folks are worried ... it has some foreign implications ... CH- C.J. Warren is a mistake ..." LBJ-"need CIA experience ..."CH-"I don't know if the right wing was in this or not."

HALE BOGGS-D,LA-HB "Cong. Goodell on floor complaining about 2 investigations (Judiciary and HUAC). WC. HB "two will be appointed by you" LBJ "aren't they all appointed by me?" HB "yes."

ADAM CLAYTON POWELL-D,NY-LBJ "Did I do all right on Civil Rights?"

JOHN J MCCORMACK-JM "We need Secret Service for Jackie-Repubs, C. Halleck opposed"-discussed Cotton Bill, WC -LBJ "I don't want JOE, J.E.Hoover does not like McCloy." JWM "No northerners???"

GERALD FORD-R,MI-WC-LBJ-"I want somebody who knows CIA over in your shop ..."

ADIVSORS

ABE FORTAS-WC-AF "Gen. Norstad" LBJ-"what about McCloy instead?" AF "OK, looks like we're stuck with Boggs."

ERIC GOLDMAN-PROF-LBJ advisor-EG-"I was impressed by your speech and I am at your disposal."

T. WADDY BULLION-LBJ tax atty, LBJ talks private business, FCC, Lady Bird.

JAMES HAGGARTY & BOB KINTNER, Pres. NBC,-LBJ-"I had Bob Anderson in and the General [Ike] and we discussed the sound dollar ..."

HORACE BUSBY-frugality, Alliance for Progress, LBJ-"we're carrying on the Alliance for Progress ..."

ROBERT ANDERSON-R, Treas Secy under Ike--LBJ-"Ike and I were just talking about you ... would like to meet with you tomorrow" Tax Bill, Civil Rights Bill-LBJ-"JFK was killed and people in Mississippi were killed... they'll be in streets ... I'll tell the Repubs you're the party of Lincoln, sign discharge ..."

TED SORENSEN-St. of UN. Speech, budget, Tax Bill, de Gaulle, D.Dillon, JK Galbraith, Ribicoff-LBJ-"I apologize for being late ... I just got Doug Dillon out of here (that's on the budget)."

ARTHUR GOLDBERG-LBJ "help share the heavy thinking ... Repubs are more united than the Dems ... Mrs Kennedy's request with the Russian Ambassador ... [?].."

LARRY O'BRIEN-Pres advisor-Wheat deal, LBJ-"we're in up to our ears ..."

JESSE KELLAM-LBJ Adv.-LBJ "I want to bring Erhard to LBJ ranch" JK talks with LBJ on Texas business affairs.

RICHARD MAGUIRE-Aide to JFK-RM-"I knew JFK since 1946" LBJ-"I need your advice, we're in same family."

EUGENE ROSTOW (To Bill Moyers) WC "name Nixon, Tom Dewey, [per Spartacus website] indications were that Rostow was speaking for a group of people…did not say who was with him when he called."

BILL MOYERS-LBJ advisor-LBJ "give him [?] information about our country and about other members of the delegation…so he doesn't think we bumped him off…"

LABOR LEADERS

DAVID DUBINSKY-Pres ILBWU- DD.. "you have a lot of friends and I'm one of them."

ALEX ROSE-Labor Leader-Liberal Party Politician in New York, offered encouragement.

GEORGE MEANEY-Pres AFL-CIO- GM "we're right behind you…I'm in a state of shock…"

WALTER REUTHER-UAW-WR-'I'd like to come by for a chat … if you need anything, let me know."

DAVE MCDONALD-Pres. United Steelworkers-Tax Bill, discharge petition on Civil Rights Bill-DM-"I'll get my legislative people up there right away."

CIVIL RIGHTS LEADERS

DR MARTIN LUTHER KING-Civil Rights Bill, LBJ-"I'll need your help."

WHITNEY YOUNG-Tax bill, Civil Rights Bill, WY "what about an invite to funeral and for CORE?" LBJ-"RFK will work it out."

A PHILIP RANDOLPH-Civil Rights Bill, discharge petition for bill.

CABINET AND OTHER OFFICIALS

WILLIAM MCCHESNEY MARTIN-Chmn of Fed Res Bd, LBJ "I don't know much about your FRB shop, are markets ok now?"

DEAN RUSK-Discusses Halaby & Moscow-Civil Air, WC LBJ "too many Republicans?" DR-"No." Halaby & Rockefeller are connected.

ALLEN DULLES-Recording starts in mid-conversation, WC-LBJ "it's a 'court of inquiry'"-AD what about my prev job?" LBJ-"that's ok.'

J EDGAR HOOVER-Alex Hidell,Texas Atty. Gen.,WC, JEH "I don't like McCloy," General Norstad is discussed as a possible WC member. JEH "I have an armored car, you don't" Discusses Rubenstein lie detector, that LHO got $6500 from Cuba.

DWIGHT EISENHOWER-Ike's message was delivered through McGeorge Bundy and Dean Acheson, no tape.

MCGEORGE BUNDY-Nat.Sec.Adv.-MB "You should meet de Gaulle, Erhard,Hume,-Mikoyan & explain U.S. position[on?]…MB "see de Gaulle 1st…he's the oldest…"L-

BJ-"that bothers me…I thought I'd sandwich him in…" (Against Bundy's recommendation, LBJ wants to visibly snub de Gaulle).

HERBERT HOOVER-Per Allen Hoover HH's son, "I can't say he's sad but he's extremely sorrowful."

JOHN MCCONE-CIA Dir-JM "I had a call from Mexico City and Alvarado his recanted his story [about LHO receiving $6500 from Castro." call was declassified 4-17-1995.

ROBERT S MCNAMARA-RSM "We're you calling me, sir?' LBJ-"call him when you're alone…must have been a mistake.." [Call was treated by transcribers as wrong number].

CORPORATE LEADERS

G KEITH FUNSTON-Pres. NYSE, LBJ-"It was good to close markets when you did."GKF "Tax Bill, Civil Rights Bill, I think confidence exists in markets."

DON COOK-head of SEC, CEO AEP, offered Treas Secy by LBJ 1965 LBJ-"We need a good man in Vietnam"-DC-"Fed Res Bd & Treas. Should be close."

ED WEISEL-CEO Paramount Pictures-EW "Tax Bill, Foreign Aid … talk to 'Bobby' [RFK?], we don't want panic…"

FRED KAPPEL-CEO AT&T-LBJ "Take your committee and give me the benefit of their wisdom…we must preserve the system…"

MEDIA

ROSCOE DRUMMOND-Christ Sc Monitor, LBJ "thanks" RD-"the hand of God is in it."

GENE PULLIAM-Owned papers in Ind and Az-GP-"congrats on your speech."

LOUIS SELTZER-*Cleveland Press*, LS-"great speech."

RUSSELL WIGGINS-Ed. *Wash Post*, Phil Graham and Sam Rayburn were discussed in general.

BEN MCELWAY-Ed. *Wash Star* LBJ- "this thing came upon me."

WALKER STONE-Scripps-Howard, let's talk on Friday.

DR FRANK STANTON-Pres. Of CBS, LBJ "Lady Bird says we need smart people."

OTIS CHANDLER-Pres. *L A Times*, mentions Bob Anderson & Ike, first use of word "assassination." (For some disgusting reason, LBJ referred to the assassination as "the Dallas thing." prior to this call).

KATHERINE GRAHAM-Publ *Wash Post*-"hello dearie" rest of tape is blank.

DAVID LAWRENCE-*US News & WR*- "jot down ideas-I just need your help.."

HENRY LUCE-Publ. of Time-Life-call cut off by receptionist.."he is with Mr. Johnson…"-operator.

JOSEPH ALSOP [very long and intense call] Columnist for Wash Post-Heavy discussion on WC-JA "You can't have it done in Texas!! … Dean Acheson and I believe … the left won't believe the FBI" LBJ "the lawyers and the Council just hit the ceiling…"

SAM NEWHOUSE-Owns Vogue, Vanity Fair-LBJ "I had this thing fall in my lap…say hi to Ed Weisel."

WILLIAM S WHITE-*N Y Times*-WSW-"I heard your speech and I cried."

Regional Politicians

JAMES FARLEY-relations w/Vatican 1933, HST appointed to Hoover Commission.

FRANK CLEMENT-Gov. of Virginia, you're wonderful.

FERRIS BRYANT-Gov of Fla. Cape Kennedy, science cmte.

JOHN BAILEY-head of DNC, "call me" "thanks"

PAT BROWN-Gov. of CA, PB-offer of help, LBJ-"you'd be a tower of strength."

RICHARD J DALEY-Civil Rights, Tax Bill, opposes Cotton Bill.

PHILIP HOFF-D,Gov. of Vermont-go to (Communist) Zanzibar for independence day.

ALLEN SHIVERS-D, Gov of Texas, I'm in over my head, you're mighty nice, etc.

JOHN PASTORE-D,Gov of R.I.-LBJ-"Let me tell you how much I love you"[yuck].

KARL ROLVAAG-D,Gov of Mn-mentions James Teague-unknown person.

PATRICK LUCEY-D,WI Chmn Wisc Dem. Party "Wisc has shown its affection for you...here's Rolvaag."

GEORGE ROMNEY-R,Gov Mich-We are fortunate to have a person of such great experience.

JOHN REYNOLDS,D, Gov of WI, LBJ "Look after things for me."

Science related

JEROME WEISNER-JW-"The AEC would like to put out a statement saying you're going to make the Oppenheimer award."

GEN DAVID SARNOFF-DS-"I'm praying for you."

JAMES WEBB-NASA CEO-JW-"problem w/military, McNamara wants Gemini transferred to the Air Force...can we push moon into 1970's?"

Miscellaneous and Unknown

NELLIE CONNALLY-LBJ "take care of Uncle John.'

LUCIA ALEXANDER-sister to LBJ, LBJ-"please refer reporters to my press secretary," (part of call was "sanitized").

MRS J D TIPPIT-LBJ-"Condolences to you and your children."

LOU DRESSCHLER-unknown-foreign visitors.

Notes:

The Kennedy Assassination Tapes, by Max Holland.

https://www.maryferrell.org/pages/LBJ_Phone_Calls.html

Chapter 26

BARON WERNHER VON BRAUN AND HIS BEST FRIEND WALTER DORNBERGER

The majority of the following information deals with background facts about General Dornberger which are not material to the overall purpose of this book. Therefore, this author has quoted in places from the website [en.wikipedia.org/wiki/Walter_Dornberger] which represents the most concise source of general information about General Dornberger as well as many other sources.

Walter Dornberger had been the top leader of ex-Nazis in post WWII captivity and he was the supervisor to Oswald babysitter Michael Paine. Also, he was the long-time best friend of Baron Wernher von Braun, who some authors accuse of being complicit in the JFK assassination.

Walter Dornberger was a Major General in the German Army. He was born on September 6, 1895. He died on June 27, 1980 at age 84. He was born in Giessen, Germany and served in both World Wars. In the First World War he was captured by U.S. Marines and was a POW for two years, during which he made repeated attempts to escape. Dornberger studied engineering at the Berlin Technical Institute..

In the 1920's Dornberger completed an engineering course with distinction at the Berlin Technical Institute. *In the Rocket and the Reich: Peenemunde and the Coming of the Ballistic Missile Era*, by James Neufeld, (hereinafter R&R) the author picks up the history of the German rocket program at page 8 with an early pioneer with a rocket background working in the Reich Defense Ministry of the Weimar Republic in 1929. This pioneer was named Karl Emil Becker, who began to investigate the rocket in 1929. Three army veterans younger than Becker would soon emerge as the central figures in the administration of the program: Erich Schneider, Walter Dornberger and Leo Zanssen. All three were products of a "study officer" program that was founded by Becker.

Son of a pharmacist from the southwest German city of Giessen and a veteran of heavy artillery units on the Western Front, Dornberger would become a masterful salesman, administrator and political infighter for the rocket program. A space flight enthusiast, he read a very early rocket genius Hermann Oberth's *Wege* around the time of its appearance in 1929. He began work in Becker's section in 1930, purportedly with the assignment of looking into liquid-fuel rocketry, but until 1936, his main area of concentration was small battlefield solid-fuel rockets.

In the Spring of 1930, Dornberger graduated after five years with an MS degree in mechanical engineering from the Technische Hochschule Charlottenburg in Berlin. In 1935, Dornberger received an honorary doctorate, which Col. Karl Emil Becker arranged as Dean of the new Faculty of Military Technology at the TH Berlin.

ROCKET DEVELOPMENT

The most famous German rocket scientist was, of course, Wernher von Braun. The very first "dreamers/scientists" regarding the German rockets were Oberth and Rudolph Nebel. Oberth had been involved with the best early sci-fi movie call *Frau im Mond* (Woman in the Moon) and the props for the movie and its ideas gradually developed into an actual scientific endeavor.

A famous picture taken on July 23, 1930 included Wernher von Braun and ushered the young rocket genius onto the stage of rocket design, never again to leave until man walked on the moon thanks to his contributions. Wernher von Braun and Walter Dornberger, also became best friends and collaborators for most of the remainder of their lives.

Wernher von Braun was prized by the rocket group from the beginning because of his title as a Baron and his aristocratic background and bearing. One could compare this "halo effect" to that of the Red Baron (von Richthoffen). Nothing in Germany could quite equal the status of the landed Prussian aristocracy and von Braun was valued for this at least as much as the technical abilities which he also possessed in abundance.

In April 1930, Dornberger was appointed to the Ballistics Council of the German Army (Reichswehr) Weapons Department as Assistant Examiner to secretly develop military liquid-fuel rockets suitable for mass-production that would surpass the range of artillery.

As early as 1932, Walter Dornberger and his friend Wernher von Braun tried to launch as successful rocket but the motor exploded after von Braun tried to light it using a long pole. This was somewhere in the location of a Rocket Test Field.

Dornberger was in his last military command in 1934 which was a rocket training battery. He had begun working for the Army Weapons Department on rocketry in 1933.

In 1934 the interim rocket facility in Germany, the VfR, folded. In 1934, Joseph Goebbels banned all discussion of rocketry that suggested uses of the missile as a weapon. Part of this attitude was due to problems between the Army and the Nazis. Then in 1934, Rudolph Nebel, who had been trying to move forward with rockets, was imprisoned by the Gestapo. In 1934, Dornberger told a now-famous rocket expert named Arthur Rudolph that they must work together. (Rudolph went on to supervise the Saturn 5 U.S. moon-rocket program).

During this time, the main line of rocket development was that advocated and run by the ideas of Wernher von Braun. Von Braun was always adamant about the use of liquid oxygen in the missile as opposed to nitric acid, which was much more dangerous to work with.

In March of 1935, Hitler renounced the Versailles Treaty and began to re-arm Germany. "23 year old Wernher von Braun wrote a position paper that must be regarded as Peenemunde's birth certificate," according to Neufeld, page 6. Peenemunde was to be established on a remote island on the coast of the Baltic Sea in the far north of Germany. The base was to be shared with the Luftwaffe for their weapons development.

There was incredibly fast scientific research and progress at Peenemunde and Neufeld attributes this to lavish funding. Dornberger was constantly battling for government control of the rocket production as opposed to using private industry to build and operate the facilities. This was a philosophy which dominated, even when the Germans moved to the Redstone Arsenal in Alabama and began producing missiles for the United States. Hence, Cape Canaveral was in public, not private, hands. This came, in part, from the Prussian tradition of the military officer corps.

Dornberger was transferred to the sprawling, newly built Peenemunde Test Facility in May, 1937.

As vividly described by Michael J. Neufeld in *Rocket and the Reich* at page 118:

> On a rainy day in March, 1939, von Brauchich brought Hitler to Kummersdorf [a proving grounds] which was a short distance from Berlin. (The Supreme Commander never set foot in Peenemunde). The two were accompanied by Becker and were met by Dornberger, Thiel and von Braun. The Fuhrer watched firings of the 300 and 1000-kg-thrust motors ... but his expression scarcely changed. When von Braun explained the workings of the liquid-fuel rocket using a cutaway A-3 [precursor of the V-2], Hitler listened closely, but then walked away.... Hitler gave the group only a backhanded compliment: "Well, it was grand!"
>
> On August 20, 1941, Dornberger and von Braun met the Fuhrer at his Wolfsschanza ("wolf's lair") headquarters in East Prussia. Dornberger began by showing a V-2 propaganda movie.
>
> "Finally, on October 3, at two minutes before four in the afternoon, the ...V-2 lifted off and arced out over the Baltic on a perfect Fall day. The rocket, which carried on its side a *Woman in the Moon*

logo, continued straight on its course until all that was visible was a glowing dot ... on the roof of the guidance division's Measurement House, Dornberger and Zanssen wept and hugged each other with joy."

That night, at the gala celebration in the Officer's Club, Dornberger delivered a moving speech in which he stated that "the space ship is born." There is little doubt about of his enthusiasm for Hitler and the system.... In the wings, the power brokers were gathering ... but a sample of twenty-eight prominent Peenemunde engineers and scientists shows that thirteen or fourteen became Party members and four, including von Braun, were in the SS, according to Neufeld at p. 179. A few, like Arthur Rudolph (a member since mid-1931) were ideologically committed Nazis, but the survey confirms the impression that von Braun was fairly typical.

Von Braun was known to have worn his SS uniform only once, and that was when Himmler ordered him to do so.

In March and April of that year [1943], the thirty-one-year-old Technical Director [von Braun] also used his rank, as he needed to, when applying to the SS Race and Settlement Office for permission to marry. (For unknown reasons, the marriage to a Berlin physical education teacher never took place).

Because the Commander of Peenemunde, Colonel Leo Zanssen [a close ally of Dornberger] was a Catholic and was [therefore] politically suspect, the local SS [thought he was part of a conspiracy involving some local Catholic priests]. According to a report ... Zanssen was an old-fashioned officer out of touch with the common man and National Socialism. Zanssen was not outspoken religiously; his wife and children were in fact Protestant.

When the Nazis came to power, he [Zanssen] even made his children stand up at the dinner table and sing the Party anthem, the "Horst Wessel Song."

In short order Dornberger discovered who was behind the accusations [against his friend Zanssen]: Stegmaier [with help from a sadistic private enterprise interloper named Gerhard Degenkolb's cronies]. Dornberger was angry with Stegmaier.

On July 7, 1943 Dornberger and von Braun were suddenly called to East Prussia to meet the Fuhrer... [on June 3, 1943]... Dornberger received a promotion to Brigadier General.

For the first time Hitler saw the impressive images of a V-2 launch. Von Braun narrated the film; Dornberger lectured and showed models of the deployment systems to the visibly fascinated Fuhrer... In any case, Hitler emerged from the meeting intoxicated by the missile and told Speer [the overall armaments minister] to push its production as fast as possible. Hitler also granted the minister's request (originating from Dornberger) that Wernher von Braun receive the prestigious title of Professor. The Fuhrer was amazed at von Braun's youth and so impressed by his talent that he made a point of signing the document himself.

Dornberger was given roles in the management of both the V-1 and v-2 programs in 1942. It took three launches of the V-2 to get the first success. Dornberger and von Braun were flown to Hitler's "Wolfsschanze" with a film meant to impress Hitler. According to a speech made by Dornberger at Peenemunde, the era of space travel actually began with that launch which ushered in a new era.

In *Blowback: The First Full Account of America's Recruitment of Nazis and its Disastrous Effect on The cold war, Our Domestic and Foreign Policy*, by Christopher Simpson, Simpson presents at page 28, a slightly different and intriguing story of the events in question:

> And in March 1943, a terrible blow fell: Adolph Hitler had a dream in which Dornberger's pet project, the giant liquid fueled V-2 rocket, failed to cross the English Channel. (Hitler then put the V-2 at a low priority). But General Dornberger was nothing if not determined. He requested and got a private audience with Hitler during July, 1943 ... Dornberger personally convinced Hitler to authorize the construction of a giant underground factory near Nordhausen ...

At least 20,000 prisoners – many of them talented engineers who had been singled out for missile production because of their education were killed through starvation, disease or execution during the course of this project.

Adolph Hitler said to Dornberger "I have had to apologize only to two men in my whole life. The first was Field Marshal von Brauchitsch. I did not listen to him when he told me again and again how important your research was. The second man is yourself. I never believed that your work would be successful.

Later in the War, in January, 1944, Dornberger began working on anti-aircraft rockets both as an artillery commander as well as with authority to develop anti-aircraft rockets.

Because the missile base at Peenemunde had been exposed to serious Allied air strikes which had crippled it badly, a new missile factory was built in the German mountains, underground, in an abandoned gypsum mine. The facility had been largely staffed by slave labor and is called Nordhausen-Mittelwork-Dora in various descriptions. Apparently thousands of slave laborers were worked to death and when Allied troops liberated this place, there were corpses piled high and very emaciated bodies were being burned four at a time in a camp crematory.

Following the defeat of the German Army at Stalingrad, every officer in the German Army realized that this was the beginning of the end and the war was going to be lost. Hence, the rocket scientists began to develop a strategy of preparing to essentially auction off their services to the highest bidder between Britain, the Soviet Union, the U.S. Military and even, incredibly, General Electric!

On 12 January 1945 on Dornberger's proposal, Albert Speer replaced the Long-Range Weapons Commission with "Working Staff Dornberger." Then the scientists began their travels to the remote areas of the German Alps where they arranged to meet with the Allied military recruiters

In her book *Operation Paperclip: The Secret Intelligence Program that Brought Nazi Scientists to America*, Annie Jacobsen, states:

> "Von Braun was willing to concede…the war… He needed a bargaining chip to use against the Americans after his was captured. Von Braun told Tessman and Huzel [two fellow compatriots that] Dornberger would also be part of this team. On April 1 [1945] Dornberger received an order [from SS General Kammler] demanding that Dornberger evacuate his staff from Mittelwerk … and Dornberger and his staff drove themselves… [the news came] Our Fuhrer, Adolph Hitler… fell for Germany this afternoon… But Hitler's death spurred von Braun to action. Von Braun approached General Dornberger [to deal with the Americans]. I agree with you, Wernher, Dornberger was overheard saying that's right. It's our obligation to put *our baby* into the right hands.

This is essentially the most significant line in the entire effort the author has made to present the personality and history of Walter Dornberger. But more important is the sheer irony that these two somewhat eccentric scientists saw themselves as (presumably) both the father and the mother of arguably the most important military invention in world history, surely at that time. Keep in mind, the Soviet Union was quickly able to imitate U.S. technology to create the atomic and hydrogen bombs. The Soviets were never able, however, to create a satisfactory, secure ICBM delivery system, despite the best efforts of such a genius as Sergei Korolev, the top Soviet missile engineer.

It is obvious to the author, that the experience of these two (partially evil) geniuses at this time and in this situation, gave them the very pinnacle of power perhaps for the whole planet. After this, everything else, even the launching of men to the moon under their supervision, was possibly an anti-climax. (And for this reason, the psychology of this will be examined in light of the events in Dallas on November 22, 1963). As stated above, there was no other way to get the missile technology than through the efforts of the Nazi scientists. And this technology was absolutely essential to avoid the possible annihilation of our entire country. So it is easy to see that the leverage possessed by these scientists would, in stark terms, trump any considerations about the possible murder of a political leader, should it ever come to that.

Beginning in February, 1945, Dornberger and his staff migrated from Schwerdt on the Oder River in Germany to a place called Bad Sachsa (still in Germany), and thence in April, 1945 to Bavaria which was being occupied by American troops, safely away from the advancing Russians. They were fleeing the slave labor camp at Mittelwerk-Nordhausen, site of the slave labor atrocities. Dornberger had hidden technical papers near Bad Sachsa to use as bargaining chips.

In *The Paperclip Conspiracy: The Hunt for the Nazi Scientists*, Tom Bower describes the scene as follows:

> Commander Henry Schade of the American Naval Technical Mission arrived at Oberammergau on May 1, 1945. He was looking for Dr. Herbert Wagner, designer of the Hs293 [German] guided missile bomb. Richard Porter, an employee of General Electric on contract to Army Ordnance arrived with CIOS [military intelligence] soon after. Wernher von Braun claimed he withheld information to get an offer. As part of their bargaining tactics, Wernher von Braun and Dornberger decided to maintain military style control over the team. That did not pass unnoticed by American intelligence officers. Dornberger and von Braun were in a position to bargain ... to exercise pressure and attempt to blackmail. "Security clearance of the group as such was an obvious absurdity" [which was the conclusion of Colonel Holger Toftoy, Chief of Army Ordnance who was there to fulfill a quota of 100 scientists to be recruited for the Army].
>
> At the eleventh hour, ... right before boarding the train, General Dornberger confessed to having hidden his own stash of papers, an ace in the hole had Dornberger been double-crossed by Wernher von Braun ... General Dornberger told Staver that he had buried five large boxes in a field near the spa town of Bad Sachsa... in a last-ditch effort to find Dornberger's stash, Staver and Porter [a representative of General Electric] sent out on a find mission... finally they located Dornberger's metal-lines cases, which contained 250 lbs of drawings and documents.
>
> At the Haus Ingeburg ski resort, Wernher von Braun and General Dornberger had selected a small team, including Herbert Axter, Hans Lindenberg, Dieter Huzel and Bernhard Tessman.
>
> A small group around Dornberger ended up in a mountain resort hotel high up on the former Austrian-German border. Von Braun joined them later in April with [Dieter] Huzel and [Bernhard] Tessman who had buried Peenemunde's archive in a mine northwest of Mittelwerk.

[U.S.] Ordnance's Special Mission V-2 also managed to ferret out the location of the Peenemunde archive.... A Soviet team including Sergei Korolev [the man who turned out to be the "von Braun" of the Soviet space program] was sent to investigate Peenemunde.

See Tom Bower, Jacobsen p. 67 and Neufeld, p. 265 regarding the quoted information.

Near the the time when Germany surrendered, and Hitler committed suicide in Berlin, on May 2, 1945, both von Braun and Dornberger met up with American troops near the Austrian village of Schattwald and were thence taken to the German town of Reutte. (Some reports say they were actually captured by General Patton's forces in Czechoslovakia)

As detailed by Annie Jacobsen in *Operation Paperclip* beginning at page 66, she writes:

> Von Braun and Dornberger were not captured.... So confident were they as to their future use by the U.S. Army that they turned themselves in ...
>
> Wernher von Braun and Dornberger sent Magnus von Braun [the English-speaking younger brother of Wernher] down to the U.S. base to make a deal. The CIOS [part of U.S. Intelligence had a] Black List for rockets research [which] included one thousand names of scientists and engineers ... and Wernher von Braun was at the top of that list.
>
> Some in the U.S. Division of CIC [an intelligence team] found von Braun's hubris appalling...so confident were von Braun and Dornberger about their value to the U.S. Army, they demanded to see...Ike.
>
> On July 6, 1945 JCS [Joint Chiefs of Staff, American] finally approved [without telling President Truman] of the Nazi scientist program. It was 1) for use against Japan, 2) no war criminals were allowed, and 3) the exploitation of the scientists was to be temporary.
>
> Because the rocket scientists were so valuable, if not absolutely necessary to the future defense of the United States, hardly any of these scientists were prosecuted at Nuremberg and, in fact, up to perhaps thousands, if you include medical, chemical and other scientists were brought to the United States, as well as some to Britain and the Soviet Union. The program in the U.S. was first called Operation Overcast and later, Operation Paperclip.

Per Neufeld, p. 269:

> The British however, had one special request. They developed a plan to construct the necessary facility on the Baltic to actually

test-fire four V-2 missiles. For this purpose, the Americans agreed to loan their captured German Scientists. After the test launches, however, a problem occurred.

The one person [U.S.] Ordance could not get back from the British was Dornberger (see Neufeld, p. 269). According to a U.K. interrogator, the former rocket General had "extreme views on German domination, and wishes for a Third World War." Moreover, the British were determined to try Dornberger in Kammler's place for indiscriminate V-2 attacks on civilians. They kept him in a POW camp until 1947.

Per Neufeld, p. 269:

Because of the narrow focus of war crimes investigations, the rocket general also avoided trial on the one charge that could have stuck: complicity in the exploitation of slave labor. (see also *Blowback*, by Christopher Simpson at p.27-39).

Continuing Jacobsen p 66 and Neufeld p. 269:

At an internment camp after the war known as "CSDIC Camp 11" the British bugged Dornberger, who in conversation with General major Gerhard Bassenge (COG Air Defences, Tunis & Biserta) said that he and Wernher von Braun had realized in late 1944 that things were going wrong and consequently was in touch with the General Electric Corporation through the German Embassy in Portugal, with a view to coming to some arrangement.

As stated in Jacobsen, p. 84:

Heinrich Himmler and Adolph Hitler were dead. Speer was in custody; also Otto Ambros, Wernher von Braun, Walter Dornberger and Arthur Rudolph were in custody, working toward a U.S. Army contract. George Rickhey had a job in London.

In his book *The Paperclip Conspiracy: The Hunt for the Nazi Scientists*, Tom Bower, (at p. 127) adds even more background about the nature of the relationship between the Nazi missile scientists:

Three Peenemunde scientists, all anti-Nazi's who had refused American contracts, confided to Osborne [a British interrogator] that the rocket team's strict hierarchical structure under Dornberger, [Herbert] Axter and Wernher von Braun had remained intact despite the German surrender. Before every interrogation, each German was carefully briefed by Dornberger, Axter and von Braun about what could and could not be disclosed. Osborne also discovered that those scientists who criticized or failed to obey Dornberger's edicts were punished.

It has to be asked, at this point, about these Nazi's rigid disciplinary system. They clearly had this system in place just before they were brought to the U.S. They were brought in numbers that reached at least into the high one-hundreds. Further, their team retained a virtual monopoly control in the divisions of NASA in Huntsville under von Braun (production) and Cape Canaveral (launching) under Kurt Debus. When exactly did this rigid militaristic disciplinary system disappear? Sorry I had to even ask!

Still more background on Walter Dornberger is provided by Annie Jacobsen in *Operation Paperclip* (at p.178):

> "Walter Dornberger was definitely the most hated man in the camp," Sergeant Ron Williams, a prison guard recalled. "Even his own people hated him. He never went out to the local farms to work like other prisoners. Wherever General Dornberger went, he required an escort. The British feared that other prisoners might kill him.
> Arriving at Wright Field in the summer of 1947 was General Walter Dornberger, newly released [from Britain]. Before turning him over to the Americans, the British labeled him "a menace of the first order" and warned their Allied partners of his deceitful nature. While holding Dornberger for war crimes, British intelligence had eavesdropped on him and recorded what he said. When Americans listened to the secret audio recordings, they too, concluded that Hitler's former "chief of all rocket and research development... had an untrustworthy attitude in seeking to turn ally against ally." Still, Dornberger signed a Paperclip contract, on July 12, 1947, just weeks after his release from prison. Dornberger's skill at manipulation was put to use by Army Ordnance, which had him write classified intelligence briefs. America needed to develop missiles regardless of what any naysayers might think Dornberger believed.

Of the *Paperclip Conspiracy,* (at p. 135) Tom Bower provides further perspective from the British point of view quoting from information provided by the British:

> Dornberger is a regular soldier of 30 years of service. [He began his career working around the famous "Paris Gun" which shelled Paris from 70 miles away in 1917], is a first rate technician and wields great power over his subordinates including Wernher von Braun...I am convinced that Dornberger is a most dangerous man and should...be...prevented to have contact with his former Peenemunde subordinates.

Bower continues regarding the British position in re Dornberger:

> ...the conviction that all Germans were dangerous was still deep seated among officials whose task for nearly six years had been to preserve the nation's [Britain's] internal security. For both the JIC [the British Joint Intelligence Committee] and the Home Office [British office in charge of law, order and immigration], the insuperable obstacle was that a brilliant German scientist would inevitably become "indispensable" and therefore dangerous.

Bower presents the counter-argument:

> Like Wev [the American officer in charge of the scientists] most believed that "beating a dead Nazi horse" served little purpose and was, in fact, self-defeating. Former Nazi's were proving themselves willing and able allies against Communism, which was jeopardizing the entire world. There was, they felt, a sharp distinction between political subversion (because Nazis believed in totalitarianism) and outright espionage.

The reader is invited to make up his or her own mind on this issue. In another interesting sidelight Bower reports the following about a Nazi named Kurt Debus:

"Debus had not deliberately denounced him [i.e. one of his German colleagues] but had been compelled to report their conversation to the Gestapo under his oath as an SS man."

As mentioned above, Kurt Debus went on to head the launching function of the NASA program at Cape Canaveral and was highly decorated by the U.S. Government for this service.

While Dornberger sat in jail, U.S. Army Ordnance conveyed across the ocean nearly 120 select Peenemunders ... von Braun had already departed for the U.S. by airplane with six others in September 1945.

In Simpson, *Blowback,* Dornberger himself did not experience the immigration difficulties that Wernher von Braun did. He was permitted to enter the U.S. in 1947 without State Department opposition ... much to the dismay of the British, who had been, after all, the targets of Dornberger's rockets ... the British held Dornberger for two years as a P.O.W. following the war and tried to bring him up as a war criminal. Dornberger got into the U.S. because he never joined the Nazi party.

The U.S. Air Force, it is now known, secretly brought Dornberger to this country in 1947 and put him to work on a classified rocketry program at Wright Field (now known as Wright-Patterson AFB) near Dayton, Ohio. By 1950, he had gone into private industry with Bell Aircraft and he eventually rose to be a Senior Vice-President of the Bell Aerosystems Division of the massive multi-national Textron Corporation. There he specialized in company liaison with U.S. military agencies..

As detailed by Neufeld in Rocket and the Reich, beginning at page 270 and then on page 271:

> They were sent to Fort Bliss [in El Paso, Texas]. Their chief role was Project Hermes, with General Electric ... Operation Paperclip replaced Operation Overcast in March 1946.
>
> The Nazis were rationalized ... because the German's technical expertise was seen as indispensable. In 1950 the group was transferred by the U.S. Army to the Redstone Arsenal in Huntsville, Alabama where they became the premier rocket development group in the United States. Their arrival in the States had in fact changed the whole balance of Army rocket activities, since the Germans displaced the smaller groups that had begun to flourish in WWII, like the Jet Propulsion Laboratory in Pasadena, California.

In her book ,Secret Agenda: The United States Government, Nazi Scientists and Operation Paperclip; 1945 to 1990, Linda Hunt (at p. 52) uncovered more information about the Fort Bliss sojourn of the German Scientists.

"Meanwhile, the lax security over Paperclip personnel became so obvious that even visitors to Fort Bliss complained. One War Department intelligence officer, Colonel Frank Reed was shocked that [Major James] Hamill [responsible for the scientists] ...made no serious checks on the German's loyalty...Reed's concern about security was heightened because he had just returned from visiting Saint Louis, France, where a comparable group of German rocket engineers worked for the French government. While there, the French commandant told Reed he suspected the Germans under French control were receiving orders from Germany and working toward a re-emergence of the Third Reich."

In the period after von Braun arrived at Fort Bliss, but before the arrival of Dornberger, Hunt reports another incident at p. 52 regarding the Germans:

"All of a sudden, word came down that Wernher von Braun had been caught sending a map overseas to General Dornberger and concealing information from U.S. officials. It was an incident ... similar [to a 1945 plot] when asked about documents, von Braun told the Army he knew nothing about their location. Dornberger later told von Braun's brother that Army officers didn't trust Wernher von Braun and that officers had even told him that von Braun had lied to them. Von Braun then sent a map to his family in Europe showing the location of a burial place where sketches stuffed in a cigarette box were hidden. He told them [his family] to deliver the map to Dornberger's wife, since the General [Dornberger] was still being held in a British POW camp. The way this scheme was supposed to work, the documents then would be located and given to German scientists who would turn them over to Wernher von Braun when they arrived in the U.S. under Paperclip. [The officers said Wernher von Braun would use the documents as a bargaining chip]. The plot was abruptly halted when Army Officers confiscated the map from Dornberger's wife. Then the officers finagled Dornberger's release from the British and flew to Germany to look for the missing documents in a forest under Dornberger's direction. [The sketches turned out to be ruined]."

Post WWII

Once the British had seen the testing of the V-2, Dornberger was taken to London, interrogated and imprisoned. The British acted out of vengeance over Dornberger's role in the horrific V-2 attacks. But the British had also seen Dornberger in action as the "informal leader" of all the imprisoned Nazi's at his facility. They feared this leadership role as an ongoing security threat.

But Dornberger was soon to be released to the Americans. He worked in the U.S. for the Air Force. Then he went to work as a Vice President of Bell Aerospace which was headquartered in Buffalo, New York with a facility in Dallas. Dornberger's projects at Bell Aerospace were mostly esoteric failures, including the never-built Dyna-Soar craft and a nuclear propelled air-to-surface missile. One noteworthy recruit landed for Bell Aerospace by Dornberger was a rocket pioneer named Krafft Arnold Ehricke.

Jacobsen, reports regarding Dornberger(at p. 262): "Russia strives now only time to prepare for war before the United States," Dornberger wrote in a classified budget pitch financed by the Ordnance Department in 1948. "The United States must decide on a research and development program that will guarantee satisfactory results in the shortest possible time and at the least expense. Such a program must be set up even if its organization appears to violate American economic ideals and American traditions in arms development" Dornberger wrote.

At least it could be said that Dornberger remained true to his totalitarian-leaning principle, that is, his belief that democratic ideals and traditions could be ignored in the quest for military supremacy. That the U.S. Army condoned Dornberger's idea appears to have never been made public before; his pitch was presented to the Ordnance Department officials at the Pentagon. A copy of the classified document was found in 2012 in Dornberger's personal papers, kept in a German state archive.

We can continue on to what else is known about the career of Walter Dornberger in the following years in which he worked toward the United States goals in weapons development.

Neufeld reports (at p. 27):

> At Huntsville [the U.S. missile facility] one of the keys to the German's success was the "everything under one roof" approach developed at Kummersdorf and Peenemunde under the direction of Becker and Dornberger. It proved very compatible with the U.S. Army's "arsenal system" of in-house development. Under von Braun's leadership the German-dominated group successfully developed the nuclear-tipped Redstone and Jupiter Missiles in the 1950's. The Redstone-which was really just a much-improved A-4 [V-2] became the vehicle that put the first American satellite and first American man into space. Finally under NASA aegis, after 1960, the Peenemunders crowned their success with the phenomenally reliable Saturn vehicles, which launched Apollo spacecraft into orbit and put humans on the moon.

Of any of the authors quoted about. Jacobsen offers the most details about the role of Dornberger's career in the U.S. after WWII. She says:

> Within two years of his arrival in the United States, Dornberger had transformed from public menace to American celebrity. In 1950, he left military custody at Wright-Patterson Air Force Base to work for Bell Aircraft Corporation in Niagara Falls, New York, quickly becoming Vice-President and chief scientist. His vocation was now to serve as America's mouthpiece for the urgent need to weaponize space. Dornberger was given a Top Secret security clearance and a job consulting with the military on rockets, missiles and the future of space-based weapons. In his desk diary, housed in the Archives of the Deutches Museum in Munich, he kept track of his cross-country business trips with an engineer's precision. He attended "classified meetings" at U.S. Air Force bases including Wright-Patterson, Elgin, Randolph, Maxwell and Holloman, as well as at Strategic Air Command headquarters, in Omaha, Nebraska and at the Pentagon. He also became a consultant to the Joint Chiefs on Operation Paperclip, visiting the inner circle in the Pentagon to discuss "clearance procedures" and the "hiring of German scientists." As a Paperclip scout, in 1952 Dornberger traveled with what he called "Pentagon Brass" to Germany to "interview German scientists and engineers [in] Frankfurt, Heidelberg, Wiesbaden, Stuttgart, Darmstadt and Witzenhausen."

In his desk diary Dornberger also detailed an ambitious schedule of public appearances, carefully noting the places he traveled and the people he met with. They were the kinds of engagements usually reserved for Congressmen. Throughout the 1950's, he jetted from one event to the next, lecturing at dinners and luncheons and sometimes week-long events. His speeches were always about conquest with titles like "Rockets-Guided Missiles: Key to the Conquest of Space," "Intercontinental Weapons Systems" and "A Realistic Approach to the Conquest of Space." He orated to anyone who would listen: the Men's Club of St. Mark's Episcopal Church, the Boy Scouts of America, the Society of Automotive Engineers. When the Rochester Junior Chamber of Commerce hosted General Dornberger for a women's luncheon in the spring of 1953, the local press covered the event with the headline "Buzz Bomb Mastermind to Address Jaycees Today."

Dornberger became so popular that his memoir about the V-2, originally published in West Germany in 1952, was published in America in 1954. In these pages, Dornberger was able to re-engineer his professional history from that of warmongering Nazi General to beneficent science pioneer. According to Dornberger, the research and development that had gone into the V-2 at Peenemunde was a romantic, science laboratory-by-the-sea affair. There was no mention made of the slave labor facility at Nordhausen or the slaves at Peenemunde. The book was originally titled *V-2: The Shot into Space* (V-2 Der Schuss in All)...

In 1957, Dornberger seemed to have found his true post-Nazi calling, attempting to sell Bell Aircraft's BoMi (bomber-missile) to the Pentagon. BoMi was a rocket-powered manned spacecraft designed for nuclear combat in space. Occasionally, and behind closed doors, usually at the Pentagon, Dornberger faced challenges. He was once pitching the benefits of BoMi to an audience of air force officials when "abusive and insulting remarks" were shouted at him, according to Air Force historian Roy F. Houchin II. In that instance, Dornberger is said to have turned on his audience and insisted that the BoMi would receive a lot more respect if Dornberger had had a chance to fly it against the United States during a war. There was "deafening silence" in the room, Houchin noted.

In 1958, the FBI opened an investigation into General Dornberger based on an insider's tip that he might be engaged in secret discussions with Communist spies. The special agent who interviewed Dornberger did not believe he was spying for the Soviets but honed in on Dornberger's duplicitous nature. "It is believed that subject [Dornberger] could carry on satisfactorily in the role of a double-agent." Dornberger was a cunning man, and this quality, coupled with his scientist's acumen, served him. No matter what the circumstances, Dornberger always seemed to come out on top.

Jacobsen P.409 "In October 1958...the Aero-Medical Association convened...General Dornberger delivered a speech." At page 538 of Jacobsen, *Operation Paperclip* in an end- note] it reads as follows: "In Dornberger papers housed at the Deutches Museum... In one [manuscript] on the use of slave labor, Dornberger cites Himmler as having said to him '[the] power of Germany [meant] a return to the era of slavery.' To this Dornberger says he wondered aloud if other nations might object, to which Himmler said, "after our victory they will not dare."

In *Blowback* by Christopher Simpson, another Dornberger contribution is described at p. 64:

> Walter Dornberger added fuel to this fire (of the perception of the USSR) in 1955 by publishing alarming speculation that the Soviets might attack from the sea, using shorter-range missiles deployed in floating canisters off the coast of the U.S. He was deeply involved in the U.S.'s own ICBM program at this point and his opinions were given considerable weight in public discussion.

So now, after looking at all of the above voluminous background on Walter Dornberger, what can we conclude? Dornberger was most likely the engineering supervisor of Michael Paine who worked at Bell Helicopter in Dallas. And Michael Paine, of course, was the man who abandoned his own home and separated from his wife Ruth at the precise time that Lee Harvey Oswald needed a place to live, just weeks before the Kennedy assassination. The day after the assassination, Paine and his wife were reconciled and Michael Paine moved back into his house.

According to the *Torbitt Document*, discussed earlier, Walter Dornberger was involved in the Kennedy assassination cabal and his job was to get Michael Paine assigned to the position in the Bell Helicopter Company where Paine could be required to participate.

The following appears in an article published by "Lupo Cattivo." As is obvious by the nature of the claims by Cattivo, this information is not thoroughly vetted, but it is in general consistent with all other known assassination research:

> Ruth's husband, Michael Ralph Paine, from which they live separately, but is in frequent contact, works in the Carswell Air Force Base in Fort Worth, armament and electronics department, performs the maintenance work for the B-52 bomber's [atomic missile]... Paine's military intelligence service name is Charles Melvin Coffey. His family has relations with the United Fruit to Rockefeller and Gibraltar Steamship, the CIA offered ships for the Bay of Pigs operation. *Paine is a cousin of the United Fruit-director Alexander Cochrane Forbes and the United Fruit President Thomas Dudley Cabot.*
> Father George Lyman Paine married after his divorce, the Trotskyite Frances Drake, so he gets close contacts with this scene and probably works as a CIA informant. George Paine was the lov-

er of Allen Dulles, [???] Mary Bancroft, friends. Ruth Forbes was previously married to Arthur Young, who is in correspondence with Dulles. Young was one of the founders of the Bell Helicopter, where the Nazi Walter R. Dornberger is Vice- President. Dornberger was responsible for the operations of the V2 rockets into London and [was accused and] should hang for mass murder in Nuremberg. In 1950, he was brought to the United States contrary to the protests and warnings of the British Joint Intelligence Objectives Agency of the [British Government].. Michael Paine also spent seven years working for Bell Aircraft.

Following retirement, Dornberger went to Mexico and later returned to Germany, where he died in 1980 in Baden-Wurttemberg.

Before we conclude this chapter, there is a fascinating and revealing description of Wernher von Braun quoted from James Webb. (a man who knew von Braun) in the book *The Man Who Ran The Moon: James Webb, JFK and the Secret History of Project Apollo* by Piers Bizony (at p. 48):

> Another fascinating aspect of von Braun's complicated character, and one that still preoccupies historians of the Nazi era, was his essential respect for chains of command. He would obey orders and show absolute public loyalty to whomsoever his masters were at any given time. Nevertheless, he somehow managed to pursue his own course within this outer appearance of compliance. In a sense, this made him a trickier fellow to deal with than if he had merely rebelled outright at any initiative from NASA headquarters that he didn't like. "He had the instinct and intuition of an animal," Webb observed of him, "What's going on here, the wind's bringing me a new scent?" Wernher had a remarkable sense of what his audience wanted to hear.

According to Bizony, James Webb and two others, formed the entire upper management of NASA. Reporting to these three were four separate segments of NASA .

As described in the book by Bizony, there was a swift re-ordering of some aspects of power in Washington in 1961. Power was moved from the four field centers to Washington, where the Washington Headquarters had four parts, each supervising one of the four field operations. The roles of the four field centers were (1) advanced planning, (2) manned space flight control, (3) space science and (4) communications. Thus, the regional power-brokers were now under the control of Washington, which included former Nazis von Braun at Huntsville, Alabama and Kurt Debus at Cape Canaveral in Florida. James Webb and Hugh L. Dryden would represent NASA in Congress and at the White House. The latter two were, of course, Americans by birth and not affiliated with the recruitment of the German scientists after the War.

And according to Bizony, Webb reported directly to President Kennedy regarding every major thing that happened in the NASA program during Kennedy's entire term in office.

Contrast this to a statement in an article by Alan Wasser.[57] There, Wasser states "Once President, Kennedy put Vice-President Johnson in personal charge of the space program."

This information reported about Johnson and his role in the Space Program seems to be directly contradicted by Piers Bizony in his book covering, in depth, the administration of NASA.

This question becomes important because some writers accuse Lyndon Johnson of being the mastermind of the Kennedy Assassination. If this were the case, Johnson would have no significant staff to use in carrying out any plot, because if, as Vice-President (because his every movement is thoroughly documented) he would not have an opportunity to meet to plot an assassination with anyone but his own staff in the normal course of business.

So if Johnson were actually in charge of NASA (which was, after all, the space program), then he could have conceivably conspired with von Braun, or Debus or other NASA employees or scientists. (It should be mentioned that Jim Garrison, in his book *On The Trail Of The Assassins*, clearly states that he felt that NASA, through their New Orleans facilities, was complicit in the assassination).

Based on the information presented by Bizony, Johnson's involvement in this manner would clearly be unlikely, if not impossible. But what about some other role involving Werhner von Braun or Walter Dornberger? As discussed in prior chapters, the *Torbitt Document* implicates both of them in the Kennedy assassination.

In the case of Wernher von Braun, anything could be possible. He is one of the most mercurial figures in the whole history of the period. He seemed to willingly join the SS, join the Nazi party and had no particular problems with the issues of slave labor, genocide or any of the other that were going on around him. Further, his role in the missile program was always one of a public relations man, rather than that of a scientific purist or introverted technician. So if we ask, could von Braun have entered into a plot to assassinate the elected President, the answer is probably yes, without much problem.

Of all the putative suspects in the Kennedy assassination case, the role of Dornberger comes closest to defying analysis by merely examining his character and his circumstances. One problem in this analysis is the case of Arthur Rudolph. This case is pathetically recounted in the book *Gestapo USA: When Justice Was Blindfolded*, by Sr. Lt. Colonel William E. Winterstein.

Col. Winterstein was the commander of the German scientists at Fort Bliss for a period of time. One of the most prominent scientists, Arthur Rudolph, after serving NASA for many years and being highly decorated, was deported back to Germany in 1983, 35 years after he came to the U.S, on grounds that he had employed slave labor during WWII.[59]

Reading between the lines of the Winterstein book, one does *not* get the impression that the German scientists were a group of arrogant, un-principled believers in fascism who were just using the United States as a place to live (and escape from their notorious past), while indulging their special interest in rockets and space.

The facts seem to be more like this: the Germans had a stranglehold on the U.S. missile program and the Moon program through their role at Huntsville(von Braun) and Cape Canaveral (Debus) through NASA. They also had a close relationship over the years with the powerful Lyndon Johnson, even if he were not their actual superior at the time.

However, the utility of their stranglehold seems to have been more defensive than offensive. In fact, some said that once the Moon had been reached, the German scientists lost their "protection" by circumstances and hence became prey to the Nazi hunters and Arthur Rudolph was actually overtaken by the Nazi hunters and he lost both his citizenship and his new homeland.

Of course this situation is a two sided coin. On one side, the scientists were indispensable to the most important (by far) of the nation's weapons programs. Thus, they were in a position to plot and act in an aggressive and conspiratorial manner, especially if they had maintained that rigid military hierarchical discipline which they brought with them to this country.

But the other side of the coin is that they were living in fear of deportation at the hands of the equally powerful Nazi-hunters, backed by Israel. So they were also vulnerable to the grossest type of blackmail.

The question becomes particularly interesting when one examines the character of Dornberger. During his career in Nazi Germany, he never joined the Nazi Party, much less the SS. This was probably due both to religious scruples or affiliations and to his loyalty to his Regular Army compatriots of 30 years. (The historical record does not disclose the religion of Dornberger, though he acted decisively to protect his Catholic friend who was in trouble with the Nazis).

Once he was established in the U.S., his practice of speaking before the Jaycees and the Boy Scouts seems to belie any association with radical right-wing extremists. Dornberger was, however, a true realist about weapons and geopolitics. If Dornberger perceived that either Eisenhower, Kennedy or Johnson were jeopardizing the integrity of the missile or any other crucial defense program, he probably would have been in favor of the assassination as a matter of necessity. (The murder of a President would not cause these Hitler associates to lose any sleep out of guilt. We know that for sure). And that could have (conceivably) been a perfectly good call, a matter of which we will never know the answer for sure.

The other aspect of his career that comes into play is the fact that the demented Nazi SS fanatics like Himmler or Kammler were always more of a hindrance rather than a help to weapons development. Even Hitler was constantly jeopardizing the German technological weapons programs with his nightmares, depression, paranoia and all the rest. For this reason, it is hard to imagine Dornberger in league with the assortment of Czarist Cavalry, European Monarchist pretenders, Ukrainian Nazi collaberators and the others who were central to the plot in Dallas. Dornberger could likely have been the agent who made arrangements with Michael Paine for housing Lee Harvey Oswald. This could have been because of his long, close friendship with von Braun, or because of blackmail over a possible deportation, either of himself or his friends.

Dornberger likely felt a lifelong distaste for the U.S. Government because it had, after all, pretty much temporarily destroyed his beloved Germany. This was a feeling shared by virtually every top Hitler associate.

It also deserves mention that at least three very major figures in the assassination history, namely Thomas J. Dodd, Allen Dulles and John J. McCloy all had hands-on experience dealing with the Nazi problem in Europe. This raises further suspicion around the major former Nazi's in the U.S., especially the scientists.

Unfortunately, unlike other parts of the "conspiracy theory" universe, like blaming the French Mafia or OAS, or J.Edgar Hoover, or the American mafia, it is not really possible to exclude Dornberger through in-depth study of the person or the circumstances. We will have to await the possible further release of classified documents to resolve the enigma of Walter Dornberger and his lifelong friend, Baron Wernher von Braun.

Notes:

The following are the reference works cited in the above chapter:
In the Rocket and the Reich: Peenemunde and the Coming of the Ballistic Missile Era, by James Neufeld.

Blowback: The First Full Account of America's Recruitment of Nazis and its Disastrous Effect on The cold war, Our Domestic and Foreign Policy, by Christopher Simpson.

Operation Paperclip: The Secret Intelligence Program that Brought Nazi Schientists to America, by Annie Jacobsen.

The Paperclip Conspiracy: The Hunt for the Nazi Scientists, by Tom Bower.

Secret Agenda: The United States Government, Nazi Scientists and Operation Paperclip; 1945 to 1990, by Linda Hunt.

The following appears at:[http://www.US-politik.ch/teil7.htm] Published by "Lupo Cattivo" which is a European-based blog claiming to be similar to Wikileaks [search for "Walter Dornberger" "James O. Eastland" OR "James Eastland"] and select Translate:

The Man Who Ran The Moon: James Webb, JFK and the Secret History of Project Apollo by Piers Bizony See also the article cited in the text by Alan Wasser dated 6-20-05, read on 3-8-15 on the website [www.thespacereview.com/article/396/1].

Gestapo USA: When Justice Was Blindfolded, by Sr. Lt. Colonel William E. Winterstein.

Chapter 27

JAMES O. EASTLAND
AND THE JFK ASSASSINATION

This chapter deals with information on the life and motivations of James O. Eastland. There has never been a definitive biography written about Eastland although he was a dominant figure in the 1950's and 1960's. There is, however, a good basic beginning to be found on his Wikipedia page [en.wikipedia.org/wiki/James_Eastland] which will serve as our beginning basis for facts about Senator Eastland.

THE EARLY LIFE AND CAREER OF JAMES O. EASTLAND

James Oliver Eastland was born November 28, 1904 in Doddsville, Mississipppi which is located in the delta region. He was a dominant force in the U.S. Senate, as a powerful Democrat who served in 1941 and again from 1943 until his resignation December 27, 1978. For 31 years, from 1947 to 1978, he served alongside John Stennis, also a Democrat. These two, for a time, became the longest serving two-person state delegation in the Senate in U.S. history. Their record was subsequently surpassed, however, by the duo of Strom Thurmond and Ernest Hollings of South Carolina who served together for thirty-six years. At the time of his retirement, Eastland was the most senior member of the Senate. He compiled a record in support of the Conservative coalition.

The grandfather of James O. Eastland had ridden with Confederate guerrilla General Nathan Bedford Forrest in the Civil War.

The family of James O. Eastland were wealthy plantation owners in Sunflower County Mississippi. Eastland was the son of Woods Caperton Eastland, a lawyer and cotton planter, and Alma Teresa (Austin) Eastland. In the Senate, Eastland was an ardent segregationist. He came by this attitude due, no doubt, to the abysmal social conditions in which he was reared. Lynchings of blacks was a frequent occurrence in Sunflower County. Eastland was born just nine months after the lynching of Luther Holbert and his wife on the Eastland plantation in 1904, an event which was led by Eastland's father, a pharmacist as well as a planter. Holbert was not hanged, but rather burned at the stake because he was accused of murdering James Eastland, the uncle and namesake of Senator Eastland.

Some Sunflower County observers say that there were lynchings most Sundays on the Eastland plantation, carried out by Eastland's father.

The NAACP compiled statistics showing that in the first three decades of the 1900's, in the 17 counties lying in whole or in part in the Mississippi Delta region of Mississippi, there were 66 lynchings. This was out of a total of 188 confirmed lynchings in the entire state.

In 1905, young James Eastland moved with his parents to Forest, Mississippi where he attended the segregated public schools. Woods Eastland was active in politics and served as a district attorney.

Growing up in an atmosphere of racial violence left Eastland with a doctrinaire racist attitude typical of the South at the time. According to a statement attributed to Eastland, he claimed "that only the purest of white blood flowed through the Eastland family veins. I know that the white race is a superior race. It has ruled the world. It has given us civilization. It is responsible for all the progress on earth."

Eastland attended the University of Mississippi (1922-1924), Vanderbilt University (1925-1926), and the University of Alabama (1926-1927) before studying law with his father and attaining admission to the bar. While a lawyer in rural Mississippi, he served one term in the state House of Representatives from 1928 to 1932

In the 1930's, Eastland took over his family's Sunflower County plantation, and eventually expanded it to nearly 6,000 acres (9.3 square miles). Even after entering politics, he considered himself first and foremost a cotton planter. While agriculture was becoming mechanized, he still had many African-American laborers on the plantation, many working as sharecroppers.

Eastland was first appointed to the Senate in 1941 by Democratic Governor Paul B. Johnson, Sr., following the death of Senator Pat Harrison. Johnson first offered the appointment to Eastland's father, who declined and suggested his son. Johnson appointed James Eastland on the condition that he not run in the special election for the seat later in the year. Eastland kept his word and the election was won by 2nd District Congressman Wall Doxey.

In 1942, however, Eastland ran for the Senate on his own initiative and was one of three candidates who challenged Doxey for a full term. Doxey had the support of U.S. President Franklin D. Roosevelt and Mississippi's senior U.S. Senator, Theodore G. Bilbo, but Eastland defeated Doxey in the Democratic primary. In those days, winning the Democratic nomination was tantamount to election in Mississippi. It was a one-party state dominated by white Democrats since disenfranchisement of African-Americans with the passage of the 1890 state constitution, which used poll taxes, literacy tests and grandfather clauses to exclude them from the political system. Eastland returned to the Senate on January 3, 1943.

The racism of the Mississippi Delta in that era was not just limited to that locale. Senior Senator Theodore Bilbo was said to have ties to an outside organization with direct Nazi ties. On the other side of the ledger, there was civil rights leader Fannie Lou Hamer, who was also a singer, storyteller and organizer of anti-segregationist efforts.

Once Eastland went to Washington, FDR and Eastland developed a working relationship that enabled Eastland to oppose New Deal programs unpopular in Mississippi while he supported FDR's agenda on many other issues. Eastland was effective in developing this type of arrangement with presidents of both parties during his long tenure in the Senate. As a result he gained major federal investment in the state, such as infrastructure construction including the Tennessee-Tombigbee Waterway, and federal relief after disasters such as Hurricane Camille.

President Eisenhower feared Eastland and let him dispense Republican patronage. Author Robert Sherrill in *Gothic Politics* repeated a noteworthy quote: "Eastland has been called 'a mad dog loose in the streets of justice.'" This evaluation of Eastland undoubtedly sprung from the brand of hate that Eastland brought with him from the violent territory of Sunflower County, Mississippi from whence he came.

In 1956, Eastland was appointed as chairman of the Senate Judiciary Committee. Under the Senate's seniority rules, he was next in line for the chairmanship and there was no significant effort to deny him the post, which he held until his retirement. He was re-elected five times, facing concerted GOP opposition only twice and not until the late 20th century, at which time party politics were shifting after passage of civil rights legislation that enforced constitutional rights for minorities.

As an illustration of the formidable power wielded by Eastland when he was at the height of his influence in Washington, we can quote from Senator Edward Kennedy's book *True Compass: A Memoir* where Kennedy wrote the following about Eastland:[8]

> As for the committee assignments, I knew who it was I needed to go to. Senator James O. Eastland of Mississippi was chairman of the Senate Judiciary Committee, but this does not begin to express this man's influence on Capitol Hill.
> [At pp.192-194] If you were to visit his office during the day, more often than not you would find his desk covered with oil maps. There would be oilmen in there from Mississippi and the Gulf areas, and they'd all be bent over these maps absorbed in oil deals that they were working out. These oil meetings would go on for the better part of a week. Everything that happened on that committee [Judiciary] in fact happened after 5 P.M. That's when Eastland

would invite his people in for a drink. Everett Dirksen of Illinois would come in an drink with him, and Richard Russell, and Hugh Scott of Pennsylvania, John McClellan of Arkansas would stop in but didn't drink.

These men had little use for other committee members-people such as Charles "Mac" Mathias of Maryland, or Phil Hart of Michigan, whom I've always thought of as the conscience of the Senate at that time.... I worked with James Eastland; in fact, the two of us became friends.

In humbly requesting if not begging for his initial Senate committee assignments, Eastland told Sen. Edward Kennedy: "... you've got a lot of Eye-talians [in your state]... you drink that drink, [the straight whiskey] so you're on the Immigration Committee. You Kennedy's always care about the Negras ... so you're on the Civil Rights subcommittee ... I think you're always caring about, you know, the Constitution ... so I'll put you on the Constitution Subcommittee."

In the late 1950's and early 1960's, Eastland was engaged in activities which were both secretive and subversive. These were typified by the actions of the KKK and other similar extremist groups in Mississippi at the time.

The notorious Southern Manifesto, which had to be signed by southern segregationists to prove their bona fides was drafted by James O. Eastland on March 12, 1956. The first White Citizens Council was formed on July 11, 1954 in Indianola, Mississippi, the county seat of Sunflower County.

In Sunflower County, 68% of the population were African-Americans. On Eastland's plantation, blacks got $.30 per hour, some had no toilets and slept 4 to a bed. The nearest toilet was 3 miles away. Eastland grossed $250,000 per year on his 5,800 acre plantation.

Eastland was known for his strong opposition to the civil rights movement. When the Supreme Court issued its decision in the landmark case *Brown v. Board of Education of Topeka, Kansas* 347 US 4983(1954), ruling that segregation in public schools was unconstitutional, Eastland, like most Southern Democrats, denounced it.

In a speech given in Senatobia, Mississippi on August 12, 1955, he said:

> On May 17, 1954, the Constitution of the United States was destroyed because of the Supreme Court's decision. You are not obliged to obey the decisions of any court which are plainly fraudulent sociological considerations.

Eastland testified to the Senate ten days after the Brown decision came down:

The Southern institution of racial segregation or racial separation was the correct, self-evident truth which arose from the chaos and confusion of the Reconstruction period. Separation promotes racial harmony. It permits each race to follow its own pursuits, and its own civilization. Segregation is not discrimination… Mr. President, it is the law of nature, it is the law of God, that every race has the right and the duty to perpetuate itself. All free men have the right to associate exclusively with member of their own race, free from governmental interference, if they so desire.

Three civil rights workers, namely Mickey Schwerner, James Chaney and Andrew Goodman, disappeared in Mississippi on June 21, 1964. Almost every American living at the time knew of this tragic situation. In regard to this murder Eastland reportedly told President Lyndon Johnson that the incident was a hoax and there was no Ku Klux Klan in the state. He suggested that the three had gone to Chicago. [From the Johnson tapes]:

> Johnson: Jim, we've got three kids missing down there. What can I do about it?
> Eastland: Well, I don't know. I don't believe there's…. I don't believe there's three missing.
> Johnson: We've got their parents down here..
> Eastland: I believe it's a publicity stunt…

Johnson once said, "Jim Eastland could be standing right in the middle of the worst Mississippi flood ever known, and he'd say the niggers caused it, helped out by the Communists."

THE MISSISSIPPI SOVEREIGNTY COMMISSION, WHITE CITIZENS COUNCIL AND THE KLAN

A topic which is shrouded in a certain sinister type of mystery is the Mississippi State Sovereignty Commission. The idea of a CIA-type organization operated by a state government would have to be considered unusual by most Americans to say the least.

The Mississippi State Sovereignty Commission was a secret state police department operating from 1956 to 1977 with the goal of suppressing the civil rights movement and maintaining segregation. The commission kept files, harassed and branded many people as communist infiltrators. They had agents who were retired FBI, CIA and military intelligence employees or agents. The files of the Mississippi Sovereignty Commission grew to be much larger and extensive than one would imagine. One reason for this is the Commission probably needed something to do which would be non-controversial and not land them in either a State or Federal penitentiary.

The Sovereignty Commission cooperated closely with the White Citizens Councils. When Ross Barnett became Governor of Mississippi in 1960, the Sovereignty Commission began funding the Councils with the full approval of the Mississippi legislature. Along with the White Citizens Councils working in the cause of segregation was the Ku Klux Klan. Most of Mississippi's Klan activity took place in the Southern counties of the State. In the racist ecology of Mississippi, the White Citizens Council was made up mostly of middle-class segregationists while the Klan was considered the province of the blue-collar racists.

From his taking a job working for the NAACP in 1954 until a March 1961 sit-in in the Jackson, Mississippi public library, Medgar Evers had been, almost singlehandedly, the entire civil rights movement in Mississippi.

The Links Between James O. Eastland and the Kennedy Assassination

One of the basic premises of our research is that the Senate Internal Security Subcommittee was linked to the JFK assassination. James O. Eastland was the official chairman of that committee. Ergo, Eastland is linked to the assassination. There is, however, a missing link in that logic. That is because Eastland delegated his active chairmanship of SISS to Sen. Thomas J. Dodd (D,CT). So what evidence is there that Eastland was "in the know" regarding the JFK plot? In 2015, this issue was resolved beyond any doubt by the publication of the book *General Walker* by Dr. Jeffrey Caulfield. But outside of the book by Caulfield, there is some linkage from the assassination to Eastland based on the circumstances of the "Bayo-Pauley" raid which was explored in a prior chapter on SISS. We know that after that anti-Cuban operation, the mercenary soldier of fortune Gerry Patrick Hemming stated that he went on from Florida to Washington to meet with James O. Eastland.

In her book *Where Rebels Roost* (WRR), author Susan Klopfer presents other linkages leading from Eastland to the JFK assassination. WRR is the definitive work on the subject of Mississippi segregationists. Author Klopfer is possibly the most outstanding and admired historian to research and write about the events in that troubled period. So, Klopfer's inclusion of the JFK material in her masterwork is almost enough to prove the connection between Eastland, other violent associates of Eastland and the murder of JFK. To back up the above statement, let's look at Klopfer's evidence against Eastland.

Medgar Evers Is Assassinated

On June 12, 1963, civil rights leader Medgar Evers was shot by a sniper from a distance of 150 yards. A man by the name of Byron de la Beckwith of Greenwood, Mississippi was charged as the killer. Greenwood is about 30 miles east of Indianola. By 1963, Medgar Evers was in first place on a "death list" which was being circulated in the State of Mississippi.

As an illustration of the level of violence in the minds of Mississippians at the time of the murder of Evers, the following story was circulating, though never verified. According to this rumor, the FBI made a plea-bargain with a gangster named Gregory Scarpa up north in New York. Scarpa was then brought to Mississippi and Scarpa, being a veteran mobster, was able to kidnap and torture a known member of the White Citizen's Council until he revealed the identity of the murderer of Evers, de la Beckwith. (This story is reported by author Klopfer at p. 399).

Byron de la Beckwith was active in Greenwood's White Citizen's Council. In May, 1966, he had applied for a position with the Mississippi Sovereignty Commission but was not hired. According to the FBI, many years later, it was rumored that the murder of Evers had been ordered by the Klan.

GENERAL WALKER, MISSISSIPPI AND THE JFK ASSASSINATION

Focusing again on the JFK assassination, we have the following digression mentioned by author Klopfer in *Where Rebels Roost*. "In the fifth volume of the 26 volumes of evidence published by the Warren Commission, there is proof that the John Birch Society cell of which General Edwin Walker was a member, was used as a vehicle for bringing military intelligence agents from Munich, Germany to Dallas to operate at the field level in the assassination of JFK. The source for this information is a published lecture given by Mr. David Emory.

There are not many specifics on the Walker-Munich connection in the JFK assassination histories. It should be pointed out that there is one direct connection between General Edwin Walker and Eastland's Mississippi. This came in September, 1962 when Walker figured prominently in segregationist violence at Ole Miss.

This insurrection was caused by the admission of James Meredith to the University of Mississippi. During the insurrection, Walker was in Oxford and rendered some encouragement to the rioters. One can read about the events at "Ole Miss" and conclude that Walker's actions were very limited and his involvement was grossly exaggerated by the Kennedy administration. Walker was heard to say to the Mob "good going, boys" However, the mere presence of such a well-known militant would be expected to inflame rioters just by itself. Ultimately, Walker was charged with sedition and insurrection and was held for 90 days in a psychiatric ward as a result of his actions at Oxford in September, 1962.

In April, 1963, the alleged attempt by Lee Harvey Oswald on the life of General Walker took place in Dallas. So Walker's connection to, (but not necessarily guilt in) the JFK assassination can scarcely be denied.

Author Susan Klopfer offers the following information which is relevant, in part, to Mississippi and the JFK assassination, though focusing on the research of John Bevalaqua and the immediate subject of his research, a millionaire by the name of Wycliffe P. Draper. Draper is a popular target of anti-conservative writers because of his identification with and funding of eugenics. Draper funded many "oddball" conservative causes including not only eugenics, but the promotion of a "back to Africa" movement for African-Americans, as well as the legitimate research done by the University of Minnesota in their well-known studies of identical twins reared separately. Draper funded much of the research in the best selling book *The Bell Curve*.

In a more sinister vein, Draper also funded the Mississippi Sovereignty Commission in 1963 and 1964. The MSC attorney referred to Draper's contributions as coming from "The Wall Street Gang." Coincidentally, 1963 and 1964 were years of great import in the TX-MS-LA region, featuring the assassinations of Medgar Evers and JFK and the questionable activities of General Edwin Walker and the murder of the three civil rights workers, Goodwin, Chaney and Schwerner in 1964.

Researcher John Bevalaqua had been investigating the Kennedy assassination and Wickliffe P. Draper for almost 20 years. Wycliffe Draper had direct ties to the Nazi movement. Bevalaqua offered some interesting observations in December, 2009 at a well-known website, including the following:

> Draper was linked to the Medgar Evers, Jr. murder via Senator James Eastland, from Mississippi, who headed up the Draper Genetics Committee for the Senate Internal Security Subcommittee. Evers' killer was KKK and NSRP member, Byron De La Beckwith, who was visited often in jail after he was arrested for the murder of Medgar Evers, Jr. by Maj. Gen. Edwin Walker who had organized and led the riots at Ole Miss when James Meredith attempted to enroll there as the first Afro-American student.

Thus General Walker, by visiting Evers' murderer in prison, knowingly linked himself to the cause of the militant segregationists in Mississippi, the subject of Klopfer's writing.

Many experts on the JFK assassination are willing to connect the assassination, at least in part, to the KKK and segregationist activities. They might do this, if for no other reason, than the reliance on political violence by the KKK, the NSRP and the other segregationist groups of that period. There is also the close physical proximity of the Mississippi Delta, New

Orleans and Louisiana, and Texas; Dallas, in particular. These are the locations where the Kennedy tragedy played out and also the travesty of Goodwin, Chaney and Schwerner

Maj. Gen. Edwin A. Walker was specifically named by Jack Ruby, who shot Lee Harvey Oswald, in his Warren Commission testimony as being directly involved in the assassination of President John F. Kennedy.

THE GUY BANISTER CONNECTION TO MISSISSIPPI AND THE JFK ASSASSINATION

Author Susan Klopfer wrote in *Where Rebels Roost* that "Banister was later linked to Lee Harvey Oswald and Mississippi's Senator through involvement with Eastland's Senate Internal Security Subcommittee or SISS (sometimes called "SISSY"), and the same information can be found in *The Emmett Till Book,* by Susan Klopfer and another excellent book by Devery S. Anderson, *Emmett Till: The Murder That Shocked the World and Propelled the Civil Rights Movement.*

The quotes by Klopfer referring to Guy Banister need some clarification. Guy Banister was a private investigator in New Orleans in the early 1960's. But the term private investigator does no justice to Banister. He could be more aptly described as a traffic controller for most or all covert operations by spy agencies in the South, or even having a major role in worldwide conspiracies of the 1955-1965 era. Banister is credited by some writers for handling the payoff money for attempted assassinations of French President Charles de Gaulle.

The next paragraph is of great note because, unlike much JFK information and rumors, it was published in an well-circulated newspaper at the time it occurred. The only difficulty with the article is that it apparently confuses the HUAC committee with the SISS committee. It also apparently misidentified SISS counsel Robert Morris as Robert Morrison. Robert Morris had actually served both McCarthy and SISS as staff and/ or counsel at separate times.

The actual quote of the article by Klopfer is as follows:

> The *New Orleans Times-Picayune* on March 23, 1956, reported that [Robert] Morrison [a former chief counsel for Sen. Joseph McCarthy] and Banister traveled to Greenwood, Mississippi, to confer personally with Senator Eastland for more than three hours. 'Describing the conference as completely "satisfactory," Morrison told the reporter that "Mr. Banister has complete liaison with the committee's staff which was the main object of our trip."

In the same vein;

Another Eastland operative, private investigator John D. Sullivan had worked under Banister [both in the FBI and privately] and as a private self-employed investigator often did work for hire for the Sovereignty Commission, the White Citizen's Councils, of which he was an active member, and for Eastland's Senate Internal Security Subcommittee [SISS], as had Banister and Lee Harvey Oswald.

The next quote by Susan Klopfer is one of the most direct and significant quotes in all of the JFK assassination literature:

> Some twenty-nine years later, in testimony before the Kennedy Assassination Records Review Board during a Dallas hearing on November 18, 1994, the late Senator Eastland was directly implicated in the president's assassination by one of the author/theorists invited to testify. He said "Lee Harvey Oswald was quite possibly an agent of the Senate Internal Security Subcommittee and he was doing the bidding of [Senator Thomas J.] Dodd, Eastland and Morrison [Morris??]," author John McLaughlin swore,[presumably under oath]. (See Klopfer, *Where Rebels Roost*, p. xxvi).

THE LIFE OF JAMES O. EASTLAND IN THE PERIOD AFTER NOVEMBER 23, 1963

Eastland, along with senators Robert Byrd, John McClellan, Olin D. Johnston, Sam Ervin, and Strom Thurmond, made unsuccessful attempts to block confirmation of Thurgood Marshall, an African-American, to the Federal Court of Appeals and the US Supreme Court.

Eastland, like most of his southern colleagues, opposed the Civil Rights Act of 1964, which prohibited segregation of public places and facilities. Its passage caused many Mississippi Democrats to support Barry Goldwater's presidential bid that year, but Eastland did not publicly oppose the election of Lyndon Johnson. Four years earlier he had quietly supported John. F. Kennedy's presidential campaign, though Mississippi voted that year for unpledged electors. This support for Kennedy, despite JFK's primary heated battle against LBJ in 1960 for the Democratic nomination, could be considered relevant in re the JFK assassination. This would indicate that Eastland was not an inveterate hater of the Kennedys. Although Goldwater was soundly defeated by incumbent Lyndon Johnson, he carried Mississippi with 87 percent of the popular vote (his best showing in any state).

This strong showing by Goldwater was largely because of white opposition to LBJ's Civil Rights Act of 1964. This raises the obvious question: if Mississippi strongly rejected LBJ in 1964, why would Eastland (if he did) participate in the murder of JFK only to have made LBJ president? This was an outcome which quickly went sour as Mississippi turned against LBJ in favor of Goldwater less than a year later in the 1964 elections. As one of the two or three most powerful Democratic Senators at the time, Eastland must surely have known about LBJ's deep-down pro-civil rights and pro-welfare beliefs and policies, i.e. The Great Society.

In 1966, freshman congressman Prentiss Walker ran against Eastland. Walker was the first Republican to represent Mississippi at the federal level since Reconstruction and the beginning of the late 19th century disenfranchisement of blacks. This was one of the early campaigns where the Republican Party worked to attract white conservatives in the South to its ranks. Following the lead of national Democrats, who supported civil rights legislation in 1964 and 1965, most African Americans in the South began to vote with the Democratic Party on national candidates. Republican Congressman Walker's defeat was judged as "very devastating" to the growth of the Mississippi GOP.

Eastland was often at odds with Johnson's policy on civil rights, but their friendship remained close. Johnson often sought Eastland's support and guidance on other issues, such as the failed nomination of Abe Fortas for Chief Justice of the Supreme Court in 1968. In the 1950's, Johnson was one of three Senators from the South who did not sign the Southern Manifesto, but Eastland and most Southern Senators did, vowing resistance to school integration. Actually, Eastland *wrote* the Southern Manifesto. The fact that LBJ was not asked to sign the Southern Manifesto is often cited as proof that LBJ had irrevocably "resigned' from the conservative Southern coalition at that moment and was never considered part of the Southern segregationist bloc thereafter.

During his presidency, JFK had dealings with the powerful Eastland regarding White House-Senate business. Contrary to popular opinion, Eastland did not use the appointment of a man named Harold Cox to a federal judgeship as leverage against John F. Kennedy's appointment of Thurgood Marshall to a federal judgeship. Cox was nominated by Kennedy more than a year before Marshall came up for consideration and his nomination resulted from a personal conversation between Cox and Kennedy. The president, not wanting to upset the powerful chairman of the Judiciary Committee, generally acceded to Eastland's requests on judicial confirmations in Mississippi, which resulted in white segregationists dominating control of the Federal courts in the state.

During his later years, in the face of increasing black political power in Mississippi, Eastland avoided associating with racist positions. He hired black Mississippians to serve on the staff of the Judiciary Committee. Eastland noted to aides that his earlier position on race was due primarily to the political realities of the times, i.e., as a major political figure in a southern state in the 1950s and 1960s

The GOP did work to elect two House candidates, Trent Lott and Thad Cochran, who later became influential U.S. senators from the state. Recognizing that Nixon would handily carry Mississippi, Eastland did not endorse the national Democratic candidate, George McGovern of South Dakota, who was an extreme liberal. Four years later, Eastland supported the candidacy of fellow Southern Democrat Jimmy Carter of Georgia, rather than Nixon's successor, President Gerald R. Ford, Jr. Eastland's former press secretary, Larry Speakes, a Mississippi native, served as a press spokesman for Gerald Ford and U.S. Senator Robert J. Dole in the latter's vice-presidential campaign on the Ford ticket During his last Senate term, Eastland served as President pro tempore of the Senate, as he was the longest-serving Democrat in the Senate.

In 1972, Eastland was reelected with 58 percent of the vote in his closest contest ever. His Republican opponent, Gil Carmichael, an automobile dealer from Meridian, was likely aided by President Richard Nixon's landslide reelection in 40 states, including 78 percent of Mississippi's popular vote. However, Nixon worked "under the table" to support Eastland who was a long-time personal friend. Nixon and other Republicans provided little support for Carmichael to avoid alienating conservative Southern Democrats.

When he considered running for re-election in 1978, he sought black support. He won the support of Aaron Henry, civil rights leader and president of the NAACP, but he ultimately decided not to seek re-election. Due in part to the independent candidacy of Charles Evers siphoning off votes from the Democratic candidate, Republican 4th District Representative Thad Cochran won the race to succeed Eastland. Eastland resigned two days after Christmas to give Cochran a leg up on seniority. After his retirement, he remained friends with Aaron Henry and sent contributions to the NAACP, but he publicly stated that he "didn't regret a thing" in his public career.

Anti-Communist Efforts

Eastland served on a subcommittee investigating the Communist Party. As chairman of the Senate Internal Security Subcommittee, he subpoenaed some employees of the *New York Times*, which was at the time taking a strong position on its editorial page that Mississippi should adhere to the Brown decision. The SISS operated largely in secret. The members apparently feared no one or nothing when it came to anti-Communist zeal. The following is due to the vast increase in the influence of journalists, but in 1956, 29 out of 35 witnesses called in executive session by SISS and 14 out of 18 called in open session were past or present staff of the *New York Times*. The *Times* countered in its January 5, 1956 editorial:

Our faith is strong that long after Senator Eastland and his present subcommittee are gone, long after segregation has lost its final battle in the South, long after all that was known as McCarthyism is a dim, unwelcome memory, long after the last Congressional committee has learned that it cannot tamper successfully with a free press, the *New York Times* will be speaking for [those] who make it, and only for [those] who make it, and speaking, without fear or favor, the truth as it sees it.

Jay Sourwine, Chief Counsel for SISS, along with Eastland charged a witness that appeared before SISS, Robert Shelton, with contempt of Congress. The case went to court. The attorney for Shelton was Joseph L. Rauh, Jr. Rauh was an elite attorney with formidable skills. Rauh brought Sourwine and Eastland before the court as hostile witnesses. Sourwine was embarrassed due to misrepresentations he had made. James O. Eastland fared even worse than Sourwine. On 77 questions, Eastland answered "I don't know" or "I don't recall." Eastland was forced to claim that he could not remember even one detail of his hearings against the *New York Times*, though the hearings had lasted for months.

Like Joe McCarthy, whose reputation plunged after the Army-McCarthy hearings, Eastland "noticeably limped [after] his encounter with [attorney] Rauh…too many people in Washington could answer the questions… [where Eastland] 'couldn't remember.'"

Eastland subsequently allowed SISS to become dormant as issues such as the perceived threat of Communism receded. However, Eastland was a staunch supporter of FBI Director J. Edgar Hoover, and shared intelligence with the FBI, including leaks from the State Department. Hoover received intelligence that Eastland was among members of Congress who had received money and favors from Rafael Trujillo, dictator of the Dominican Republic. Eastland had regularly defended Trujillo from the Senate floor. Hoover declined to pursue Eastland on corruption charges – but accepting money from foreign officials is illegal. Like all the other confidential information Hoover gathered on members of Congress, Hoover could well have used this information against Eastland if he had the chance.

In his last years in the Senate, Eastland was recognized by most Senators as one who knew how to wield the legislative powers he had accumulated. Many Senators, including liberals who opposed many of his conservative positions, acknowledged the fairness with which he chaired the Judiciary Committee, sharing staff and authority that chairmen of other committees jealously held for themselves. He maintained personal ties with stalwart liberal Democrats such as Ted Kennedy, Joe Biden and Phil Hart, even though they disagreed on many issues. Following Johnson's retirement from the White House, Eastland frequently visited Johnson at his Texas ranch.

Eastland died on February 19, 1986. The law library at Ole Miss was named after Eastland until 2012. This caused some controversy in Mississippi, given Eastland's earlier racist positions, but the University benefited financially from Eastland's many friends and supporters, as it has done from other political figures.

James Eastland was the most recent President pro tempore to have served during a vacancy in the Vice Presidency. He did so twice during the tumultuous 1970's, first from October to December 1973 following Spiro Agnew's resignation until the swearing-in of Gerald Ford as Vice President, and then from August to December 1974, from the time that Ford became President until Nelson Rockefeller was sworn is as Vice President. During these periods, Eastland was second in the presidential line of succession, behind only Speaker of the House Carl Albert.

Following his death, the extensive papers of James O. Eastland were bequeathed to the Ole Miss Law School in Oxford, Mississippi. The Ole Miss Law School was re-named the James O. Eastland College of Law. Eastland's papers were locked in a room and thereafter, absolutely no researcher or historian was granted any access to the papers.

When our often-mentioned author Susan Klopfer requested access to the files, she received a letter from the Law School librarian stating "in response to your Freedom of Information Act (FOIA) request, that the Eastland records are private and hence not subject to FOIA." In August, 2004, the Law School transferred the records to the Archives and Special Collections of the J.D. Williams [Ole Miss] Library. According to one researcher who was finally allowed to inspect them, the records had been "sanitized."

The Law School of the University of Mississippi no longer bears the name of James O. Eastland, his name having been taken off the school for reasons which are not available even on the Internet from any source. One can only assume that something came up which would make that name detrimental to the school or generally. Eastland's name is still seen on dedication monuments on Interstate 55 north of Jackson, which is named the James O. Eastland highway. Incidentally, according to author Klopfer the papers of Senator John Stennis, Eastland's segregationist Senatorial papers from Mississippi, also remained sealed as of 2005.

The final item about James O. Eastland which we can report is a quote in an oral history for which Eastland was interviewed in 1975. This oral history is in the possession of the Lyndon Baines Johnson Library. In this interview, Eastland was asked about the Warren Commission. He stated at p. 9 "...I had no contact at all with the Warren Commission. The President called me in advance and told me what he planned to do...It was a good procedure. I think their conclusions were wrong. I think that some foreign country, the ruler of some foreign country, was behind the Kennedy Assassination."

Your writer gladly accepts this endorsement by Eastland of the thesis of The Three Barons.

Notes:

This author has quoted extensively from [en.wikipedia.org/wiki/James_Eastland] last edited 09-08-2017, retrieved 09-21-17. This represents the most concise (and one of the few available sources) of general information about James O. Eastland.

Another source of information on the subject is:
Marjorie Hunter "James O. Eastland is Dead at 81, Leading Senate Foe of Integration" *New York Times*, February 20, 1986.

The following book, cited in the text, is one of the classics on civil rights in Mississippi:
Where Rebels Roost: Mississippi Civil Rights Revisited by Susan Klopfer with Fred Klopfer and Barry Klopfer (Lulu.com 2005).

Gothic politics in the Deep South: Stars of the new Confederacy (1969) by Robert Sherrill. The "mad dog" quote is found at page 177.

True Compass: A Memoir (2009) by Edward Kennedy.

For a source regarding living conditions in Sunflower County, see:
Eyes on the Prize: America's Civil Rights Years, 1954–1965, (1987) by Juan Williams.

WhiteHouseTapes.org :: The secret White House tapes and recordings of Presidents Kennedy, Johnson, Nixon, Roosevelt, Truman, and Eisenhower regarding the LBJ conversation with Eastland about the missing civil rights workers.

For the quote about Eastland blaming a flood on black people, see:
Robert Kennedy and His Times (2002) by Arthur Schlesinger, Jr. p. 234.

For a commentary on the Mississippi Sovereignty Commission, refer to:
Susan Klopfer [a JFK author] in an article entitled "Mississippi Sovereignty Commission, State Government Funded Racist Department" on 1-1-10, read on 2-14-15. [mississippisovereigntycommission.blogspot.com/2010/01/Mississippi-jfk-links.html]

General Walker and the Murder of President Kennedy: The Extensive New Evidence of a Radical-Right Conspiracy (2015) by Jeffrey H. Caulfield M.D.

From a lecture given by Mr. David Emory and reprinted in a writing entitled Conspiracy Nation Vol.I No.92, of an uncertain date: www.textfiles.com/conspiracy/CN/cn1-92.txt

For background on the riots at Oxford, Mississippi in 1962, see: *An American Insurrection: James Meredith and the Battle of Oxford, Mississippi, 1962 (2003)* by William Doyle.

The book which is associated with Draper and mentioned in the text is:
The Bell Curve: Intelligence and Class Structure in America (1994) by Richard J. Herrnstein and Charles Murray.

The Bevilaqua citation is from: https://deeppoliticsforum.com/forums/forumdisplay. php?4-JFK-Assassination

As mentioned in the text, see:
The Emmett Till Book (2005) by Susan Klopfer.

Emmett Till: The Murder That Shocked the World and Propelled The Civil Rights Movement, (2015) by Devery S. Anderson

For the information on Guy Banister, see:
The Man Who Knew Too Much, by Dick Russell, at p.396.

The article by the *Times-Picayune* quotes can be found as independently reported in the March 23, 1956 issue of the *New Orleans Times Picayune*.

For data on the electoral issues described in the text, see:
Dave Leip's Atlas of U.S. Presidential Elections - Data Graphs.

"Challenging the Status Quo: Rubel Lex Phillips and the Mississippi Republican Party (1963-1967)", *The Journal of Mississippi History*, XLVII, No. 4 (November 1985), p. 256.

On the Abe Fortas nomination, see:
Abe Fortas (2008) by Laura Kalman Yale University Press.

For background about the aggressive treatment of the New York Times, see:
Gothic Politics, Sherrill p. 198. *New York Times* countered in its Januuary 5, 1956 editorial.

For the story of Eastland's disgrace due to his testimony in the legal case, see:
Gothic Politics, Sherrill p. 202.

Regarding the allegations relating to Trujillo, see
Enemies (2013) by Tim Weiner.

Chapter 28

EASTLAND AND THE
NEW ORLEANS SCEF RAID
IN OCTOBER, 1963

BRIEF HISTORY OF THE SOUTHERN CONFERENCE EDUCATIONAL FUND-SCEF

The book *General Walker* by Dr. Jeffrey Caulfield is probably the best single book on the JFK assassination. And in that book, the climax is the October, 1963 raid on the offices of the Southern Conference Educational Fund, more commonly known as SCEF. Most people have never heard of SCEF or its president, James Dombrowski. Yet Dombrowski was a person who was central to the rise of the civil rights movement in the South. Among white people, he was probably the most central of anyone. In the summer of 2016, working under the direction of another JFK researcher, I had the distinct pleasure of going through all 17 boxes of the James Dombrowski papers, which are in the Wisconsin Historical Society archives. This was a unique experience for this author and the first with personal papers of a famous figure. What I found made it well worth the time.

James Dombrowski was born on January 17, 1987 in Tampa, Florida. His ancestors had come from the Germany-Poland area before the Civil War and they were Lutherans. His father, John Dombrowski, had moved to Tampa, Florida and set up a jewelry store in around 1890. Dombrowski graduated cum laude from Emory University. He also attended Union Theological Seminary and Columbia University, both in New York City. He received his Ph.D. from Columbia in 1933. Dombrowski studied under famous theologian Reinhold Niebuhr and the progressive Methodist clergyman Harry F. Ward.

When he graduated from Emory, he was offered an excellent job by the Coca Cola Company. In Dombrowski, two contradictory motivations were combined: he was a natural businessman and manager, but he also was a natural-born religiously oriented altruist whose main drive in life was to be a good person and to do positive things for others. When he became CEO of the Southern Conference Educational Fund, he combined his genius for management with his altruistic ideals.

The trouble for James Dombrowski was that the South was not ready for a person with his particular genius, because he became focused on helping the laboring man and the African-Americans.

The SCEF had been a branch of the Southern Conference for Human Welfare which was established in the South in 1938. This organization was a sort of bridge from the New Deal enlightenment in civil rights to the post-war beginnings of grass roots civil rights movements in the South.

Dombrowski had begun his career affiliated with the Highlander Folk School in Monteagle, Grundy County, Tennessee, which had been founded in 1932. Even at the date of this writing, there are signs around Moneagle denoting the location of this famous institution as one passes through Tennessee on Interstate 24. The school was modeled after similar schools in Scandinavia. Amazing as this sounds today, the Highlander School's curriculum was geared to teaching children about labor organizing from the time they were young. Today, such a school would not survive for very long, but back in the 1930's and 1940's it succeeded fairly significantly and was well-known. Dombrowski's teaching there was on the subject of "Union Problems."

On December 12, 1941, Dombrowski telephoned a woman named Virginia Durr. She was the sister-in-law of Hugo Black of Alabama who later became a Supreme Court Justice. Dombrowski wanted to apply for a job with the Southern Conference on Human Welfare (SCHW) and Virginia Durr was the leader of that organization.

Dombrowski was hired and his employment proved to be good for him and for the SCHW. He had powerful allies in the progressive community. On January 3, 1942 Dombrowski left the Highlander School and moved to Nashville, the headquarters of the SCHW.

Dombrowski had a special relationship with a New York heiress named Ethel Clyde. She lived in luxury at a Manhattan apartment and used her substantial inherited wealth to further liberal causes such as Dombrowski's pro-labor and pro-African American efforts in the South. As we shall see, she also socialized with alleged Communist mole Alger Hiss.

The major patron of the SCHW was Franklin D. Roosevelt. Its guiding force was Virginia Durr and its most famous member was Supreme Court Justice Hugo Black.

The first meeting of SCHW was on November 29, 1938 in Birmingham, Alabama. Another original supporter was Eleanor Roosevelt.

The biggest complaint against James Dombrowski was that he was soft on Communists. This criticism followed him his entire life and wound up placing him in the clutches of James O. Eastland and even into the vortex of the assassination plot in New Orleans in October, 1963. Although Dombrowski was nowhere near to being a Communist, he insisted that anyone should be entitled to believe in Communism if he so choose. America is a free country, Dombrowski believed. So, you can't persecute someone for their beliefs, no matter how unpopular they might be.

The FBI began a file on Dombrowski from the very beginning. The FBI noted that Dombrowski was classified by his draft board as "someone deserving custodial attention in case of a national emergency." Scary!

Noteworthy throughout this discussion, is the participation and commentary on these activities emanating from famous Swedish sociologist Gunnar Myrdal. It is noted elsewhere in another chapter that Walt W. Rostow (who was most likely one of the JFK assassination plotters) and a staff member of the National Security council for a time, had also worked for Myrdal in Europe as a young man. FDR's advisor Dr. Ralph Bunche was an assistant to Myrdal during the research phase for Myrdal's nationally famous book, *An American Dilemma.*

Bunche was involved with the group that was promoting the SCHW.

In 1943, Dombrowski conceived the idea for an SCHW periodical called The *Southern Patriot.* This periodical would be the main platform for Dombrowsky from that early date up to 1963 and beyond.

In 1945, the segregationist Senator from Mississippi, Theordore Bilbo, denounced SCHW from the Senate floor. While Dobrowski had been concentrating on the finances of SCHW, it elected a new president, Clark Foreman, who was the New Deal specialist on civil rights. Foreman blasted back in print against Bilbo. In 1946, the Congress of Industrial Organizations (CIO) began a campaign to organize unions in the South. Unlike the rival American Federation of Labor (AFL), the CIO had leaders who in some cases were openly Communist.

At this time, the SCHW was under pressure from the IRS because of their political acitivity. This threatened their tax status as a charity. So for tax purposes, the SCEF was formed as a charitable foundation and James Dombrowki became the leader of SCEF. In a fateful decision, Dombrowski changed the residence of the SCEF from Nashville to New Orleans because a large convention was going to be held in New Orleans. That was where the headquarters of SCEF was to remain.

In June of 1947, the House Un-American Affairs Committee (HUAC) under its chairman J. Parnell Thomas condemned SCEF as a Communist front. From this time Dombrowski became tainted for being Communist, simply because he refused to exclude Communists from SCEF activities. Personally, he was not Communist or even socialist, although he did join the Socialist Party for a time when he was in Divinity School.

In May of 1948, the old SCHW was terminated. In 1947, Dombrowski headed north. He visited the University of Chicago where Chancellor

Robert M. Hutchings had grant money available. Then he went to New York. There, public relations genius Edward L. Bernays gave him some public relations advice which carried SCEF for many years. He said to concentrate on schools, housing, courts, recreation, health care and other social institutions. Dombrowski also met with his long-term financial backer Ethel Clyde. Back in New Orleans, Dombrowski began to focus on the issues of schools.

Adding to the public relations advice from Edward L. Bernays, Dombrowski felt that SCEF should agitate and organize. He began hammering away at segregated schools and segregated health care. The SCEF was often referred to as "the conscience of the troubled South." Following advice from his former teacher, theologian Reinhold Niebuhr, Dombrowski began to advocate non-violent resistance.

In November, 1950, the IRS threatened to revoke the 501(c)(3) status of the SCEF. The decision on that matter went up to the Chief Counsel of the IRS. In January, 1952, in his Southern Patriot newsletter, Dombrowski published a picture of a Coca-Cola machine with a "white" spigot and a "colored" spigot. This picture was reproduced and published around the world, even as far away as India.

It was at this point that SCEF began to enter the world of the JFK assassination conspiracy. On March 5, 1954, SCEF officer Aubrey Williams was working on his Alabama farm when he was served with a subpoena to appear before SISS, then chaired by Senator William Jenner of Indiana, an extreme right-wing Republican. Also subpoenaed were Dombrowski, Virginia Durr (sister-in-law to Hugo Black of the Supreme Court), and even Miles Horton of the Highlander School in Tennessee got a subpoena. In the past, James Dombrowski had been cooperative in testifying before the Dies Committee. It was announced that these hearings would be chaired by Mississippi Senator James O. Eastland, a member of the Democratic minority. SCEF officer Aubrey Williams had a lot of friends. As a result of his contacts in Congress, not a single Repubican member of SISS came south for the hearings with Eastland.

Senator Eastland arrived in New Orleans with counsel Richard Arens along with two paid informants, both claiming to be ex-Communists. New Orleans became, for the first time, a SCEF battleground. The defendants had excellent volunteer lawyers. Both Virginia Durr and her husband Clifford (who was a top-flight lawyer himself) were in New Orleans as was heiress and Dombrowski backer Ethel Clyde. James O. Eastland announced that cross-examination of witnesses would not be allowed.

Local witnesses from New Orleans denounced Dombrowski as a Communist. When Eastland asked Dombrowski for a members list, Dombrowski replied that SCEF had no members, only subscribers to the Southern Patriot as well as contributors. When James O. Eastland demanded the list of contributors, Dombrowski refused, pointing out that the list had not been included in the subpoena. The two argued for an hour on that issue. At one point, Dombrowski was questioned for five straight hours.

During lunch, Dombrowski's financial angel Ethyl Clyde was sitting next to Virginia Durr's lawyer. She told him he should join the Communist Party, because it had been good for her own health. Two different witnesses claimed Clifford Durr was a Communist. James O. Eastland was happy to link Durr and his brother-in-law Justice Hugo Black (who was from Alabama) to Communism. When an informant by the name of Paul Crouch labeled Virginia Durr to be a Communist, her husband (an attorney) Clifford Durr lunged at him, threatening to kill him and had to be restrained.

Back in Washington, the friends of SCEF officer Aubrey Williams went into action. Hubert Humphrey and Paul Douglas, both Northern Democratic Senators wrote letters of support. In the Senate, minority leader Lyndon Johnson devoted an hour of his time to "go into detail about the issues" in the hearings.

Then on May 17, 1954 a bombshell fell. The Supreme Court handed down the decision in *Brown vs. Board of Education*. Soon, Dombrowski traveled the South organizing compliance conferences following up on the Brown decision. The FBI and their legion of informants also traveled the South. White Citizen's Councils sprung up all over the South. By the end of 1956, they claimed 300,000 members.

However, all was not great for the SCEF at that time. In the bus boycott in Birmingham, Alabama led by Dr. Martin Luther King in 1956, King decided to exclude the SCEF. Quoting King, "the SCEF was supposed to be Red."

Not only had the NAACP excluded the SCEF but the recently formed AFL-CIO maintained a list of subversives and the SCEF was on it. Dombrowski wrote at the time that he would welcome a showdown (which could be in hearings in Washington D.C.) to clear up the record. He felt that the SCEF had been "put out on the street" by the Eastland-SISS hearings.

In March 1956, SISS, under its chairman James O. Eastland, again visited New Orleans to hold hearings. The topic was "Scope of Soviet Activity in the United States." The first witness was Herman Liveright, a program director for WDSU in New Orleans. Liveright was questioned on March 10, 1956 by the ever-present Judge Robert Morris who we have discussed in a number of prior chapters. Morris asked Liveright "Are you a Communist?" Liveright took the Fifth Amendment. Later, the wife of Liveright was called as a witness and browbeaten when she refused to say if she was a Communist. (On February 6, 1957, Robert Morris told a

Federal Court that Liveright had been sent to New Orleans to take over the direction of Communist activity in New Orleans). Liveright was sentenced on 14 counts of contempt of Congress, but the Supreme Court of the U.S. overturned the conviction on May 21, 1962.

Following these hearings, Mayor de Lesseps Morrison of New Orleans ordered Police Superintendent Guy Banister to conduct an investigation of Communist activity. Morrison arranged a meeting between James O. Eastland, Guy Banister and himself in 1956. At the meeting which was held in Greenwood, Mississippi, the three men conferred for over three hours. They discussed cooperation between SISS and the City of New Orleans to investigate subversion. Louisiana "Godfather" Leander Perez offered his assistance. Perez was a wealthy former judge and virtual dictator of Plaquemines Parish, a rural backwater southeast of New Orleans.

Leander Perez requested to James O. Eastland that he investigate James Dombrowski as well as the NAACP. On April 6, 1956, more hearings were held. Despite most or all of the witnesses pleading the Fifth Amendment, issues arose which were sent to the FBI in Washington for further investigation. Eastland's most desireable target for his hearings was Hunter Pitts O'Dell, a civil rights leader and admitted Communist. Police Assistant Superintendent Guy Banister ordered Sergeant Hubert Badeaux to arrest O'Dell, but O'Dell was not to be found. So they searched his apartment and found a trove of Communist literature.

O'Dell was questioned by SISS in Washington on April 12, 1956 by counsel Robert Morris. He was interrogated again on July 30, 1958 by HUAC. After the finale of his New Orleans hearings, James O. Eastland published the report entitled "Scope of Soviet Activity in the United States, 1956" in which there was no evidence at all of any such activity. Next, in 1957, James O. Eastland began more hearings for SISS in the South, this time in Memphis, Tennessee. SCEF was the most important subject. He also held hearings in Miami and Charlotte, North Carolina in 1957.

The states began to set up "little FBI's" such as the Louisiana and Mississipi Sovereignty Commissions and the Louisiana Legislative Committee on Segregation. On March 6-9, the State of Louisiana Joint Legislative Committee held public hearings on subversion. They used files from SISS and HUAC as well as other information. Guy Banister testified. Banister claimed to be an expert on the Communist Party, citing his experience with the FBI. Banister also claimed to have set up the intelligence unit of the New Orleans Police Deparment. Manning Johnson testified on Communism. Johnson had been a Communist and had lived in the Soviet Union. Another ex-Communist witness who had lived in the USSR was Joseph Kornfeder, who testified to the Joint Legislative Committeee on March 7, 1957. These witnesses made outlandish claims that, basically, the civil rights movement was entirely Communist. Kornfeder claimed that half of the Communist agents trained in the Soviet union over the last 30 years were black.

Author Jeffrey Caulfield believes evidence proves that Hubert Badeaux, a member of the Louisiana segregationists, was grooming Lee Harvey Oswald as in infiltrator and informant before, during and after his military career and defection to the Soviet Union. While this could have been possible, there are two problems with Dr. Caulfield's theory. First, would a police official put all his eggs in the basket of Oswald who would have been 15 years old when he was in the Civil Air Patrol and when he began to write letters to Communists? It's possible, but it would me more credible if Badeaux would have recruited multiple teenagers to become informants in the future.

Caulfield cites a letter written April 27, 1957 from Hubert Badeaux to right-wing legislator Willie Rainach which said, "I have been in contact with an out-of-town person, which I have been grooming to come here to take over the establishment of infiltration into the University and intellectual groups, I will tell you in detail about that when I see you in person."

Oswald had enlisted in the military on October 24, 1956. So Badeaux would be waiting until June 1, 1962 when Oswald returned from the Soviet Union. Even then, Oswald first went to Fort Worth, Texas, not New Orleans. He didn't return to New Orleans until April 24, 1963. So Badeaux would have waited 9 years for Oswald to ripen into an informant in New Orleans. Badeaux could have generated hundreds of informants during that time period. There was nothing special about Oswald in that regard. If Badeaux had been grooming someone long-distance for a future role as an informant in New Orleans, how much would Badeaux be able to pay an informant? $50 per month? Would Oswald want to spend 9 years grooming himself for a $50 per month job? What if Oswald found a better job for more money and decided to do something entirely different?

Where would that have left Badeaux?

The second problem is that Dr. Caulfield believes what every other assassination researcher believes; i.e. that Oswald was only pretending to be a Communist. That just isn't the case. If one reads the book *Brothers in Arms* by Guy Russo and Stephen Molton, the authors prove beyond doubt that Oswald was a real Communist. Oswald wrote manuscripts on the subject of Communism. Assassination authors virtually never claim to have read any of them. Russo and Molton demonstrate that Oswald could not have devoted all the obvious time that would be necessary to master the subject of Communism just to be a fake Communist. This is in addition to the fact that he began writing letters to Communist groups at age 15. That kind of double-dealing is beyond the mental capabilities of even a very bright 15-year-old which Oswald was not.

In 1957, looking to build more depth in SCEF, it welcomed Carl and Anne Braden to its staff. Carl Braden had been sentenced to 15 years in prison on sedition charges for helping a black person buy a home in a white neighborhood. He was saved from that fate by the U.S. Supreme Court. In 1958, Dombrowski and SCEF officer Aubrey Williams were in Washington meeting with the Civil Rights Commission, the Justice Department and a group of Congressmen.

In 1958, HUAC announced hearings to investigate Communist infiltration in the South. Both Carl and Anne Braden were subpoenaed for hearings on July 38, 1958. At this time there was a group called The Committee To Abolish HUAC. The anti-Communist right felt that this group was essentially Communist, although the group was actually interested in freedoms of speech, beliefs and association along the lines of the ACLU. The Chairman of HUAC at the time was Congressman Edwin Willis. In her book *Me & Lee*, the lover of Lee Harvey Oswald, Judyth Vary Baker presented circumstantial evidence that Congressman Edwin Willis was involved with the horrendous weaponized cancer project along with Baker, Lee Harvey Oswald, Dr. Alton Ochsner and the others.

At the HUAC hearing, both Carl Braden and Fred Wilkinson appeared to testify. Wilkinson was head of the "abolish HUAC" association. When Wilkinson began to challenge the legality of HUAC, the hearings quickly adjourned. But things were getting more serious in Washington. On August 12, 1958, the full House of Representatives voted to hold Carl Braden and Fred Wilkinson in contempt of Congress. Federal Judge Boyd Sloan sentenced both to one year in jail, but they were freed based on their appeal to the U.S. Supreme Court. But on February 27, 1961, in a 5-4 decision, the U.S. Supreme Court upheld their convictions.

James O. Eastland held a SISS hearing on March 18, 1959 on the subject of Red propaganda going through the Port of New Orleans, destined for Latin America. This was the *third* set of hearings on Communism that had been held in New Orleans; two by SISS and one by HUAC in 1957. Meanwhile, Judge Leander Perez testified to the Senate Judiciary Committee in Washington on the subject of Communism and civil rights. Eastland was also Chairman of the Judiciary Committee, which was the "parent" committee of SISS.

Dr. Caulfield discovered a very important connection regarding SCEF. In a Guy Banister file dated August 27, 1959; there was proof that Banister had infiltrated Dombrowki's SCEF office in New Orleans. A man named Allen Campbell burglarized the SCEF office under instructions from Banister. LUAC (the Louisiana Un-American Activities Committee) held hearings in 1961 that resulted in the firing of an English professor at LSU who wrote a letter in support of civil rights and was a member of the ACLU and the NAACP.

THE THREE BARONS AND THE JFK ORGANIZATIONAL CHART

On October 1, 1960, the State of Louisiana set up the aforementioned Legislative Committee on Un-American Activities (LUAC). The chairman was James Pfister, a segregationist Louisiana legislator (who had a close relationship to Clarence Manion, long-time Dean of Notre Dame Law School and a charter member of the John Birch Society). Guy Banister applied for a position at LUAC. Staff from the Louisiana Sovereignty Commission were assigned to assist LUAC. Banister was hired as an investigator.

ROBERT MORRIS, LUAC AND LEE HARVEY OSWALD'S FPCC IN 1963

LUAC held a hearing on April 24, 1963. Two witnesses testified about Communist literature in New Orleans. Robert Morris, former counsel of SISS, testified next. He shared his work history with the Committee with regard to his role as a Naval Intelligence officer in 1941. As part of his job, he attended a Communist rally in New York City. Importantly, Morris warned LUAC about the Fair Play For Cuba Committee (FPCC) whose only member in New Orleans in 1963 was Lee Harvey Oswald.

Basically, one has to conclude that Morris knew Lee Harvey Oswald either indirectly or maybe in person. If Morris testified under oath about the FPCC in New Orleans, what other conclusion could one reach?

Senator James O. Eastland had been investigating the FPCC in SISS hearings beginning in 1960. Out of eight hearings, five were held during the time when Lee Harvey Oswald was active in contacting Communist groups which included the FPCC. Oswald actually wrote to the Socialist Worker's Party trying to entangle them with the FPCC. Dr. Caulfield points out that the witnesses against the FPCC had not been to the Soviet Union. In the past, turncoat Communist witnesses before SISS, HUAC and the McCarthy Committee had usually been to Russia. This is an important argument when we evaluate Oswald as possibly working for SISS. Eastland would have welcomed Oswald as an informant, infiltrator and witness. Oswald's history in the USSR would be crucial to Eastland's task.

In October, 1961, there had been a "school" on anti-Communism held in New Orleans. Guy Banister, Robert Morris and Herbert Philbrick were in attendance. (As mentioned elsewhere, the name Herbert Philbrick pops up at a very high level in statistical analysis of the assassination). HUAC investigated the FPCC in 1962. To restate the facts regarding Willis, in *Me & Lee*, Judyth Vary Baker implicates HUAC chairman and Louisiana Congressman Edwin Willis in the assassination plot.

Upon returning from Russia, Lee Harvey Oswald began correspondence with the Socialist Workers Party (SWP). He wanted to start a Dallas chapter but was refused. He also communicated with a number of other Communist related groups. He was seeking to manufacture evidence that he had actually done photographic work for the Communist Party.

On February 8, 1963 Eastland held a hearing on the FPCC where he used letters from SCEF officers Aubrey Williams and Carl Braden to forge a link between FPCC and SCEF. On February 14, 1963 at an Eastland hearing on FPCC, the start witness was V.T. Lee. As most readers familiar with the JFK history will recognize, V.T. Lee was exchanging letters with Oswald during this period. In March, 1963 while hearings about the FPCC were ongoing, Oswald ordered his rifle. As Dr. Caulfield points out, the Warren Commission found that LHO may have handed out FPCC literature in Dallas in April, 1963. In April, 1963, the FPCC sent literature to Oswald while he was still living in Dallas. In May, 1963, Oswald again wrote to FPCC head V.T. Lee. This time it was about his, Oswald's, opening an office in New Orleans which went against the instructions he received from Lee.

At this point, Caulfield injects evidence produced by Jim Garrison that ex-Marine and Oswald buddy Kerry Thornley was impersonating Oswald in New Orleans. So, even as of May, 1963, the circumstantial evidence seems clear that Eastland and Oswald were working together with regard to the issue of the FPCC. If Thornley was involved, then there were other U.S. Government agencies involved as well. This would be because Thornley (Oswald's buddy from long ago in the Marines) was essentially stalking Oswald for some unknown reason, which could only have been a mission for some "deep cover" intelligence operation.

The reader may have read that Thornley was not only Oswald's acquaintance in the Marines, but also (for some bizarre reason) had written a book about Oswald years before 1963. That could only be the case if Thornley had become an expert on Oswald so he could impersonate him at some later date. All of this smacks of the "false defector" program in action.

In June 1963, SISS Chairman James O. Eastland was doggedly working to link the FPCC and SCEF to the Communist Party. On August 9, 1963, the famous brawl involving Cuban Carlos Bringuier and Lee Harvey Oswald occurred on the streets of New Orleans. Not only were SISS and HUAC investigating Communists in Septermber, 1963, but the old McCarthy Committee (the Permanent Subcommittee on investigations) was interviewing crusty old Communist turncoat Louis Bundez on the subject of Corliss Lamont, the NAACP and the Committee to abolish HUAC with which James Dombrowski was involved. Your author found a listing of members of the Committee to Abolish HUAC among Dombrowki's personal papers.

On August 16, 1963, Oswald was again handing out FPCC literature, this time in front of the International Trade Mart. On August 28, Oswald wrote the the Central Committee of the Communist Party, discussing the

FPCC and events in New Orleans. At this same time, Oswald gave people his business address, which was actually the address of the New Orleans African-American newpaper, *The Louisiana Weekly*. Because James Dombrowski of SCEF was the preeminent white civil rights figure in New Orleans at that time, he and SCEF had a close relationship with the newspaper. Also at this same time, Oswald appeared at the famous black voter registration drive in Clinton, Louisiana.

On November 14, 1960, just seven days after the presidential election, U.S. Marshalls forcibly integrated the New Orleans schools. On May 19, 1961, Dombrowski was called to Montgomery, Alabama by the Reverend Ralph Abernathy and other leaders to assist Freedom Riders there. Clifford and Virginia Durr were there along with other staunch supporters of SCEF. A car belonging to the Durrs was turned over and set on fire. Meanwhile, inside a church, Dr. Martin Luther King was giving a speech.

The Freedom Riders headed on to New Orleans. In Montgomery, Attorney General Robert F. Kennedy dispatched 400 federal marshalls to protect demonstrators. JFK's personal representative there was clubbed unconscious. At this point the Bradens acted to ally the SCEF with such other groups as the Student Non-Violent Co-ordinating Committee (SNCC) and the Southern Christian Leadership Council (SCLC). Carl Braden of Dombrowski's SCEF had strong ties to Labor. He got the Teamsters to contribute to SNCC. Bob Zellner, a graduate of a Methodist school called Huntington College was hired by SNCC. He, in turn, urged the Students for a Democratic Society (SDS) to start an organizing drive in the South. SDS was, in its day, considered a violent and dangerous group by many. Governor George Wallace of Alabama ordered Zellner arrested but was found to lack the legal authority.

When Zellner and SNCC marched on the City Hall in McComb, Mississippi, Zellner was beaten, his eyes gouged, and he was kicked unconscious. In nearby East Baton Rouge, Louisiana, Zellner and SNCC volunteer Charles McDew were jailed and charged with criminal anarchy. By mid-1962, SCEF was working with the National Lawyers Guild, which was considered to be a subversive group by Southern segregationists.

Around the time of the anti-Communist activity of James O. Eastland and SISS, the Louisiana legislature enacted tough new laws aimed at subversive activities and Communist propaganda. The impetus for these laws came from the wealthy quasi-dictator of Plaquemine Parish, Judge Leander Perez. The first announcement about these laws came on May 11, 1962.

According to Dr. Caulfield, the planning for the raid on SCEF which was attendant to these laws, began as early as July, 1962. He says that in an affidavit in a later proceeding, SISS Chief Counsel J.G. Sourwine admitted to being involved in SCEF raid-planning before July, 1962. If that is true, then the timing coincides exactly with the activities of Senator Dodd and General Julius Klein in co-operation with General Reinhard Gehlen of West German intelligence and the overall plan of the JFK assassination. Dodd and Eastland shared the chairmanship of SISS. Obviously their activities would have to be in tandem.

Dr. Caulfield believes that the hearings held on July 31, 1963 were also part of the plans for the SCEF raid. The subject of the hearings was JFK's proposed Civil Rights Act and the hearings focused on Communists within the Civil Rights movement. Robert F. Kennedy had recently denied the presence of Communists on the Staff of Dr. Martin Luther King. Senator Strom Thurmond, a strong segregationist, is one of several such Southern Senators whose names are not usually seen in the assassination literature. Others are Senator Richard Russell of Georgia and Senator John Stennis of Tennessee.

But in on August 24, 1963, Thurmond began inserting anti-Communist propaganda into the Congresssional Record which blamed Communism for the increasing civil rights pressure in the South. This even included specific statements about SCEF officer Carl Braden. Dr. Caulfield suggests that this was because Thurmond was by then aware of the plan for the SCEF raid and the legal attack against SCEF. If so, Thurmond's knowledge likely did not include any inkling about the JFK assassination plot. Apparently Richard Russell, John Stennis and Strom Thurmond never had any JFK blood on their hands. In the opinion of the author, this fact can be inferred because of their reputations for favoring "law and order" instead of lynchings and terror. By their actions after the assassination, Russell and Stennis seemed to favor exposing the truth about the assassination.

After the bombing of the Sixteenth Street Baptist Church on September 15, 1963, Alabama Governor George Wallace made an appearance on the television show *Today* where he blamed the bombing on agitators and on the Kennedy Administration. Especially significant to our story, he displayed pictures of SCEF officers Anne Braden and Carl Braden; also SCEF chief James Dombrowski. Wallace cited the hearings of Eastland in 1954 and the HUAC hearings in 1958. This connection to violence on September 15, 1963 mirrored the tongue-slashing of witness Stanley Holden of the Otepka hearings around the same time. Incidents of violence were beginning to escalate on the part of perpetrators and their opponents. Of course, this escalation led up to the assassination.

In order to move forward with their plans for SCEF, in August 1963, the Louisiana segregationists decided to stage a raid to get the list of supposed Communist supporters rather than rely on the power of the subpoena. They met together with SISS counsel J.G. Sourwine to plan this raid.

On October 4, 1963, over 50 attorneys who were members of the National Lawyers' Guild were in New Orleans for a conference together with the SCEF. Just after 3 P.M. that day, police broke into Dombrowski's office with pistols drawn. The police boxed up all of the SCEF records. These police raiders included the Louisiana State Police Bureau of Identification led by Major Russell Willie. Also involved was New Orleans Police Intelligence represented by Major Presley J. Trosclair. And last but not least was Frederick B. Alexander, the staff director of the Louisiana Joint Legislative Committee on Un-American Activities (LUAC).

The raiders carried away 73 boxes of SCEF records. Although SCEF was a foundantion and therefore had no actual members, the raiders found a mailing list for an organization called New Orleans Committee for Peaceful Alternatives. (Dr. Caulfield, in *General Walker*, presents evidence that Lee Harvey Oswald had infiltratied that group). Some of the Louisiana State Police involved in the raid were, at the time, assigned to the staff of the Louisiana Sovereignty Commission.

At 11:45 P.M. on October 4, 1963, the Counsel for LUAC Jack Rogers called SISS counsel J.G. Sourwine in Washington. Rogers described what had been found. He called Eastland who then ordered a subpoena for the SCEF records. The subpoenas were dated on October 4, 1963 which proved that Eastland had involvement before the fact of the raid, but he denied it. James Pfister, chairman of LUAC blamed the SCEF raid on the anti-Braden press statements of Alabama Governor George Wallace.

James Dombrowski and his lawyer Ben Smith were arrested. Smith and his law partner Bruce Walzer were arrested and charged with being members of the National Lawyer's Guild, a subversive group and that they hadn't registered as such. Back at the NLG convention, the 50 lawyers who were assembled went wild with anger. Such nationally prominent lawyers were in attendance as Arthur Kinoy and William Kunstler, who would eventually gain national fame.

The SCEF raid made page one headlines as far away as Los Angeles. Jack N. Rogers, who was chairman of LUAC, held a press conference. He said the raid had been sparked by Governor George Wallace of Alabama who said on TV that Dombrowski and the Bradens were "the cause of racial agitation in his state."

LUAC counsel announced the theory of the LUAC case against SCEF. He alleged that SCEF was a "holding company" for all Southern civil rights groups. As such, if you proved that SCEF was involved with the Communist Party, that would apply to all the "affiliated" civil rights groups that SCEF supported, either verbally or financially.

Thus, under the state Communist Control acts, virtually all southern civil rights groups could be legally abolished as Communist.

SCEF leader James Dombrowski spoke out against the raid and prosecutions. He said that if the Communist Control Act remained in force and applied, that no citizen or lawyer would come to the aid of the blacks because they would be afraid of a conviction for subversion.

Acting on the advice of his noted lawyer Arthur Kinoy, Dombrowski filed a civil rights suit against Eastland. The judge in the criminal case was J. Bernard Cocke. In this criminal proceeding, a policeman testified that an informant had supplied information that the SCEF was subversive. Under cross-examination, he refused to give the name of the informant. That informant was probably Lee Harvey Oswald.

Judge Cocke ordered LUAC to bring into court every item seized in the raid. Failing that, the judge quashed the arrests citing insuffient evidence and accused LUAC of having based the arrests on their own conclusions rather than upon the evidence. Outside the courtroom, Representative James H. Pfister, chairman of LUAC held a press conference. He said that on the following Tuesday, both he and Jack Rogers, chief counsel of LUAC, would appear before SISS at a public hearing. Before this press conference, no one had known that James O. Eastland was involved in the raid. It was also revealed that J.G. Sourwine, Chief Counsel of SISS came to New Orleans the day before with blank subpoenas.

Federal Judge Robert A. Ainsworth ordered SISS to keep the records inside the boundaries of Louisiana. But overnight, SISS absconded with the records, taking them across the river to Mississippi and thus out of the jurisdiction of the Louisiana Federal District court. Although in Birmingham on business, Dombrowski returned to New Orleans on November 14, 1963 where a grand jury was convened to investigate SCEF. The Federal Court was asked to quash the State proceedings which, at that time, would have been totally against both Federal Statutory law as well as Federal precedent. The issue before Judge Ainsworth was whether the Louisiana Communist Control act was constitutional. In a decision by a three-judge appeals panel on December 9, 1963, one judge thought the law unconstitutional but the majority upheld the Louisiana anti-Communist law.

District Attorney Jim Garrison was on the side of the prosecution, but he agreed to delay the prosecutions of Dombrowski and others until the Supreme Court of the U.S. heard the appeal. Recall that Dombrowski had also filed a civil suit based on the Civil Rights Act against James O. Eastland. In that case, the U.S. Supreme Court ultimately decided that James O. Eastland was immune from suit because he was a member of Congress acting in his job. However, Chief Counsel of SISS J.G. Sourwine was not held to be immune and he was required to defend himself in court and suffer possible liability if he lost.

In a case which became a landmark, in April, 1964 the U.S. Supreme Court in Dombrowski vs. Pfister, struck down the Louisiana Communist Control Act in a 5-2 decision with two abstentions. One abstention was Justice Hugo Black, who abstained on the basis that his in-laws had been founders of SCHW, the predecessor of SCEF. With only five justices against the Communist Control Act, a switch by only one Justice could have thrown the entire civil rights movement into oblivion.

Equally important in the case was the ending of the "doctrine of abstention." This required Federal Courts to await the outcome of State proceedings until reviewing or altering them. This was a major fundamental earthquake in the relationship between State and Federal courts. Finally, approving Dombrowski's civil case against the raiders of SCEF was also a landmark decision. It is remarkable that a Federal Judge would allow a suit for damages against the Chief Counsel of a Senate Committee when he was in the process of doing his job in that capacity. One has to wonder whether the precedent in the case by Dombrowski against Sourwine has ever been followed by Federal Courts or was it unique to this explosive case.

The wheels of justice turn slowly. But in the case of the SCEF raid, the Federal Courts moved like lightning. When they instantly intervened to halt the SCEF raid trainwreck in New Orleans, there could only have been one reason. Their actions totally ignored the ironclad doctrine of abstention which was both a statute and in total precedence without exception. The Federal Judge involved had to know that there was an overwhelming national security issue behind this raid and the aftermath. In the opinion of this author, it was very likely that the Judge was quietly told that this raid might be part of a plot to murder a high official (or some story close to that) and if this case blew up in the papers, when that happened, then the cat would be out of the bag and this would spell disaster.

According to Dr. Caulfield, James Pfister, Chairman of LUAC was the first to tip his hand about the larger intent of the SCEF raid. According to Caulfield, "everyone involved with the creation of LUAC had ties to [Jim Garrison suspect Guy] Banister and nearly everyone involved in the SCEF raid had ties to the Banister operation." Pfister announced that LUAC would be investigating the connection between SCEF and Oswald's FPCC.

Major Russell M. Willie testified to the House Select Committee on Assassinations in 1978. He stated he was employed by the Louisiana State Police and the Louisiana Sovereignty Commission. When testifying before LUAC, Major Willie stated that he had an informant who provided him with evidence that SCEF was subversive. This informant, by process of elimination, had to be Lee Harvey Oswald. At the hearing, Willie refused to name the informant. As every JFK assassination buff knows, Lee Harvey Oswald was the only member of the FPCC in New Orleans. And there was no other known connection between the FPCC and SCEF other than what may have occurred between Oswald and SCEF in New Orleans. Pfister announced this intention on November 28, 1963. In the famous midnight press conference at the Dallas jail when Oswald went before the press (on the night of the assassination inside the Dallas jailhouse), even Jack Ruby demonstrated that he knew Oswald was connected to the FPCC. He stood up and corrected District Attorney Henry Wade when Wade forgot the name of the organization with which Oswald was connected. Ruby yelled out "FPCC!"

Dr. Caulfield does disclose that the Chairman of LUAC, Jack Rogers did display a letterhead from the Los Angeles Chapter of the FPCC showing that Carl Braden (an officer of SCEF) was the "Honorary Co-Chairman." There were two sides to the story regarding Socialism/Communism in the U.S. As mentioned previously, when this author examined the personal correspondence of James Dombrowski, it was shocking to see that Dombrowski's life-long financial backer Ethel Clyde would boast about hosting the infamous accused Communist spy Alger Hiss at an event at her apartment.

SISS Chief Counsel J.G. Sourwine stated in a court affidavit in 1964 that he had studied SCEF. He included not only SCEF but other groups that were connected to SCEF (presumably SNCC, SCLC, CORE, NAACP, ACLU, National Lawyers Guild and most of all Oswald's FPCC). He described all of these (without naming them) as being dominated by a foreign power, i.e. the Soviet Union. In a prior chapter we examined the views of Judge Robert Morris, a Chief Counsel of SISS. We can see that the Chief Counsel of SISS in 1963, J. G. Sourwine held the same broad-based, irrational viewpoint on Communism and the alleged danger of Communism in the U.S. And in this instance, the Red Scare tactic was being turned against all of the civil rights community.

The entire thesis of *General Walker* by Jeffrey Caulfield, M.D. was that Oswald was being guided like a puppet to put his "dirty Communist fingers" on each and every group which Eastland and his friends despised. To the Warren Commission, Oswald was seemingly performing random actions. One instance was his appearance with CORE in Clinton, Louisiana. Another was his protesting against the New Orleans Committee for Peaceful Alternatives (NOCPA). Still another was his correspondence with the Socialist Worker's Party and the Communist Party USA. And then there were the backyard photos with Communist newspapers in his hand and his attendance at an ACLU meeting with babysitter Michael Paine.

Caulfield raises a crucial issue. When Lee Harvey Oswald was 15 years old, he allegedly wrote a letter to the Young People's Socialist League in New York. How would a 15-year-old find out about such an organization? This author can share from personal experience back in the 1950's and

1960's, there were nationwide drives by both left-wing and right-wing groups to ensnare young people in various youth organizations. In your author's own recollection, parents warned their children not to join such groups for fear of being blacklisted by employers for the rest of their life. It was scary.

On page 768 of *General Walker*, Dr. Caulfield shares the fact that he discovered some revealing correspondence. In it, Carl Braden, (an officer of SCEF) was writing letters to the Socialist Party/YPSL. Why would an adult be writing to a Young People's Socialist League? Answer: To further the effort to approach and ensnare young people, logically, in his own community. So the question of how Oswald would have found out about a Socialist/Communist youth group is an easy one. He was obviously approached to join the group by an adult Socialist/Communist. Much, much less likely was that he was enlisted as an informant by LUAC.

Never send a boy to do a man's job. Dr. Caulfield readily connects Oswald with David Ferrie while Oswald was in the Civil Air Patrol. But a 15-year-old would make a terrible witness to appear before SISS to prove the danger of a pending Soviet takeover. Even if you convinced a 15-year-old to become a fake Communist, in what way could you use him? An informant? A witness? And why only Oswald and not others? Oswald was not a prodigy. Wouldn't others have remembered such activities going on the the Civil Air Patrol? (Granted, the CAP was entirely political in purpose).

To believe this theory, you would have to believe the inclusion of the entire anti-Communist, anti-civil rights establishment from James O. Eastland, to Leander Perez, to the New Orleans Police Intelligence Department, to the Sovereingty Commission and LUAC; the plans of all these villians would be put in the hands of a single 15-year-old and they would all be willing to wait 9 years for the payoff.

The fact is, some unknown person, maybe a teacher, maybe Oswald's Jesuit cousin, maybe a next-door neighbor; somebody put Oswald up to becoming a junior league Communist and they succeeded. Oswald would remain either a full-blown or at least a half-hearted Communist until the day he died. And like many other Communists, he exploited his knowledge for financial gain, even if it turned out to be a very small gain in the end.

And in addition to carrying the LUAC on his back, Oswald also worked in a project to allegedly weaponize cancer together with top New Orleans doctors. And on top of that, he helped Senator Thomas Dodd and his Juvenile Delinquency Committee investigate Seaport Traders for selling mail-order weapons. These facts, though true, seem to be straight out of Marvel comics. Knowing all this, on 11/22/63, why didn't Oswald just jump off the Book Depository wearing his red cape and just fly away?

Dombrowski biographer Frank Adams tells us that LUAC published three reports on the above facts. They found that SCLC and SNCC were "substantially under the control of the Communist Party." Jack Rogers, the lawyer for LUAC stated that over 200 civil rights groups were under investigation as being Communist. Eventually, on April 26, 1965, as mentioned before, the Supreme Court of the U.S. struck down the Louisiana Communist Control Act because it was unconstitutionally vague.

James Dombrowski left the SCEF in December, 1965. He died May 2, 1983.

Notes:

As documented in references in the text of this chapter, four sources are relied upon for the information in this chapter. The are:

James A. Dombrowski Papers, State Historical Society of Wisconsin, Madison, Wisc. Referred to as Dombrowski Papers.

General Walker and the Murder of President Kennedy: The Extensive New Evidence of a Radical-Right Conspiracy (2015) by Jeffrey H. Caulfield, M.D.

James Dombrowski: An American Heretic, 1897-1983 (1992) by Frank T. Adams.

Brothers in Arms: The Kennedys, the Castros, and the Politics of Murder (2008) by Gus Russo and Stephen Molton.

Me & Lee: How I Came to Know, Love and Lose Lee Harvey Oswald (2011) by Judyth Vary Baker, p.288.

Chapter 29

BIOGRAPHER WILLIAM J. GILL AND HIS WIFE, THE NAZI MATA HARI

Before we examine the very interesting facts and issues raised in *The Ordeal Of Otto Otepka*, by William J. Gill, hereinafter Gill, we must first find out what we can about the author himself. But a bit of information which was recently discovered at the last moment by this author is that William J. Gill was married to a woman known as the Countess von Podewils, who was of the German nobility.

The starting point would be the information presented on the fly-leaf of *The Ordeal Of Otto Otepka*, which is to the effect that Gill has been a journalistic prize-winner and has been a correspondent for such publications as *Life, Saturday Evening Post, Reader's Digest, National Geographic* and others. He also won a "Golden Quill" award from a journalism honor society. He is also identified as a co-author with F. Clifton White, of *Suite 3505: The Story of the Draft Goldwater Movement* (Arlington House, 1967).

This paragraph on the fly-leaf makes Mr. Gill appear to be mostly politically neutral; after all, the *Saturday Evening Post* and *Reader's Digest* were, and have been ever since, considered the paragons of America, somewhat like apple pie. Who can forget all the brilliant Norman Rockwell covers for the *Post*? So Mr. Gill seems to be a kind of Norman Rockwell who is working with the printed word.

So what else can we find in print about Mr. William J. Gill? A slightly more revealing excerpt of Mr. Gill's political opinion is found in a review which he drafted regarding a Kennedy assassination book entitled *Final Judgment: The Missing Link in the JFK Assassination Conspiracy* by Michael Collins Piper.

In Piper, *Final Judgment*, the blame for the Kennedy Assassination is placed on Israel and/or Zionists. This is a novel theory, when compared to the many other hypotheses regarding J.F.K. Mr. Gill states in a review of *Final Judgment:*

"I think you've pinned the tail on the donkey. In my estimation, *Final Judgment* ranks as the most important book of the 20th Century."

Either the entire world has passed this unparalleled theory by, or Mr. Gill must be greatly exaggerating the importance of this book. William J. Gill is described in a brief bio which appears with this quote as follows:

(The former executive director of the Allegheny Foundation and author of such books as *Trade Wars Against America, The Ordeal of Otto Otepka* and *Why Reagan Won*. Gill was a journalist with UPI and the *Pittsburg Press* and also wrote for *Life, Fortune, The Saturday Evening Post, Reader's Digest* and *National Geographic*.)

One extremely intriguing item which went along with the rave review of the *Final Judgment* was the review that appeared alongside the review by Mr. Gill. This second review reads in part:

> As one who has read over 200 Books on the JFK assassination, and engaged in research both as an individual and as part of various teams, I can say ... that Piper's book is now the definitive work on the JFK assassination ... Michael Collins Piper has struck gold. Herbert L. Calhoun, PhD.
> (Dr. Calhoun retired as deputy division chief of the Policy, Plans and Analysis Office of the State Department's Bureau of Political-Military Affairs and formerly served for the U.S. Arms Control and Disarmament Agency).

An important fact is that the State Department has such a bureau. Maybe it's just a coincidence, but we will see that this man's bio reads exactly as if it had jumped from the pages of *The Ordeal of Otto Otepka*, by Mr. Gill, because of his affiliation with the State Department.

In an internet posting, author Michael Collins Piper relates the following about Gill: "Bill Gill was also very entwined with the CIA and military intelligence and over the years he was involved with a number of ventures involving matters of special interest to the Mossad. He was one of those old-time Cold Warriors who used to buy the idea that Israel was a valuable Cold War asset – but Bill was privately VERY ANTI-SEMITIC. And – Tim Gratz will love this – Bill was married to a German countess who was the god-daughter of Eugenio Pacelli, later to become Pope Pius XII – so-called "Hitler's Pope."

In 1970, in the trade magazine *Broadcasting: The Business Weekly of Television and Radio*, the following article appears, in part:

> An alternative to television network news coverage will be offered by a new TV-news programming service, scheduled for introduction next fall. Aimed at countering what was termed "one-sided slanting" and "bias" of network news coverage, the new service-News Perspective International-has been in the works in Washington for about a year.
> William J. Gill, author, reporter and former T.V. producer N.P.I. president said last week news directors around the country had

told him several months ago of their dissatisfaction with the network-news product. To confirm this sampling, Mr. Gill commissioned William T. Gladmon of Vienna, Va. to conduct a "National Television News Survey."

Questionnaires with seven questions were sent to every TV station in the country-except the 15 owned by the ABC, CBS and NBC networks.

In his covering letter to the TV news executives, Mr. Gladmon asked "whether you believe there is room within the television industry for a regular program that would objectively present national and international new without the "strong leftward bias that Howard K. Smith and others claim predominates the network news shows." He said newspapers would also be offered a newswire service.

NPI was incorporated last summer in the District of Columbia with a declared capitalization of $5 million. Mr. Gill would not disclose the source of the funding."

Apparently during this period when Mr. Gill was serving as a moderate-to-conservative journalist, he also was working the Allegheny Foundation: the article in "Broadcasting" magazine continues:

Mr. Gill's latest book [which was published in January, 1970] is *The Ordeal of Otto Otepka*. He has served as United Press correspondent and reporter with the *Pittsburg Press* and as writer and co-producer in 1963 of a series of documentaries on KDKA-TV Pittsburg.

Most recently he was in charge of the Allegheny Foundation for T. Mellon & Sons, Pittsburg. Mr. Gill in 1967 collaborated with F. Clifton White, campaign manager for New-York's Republican-Conservative Senator-Elect James Buckley, on the book *Suite 3505* about the 1964 presidential campaign.

And this connection to the Buckley's of course connects Mr. Gill at least in some way or other to the CIA. William F. Buckley co-operated very closely with his brother Senator James Buckley. It is well known by assassination researchers that William F. Buckley started right out of Yale University working for the CIA in Mexico City. Mr. William F. Buckley was also a founder of Young Americans for Freedom, or YAF. This organization took off like a meteor in 1963 around the time of the Goldwater movement.

By searching the internet, a great deal of information about William F. Buckley is available.

The import of the information is to the effect that Mr. Buckley was involved in producing disinformation regarding the famous assassination of Chilean diplomat Orlando Letelier. This occurred on September 18, 1976.

If you take that as fact, that would put Mr. Buckley as supporting the interests of Chilean dictator Augusto Pinochet, the convicted war criminal, even in 1976. Mr. Buckley began officially working with the CIA in 1951.

Getting back to William J. Gill, it is apparent that Mr. Gill was not operating in the moderate or "middle of the road" circles that would be implied by his relationship with *Reader's Digest*, UPI, *National Geographic* and *The Saturday Evening Post*.

The final topic regarding the career and politics of Mr. Gill is regarding the Allegheny Foundation, of which he was executive director and its parent, The Scaife Foundation:

The Scaife Foundations are actually a group of four foundations which include the Allegheny Foundation, The Carthage Foundation, The Sara Scaife Foundation and the Scaife Family Foundation all of which are based in Pittsburg, PA. Richard Mellon Scaife (July 3, 1932-July 4, 2014) was an American billionaire, a principal heir to the Mellon banking, oil, and aluminum fortune, and the owner and publisher of the *Pittsburgh Tribune-Review*. In 2005, Scaife was number 238 on the Forbes 400, with a personal fortune of $1.2 billion. By 2013, Scaife had dropped to number 371 on the listing, with a personal fortune of $1.4 billion.

Scaife was also known for his financial support of conservative public policy organizations over the past four decades. He provided support for conservative and libertarian causes in the United States, mostly through the private, nonprofit foundations, now controlled by his daughter Jennie and son David. More details about these foundations can be found at groups.google.com.

William J. Gill worked for Scaife's charitable foundations 30 years ago. Gill took a trip to Vietnam on foundation business and when he returned submitted an expense account that included charges for laundering his shirts during the trip. Scaife refused to pay for laundering and wrote a memo that Gill could never throw out: The memo was to the effect that Scaife would not agree to pay $8.00 for Gill's cab fare.

As will be discussed in a later chapter, Gill was apparently head of the Catholic War Veterans and on the board of the American-African Relations group at times during the 1950's and 1960's.

Because William J. Gill was both a close associate of CIA operative William F. Buckley as well as married to a German Countess, this puts Gill right in the middle regarding inside information about the JFK assassination. His biography fits like a glove with the special interests whom we have proven by our research to be responsible for the assassination.

Notes:

The Ordeal Of Otto Otepka (1969), by William J. Gill.

Suite 3505: The Story of the Draft Goldwater Movement (1967), by William J. Gill and F. Clifton White.

Final Judgment: The Missing Link in the JFK Assassination Conspiracy (2000), by Michael Collins Piper.

To find the review by Herbert L. Calhoun, see: https://mark1marti2.wordpress.com/2011/09/12/mark-dankofs-final-word-on-michael-collins-pipers-final-judgment-on-israel-and-the-assassination-of-jfk/

For the quote about William J. Gill made by author Michael Collins Piper, see: http://education-forum.ipbhost.com/topic/6130-michael-collins-piper-final-judgment/

See the link below for Gill's obituary in the Washington post which verifies his marriage to Countess von Podewils. https://www.washingtonpost.com/archive/local/2003/09/07/author-book-shop-owner-william-gill/584b3b0c-26a7-4b64-970b-ace27c24e66f/?utm_term=.afed7a3828c7

Mr. Gill in 1967 collaborated with F. Clifton White, campaign manager for New-York's Republican-Conservative Senator-Elect James Buckley, on the book *Suite 3505.*

The quote about the proposed news service can be found at;[americanradiohistory.com/Archive-BC/BC-1970/1970-12-21-BC.pdf]

At the following website: [Spartacus –Educational.com/JFKbuckleyW.htm] more information regarding the intelligence role of Mr. William F. Buckley can be found.

For background on the Scaife Foundation, see: [www.snipview.com/q/Scaife%20Foundations] [search "william j gill" "allegheny foundation']

And at: [en.wikepedia.org/wiki/Richard_Mellon_Scaife]

More details about these foundations appear at: [https://groups.google.com/forum/#topic/alt.politics/democrats.d/_C50j3UIrUO]

Chapter 30

OTTO OTEPKA, SISS AND THE JFK ASSASSINATION

THE BACKGROUND OF OTTO OTEPKA

In her updated assassination history, noted JFK author Professor Joan Mellen presents a great deal of significant new research on the subject of State Department Security Analyst Otto Otepka.

Joan Mellen was apparently the last historian to interview Otepka just prior to his death in 2010. Based on her April 2006 interview, Mellen broke some very important new ground in regard to Otepka. In the interview, Otepka went as far as to suggest that the reason he was hounded out of his Security job at the State Department by Robert Kennedy and others was because of his ongoing investigation of defector Lee Harvey Oswald.

In this chapter, the focus will be on Otto Otepka and his relationship, not only with his employer the State Department, but more importantly, his relationship with the Senate Internal Security Subcommittee, a/k/a SISS. As we have said before, an understanding of the role of Joe McCarthy, the role of Otto Otepka as well as the role of the Senate Internal Security Subcommittee are absolutely necessary to properly understand the assassination of President John F. Kennedy.

Your author was in his early teens in 1963 and was very interested in current events. And the name Otto Otepka was in the headlines of the period. That part is basically true. Otepka had become the focus of an important Senate investigation back in the early 1960's. Although the real connection of Otepka to the Congress was close, Otepka was neither a Teamster, nor an Iron Curtain related spy. He he was, in fact, a somewhat hapless employee of the U.S. Government.

It is clear that the dynamic forces which caused the JFK assassination were the desperate attempt of the reactionary forces of anti-Communism to preserve their privileges in the democratic capitalistic countries of the West. Many Americans are still around who lived during that period. It is stunning and disheartening, however, that the majority of facts which determined the events from 1945 to 1963 in U.S. history were, and are still, so well hidden that it takes literally years of research to dig out the truth about what was actually going on behind the scenes at the time.

There were any number of events which highlight the hidden collision between religion, democracy, nuclear security, the press and very wealthy individuals which together gave birth to all the hobgoblins of Communophobia. But more than anything else, the key to understanding those events is to study and understand the fundamental attempt by those hiding in secrecy, to weaken and destroy the office of the President, the elected majority of Congress, legitimate law enforcement agencies, honest judges, justices and the traditionally non-political officers of the military.

So let's look at Mr. Otto F. Otepka as a prime example of a front-line soldier in this vicious war for control of the United States Government, which would be for nothing less than control of the entire planet Earth itself.

Otto F. Otepka was Deputy Director of the United States State Department's Office of Security in the late 1950s and early 1960s. He was fired as the State Department's chief security evaluations officer on November 5, 1963. He lost his job because he had allegedly furnished classified files to the United States Senate Subcommittee on Internal Security. Significantly, this firing came only 17 days before the JFK assassination.

Otto Otepka was important because he was literally almost *the only point man* and insider in the battle for control of the U.S. State Department. The reader can better understand this battle for control of the State Deparment by trying to understand the actual situation in 1960.

To conservatives who were hold-overs in the Federal Government and who still represented the Eisenhower administration, it was disturbing to think that JFK and his liberal Democratic friends could gain control of U.S. foreign policy. If this were allowed to happen, it would reverse all the hard work done by Allen Dulles as Director of the CIA, by John Foster Dulles as Secretary of State, and not to mention the fervent and nasty victories (if you could call them victories) by the Red-baiters such as Joe McCarthy, Richard Nixon, HUAC and all the rest during almost the entire decade of the 1950s.

If we examine the situation of Otepka in the State Department, we can learn about the tactics of these conservative anti-Communists like Joe McCarthy and the Dulles brothers who wanted to impose their party line on the country, despite the fact that they represented only a minority of the opinions that Americans actually held on the issue.

These extreme anti-communists were a minority of the membership of Congress, a minority of the Federal Judiciary and certainly a minority of members of the military and employees of all levels of government. But they were mostly wealthy, most were rigidly religious, and some were in control of key media outlets. They perceived that their rights and privileges were not just called into question, but that their backs were actually to the wall at the most fundamental level.

So where did Otto Otepka fit into this picture? Otto Otepka was born in Chicago on May 6, 1915. In 1963, he was about 47 years old. Otepka was a very typical American. He attended Harrison Technical High School in Chicago. After his high school graduation, Otepka continued his education while employed by the U.S. Government starting in 1936. His first position in the government was with the Farm Credit Administration. Otepka received his law degree in June, 1942 by studying in night-school, from Columbus College, now merged with Catholic University of America. The first month following his college graduation, he left the Bureau of Internal Revenue where he had worked for three years and went on to new challenges.

When World War II broke out, Otepka worked as a personnel classification specialist for the United States Navy. After an honorable discharge, Otepka moved to the U.S. Civil Service Commission as an investigator in 1946. At the Civil Service Commission, Otepka worked almost exclusively on what were being described as "loyalty cases." In this context, the word "loyalty" basically meant the analysis of whether a person was a believer in the American form of government or whether he held beliefs which were considered Communist or in other ways extreme. It was felt that "loyalty" questions could compromise the employee's ability to perform his job in the government.

The definitive work on the case of Otto Otepka is a book entitled *The Ordeal Of Otto Otepka* by William J. Gill. We introduced Willam J. Gill in the previous chapter. In this book about Otepka (which we will sometimes shorten to "*OOO*"), author Gill tells us that Otepka was appointed Technical Advisor on Loyalty in the Central Office Investigations Division of the Civil Service Commission in 1947.

The Beginnings of Anti-Communism and the Issue of Security

There are at least five terms that describe the legal issues at play in the era of the Red Scare. These terms are 1) espionage, 2) sabotage, 3) loyalty 4) security and 5) sedition. For most of America's history, anti-spy efforts were mainly directed against the problems of espionage and sabotage. Law enforcement tended to focus on these things rather than the more vague and amorphous problem of loyalty, security and sedition.

There had been some very notorious instances of sabotage. The most famous was the "Black Tom" explosion in New York City during World War I, where people were killed and a huge portion of the port facilities in New York had been destroyed. And this was just one act by an enemy saboteur.

The concept of espionage needs little illustration. The Rosenbergs, who sold U.S. atomic secrets to the Soviet Union, were espionage artists who did great damage to our country.

After we consider sabotage and espionage, we next consider "loyalty" which has also been known as "sedition." We have all heard of the Alien and Sedition Acts of the late 1790's. So the battle against "disloyalty" or "sedition" also has a long history. But there are many more problems with the enforcement of "loyalty" than battling outright "sabotage" or "espionage." A flare-up of fear surrounding the issues of loyalty and sedition had occurred at the time of the famous Palmer Raids in 1919. These raids, which were carried out by the Justice Department, were directed against leftists and Anarchists.

But following the Palmer Raids, the powerful Attorney General Harlan Fiske Stone issued an edict to the FBI that every American should be aware of. He decided that the FBI could only investigate persons who were suspected of violating a *specific Federal statute*. This policy eliminated political witch hunts. Further, this required a hands-off policy regarding those who merely held unpopular beliefs. Remarkably, even though J. Edgar Hoover is often dismissed as a thug, it is important to remember that Hoover observed this hands-off policy laid down by Stone long after Harlan Fiske Stone was no longer Attorney General. This policy was the standard during the entire period between the World Wars.

It was only when the Soviets along with the U.S. and the U.K. had defeated Hitler that "security" and "loyalty" questions began to emerge, directly targeted against Communism. It could fairly be said that the U.S. government did not attack those who were sympathetic to the Nazi's in the same way it targeted Communists or Communist sympathizers. In this context, it should be kept in mind that there was no real possibility that Communists could ever take over the United States.

The drastic methods of slander and blacklisting used by anti-Communists such as Joe McCarthy and his supporters were actually targeted at influencing U.S. foreign policy toward other countries. As we look into the particular battles over the issue of anti-Communism, this will become increasingly clear.

When it comes to the relationship between between our government and any particular religion, it is the dogma of American civics and education that religion is *transparent* to the U.S. Government. In that sense, religion is *invisible*. Religious freedom is the watch-word. And to enforce religious freedom, it is considered necessary to be color-blind to religious issues as such.

But when the epic battle against Communism began in earnest in 1945, the role of various religions came up to front and center. The American public was told that Soviet Communism was "atheistic." According to the extreme anti-Communists like McCarthy, that was all anyone needed to know. Whether the Soviet attitude toward religion was any different from our Constitutional ban on establishment of religion was never considered. Americans never knew that Stalin was at one time a student in a religious seminary. Having described the facts and forces of anti-Communism in the 1950's, let us look at the situation of Otto Otepka and see how the battle against Communism, influenced in part by religion, affected him in his quest to instill "loyalty" into the State Department.

OTTO OTEPKA JOINS THE STATE DEPARTMENT BATTLE OVER LOYALTY AND SECURITY

Beginning with his job as State Department Security Evaluator during the McCarthy era, Otto Otepka was one of the most important frontline players, especially following the fall from grace and then the death of Senator Joseph McCarthy in 1957.

Otepka, like McCarthy, had attended a Catholic university. During the period from the middle 1950's to the late 1960's, Otepka, like McCarthy, became involved in the furious bureaucratic war against his superiors at State around the issue of loyalty, the same superiors who were targeted by McCarthy.

Otepka always claimed that he was motivated by a slavish adherence to all the rules. There were several key statutes, regulations, and executive orders which governed State Department Security. Otepka's job was to weed out subversives (and also homosexuals, alcoholics, and other "high risks") from the State Department by following these laws and rules.

However, when we examine Otepka's application of his vaunted rules, it becomes painfully clear: *Otepka's subjective judgment was the "rule."*

In the book named *Despoilers of Democracy*, by Clark Mollenhoff, at p. 244, (hereinafter DOD) says that Otepka considered himself at that point to be a moderating force in this bureaucratic battle against Communism. On June 15, 1953, Otto Otepka transferred from the Civil Service Commission to the Department of State.

In this struggle, Otepka had been recruited by R.W. "Scott" McLeod. McLeod had been brought into the State Department by the new Secretary of State, John Foster Dulles, to be a hatchet-man for for the vociferous anti-Communist faction at State, which was actually a numerical minority of the State Department employees. In this effort, Otepka began his work as a security evaluator.

Otepka and Scott McLeod were mentioned in a magazine called *The Reporter*, in an article titled "Big Brother at Foggy Bottom," which described the new policies under Eisenhower's Executive Order 10450 (which elimiated the distinction between "loyalty" and "security"), and the reaction of State employees to it. As it worked out, in at least one atypical case, Otepka found himself actually engaged in a behind-the-scenes struggle *against* that "most powerful man in America," Senator Joe McCarthy.[3] The battle was joined in 1953 when the Senator put the heat on the State Department to fire a man named Wolf Ladejinsky.

It is important to understand the process where conservative Democrats and Republicans wanted to wrest control of the State Department away from Liberal Democrats and the thousands of career diplomats who populated the State Department bureaucracy.

THE STATE DEPARTMENT SECURITY CASE OF WOLF LADEJINSKY

Ladejinsky was an influential agricultural economist. He had served in the Department of Agriculture, the Ford Foundation and the World Bank. His focus had been on the Far East. Among other things, Ladejinsky would become an advisor to South Vietnam leader Ngo Dinh Diem, from 1955 to 1961. Ladejinsky's specialty was land reform.

Land reform was the practice of taking of estates from wealthy landlords, carving them up and then transferring them to peasant farmers. Such land reform was actually an important issue in the American Revolution, but most Americans don't realize it.

Ladejinsky considered land reform to be one of the most effective ways to battle and co-opt Communism. Ladejinsky was actually a strong anti-Communist. The catch was that he thought pro-American anti-Communists could essentially win a "bidding war" against the Communists in China by promising even more to the peasants than the Communists promised.

This question of outbidding Mao Tse Tung for the hearts of the Chinese peasant could never really be mentioned or seriously discussed. The plan of taking land from landlords and gifting it to tenants was something that wealthy Americans would consider subversive *per se*, regardless of its potential as an anti-Communist strategy. Any strategy which involved a "bidding war" to win over the Asian peasant, (effectively out-bidding the Communists in the eyes of the peasant), would never even be remotely considered by McCarthy and his backers, even if it actually would work!

In 1953, McCarthy demanded that the State Department fire Wolf Ladejinsky. In addressing the demands of Senator McCarthy, Otepka became involved in the security evaluation of Wolf Ladejinsky.(see DOD p.245) The evaluation of Ladejinsky had convinced Otepka that he was not a subversive. But soon thereafter, Ladejinsky had his security clearance revoked by others besides Otepka.

Otto Otepka had cleared Ladejinski while the latter was at State. But Ladejinsky was transferred to the Department of Agriculture, which was run by Secretary Ezra Taft Benson, a militant conservative (even by Eisenhower standards), possibly *the* most extreme right-wing person in Ike's administration.

Ladejinsky was quickly fired by Benson. Benson considered Ladejinsky a "security risk" despite lack of any hard evidence against him. The reason was that, at the time, Ladejinsky had three sisters living in the Soviet Union and that he supposedly had a clearance from the Communist Party to work certain places. It was alleged that Ladejinsky was a member of two supposedly Communist front organizations. One of these was a small book store, Ladejinsky merely had his name on a customer list. That was only because he had purchased a book at that store and nothing more.

The press set upon President Eisenhower about the case of Ladejinsky. The focus of this criticism was that Harold Stassen, (the former Republican Governor of Minnesota) had named Ladejinsky to the Foreign Operations Administration to direct land reform in South Vietnam. In that post, Ladejinski had enjoyed an even higher level of security clearance than at State. (The issue of land reform in South Vietnam, as we can now see in light of history, would probably be the most contentious of any possible issue in the entire U.S. Government).

Another issue regarding the loyalty of Ladejinsky was his association with an entity called Amtorg. Amtorg was the Russian trading agency. Even famous author James Michener had written that Ladejinsky was considered "Communism's most implacable foe in Asia." Ladejinsky was still fired.

Author William J. Gill claimed that he himself, as Otto Otepka's biographer, had at least one thing in common with Otepka: Gill claimed to be opposed to merely throwing mud on people for political gain. Gill portrays Otepka as a man totally functioning on laws, rules and regulations and not merely following emotion or a political agenda. Though probably true to some extent, as we shall see, Otepka was seemingly more motivated by allegiance to powerful conservatives. This would include Senators from both parties that made up the membership of the formidable Senate Internal Security Subcommittee.

But prior to 1960, in addition to the Ladejinsky case, Otepka had been involved in two other of the most important cases in his time involving State Department security.

THE STATE DEPT. SECURITY CASE OF JOHN STEWART SERVICE

Following on the heels of the Ladejinsky case, came the case against a man named John Stewart Service. This case was purely an example of the "let's kill the messenger" point of view. As we shall see, the supporters of John Stewart Service could truthfully point to him as a perfect example of a dedicated, life-long State Department employee. But it was exactly this type of person who was being hounded out of government for the political advantage of persons like Senator Joe McCarthy.

John Service was born in the Sichuan province of China, the son of Protestant missionaries. Later, he attended high school in Berkely, California and graduated from Oberlin College in Ohio. Starting in 1933 he served as a clerk in the American consulate in the capital of Yunnan province. He got several promotions. As time progressed, Service was eventually promoted to Second Secretary at the U.S.Embassy in China.

Service had spoken very critically against Chiang Kai-shek and his Kuomintang forces. Because of his knowledge of China, he was sent on a fact-finding mission to scout the Chinese Communists under Mao Tsetung. He met with Mao and Zho Enlai, the Secretary of State under Mao. In his reports about the Chinese Communists, Service praised the Communists as "democratic." He continued to criticize in writing the Nationalists and Chiang Kai-shek as "corrupt and incompetent."

Service along with others believed that Mao would triumph in the struggle against Chiang. They suggested that Chiang could join with the communists to form a coalition government. Most Americans have no idea how close China came to getting this coalition government, due mostly to the personal involvement of General George C. Marshall. The reader should know that colonial imperialist governments like those of Britain and France were interested in playing one side in China against the other as they always did in colonial-type situations. Diplomats of this stripe felt that, in hindsight, such a policy and especially a coalition government in China would have avoided not only the Korean War but also the Vietnam War.

The new U.S. Ambassador to China, Patrick Hurley, tried for unity in China but he failed. Hurley eventually came to support Chiang's view exclusively.

A faction in the U.S. called the "China Lobby" was started, some of whom were former Protestant missionaries in China (like John Birch of the John Birch Society).

The members of the China Lobby lived in a kind of dream world. In the 1950's and1960's these people demanded that the U.S."turn Chiang Kai-shek loose on the Communists." They were pretending that Chiang, who was exiled in Taiwan, could simply walk in and destroy the Communists who had just defeated him with very little problem.

It was against this background that John Stewart Service returned to Washington in 1945. He was soon arrested as a suspect in the Amerasia Case. *Amerasia* was an allegedly Communist foreign policy magazine. He was accused of passing confidential U.S. materials from his time in China to the editors of the *Amerasia* magazine. However, a grand jury declined to indict Service, finding that the materials were not sensitive or classified and were of a kind commonly released to journalists.

Eventually, five years later, Service was dismissed from the State Department after Joe McCarthy accused him of being a Communist. Service challenged the dismissal in court. Ultimately, the U.S. Supreme Court ruled in his favor and he was reinstated. Service then had three more overseas assignments under MacArthur in Tokyo and in New Zealand up to 1949. But while back in Washington, he was wire-tapped and framed for an alleged security violation involving *Amerasia* magazine.

FBI investigators broke into the offices of *Amerasia* and found hundreds of government documents, many labeled "secret," "top secret," or "confidential." Service was arrested as a suspect regarding these documents. A grand jury refused to indict Service by a vote of 20-0. Service was subjected to loyalty and security hearings every year from 1946 to 1951 with the exception of 1948. In each hearing, he was cleared.

In 1959, he was given a new security clearance. Loy Henderson, the Undersecretary of State for Administration approved the clearance. Henderson's qualified approval allowed Service to continue his career. The State Department found a lesser position for him which did not require Senate confirmation. But for the rest if his career, despite excellent job reviews, the State Department refused ever again to promote him.

We have examined the cases of Ladejinsky and Service to illustrate the nature of the war that was being waged nonstop from WWII right up to the JFK assassination and beyond between ultra-conservatives and the State Department.

THE STATE DEPT. SECURITY CASE OF JOHN PATON DAVIES

John Paton Davies, born in Sichuan, China and a graduate of the University of Wisconsin, Madison, joined the Foreign Service in 1931. He was a member of a fact-finding mission about Mao and the Communists in China called the "Dixie Mission." The U.S. Government and specifically the State Department was wrestling with the question of the best policy by which to approach the major unresolved question of China.

John Paton Davies went on to serve under U.S. General Stilwell, General Albert Wedemeyer and General Patrick Hurley: all three assignments were in China. After World War II, Davies served on the State Department policy staff as well as for the U.S. High Commission for Germany. John Paton Davies spent the whole time fighting the slander directed at him by the extremists in the China Lobby.

Another whipping boy of the China lobby was an organization called the Institute of Pacific Relations. In his book *The Anglo-American Establishment*, author Carroll Quigley states that the case of John Paton Davies became intermixed with the case of the Institute of Pacific Relations. The Senate Internal Security Subcommittee had a virtual vendetta against the Institute of Pacific Relations. Author Quigley states that the Institute had roots with Wall Street and the British Commonwealth, among others groups. It was supported by the Wall Street investment bank of J.P. Morgan and other similar organizations and individuals. But there were allegations floating around that the IPR was dominated by Communists.

The Senate Internal Security Subcommittee spent an entire year investigating the IPR. In 1952, McCarthy also began attacking the IPR. It is unclear when J.P.Morgan and the Rockefeller and Carnegie foundations withdrew their support and left the IPR or if they ever left at all. As of this writing, information about the IPR is still very hard to come by.

It is in connection with the case of John Paton Davies of the State Department that Security Officer Otto Otepka came into this picture. It was claimed by his enemies that Davies had knowingly delivered papers to Communist agents in order to help assure the downfall of Chiang Kai-shek.

Otto Otepka had ruled that Davies was not a security risk. The Davies case had gone before an independent Security Hearing Board at the State Department. That board voted 5-0 for Davies to be fired. Secretary of State John Foster Dulles, Ike's appointee, relied on certain findings by Otepka to uphold the firing. After this controversy, John Paton Davies was in security limbo and was not eligible to be rehired by the State Department until January 1969, when he was hired as a consultant on disarmament.

After the Davies case, the U.S. Foreign Service Corps developed hostility to Otto Otepka. Also, as a result of these controversial security issues at the State Department, a right-wing hatchet man named Scott McLeod was installed at State. He was a close ally of Otto Otepka and was subjected to severe criticism in some quarters.

THE BATTLE FOR STATE DEPT. SECURITY UNDER IKE

On April 25, 1954, Otepka was promoted to Chief of the Division of Evaluations by Ike's hatchet man Scott McLeod. In his work, Otepka emphasized linking any finding of security problems to the name of the individual who made the call with regard to the clearance. Otepka believed in accountability. If these decision-makers could merely pass into anonymity, Otepka believed that the framework of Internal Security would collapse like a house of cards.

In defense of the objectivity of Otepka, it should be said that he sometimes disagreed with his superiors in the Eisenhower Administration. Author Clark Mollenhoff, one of the best investigative reporters of his era, wrote critically about this security system at State. In his book DOD at p. 245, Mollenhoff pointed out that it is difficult to justify a system where a mid-level bureaucrat like Otto Otepka could, essentially, be the last and only chance to head off a major foreign policy and national security disaster. (See DOD p. 39) We will soon see how this flimsy system arguably led to disaster in the rise of Fidel Castro in Cuba.

Mollenhoff suggests that Otepka was justified in many cases to bypass his superiors regarding security decisions. Otepka had multiple devious techniques to be able to "go around" his superiors at State. One way was to refer matters to the Personnel Department at State. Another more drastic method was to secretly inform the Senate Internal Security Subcommittee. It was Otepka's tactic of approaching the Senate Internal Security Subcommittee where he ran into a hornets nest. And this is what connected Otepka to the JFK assassination.

Because of conflict with Congress, President Truman had issued Executive Order 9835. This well-known order prohibited a Federal employee from providing classified information to any Congressional Committee. Part of Truman's rationale for this was that: because of its diverse and loose structure, the Congress could not keep sensitive information secret. Further, Truman felt that it was he and not the Congress who was accountable for the actions of the employees in the executive branch. According to this belief, he felt that Congress would mostly be an interference in carrying out foreign policy.

However, following the election victory in 1952, the Eisenhower Administration moved in the opposite direction. With Executive Order 10450, Ike made things tougher on alleged violators of security. Order 10450 abolished the existing distinction between "loyalty"and "security."

We now bring in Otepka biographer William J. Gill and his opinions regarding controversy surrounding Otto Otepka. In *The Ordeal of Otto Otepka*, the viewpoint of author Gill represents the attitude of the Taft-Eisenhower-Dulles conservatives of the 1950's. This is true with regard to the crucial issue of U.S. foreign policy in general and the State Department in particular.

In a duplicitous manner, Gill faults the FBI, the CIA and other intelligence agencies because in the 1950's they drew a distinction between a Communist and a Socialist. Gill agrees on one hand that they *should* make that distinction. But in the very next sentence he says that Socialism is international in nature and that the Soviets always prefer to recruit espionage agents from among the Socialists. Gill seems to imply here that he would be perfectly okay if the U.S. Government fired Socialists because of their political beliefs.

The case of Otto Otepka and his risky relations with the SISS committee is crucial to understanding the assassination of JFK. The battle between State and SISS was the extreme front line of this battle and Otepka was the solitary soldier on watch that came under the most fire and was most exposed in this epic confrontation.

This conflation of Socialism and Communism shows that Gill, in most respects an excellent journalist, nevertheless both insults and attempts to mislead the reader. Thus Gill, although generally an objective journalist, fails to resist the temptation to make such an equation between Socialism and Communism. Gill even goes so far as to suggest that a purely legal view of this loyalty-security controversy is fundamentally detrimental. Gill faults William Blackstone. Blackstone was the British jurist who penned the monumental Blackstone's Commentaries. Blackstone is one of the cornerstones of English common law. And the Constitution states that the English Common Law will be the law of the United States. Gill is not impressed. Thus, he dismisses the entire English Common Law as being a hindrance in the battle against Communism and subversion.

THE ESTABLISHMENT OF THE LAWS AGAINST COMMUNISM IN THE MCCARTHY ERA

The Internal Security Act of 1950 provided for registration of Communists or Fascists who wished to overthrow the U.S. Government. It was to monitor the enforcement of that Act that the Senate created the Senate Internal Security Subcommittee, known both as SISS and as the McCarran Committee.

Many, perhaps most departments of the Federal Government, had officers who were in charge of weeding out Communists, homosexuals, alcoholics and certain other types of people. It was felt back then that these people were considered dangerous, either because they were actually subversive or that they were exposed to the threat of blackmail because of their unpopular life-style. As far as it is known to this author, this concept of security was new on the scene in this era of the Red Scare. Of course you could cite the Palmer raids of 1919-1920. And before that, there were the Alien and Sedition Acts in 1798 under the second President, John Adams. But the McCarthy era security laws and practices were of a different source and genesis.

The key to understanding these issues is to recognize that the Red Menace was not really a menace to the United States itself. Like the United Kingdom, France, West Germany, Scandinavia and other stable Western democracies, there was little risk of Communism taking over and establishing a Communist dictatorship of the type under Lenin or Stalin. Although the Communist Party was allowed to be on the ballot in the U.S. as late as the 1940's, it never drew more than 100,000 votes out of, for example, the 24 million who voted in 1948.

The Red Scare scenario came from the fear of Communism taking over in other countries. And these were the countries which happened to be poorer than average or were already under the thumb of an oppressive government. Whence came the fears of the Vatican regarding the threat of Communism in Italy, Spain and Latin America. And there was the fracas over the loss of China to the Communists. There was also vulnerability in countries like the Philippines, Vietnam, Laos, Cambodia, Indonesia, Africa and the remnants of the British Empire.

And so after WWII, the struggle began for control of the foreign policy of the United States. This struggle led directly to the assassination of President Kennedy. Related to this were the fluid, developing twin concepts of "security" and "loyalty" which were at work in the day-to-day job of the State Department Security Analyst Otto Otepka.

To shine a light on the amorphous concept of Otepka's definition of security, we can cite the following statistics. The SY (State Department Security), in reviewing the files of 10,000 employees, had made a list that numbered 1,943 persons, all of whom had "some form of derogatory information" in their files. As previously stated, this included suspected Communists, homosexuals and alcoholics, to name a few of the suspect traits and categories. Otepka boiled this list down to 858 of his fellow employees who deserved future monitoring.

Otepka was considered to have an attitude which represented Eisenhower. Upon the election of John F. Kennedy, things drastically changed. Following the 1960 election, Otepka was confronted in December 1960, during a private meeting by Robert F. Kennedy and the new Secretary of State, Dean Rusk. To Otepka, this meeting was hostile and ugly and posed a threat to his ability to to do his job as it had been done under Eisenhower.

Otepka worried most about the attitude of Robert Kennedy. In discussing the desire on the part of Robert Kennedy to obtain a security clearance for future Presidential Advisor Walter W. Rostow to work in the State Department if that became necessary, Otepka stated that such a clearance would not be granted. His main reason being that Air Force intelligence had in the past refused Rostow a security clearance and also that Rostow's family had a Russian connection. In this tense meeting, the impulsive RFK would summarily dismiss the Air Force intelligence men as "jerks."

But when it came to the controversy which swirled around the lonely soldier Otto Otepka, there was more, much more to the story.

OTEPKA INVESTIGATES LEE HARVEY OSWALD

As portrayed in her book *A Farewell To Justice: Jim Garrison, JFK's Assassination, and the Case That Should have Changed History* (FTJ), author Joan Mellen was the last JFK assassination researcher to interview Otto Otepka. Ms. Mellen discovered that as of June 30, 1960, during the Eisenhower Administration, the Office of Security of the U.S. State Department began to investigate a list of supposed defectors to the Soviet Union and on that list was the name of Lee Harvey Oswald. Also involved in this investigation was the Office of Intelligence Resources and Collection, Bureau of Intelligence Research of the State Department.

On December 5, 1960 Otto Otepka was informed by the Intelligence Collection and Distribution Division of the State Department that his department, the Office of Security, would handle the investigation of persons on that list of defectors who were potential intelligence agents. The job of Otepka was normally not to investigate just anyone, but rather *State Department employees*. Were these defectors nominal State Department employees? Could they be spies attached to embassies in the same way that CIA spies sometimes masqueraded as attachés at U.S. Embassies? We know for certain that Otepka was (for some reason) investigating Lee Harvey Oswald at a very early date, long before the name Oswald was to become one of the most famous in American history.

The reader might ask, why did the State Department have a Bureau of Intelligence Research? It's not as if the U.S. Government had a shortage of agencies examining intelligence issues. The FBI, the CIA, the NSA, Army Intelligence, Naval Intelligence and even the Police Departments in major cities were all heavily involved in intelligence. So why the State Department, too? Author Mellen states that Otepka's mission was to determine if persons on this defector list had any connection to State Department employees.

Of course, the State Department had a passport office. It would probably have some interest in persons who might be involved with foreign governments. But it is not clear why the State Department would undertake to monitor the activities of persons like Oswald who might be spies. That would seem to be the duty of the FBI, the CIA or military intelligence. And we know that after he returned to the U.S. from the Soviet Union, both Oswald and his wife were followed by FBI agent James Hosty.

It strikes this writer that the duty of investigating a list of defectors implies that this program was somehow connected to activities of the State Department, probably through foreign embassies. We know that, for instance, when Oswald defected to the USSR, the U.S. State Department for some reason that is unclear, held up his paperwork without honoring his request to renounce his U.S. citizenship. This made possible his easy return to the U.S. The excuse for this was that they were being big-hearted and felt sympathy for Oswald, i.e. that they were protecting Oswald from himself. However, it might also have been the case that while Oswald was living in the Soviet Union, he had been passing information to the U.S. through the U.S. Embassy or a consulate. When Oswald was in the Soviet Union he worked in an electronics factory. At that time, the U.S. had intelligence departments gathering information about the state of Soviet industry. A former CIA agent once hinted at that gathering of information on electronics by Oswald, when he went about explaining all of his duties while over in Russia.

It is well known to anyone interested in JFK assassination research that when Lee Harvey Oswald returned to the U.S. following his defection, he was given a loan from the State Department to pay the expenses for both himself and his family to travel back to New Orleans. Those funds must have been legally available for such purposes. It is also true that Oswald, upon his return from the USSR, was put in contact with private parties and that some of these parties had connections to right-wing interests. Thus, it seems likely that if there were a string of double agents being run at that time that U.S. embassies would have been involved and that might be the reason for the State Department to be maintaining a file of Oswald.

When one reads about the FBI Counter Intelligence and British S.O.E. during World War II, one sees that these agencies were each running a string of double agents. The reason that both of these agencies were interested in having a number of such agents was to benefit from economies of scale. In other words for example, all of these double agents needed a mail drop and short-wave communications with a home base. Multiple agents could all use the same mail drop and the same means of communication. Thus, the U.S. and the U.K. benefited in these efficiencies in maintaining double agents in Germany during World War II.

The Kennedy Administration Begins as Otepka Meets Robert F. Kennedy

On a day in December 1960, in a 7:00 P.M. special meeting between Otepka, Dean Rusk and Robert Kennedy in Otto Otepka's office, Robert Kennedy came quickly to the bottom line: Kennedy wanted to know whether Otepka would clear W.W. Rostow for employment at the State Department on grounds of security. On two previous occasions, in 1955 and 1956, Otepka had declined to approve Rostow for State Department employment. (FTJ p. 431).

"What kind of security problem would be encountered," Rusk asked. The case against W.W. Rostow was threefold: *first,* because Rostow had a history of close associations with persons who were Communist Party members, some proven to be Soviet espionage agents, *second,* because two of his aunts were members of the Communist Party in the 1940's, and *third,* Rostow's father was a native of Russia and had been a Socialist there prior to the first Communist revolt which occurred in 1905. The elder Rostow continued as a Socialist activist when he came to the U.S. in 1905. The U.S. Air Force Intelligence had declared Rostow a "security risk," a very serious charge in that field. Otepka indicated he would not clear Rostow. When he said so, Robert Kennedy exploded, saying "those Air Force guys are a bunch of jerks, they're nuts!" As a result of Otepka's rejection, instead of working at the State Department, W.W. Rostow became an advisor at the White House, where he would head up the Staff of the National Security Counsel. The State Department had no control over security clearances at the White House.

The almost unbelievable sequel to these events is that Rostow, after being rejected by Otepka, went on to become the sole author of U.S. Foreign policy. He was the architect of the Vietnam War policy which divided Americans from 1963 to 1975. Vietnam was by far the most dominant issue in U.S. politics for that entire period. But Rostow's clearance and thus his ability to work for the U.S. State Department hung from the tiny thread that was the *personal opinion* of Mr. Otto Otepka.

It is argued in some sources that it was the emphasis on correct legal procedures that got Otto Otepka into instant trouble with the incoming Kennedy administration. But we also see that the negative decision on the Rostow clearance was not because of something that was carved in stone in rules and regulations of the State Department. Rostow was not personally accused of anything. Would the written regulations of the State Department require that if your relatives were involved with Communism, that you would be fired?

Not likely. The guilt of Rostow was based on the alleged pro-Communist acts of his relatives and acquaintances. So Otepka's decision did not really amount to "going by the book." It was rather the same old guilt by association as practiced by Joe McCarthy. If an investigator such as Otepka can consider anything he wishes to be classified as subversive, he is not "going by the book." Instead, he is writing his own book every time he makes a decision.

Since Otepka was a long term, experienced security officer, with 25 total years in the U.S. Government, he felt he knew pretty well what the challenges were in enforcing security in the State Department. In 1960, in an evaluation of Otepka himself, he was commended for his knowledge of laws, regulations, rules and procedures in all aspects of security. The evaluation also mentioned that he was especially knowledgeable about Communism and its dangerous role in subversion in the United States.

THE BLUNDER OF WIELAND OPENS THE DOOR TO CASTRO

So now we will look into the biggest mistake of all from this era regarding the Communist menace. This would be the question of "who lost Cuba?" And the one person who, more than anyone else got the blame was a State Department representative named William Wieland.

In a press conference on January 24, 1962, a veteran journalist named Sarah McClendon confronted President Kennedy about the case of William Arthur Wieland. Reporter McClendon described Wieland as a well-known security risk who had apparently been put on a task force to reorganize the [State Department] Office of Security. It came to light that the Senate Internal Security Subcommittee (SISS) had been investigating State Department employee William Wieland for over a year. Kennedy had replied to the question by Sarah McClendon by saying that Wieland was cleared on grounds of security. In fact Otto Otepka had refused to clear Wieland. SY (Security) Director William O. Boswell, Otepka's immediate boss and Roger Jones, Deputy Undersecretary for Administration had both confronted Otepka and demanded that Otepka clear Wieland immediately.

The Wieland situation was up in the air for months. SISS was involved (in the person of acting chairman Senator Thomas J. Dodd of Connecticut). Secretary of State Dean Rusk told Dodd that he, Rusk, had personally cleared Wieland. Rusk had not. This interaction between Rusk and Dodd represented the security "war" that had erupted due to the conflict between SISS, Dean Rusk and the Kennedys. But who was the subject of this dispute, William Wieland? See: [http://havanaschooleng.blogspot.com/2012/05/cuban-conspiracy-nine-wielands-case-i.html] Viewed 3-19-15, hereinafter "havblog."

Wieland joined the State Department in 1941, and in 1957, he had reached the high position of Director of the Bureau for Mexico and the Caribbean of the Undersecretary of State for Latin America. The problem was that Wieland's long career in the State Department apparently had both begun and developed without the required security clearances. In addition, Wieland had never even managed to present the necessary identity documents to begin work of the Department. Nobody knew for sure what his real name was. Wieland sometimes appeared as William Arthur Wieland, at other times as Arturo Montenegro and still others as William Montenegro. These questions about Wieland led to the investigation of sensitive foreign policy decisions in which Wieland was involved.

Wieland was regarded as the man responsible for the overthrow of Fulgencio Batista in Cuba. But after that, he was also a central player in the rise and consolidation of power by Fidel Castro. Members of SISS and several State Department officials who testified before SISS were suspicious about Wieland. They found that Wieland was the main instigator of the suspension of arms shipments to General Batista's government. This had set the stage for the fall of Batista and the rise of Castro.

As Director of Mexican and Caribbean affairs in the State Department, Wieland was able to recommend policies whenever he wanted toward any country of the region. He also had considerable influence with his boss, Roy Rubottom, the Undersecretary of State for Latin America, on how to implement these policies.

In addition, Wieland, was pointed to (by some) as the *mastermind* of the international media manipulation that shaped the image of Fidel Castro. Castro was first heard of as a little known guerilla leader in the mountains of Cuba. He was cast in the media as a modern-day Robin Hood. Apparently, Wieland had much to do with a famous interview by Herbert Matthews, the star reporter of the *New York Times*. Matthews met with Fidel Castro when Castro was still fighting in the Sierra Maestra mountains against Batista. In addition, along the same lines, there was a pro-Castro CBS television documentary where Castro's guerrillas in the mountains of eastern Cuba were portrayed in a favorable light.

Wieland had also managed to replace Arthur Gardner, the American ambassador who was sympathetic to the Batista government, with Earl E.T. Smith, who would play an important role in the fall of the Batista regime. The final bottom line with regard to Wieland and his support of Castro, came on an important plane flight. In August 1959, Ambassador to Mexico Robert C. Hill told SISS that he was trying to get the word to President Eisenhower about Castro's true colors. Hill tried this by informing Presidential advisor Milton Eisenhower about the bad side of Castro. Milton Eisenhower was acting at that time as the White House advisor on Latin America. On the plane flight in question, Mr. Raymond Leddy, political counselor to the American Embassy in Mexico City and Colonel Benoid Glawe, the embassy air attaché had both told Milton Eisenhower that Castro was a Communist. Wieland, being on the same flight, shouted that these men were lying, so Milton Eisenhower would not listen further to any discussion on the Castro issue.

Around this same time, the SISS began an investigation of Wieland. The overall purpose of SISS was to help enforce the Internal Security Act of 1950.

It is the job of the Senate to pass legislation. But also through the committee system, Congress is allowed to gather information to enable it to pass appropriate laws. However, the Supreme Court has held that Congress has no power to investigate simply to investigate. The investigations by Congress have to have at least some connection to legislating and legislation, or for purposes of presidential and other appointments and similar issues.

Another, more controversial theory regarding committees of Congress would allow them to monitor the Executive to see whether the Executive is doing its job and enforcing the laws. Some scholars have argued that this function of monitoring the executive branch is really not appropriate according to the separation of powers unless the Senate might be putting a President on trial for "high crimes and misdemeanors" preparatory to impeachment.

The dichotomy of freedom versus security would, as we shall see, go on to cause the rift between reactionary forces in Congress and more pragmatic individuals within the executive branch. There were moderate, non-political individuals and bureaucrats in the Roosevelt, Truman, Eisenhower and Kennedy Administrations. These moderates (which could well have included Rockefeller-affiliated Republicans of the day) were charged with actually making things work on a day-to-day basis. They tended to favor expediency regarding such issues such as "atoms for peace," "open skies policies," arms control, the Test Ban Treaty and summit meetings. One could even throw into that category the pragmatic policies which attempted to solve the Korean and Vietnam wars. However, in Congress there were some right-wing extremists who favored dogmatic responses.

OTEPKA BATTLES THE KENNEDY ADMINISTRATION OVER STATE DEPARTMENT SECURITY

Author William J. Gill states in *The Ordeal of Otto Otepka*, that the preeminent interest of Robert Kennedy was the State Department. It is generally agreed by historians that the JFK administration was oriented most strongly to foreign policy.

Despite this heavy emphasis, it seems strange to this author that State Department security was placed in the hands of a single middle-level bureaucrat like Otekpa, to the exclusion of the Secretary of State, the head of the Security Department and even the President himself. The concern of RFK about the clearance for Walter Rostow was only one example of conflicts between the White House and State Department bureaucrats over the State Department security issue (see DOD p. 242).

Otepka had been working in security during the transition between what we can call *the two Robert Kennedys*. It was the *old* Robert Kennedy who was Assistant Counsel and close personal friend for life to Joe McCarthy, working in McCarthy's outlandish Red-baiting crusade. It was the *new* Robert Kennedy who Otepka would view as a coddler of Communists. In 1961, the Kennedys would synthesize their experiences with Communism and change themselves into the leaders at the forefront of the effort to achieve detente with Communism on a world-wide basis.

JFK had always represented big-city bosses, some of the more conservative labor leaders and, quite importantly, leaders from the South. When it came to his brother Bobby, Gore Vidal had described RFK as "a dangerous, ruthless man." On issues related to McCarthy, (as a Senator), JFK had joined Joe McCarthy to harshly criticize such diplomats as Owen Lattimore and John K. Fairbank who were typical Joe McCarthy targets. As recently as 1955, Robert Kennedy, acting as Chief Counsel of the Government Operations committee, drew up a report castigating the the military over subversives in Fort Monmouth, New Jersey. This allegation about Communists in the Army was considered one of McCarthy's most extreme accusations.

Amazingly to the student of history, there was a specific day when JFK switched from "tough" to "soft" on Communism. This was right after the 1956 Democratic Convention. Eleanor Roosevelt had accused JFK of being "soft on McCarthyism." According to Gill, it was JFK's aide Theodore Sorensen, historian James Schlessinger, Jr. and economist John Kenneth Galbraith who turned JFK around to Liberalism.

In June, 1959, JFK dined with a group of Harvard-type Liberal intelligentsia (see OOO p 60). This was the apparent date of JFK's "conversion to Liberalism." Soon after, JFK's first Liberal act was to vote against confirmation of Lewis Strauss to be Secretary of Commerce. Liberals had a vendetta against Lewis Strauss because he had been head of the Atomic Energy Commission when the the AEC denied a security clearance to Robert J. Oppenheimer. This was done, despite the fact that Oppenheimer had given the U.S. Government the "gift" of the the atomic bomb.

In his Lone Ranger quest to fend off Communists in the State Department, Otepka had begun informing to SISS whenever he was unable to deny clearances to suspected security risks by any other means.

And when we look at the new Secretary of State under JFK, Dean Rusk, we find that Rusk had testified to SISS repeatedly during the period from just four weeks prior to Dallas on October 21, 1963 to sometime in 1965. However, when the JFK administration took over from Ike, Otto Otepka had come under fairly severe persecution because of his rigid approach to security. Rather than Dean Rusk, the blame for the persecution of Otepka was put on William J. Crockett, Deputy Under Secretary for Administration in the State Department. On October 21, 1963 Rusk appeared before SISS, with 7 of the 9 Senators present:these were Dirksen, Dodd, Ervin, Hruska, Keating, McClellan and Scott.

RUSK AND WALTER W. ROSTOW, THE ANGLOPHILES AT STATE

The politics of Secretary of State Dean Rusk were generally opaque. It seems that Rusk had worked very hard to disguise his politics. Author William J. Gill in *OOO* analyzes Rusk's politics, not as pro-Communist or anti-Communist, but rather as Anglophile. Like many of the more sophisticated historians, Gill analyzes Rusk as mostly influenced by his extensive period of study in England and Europe. Gill would claim that Rusk was functioning more along the ultra-high level guidelines unique to Rhodes-scholarly Anglophiles like himself and W.W. Rostow.

Coming from humble beginnings on a tenant farm in Georgia, Dean Rusk had indeed gone on to become a Rhodes Scholar in England,. He studied there for three years. In his final year he won the "Cecil Peace Prize." worth 100 British pounds. Then he had gone on for further studies in Germany. (Interestingly, there is no record of Rusk ever having commented on what he experienced in Germany during the rise of Hitler).

We have already explained the extreme importance of the China issue to many public and private individuals in the U.S. We note that during World War II, Rusk worked in Army Intelligence (G-2) in the British Empire section, of which he became Chief. So in that crucial period, Rusk had been up to his eyeballs in the China issue. All of the State Department "China Hands" we have mentioned previously in this chapter were fellow China experts or persons with experience in China like Dean Rusk.

By 1943, Rusk was on the staff of Gen. Joseph Stilwell. Rusk became Deputy Chief of Staff for the entire China-Burma-India theater. While Rusk was in China, also present were "old China hands" John Stewart Service, John Paton Davies, John K. Emmerson and Owen Lattimore. Rusk was secretly the architect of a proposed plan to arm 1 million Communist troops and put them under General Stilwell, a plan that was rejected by Chiang Kaishek. As we have stated before, the policy of "divide and conquer" was the hallmark method of the British Empire and its advocates. So in this regard, Rusk was possibly doing the bidding of the U.K. as well as the U.S. in China.

Stilwell was succeeded by conservative Gen. Albert C. Wedemeyer and ambassador to China Patrick J. Hurley. Rusk was suggested [though never proven] as the author of a famous report entitled "the 1949 White Paper on China" which, per Gill, paved the way for the victory of Mao Tse-Tung.

Rusk was ordered back to Washington where he became Assistant Chief in the Operations Division of the War Department's General Staff. Rusk was a protégé of General George C. Marshall. Among other cohorts of Rusk were soon-to-be Secretary of War Robert Patterson and Under Secretary of the Army John J. McCloy. This close connection with Patterson and John J. McCloy is very telling. McCloy, of course, effectively ran the Warren Commission. Patterson worked closely during the WWII with James Forrestal. In the opinion of your author, this "Forrestal connection" included some people involved in the JFK assassination. This connection is presented in more detail in other chapters.

After leaving the Army in February, 1946, Rusk became Assistant Chief of the Division of International Security Affairs. The new Secretary of State George C. Marshall named Rusk Director of the Office of Special Political Affairs, a post just vacated by Alger Hiss. Hiss, of course, was later proven to be one of the rare *actual* Communists or former Communists in the State Department. Hiss was exposed in that role by Richard M. Nixon, then a member of the HUAC committee.

In December, 1952, things were happening at the SISS. On December 16, Carlisle H. Humelsine, then Deputy Undersecretary of State in charge of security, was questioned by Jay Sourwine before SISS. Humelsine claimed to SISS that there had been a definite effort by the State Department to recruit American Communists for work at the U.N. So we see, (at that early date) when Joe McCarthy was at his zenith, SISS was already involved with trying to supervise or possibly even run the State Department, even after the election of a Republican President.

Regarding Chiang Kai-shek, the U.S. cut off further weapons for him, and he quickly lost the South and West of China to Mao Tse-tung. Rusk likened the Communist takeover of China to the American Revolution. Credit for the White Paper on China went to Philip Jessup, a former Chairman of the Institute of Pacific Relations. Jessup was allegedly involved with five Communist fronts. Rusk, during this time, was the most important voice in advising President Truman to intervene in the Korean War. Also at this time, General MacArthur sensed something was wrong in Washington. MacArthur said, "There was a tendency towards temporizing rather than fighting it through." (OOO p. 77).

On November 6, 1950 in Korea, General Douglas MacArthur had discovered that 200,000 Chinese troops were massing just north of the Yalu River. MacArthur ordered the bridges across the Yalu River to be bombed. But according to the memoirs of Harry S. Truman called *Years of Trial and Hope*,

Truman says he revoked MacArthur's orders to bomb the bridges because Assistant Secretary of State Dean Rusk cited an agreement *with Britain* not to go near the Yalu River without consulting with them. Note the advocacy for Britain on the part of Dean Rusk. This was only the latest example of Rusk being involved with Britain, perhaps to the detriment of U.S. security.

On April 11, Truman removed MacArthur from his command, and the memo to that effect delivered to MacArthur was, according to *Look* magazine, written by Dean Rusk. In December 1951, Rusk resigned from the State Department. After his resignation, Rusk went on to become President of the Rockefeller Foundation. Five months before Rusk resigned from State, his close advisor, Oliver Edmund Chubb, was proven to have close relationships with subversives. The month Chubb was declared a security risk by a State Department Board, SISS began a year-long investigation of the Institute of Pacific Relations. In July, 1952, SISS issued its report which said that IPR had been "an instrument of Communist policy, propaganda and military Intelligence."

So we see that, as previously mentioned, the Institute of Pacific Relations was on the hot seat. This was despite the fact that both the Rockefeller and Ford Foundations were funding IPR. As we have noted, to this day there is a dearth of available objective information about the Institute of Pacific Relations.

The implication of the SISS versus IPR controversy, was that the British Commonwealth nations along with the Rockefeller interests were at that time considered too soft on Communism by the right-wing anti-Communists who were in control of Congress. At least that's what they felt when it came to the issue of worldwide Communism. This could have logically arisen because of the natural British concern over the eventual fate of the British Empire *vis a vis* Communism.

THE BATTLE BETWEEN OTEPKA AND SISS AGAINST RUSK AND ROBERT KENNEDY INTENSIFIES

At this time, Gill claims that there were Communists in the U.S. Government masquerading as Liberals. (For some reason author Gill capitalizes Liberal but conservative is left in the small case). SY (State Security) Director William O. Boswell who was one of Otto Otepka's superiors, was quoted thus: "once... [Boswell] told Otepka that he intended to eradicate the "the McLeod image" from SY. McCleod, as described previously, was an Ike/McCarthy anti-Communist hatchet-man at State.

Gill claims that, by 1961, it had become harder and harder to find real security risks in the government. (OOO p. 88). The obvious question here was, could it be because there were *actually fewer security risks?* Gill claims that this was due in large part to the paucity of new defectors from the American Communist Party. But the fact was, in 1961, the majority of members in the American Communist Party were paid FBI informants. The FBI, therefore, was the major funding source for the Communist Party at that time. Coming full circle back to SISS, all of this was bad news for people who had turned the Red Scare into cash in the bank such as Senator Thomas J. Dodd, permanently acting Chairman of SISS.

The reader might wonder, why are we going so far afield from our effort to understand the assassination of JFK? It comes down to this: the whole direction of U.S. history from 1945 to 1963 was pointed to battling world Communism. And the front line players in this epic battle were people like the "China hands" which included both Dean Rusk and John Paton Davies, and Senators McCarthy, Thomas Dodd, James O. Eastland and Pat McCarran, founder of SISS. The three main anti-Communist Committees, HUAC, SISS and the McCarthy Committee were the springboards for such influential politicials as McCarthy and President Richard M. Nixon. And even more importantly, there were actual fingerprints of SISS, HUAC, SISS Chairmen James O. Eastland and Thomas Dodd all over the JFK assassinatin. *Is that direct enough?* (Stay tuned!)

To comprehend the dynamics that drove the JFK assassination, one has to be aware of the continuous existential battle from 1945 to 1963 between the Congress and the Presidents. The most famous evidence for that internecine war is the warning by Ike about the "military-industrial complex." That statement by Ike gives a clue as to what all of this is about. To many people intimately involved in the battle against Communism and the USSR, from the Ukraine to Taiwan, their backs were against the wall. Just imagine what it would have meant to the Vatican, for example, if the Soviet Communists had taken over Italy! And because of their strong and numerous Communist Party, Italy was one of those countries teetering on that dangerous brink, ready to fall into the abyss.

So the battle between Otepka, Rostow, Rusk and SISS for the soul of the State Department raged literally right up until November 22, 1963. One has to gain insight into this epic struggle to appreciate the dynamics of the murder of JFK.

MORE ON WALTER W. ROSTOW

Early in 1960, the attempts to exile Otepka were begun by his superiors John W. Hanes (who also owned the Hanes underwear company) and SY Director William O. Boswell. After the 1960 elections the pressure against Otepka increased. Although denied clearance to work at the State Department, Walt Whitman Rostow was making an impact as a Presidential advisor at the White House. As an example of the way Rostow thought, he stated at one point "he does not believe that the United

States has the right to preserve its own 'nationhood.'" Rostow's anti-nationhood bias was a product of the unique experiences in his career.

Walter W. Rostow had graduated with a bachelor's degree from Yale, and studied in England as a Rhodes scholar. Rostow studied at the Balliol College within Oxford University which was considered the most liberal of all the Oxford Colleges. After Oxford, Walter Rostow returned to Yale for his PhD. During World War II, like Dean Rusk, W.W. Rostow capitalized on his Oxford background by serving with the OSS in Britain.

Rostow returned to England in 1946 as a professor of American history. Then he went to Switzerland working directly for Swedish sociologist Gunnar Myrdal. Myrdal went on to eventually hire Rostow's brother Eugene Debs Rostow. Walter Rostow would come to the State Department in 1967. Ultimately, it was finally disclosed that Rostow was the originator of President Eisenhower's "Open Skies" proposal, which sought to allow the U.S. and the USSR to inspect each other's attack potential from the air. This was exactly the type of moderate policy that SISS and the ultra-conservatives might consider an act of treason.

Most of the steps taken by Kennedy and Johnson towards disarmament originated at the Pugwash conference. It was so-called because the first such meeting had been held at a place called Pugwash in Nova Scotia. The meetings were organized by Cyrus S. Eaton, a wealthy friend of Krushchev. The major initiatives from that conference were the the renunciation of a first-strike nuclear strategy, the ban on nuclear weapons in space and the 1963 Treaty of Moscow, also called the Limited Test Ban Treaty. SISS tried to interfere with this meeting, complaining that some of the attendees were Communists. (This was not surprising at a meeting of U.S. and Soviet officials).

It was the Limited Test Ban Treaty that most rankled SISS. In 1961, Kennedy took his foreign policy advice from White House advisors Walter W. Rostow and McGeorge Bundy. But apparently, Rostow and Bundy had to rely on information and opinion from the State Department. After all, there could be no substitute for the all the nearly 9000 State Department employees spread around the world in U.S. Embassies and Consulates. In early 1961, Walter Rostow became the chief of the State Department's Policy Planning Council. In the words of President Kennedy to Rostow when he sent Rostow from the White House to the State Department: "Over here in the White House we have to play with a very narrow range of choices. We are pretty much restricted to the ideas coming out of the bureaucracy. We can't do long-range planning; it has to be done over there [at State] I want you to go over there and catch hold of the process at the level where it counts." (OOO p. 88).

As early as November 1961, there began the effort to remove Otto Otepka from his position as Deputy Director of the Office of Security. SISS and the Administration quickly became involved in a conflict about the administrative changes to SY. A journalist at the Hearst newspapers reported that there was an effort being made to abolish the jobs of 25 State Department Security officials.

THE BATTLE BETWEEN SISS AND STATE BECOMES WAR

It was in the context of this reorganization that on November 16, 1961 Otto Otepka was first called to testify to SISS. Otepka was joined before SISS by Elmer Hipsley and Harris Huston, two veteran State Department security officials. One of the most crucial changes proposed by the top people at State Security was the transfer of the place where security and intelligence reports were processed at the State Department. The Evaluations department had for years been the initial recipients at State for the reports from the FBI, CIA and other Intelligence agencies. This duty would now lie in the Intelligence Research Bureau, which was not even a part of the Security Department at State, and was considered a dead-end. The good thing for Otepka in the proposed reorganizations was that he was put in charge of Evaluations. At around that time, Scott McLeod, the Eisenhower anti-Communist hatchet-man, died of a heart attack. The big issues at this time were the status of Otepka's job, SISS, Jay Sourwine (Chief Counsel of SISS) and Ben Mandel, (head of research at SISS).

Beginning in December, 1960, following an important conference between Robert Kennedy, Dean Rusk and Otepka, procedures at the State Department were adjusted in order to route close cases around Otepka so he would never see them. After that meeting with Rusk, Otepka and RFK, over a fourteen-month period, Dean Rusk would write up as many as 152 "security waivers." which allowed hiring without the normal FBI background checks.

During the entire Eisenhower administration, such peremptory emergency clearances were only granted five times. These were clearances of relatively high ranking officials. In February 1962, Otepka went to see Boswell, informed him about the waiver problem and Boswell replied that these were done "on the prerogatives of management."

On March 8, 1962, Boswell, Jones and Otepka all testified to SISS. Otepka revealed that some clearances had even been backdated. It came out later that all the 152 "waivers" had been personally authorized by Secretary of State Dean Rusk. In defense of Rusk, it should be said that Rusk would not have wanted to sneak practicing Communists into the State Department and certainly not suspected spies. So these 152 waivers were probably issued to speed along the hiring process. Gill claims that the problem of doing this meant once you hired someone, a subsequent background check would not matter because it was difficult to get rid of employees once they were on the job. This was possibly due to Civil Service protections and procedures.

This again, reveals the real agenda of SISS and their ally Otto Otepka. If a subsequent background check turned up espionage or Communist Party membership, that person would very quickly be fired. What SISS and Otepka were really arguing was that post-hiring background checks would not be able to produce any hard evidence to exclude or dismiss the new hire.

At this point we are reminded of author Gill's condemnation of Blackstone and the common law. In the mentality of Otepka and SISS, the law didn't guarantee valuable rights. The law (the entire law!) served only to shelter Communists. Their objections were often based on such things as a candidate having an aunt or uncle who was sympathetic to Communism, or a person bought a book at a bookstore which offered books about Lenin or Stalin.

In any kind of fair process such as a hearing before the Civil Service Commission, the SISS-Otepka kind of guilt-by-association evidence would not hold up. And further, what SISS (along with Otepka) really wanted was a veto power, exercised by conservatives in Congress, or perhaps even private citizens over the hiring process for the State Department. Apparently this veto power could be based on liberal versus conservative politics. That, of course, is not the way our government was set up. Under the Constitution, the Congress passes laws and the Executive hires people for the executive branch alone, except for certain high offices where confirmation by the Senate is required.

One could therefore ask the following question: if people like Dean Rusk were subject to confirmation by the Senate, why wasn't the Senate able to weed out, in the confirmation process, officials who were destined to be found "soft" on Communism? Keep in mind, the entire Senate could not have been kept in the dark about the activities of SISS. The situation was undoubtedly the opposite. The Senate was obviously too divided or disorganized to carry out the political dirty work which individuals like McCarthy and Senator Dodd of SISS wanted them to do.

In 1962, there was publicity in the print media about a "grand design" being promoted by Walter Rostow. The details of this design are not pertinent to the analysis of the Rusk vs. SISS confrontation. However, a statement and summary of the issue by Senator Everett Dirksen, a crucial SISS member, seems to sum up the concepts of Rostow best. "The core of Mr. Rostow's proposal," said Dirksen, "is an assumption that the Soviet Union and its Communist masters are 'mellowing'; that Russia is becoming a mature state; that if we are only nice to the Soviets they will drop all their suspicions of the free world and peace will finally bloom."

There were some who were fearful that Robert Kennedy was quickly being educated about foreign policy so that he could attempt to micro-manage foreign relations. This would add to the already long RFK list, which included the micro-management of the murder plots against

Castro, the prosecution or deportation of the Mafia, and the civil rights activity of the Justice Department in the South.

There were allegations that, while traveling abroad, RFK personally decided to transfer Dutch New Guinea to Indonesia's Sukarno. This was in early 1962. Some would say that in addition to foreign policy, RFK at that time was also planning to micro-manage the hiring and security clearance problem at the State Department. The reader should take note. It was apparently on or around this time that the polarization in the executive branch began.

Author Gill, with justification, analyzes this divide as follows: a Rostow-Rusk agenda was pitted against the agenda, of the Kennedy brothers. Gill seems to emphasize, quite correctly, the fact that both Rusk and Rostow had studied for many years in such places as Britain, Germany, Switzerland and elsewhere in Europe. They had therefore absorbed an Anglophile and a one-world-government philosophy that would soon rear it's ugly head in the form of the Vietnam War. Why did the Rusk-Rostow philosophy predominate?

The answer to this question is an easy one. Why did Abe Lincoln appoint his political rivals to his cabinet as did President Obama in a later era? JFK would never have done that. JFK was much more high-handed than Abe Lincoln. Let's face it. The Kennedys would change their colors like chameleons. They were apparently operating on the advice of the patriarch Joseph P. Kennedy, who retained the ability to communicate even after his 1961 massive stroke.

President Franklin Roosevelt finally gave up on the idea of Joseph P. Kennedy being part of the Roosevelt government. FDR felt that Kennedy was too unpredictable and inconsistent in his opinions to be trusted. Because of their lack of a true compass, the Kennedy administration was becoming a case of "putting out fires" everywhere; in place of action came reaction.

U.S. FOREIGN POLICY, SISS AND THE MICRO-MANAGEMENT BY ROBERT KENNEDY

It is not surprising that the Kennedy brothers were trying to personally manage virtually everything in the government. Even worse was the fact that it was RFK, the one of the two who most lacked any particular philosophy, who became the one with his fingers in the greater number of pies. It is a sign of a tremendously weak government where close family members were the only ones to be trusted and even more importantly, the only ones to be consulted. (We are seeing this dilemma in the current Trump administration at the date of this writing).

The ultimate absurdity, if true, is the strong possibility that RFK might have been personally entangled with Lee Harvey Oswald while working on one of his covert projects. One source for that is Otto Otepka, who believed that his investigation of Oswald was of personal concern to RFK. Otepka even believed that his dogged following of the LHO case could have been the actual reason for his subsequent persecution by the Kennedy administration. Another source of information about a possible Oswald-RFK connection is that provided by Judyth Vary Baker regarding the anti-Castro weaponized cancer project in New Orleans. Apparently, the murder plots against Castro, known as Operation Mongoose, were personally supervised by RFK.

THE FINAL SHOWDOWN BETWEEN JFK's MASSACHUSETTS MAFIA AND SISS

On April 16, 1962 a man named John Francis Reilly took over as head of the Office of Security in the State Department from William O Boswell. In a later hearing on the Otepka case, Reilly testified that he was recommended for his new job by Andy Oehmann who was Executive Assistant to Attorney General Robert Kennedy. In addition to John Francis Reilly, there was a team of people from Massachusetts with connections to the Kennedy clan who were hired at State. One would be Joseph E. Rosetti, who had worked in JFK's Congressional office. Another would be Robert J. McCarthy, also from Massachusetts. Still another would be Charles W. Lyons who had worked as an evaluator under Otepka. The fourth would be David L. Belisle, also from Massachusetts. Author Gill refers to this group as the Massachusetts Mafia.

After the arrival of these administrators, there was an immediate attempt to lure Otepka away from his job by sending him to the War College, which was sometimes considered an honor by employees at State. Otekpa refused the War College offer. But, important to the Otepka story was the fact that even such a seemingly minor personnel decision was met with a letter from Senator Karl Mundt. Mundt was an extreme conservative who had served in both Houses of Congress during a long career; a member of SISS, and had been closely involved with State Department issues. Mundt had even been involved with the Alger Hiss case fifteen years prior as a member of HUAC. The letter from Mundt was sent to Roger Jones, the Deputy Undersecretary for Administration. Mundt expressed disapproval of the treatment of Otepka, and raised the specter of possible future Soviet penetration of the State Department.

Two days later, Roger Jones was called to appear in front of SISS. Jones was pointedly questioned about the seemingly minor issue of Otepka's job description. The message from SISS was clearly "hands off Otepka." The next security controversy at State was the advent of the "short form report" which eliminated many of the questions on the prior required longer-form report. With the new report, the person who was the investigator had to summarize any negative information against an applicant and even pass over negative information in the process of boiling down information to fit onto the short form. Otepka felt that this turned the front-line investigator into an evaluator.

The next controversy regarding Otepka and his role at State was the case of Harland Cleveland. Cleveland was Assistant Secretary of State for International Organization Affairs. Like Dean Rusk and Walt Rostow, Harland Cleveland had studied in England as a Rhodes Scholar. Gill describes Cleveland as a "peace-nik." In an interview, Cleveland had asked Otto Otepka "what are the chances for Alger Hiss [being rehired]"? Cleveland's main duties revolved around the United Nations. Cleveland wished to begin an Advisory Committee for employment of people in the United Nations. This committee, like many of the other State Department security cases, came under much discussion at State. Generally, there was a desire on the part of many people to get more and better candidates to work at the U.N.

Another example of the role of SISS in investigating seemingly minor issues was the case of Povl Bang-Jensen. The connection to the U.N. led to a situation surrounding the possible murder of a Danish diplomat in New York named Povl Bang-Jensen. Jensen had refused to name certain people who had been involved in the 1956 Hungarian uprising. SISS had investigated the mysterious death of Bang-Jensen. Part of the story involved possible information revealing Soviet agents who were infiltrating the U.S. Government. SISS had issued a report sharply questioning the New York police in their finding of suicide in the Bang-Jensen case.

Cleveland Advisory Committee on International Organizations member Leonard Boudin wrote to the NY Times ripping SISS. Andrew Cordier (in re U.N) and Ernest Gross [former SD legal advisor] were close friends of Alger Hiss. Otepka denied approval to Cordier and Gross for the new Committee possibly because of the murder of Bang-Jensen over the issue of the Hungarian revolt and the matter of 80 political refugees. Otepka said SY now had no jurisdiction over UN employees because of the 1953 decision by Ike to setup the "International Employees' Loyalty Review Board."

In October, 1962 at the height of the Cuban Missile Crisis, SISS issued its 202 page report on Otepka's case. The report cited 1) Otepka's difficulties with the Office of Security, 2) deliberate subversion of the law in issuing passports to Communists, and 3) discussed the mysterious career of William Arthur Wieland who some had blamed for the rise of Castro in Cuba. The SISS report was signed by all 9 members: Dodd (D,Conn) Chmn Eastland(D,Miss), Olin Johnson (D,SC), Sam Irvin (D,NC), John McClellan (D,AR), Ev Dirksen, Min Ldr (R,IL), Roman Hruska (R,NE), Ken Keating, (R,NY), and Hugh Scott, (R,PA). In an unusual move, SISS demanded that Otepka at least be named to his old position entitled Deputy Director of the Office of Security. This was a confrontational report because it asserted the right of Congress to decide on the employment of someone in the Executive Branch who was not subject to the Senate Confirmation process. This demand was all the more unreasonable because of the secretive nature and procedures of SISS.

Even with the requirement of confirmation by the Senate of Cabinet members and other select high officials, the process is open and public. If Senators have objections to such a high-level appointment, those objections have to be raised directly to the appointee in public. The process asserted by SISS is essentially the right to demand the hiring or firing of any Executive employee, even to the level of clerks and secretaries. Also suggested by the SISS report is that the properly constituted management of the State Department is not qualified or capable of enforcing policies in the area of security. Logically, there seems little difference between the SISS proposal and the proposal of turning over to SISS (a committee that operates in secret) of the entire operation of each and every department of the Federal Government if SISS so desired.

It is at this point where it becomes apparent that SISS is either drunk with power or sincerely feels that it is standing alone against an imminent and likely takeover of the United States government by pro-Communists or subversives. These demands by SISS went far beyond any activities and methods of Joe McCarthy. McCarthy operated by publicly slinging mud at those he suspected of subversion. McCarthy never demanded the right to dictate the management structure of the State Department nor asserted the right to decide who to hire and fire there.

As we examine the list of which Senators were chosen to serve on SISS, as was mentioned in a previous chapter, we see that in thus constituting this subcommittee, the entire Congress effectively signed off on a plan to allow the extreme right-wing members of the Senate to do a hatchet-job on the Kennedy Administration. If SISS did not get its way on the issue of perceived subversion, then at what extreme would they stop to solve this perceived problem? It is very likely that SISS felt justified in cooperating in some way with the assassination of JFK.

Ms. Frances Knight became the head of the Passport Office back in 1955. In 1958 the Supreme Court held that a person could not be denied a passport without due process of law. In 1961, the Supreme Court upheld the requirement that Communists must register. The Internal Security Act of 1950 had prohibited the issuance of a passport to Communists.

In January, 1962, Dean Rusk approved a rule which gave people the right to confront those accusing them of being Communists. Miss Knight as head of the Passport Office was, by this rule, forced to issue passports to Communists or else allow the Communist to have access to secret FBI and CIA files which they would be entitled to use in their defense. Miss Knight, like

Otepka, had testified before SISS on this issue. Author Gill is again decep-
tive when he replaces the word "Communists" in his reporting to "dangerous
espionage agents," in describing exactly who should be denied a passport
under the above laws. Miss Knight was strongly opposed on her policies by
Abba Schwartz, Administrator of the Bureau of Security & Consular affairs
and by Department of State Attorneys Chayes and Lowenfeld.

Per author Gill, the person who was most engaged in promoting more
lax passport rules was Robert Kennedy.(RFK again!!). (OOO p. 156).
According to historian Arthur Schlesinger, Jr. the two persons who first
recommended loosening the passport rules for Communist travel were
Averell Harriman and George Ball. Gill describes "the growing army of
domestic spies, saboteurs and professional agitators dedicated to the destruction of the American society."

The passport procedures as well as those relating to loyalty and security became the object of SISS inquiries. This story seems to get more
bizarre as it unfolds. SISS, a group of nine hand-picked, right-wing Senators wanted to place its judgment in place of decisions of the elected and
Senate-confirmed officials in the Executive Branch, as well as in place of
decisions of the U.S. Supreme Court. And almost all of the SISS activity
was being conducted in secret. With clandestine enemies of democracy
like the furtive SISS, you didn't need Communists to destroy our democratic traditions. SISS would take care of that job themselves. And of
course, according to Otepka biographer Gill, the law is an ass.

The drastic steps being taken by SISS cannot be explained in terms
of a real, credible threat of a Communist takeover of the U.S. In the judgment of this author, the SISS policy was not considered necessary to protect against a home-grown threat by Communists against the U.S. It is
much easier to understand the Red Scare tactics of SISS when viewed as
a policy designed to protect from Communism such Catholic-oriented
countries as Italy, France and even French Indochina. And the concern
was much the same regarding the rest of the far-flung and soon-to-disap-
pear empires of France, England, the Netherlands, Belgium and Portugal.

There are several vantage points from which to evaluate the security
rules as interpreted by Otepka. *First,* to be acceptable as a rule, regulation
or law, the rule has to serve to notify the person who must abide by the rule
as to the specific behavior allowed or prohibited. The Otto Otepka type of
rule states that an employee of the State Department cannot do anything of
which Otto Otepka does not personally approve, even after the fact. That is
not a legitimate rule. *Second,* a rule generally applies to behavior of the person subject to the rule. In our legal system, a person is not normally penal-
ized for the behavior of another person acting independently, not involved
in an agency relationship, unless we are talking about a parent being responsible for the behavior of a pre-adolescent child. *Third,* when a person is de-

prived of a government job, there is in many cases the right of due process of law. This might go doubly for the due process right of a person seeking a passport, or a person being deported or deprived of his citizenship. Otepka supposedly loved rules and regulations, but apparently despised the due process of law. Author Gill even suggests that the thousand-year history of English common law was a gigantic mistake, misguided, just so much time and effort, *wasted*. (This disrespect for U.S. law could have come from Gill's wife, who was a veteran Nazi and a Nazi spy).

At this crucial time when SISS was confronting the State Department on issues of security, loyalty and passports, the first proven advanced knowledge of the JFK assassination plot was recorded, spoken by Florida Mafia kingpin Santos Traficante in September, 1962.

Only four months after he was hired, Francis Reilly was promoted to a job which was created for him titled Deputy Assistant Secretary of State for Security in August, 1962. During these months, Senator Thomas Dodd was acting Chairman in charge of SISS. Although James O. Eastland was the actual Chairman of SISS, he hardly ever attended meetings. Instead, Eastland allowed Dodd to function as temporary chairman. The reason Eastland stood aside for Dodd is not completely clear. Possibley it was that a northern Democrat would be free of the likely stigma that existed in some circles because of the segregationist image of most southern Democrats, especially Eastland.

Another interpretation might be that the Northern Catholic faction of the Democratic party powers actually held sway over the Southerners in Party dynamics. They might have demanded this role for Dodd. Even more sinister is the possibility that ex-Nazis acting through Senator Dodd and Julius Klein had bribed enough Senators to make possible the powerful role that Dodd had assumed. (There was ample circumstantial evidence of such bribing of Senators which came up in the Dodd censure hearings).

It was at this time in August, 1962 that the anti-Otepka activities of Reilly increased. Otepka's secretary was harassed. Reilly chose David Belisle to serve as his chief of staff and to help in the effort to thwart Otekpa in his security duties. Mrs. Eunice Powers, Otepka's secretary was harassed. Three evaluators began to cooperate with Reilly and Belisle. They were Frederick Traband, Joseph Sabin and Carl Bock. Under new procedures, investigators effectively became the evaluators. During this period, Reilly testified directly to SISS on security matters. Specifically, Reilly lied to SISS about Otepka's handling of the controversial Wieland case. Reilly claimed that Otepka had removed himself from the controversial case, which was not true.

The Wieland case was given to Robert McCarthy, an investigator. In the same month, Reilly removed Otepka's name from the list of SY officials who could be contacted by the FBI. As a result of the less detailed clearance procedures, the Civil Service Commission began to complain that the State

Department security reports were lacking information (regarding the employee) which was needed by the Commission itself to function.

In the spring of 1963, pressure mounted for Otepka to resign from the State Department and it seemed to increase exponentially. Robert McCarthy was from Massachusetts and boasted of his connections with the Kennedys. He had an offer brought to Otepka's attention that he might be considered for a post as Ambassador. When Otekpa declined, McCarthy voiced surprise to his co-workers, asking them what they thought might be used to further tempt Otepka to leave his security position. In 1962 SISS had issued its report asking for changes to State Department security procedures, but Otepka realized that Dean Rusk had no intention of implementing the SISS recommendations.

Otepka had indeed considered resignation. The person who dissuaded Otepka from resigning was Jay Sourwine, the counsel to SISS. Toward the end of 1962, Otepka and Jay Sourwine were having lunch together once or twice a month. Experts on Congressional Committee procedures say that it is considered *unethical* to approach a member of a Congressional committee "on the side," ie. outside the regular hearings process.

OTEPKA BEGINS HIS INSUBORDINATION: SISS VS. THE KENNEDY ADMINISTRATION

Jay Sourwine told Otepka that his resignation could lead to an irreparable breakdown of security, not just at State, *but thoughout the Federal Government.* The relationship of Otepka to Jay Sourwine of SISS became the focus. We have seen that Sourwine was likely becoming personally involved with Lee Harvey Oswald at this time in New Orleans in the FPCC case. Otepka first talked to SISS in August, 1961. Otepka was aware at that time that the State Department did not want him to be meeting like this with Sourwine. Truman's directive 9835 of 1948 banning revelation of classified material to Congress was still in effect. Sourwine knew, however, that the State Department could not afford politically to completely prohibit Otepka from testifying. In February, 1963, Otepka received notice through State Department channels that he was to testify to SISS again. During the next two months, Otepka was to testify four times before SISS. The hearings were secret and closed. When presiding at one hearing, Senator Everett Dirksen questioned Otepka about reprisals he might have encountered. After a short period of questions, Otepka laid out the entire scenario of reprisals he had encountered from management. Otepka reported to SISS that Evaluations Division had been stripped of intelligence gathering and he discussed the new "short-form" evaluations.

Sourwine inquired into the Advisory Committee on the Arts under Bureau of Cultural affairs on which proposed members would include Archibald MacLeish, Melvyn Douglas, Agnes DeMille and George Seaton. Later names added to the Advisory Committee were Marian Anderson, Roy E. Larson, Chairman of the Executive Committee at Time, Inc., Peter Mennin, President of Julliard, and Warner Lawson, Dean of Music at Howard University. An obstacle arose when Archibald MacLeish and actor Melvin Douglas (husband of Nixon Senate opponent Heleg Gahagan Douglas who had been labeled by Nixon "The Pink Lady") refused to fill out the State Department employment form and security questionnaire. Otepka said Douglas could clear his name in this process, but he refused. Archibald MacLeish had been a speech writer for FDR and was called the "Bard of Harvard Yard." The SD Personnel department refused both Douglas and MacLeish, but Otepka was ordered to henceforth send no security files to the State Department Personnel staff.

In his March 1963 final appearance at SISS, Otepka discussed 1) Dean Rusk's abbreviation of the security clearance process and 2) Harlan Cleveland's advisory committee trying to reestablish a policy of placing Americans in U.N. jobs without first subjecting them to field investigations by the FBI. When asked about the topic of waivers, Otepka said that 398 waivers were issued to clerical and secretary personnel; only Dirksen and Roman Hruska had attached any real importance of these issues.

In the opinion of this author, at this point, the debate between the State Department and SISS about the Otepka situation had begun to focus increasingly on trivial issues. Questions were being raised as to whether certain people could serve on an arts advisory council. The only objections were that they had flirted with Communism twenty years in the past.

The question as to which Americans could be approved for work at the U.N. was of very little importance when compared to the 1940's era issues such as "who lost China?" When examining the state of mind of Senators Dodd, Dirksen and the others, the real fear seemed to be that the tradition of McCarthyism would entirely die out.

If the tradition of McCarthyism were forgotten, those who tended to agree with Adlai Stevenson and Eleanor Roosevelt could go about their business without fearing Congress. This would reduce the carefully crafted power of the Congressional alliance between southern segregationists and conservative Republicans. And in the view of these conservatives, that could lead to a policy which was agnostic and neutral on Communism overseas. Probably of equal importance was the dawning realization that America could be facing 24 years of Kennedy brothers' presidencies!

After three SISS appearances, Otepka became the target of clandestine surveillance in his workplace. On March 24, 1963, Otepka came in late to work and his office was invaded by David Belisle and Terence Shea, who were there to install wiretapping devices. In mid-March, Reilly had ordered expert Russell Waller to crack Otepka's safe. Otepka's trash was searched daily by Rosetti, Belisle, Terry Shea, Robert McCarthy, and Fred Traband. All of the above failed to turn up anything against Otepka. So Reilly and his allies decided to frame Otepka for a crime.

TONGUE SLASHING AND THE COUNTDOWN TO THE MURDER OF JFK

Otepka's phone was tapped, but there were problems with the tap, so Stanley Holden, a State Department expert on electronic surveillance, removed the tap. In April 1963, Otepka invited expert Russell Waller to listen to his phone and Waller said "your phone is bugged." On April 25, John Reilly testified before SISS. Senator Dodd, who had been less involved than he normally was, was at first favorable to John Reilly. But Dodd quickly realized that there had been an escalation of the conflict between SISS, the State Department and Otepka and that Reilly had been lying to SISS. (Keep in mind that at this same time, the "Battle of New Orleans" was occuring between SISS, LUAC, Eastland, Sourwine and SCEF and this involved Lee Harvey Oswald in a direct role). Ben Mandel, the Research Director of SISS, trying to play the peacemaker, called Otepka and asked him to effectively make peace with Reilly. Otepka informed Chief Counsel Jay Sourwine about the phone call from Mandel. When Otepka was given a transcript of Reilly's secret testimony, he saw that Reilly had lied to an even greater extent than before. Then Otepka met with Sourwine. At this point, it almost seemed to the parties that this feud over State Department Security was careening out of control.

The following is a summary of the things that happened to Otepka during this bureaucratic struggle with his superiors.

1. His office was bugged.

2. His telephone was tapped.

3. He was put under physical surveillance even at home.

4. His desk was ransacked.

5. He was beset with various security personnel.

6. His secretary was transferred without any reason.

7. He was denied access to any secretarial services.

When all of the above became known to his co-workers, they started to shun and avoid him. The next step is that the State Department tried to fire him because he had turned over classified documents to SISS, which may or may not have been a violation of law.

Toward the end of May, 1963, SISS called Reilly back again to testify. The SISS-State quarrel descended to an even lower level. Reilly claimed that "Otepka had a tendency to dwell in the past," had taken his demotion in a way which showed Rielly that "He seems emotionally overwrought on that topic and said that "He does not strike me as being a balanced individual."

Sourwine indicated that over the years he had seen many anti-Communists branded as insane or emotionally unstable. The situation had descended to the low levels witnessed in the heyday of Joe McCarthy. *"I've been wondering if this was coming,"* Sourwine noted. Sourwine said that he had expected the charges of emotional imbalance to enter the discussion in discrediting Otepka and (by implication) SISS itself.

Sourwine called Otepka on May 23 and asked for a meeting. Otepka knew he had to tell SISS the whole story because the top State Department officials would never force a Reilly retraction of his lies about Otepka. Otepka told interviewers in later years that he feared a possible Kim Philby situation in the State Department if security rules were not observed. (Kim Philby was an actual Soviet spy who infiltrated government at a very high level). Otepka actually feared that if he did not stand up for proper security procedures, that such procedures could disappear throughout the Federal Government.

Otepka had discovered a mysterious man in an unfamiliar car parked in front of his house on a full-time basis. Police found that this stranger was Eric Eisenberg, an employee of a private detective agency. Two officers, including Deputy Assistant Secretary John F. Reilly, perjured themselves before the Senate Internal Security Subcommittee and had to resign in November 1963. However, Senate efforts notwithstanding, Otto Otepka was relegated to a meaningless position before his termination. So were some of his colleagues who had backed his efforts.

At this point, author Gill expands the context of the SISS-State feud to the overall political situation in mid-1963. Per Gill, John F. Kennedy had decided at that time to formally adopt the Rostowian policies of convergence and détente. On June 10, 1963, President Kennedy delivered his tremendously famous speech at American University. Kennedy said that he had a formula which would bring peace for all time. Kennedy asked that all Americans examine their attitudes toward the Soviet Union. The President warned Americans "not to see only a distorted and desperate view of the other side, not to see conflict as inevitable, accommodation as impossible." Kennedy called on his countrymen to "help make the world safe for diversity."

Per author Gill, this was a far cry from the Wilsonian promise to make the world safe for democracy. "Let US re-examine our attitude toward the Soviet Union," Mr. Kennedy reiterated and that the move toward peace "would require," he said, "increased understanding between the Soviets and ourselves…increased contact and communication." It was at this point that President Kennedy brought up the possibility of a Test Ban Treaty with the Soviets. Krushchev later told Averell Harriman, the chief U.S. test ban negotiator, that it was "the greatest speech by any American

President since Roosevelt." This focus on the doctrine of "convergence" with the Soviet Union was set forth not only in *The Ordeal of Otto Otepka*, but also reported by Col. L. Fletcher Prouty in his book *JFK: The CIA, Vietnam and the Plot to Assassinate John F. Kennedy*. Col. Prouty had a Pentagon job which placed him right in the eye of this developing hurricane in Washington and the information in his book completely corroborates the 1963 situation that we have just described.

Reilly approved a change to security regulations to permit the hiring of previous employees who had been banned on security grounds. Leo Harris, an assistant counsel in Abram Chayes' Office admitted that this change was to permit the return of John Paton Davies to State. Otepka saw Dean Rusk as a representative of the old pro-Mao cabal. Otepka felt that bringing back John Paton Davies would open the floodgates to even worse potential employees. Otepka had handled the Davies case himself years before. There was proof that Davies had improperly delivered secret U.S. documents to Communist agents in the days of Chiang Kai-shek's China. A SD hearing board had unanimously determined Davies to be a security risk. Davies, now in Peru, had been running a furniture business which was possibly a front for the CIA and he also had secretly been communicating with the administration and advising the U.S. government about the Alliance for Progress.

Otepka refused a clearance for Mrs. Patricia Glover Barnett, stating "I was not in any way influenced by the fact that Senator McCarthy once charged her with … close contact with Soviet agents." In another perplexing situation, the Rockefeller Foundation had given Robert Barnett, her husband, four separate grants, despite the fact that he was declared to be a security risk by the State Department. The broad outlines of a situation like that appears to be some sort of confrontation between the wealthy Eastern establishment types like the Rockefeller family on the one hand and on the other the conservative Republican-southern Democrat coalition in Congress which would also include the Catholic anti-Communist activist lobby and even European fascists.

Considerable pressure was brought to bear in the case of the issuance of a special clearance to Abba Schwartz, czar of the Bureau of Security & Consular Affairs and a protégé of Adlai Stevenson. Otepka found security concerns with Schwartz. Schwartz had recently helped Abram Chayes, Nicholas Katzenbach and Bobby Kennedy subvert the law with regard to issuing passports to Communist agents. For these and other services rendered the Kennedy's, Schwartz was rewarded with Scotty McLeod's old job in the Department of State. Schwartz had trouble getting confirmed by the Senate in 1962 when he was ripped by Strom Thurmond.

In May, 1963, Otepka uncovered actual evidence of a decision by Rusk to totally scuttle security procedures in the State Department. Otepka's revelation about Secretary Rusk's wholesale issuance of waivers in 1961-62 had created too many problems. It had now been decided to avoid a repetition of the waiver scandal by scuttling the security regulations entirely. Obviously, this decision had to be made at a very high level.

Many months earlier, based on private sources, President Kennedy had tipped off the State Department that there may have been a major infiltration of Latin American Communists into various agencies in Washington, D.C., including the Organization of American States. On June 18, 1963, SISS summoned Reilly-Belisle and company to testify about the spying being directed against Otepka. Senator Edward Kennedy was in attendance to try to protect Reilly and his Massachusetts cohorts.. This was the only time Edward Kennedy had appeared in the SISS hearings. Senator Edward Kennedy was a member of the parent Judiciary Committee. Because of this fact, Kennedy had a legal right to attend (but not vote) at any hearing of a Judiciary subcommittee which included SISS. Attendance by Edward Kennedy at the SISS hearing could indicate he was hearing things through the grapevine about this dangerous situation.

The spying on Otepka became known throughout Washington. When the pro-Kennedy State Department officials testified about the various wiretapping and surveillance measures taken against Otepka, they all denied any knowledge of it. Sourwine kept the focus on the safecracking job. Joe Rosetti had already established the fact that he was Chief of Domestic Security Division, but Sourwine inquired as to the duties which went with Rosetti's job. Incredibly, Edward Kennedy interrupted the witness to ask: "Does he have the competency to know that? I just did not know whether the witness understands the full responsibilities of the Division Chief. Maybe he does, but I just want to know that, if he does know and understand what those responsibilities are or not."

The most important fact of all emerged when it became obvious that Rusk was fully prepared to defy SISS or the whole United States Senate if necessary. (Query whether Rusk was conferring closely with his Rockefeller backers in this controversy?) Reilly must have known this or sensed it. If he had lacked confidence in his being backed by Rusk, and therefore of his backing by the Kennedy's, Reilly would never have gone totally against SISS as he did shortly thereafter.

On Thursday June 27, 1963, Otepka was transferred to the job of preparing guidelines for evaluators and updating and reviewing the Office of Security handbook. This removed Otepka from his work for State Department Security. Otepka's files were seized. These files contained up to 20 years of security clearance information about many State Department employees. Nine other SD employees were summarily transferred out of their jobs by John Reilly, who was acting under the orders of men who were determined to carry out a hidden revolution in the State Department and thus in U.S. foreign policy. The dead giveaway about the intentions of Otepka and his supporters lies in this claim of "revolution." In making this characterization of a "revolution," author Gill reveals that the Otepka-State Department battle was not really anything to do with true security issues such as espionage or criminal activities of employees. By describing the situation thus, Gill equates the control of the security clearance process to control of State Department policy.

Actually, Otepka and his allies in SISS felt that they could and should be in control of State Department policy. For SISS, an Adlai Stevenson or Eleanor Roosevelt-type philosophy equated to being a Communist. Obviously, the control of foreign policy properly belonged in the hands of leaders duly elected or confirmed for that purpose.

What was never appreciated by observers at the time and especially not appreciated by JFK and RFK was the following fact: there were some overseas-based anti-Communist, monarchist, colonialist and related interest groups who were willing to commit murder to prevent a middle-of-the-road policy from becoming American foreign policy. Most importantly, this interest group was populated with ex-Nazis left over from World War II who were apparently organized and financed on a world-wide basis. And the reader must not forget the huge potential role of NATO in this epic confrontation. Of course, NATO itself was, in 1963, under the control of ex-Hitler associates. This emerging middle-of-the road policy was favored by professional foreign policy experts. Further, since this conflict over policy pitted the Congress against the Executive, then these desperate foreign anti-Communists had the perfect opportunity to sponsor a Presidential assassination. There could be guaranteed cover coming from the Republican-Southern Democrat coalition. It would be this coalition of Republicans and Southern Democrats that would soon turn up and populate the Warren Commission.

The members of SISS, who soon became allied with the plotters of the assassination, put forth the issue of the Nuclear Test Ban Treaty. This was the political football which could be kicked back and forth as camouflage for the real issue. It could be put forth as a litmus test for pro- versus anti-assination partisans. But the real issue was the control of U.S. foreign policy. Even among the handful of people privy to Otepka's fate there were not more than a few who understood fully the connection between the Treaty of Moscow and what happened to Otepka. *"President Kennedy never grasped it, nor his brother Bobby. Dean Rusk knew, of course and certainly Walt Rostow."* This is a verbatim quote from Gill's book at page 283.

Here author Gill lays down his cards. Gill properly attributes the possession of foreign policy power and the struggle for this power at this time to Rusk and Rostow, over and above the power of the disorganized duo of JFK and RFK. This attribution follows the fact that both Rusk and Rostow had spent most of their early formative years studying in England

and Europe. Their loyalty to the ideas absorbed at Oxford would simply overwhelm their loyalty to American democracy, plain and simple.

The last week of July, 1963, Otepka learned that he was under investigation by the FBI for alleged violation of the Espionage Act. The reader should note the lack of any involvement by the FBI up to this point in the story. Mrs. Eunice Powers, Otepka's former secretary, was questioned about Otepka's activities. She was called back by the FBI to sign a statement regarding her knowledge of Otepka's association with Jay Sourwine. On August 14, 1963, it became the turn of Otto Otepka to himself be interviewed by the FBI. There were two FBI agents, Robert Byrnes and Carl Graham who conducted the interrogation of Otepka. The agents explained that it was a "higher authority" in the Department of Justice who had ordered the investigation of Otepka. This phrasing would indicate that the Attorney General, RFK,(and not J. Edgar Hoover) had instigated the case against Otepka. The questioning of Otepka took three days. Otepka did not deny his close association with Jay Sourwine. Otepka was shown certain papers which apparently had once contained classified labels, but the classified labels had been clipped off.

Otepka was permitted to draft his reply to the charges of handing over classified materials to unauthorized persons. Otepka cited a law establishing the right of all Civil Service personnel "to furnish information to either house of Congress or to any Committee or member thereof." On Friday morning at about half-past twelve, Otepka was asked to testify again to SISS. But by this time, Dean Rusk had issued a prohibition forbidding anyone in the State Department from providing information to SISS without advance permission from William Crockett, the Deputy Undersecretary of State for Administration. This prohibition would remain in effect for two years. But there were three State Department officials who SISS desired to hear from and to investigate. This trio was John Reilly, Elmer Hill and David Belisle. For six more weeks nothing transpired regarding the Otepka case.

SISS believed that Dean Rusk and Robert Kennedy would agree to work out a suitable compromise in the Otepka case. On September 22, 1963 Otepka was given a termination letter from the Chief of the Personnel Operations Division at the State Department. It listed thirteen charges against Otepka. The charges alleged violation of the Truman directive 9835 prohibiting the release of classified information to the Congress. Otepka was also charged with mutilation of classified documents, among which was a memo to McGeorge Bundy at the White House.

At the same time that Otepka was handed his termination letter, the Senate was ending debate of the Nuclear Test Ban Treaty. The campaign in favor of the Nuclear Test Ban Treaty was run by Robert Kennedy in a very ruthless manner. It was claimed by opponents that FBI and CIA files were used to blackmail some senators.

A true discussion of the Nuclear Test Ban Treaty (NTBT) would begin with the fact that the Eisenhower Administration had agreed to a test ban moratorium in 1958. Author Gill would characterize the proponents of the NTBT as far-leftists and wishful thinkers. According to critics, the Eisenhower moratorium had allowed the Soviets to catch up and surpass U.S. [nuclear weapons] science. Supposedly, Khrushchev wrote to Kennedy saying "the time has come to put an end…to nuclear tests." "This has become a giveaway" said Everett Dirksen. Senator Dodd was expected to lead the opposition to the NTBT. Dodd, however, switched sides and called for a "limited test ban."

The list of those who in the end opposed the NTBT reads like a "who's who" of ultra-right partisans. In this regard, Gill mentions General Curtis LeMay, the Air Force representative on the Joint Chiefs of Staff. The most well-known opponents in the end were Dr. Edward Teller, and several military men, among them Lewis Strauss, Admiral Arleigh Burke and Admiral Arthur Radford. General Thomas Power, still the head of the Strategic Air Command, was the only active-duty officer to oppose the treaty publicly. With this, he [Power] forfeited his expected promotion to the Joint Chiefs of Staff. In the Senate debates, opponents were Strom Thurmond, Barry Goldwater, Richard Russell (Chairman of the Armed Services Committee), John Stennis, and Frank Lausche of Ohio, the only Northern Democrat who opposed it. The bill passed 80-19. Notably, author Gill neglects to mention that the NTBT in the end outlawed only *above ground* testing. As we know now with the benefits of hindsight, underground testing proved to be more than adequate in creating ever-more destructive nuclear weapons.

Upon contemplating the cost of hiring a lawyer, Otepka was told by SISS that they would find the money to pay for his lawyer although they never lived up to that promise. One of the press officers of State had publicly confirmed the charges against Otepka on September 26, 1963. Strange things began to happen. News of the charges against Otepka was released in, of all places, Dallas, Texas. Dr. Robert Morris, the President of the University of Dallas and a former chief counsel of SISS was the person who released them.

Perhaps most importantly, Chairman Eastland, heretofore silent regarding SISS, stated in the press "The powers of Congress are at stake, and I intend to protect Mr. Otepka by every means at my command." Rusk had always, to this point, refused to appear before SISS. Dodd flew to New York [where Rusk was] to deliver a subpoena. SISS source George Pasquale told them that Stanley Holden had told him of the plot to bug Otepka's office. All of this activity creates the picture of frantic desperation.

By far the most important event in the SISS-State drama occurred on October 3, 1963. On that day, the day after Dodd confronted Rusk in New York, Stanley Holden suffered a mysterious "accident." Like Otepka, Holden had been under clandestine surveillance for some time. Holden had been the chief of the State Department's electronics unit. Holden had investigated the surveillance and had followed bugging wires to a point very close to the office of Elmer Hill, another electronic surveillance expert at the State Department. Holden and Joe Rosetti had gone to John Francis Reilly's office to confront him regarding the surveillance. Reilly denied knowing anything. It was on this same October 3 that it was established that Reilly knew for a fact that Holden had been feeding information to Otepka.

It was at this point that George Pasquale called Holden's home. Holden's wife told Pasquale that Thursday afternoon Stan had suffered a severe face injury. His face *and tongue had been badly cut.* Stitches had been required. Mrs. Holden refused to give Pasquale any information on the cause of the accident. There were soon reports that Holden had been beaten up by the Reilly faction in order to prevent him from testifying to SISS. With the painful tongue injury, Stanley Holden could not talk about anything that day. On top of his injuries, Holden was confronted in his own home by Robert J. McCarthy. McCarthy was a Kennedy loyalist and investigator. There, McCarthy screamed at Holden, "Don't you have any loyalty at all?"

The injuries to Stanley Holden are treated by some as just another background fact regarding the State-SISS confrontation. However, Holden's injuries were more than business as usual. One would have to go back to the caning of Senator Charles Sumner by Representative Preston Brooks in 1856 to find an example of a similar act of violence between participants in the operation of the Federal Government. (There were later, of course, numerous witnesses who died violently just prior to giving testimony before the House Select Committee on Assassinations). But the violence involving Stanley Holden was different in that it was open, notorious and occured in an epic confrontation between the Executive and the Legislative branches of the U.S. Government.

A mere six weeks later, the President of the U.S. lay dead, a victim, apparently, of what would be a cycle of violence, possibly hastened by the attack on Holden. This event, in addition to the JFK assassinatin, could have combined with the growing frequency of extremist church bombings and the insurrection against integration at Ole Miss to fuel passions. Perhaps beginning in these three weeks in 1963, one could date the real start of the violence of the 1960s.

There is something about the attack on Holden that bears the personal brand of Robert Kennedy and his aide and assistant, Walter Sheridan. Robert Kennedy was constantly acting with the desire never to be outdone. From the perspective of your author, this attack on Holden would fit perfectly into the events whereby certain people might become desperate enough to murder a President. Apparently the specter of U.S. foreign policy reverting to the control of people like Franklin and Eleanor Roosevelt, (albeit moderated by Walter Rostow and Dean Rusk), was way too much to take for men like James O. Eastland and Everett Dirksen. These conservatives were looking at a future whereby the State Department would become agnostic on the issue of Communism. The looming situation which could find officials like Adlai Stevenson, Senator Paul Douglas and Eleanor Roosevelt even partially in control State Department policy, was just too much for the conservatives of both parties in Congress.

After the confrontation between Senator Dodd and Dean Rusk, Rusk worked with Undersecretary of State George Ball to come up with a reply to the committee. As a defensive measure, Rusk came up with a demand that SISS give him access to all the information in the possession of SISS. JFK was confronted with the Otepka issue in an October 9 press conference. Kennedy replied that the matter would go from Rusk to the State Department, then to the Civil Service Commission and finally, into the courts. On October 21, 1963, just four weeks prior to the assassination, Rusk finally appeared before SISS. Seven of the nine members of SISS were present. Rusk testified that "the Department of State, like any foreign office in any important country, has real security problems." Rusk listed four major issues:

1. The Otepka case.

2. The new passport regulations.

3. The reorganization of Abba Schwartz's Bureau of Security and consular affairs.

4. Certain aspects of the security practices within the Department.

Not under oath, Rusk said "I can assure you, however, that the charges were not brought [against Otepka] in retaliation for Mr. Otepka's testimony before this Subcommittee, nor do they mark any attempt by the Department to interfere with the work of the subcommittee."

Rusk claimed substantial compliance with the 1962 SISS recommendations, citing that only six waivers had been issued since the SISS recommendations. Rusk cited the decision that all FBI and CIA reports dealing with counter-intelligence be sent directly to the Bureau of Intelligence Research to help information to flow to the highest level. Rusk demanded that before any SISS hearing, the Chairman should send to State a statement of the scope and nature of the inquiry. Author Gill presents one of his rare openly biased conclusions, saying that the request of Rusk of advance notice of issues was an attempt to "control all witnesses and any information the subcommittee would receive from his department."

This statement by Gill goes directly against the existing Supreme Court cases which required the witness before Congressional Committees to have notice about what the issues were regarding his testimony as a matter of due process, so he could know to which questions he could legally be required to respond. This prohibited wide open "fishing expeditions" which, under statute, could lead direcly to criminal prosecution. In effect, the witness, under these circumstances, should be entitled to know, in advance, of what criminal liabilities [if any] he might be facing. Rusk cited the 1948 Truman directive number 9835. Rusk also raised the specter of Joe McCarthy, because of which, Senators were afraid of being branded "McCarthyites."

Senator McClellan protested, "I don't see any reason why there is such a great secrecy between the Executive Branch and this committee?" McClellan mentioned "arbitrary attitudes" which he would oppose. When asked if Otepka had been dismissed because of his cooperation with SISS, Rusk said, "It was nothing to do with it."

Senator Hruska got Rusk to admit that the formal charges against Otepka involved matters supplied to SISS by Otepka. Rusk then threw up the accusation made about the Department of trying to rehire Alger Hiss. Otepka compared himself to a prisoner in a burning prison having to choose between being burned alive, or hanged because of the escape. (OOO p. 306). On October 31, ten days after Rusk's appearance, a brief letter signed by all the members of SISS was sent to Rusk, handled by Eastland, defending Otepka to the hilt. On November 5, 1963, Otepka was handed his "final" dismissal.

Dean Rusk, with the support of the Kennedy brothers, had thrown down the final gauntlet. The State Department had shown that it would bend the security laws any way they wanted, and they would hire security risks whenever they wished. Author Gill extends this policy quite a bit by saying that State would also push for convergence with Communism and sacrifice anyone in the construction of the "Rostowian dream."

Tom Dodd did not get along very well with the Kennedys. But because of party dynamics, he could not afford to come out into an open feud with the Kennedys. Dodd, being a Northern Liberal, would have a unique roll in the Otepka controversy unlike his fellow Senators from the deep South. Bluntly, before a Senate Chamber mostly full, he declared [the firing of Otepka] "an affront to the Senate and a denial of its powers." Dodd argued regarding the statute that gave the right of any Civil Service employee to turn over information to Congress. The reign of Bobby Kennedy in the Justice Department had made many in Congress fearful of wiretapping and surveillance. In Massachusetts, testimony had claimed that an agency of the Justice Department had permanently tapped the central phone exchange throughout Washington D.C.

In the three weeks prior to the JFK assassination there was a great deal of activity regarding the Otepka case, including the issue of wiretapping. It should be noted that in the SISS hearing on November 19, 1963, Senator James O. Eastland exercised his prerogative and chaired the hearing. A small number of newpapers had been following the story all along. One of these journalists was Clark Mollenhoff, who later wrote and published a book dealing with the Otepka case.

The *New York Times* covered the dismissal of Otepka on its front page. Dean Rusk accepted the resignations of Reilly and Hill yet David Belisle was spared being fired on the grounds that his testimony only involved the reporting of hearsay, not factual knowledge. There were questions emerging as to what the political support for Dean Rusk was on the part of President Kennedy. Some speculated that Rusk was quickly becoming a political liability for Kennedy.

Author Gill stops the action in the Otepka case on November 22, 1963. He begins a diversionary discussion of the role of Otto Otepka in the investigation of Lee Harvey Oswald prior to his, Otepka's exile. We will summarize this background on the Otepka-Oswald connection as related by authors Mellen and Gill. Picking up on our prior discussion, we have seen that as early as June 1, 1960, the State Department Office of Intelligence Resources and Collection, Bureau of Intelligence Research began an investigation of certain defectors to the Soviet Union. On December 5, 1960, Otepka was asked to start work on a study of these American defectors. Otepka was asked to find out if they had any connection to employees or applicants for employment in the State Department. One of the names on that list was Lee Harvey Oswald.

Author Gill wondered whether, if Otepka had completed that study on Oswald, perhaps Otepka could have foiled the assassination. Despite the fact that the State Department testified that the typical wait time for an American to get a visa to travel from Helsinki, Finland to the Soviet Union was one to two weeks, Oswald got his in two days in October 1959. There were questions on why the U.S. Embassy in Moscow kept Oswald's passport handy for him to flee back to the United States. Otepka would have raised the question as to who at the State Department was involved in approving the loan of $435.71 from the State Department which Oswald used to finance his return to the U.S. According to Gill, in June 1963 Oswald was granted a visa to return to Russia authorized by Abba Schwartz on one day's notice. (OOO p. 326).

In writing about these events relating to Oswald, Gill is suggesting that under different rules, Otepka could have foiled the JFK assassination. This implies that Otepka would have had a continuing duty to monitor Oswald as well as any number of other defectors and/or possible spies. It is an apparent fact that Otepka had kept a file on Oswald in his safe and which disappeared when his safe was burglarized by State technical security officials. That seems to clash with what Gill has told us about Otepka's function as being to investigate State Department employees. For what purpose was Otepka keeping the file on Oswald as an active one? Is Gill implying that Oswald would have been discovered as having a relationship to a State Department employee or applicant? We know that Agent James Hosty of the Dallas FBI was monitoring Oswald. Why would Otepka in the State Department be monitoring Oswald?

One of Johnson's closest friends in the Senate was Senator Thomas Dodd. "It [the assassination] blotted out the Otepka case at the very moment that it threatened to blow up Dean Rusk's Department of State."

It is apparent to this author that William J. Gill had real-time intelligence connections in 1963 and that Gill knew that the timeline of the Otepka case exactly followed the timeline of the JFK assassination. Since your author has recently discovered that Gill was married at some point to a German Countess, he could very likely have been spoon-fed the inside information on the assassination from German sources). Further, let's just look at the group of conservative Senators of both parties that JFK, Rusk and RFK were battling in the Otepka case. This group would include James O. Eastland, Richard Russell, Everett Dirksen, Sam Ervin, Thomas Dodd and the rest of their close allies. In the injuries suffered by Stanley Holden, the Otepka case had turned violent. Natural inhibitions against wholesale indiscriminate wiretapping had disappeared and were replaced by a feeling of suspicion revolving around surveillance.

Gill acknowledges that the Kennedy assassination had resolved, at least in both the short and intermediate term, the incipient, creeping agnosticism on the issue of international Communism. The plight of Otto Otepka and his dispute with the executive branch would be put on hold for at least five more years thanks to the tragic assassination of JFK. The administrations of LBJ and Nixon put an immediate halt to the advance of the "intelligentsia" who had come together in the three brief years of the JFK administration.

Immediately after the assassination, Lyndon Johnson could count on his friends Thomas Dodd and James O. Eastland who ran SISS to cover up the Otepka case and to try to fix the security problems. "Dean Rusk would prove the most durable [among Kennedy holdovers] of all, though before President Kennedy's assassination, his position was easily the shakiest, next to Johnson's…"

Almost the entire record of the Otepka case was established before the JFK assassination. Some weeks before Otepka's final SISS testimony, he had received an invitation to appear before the 1964 Republican platform committee at the San Francisco convention. When Otepka asked the State Department for permission to appear, he was denied approval.

It is a monument to the importance to LBJ of SISS, that Senator Thomas Dodd was brought to the White House by LBJ for the purpose of announcing his choice for his Vice-President. Senator Dodd and Hubert Humphrey were both touted as the last two possibilities for LBJ's V.P. To this author, the [fake] consideration given to Dodd by LBJ for V.P. is another confirmation of the linkage between the Otepka case and the JFK assassination. Senator Dodd himself would have proved utterly incompetent to even function in a nationwide campaign for the Democratic ticket. LBJ, being an astute evaluator of people, would have known this better than anyone. The totally symbolic "courtship" of Thomas J. Dodd for V.P. was an acknowledgment by Johnson that he was ready to reward all of the people who had helped set up as well as cover up the JFK assassination. Dodd had enjoyed the Presidential limelight. He had secured the highest recognition he could expect for many services which he had rendered. The highest of these services was his playing the role as "Joe McCarthy, phase II," i.e., uniting the John Birchers, the Southern Segregationists and the Northeastern Catholic anti-Communists like Dodd himself.

AS LBJ ASSUMES POWER, OTTO OTEPKA RECEDES INTO HISTORY

But the issue of security at the State Department became a moot point with the accession of LBJ. Like President Truman before him, LBJ came from an atypical southern State. Missouri and Texas were both geographically part of the south, and were dominated by the very large cities of Dallas, Houston, St.Louis and Kansas City. The multitude of connections that were enjoyed by LBJ (especially in his home state of Texas) totally eclipsed the miniscule number of truly loyal colleagues who could assist JFK and RFK. Both Truman and LBJ, as Senators, had focused only on the pork-barrel issues and on the institutional side of the Senate. As LBJ would soon demonstrate, he didn't really know of, or care about, the quality of information and analysis of foreign policy. The Vietnam War fiasco stands as a testament to that reality. LBJ simply did not care about normalizing relations with China, Russia, Cuba or anywhere else. Because of this quality in LBJ, State Department security became irrelevant. LBJ would take his foreign policy advice from his former colleagues in the Senate or possibly from people like J.Edgar Hoover, the Pentagon or the CIA.

Immediately following the 1964 election, LBJ asked the Congress for a 90-day hiatus so he could launch his Great Society, but this hiatus included any action on the case of Otto Otepka. Some people were puzzled about Dodd's turnabout on the Otepka case. But the key to that turnabout was Dodd's personal support for his friend LBJ. Dodd would not even release transcripts of Otepka's testimony for four years. Some in Washington compare Dodd's turnaround on Otepka to his famous turnaround on the Nuclear Test Ban Treaty. Soon it was clear that Dodd was prepared to sell out Otepka. He called him a prima donna. This defense of Rusk and the State Department was the exact opposite of the threats against Rusk's State Department only a year earlier on the Senate floor while Rusk was working for JFK.

Gill, too, flip-flopped in his opinion of Senator Thomas Dodd. Gill describes Dodd's anti-Communist posture as mostly mere rhetoric. As evidence, Gill returns to his shibboleth, the Nuclear Test Ban Treaty. The promotion, by Gill, of the Test Ban Treaty as a litmus test of anti-Communist resolve, has simply not stood the test of time. In fact, the Nuclear Test Ban Treaty has, since the 1960s, stood as the shining example of the triumph of good sense over the sleazy side of the professional anti-Communists, which promoted Communophobia-for-hire. According to Gill, the Nuclear Test Ban Treaty was an issue where the future of the United States was at stake. No matter the fact that the atmospheric testing was putting radioactive Strontium 90 fallout into the milk of baby bottles all over the world. No matter the fact that the U.S. Government produced, over the years, 66,000 nuclear weapons, Test Ban Treaty or no Test Ban Treaty.

The parents of Thomas J. Dodd were devout Roman Catholics, and they sent their son to Catholic Providence College in nearby Rhode Island. Dodd was elected to the U.S. Senate in 1958. Upon his election, Dodd immediately set himself up as the pillar of anti-Communism.

Dodd was active both on SISS and his Senate Juvenile Delinquency Subcommittee of which he was also chairman. Seemingly out of nowhere, Dodd was the subject of an inexplicable large-scale mutiny of his staff. Dodd's speechwriter, James Boyd, organized a massive campaign against his own boss. His staff employees kept their own hidden set of books where they tracked Dodd's often clandestine income. Then his staffers, acting in total concert, borrowed and photocopied an estimated 3000 pages of documents from his private Senatorial files.

Because of this extreme "mutiny/investigation" and the collusion with his staffers with some key journalists, Dodd was censured by the Senate for financial corruption on June 23, 1967 by a vote of 92-5. His staffers wound up being fired because of their actions, and their careers went down the drain.

Was Otepka, as being allied to Dodd, on the financial take along with Dodd? The gorilla in the room is the fact that out of 5 Senators censured in recent history, two of them were McCarthy and Dodd, both of whom were Catholic activist anti-Communists elected from states in the north.

As a part of an unusual situation surrounding the Rostow brothers, in April 1966, LBJ brought Walter Rostow back from the State Department to the White House, and at the same time installed his brother, Eugene Rostow as number-three man in the State Department. All the while, Otto Otepka considered these two men as major security risks who should be legally forbidden to work in even the lowliest posts in the U.S. Government. There seems to be something illogical about this entire situation. Did the concept of "security" followed by Otepka have anything at all to do with actual security? There was another man who continued to give Otepka encouragement and that was Strom Thurmond. (OOO p. 401).

Senator Eastland, backed by Dirksen, Hruska and Dodd, introduced the first of several bills designed to overhaul SY. None of the bills became law.

In the fall of 1965, the State Department named a retired judge to be the hearing officer in Otepka's State Department hearing. Reports surfaced that LBJ had ordered administration officials to settle the case as soon as possible. Otepka's hearing began in June 1967. Otepka and Roger Robb, his attorney, continued to protest the closing of the coming hearing to the press. The State Department's hearing into the dismissal of charges leveled against Otepka was to last four weeks. In total, only three witnesses testified: Otepka, Sourwine and Reilly.

Robb stated "the evidence will show that these charges (against Otepka) were the culmination of a conspiracy, beginning as early as 1960, to get rid of Otepka by a relentless campaign of harassment and reprisal, by surrounding him with unfriendly and disloyal associates, by wiretapping, by clandestine surveillance ... and finally on the part of his immediate superiors, by perjury.

One long-standing issue brought out in the hearing by Otepka, was the transfer of the duties regarding reports received from other intelligence and law enforcement agencies over to the bureau of Intelligence and Research at the SD. Otepka claimed to know that in that bureau of Intelligence Research, there was a large concentration of officials who had records of activities and associations with Communists.

Should the reader believe that there were Communist sympathizers who might be running the Intelligence function of the State Department? This contention by Otepka would seem to automatically impugn the top officials at the State Department. If Otepka actually had any evidence of such Communist infiltration, why couldn't he just write a letter to the highest officials in the State Department and they would take care of the problem? What about the FBI? Was J. Edgar Hoover covering up for State Department Communists, too? And if Strom Thurmond was a continuing supporter of Otepka, why couldn't Otepka just hand the list of Communist-affiliated workers at the State Department to Thurmond and then Thurmond would have raised the issue through proper channels?

The concept of guilt by association, not provable in the light of day, goes totally against the Constitution. It also contradicts our traditional American concept of fairness and justice as well as the rest of our laws. Otepka's concept of security was, in itself, the major challenge to true American security. When Otepka said he put his love of county ahead of orders from his supervisors, it begs the question. What would our country be like, if the Otepka theory of government ever came to be? Outraged at his own phone being wiretapped, Otepka would eagerly turn around and persecute people using the fruits of illegal and clandestine wiretaps.

Harry Truman's motto emblazoned on his desk was "The Buck Stops Here." Otepka always maintained that Truman's motto should have been on his, Otepka's desk. If Otepka had such a low opinion of the value of laws, and of duly elected or appointed officials, then Otepka and his gang would think nothing of (at least) tacitly supporting the murder of a President.

At a later hearing about the Otepka case, the hearing officer kept asking him to identifiy the people who were out to get rid of him. Referring to the Senate subcommittee's record, Otepka first named Boswell and Roger Jones. Then the following exchange took place:

> **Jaffe**: Who else [that was out to get you] entered your mind?
>
> **Otepka**: [after another sentence] Otepka answered: "The person was Robert Kennedy."

Rusk, in denying Otepka his appeal within the State Department, wrote: "I therefore decide that disciplinary action is required in this case and hereby direct that the following actions be taken with respect to Mr. Otto F. Otepka: a) That he be severely reprimanded, b) The he be reduced in grade from GS-15 to GS-14, c) That he be transferred to duties which do not involve the administration of personnel security functions.

In the first week of January, 1968, SISS finally issued its long-awaited official report on the Otepka matter. Released in four separate volumes over an eight-day span, the report was virtually ignored. In April the Civil Service Commission issued a ruling upholding Secretary of State Rusk's reprimand and demotion of Otepka. Otto Otepka, perhaps more acutely than any other man, understood the central tragedy of the deaths of John and Robert Kennedy.

Those who held a viewpoint similar to Otepka might have argued that Lyndon Johnson's appointment to the Supreme Court of Abe Fortas was the most flagrant flaunting to date of the nation's internal security laws. This was because Fortas had been close friends with Alger Hiss and Harry Dexter White in 1945, Fortas is said to have helped Alger Hiss and Harry Dexter White draft the U.N. Charter, both Hiss and White were proven at least at one point to be actual Communists.

Nixon appointed Henry Kissinger, Harvard Professor and former advisor to Nelson Rockefeller, to replace Walter W. Rostow. Undersecretary of State Nicholas Katzenbach issued a memorandum summarily restoring a security clearance to John Paton Davies, the China cabalist who for fifteen years had been classified as a security risk.

Nixon's Secretary of State upheld the prior findings of Dean Rusk and refused to favor Otto Otepka. SISS in the person of Everett Dirksen, worked out a compromise: Ottepka would be appointed to the Subversive Activities Control Board. The *New York Times* came out against Otepka and labeled him "a member of the John Birch Society and also an anti-Semite." On April 15, 1969, the Senate Judiciary Committee conducted a hearing on the President's appointment of Otepka to the SACB and Senator Dirksen volunteered to testify. Senator Edward Kennedy, taking his cue from the *Times* and perhaps a memory of his brother Bobby, launched a final assault against Otepka during the Judiciary Committee's deliberations. Kennedy and three other Senators, Quentin Burdick of South Dakota [sic s.b. North Dakota], Philip Hart of Michigan and Joseph Tydings of Maryland had Otepka recalled to Capitol Hill twice to answer a series of silly questions about his alleged connection to the John Birch Society and a group known as the Liberty Lobby. Kennedy... quickly zeroed in on a meeting Otepka had attended as a guest in San Diego in March, 1965. He demanded to know with "what organization" the man who invited Otepka was connected. Otepka replied that the man was "connected with the United Republicans of California." The full Senate voted 61-28 to confirm Otepka's appointment to the SACB. By the late 1960's there was a Congressional hearing into the dismissal of Otepka but in the end Otepka was never returned to his previous station. In 1958 under John Foster Dulles, he was given the State Department Meritorious Service Award. Otepka retired in 1972 and moved to Cape Coral, Florida in 1975. He was a member of the Association of Former Intelligence Officers, which also included former CIA agents and bureaucrats.

One of his last, if not *the* last, interview, was granted to JFK assassination research author Joan Mellen in Florida in 2006, just prior to his death. It is recounted in her excellent book *A Farewell To Justice: Jim Garrison, JFK's Assassination and the Case That Should Have Changed History.*

Notes:

Nearly all the information in this chapter can be verified by referring to: *The Ordeal Of Otto Otepka,* (1969) by William J. Gill, sometimes abbreviated as OOO.

Another excellent source on the subject of Otto Otepka is: *Despoilers Of Democracy: The Real Story Of What Washington Propagandists, Arrogant Bureaucrats, Mismanagers, Influence Peddlers, And Outright Corrupters Are Doing To Our Federal Government* (1965), by Clark R Mollenhoff, sometimes abbreviated as DOD.

For information on Ladejinsky, see: [Wikipedia Wolf Ladejinsky]

For information on John Stewart Service, see: [Wikipedia: John Stewart Service]

For information on John Paton Davies, see: [Wikipedia:John Paton Davies]

Anglo-American Establishment (1981) by Quigley Carroll, see page 50.

399

A Farwell To Justice: Jim Garrison, JFK's Assassination, and the Case That Should have Changed History (2007), by Joan Mellen, sometimes abbreviated as FTJ.

For information on William Wieland, see: [http://havanaschooleng.blogspot.com/2012/05/cuban-conspiracy-nine-wielands-case-i.html] Viewed 3-19-15.

Memoirs: Years of Trial and Hope (1956) by Harry S. Truman.

Chapter 31

IMPORTANT ISSUES IN INTERNATIONAL RELATIONS IN 1963

THE GENERAL ANALINE AND FILM CASE

Klein: "I am always accused of being a representative working for the return of confiscated German property which is not true and that I am a front for IG Farben [an accusation made by Senator Smathers in an op-ed] which is also not true." (per General Julius Klein in testimony before the U.S. Senate, 1963)

General Julius Klein was the bagman who was apparently bribing U.S. Senators and furiously meeting with assassination suspect Senator Thomas Dodd in the few short weeks before the assassination. And General Klein, as shown in the above testimony he gave before Congress, was allegedly representing IG Farben. Farben was behind the front of ownership of General Analine and Film at the time GAF was seized as enemy property in World War II under the Trading With The Enemy Act. *Der Spiegel*, the top German newsmagazine claimed, in an article on October 4, 1963 that Klein represented "a half dozen of the largest German automotive, heavy industrial and pharmaceutical companies operating in the United States."

As has been referred to previously, the German Government had been engaged in spying in the U.S. continuously since at least 1890. It was in that year that a chemist named Walter Theodore Scheele came to the U.S. Scheele had been in the German military and achieved the rank of Captain. After this, he came to the U.S. in 1890 but he was kept on the military payroll and was paid $1500 per year, which would be almost $40,000 in 2016 money.

While he was on the German payroll, he worked on creating explosives for the German military. In the book *The Secret War Against the United States in 1915*, by Heribert von Feilitzsch, the author describes in great detail the intricate German spy network in the U.S. beginning in the 1890's and continuing on without interruption ever since, likely to this very day. German spies were paid through Bayer Company and Hamburg-American Cruise Lines. One of our three Barons, General Charles Willoughby, probably came to the U.S. as a German spy in 1910 and joined the U.S. military.

What most Americans never appreciated is the fact that in Germany, the line between government action and private industrial action was much more blurred than in the United States. Germany encouraged the existence of giant industrial cartels. This was exactly the same thing that our American anti-trust laws were invented to eradicate and prevent.

In the World War I era, there was a German industrial behemoth called the "Bix Six." The Big Six was a conglomerate of the largest chemical companies in Germany. Although it was ostensibly working with the ordinary chemical color dye industry, the invention and production of various color dyes involved such advances in chemistry that a whole new world of chemicals was opened up as a result. The German government and the chemical cartel threw huge resources in to this effort because they knew two things. First, advances in chemicals would lead to powerful new explosives for bombs and munitions. Second, they knew this research would also lead to the production of artificial rubber and artificial fuels from coal which would make Germany independent from the rest of the world and allow Germany to wage war without the fear of a British or other naval blockade.

For an apt comparison, one should look at the major U.S. defense contractors such as Lockheed, General Dynamics and Bell Aerospace. They were quasi-governmental. They guarded the American defense secrets which secured our survival as a nation. The famous Lockheed Corporation "Skunk Works" led by engineer Clarence "Kelly" Johnson would be an example. The Skunk Works designed the U-2 spy plane and the SR-71 spy aircraft. It was a quasi-governmental operation because its funding depended almost entirely on the U.S. government and most of its discoveries could not be shared with other countries.

During the World War I era, the U.S. Congress passed the Trading With The Enemy Act. This allowed the Federal Government to seize and hold onto German and other foreign assets after war was declared against Germany. These assets became the property of the Alien Property Custodian.

During the lead-up to World War II, this act had never been repealed. FDR used it to seize property owned by citizens of Denmark and Norway after those countries were invaded by Germany in April 1940. Then, when war was declared following Pearl Harbor, the U.S. Government seized the ownership of General Aniline & Film in February, 1942. It was the largest company seized under the Trading With The Enemy Act. At the time, it owned over 3900 patents on chemical processes. All told, the WWII Alien Property Custodian owned assets worth $800 million, which would be $15 billion in 2016.

General Aniline was technically owned by a Swiss corporation called Interhandel. The U.S. acted against General Aniline (now GAF) on the theory that Interhandel was just a front for IG Dyes which most Americans would recognize by the name IG Farben. This dispute was held up and delayed in court the entire time GAF was owned by the U.S. Government Alien Property Custodian. According to author Sidney Jay Zabludoff, General Aniline was transferred to a Swiss holding company IG Chemie. IG Chemie in turn owned the shares of the U.S. company General Aniline and Film Corp. A man named Albert Gadow had a "repurchase agreement" whereby he could, at any time, repurchase the shares of General Aniline. Gadow, in turn had an agreement that he could sell those shares to no one but IG Farben. So IG Farben, in reality, owned or completely controlled General Aniline & Film Corp.

GAF was a main competitor of du Pont for chemicals, Kodak for film and Xerox for the photocopy business. Those of us who were of age in the 1950's and 1960's can appreciate the central role of du Pont, Kodak and Xerox. These were essentially monopolies and if their main competitor, GAF, were owned by the U.S. government, the stakes in this situation would be astronomical.

The most controversial part of the story of GAF was the collaboration of Standard Oil of New Jersey (now known as Exxon) with Hitler's Nazi government during World War II. The entire issue of the Trading With The Enemy Act and the very existence of the Alien Property Custodian has essentially been suppressed in American history. There were many obvious conflicts surrounding it and it made the leaders of American industry such as du Pont and Standard Oil look very bad. The father of George H.W. Bush owned the Union Banking Corporation which was seized by the government under the Trading with the Enemy Act.

The alien property was being held in order to sell it and use the money to settle claims against Germany by those who had grievances against Nazi Germany. In 1954, Senator Everett Dirksen, introduced a bill which would demand return of the alien property to the former owners. Eisenhower's Secretary of State John Foster Dulles testified in support of the Dirksen Amendment. This testimony and the position of Dulles on this issue shocked the world. Many other countries were still holding on to German assets seized during and after the War.

But with backing from Ike's Department of Justice, the Dirksen Amendment was defeated.

When John F. Kennedy was elected, negotiations to return the GAF ownership to Interhandel and thus IG Farben continued. There was a secret meeting involving the negotiators for Interhandel. These negotiators were Robert A. Schmitz and Charles E. Wilson. Schmitz had worked on the GAF-Interhandel case most of his life and Wilson was thought to have the inside track with the Eisenhower Administration.

Significantly, this secret meeting involved JFK's father Joseph P. Kennedy and his new Treasury Secretary C. Douglas Dillon and it took place in Palm Beach, Florida. Nothing came from the meeting.

In 1961, the attorney for Charles E. Wilson, Charles Spofford, met with the Assistant Attorney General in charge of Alien Property, William

H. Orrick. By this time, the Union Bank of Switzerland was the nominal owner of the majority of Interhandel and Union Banks representative Alfred Schaefer became the CEO of Interhandel. Shaefer was at the meeting with Wilson, Spofford and Orrick. According to Orrick, Schaefer launched a verbal attack against the U.S. Government and its role in the case. As a result, Orrick ordered Schaefer to leave his office.

The next move was made by Alfred Schaefer. Returning to Europe, Schaefer hired Prince Stanislaw Radziwill to represent the interests of Interhandel with the administration of John F. Kennedy. Of course, Prince Radziwill was married to the sister of the First Lady, Jacqueline Kennedy and Radziwill was not a lawyer.

Prince Radziwill sent a letter to Attorney General Robert F. Kennedy requesting a meeting between RFK and the abrasive Albert Schaefer. The letter was enclosed in an elaborate set of envelopes bearing the royal Radziwill family coat-of-arms or seal. RFK responded, mentioning that his staff was totally set against the proposed settlement for the sale of GAF to its former owners or to allow them to share in the proceeds of a possible sale of the GAF company.

In late 1961 and early 1962, RFK was getting closer to a deal in the GAF case, which would provide for sharing the proceeds of sale with the U.S. government. The role of Prince Radziwill was kept almost totally secret and away from the press due to a fear of public outrage and criticism which would follow.

The negotiations dragged on into 1962. In mid-1962, Orrick left the Justice Department for the Department of State. Assistant Attorney General Nicholas Katzenbach then took charge of the GAF negotiations. Katzenbach immediately decided that if GAF could be sold at public auction, that would blunt much of the criticism which would come with a settlement.

In order to sell GAF at public auction, an amendment was necessary to the Trading With The Enemy Act. Kenneth Keating, the Republican Senator from New York, had introduced such an amendment in 1962, but Interhandel had succeeded in blocking it. In fact, the Justice Department had been trying for decades to get such an amendment passed. Katzenbach persuaded Interhandel to stop blocking the Keating amendment and the bill then passed, which allowed a sale without court approval. President Kennedy signed it on October 22, 1962.

The *New York Times* predicted that the bill would only open a new and tangled chapter in the GAF case. One problem was that there were tax claims of $24 M against GAF. Katzenbach insisted that the tax claims be counted against the cash that was being received from the sale by Interhandel. If there were a sale as allowed by the new law without court approval, Interhandel would have fought the new law on Constitutional grounds in the U.S., then appealed to the international court in the Hague. When the settlement and sale agreement was announced, JFK was grilled about it at a press conference. A questioner asked whether the U.S. Government theory that I G Farben owned Interhandel and thus also GAF was erroneous. Or, it was asked, was JFK giving in to pressure from the Swiss Government?

In Congress, Democratic Representative John Dingell, a high-ranking member of the House Interstate and Foreign Commerce Subcommittee railed that Interhandel did not have a nickel coming to it. Republican Willard S. Curtin of the same subcommittee said that "splitting the baby" was just wrong.

On December 20, 1963, a stipulation of settlement was signed by the Department of Justice and also Interhandel which provided for the sale of GAF to the public and the splitting of the proceeds per the prior agreed percentages. In April 1964, the Federal U.S. District Court was asked to approve the settlement, which it did, and the Court authorized the sale.

Criticism of the agreement mounted. Columnist Drew Pearson pointed to the clandestine visit of the Interhandel representative to the Joseph P. Kennedy home in Palm Beach right after the 1960 election. The rank and file lawyers at the Department of Justice who had worked on the case were unanimously opposed to the settlement. Robert Kennedy, as Attorney General, had appointed William Payton Marin as Vice-Chairman of the GAF board. Marin was the principal legal counsel for Joseph P. Kennedy. Marin quickly became the dominant figure on the board of GAF. Drew Pearson then dropped the bombshell—a memo in Justice Department files which referred to the involvement of Prince Radziwill.

In July, 1964, when RFK was going to run for the Senate from New York, the Jewish War Veteran's organization asked an official of the Justice Department whether any of the proceeds of the GAF sale would wind up in the pocket of any former Nazis. The reply was no.

On March 9, 1965 the General Aniline and Film stock was sold at the largest competitive auction in Wall Street up to that date. The winning bid was over $320 M, or $2.5 B in 2016 dollars.

On December 13, 1974, GAF which was now legitimately owned by Americans, together with BASF, Bayer, DuPont and five other companies pled guilty to a criminal conspiracy to fix the prices of dyestuffs in the United States. On April 1, 1978, the public was told that the GAF dyestuff plant at Rensselaer, New York, originally built by German Darl Duisberg, was sold to BASF a German company and the world's largest chemical company. The plant had been seized by the Alien Property Custodian in both World War I and World War II.

Only time will tell if history will repeat itself a third time. The question for our analysis here is whether the GAF case factored into the JFK assassination. Part of the arrangements for the sale of GAF involved the appointment of an advisory committee which was made up of seven persons. Three were officers of GAF. The chairman of the committee was Donald C. Cook of New York, who was President of American Electric Power Company. On November 30, 1963, Lyndon Johnson and Donald C. Cook participated in a lengthy phone call. During the call, Johnson discussed such personal issues as whether Cook's son would want to date one of LBJ's daughters. Cook also informed LBJ that he would like LBJ to meet with a group of men to discuss some issues which were not explicitly mentioned. LBJ agreed to a very hasty meeting which would take place within a week.

He may have appointed Don Cook to the advisory board for the GAF sale because of a prior friendship. Or Cook may have been calling to pressure LBJ to finalize the GAF deal where JFK and RFK had balked. Circumstantial evidence can be found in the fact that the sale was approved in December, 1963. This was less than four weeks after JFK was assassinated. It would seem like Cook was calling for the same purpose others were calling LBJ immediately after the assassination: he may well have wanted an affirmation to confirm that he would see the desired result for one of his (German) friends' efforts in helping to further the assassination.

One theory which could be suggested is this: as long as GAF was owned by the U.S. Government, it would be very difficult to involve GAF in price-fixing with DuPont, BASF and Bayer in the sale of chemicals in the U.S. When GAF was sold at auction, it brought $2.6 billion in 2016 dollars. But there would be additional profits that would accrue if the old German theory of cartelization and price fixing were to include GAF. Those extra profits could have far eclipsed the $2.6 B from the GAF sale. Those illicit profits could have mounted into the $50 billion range. The greater the financial stakes involved in the case of GAF, the larger role the GAF case would have played in the JFK assassination. If great enough, GAF could have been the actual proximate cause of the assassination itself.

The most important takeaway from the General Aniline and Film case is the degree that the Old World values and personages had penetrated into the JFK administration. Prince Radziwill had been paid off to insert himself into the biggest case involving ex-Nazis and German industrialists. No other president had invited the Old World into his administration like JFK did.

In the 1930's, JFK along with his father Ambassador Joseph P. Kennedy was over in Europe literally slow-dancing with the future Queen Elizabeth. The mother of Jackie Kennedy had an affair with the ridiculous pretender George de Mohrenschildt. Jackie's sister married Prince Stanislaus Radziwill. De Mohrenschildt was the person in Dallas in closest association to the assassination aside from Oswald. Baron George de Mohrenschildt and Prince Radziwill had almost identical resumes.

Old World "nobility" would mean nothing to Truman, Eisenhower, Nixon, Ford or Carter. It was not until President Ronald Reagan paid his famous visit to an SS cemetery in Germany when these Old World issues next penetrated into the life of a President in a personal way. It was JFK's (and his family's) perverse fascination with this Old World junk that left the door wide open to his own assassination. Shame on *him!*

KENNEDY, ADENAUER AND U. S.-WEST GERMAN RELATIONS

The relations between West Germany and the United States were not the best in 1963. There were several issues that were front and center in this regard. First, the U.S. needed German soldiers to be a part of the plan to resist a possible Soviet attack or takeover of the remainder of Europe. Second, the borders of post-World War II Germany had not been made final. There were 10 million refugees in Germany who had been displaced from the lost eastern territories. They were hateful about this issue of Germany's eastern boundaries. It was these refugees, through their leaders, who were very high up on the list of facilitators of the JFK assassination.

There is an excellent book covering this topic. It is called *Adenauer and Kennedy: A Study in German-American Relations 1961-1963* by Frank A. Mayer. In his book he describes how Eisenhower set forth the U.S. policy toward Germany in 1953. It was:

1. An integrated European Union.

2. Working to reduce Soviet policy influence throughout all of Germany.

3. A *peaceful* road to a united Germany.

4. A healthy economy for Germany within the EU.

5. Maintenance of Western control of West Berlin.

In return for West Germany joining NATO, the western allies promised a reunification of Germany by peaceful means. But despite the above policies, West Berlin was still not under the control of the West German Government in Bonn.

Adenauer placed German reunification as a requirement before he would agree to accept the new post-war German borders, i.e. the Oder-Neise Line. In 1957, there was a joint declaration by France, the U.K., the U.S. and West Germany affirming the policy of a peaceful re-unification of Germany.

As mentioned elsewhere in our study, the U.S. elections of 1958 brought about a revolution in power in Washington, D.C. The Northeastern Democratic liberals gained much more control in the Senate. As a consequence, J. William Fulbright became the chairman of the Senate Foreign Relations Committee and Mike Mansfield of Montana became the Majority Leader of the Senate. Both Fulbright and Mansfield favored a dialogue with Moscow on security issues. To these liberals, the unification demands of West Germany were a barrier to direct disarmament talks with Moscow.

Another issue was the policy of the U.S. military strategy. Eisenhower believed in "massive retaliation." In other words, if the Soviets attacked in Europe, there would immediately be a nuclear war. This was much less expensive than maintaining a huge standing army in Europe to battle the Soviets using conventional military means.

On March 15, 1960 Eisenhower re-affirmed the primacy of German re-unification. The big question for that year was whether a newly-elected JFK would also recognize such a priority. Mayer quotes historian Richard Reeves who wrote about JFK as "a professional politician who reacted to events...careless and dangerously disorganized...living in a race against boredom." While a Senator, JFK had dismissed Chancellor Konrad Adenauer as "a shadow of the past." He also said that German re-unification was "many years away."

Importantly for our prior discussion of the National Security Council, Mayer reports that Walt W. Rostow as a powerful figure in JFK's National Security Council tried to persuade JFK to set up an explicit formalized policy system. Instead, JFK abolished Ike's Operations Co-ordinating Board and started using *ad hoc* committees drawn from the White House team. This was no small matter.

The National Security Council as well as its Operations Co-ordinating Board had been foisted on the Presidency by villainous types like interfering Wall Street bankers and ex-President Herbert Hoover. In this study you will find that Herbert Hoover was not content to stop his political activities after having wrecked the U.S. economy during his Presidency and drastically worsening the cataclysmic Great Depression. In the 1950's, he set about to wreck the Office of the President through the Hoover Committee. Most people regarded Hoover as a sort of genius. A student of the JFK assassination only finds Hoover to be a genius at trying to wreck things; like for instance the Presidency, both while in the office and later, right up until his death in 1964 at age 90.

So in 1961, JFK began struggling with the bizarre product of the Hoover Commission, the National Security State. Ike had called it "the military-industrial complex." That complex included the Secretary of Defense who was a statutory mandated member of the four- or five-person National Security Council. Mayer reports at page 9 that under JFK, all cables to the Secretaries of Defense, State and the CIA Director were read first by National Security Advisor McGeorge Bundy and his Deputy W.W. Rostow. This presumably meant that the cables could be put by them on an indefinite hold or bounced back to the sender. That point is not entirely clear.

As a judgment which literally had fatal consequences, Mayer reports (at p. 8) that the Administration of JFK was more inclined toward West Berlin Mayor Willi Brandt of the Social Democratic Party in Germany, than to Chancellor Konrad Adenauer. JFK snubbed Adenauer by inviting Willi Brandt to visit the White House before the first visit of Dr. Adenauer in 1961. JFK and Pope John XXIII both believed in dialogue with the East. Senator Thomas Dodd declared that *his* President JFK and *his* Pope John XXIII "had each inflicted 50 years' worth of damage." Just try to figure that one out.

Early on, the JFK White House decided that the phrase "German re-unification" should never be used by JFK. Dean Rusk felt that a conventional military response to Soviet aggression should be tried before a nuclear exchange. This went against Ike's belief in "massive retaliation." This went against the wishes of Germany which felt it would be sacrificed in a conventional war and, further, it was unable to possess nuclear weapons to threaten its own "massive retaliation."

JFK felt Adenauer was pro-Nixon in the 1960 election. Dean Rusk felt that Adenauer's desire for German re-unification was unrealistic and that Adenauer was diplomatically inept. Former Secretary of State and diplomatic elder statesman Dean Acheson thought that the Bay of Pigs fiasco destroyed all faith in the Kennedy Administration on the part of the European Allies because of its disastrous results.

Meanwhile, Chairman J. William Fulbright of the Senate Foreign Relations Committee and Senate Majority Leader Mike Mansfield were promoting the idea of Berlin as a "Free City," i.e. 50% Communist. JFK's White House thought that Adenauer had too much influence on U.S. foreign policy. Noteworthy for our JFK assassination analysis, a committee on Berlin and Germany was formed which included both Treasury Secretary C. Douglas Dillon and Paul Nitze. Both of these men were under the total financial control of their sometime boss, Clarence Dillon, owner of Dillon, Read investment bank. Dillon controlled how much money, if any, they would ever get from the accumulated profits and partnership interest in Dillon, Read. Clarence Dillon very likely played a role in the assassination, mostly because he had the motive, means and opportunity, as this situation amply demonstrates.

Author Mayer quotes historian Ernest May, who said that Chancellor Konrad Adenauer was one of the most influential people inside the American Government. Due to the power and position of Germany in the Cold War, that scarcely needed saying. Of course, West Germany and Adenauer gained effective military control of NATO around this time by placing NATO under the control of former Hitler general staffers. In 1961, Adenauer disavowed a new list of American positions on re-unification and treatment of the East German government in European negotiations.

JFK and Adenauer met for the first time in a meeting at the White House in November 1961. At the meeting, Adenauer promised that West Germany would not begin to "flirt" with the Communist Eastern Bloc.

But then JFK decided to broaden the negotiations without consulting the Western allies. He now wanted to discuss the following:

1. A West German (FRG) and East German (GDR) mixed commission to work out issues about Berlin.

2. A nuclear non-proliferation agreement.

3. A NATO-Warsaw Pact non-aggression treaty.

At about this time, the idea was floated suggesting a United Nations role in running Berlin. In a possible show of JFK's unfortunate tendency to double-cross, he suggested negotiating with Khrushchev about the above points. JFK had promised the West Germans that the above issues would be off-limits. This new agenda would diminish the importance of NATO and would also recognize the status quo of the "Iron Curtain."

On April 13, 1962, there was a meeting in Bonn between Paul Nitze, the Assistant Secretary of Defense for International Security, the U.S. Ambassador to West Germany Walter Dowling and Konrad Adenauer. Adenauer expressed shock at recent developments. In the meantime, a new idea was being floated. This proposal would create a commission to deal with the issues of access to West Berlin and would consist of members from Sweden, Austria and Switzerland.

Anger arose from the discussions. Adenauer thought the U.S. was going soft. In the heat of the discussions, JFK demanded that the West Germans recall their ambassador Wilhelm Grewe. The new West German ambassador Karl Heinrich Knappstein was privately dressed down by JFK as no other western ambassador had ever been. Charles de Gaulle opposed British entry to the EU on 1-14-1963, calling the UK a "Trojan horse" for the United States. In response to the open hostility, JFK made the ultimate threat against Bonn and de Gaulle: that the U.S. would just turn their back, withdraw the nuclear umbrella and allow to Soviets to "have at it" and take over the rest of Europe.

On January 22, 1963, West Germany and France signed the Élysée Treaty in Paris. This Treaty established a new foundation for relations between France and Germany, who had fought wars over many centuries. The Germans claimed it was a good thing and represented a positive reconciliation between enemies.

But officials in the U.S. were very concerned because the Treaty deliberately declined to mention NATO. This omission was interpreted as a slap against NATO. In general, the treaty also represented an overall threat that existed ever since the end of World War II. That threat was that France and Germany would get together and "go it alone." That meant that they would try to plan a defense of Europe whereby they did not need the help of the U.S. and the U.K.

One outcome of the Treaty was the establishment of a Franco-German military brigade. This brigade was not actually established until 1987, but was still in existence in 2016.

The bottom line for U.S.-West German relations at the time of the JFK assassination was that there was a great deal of "rocking the boat" going on about West Berlin and German reunification. General Julius Klein, whose activities are discussed in several other chapters, was pressuring Senator Thomas Dodd to introduce a Senate Resolution calling for German reunification. But the over-arching issue was the personality of Chancellor Konrad Adenauer. Adenauer was considered by some historians to be a "mean old man." It was not so much that Adenauer personally disliked or distrusted JFK. But Adenauer was ruthless. He clearly believed that JFK's policies toward the two Germanys and toward the Soviet threat were inept or even dangerous.

General Julius Klein was the bagman for much of the money involved in the JFK assassination through bribery of Senators and probably other things. General Klein's main contact and most powerful supporter in West Germany was Adenauer. But Adenauer was not an ex-Nazi and his respect in Germany was based on his stable performance in office while surrounded by chaos. Would Adenauer have jeopardized his legacy by being a party to assassination and murder? This remains a question mark.

Adenauer resigned as Chancellor on October 16, 1963. His successor was Chancellor Ludwig Erhard. Erhard was the first foreign leader to meet with LBJ after the assassination. He was quickly invited to the LBJ ranch. It would appear that Adenauer resigned just four weeks before the assassination so that he would not go down in history as a party to murder.

It seems ridiculous to even state the obvious. Adenauer was surrounded by a large number of ex-Nazis in his government who had already murdered at least 12 million people. What if JFK were victim number 12,000,001?

ISRAEL'S NUCLEAR PROGRAM

Some assassination authors have theorized that the assassination of JFK happened because he was trying to prevent Israel from getting the bomb and that Israel retaliated against him.

In June, 1945, 17 Jewish-American millionaires met at the home of the wealthy Rudolph S. Sonneborn on 57th street in New York City. A group was formed to further the establishment of the State of Israel. It was given the code-name "The Sonneborn Institute." In the JFK assassination research, two very prominent names belonged to this Institute. One was Louis Bloomfield, a Canadian lawyer and businessman who was considered the leader of the Canadian Jewish community. Significantly, the Sonneborn Institute was called a "North American" group, not an American one. The other famous member was General Julius Klein.

Physicist Robert J. Oppenheimer was basically the inventor of the atomic and hydrogen bombs. (Thanks a lot). In 1952, he paid a visit to Israel. On May 12, 1955, France contacted the Israeli ambassador and took the first step in setting up a long-term cooperation agreement between Israel and France to develop nuclear weapons. Israel had the Jewish physicists, but France had the North African territory and the Pacific Islands upon which to test bombs which could not be done in tiny Israel.

In 1956, Israel made an agreement with the U.K. and France. Israel would get a nuclear reactor capable of creating weaponized plutonium if they would agree to help in the seizure of the Suez Canal from Nasser's Egypt. This was the Suez Crisis of 1956. By 1959, the Israelis had a 40 megawatt nuclear reactor which could produce enough plutonium for 4 or 5 bombs per year.

For the JFK researcher, it is significant to note that the French Minister of Atomic Energy was Jacques Soustelle. He was considered a friend of Israel. Soustelle is frequently mentioned by assassination authors as being involved in the assassination. Soustelle was actually a close political ally of General Charles de Gaulle and his affiliation with the OAS, if any, is a complex issue in itself. Soustelle had, at least, some relationship with the OAS and a history of affiliation with British Intelligence. When the French-Israeli nuclear program kicked into gear, Israeli leader Shimon Peres and scientist Joseph Shalheret decided to bypass the French Government and go directly to Jacques Soustelle.

The Israeli nuclear program was generally called Dimona after the name of their nuclear reactor. A secret fund-raising for the Israeli bomb was conducted from 1950 to 1960 in the U.S. and raised over $40 M. American lobbyist Abraham Feinberg was a leader in the fundraising. He was a confidante of Truman, Kennedy and LBJ. Feinberg asked for a list of the members of the 18 Sonneborn Institute members. The only names revealed were Samuel Zacks, Louis Bloomfield, Bernard Bloomfield, Samuel Bronfman (all four were Canadians) and Henry Morganthau (former U.S. Treasury Secretary). All the rest of the donor list is still secret today. Also donating were the British and French Rothschilds.

For the nuclear program, Israel purchased ingredients from Norway, but had to supplement this with more material from the U.K., which was approved by the British Government. American intelligence was officially informed of the existence of the Israeli nuclear program by a University of Michigan professor in December 1960.

When President Eisenhower first found out about a possible Israeli nuclear program, he called a meeting in his office. Present at the meeting were Secretary of State Christian Herter, Allen Dulles of the CIA, John McCone of the Atomic Energy Commission and Robert Anderson, Secretary of the Treasury. Ike wanted to know where the money had come from. The list of contributors that was assembled has been kept secret ever since. Ike was most worried about a "domino effect" which would lead to nuclear proliferation.

When JFK entered office, he met with David Ben-Gurion. The chemistry between the two was not as good as the LBJ-Levi Eshkol, Nixon-Golda Meir and the Clinton-Yitzhak Rabin chemistry. It is significant to note that as of 1962, the Mossad had no unit which was involved in operations. The Mossad was only engaged in collection of intelligence. Israeli General Meir Amit was head of Israeli military intelligence. On April 1, 1963, Prime Minister Ben-Gurion named General Amit to head the Mossad. Following that appointment, Amit went to West Germany to meet with the head of West German intelligence, General Reinhard Gehlen.

In December, 1962, JFK met with Golda Meir in Palm Beach, Florida. Golda Meir then went to see Ben-Gurion to tell him that Israeli soldiers were being trained in West Germany, as was reported by the German News Agency. It was revealed that German Defense Minister Franz Josef Strauss and Shimon Peres had made this agreement.

Israel attained nuclear capability in the second half of 1966. According to U.S. sources, as of 1967 they had two bombs.

So what is the conclusion which should be reached regarding the relationship between the Israeli nuclear program and the assassination of JFK? Most importantly, there were names involved in the history of the Israeli nuclear program which are also found in the JFK assassination literature. Examples are Major Louis Bloomfield, General Julius Klein, General Reinhard Gehlen and Frenchman Jacques Soustelle. But there is no information whatever regarding any particular attitude or policy which ties John F. Kennedy to the Israeli nuclear program. That statement also applies to any information whatsoever linking the JFK assassination to Israel, Israeli intelligence or the Israeli Mossad.

These were the three most important international issues in 1963 which affected or could have affected the JFK assassination. The conclusion to be reached was that it was the foreign policy tension between the U.S., JFK, West Germany and Adenauer, which were the precipitating cause of the assassination.

Another fact was very important. The West German "Shadow Ambassador" General Julius Klein almost certainly represented the giant German chemical company I G Farben. Klein was the "bag man" for bribing U.S. Senators and for dealing with the public relations challenges surrounding the assassination events from the standpoint of the West German ex-Nazis who were involved. As stated above, the GAF case was settled in December, 1963. The settlement, as alleged by Senator George Smathers, might well have put millions (billions in 2016 dollars) into the pockets of ex-Nazis.

There was also a possible issue of unclaimed "dormant" accounts never repaid to the Jews by German banks. Klein stated that he only "got into trouble" when he began to fight for Hermann Abs. Abs was a former Nazi-affiliated banker under Hitler and was CEO of Deutsche-Bank both before and after World War II. Abs was on the itinerary of Senator Thomas Dodd and General Klein whenever either of them visited West Germany. They both went there often.

It would be impossible to disentangle the relationships between Klein, Senator Thomas Dodd, IG Farben, Chancellor Konrad Adenauer, General John B. Medaris, Roy Cohn and on and on and on. Suffice it to say that the international situation in the broadest sense was what brought on the assassination of JFK. This factor was at least co-equal to the factor of the exploding Civil Rights movement in the South. This mix led to the assassination of John F. Kennedy.

Notes:

This is the source for the opening quote from General Julius Klein:
Activities of Nondiplomatic Representatives of Foreign Principals in the U.S.: hearings before the United States Senate Committee on Foreign Relations, Eighty-Eighth Congress, first session. PT.1-13 by United States. Congress. Senate. Committee on Foreign Relations. Published 1963.

The Secret War on the United States in 1915: A Tale of Sabotage, Labor Unrest, and Border Troubles (2015) by Heribert von Feilitzsch.

Cited in the text by reference to Zabludoff: *The Plunder of Jewish Property During The Holocaust: Confronting European History*, edited by Avi Baker, Chapter 7 "German Assets in Switzerland At The End Of The Second World War," written by Sidney Jay Zabludoff, p. 136.

President Kennedy: Profile of Power, by Richard Reeves, quoted by Mayer at page 7 of *Adenauer and Kennedy*.

Referred to in the text is: *Adenauer and Kennedy: A Study in German-American Relations 1961-1963* by Frank A. Mayer.

A valuable resource for the issues presented in this chapter is: *The United States and Germany in the Era of the Cold War, 1945-1968: A Handbook, Vol. 1: 1945-1968* by Detlef Junker (Editor), Philipp Gassert (Editor), Wilfried Mausbach (Editor), David B. Morris (Editor).

Der Spiegel, 10-4-63 is the date for a very important article which sits in the middle of the JFK assassination information, based on its timing and subject matter. One can find it on the internet by searching on the name and General Klein as search terms, or find it in a major library such as the Memorial Library at the University of Wisconsin-Madison.

The best source for Israel and the Bomb is: *The Bomb in the Basement: How Israel Went Nuclear and What That Meant for the World*, by Michael Karpin.

Chapter 32

SENATOR THOMAS J. DODD AND THE JFK ASSASSINATION

The guilt of the Senate Internal Security Subcommittee in the assassination is shown by Dr. Jeffrey Caulfield in *General Walker*, and again by William J. Gill in *The Ordeal of Otto Otepka*, which is explained above in a prior chapter. Since Senators James O. Eastland and Thomas J. Dodd essentially shared the chairmanship of this committee, their guilt is undeniable.

Thomas Joseph Dodd was born May 15, 1907. Dodd was a United States Congressman and later the Senator from Connecticut. He is the father of two sons well known in their own right as dedicated public servants. One was U.S. Senator Christopher Dodd and the other was Thomas J. Dodd, Jr. who served as the United States Ambassador to Uruguay from 1993-1997 and to Costa Rica from 1997-2001.

Dodd was born in Norwich, New London County, to Abigail Margaret O'Sullivan and Thomas Joseph Dodd, a building contractor. All four of the grandparents of Senator Dodd were immigrants from Ireland. His paternal grandparents were farmers in the Housatonic River valley with large commercial tobacco leaf farms located near Kent and New Milford. He graduated from Saint Anselm College's preparatory school which was run by Benedictine monks in Goffstown, New Hampshire, in 1926. He then graduated from Providence College [a Catholic religious college] in 1930 with a degree in philosophy, and from Yale Law School in 1933. In 1934, Dodd married Grace Murphy of Westerly, Rhode Island. They had six children.

Dodd served as a special agent for the Federal Bureau of Investigation in 1933 and 1934. The highlight of his FBI career was his participation in the famous but unsuccessful attempt to capture John Dillinger at Little Bohemia Lodge in northern Wisconsin. He was then Connecticut director of the National Youth Administration from 1935 to 1938. The National Youth Administration was a New Deal program begun by the Administration of FDR.

Dodd was the subject of a biography written by his former speechwriter James P. Boyd. In addition to being a very good writer, he was credited by his associates as being a very intelligent person, and was often described as such. His book about Dodd was called *Above The Law*, which we will refer to as (ATL).

When World War II broke out, Tom Dodd was unable to serve in the armed forces because he was over 30, was supporting a family and had some disqualifying medical conditions. Dodd instead chose to work as a public prosecutor which he looked upon as duty he owed to his country.

He was assistant to five successive United States Attorneys General (Homer Cummings, Frank Murphy, Robert Jackson, Francis Biddle and Tom Clark) from 1938 to 1945. Most names on that list are well known to historians of the period, having gained fame as jurists or in other offices.

As a special agent for the Attorney General, Dodd was basically a trial-level federal prosecutor. He worked primarily on criminal and civil liberties cases, including the prosecution of the Ku Klux Klan in the 1930's. In 1942, he was sent to Hartford to prosecute a major spy ring case in which five men (Anastasy Vonsyatsky, Wilhelm Kunze, and others) were accused of violating the Espionage Act of 1917 by conspiring to gather and deliver U.S. Army, Navy and defense information to Germany or Japan. Four of the five pled guilty; Dodd tried and won the conviction of the fifth man, Reverend Kurt Emil Bruno Molzahn. Dodd played a major role in obtaining the conviction of the "American Fuhrer" Fritz Kuhn and also other German-American Bundists (Nazi sympathizers)(The Case Against Congress, hereinafter CAC, p. 37).

Dodd was involved in a particularly noteworthy prosecution involving a problem which concerned the top leaders at the Teheran Conference during the war. The case in question began when Stalin was complaining to President Roosevelt about some communications cable which was defective. When the President first heard this, he thought it was just Stalin being overly particular. However, the next party to complain about the wire was General Eisenhower. Dodd got the FBI involved, then he tried officials of Anaconda Wire and Cable Company and gained their conviction for defrauding the U.S. Government.

Following his success in these wartime prosecutions, Dodd became vice chairman of the Board of Review and later executive trial counsel for the Office of the United States Chief of Counsel for the Prosecution of Axis Criminality at Nuremberg, Germany, in 1945 and 1946.

Dodd considered the likely political benefit for his future career when he took this job in Nuremberg at the War Crimes tribunal. The post involved major inconvenience because he would be required to be absent from his family during the trials. Dodd would also be away from Connecticut politics for the duration.

There was some criticism of the concept of the Nazi war crimes. "Mr. Republican" Robert Taft of Ohio felt that the war crimes as alleged violated the provision in the U.S. Constitutional prohibiting *ex post facto* laws. (ATL

p. 11). These were laws which created a crime after the fact, or operated ret-roactively. Despite this type of criticism, Dodd saw the duty of prosecuting war crimes as a potential benefit to his future political career.

The defendants in the trials would be the top Nazi leaders during the Third Reich. Justice Robert H. Jackson of the United States Supreme Court would be in charge of the U.S. portion of the prosecutions. The other countries involved in the prosecutions would be the Soviet Union, the United Kingdom and France. Thomas Dodd had a great admiration for Justice Jackson, a man who was universally respected. Because of Dodd's enthusiasm for the job, Justice Jackson soon promoted him to the position of Executive Trial Counsel, which made him the number two prosecutor in the United States delegation. The Nuremberg Trials involved cooperation among the four victorious powers and lasted eleven months.

Thomas J. Dodd always declined to discuss anything related to his experiences or his role in the Nuremberg Trials. However, there is much information available from other sources about the specific duties performed by Dodd. Dodd had such duties at the Nuremberg Trials as cross-examining defendants Wilhelm Keitel, Alfred Rosenberg, Hans Frank, Walther Funk, Baldur von Schirach, Fritz Sauckel and Arthur Seyss-Inquart. In addition to cross-examining witnesses, Dodd drafted indictments against the defendants, showed films of concentration camps, provided evidence of slave-labor programs and presented evidence of economic preparations by the Nazis for an aggressive war.

Dodd showed, through his evidence, that Ukrainian Overlord Erich Koch and defendant Polish Overlord Hans Frank were responsible for the plan to deport one-million Poles for slave labor. Dodd also showed evidence that defendant Walther Funk turned the Reichsbank into a depository for gold teeth and other valuables seized from the concentration camp victims. Dodd showed a motion picture of the vaults in Frankfurt where Allied troops found cases of these valuables, containing dentures, earrings, silverware and candelabra. Dodd also showed many gruesome items of evidence, such as a shrunken, stuffed and preserved human head of one of the concentration camp victims that had been used as a paper-weight by the commandant of Buchenwald Concentration Camp.

All but one of the defendants had claimed innocence, including Hermann Goring, whom Dodd had charged with ordering Reinhard Heydrich to set the Holocaust in motion. In addition to prosecuting the individual defendants, Dodd demanded in his summation to the Tribunal that all six of the indicted Nazi organizations be convicted of crimes against humanity, despite the arguments that they were too large, were just part of a political party or other such defenses. These six organizations are the Leadership Corps, the Reich cabinet, the Gestapo, the Storm Troops (SA), the Armed Forces, and the Elite Guard (SS). Dodd said that these organizations should not escape liability on the grounds that they were too large, part of a political party, etc.

As a result of his vigorous prosecution of the various Nazi officials, Dodd was able to obtain a sentence of death by hanging for twelve defendants and life in prison for three more. Three were found not guilty. Dodd was apparently affected by his experience prosecuting the Nazis. Or perhaps he felt that there was some information he had as a result of his experience which might be sensitive for some reason. Dodd never discussed his experience at Nuremberg. This silence even obtained when Dodd was asked for information by reputable historians.

Dodd was given several awards in recognition of his work at the Nuremberg trials. Jackson awarded him the Medal of Freedom in July 1946 and President Harry Truman awarded him the Certificate of Merit, which Jackson personally delivered to him in Hartford in the fall of 1946. Dodd also received the Czechoslovak Order of the White Lion. In 1949, the Polish government had intended to award Dodd with a badge of honor called the Officer's Cross of the Order of Polonia Restituta. Dodd rejected the medal due to his commitment to human rights and his views that the Polish government was imposing a tyranny similar to that imposed by the Nazis.

Surprisingly, during the period after Nuremberg, Dodd repeatedly voiced his support for the theory of one world government. (CAC p. 37). He became president of Connecticut's United World Federalist group. Dodd did this despite the fact that the theory of one-world government presented a challenge to U.S. sovereignty. Some could associate this with the movement toward the New World Order, the precise meaning of which is often unclear.

The question as to why Dodd so quickly became an ardent anti-Communist remains an interesting one. It is a fact, however, that several of those in public life who had face-to-face experience in dealing with Nazi's after World War II, went on to became major players in the Communist-Nazi-Democracy struggle.

One such example was John J. McCloy. McCloy was High Commissioner for Germany and was, according to some, the person who, for all practical purposes, ran the Warren Commission. Another was Allen Dulles, who had negotiated with Nazi scientists and recruited the Nazi spy chief Reinhard Gehlen to serve in U.S. Intelligence. Dulles also worked closely with McCloy to run the Warren Commission. In retrospect, these duties were among the most crucial for U.S. national security in the era of virulent anti-Communism in the 1950's and 1960's.

Upon returning to the U.S., Thomas J. Dodd began the practice of law .He practiced law privately in Hartford Connecticut, from 1947 to 1953. He also moved quickly into Connecticut politics. In the election season of 1948, Dodd entered the race for Governor of Connecticut. Dodd was opposed for that office by Connecticut party boss John M. Bailey. One of Dodd's political handicaps was his sudden and extreme obsession with the issue of Communism and Communists. He charged that the Connecticut Democratic ticket was headed by Communists. As discussed in another chapter, the anti-Communism of Joe McCarthy could be traced to one single dinner date with some anti-Communist activists. With Senator Dodd, the root of his singular crusade against Communism is less certain.

In the 1952 election, Thomas Dodd was elected to the House of Representatives. He served two terms. In 1956, he ran for the Senate and lost. He lost that 1956 bid to Prescott Bush, father of President George H.W. Bush. In 1958, however, he was elected to Connecticut's other Senate Seat and was then re-elected in 1964.

Before becoming a U.S. senator in 1958, Dodd was hired to lobby for Guatemala in the United States for $50,000 a year by dictator Carlos Castillo Armas. According to the North American Congress on Latin America, Dodd "had perhaps the coziest relationship with the Castillo Armas government." After a short trip to Guatemala in 1955, Dodd urged the House of Representatives to increase aid to the Central American country. Dodd's amendment in that regard passed and Guatemala received $415 million in US aid in 1956.

Only rarely would Dodd attend the working meetings of the major committees he had once coveted and to which he had won appointment: Foreign Relations, Judiciary and Aeronautics and Space Sciences. Dodd apparently had a strong preference for clandestine secret subcommittee work, a preference which he had in common with the Kennedy brothers, especially Robert Kennedy. Sounding the same note, Dodd stated at one point that there were only two jobs for which he would leave the Senate. The first was FBI Director and the second was head of the Central Intelligence Agency.

In 1960, after first being elected to the Senate, Dodd launched an attack against his party leaders Mike Mansfield of Montana and J. William Fulbright of Arkansas on the grounds that they were too soft on the Soviets. As a Senate newcomer, Dodd was immediately identified as an LBJ man and was labeled by journalist Drew Pearson as a "bargain basement McCarthy." Around the same time period, Dodd attacked TV journalist-producer Howard K. Smith of ABC. Dodd rebuked Smith because he put together a TV program resurrecting and defending Alger Hiss. In 1961, Dodd visited the Congo to investigate the civil war caused by the secession of the province of Katanga. At this time, the assassination of Patrice Lumumba, leader of the Congo was on the agenda of the CIA. Lumumba was killed, but the question of who sponsored his murder has never become clear. As chairman, Dodd brought respected citizens such as physicist Linus Pauling and businessman Cyrus Eaton before the Senate Internal Security Subcommittee.

The following is a list of Senator Dodd's regular Senate office staff:

1. Michael O'Hare, financial

2. Dave Martin, foreign affairs

3. Gerry Zeiller, municipalities and industries

4. Marjorie Carpenter, secretary

5. James Boyd, speech writer

6. Doreen, dictation

For the Senate Juvenile Delinquency Subcommittee, the list included the following:

1. Carl Perian, staff director

2. George Gildea (unknown title)

3. Al Morano (unknown title)

As mentioned above, Dodd never discussed his activities as a prosecutor at Nuremberg. One explanation could be that he suffered some sort of PTSD reaction. Another would be that his actions had involved trade-offs and compromises which would be hard to explain to anyone who was not involved. As mentioned in a later chapter, one key defendant whose lax treatment by the Nuremberg tribunal would become controversial was Adolf Heusinger, (one of Hitler's top advisors). Dodd could have been involved in that question or other similar controversies.

Still another theory was that he was prosecuting Nazi's at a time when his jurisdiction, Connecticut, was rife with Russian Fascists and other European extremists and likely Nazi sympathizers. It is not known for certain why Senator Thomas Dodd returned from Germany as an extreme anti-Communist when he had never shown any strong interest in the topic prior to that service

James Boyd in *Above The Law*, describes the scenario, and we paraphrase, regarding people who visited Dodd's office for the purpose of influencing him and his staff: (ATL p. 34).

Gerry Zeiller was the specialist on issues involving local government such as funds for urban renewal. Close by was Dodd's foreign affairs section, led by Dave Martin who was described by at least one source as having a conspiratorial look. Into Dodd's office came such people as Black African ambassadors, persons who had fled Cuba for political reasons, bishops of the Eastern Orthodox persuasion who were distinguished by their full beards and last but not least, aristocratic pretenders from Czarist days. It is noteworthy that the leader of the Russian Fascist organization in the U.S. was Anastase Vonsyatsky who operated out of Putnam, Connecticut in the 1930's. It was Dodd himself who had prosecuted Vonsyatsky under the Espionage Act of 1917 in 1942.

Dodd took numerous trips to Florida during his term in the Senate. The expenses for these trips were charged to the Senate Internal Security Subcommittee. He claimed that the nature of the trip would be to interview witnesses in connection with subcommittee hearings. These trips to Florida seemed mysterious and questionable even to his staff, who were presumably aware of his activities. Comparing notes, there was no staff person on Dodd's payroll who knew exactly what went on in Florida. The staff considered the trips in some way suspicious.

Senator Dodd's staff had always believed that his speech-making on the topic of anti-Communism was idealistic on his part. Eventually, though, the staff found out that Dodd was being paid handsomely by wealthy right-wing extremists. Dodd's total estimated take as calculated by his staff over a period of five years for his anti-Communist activities was $50,000.

Senator Dodd shared with at least one person that, when he had campaigned with John F. Kennedy in 1960, he had become very uneasy about the penchant of JFK for diving into throngs of his admirers in order to shake their hands. Dodd had accurately observed that Kennedy was reckless concerning his own physical safety on the campaign trail.

According to Dodd's biographer Boyd, (ATL p. 68), Dodd had diverted campaign funds to pay for his daughter's wedding in October, 1963. Her wedding had cost $6,000. Boyd also reports that in October, 1963, Dodd was in financial trouble both with private creditors and the IRS. According to Boyd, Dodd owed $12,000 in back taxes to the IRS and the IRS was hreatening Dodd as of 1963 with a further audit.

Based on the circumstances surrounding this situation, it could be said that the confrontation between the Kennedy brothers against SISS and chairman Dodd reached a crescendo in October, 1963. Considering all of these facts, one could question whether the IRS was being used at this time against Dodd for political reasons. Threat of prosecution could have been part of the gunpowder leading to the explosion of hostility that was occurring in that fateful month in 1963.

Dodd staff member David Martin was involved at this time in a special effort. His task was to reach out to Connecticut's many Eastern European ethnic groups. It was assumed by Dodd's staff that these people of

Eastern European descent were dealing with Dodd on the issue of hard-line anti-Communism.

By contrast, there were many political issues with which Senator Dodd was involved which were very *pleasing* to the liberal side of the Democratic Party. Examples of such issues which Dodd would champion were internationalism, support for organized labor and help for the underprivileged and for racial minorities. In order to bolster his Northern Liberal image, he put forth his record of flawless support for the progressive agenda of the Kennedy-Johnson Administration. Also on this list of liberal issues were his support of the Nuclear Test Ban Treaty, leadership on civil rights and also his lifelong support of the Democratic Party. He did not have to pretend to be both liberal and conservative; he was naturally fragmented.

In Connecticut, Dodd's candidacy was supported by a mixture of both liberal and conservative groups and interests. On the conservative side were Young Americans for Freedom [YAF]. On the liberal side was Americans for Democratic Action (ADA). One of Dodd's committees was composed of prominent liberals like Elmo Roper, Eugene Rostow, and Norman Cousins, and another one included famous conservatives like Mrs. Kermit Roosevelt, Admiral Redford, and Taylor Caldwell.

Dodd's largest single contributor was the AFL-CIO. This situation would seem to prove that it was possible for a Senate candidate like Dodd to walk down the centerline of politics, supporting causes that were liberal as well as conservative and thus fill his campaign coffers with cash from both sides. Why wouldn't more Senate candidates figure this out and do likewise? The answer to this question may be the following proposition: if a candidate takes money from a contributor, the contributor might react more strongly to a perceived betrayal than to perceived support. A cascading sense of betrayal may be the reason that Dodd wound up in the small group of Senators, McCarthy included, who were censured for their deeds by the Senate.

The following situation paints a remarkable picture of Dodd as either incredibly weak or lacking a moral compass. Senator Dodd had led a campaign and a lawsuit against Jimmy Hoffa. However, in late 1963, Senator Dodd did a 180-degree turnaround on the issue of Jimmy Hoffa and the Teamsters. After late 1963, Dodd actually began to refer to the Hoffa criminal case as *"persecution"* of Hoffa by the Kennedys. But by then, LBJ had become the President and Dodd may have begun buttering his bread on the other side.

Immediately prior to the 1964 Senatorial election, Dodd's staff began to covertly investigate him for the alleged reasons of corrupt financial practices. By December, 1964, the staff had proved that Dodd had siphoned off $200,000 from the campaign for his personal use. Around the same time, Dodd's relationship with other Senators began to suffer.

After the 1964 elections, Senator Mike Mansfield, the majority leader, canceled a Congressional junket which Dodd and his wife had been planning. Dodd denounced Mansfield for this action. However, because such an attack on another Senator was a breach of Senatorial courtesy, Everett Dirksen, the minority leader, went before the Senate and threatened to publicize Dodd's record of poor attendance and failure to attend to his other duties as a Senator. Dodd promptly apologized publicly to Mansfield.

Never in history had the Senate taken formal disciplinary action against a member for financial misconduct. James Boyd was, the speechwriter and staff member for Senator Dodd. The staff of Senator Dodd had been investigating the financial situation of Dodd. Boyd recounts some disturbing information regarding Senator Dodd and John F. Kennedy. Dodd had flown from Hartford to Washington very close to the hour of the assassination. First, Boyd relates that Dodd had claimed that President Kennedy wanted to meet him immediately after his planned arrival in Washington from Dallas. Boyd discounts this part of the story as a fabrication. Dodd's staff was, nevertheless, present when Dodd's plane arrived at the airport in Washington on November 22, 1963. Boyd states that the reasons he and the Dodd staff were bound together in their enterprise of investigating Dodd, were the repugnant statements made by Dodd upon hearing of the JFK assassination.

After his plane from Hartford had landed, Dodd was briefed on the situation. When told that Senator Smathers had just landed wearing a black arm band, Dodd said "Smathers was a friend of the old administration... I am a friend of the new administration.... We sat in appalled silence as it dawned on us that Dodd considered this a day of victory." Air Force One was due in Washington with the body of JFK at any moment. Regarding the assassination, Dodd made this almost unbelievable statement: "I'll say of John Kennedy what I said of Pope John the day he died. It will take us fifty years to undo the damage he did to the U.S. in three years." (ATL p. 106). Though biographer Boyd never said it in so many words, the conclusion is inescapable that Dodd's staff considered him complicit in the assassination.

Senator J. William Fulbright investigated Dodd's close friend and associate, General Julius Klein in mid-1963. Fulbright was the chairman of the Senate Foreign Relations Committee. During the entire era of Joe McCarthy and the era of the Otepka-Dodd relationship, the focus of the anti-Communist activities was always on the U.S. State Department. Despite this long history, the Senate Foreign Relations Committee had not investigated McCarthy or Dodd since 1950. In that year, a subcommittee of Foreign Relations called the Tydings Committee had investigated McCarthy. That being the case, why were the McCarthy and Dodd attacks against the State Department in the various hearings not investigated by the Senate Foreign Relations Committee? In 1950, the Tydings Committee had referred to McCarthy's information on Communists as "a fraud and a hoax." After that, Foreign Relations had lost its appetite for opposing the Red-baiters until 1963. The Senate had just created the Select Committee on Standards and Conduct in 1964. Very soon after that, they began to investigate Senator Thomas Dodd for ethical violations.

Dodd continued to state that the reason he was being investigated was because he was so strong in his opposition to Communists and the Soviet Union. Dodd referred to "the Soviet terror apparatus" implying that there was some relationship between the Soviets and his own censure investigation.

In a summary of the findings against Dodd, the *Washington Post* recounted "that thirteen members of the Juvenile Delinquency Subcommittee's staff were diverted to work for Dodd on matters unrelated to the subcommittee's business, that some members of the Internal Security Subcommittee staff were used as fund-raisers by Dodd, and that some Senate employees were exploited as personal servants."

The result before the Senate Ethics Committee was, among other matters, that the committee recommended "censure" of Dodd for a course of conduct between 1961 and 1965 that "is contrary to accepted morals, derogates from the public trust expected of a Senator and tends to bring the Senate into dishonor and disrepute. The committee found that Dodd's relationship with General Julius Klein was "indiscreet and beyond the responsibilities of a Senator to any citizen.".... Dodd was recommended for censure, a condemnation visited on only five Senators in the nation's history.

Ninety-two members of the Senate voted for censure. The only Senators voting in support of Dodd were Earl Long, Abraham Ribicoff, Strom Thurmond and John Tower of Texas, as well as Dodd himself, who voted no. Dodd was the only Senator in history to be censured for financial misconduct.

Beyond the Senate Ethics Committee's formal disciplinary action, other sources (such as investigative journalist Drew Pearson's and Jack Anderson's "Congress in Crisis") suggest Dodd's corruption was far broader in scope, and there were accusations of alcoholism. In response to these accusations, Dodd filed a lawsuit against Pearson claiming that Pearson had illegally interfered with his private property. (This was because Pearson had received stolen records which had been taken by Dodd's staff). Although the district court granted a partial judgment to Dodd, the appellate court ruled in favor of Pearson on the grounds that Dodd's property had not been physically abused. In 1970, the Democrats endorsed for his seat Joseph Duffey.

Dodd was criticized for beginning investigations and then halting them after getting contributions from defendants in the investigations. In particular, a major target of his investigations was the firearms industry. We have seen that Lee Harvey Oswald just happened to order his two firearms from the two mail-order gun outlets being investigated by Dodd's committee. Dodd was to investigate the gun salesmen (and to receive contributions from them) in 1961, 1963, 1964 and 1965.

In addition to his work with the firearms industry, Senator Dodd opened what became nearly three years of scheduled hearings on the effects of violence on TV. The results of the three committee staff monitoring reports of television content in 1954, 1961 and 1964 showed incidents of violence. Senator Dodd and Estes Kefauver are the two men responsible for informing the public of the effects of violence on juveniles.

Dodd played an instrumental role in the prohibition of LSD in the United States, presiding over subcommittee hearings investigating the drug's effects on youth. Notably, LSD proponent and Harvard psychologist Timothy Leary was called to Washington to testify. Leary urged lawmakers to enact a framework of strict regulation whereby LSD could remain legal and used for medical and research purposes. However, Dodd and his colleagues drafted a ban which was later adopted. This event was one of the precursors to the all-out "War n Drugs" in the 1970's.

In 1970, the Democrats endorsed for his seat Joseph Duffey, who won the nomination in the primary. Dodd then entered the race as an independent, taking just under a quarter of the vote, in a three-way race which he and Duffey lost to Lowell Weicker. Months after his defeat, Dodd died from a heart attack at his home. His son Christopher Dodd was elected to the Senate as a Connecticut Democrat in 1980.

Notes:

For basic biographical facts about Dodd, see: [en.wikipedia.org/wiki/Thomas_J._Dodd]. Information in this chapter not otherwise noted can be found at this Wikipedia address.

Most information in this chapter can be found in the following: *Above The Law: The Rise And Fall Of Senator Thomas J. Dodd* (1968) by James P. Boyd, abbreviated as ATL.

Another excellent source about Senator Dodd is: *The Case Against Congress: A Compelling Indictment Of Corruption On Capitol Hill* (1986) by Drew Pearson and Jack Anderson, abbreviated as CAC.

Of course the Dodd censure hearings, a valuable source, is cited here as: Investigation of Senator Thomas J. Dodd. : Hearings, Eighty-ninth Congress, second session ... pursuant to S. Res. 338, 88th Congress. PT. 1-2 by United States. Congress. Senate. Select Committee on Standards and Conduct. Published 1966.

Chapter 33

THE STASHYNSKY AFFAIR

Douglas N. Stashynsky
Accomplished NKVD

INTRODUCING THE STASHYNSKY CASE

The Stashynsky affair and the JFK assassination have a direct relationship, but it is a relationship which is largely overlooked. (See notes for the citation for the above headlines, articles and picture reproduced for the reader above). However, Dick Russell, author of the most comprehensive assassination book, *The Man Who Knew Too Much* (usually called *TMWKTM*), mentions the Stashynsky affair as it relates to General Willoughby and H.L. Hunt, the Dallas Oilman. (TMWKTM, p. 594-597).

Author Russell came into possession of some documents from the Douglas MacArthur Archives in Norfolk, Virginia. In 1967, General Charles Willoughby wrote to oilman Hunt, "There is no difference between Stashynsky and Oswald ... in an obvious parallel of training and planning and direction." In another memo, Willoughby wrote "The similarity with the Oswald case is irresistible ... the case should be widely publicized to remove the leftist smear on Dallas ... I recommend patriotic residents of Dallas to handle this project under your leadership."

The fact is, Agent Bogdan Stashynsky (a/k/a Stashinsky and other similar spellings) was a Russian defector who was most likely part of the plan for the JFK assassination. His activities preceded 11-22-1963 by several years. But they were apparently an integral part of the JFK plot.

Russell next describes the general outline of the story of Stashynsky. But the story begins with a man by the name of Stepan Bandera. Bandera was a famous figure in Ukrainian history, not just back in the 1950's and 1960's, but even today. Holding on the Bandera legend could be due to a backward-looking perspective of Ukrainians and other people of Eastern Europe. They are constantly looking to specific periods in history to bolster their argument that a border should be drawn in this place or that place. So, to the Ukrainians, the story of Bandera is important because to them Bandera was a patriot who fought for the nation of Ukraine. Also important is that Bandera was a collaborator with Hitler in the WWII struggle against the Soviets. This fact is used to inspire many Neo-Nazis still active in Ukrainian politics today.

On October 15, 1959, Stepan Bandera was found dead in his apartment in Munich, Germany. According to author Russell, Bandera had worked with two of the closest right-wing allies of Charles Willoughby, namely Jaroslaw Stetzko and Theodore Oberlander. Many of the followers of both Bandera and Stetzko were recruited to work for U.S. Military Intelligence and the CIA in the late 1940's to help combat the Soviets.

According to Russell there was a suspect in the death of Bandera, but that suspect was Bandera's friend Theodore Oberlander. This theory was based on the fact that Oberlander had a shady past as a Nazi. Oberlander's past was about to be exposed. Stepan Bandera had information about Oberlander that he might be compelled to reveal in some pending Nazi trials.

Perhaps the most important trial was about Oberlander being held in Communist East Germany, beyond the control of West German officials. Bandera could have wound up as a witness there and devastated the reputation of Oberlander who was, by 1959, a high West German official.

In August, 1961, Bogdan Stashynsky, a Russian citizen, defected to American officials in West Germany and immediately confessed to having killed Stepan Bandera. On top of that, he also confessed to having murdered another Ukrainian in 1957 whose name was Lev Rebet. Stashynsky claimed to have used a previously unknown type of weapon—a "gun" which squirted either cyanide or prussic acid (these are two names for the same chemical). This gun had allegedly been able to fool the coroner in the death of Rebet. Officials believed that Rebet had died of a heart attack. However, the death of Bandera was blamed on cyanide poisoning. The police had not determined who killed Bandera.

After Stashynsky defected to U.S. authorities, U.S. officials quickly turned him over to the German criminal investigators. Both of the alleged murders had occurred on West German soil. Author Russell makes an important connection. He reminds the reader that when Lee Harvey Oswald returned from the U.S.S.R., he was greeted by a man named Spas T. Raikin, a member of Bandera's Ukrainian underground.

Author Dick Russell also reports an important fact that happened over two years later. On November 26, 1964, Washington-based columnists Robert S. Allen and Paul Scott wrote in the *Philadelphia Daily News*:

> "Fifteen days before he was shot down, President Kennedy was warned that assassins were being trained to commit murders in the U.S. and England. The burden of [Congressman Charles] Kersten's letter was an effort to obtain Administration help in focusing public attention on the assassination of Stepan Bandera, the Ukrainian underground leader, by Communist agents" (*TMWKTM*, p. 596)

Also reported in this column was a claim by Congressman Kersten that a hearing on the Stashynsky-Soviet murder situation had been delayed by the Kennedy State Department. Russell then cites the article in the Ukrainian Bulletin which is reproduced above.

It would have been better if author Russell had realized that artificially placing Oswald and Stashynsky together as students of murder in the Soviet SMERSH group was a basic ploy by the JFK assassination plotters.

But Dick Russell took a wrong turn in his analysis of the information he had about Stashynsky. Russell focuses on a memo which shows that General Charles Willoughby and oilman H. L. Hunt were very interested in the cyanide "gas gun" described by Stashynsky. Also disclosed sometime in the mid-1960's was the involvement of Senator Thomas J. Dodd in the Stashynsky Affair. Dodd attempted to use Senate Internal Security Subcommittee (SISS) to frame the Russians for the murder of JFK. In this, Dodd was apparently working with the JFK plotters and former Congressman Charles Kersten in a trans-Atlantic plan which resulted in the murder of JFK. Dodd's partners in crime were West German intelligence (BND) and certain ex-Nazi's still involved in the government of West Germany.

THE KIDNAPPING OF DR. LINSE

The best author on the subject of Stashynsky and alleged Soviet assassins is Ronald Seth, who wrote the definitive book on the subject called *The Executioners*.

To understand the subject of Stashynsky, the reader must begin with the alleged kidnapping of Dr. Walte Linse in 1952. (Seth, p. 113).

Dr. Walter Linse was a prominent German lawyer and was acting President of the Association of Free German Jurists, which was in turn affiliated with the World Federation of Free Jurists. This group was anti-Communist in nature. Among the officials of this association, only the acting President, Dr. Walter Linse, was available for the Soviets to kidnap because he happened to live in the American sector of Berlin.

Four kidnappers were selected to do the kidnapping. On July 8, 1952, they grabbed Dr. Linse, forced him into a vehicle and then sped into the Soviet sector. Linse was kept imprisoned for an unknown period. In 1960, the Russian Red Cross informed the German Red Cross that Dr. Walter Linse had died in a Russian prison camp on December 14, 1953.

At the time of the kidnapping, John J. McCloy was U.S. High Commissioner for Germany in the American Sector. He protested to his Soviet counterpart about the kidnapping but the Soviet Commissioner said he didn't know anything about it.

There was a noted Soviet defector in the early 1950's named Pyotr Deriabin. He testified often to Congress, making use of his inside knowledge of Kremlin activities and methods. He testified to the SISS about the case of Dr. Linse. He stated that all of the high officials in the Soviet Union had been aware of the kidnapping of Dr. Linse.

For the next eight years, demands for information and denials went back and forth between the West and the Soviets. In New York, the Linse case was taken up by The Committee to Combat Soviet Kidnappings. The members of the Committee were Judge Robert Morris, later chief counsel for SISS; the Rev. Charles Lowry, later head of the foundation for Religious Action; Archbishop Paul Yu-Pin, at that time the head of Sino-American Amity; Metropolitan Anastasy, the United States head of the Russian Orthodox Church in Exile; Countess Alexandra Tolstoy, founder and President of the Tolstoy Foundation; Admiral Paulus Powell and General Charles Willoughby. Willoughby was one of the three major Barons involved in the JFK assassination. At the time the this committee was formed, he was the former head of intelligence for General Douglas MacArthur in the Far East and Japan.

The people listed above represented some of the key vertebrae in the backbone of the JFK assassination plot. They were part of a small inside group who perpetrated the JFK assassination.

Shortly after the formation of the Committee in 1954, there was another kidnapping, that of an anti-Communist Russian émigré leader, Valery Tremmel, who was kidnapped by SMERSH (the Russian assassination and kidnapping agency). The Committee presented evidence of this kidnaping to the United Nations Committee on Human Rights. They also investigated, arranged lectures and set up an international information service. This information service was related to The International Research on Communist Techniques, Inc.

This committee activity was typical of the tangled web of government and private covert operators involved in Eastern Europe in the 1950's and 1960's. The President of The International Research on Communist Techniques, Inc. was Vladimir N. Rudin, a writer and analyst. It's Vice-President was Eugene Lyons, a senior editor for *Reader's Digest* who had written several books on Russia. It's V.P. and Treasurer was A.G. Elmendorf, who had worked for the World Council of Churches in Greece and had also been director of the Tolstoy Foundation. Other officers were Emily Kingsberg, and Natalie Kushnir.

Four cases of Soviet acts were submitted by the Committee to Combat Soviet Kidnappings to the U. N. Commission on Human Rights. No action resulted. They did have one success: they led a campaign against Article 16 of the proposed Austrian Treaty which would have forcibly repatriated people back to the Soviet Union. The Article was eliminated.

What actually happened to Dr. Walter Linse once he was in the Soviet Union was known and it can be described as follows: Dr. Linse was first taken to the East German Police Headquarters and then to SMERSH headquarters in Karlhorst, Germany. He was interrogated by as Soviet Major General named Kaverznev, who was head of SMERSH at that location. Under interrogation, Dr. Linse revealed the names of somewhere between 21 and 27 of the secret contacts within East Germany of the Association of Free Jurists.

Soviet law allowed the torture of traitors to gain information. According to defector Pyotr Deriabin, a person under interrogation may be subjected to torture if it has been established that he has already done harm to the Soviet Union. All of the contacts that Dr. Linse revealed were arrested, imprisoned or sent to forced labor camps. Dr. Walter Linse was tried before a secret tribunal and sentenced to 25 years imprisonment.

The rendition of the story of Dr. Linse has a surreal quality. He is described as a jurist but he was apparently a spy. There is no information presented by author Ronald Seth as to who the betrayed contacts in East Germany were or if this was really a spy ring that the Soviets disrupted. The American reader could perhaps feel some sympathy for a spy who got kidnapped back to Russia, but only if we knew more about for whom he was spying.

It seems like a dangerous avocation for a Judge to be spying on East Germany and the Soviet Union, unless he was not a mere volunteer. Was Linse working for the Gehlen organization or for the CIA? How many honest judges just happen to know between 21 and 27 spies in East Germany?

There was a fundamental problem in the attitude of the U.S. Government about the type of spying which involved Dr. Linse and this Committee. This attitude assumed that the "White Russians" were the cure for Soviet Communism. In fact the "White Russians" were not the *cure* for Soviet Communism. They were the *disease* that caused Soviet Communism to come to power.

If the U.S. had sponsored pro-democracy operatives against Soviet Communism in place of the White Russians (and Nazis and other fascists), then Communism might have been established.

As in all of our chapters which deal with people like General Willoughby, the de Mohrenschildt brothers and Dr. Walter Linse, things might have been different if they were fighters for democracy. If the members of the The Committee to Combat Soviet Kidnappings were small "d" democrats, they would evoke more sympathy. For instance, with regard to Princess Alexandra Tolstoy, we know that a Princess, (should she be successful in helping overthrow the Soviets), would likely want her title back. And we know that a Princess does not run for election for her legally recognized position in societies like that of the Czar. We know that Sergius von Mohrenschildt (father of Oswald babysitter George de Mohrenschildt) was appointed Governor of the Minsk region by the Czar. *He* wasn't elected to that post, either.

We now know that when Soviet Communism finally collapsed of its own weight in 1991, democracy was attempted, but it is an open question whether it was achieved in 1991 or since. And we have to keep one important thing in mind. It was a huge mistake to admit White Russians like Alexandra Tolstoy, George de Mohrenschildt, Dimitri de Mohrenschildt or Count Konstantin Maydell to the U.S. given their fanatical political beliefs. They had so little use for democracy that they formed a major part of the backbone of the plot to murder America's elected President. That was their thanks to the U.S. for giving them asylum. And he wasn't even President of *their* country. To the day they died, their country was Russia. Maybe the JFK assassination can serve as a bad example – don't let people into the U.S. unless they sincerely believe in the Constitution – believe in America and believe in American values.

So what about Bogdan Stashynsky? The Stashynsky case was the next big case where SMERSH was blamed for murder. Unlike the case of Dr. Linse, the Stashynsky case formed part of the plot in either the assassination or the attempted assassination of the Presidents of two Western countries. Americans are blind to the plotting and machinations of those who believe in either fascism, titled nobility or non-Constitutional monarchies. But as the assassination of JFK and the attempts to assassinate de Gaulle show, neither the French Revolution nor the American Revolutions are finished. It's no accident that George Washington proudly displayed the key to the Bastille at Mount Vernon, where it hangs today. This history and the American Revolution are reasons enough that every American should be told who it was that murdered John F. Kennedy.

Bogdan Stashynsky was an ethnic Ukrainian by birth, born in 1931 in a village near modern day Lvov. His home village of Borshtshevice, however, was part of Poland at the time of his birth. His father managed a farm, worked as a carpenter and the family was a practicing Christian family, but their religious affiliation is unclear.

Prior to World War I, the village was part of the Austrian empire.

In 1939, when Stashynsky was eight, the fourth partition of Poland took place and as a result, his village became part of Russia. Two years later, when Stashynsky was ten, the Germans overran his home area and it came under the control of Hitler. So that change increased the number to five countries (Austria, Russia, Poland, Ukraine and now Germany) under whose rule some of the oldest residents of Borshtshevice would have lived.

Under Hitler, the Ukrainian state (for the first time in millennia) became independent. The pro-Nazi leader of Ukraine at that time was Jarowslav Stetzko. When the Russians prevailed over the Germans at Stalingrad and moved west into Ukraine, the family of Stashynsky became part of an anti-Russian underground. Logically, this would place the sympathies of Stashynsky with the former Nazi's who fought under Hitler against Stalin. Since Stashynsky was raised with a normal family and childhood, there is no obvious reason he would have turned against his family and village, except for unusual exigencies or circumstances.

Having studied in Lvov from 1945 to 1948, Stashynsky began his college work in 1948 studying mathematics. Stashynsky suffered some bad luck when he was riding the train between his home village and Lvov without a ticket in the summer of 1950. He was supposedly detained by the police for not having a ticket

According to his story, he was taken to a police station of the KGB. There he was confronted with the fact that his family had been helping the Organization of Ukrainian Nationalists (OUN). Stashynsky had supposedly been brainwashed by the Russians as a youth and had been told the leaders of the OUN were in the pay of the Americans. The Soviets made threats against both his family and his plan to pursue his college education. In the face of these threats he signed on to work for the KGB, the mortal enemies of his family back in Borshtshevice.

In 1949, Stashynsky infiltrated into the OUN. His family found this out and cut off his college money. Thus, he became a full-time employee of the KGB. He went into training as a spy in Kiev in 1952; since he was being taught German, he knew his future spy work would be in West Germany. According to the story that has emerged about Stashynsky, he was required to assume a false identity of a Polish man named Josef Lehmann. He was sent to Dresden in East Germany. His first actual assignment (in January 1956) in the West was to make contact with a Ukrainian spy living in Munich. Six months later, his next assignment was to meet up with an unknown man and find out facts about an upcoming Khrushchev visit to London and its relationship to the Ukrainian nationalists. He was also asked to find out if the OUN had any contact with German or American intelligence. Stashynsky worked with this "Mr. X" well into 1957 as he tried to mend the relationship between X and the KGB by using bribes and threats involving X's wife.

In addition to this assignment, Stashynsky was also asked to perform reconnaissance on American troop concentrations and to get information about a school for CIA agents in Upper Bavaria. In the Spring of 1957, he was transferred from his regular KGB assignment to the Soviet murder agency called SMERSH. In SMERSH, he was assigned to collect information about Ukrainian leader Lev Rebet, who was living in Munich. In September, 1957, he was summoned to the Soviet police headquarters at Karlhorst, Germany and was told his assignment would be to murder Lev Rebet.

At this meeting, Stashynsky was shown a new invention, a "gun" which was a tube which, according to Ronald Seth, sprayed a chemical called prussic acid. To protect himself from the effects of this weapon, the would-be assassination had to take both sodium thio-sulphate and, later, amyl-intrate. Stashynsky claimed to have tried out this weapon on a dog under instructions from his superiors. The dog died immediately.

On October 9, 1957 he flew to Munich. The plan was for him to use the gas weapon to murder Rebet. He stalked Rebet in his office building in Munich. As Rebet was ascending the stairway in his office building, Stashynsky descended the stairs. Meeting Rebet, he sprayed Rebet with the poison gun. Rebet, dead, sprawled on the stairs. Stashynsky then ran and covered a fairly long distance before he was able to throw the murder weapon into a creek known as the Kogelmuhlbach. The autopsy of Rebet was done 48 hours after the murder and the cause of death was determined to be a heart attack.

Ronald Seth relates the story about how Stashynsky supposedly began to experience guilt. Seth raises the question as to how Stashynsky could feel so guilty since he was a KGB agent of seven years' experience. The explanation for this is offered, that in April, 1957 Stashynsky had met a woman named Inge Pohl in East Berlin. Pohl lived in East Berlin, but worked as a hairdresser in West Berlin. Pohl was an anit-Communist but Stashynsky was willing to overlook this fact because he had fallen in love with Pohl.

After the alleged murder of Rebet, Stashynsky went back to being an errand boy for SMERSH and assigned to compile a list of all the writings of Ukrainian writer Stefan Popel. But in 1959, he was given a false identity, that of a German national named Hans Joachim Budeit of Dortmund. He then used his new papers to travel to Munich and spy on the home of Stepan Bandera.

In April 1959, Stashynsky became engaged to Inge Pohl. Seth (who is a renowned expert on SMERSH) questions how the KGB could have allowed this to take place? A prior murderer-agent named Nikolai Khokhlov had also been engaged and married under similar circumstances and then defected. The Khokhlov defection had caused major problems for the Soviets, so Seth wonders why they would take such a chance again. How could a murder-agent be allowed to marry an anti-Communist? Seth points out that SMERSH had files whereby they would have known the politics of every girlfriend of every *foreign* agent.

In Moscow, Stashynsky met with a high-ranking KGB officer who told him that his next assignment would be to murder Bandera. The method would be the same as that used to murder Rebet.

Seth raises another question. Stashynsky was having pangs of guilt and didn't understand why the Soviets would want to murder Bandera. Stashynsky was reportedly speculating that the Soviets might have been planning something much bigger than the Bandera murder but they weren't yet telling Styshynsky about this bigger operation.

Next, Stashynsky went on a trip which was part of the plan to murder Bandera. Trying to gain entry to Bandera's residence, Stashynsky had difficulties with the key to Bandera's house. On the next trip, he was asked to observe the lock on the door of Ukrainian leader Jarowslav Stetzko. Much later, when Stashynsky was interviewed and interrogated by Western authorities, he claimed that the Soviets had told him that Ukrainian history had been made by only four men. These were two men named Konovalec and Melnik and also Bandera and Stetzko, who were alive and known to Stashynsky. Stashynsky claimed that the murders of Bandera and Stetzko were desired in order to demoralize the Ukrainian people in their desire for independence. That was presented to him as the Soviet motive in the murders of the Ukrainians.

In August, 1959, Stashynsky was allowed his annual visit to see his parents. On October 14, 1959 he was again in Munich, stalking Bandera. He went to Bandera's apartment building and a woman walked by him who could have remembered his face. He was next to an elevator in the building but could not remember whether he had walked upstairs or took the elevator. Seth questions this lapse of memory.

Seeing Bandera trying to open his door, Stashynsky walked up to him and squirted him with the gas gun. Unlike the killing of Rebet, Bandera survived the attack but died soon afterward. Because both the deaths of Rebet and Bandera were premature and unexpected, authorities investigated the death of Bandera more closely. The cause of death was ruled poisoning by prussic acid. Glass splinters on the body were discovered (despite the addition of a filter on the murder weapon by the Soviets to prevent glass splinters). However, by then, Bogdan Stashynsky had made a successful escape back to East Berlin.

Although Stashynsky received the highest honors from the KGB, he had made up his mind to escape to the West. He later claimed that he attended the movies and a newsreel showed a picture of Bandera in his coffin, which pierced him with guilt. Stashynsky started to spend more time with his fiancée Inge Pohl. The KGB did not approve of the relationship and told him he would have to break up with the girl. Seth again questions why the relationship was still continuing despite Stashynsky's continued role as an assassin. He told his boss Alexei Alexeyevich to his face that he refused to break up with Inge. He was then interviewed by Alexander Shelepin, head of KGB. Shelepin was a V.I.P. who had once been considered to lead the entire Soviet government.

Stashynsky was then supposedly given an award called the Order of the Red Banner. This award allegedly bore the signatures of Marshal Voroshilov, Chairman of the Soviet Presidium and of its Secretary, Michail Georgadse. Stashynsky would claim that Shelepin, the would-be head of the USSR, had discussed with him his romance with Inge Pohl. He allegedly told Shelepin that Inge Pohl was a true believer in Communism (when she was the opposite). Shelepin then, according to Stashynsky, gave his consent for the marriage on the condition that Inge Pohl should visit Moscow. Another condition was that he should tell Inge Pohl that he worked for the KGB. Stashynsky visited Inge in East Berlin and went against orders by visiting West Berlin with Pohl. At that point, she suggested they should both defect to the West.

When Inge eventually visited Moscow from January to March, 1960, the couple was able to fool the KGB into believing Inge was an enthusiastic Communist. The two were married on April 23, 1960 in a Protestant religious service. Then they became residents of Moscow where Stashynsky continued his training in both espionage and English. Inge became pregnant but the authorities told the couple that their choices were abortion or adoption. Next, Bogdan and Inge discovered electronic eavesdropping devices in their apartment.

Author Seth points out that since a prior Soviet murderer had defected, it is inexplicable that the Soviets would have planned on using Stashynsky for even more missions of murder. He *suggests* that normally, in such a situation, both Stashynsky and his new bride would have been liquidated to avoid any further problems such as a defection. Next, he confessed to Inge that he was a double murderer, which supposedly just increased her loyalty to her new husband.

Stashynsky was able to get Soviet permission for Inge to visit her parents in East Germany. At this time, Stashynsky was studying at the First Moscow State Pedagogical Institute for Foreign Languages and the instructors at the Institute knew he was an agent. Seth raises another question in this regard. Drawing on his great knowledge of the tactics of espionage, author Seth questions why the KGB would allow all the people at the Institute to know of Stashynsky's role as a KGB agent? Such knowledge is usually strictly limited to as few people as possible, even concerning people's knowledge inside the KGB. And further, writes Seth, for the first time in his KGB career, Stashynsky carried identification papers bearing his actual name, Bogdan Stashynsky.

Inge was able to prolong her stay with her parents in East Germany long enough to give birth to a son, Peter. Stashynsky asked for permission to visit her in East Germany but this was refused. Next, the baby Peter died. Due to this event, his boss at the KGB granted Stashynsky permission to visit his wife in East Berlin, in part out of fear she would reveal to someone her husband's history as a KGB hit man. The KGB, per Stashynsky, suspected that his baby could have been poisoned by the Americans. This theory held that the Americans could foresee the results of the poisoning, i.e. Stashynsky's visit to East Berlin and there they could kidnap him.

(Did you notice? Our story is getting more and more far-fetched)?

At the home of Inge's parents, there had been no room for their daughter so she was living in a nearby apartment. When Stashynsky was visiting at this location, the couple slipped into some woods behind the apartment. Next, they walked to a place called Falkensee and took a taxi to East Berlin. Stashynsky showed authorities his identification with the false name Lehmann, which the Soviets had forgotten to take from him previously. Thence, they took a train to West Berlin and asked some friends to take them to American authorities. They went first to Berlin police headquarters and after claiming asylum, they were taken by the Germans to the custody of the Americans.

After 13 months in prison, Stashynsky was put on trial before the West German Supreme Court on October 8, 1962. He was sentenced to 8 years penal servitude for "aiding and abetting murder" and also treason. Per author Ronald Seth, the opinion of the court was almost unique in this case:

> 1. It named the Soviet Union as the country which was a party to the murder when the usual practice is only to name "a foreign power."

> 2. Seth uses the word "avuncular" to describe the way the court writes about Stashynsky as an individual. The reader is reminded of the definition of avuncular which is "suggestive of kindness or geniality." In their written legal opinion, the German high court seems to be saying "boys will be boys" and that Stashynsky was contrite. Contrition is not usually very important in a case of two premeditated murders.

Seth readily admits he has based his rendition of the facts on the information repeated by the German Supreme Court. When one reads the opinion in its original form, it is more complicated than presented by Seth. The fact that Stashynsky was given a very light sentence and received a ridiculous degree of clemency for a double-murder was heavily influenced by the recent history of West Germany. The court attached overwhelming weight to the fact that Stashynsky had been living in a totalitarian State and had been ordered by that State to commit the two murders. This is the "Nazi" defense which was undoubtedly very popular in West Germany at that time. The Auschwitz trial was just around the corner as were other potential trials of important German war criminals.

In a book on Soviet espionage written by *U.S. News and World Report*, the following information was reported about Stepan Bandera: 1) following World War II, the main enemies of the Soviet Union in European clandestine activities were the Ukrainian OUN and the Russian NTS; 2) Stepan Bandera had begun to work toward an independent Ukraine as early as the time of the Russian Revolution; 3) during World War II, Bandera served in French and British Intelligence; 4) after World War II he worked for U.S. Intelligence and for the Gehlen Organizion, which had first been under the CIA then became the West German BND; 5) Bandera had agents that worked in Ukraine, East Germany and Hungary. (Cited in notes as *Famous Soviet Spies*, Lowry ed.).

On April 3, 1962, after the defection of Stashynsky, the Soviets called a news conference where they presented a Ukrainian defector who had "gone East." The defector addressed the assembled journalists. His name was Osyp Werhun. Werhun had formerly lived in Munich, West Germany. Werhun stated that many Ukrainians were serving in the West German intelligence services. He said the Ukrainians were being used [by Germany] in spying on the United States, France, Austria and other Western Countries. He alleged that a Dr. Roman Hanlinger-Grau, working for the Ost-Europa Institute in Munich was running the spies in Austria. He also listed the names of other agents and intelligence organizations which were involved in similar activities. The one which is most interesting to our analysis of the Stashynsky case is "The American Committee for Liberation." In archives that have been opened at some point well after 1962, it has come to light that this agency had a CIA code name AMCOMLIB and was funded by the CIA from 1950 to 1971. Most importantly, Werhun said that Bogdan Stashynsky was a specially trained OUN member and that Stashynsky's story about the Rebet and Bandera murders was not fact, but was a "provocation." This represents the Soviet side of events in the Stashynsky case, which is very different from that of the U.S. and the West German side, which accepted the story of Stashynsky at face value.

According to an online website, (see notes), Stashynsky went to America under cover after his release from prison in 1968. Other information says he went to Panama. Another theory was that Stashynsky was given cover by South Africa in 1968 as described in the following new story (see notes for citation):

South Africa gave a convicted KGB assassin asylum and...

March 6, 1984

JOHANNESBURG, South Africa -- South Africa gave a convicted KGB assassin asylum and an assumed identity in a secret deal with the West German Security Service, a former police commissioner said in an interview.

Gen. Mike Geldenhuys, who retired last year as chief of the South African police, told the Rand Daily Mail that former Soviet hit-man Bogdan Stashynsky was supplied with a false identity and a job and underwent cosmetic surgery to change his appearance when he arrived in South Africa in 1968.

Stashynsky defected to the West in September 1961 and was sentenced in West Germany to eight years for killing Ukranian exiles Dr. Lev Rebet and Stefan Bandera in 1957 and 1959, Geldenhuys said.

"In the meantime, we were approached by the West German Security Service and asked to give this man asylum in South Africa because they were convinced it was the only country where he would be comparatively safe from KGB agents," Geldenhuys told the newspaper.

'He was able to supply our intelligence service with a vast amount of invaluable information on the structure and operations of the Russian secret service,' he said.

In 1964, Senator Dodd went to West Germany and interviewed Stashynsky. In the Spring of 1964, SISS held hearings on the Soviet "Murder, Inc." The Senator held as a hammer or threat the fact that he could have held a press conference and claimed that Stashynsky knew Oswald in the USSR or that Stashynsky worked for the Soviets, thus blaming the Soviets for the JFK assassination. This implicit threat from Dodd was used as a basis for the fear of a nuclear war arising from these allegations against the Soviets. Under this theory, the Stashynsky facts, true or untrue, would have generated public outrage and war hysteria in the American public. At any time, Senator Dodd could have held a press conference and claimed that Stashynsky knew Oswald in the USSR, that Stashynsky was part of a JFK plot, that the Soviets were responsible for the assassination, etc. So Dodd had this issue to use as a shield against any honest investigation of the Kennedy assassination.

ANALYSIS OF THE STASHYNSKY CASE: STARTING BACKWARDS

Analyzing the Stashynsky case is both necessary and crucial to understanding the assassination of John F. Kennedy. And to do this analysis, we must start at the end of the story and work backward to the beginning.

Regarding Stashynsky, the last thing that happened before the JFK assassination was the mailing of the warning letters to the Kennedy brothers from former Congressman Charles Kersten. This happened on November 7, 1963. Whether these letters were actually sent is a moot point since they were reported in the press on November 26, 1963 as fact and Kersten must have told the press or somebody else on or before that date. Kersten also testified about these letters to Congress under threat of perjury so this must have happened as stated.

The next previous event in the story was the elaborate scheme to place Lee Harvey Oswald in the company of Valerie Kostikov, the Soviet supervisor of assassinations. This allegedly took place in September, 1963, just prior to the assassination. According to most assassination authors, this meeting was mentioned in a tape-recorded phone call, but it was someone other than Lee Harvey Oswald on the call. That means it was an attempt to frame the Soviets. Kostikov, however, was actually assigned to the Soviet Embassy in Mexico City where the supposed meeting took place, according to the CIA. (see cite Mary Ferrell.org in notes).

The next previous event was the attempt of Senator Thomas Dodd to travel to Germany and interview Stashynsky in person. Dodd was acting Chairman of the Senate Internal Security Subcommittee. We will prove in later chapters that there is hardly any doubt whatsoever that Dodd and his Committee were involved with Oswald and others in the plot to kill JFK. Dodd even tried to get the *German Supreme Court* to travel to the U.S. and tell people about the Stashynsky case. This happened in mid-1963. (The German Supreme Court traveling the U.S.? Give me a break!).

The trial of Stashynsky began October 8, 1962. Unlike in America, under German law the family of a victim has a right to be represented by an attorney at the trial of the criminal, in this case the murderer of the son and husband of the Bandera family. The attorney for the Bandera family was former Congressman Charles Kersten, the same person who sent the letters to the Kennedys two weeks before the assassination. Kersten must have begun his legal relationship with the Bandera family some time before the trial, but after the West Germans decided when (or if) to bring Stashynsky up on charges. And in West German law at the time, the role of the lawyer for the victim's family was on an equal plane with the state prosecutor and made all the same type of arguments prominently before the court and in the record. (see note, Raschhofer).

The next previous event was the press conference where the Soviet Ukrainian defector claimed that Stashynsky was not who he said he was, but rather a Ukrainian provocateur. This was April 2, 1962. This press conference raises a question. If the Stashynsky defection was fake and the product of horse-trading between the KGB, the West German BND and the CIA, would the Soviets have held such a press conference? The other defector besides Stashynsky at the press conference, Osyp Werhun claimed, that Stashynsky was really a specially-trained member of the OUN. Because the Soviets were apparently co-operating in the release of "defector" Stashynsky, this does raise the possibility the Soviets were somehow complicit in the assassination. The Soviets either had foreknowledge of the assassination attempts on Kennedy or they did not. Other than the release of Stashynsky, there is no other evidence that they were involved, so the point may be moot. One could assume that there were at least some officials in the USSR that would have welcomed the disruption of the US government that would have ensued. We will only know that if there is new information released in the years to come.

Stashynsky must have actually been living in the Soviet Union for most or almost all of the time between his alleged affiliation with the KGB in 1950 and his defection on August 12, 1961. The question is, was he living in Moscow or elsewhere or was he actually living all along with his parents in or around Lvov? The Ukraine was part of the Soviet Union. The only people with access to events within the Soviet Union who could inform westerners on that question would be the Soviets or the Ukrainian OUN.

Western reporters could not go into Russia and start asking people questions.

From 1950 to 1953, Stashynsky was an infiltrator into the OUN and acted as an informant to the KGB. Only in 1953 did the KGB begin to train him as a full-time regular agent. So he could easily have actually been a member of the OUN infiltrating the KGB instead of a KGB man infiltrating the OUN. Given his family background in the OUN, one would at least expect a double-agent relationship of some kind.

An online source reports that when Bandera's body was discovered and an autopsy was performed, cyanide was found in his stomach. The gas gun was supposedly used to give a foolproof result in an autopsy which would indicate a heart attack. That ruse didn't work as planned.

Stepan Bandera probably had more people with a motive to murder him than anyone alive. He was controversial, a turncoat, and he was involved with every spy agency in Europe and the U.S. In 1959, a man named Albert Norden published a claim that Bandera was murdered by his assistant during World War II, Theodore Oberlander. Author Norden had some accurate information about Oberlander, specifically that he was the political commander of the "Nightingales," a unit which fought side-by-side with Hitler. According to Norden, Oberlander murdered Bandera because Bandera was ready to tell people about Oberlander's Nazi past. As previously mentioned, this imformation about Oberlander, who was a high West German official, could have been released in a trial which was going on behind the Iron Curtain).

Let's list the problems that author Seth finds with the official "biography" of Stashynsky only found in the legal papers and opinion of the West German Supreme Court:

> 1. According to the Court, the body of Bandera was found to have glass splinters on it from the gas gun used by Stashynsky, even though the gun had been filtered to avoid just such a problem.

> 2. How could Stashynsky have been guilt-wracked young man and also a professional assassin for the KGB (and an up-and-coming agent) for 7 years?

3. Why would the KGB allow Stashynsky to marry someone not well vetted, especially a girl who was, in fact, anti-Communist in her beliefs?

4. Why did Stashynsky supposedly not understand why the Russians would want to murder Bandera and thus come to believe they intended something much bigger? The murder of Bandera would be a huge event. This hinting about an even bigger caper smacks of prior knowledge about the murder of a Western President, i.e.de Gaulle or JFK.

5. Why was Stashynsky not able to recall if he took the elevator in Bandera's apartment when he went up to murder him? This sounds similar to the shoddy reconstruction of the movements of Lee Harvey Oswald in the Texas Book Depository.

6. An online source says that Stashynsky got a glimpse of Bandera's face turning suddenly purple and black. Another website says the victim may appear purple or red as with carbon monoxide poisoning (see notes, Brightview). If the prior victim of Stashynsky, Lev Rebet were poisoned by the same gun, wouldn't his murder have been obvious because he had turned purple?

7. Had the Soviets practiced with the cyanide gun on humans? If they had, Stashynsky would have been told about it. This would have made the Soviets seem even worse. He probably would have informed Western intelligence, but he didn't. This is a major hole in his story.

8. Why would the top men in the Kremlin put their signatures on an award certificate given to a tawdry murderer like Stashynsky. This would put their names in the record for their complicity in his murders. This sounds gratuitous. It would serve no good purpose for these high officials.

9. Why would Stashynsky be studying languages at a Moscow language Institute where the faculty and students knew him to be a KGB agent? Per Seth, this went totally against their policy of secrecy about the nature of the employment of their agents.

10. When Stashynsky defected, why would he still be in possession of false papers which had long ago been superseded? How many different sets of papers would the KGB allow him just to keep around for no apparent reason?

11. Probably most ridiculous claim is the assertion that the Soviets suspected that American intelligence might have murdered his baby in order to lure him into a kidnapping? The CIA was not known to either murder babies or kidnap people. What would the CIA do with him after they kidnapped him? Why would they kidnap him? This claim goes

against everything we know about our own American intelligence. This claim alone proves the false nature of Stashynsky's story.

12. Why did Stashynsky just happen to defect the night before the Berlin Wall went up? Why would a mere operative like him (who was being watched by the KGB around the clock) be warned that the wall was going up? Was it just a coincidence? Did Stashynsky and his wife just get lucky?

13. Why did the KGB blow the surveillance and allow Stashynsky and his wife to disappear into woods behind an apartment? The theory that her parents did not have enough room for them seems very convenient in light of the fact that they wound up staying in a place with woods behind it. Even more convenient was the fact that beyond the woods was a totally secluded wooded avenue which led, essentially, all the way to West Berlin.

14. Was Stashynsky, in the longer term, in the custody of U.S. or West German intelligence? According to one source, he fled to the U.S. following prison, but another source says West German intelligence found him cover in South Africa.

15. If this cyanide gun works as advertised in this case, why haven't we ever heard about it being used elsewhere, either before or since?

The legal case and the written legal opinion of the West German Supreme Court are even more problematic than the alleged facts. The main problems are as follows:

1. Why was the case brought in the West German Supreme Court? For reasons of practicality if nothing else, our own Supreme Court is not the place where a murder case can be initially filed. There are so many murders, that a Supreme Court would be buried in murder cases. Why was the Stashynsky case special?

2. Why did the West German court, according to Seth, depart from their normal practice of avoiding the naming of foreign governments in criminal cases? Courts everywhere have to be following precedents. Why not here?

3. Since Stashynsky had confessed, why was there even a trial or court case? Why wouldn't Stashynsky just issue a guilty plea based on a criminal complaint and appear for sentencing?

4. As asked by Seth, why did the Court describe Stashynsky in such overly favorable terms. We have discussed the fact that the Court was, in part, using the "Nazi" defense, i.e. that a dictatorship had ordered the murder, hence clemency should be exercised. But this

did not require the Court to describe Stashynsky as a nice guy who had just made a mistake and was repentant.

So what can we conclude by putting all these facts on the table? These are the inevitable conclusions:

1. The defection took place August 13, 1961. The obviously false part of the story occurred at that same time. The most fallacious part was the inexplicable granting of Stashynsky the privilege of visiting his in-laws near the border. It also includes the preposterous claim that the CIA may have poisoned the baby. And finally, it also includes the blowing of the surveillance of Stashynsky by the KGB on August 13, 1961.

2. Stashynsky was a member of OUN but he was apparently also working for the KGB. This is born out because no one has claimed that he had any other employment from 1950 to 1961. From 1950 to 1953, he had been a working member of the OUN and also an informant for the KGB, so this implies some sort of double agent status.

3. The Soviet "double defector" Osyp Werhun claimed that Stashynsky was a specially trained OUN agent. This is consistent with the above narrative.

4. The KGB and the West German BND would have certainly had conduits through whom they could exchange information. This is universal intelligence practice, both in the World War II era and since. Stashynsky may have been such a conduit.

5. The information from author Albert Norden which claimed that the Nazi Oberlander had murdered Bandera would have damaged West German credibility in the eyes of the Ukrainians. According to author T. H. Tetens, ex-Nazis were in effective control of West Germany in 1961. Certainly, the head of West German intelligence, General Reinhard Gehlen was an admitted ex-Nazi. If Stashynsky confesses, this cloud is gone. Oberlander was a member of the Bundestag for most of the period 1953 to 1965 and had been held a ministry under Adenauer.

6. West German intelligence (BND) apparently colluded with the KGB to allow Stashynsky to defect and to tell his story. This helped the BND because it removed the idea that an ex-Nazi had murdered Bandera. It helped the Soviets because they knew the BND was possibly going to use Stashynsky to create a cover story for the murder of JFK and/or de Gaulle. This would sew chaos in the Western countries.

7. Former Congressman Charles Kersten became the attorney for the family of Stepan Bandera about this time. We will find out in

the chapter following this one that Kersten had worked in "psychological warfare" in Eisenhower's National Security Council. Kersten was the preeminent American in public-private involvement with Eastern European covert activities. He was totally involved in Eastern Europe from 1946 to 1963 and probably beyond. He was prominently featured in "Anti-Bolshevik Nations" and Ukrainian publications during this entire period. His involvement represents U.S. involvement in the Stashynsky scheme.

8. Since Chancellor Konrad Adenauer was closely involved in all of these operational issues, there could have been many diplomatic favors running from the Germans to the Soviets in payment for their co-operation in the Stashynsky defection. We will never know what they might have been if they in fact went into effect. Some issues on the table at the time were German re-unification, recognition of East Germany by the West, recognition of the Oder-Neisse eastern boundary for Germany and many other issues.

With our analysis of the impending frame-up of the Soviets complete, we can move on to analyze the role of people like Charles Kersten, Reinhard Gehlen, Metropolitan Anastasy, Judge Robert Morris and others who we have already encountered.

In our chapter on factor analysis, we will also prove that between 25% and 30% of all evidence published about the assassination from the Warren Commission forward has been evidence which attempted to frame the Soviets for the JFK murder. Despite this fact, not one single assassination author has implicated the Soviets as a serious theory of the JFK assassination.

Notes:

For the place to find the above headlines and article see: *Ukrainian Bulletin* (January, 1964), p.2, also cited in Scott "Dallas Conspiracy," p. II-31.

The Man Who Knew Too Much, by Dick Russell, p. 594. (*TMWKTM*).

The Executioners: The Story of SMERSH, by Ronald Seth, passim.

Famous Soviet Spies-The Kremlin's Secret Weapon, by U.S. News and World Report and DeWitt Copp, edited by Judy Lowry, p. 98.

Ukrainian Bulletin, Vol. 15, Numbers 9-10, May 15, 1962 to May 15, 1962, p.35.

The citation for the South African newspaper article is: http://www.upi.com/Archives/1984/03/06/South-Africa-gave-a-convicted-KGB-assassin-asylum-and/8880447397200/, accessed 10-17-2016.

The citation for the Kostikov information is: https://www.maryferrell.org/pages/Valeriy_

Kostikov_and_Comrade_Kostin.html

Political Assassination; The Legal Background of the Oberlander and Stashinsky Cases (1964), by Hermann Raschhofer.

For article by Norden about Oberlander, see: http://www.brightreview.co.uk/ARTICLE-Bandera.html

On Stashynsky's face turning purple see: http://www.iwp.edu/news_publications/detail/divide-and-conquer-the-kgb-disinformation-campaign-against-ukrainians-and-jews and also on the issue of turning purple, see: brightview.co.uk.

Chapter 34

SENATOR DODD'S JUVENILE DELINQUENCY COMMITTEE AND OSWALD'S WEAPONS

It seems almost beyond belief that the assassination of a U.S. President could have been planned at least six months in advance, yet kept secret from the press, not to mention being kept secret from the President himself. Yet this is apparently what happened. We know that Lee Harvey Oswald was seen in possession of a gun in his apartment in April, 1963 and the alleged shooting incident involving General Edwin Walker also occurred at that time.

In studying the investigation of mail-order firearms by the Senate Subcommittee on Juvenile Delinquency, it seems apparent that Dodd's committee was in on the pre-planning of the assassination as early as January 1963. It should be noted that Senator Dodd represented Connecticut in which there were several firearms manufacturers including Colt Industries and Sturm and Ruger of Southport, Connecticut.

Senator Dodd chaired the Juvenile Delinquency Subcommittee. In the first half of 1963, there were multiple hearings and dozens of witnesses dealing with the issue of the interstate sale of firearms. There were two officials of the Bureau of Alcohol, Tobacco and Firearms who testified. One was attorney Thurmond Shaw and another was John W. Coggins, Chief of the Technical Branch of the ATTU. (In places, your author has taken license to call the ATTU the ATF since that is the name which it took on very soon after the assassination and most Americans recognize that name for the agency, but not the name ATTU).

One organization which was represented in the course of the hearings was the National Shooting Sports foundation. This organization included 20 manufacturers and importers of guns including Klein's Sporting Goods of Chicago where Oswald allegedly purchased his Mannlicher-Carcano rifle.

For the Senate Juvenile Delinquency Subcommittee, the list of staff included the following:

1. Carl Perian, staff director

2. George Gildea, job description unknown

3. Al Morano, job description unknown

Information supporting the following facts can be found at James Ostrowski, jfkassassinationforum.com. This article by Ostrowski summarizes the relevant facts regarding the hearings on weapons.

The two particular gun mail-order houses Dodd's subcommittee were investigating just happened to be the ones from which Oswald allegedly ordered his two weapons. First, Oswald's Smith and Wesson .38 revolver was ordered from Seaport Traders of Los Angeles and second, his Mannlicher-Carcano carbine was ordered from Klein's of Chicago. The order form for Oswald's pistol was filled out just two days before Dodd's subcommittee began hearings on the matter on January 29, 1963. Such subcommittees used data and statistics in order to determine violations of law. In the case of Seaport Traders in Los Angeles, the Committee was provided with statistics which showed a purchase in Texas made from Seaport Traders. It just so happened that one of the groups being investigated for purchasing firearms illegally was listed in Oswald's address book, which was the American Nazi Party.

By a strange coincidence, one of the investigators looking into these interstate firearms sales was Manuel Pena. Pena was a Los Angeles police Lieutenant who was later to be one of the important police officers tasked with investigating Robert Kennedy's assassination. Pena was able to trace the telescopic sight on Oswald's rifle to a California gun shop. Oswald's rifle was referred to as a Mannlicher-Carcano carbine. As mentioned in the previous paragraph, this rifle was in heavy competition with the products of the old-line weapons manufacturers in the State of Connecticut such as Colt Industries. As Senator from Connecticut, Dodd was the representative of the arms industry in his State in the U.S. Congress.

This connection made by Ostrowski between the purchase of weapons, the American Nazi party and Oswald's address book is significant. Many researchers, including Peter Dale Scott, have stated their belief that the ATTU and weapons purchases were the pretext or cover issue used to disguise the assassination plot as something besides an assassination. Since we have discussed the connection between the American Nazi Party, Dan Burros and Roy Frankhouser, it is possible to speculate that Roy Frankhouser (working for the National Security Council) instructed Dan Burros to contact Oswald and tell him to order a weapon in order to show that a member of the American Nazi Party could legally purchase a gun through the mail. That could explain why Oswald had Burros' name in his address book. Burros, Frankhouser and Oswald could all three have been working as informants at the same time while involved in such a weapons sting.

The hearings on the mail-order weapons in Dodd's committee began within two days of when Oswald filled out the order form for his revolver (although he did not mail the form until about two months later).

In the interest of accuracy, the reference in the hearings to the American Nazi Party was fairly insignificant. It read as follows:

EXHIBIT NO. 13

How To Acquire A Machine gun Legally

Federal laws covering disposal of surplus and "war trophy" machine guns and other automatic weapons have uncomfortable loopholes.

At a recent trial here, Federal Judge Harry C. Westover noted that the "choppers" can be easily obtained by the most irresponsible elements in our society.

The trial involved a former officer of the American Nazi Party, a completely crackpot outfit of homegrown storm troopers who specialize in racial and religious bigotry.

U.S. Treasury agents found a fully operative submachine gun in the local gauleiter's home.

Investigation showed a gun dealer had complied with the law in deactivating the weapon by spot welding the barrel closed before he sold it.

However, the barrel is demountable, and it was a simple matter of the neo-SS type to obtain an operable barrel. Any juvenile gang member with a little imagination and an itch for a big rumble could have done the same thing.

This exhibit was just one of many and there does not seem to be any emphasis on the American Nazi Party per se. The only other reference to the word Nazi was another paragraph which was discussing the importation of Nazi military trophies captured from the Germans during World War II. The emphasis in respect to Nazi's was the suspicion that Nazi's could obtain machine guns or bazookas and not weapons of the type purchased by Oswald.

A very significant exchange occurred in the January 29 hearing. Sergeant K.T. Carpenter, an investigator for the Board of Police Commissioners for the Los Angeles Police Department was giving his testimony.

Senator Dodd: My understanding is that the box of ammunition was shipped [by Seaport Trading of Los Angeles] with it as well [in reference to the pistol that killed a 14-year-old in Fairfax, Virginia].

Sergeant Carpenter: Yes Sir. The box which – this is hearsay on my part, but I was told that one little blank shell you see in there [in an exhibit] was the shot that snuffed out the life of a 14-year-old youth.

Senator Keating: Who got that? Was it another boy?

Sergeant Carpenter: The gun was ordered by a 17-year-old from this company in Los Angeles [Seaport]. The ammunition – I don't know where they got this, probably bought it locally.

Senator Keating: So the ammunition you don't think came from the mail-order house?

Sergeant Carpenter: I doubt that. I don't know.

There doesn't seem to be any information available as to where Lee Harvey Oswald obtained his ammunition. We know that Lee Harvey Oswald was only in possession of four bullets for his rifle. No other bullets were found at the book depository nor at his rooming house, nor at the Paine residence where he was keeping his rifle, according to all the research with which your author is familiar.

Again, no boxes of ammo belonging to Oswald for either gun were ever found anywhere. The four shells found at the scene of the murder of J.D Tipitt were from two different manufacturers. So were the bullets that killed Tipitt. In his questioning of Sergeant Carpenter, Dodd seems to be trying to solve this problem in advance. Dodd tries to put words in the mouth of Carpenter on this issue. He tries to suggest to Carpenter that he should testify that Seaport Traders ships ammunition with the pistols they sell through the mail.

Interestingly, Senator Kenneth Keating steps in and clarifies the issue. Since there has never been any information as to where Oswald bought his ammunition, it looks like this action by Keating signals that he already knew about the pending frame-up of Oswald as of January 29, 1963. We have also seen that it was the absence of Keating from a hearing that caused James O. Eastland a problem with subpoenas in his New Orleans raid on the SCEC carried out in October, 1963. All of this may mean that Keating was the lone dissenter on SISS regarding the approval of JFK's assassination.

In a further exchange:

Senator Dodd: One of these guns by Seaport Traders is the one used by the boy who was killed here?

Sergeant Carpenter: It was from this company on November 17, 1962, ... and sent to Fairfax, Virginia and I believe it was 3 days later the 14-year-old boy was killed.

Senator Dodd: I think it is important that it is in the record. Here is the gun that actually was shipped from California? To this boy in Fairfax, Virginia?

Sergeant Carpenter: Yes, Sir.

Senator Dodd: To this boy in Fairfax, Virginia?

Sergeant Carpenter: Yes, Sir.

Senator Dodd: And they shipped the ammo, too?

Sergeant Carpenter: The ammo was bought locally.

Dodd just doesn't want to give up on this issue of shipping ammunition through the mail. Throughout all the hearings from January to May, 1963, there was not one instance where ammunition was shipped through the mail with the mail-order guns, despite the efforts shown here by Senator Dodd to create such an example. The police were firm on this issue. And it is easy to see why. Shipping ammunition through the mail would be very dangerous should there be a fire at the post office or should a postal truck be involved in a fire or collision. This should be obvious. Dodd, as the leading expert in the Congress on these matters should have known this.

Carl Perian, the investigator for the Senate Juvenile Delinquency Subcommittee, had worked in that job for eleven years. He had served under five chairmen. He was an expert investigator, having investigated among other issues, the trafficking in firearms. Carl Perian had participated in many stings, including some relating to illegal narcotics coming from Mexico. Perian had agreed with Dodd's mutinous staffer, James Boyd, in providing support to the cause of investigating Dodd.

There was a very important connection between the Senate Juvenile Delinquency Subcommittee (a/k/a JDS) and Lee Harvey Oswald's weapons. In that connection, Carl Perian, investigator for the Delinquency Subcommittee, would have been directly in the middle of an apparent weapons sting which framed Oswald. James Boyd stated that when off-microphone, Carl cultivated people who would be called "beatniks," presumably non-conformists. Some of the issues which Perian had investigated would include:

1. narcotics

2. firearms

3. TV portrayals of crime, violence and depravity

4. drug pushing in Aspen, Colorado

5. inadequacy of the Border Patrol

6. corrupt Mexican officials

7. in January, 1964, the motion picture industry portrayal of crime and violence

During the period of January 29, 1963 to May 2, 1963, the JDS conducted a running series of hearings about mail-order weapons as they related to both juveniles and the general public. This testimony came, in part, from the Chief Counsel to the Bureau of Alcohol and Tobacco Tax Division of the U.S. Department of the Treasury (ATTU), John W. Coggins. Another official who testified was Thurmond Shaw, attorney for the

ATTU. The record makes reference to other officials of the ATTU who had provided information in the past and had testified before the committee.

To begin a hearing in May 1963, Senator Dodd made an opening statement. In that statement, he said that police in the District of Columbia reported that one mail-order gun surpasses all others and that is a .22 caliber revolver from Seaport Traders in Los Angeles. Seaport Traders is the firm from which Lee Harvey Oswald purchased his handgun.

We will continue to emphasize this close connection between Dodd's committees and the ATTU. The ATTU, now called the ATF, was a bureau within Treasury as was the Secret Service. Both agencies reported up the chain of command with C. Douglas Dillon, the Treasury Secretary, at the top. This partnership in the mail-order weapons probe would accomplish two things for possible assassination conspirators at Treasury and SISS.

First, it would enable both agencies to cooperate in the setting up of Oswald's alleged murder weapons. Some even suggest that Oswald could have been run as an *informant* for either SISS and/or the ATTU and Treasury. Second, it would provide a cover for both agencies meeting together discreetly. This is something that might otherwise have stood out. Third, it would explain the apparent evidence of complicity in the assassination of the ATTU and Secret Service field agents, but total lack of evidence of complicity of other agencies such as the FBI and State Department.

The testimony in these hearings centered on the use of mail-order weapons in the commission of crimes by juveniles. Just citing one statistic reported by Chief John B Layton of the D.C. police, out of 3000 juvenile arrests in 1962, only 23 involved handgun offenses. When one reads the testimony at the hearings, it is obvious that there were very few juveniles obtaining mail-order weapons, surely not enough to justify months and months of hearings. There were systems in place to prevent this. These systems for identification and proof of age were apparently functioning quite well. And the recommendations from the hearings suggested few if any changes to mail-order firearms laws and procedures would be necessary.

The actual weapons venders who were being investigated crossed the entire gamut of mail-order vendors. The weapons vendors allegedly used by Lee Harvey Oswald were not necessarily singled out in the statistics, but the name "Seaport Traders" was the only one actually emphasized by the Senators in their questioning. Seaport Traders was where Oswald got his pistol. Also, in his questioning, Dodd tried to insinuate that ammunition was sold through the mail to accompany the weapons. This suggestion was strongly denied by the witnesses. As stated previously, apparently Dodd wanted to create a false narrative which would explain how Oswald obtained his ammunition, a fact which has never been made clear ever since the assassination.

In the summer of 1963, JDS investigated "cherry bomb" firecrackers and also "M-80's" and [Dodd then] called Carl Perian and told him to stop investigating illegal fireworks manufacturers. Apparently, Thomas Dodd would begin to investigate a problem industry such as, say, firearms, fireworks or TV violence. He would then accept payoffs from those industries to quell any further investigation.

The investigator for the Subcommittee on Juvenile Delinquency was Carl Perian. He was the investigator for this Subcommittee at the time when the weapons of Lee Harvey Oswald were purchased, and they were possibly purchased either by Oswald, Perian or someone else in connection to an investigation of this Juvenile Delinquency Committee. It is absolutely necessary to the understanding of what would have transpired regarding the Oswald weapons to realize that Perian was constantly involved in sting operations on behalf of Dodd. The methods and experience of the team of Dodd and Perian can shed some light on the sources of information and the types of investigations and stings which they used in their pursuit of better legislation.

In *Timothy Leary: A Biography*, by Robert Greenfield, the author details the actual conflict between then-Senator Robert Kennedy of New York and Dodd centering around this LSD issue. Robert Kennedy chaired the Subcommittee on the Executive Reorganization of the Senate Committee on Government Operations. Dodd was still chairman of his Senate Subcommittee on Juvenile Delinquency. Leary's testimony before Dodd's Subcommittee was arranged by Dodd's long-time investigator Carl Perian. Perian then told Leary that Senator Edward Kennedy would be flying to Washington for the hearings. Edward Kennedy in fact appeared and got into an intense discussion with Leary about the positives and negatives of LSD.

In *Fear and Loathing in America: The Brutal Odyssey of an Outlaw Journalist* by Hunter S. Thompson, there is a reference to Carl Perian as an advocate of issues in the gun possession debate in 1969. In discussing a possible gun debate the author says "Carl Perian would be better: the truth is not in him; he's so crooked that he has to screw his pants on in the morning." His number one assistant was Gene Gleason, "the old *World-Telegram* crime-buster." The author also mentions Senator Joseph Tydings of Maryland as also interested in this controversy.

In the magazine *Boating* Jan-June 1976, the following information appeared:

"Rep. John M. Murphy (D. N.Y) a member of the House Committee on Merchant Marine and Fisheries Committee and its Subcommittee on Coast Guard and Navigation, became interested in these reports [on particular boats] and sent congressional investigator Carl Perian to work. Perian's sleuthing uncovered several possibly drug-related incidents, enough to convince Rep. Murphy that a real problem existed." Perian turned up 611 missing pleasure boats, probably used in the drug trade."

In *The Snail Darter and the Dam: How Pork-Barrell Politics Endangered a Little Fish and Killed a River,* by Zygmunt Jan Broel Platter, the author stated "Murphy's Chief Aide, Carl Perian ... when I'd asked about signing onto a GAO request [said] "what's in it for Murphy?" he asked. "He typically gets something when he does people favors." Representative John D. Murphy (D, NY) was widely rumored to be taking bribes." As this quote shows, Carl Perian in 1978 was still actively involved in Congressional investigating.

Notes:

The record of the hearings were published in part as: Report from the Subcommittee To Investigate Juvenile Delinquency of the Committee on the Judiciary, United States Senate, Eighty-Eighth Congress, First Session, Part 14, "Interstate Traffic in Mail-Order Firearms, January 29 and 30; March 7, and May 1 and 2, 1963, Washington DD."

Cited as Ostrowski in the text is: James Ostrowski,2-2015, [www.jfkassasinationforum.com/indexphp?topic=9161;wap2)].

On Timothy Leary, see: *Timothy Leary: A Biography,* Robert Greenfield.

Fear and Loathing in America: The Brutal Odyssey of an Outlaw Journalist, Hunter S. Thompson.

Boating, Jan-June 1976.

The Snail Darter and the Dam: How Pork-Barrell Politics Endangered a Little Fish and Killed a River, Zygmunt Jan Broel Platter.

Chapter 35

GENERAL JULIUS KLEIN

In the interest of objectivity, our discussion of General Julius Klein begins with some excellent objective biographical information about him written by author Shlomo Shafir in his book *Ambiguous Relations: The American Jewish Community and Germany Since 1945.* Shafir is an expert on American-Jewish-German-Israeli relations post WWII. His writing is devoid of any sensational information on either side of this controversial topic. He describes General Julius Klein and his activities as beginning in the mid-1950s.

Per Shafir, Klein was hired by West Germany (FRG) in an effort to improve the image of the FRG in the eyes of Jewish-Americans. Klein began in 1953 to work for the return of assets confiscated from Germany due to the war. He was involved in these issues for the next 15 years.

Klein had contacts among Democrats and Republicans, although his personal affiliation was Republican. He quickly gained the support of German Chancellor Konrad Adenauer and remained a permanent proponent of the leadership of Adenauer. In 1954 Klein served as a consultant for a committee of the Senate on military issues. Next he became a lobbyist for German industrial concerns. Israeli leaders were grateful for the benefits he tried to obtain for Israel although not all American Jews liked him.

Klein's family came to the U.S. from Germany in 1848. Although Klein was born 53 years later in 1901, he attended school in Berlin before World War I. In 1917, he volunteered to join the U.S. Army and after the war, he served as a menial member of the U.S. German military mission. Like so many other figures associated with the JFK assassination, there is a question as to why his family would send him to school in Berlin and did this represent divided loyalties between Germany and the U.S.? Or did his family have a special pipeline to business interests in Germany after 53 years in America?

According to Shafir, Klein was involved in spying on pro-Nazi groups in the U.S., which would be odd for a Jew given the principles of the Nazi party ever since at least 1923. Did he have business contacts in Germany that he used for this? Was he one of those Jews who for some reason assisted Hitler and the Nazis (or pretended to) for profit? The answers to these questions are unknown.

Klein served in the Army again in WWII in the Pacific and after the war, took charge of the Jewish War Veterans, an organization started in

1896 by Jewish veterans of the Civil War. Immediately after the war, he opposed leniency for Nazi war criminals but later reversed his opinion.

Klein started out defending a Nazi sympathizer named Friedrich Middelhauve. Klein arranged for Middlehauve to meet prominent American Jews on a trip to the U.S. in 1955. As of 1955, Klein was making frequent trips to Germany and meeting not only regularly with Adenauer but also Secretary of State Hans Globke, draftsman of the Nazi-era Nuremberg Laws which sealed the fate of German Jews.

Klein performed a valuable service for Israel in arranging for Adenauer to meet with Israeli diplomats and in 1965, helping arrange for then-Chancellor Ludwig Erhard to extend diplomatic relations to Israel. At this time, Klein admitted that he was working for the CIA but he claimed he didn't tell the CIA anything that he learned about Israel.

There were a number of things about Klein that some American Jews did not appreciate. Klein arranged for a change to the Trading With The Enemy Act which allowed the return of frozen assets to Germany. He represented a company named Rheinmetal, which had used Jewish slave labor under Hitler and refused compensation, reparations or indemnification.

Klein, a Republican, was disliked by both the Truman and the Kennedy Administrations. Kennedy especially disliked Klein because of his extremely close relationship to Adenauer. Adenauer opposed JFK's attempts to achieve a better relationship with the U.S.S.R. It is at this point that author Shafir breaks off his discussion of Klein. This was when Klein's pro-German activities almost certainly involved him in the plot to murder Kennedy, which is a topic that Shafir would never touch in his wildest dreams because of his policy of neutrality on German-American-Jewish issues.

Shafir does mention, however, that Klein was called before the Senate Foreign Relations Committee which, among other reasons, caused the German ambassador and Foreign Secretary to distance themselves somewhat from Klein, at least in official situations.

The perception of General Julius Klein varies dramatically depending on the perspective one takes on the issues at stake in the 1950's and 1960's. The biographer of Senator Thomas J. Dodd, James Boyd, presents Klein in a negative light, but in the end dismisses him as a hapless and harmless con man.

As presented by author Shafir, Klein was disliked by the Truman and Kennedy administration. By omission, Shafir implies that Klein was fine with the Eisenhower administration. This would not be surprising since Klein was an active Republican.

In *Above The Law*, Boyd also explores the background of Julius Klein from his own close-up perspective. Boyd, however, treats Klein in an enigmatic fashion. According to Boyd, Klein was surrounded by evidence of possible connections to the U.S. Joint Chiefs of Staff and the German

High Command. Klein had on display pictures of himself with Generals Eisenhower and MacArthur. His chief American public relations client was the whiskey baron Lou Rosenstiel.

Boyd described Klein as being served by a staff of military men. But what exactly was the role of these military men? It is an established fact that the P.R. firm partner of Klein was General Kenneth Buchanan, also of the Illinois National Guard. In Senate hearings Klein also divulged a relationship with retired Army General John B. Medaris. Boyd does provide names, however, of the military men to whom he refers. Boyd describes how Klein directed an important public relations firm which had offices in Frankfurt, Chicago, Los Angeles, New York and Washington.

But was this an actual firm with real clients? Boyd treats Klein as a phony and a buffoon. From other sources we can learn that Klein was anything but a buffoon. It seems very unlikely that Ethics Committee chairman John Stennis, a veteran and high-ranking member of the Senate would focus the proceedings in the Dodd investigation on General Julius Klein if he were merely a buffoon. This would be a complete waste of time and we know that for Senators, their time is precious because of all the demands of their office.

Boyd claims that Klein was a very lowly employee in relations with the U.S. Army, the General Staff, the movie industry, and had a minor role in the Illinois Republican party. Boyd also reports that Klein was booted out of the Illinois National Guard, with his commanding officer explaining that he considered Klein a "dangerous man."

Boyd relates that each time Julius Klein crossed the Atlantic, it was aboard the liner *United States*, and he occupied the stateroom reserved for the Duke and Duchess of Windsor. It seems from circumstances, that Klein was averse to air travel. Did Boyd mean to imply anything special by his mention of the Duke and Duchess of Windsor (since they were felt to be Nazi-sympathetic by some historians)?

Could the income from a public relations firm with five offices produce enough income for Julius Klein to be spending like this? Boyd continues, recounting the background and resumé of Klein as put forth by Klein and his associates. According to that narrative, General Klein had various and sundry positions and accomplishments, dating from World War I and forward.

According to Klein, he began as a thirteen year-old war correspondent in Germany. At seventeen, Klein was a soldier in World War I. At age eighteen, he had been part of the entourage of Colonel Edward M. House, who was almost the one and only advisor to Woodrow Wilson at the Treaty of Versailles following World War I. Then he was part of the United States Military Commission in Berlin. During the Capone era in Chicago, he was an editor for the Hearst newspapers. Then he became a

Washington correspondent. In the 1930's he became a Hollywood executive, earning as much as $75,000 annually. In World War II, he commanded troops in the Pacific Theater. He originated the Defense Department's first anti-subversion program. Then he was an officer on the General Staff, and an advisor to Congress on the subject of the Cold War. Then he became an author of important books and a Republican Candidate for the Senate from Illinois in 1950. Finally, as mentioned by author Shlomo Shafir, Klein was chosen as the National Commander of the Jewish War Veterans organization, which boasted 100,000 members and commanded a great deal of political leverage.

At this point in our narrative, it should be noted that the name Julius Klein prominently appears in the iconic journal article in the Executive Intelligence Review entitled "*Permindex: Britain's International Assassination Bureau,* by Jeffrey Steinberg and David Goldman. As mentioned in the discussion of Lyndon LaRouche, Steinberg and Goldman were security officers for LaRouche. They researched and wrote articles for *EIR,* and those on the subject of the assassination of President John F. Kennedy in particular. Although Julius Klein is not mentioned in the *Torbitt Document,* he is featured prominently by *EIR* and assigned major blame for the JFK assassination.

The problem with that fact is that there was a policy on the part of LaRouche to blame Jews whenever and wherever possible. On top of that, the *EIR* and LaRouche also falsely blame Britain for everything under the sun. In the article in *EIR,* Julius Klein is described as serving at some time prior to 1981 and prior to his retirement as the manager of the Swiss-Israel Trade Bank and as such was involved with British-Israeli-Mossad activities.

The above article also claims that Julius Klein was involved after 1922 with British Intelligence operations in the U.S. under Sir William Wiseman. Wiseman was a partner in the Jewish investment bank Kuhn, Loeb in New York. Next the *EIR* links Klein to the British spy agency the S.O.E., which was the equivalent of the American CIA. The above article also links Klein to FBI Division Five (the counter-intelligence department of the FBI). This Division Five connection is named by the above article as well as by the infamous "Torbitt Document" as being at the middle of the JFK assassination plot although Torbitt does not mention Klein.

Further, the article claims that Julius Klein created the Jewish War Veterans organization and that the same organization would be used as a front for the intelligence activities of Sir William Stephenson, the top British spy in the United States and Canada during and following World War II. As mentioned in a prior paragraph, the Jewish War Veterans organization was actually created in 1896 by veterans of the Civil War.

The article in *EIR* quoted above also says that, in 1948, Klein along with a group of right-wing American Jews, founded an organization called the American Jewish League Against Communism. The authors cite "strong circumstantial evidence" that the League was from the very beginning, a mere front for the combined FBI Division 5-British SOE (special operations) activities of the period. It is a fact that records of both FBI division five *and* the British SOE have by some co-incidence been sealed ever since World War II and remain so at the date of this writing.

The *EIR* also cites as further proof of their theory of the assassination, the involvement of a long-term crony of J. Edgar Hoover named Lewis Rosensteil. The *EIR* authors describe Rosenstiel as a "famous bootlegger" and that Rosenstiel provided a part of the funds to set up the organization.

EIR reports that, as if all the above were not enough, Julius Klein was credited as being the recruiter for the Permindex organization, of which Clay Shaw was an officer and board member. Clay Shaw was, of course, the defendant in the New Orleans prosecution by Jim Garrison in the Kennedy assassination conspiracy. Garrison did not mention Permindex in his 1970 book but did mention it five times in his second book written in 1988.

So this is a capsule summary of the career and activities of General Julius Klein.

Notes:

Ambiguous Relations: The American Jewish Community and Germany Since 1945 (1999) by Schlomo Shafir.

Above The Law: The rise and fall of Senator Thomas J. Dodd (1968) by James Boyd.

Executive Intelligence Review entitled "Permindex: Britain's International Assassination Bureau," by Jeffrey Steinberg and David Goldman dated 11-14-81.

Chapter 36

GENERAL JULIUS KLEIN APPEARS BEFORE THE FULBRIGHT FOREIGN RELATIONS COMMITTEE

In mid-1963, the Senate Foreign Relations Committee began hearings on "The Activities Of Nondiplomatic Representatives Of Foreign Principals In The United States." According to the official version the Foreign Relations Committee under J. William Fulbright decided to issue a report on the work of 411 companies that were affiliated as "foreign agents" with foreign governments in the U.S.A. Ostensibly, the biggest problem with these agents involved the "Sugar Lobby," which arranged for increases in price supports on sugar to the detriment of the U.S. national interest.

But in an important article in the German newsmagazine *Der Spiegel* on October 4, 1963, the hearings were discussed from the perspective of the West German Government. This article states that General Julius Klein's enemies in the Foreign Office "created the impression" that the hearings were directed at him. Based on the retrospective importance of these hearings as they applied to Klein, it would have been very easy to create such an impression, given the crucial situation with U.S.-German relations and the role played in this situation by General Klein.

In fact, the hearings were conducted, in the opinion of this researcher, in an attempt to derail what was known to Fulbright as an ongoing plot to murder the President. Many of the sessions were chaired by committee member Frank Church, who twelve years later would become an arch-enemy of the CIA and the intelligence community in general. This investigation looks in hindsight to be a foretaste of that 1975 confrontation between Church and the CIA.

Another excellent source on the Fulbright investigation of General Klein is a master's thesis in 1967 by Louis J. Haugh.

Although the biographer of Senator Thomas Dodd, James Boyd, describes General Klein as a small-time con artist, this characterization is patently absurd. The article in *Der Spiegel* describes Klein as the West German "shadow ambassador." He was also known in Germany as "foreign agent 975." He was, according to *Der Spiegel*, "the long-serving Shadow Ambassador of the Federal Republic of Germany in the United States."

As mentioned above, author Shlomo Shafir does mention that Klein was called before the Senate Foreign Relations Committee. Shafir, like other writers, admits that these hearings affected Klein and his relations with West Germany. It caused the German ambassador and Foreign Secretary to distance themselves somewhat from Klein, at least in official situations.

So exactly what was Klein's relationship with West Germany and what was Fulbright seeking in his investigation? In registering as a foreign agent, Klein identified his foreign client as Deutsch-Americanische Ausammerarbeit (German-American Cooperation), a group formed to promote the common cause of German-American cooperation. Klein claimed that he did not know who was contributing the $125,000 to $150,000 per year which his contract required.

Klein, in fact, had another German client, The Cologne Society. (Haugh, p. 101). For this society, Klein lobbied for the recovery of property seized by the United States in World War II.

The Fulbright Committee pressed Klein to reveal the names of the group members who were promoting German-American relations, which was also called the Foerderkreis (Society for the Promotion...). It was discovered that Klein wrote speeches for members of Congress that were delivered on the floor of the House without disclosure that Klein had written them.

In his testimony regarding his activities, Klein said "we also arrange proper reception for important German political, civic or business leaders who visit the U.S. and vice-versa."

When asked by the Chairman, "Who do you represent?" Klein responded "the Foerderkreis fur Deutsch-Americanische Zusammenarbeit." Klein stated that most of the members of the Cologne Society were members of the Society for the Protection of Foreign Investments. The Chairman said that on April 6, 1960, "you [Klein] filed as representing German industrialist and civic leaders. Correct?" Ans: "Yes"

Per the Chairman, "Your filing stated that the identity of your foreign principals would be provided at a later date. That was two years ago. Were they?" Ans: "I dealt with only two people – Dr. Hempel and the Frankfurter Bank. The head of the Frankfurter Bank was head of the Foerderkreis."

Klein: "the names of some [of the industrialists who Klein represented] are Brentano, Mende, Erhard, Altmeier, Social Democrats..."

Author T.H. Tetens, in *The New Germany and the Old Nazis* states "Large sections of the German press, stirred by the propaganda in the SS paper, *Wiking-Ruf,* and the *Deutsche Soldaten Zeitung,* launched an attack against the allies. Roosevelt and Churchill were almost daily branded as the real war criminals. Bundestag member Dr. Erich Mende, an influential politician in the Adenauer coalition, demanded the ultimate 'release of all war criminals…whose acts were in no way different from those committed by the U.N. troops in Korea.'"

Chairman: "Who is Mende?" Klein: "He is chairman of the present Free Democratic Party in Germany and a former top industrialist, attorney for some industrial clients we have…I know Dr. Mende quite well, I know him many, many years, he was one of my close friends when I was still on active duty in Germany, and I gave Dr. Mende a reception and a dinner in my own home in Chicago, and I was here when he was in Washington. He was the official guests of – I mean he came here officially in behalf of his party which is the coalition party of Chancellor Adenauer."

Chairman: In a memo dated 7/24/62, it says "General Klein suggested to ask Senators Humphrey and Javits to invite Erhard to make speeches."

Chairman: In a memo dated January 28, 1961, from Julius Klein to Heinrich von Brentano, "I recommend you visit Washington and also visit with Humphrey, Bridges and Javits."

Klein: "I am always accused of being a representative working for the return of confiscated German property which is not true and that I am a front for IG Farben [an accusation made by Senator Smathers in an op-ed] which is also not true."

Chairman: Quoting from the Frankfurt Bank letter which says "we are pleased to confirm that we act as payees for you in regard to any and all fees paid to you in the Federal Republic of Germany in connection with your P.R. work, activities or related orders – such payments com in from circles of trade or industry and through the Deutsche Bundesbank for account of Government Offices."

Some money which was received by the Frankfort Bank was used to pay off loans that the Frankfort Bank had made to Julius Klein, in effect transferring money to Klein for his services.

Chairman Church: The money apparently came "for account of government offices."

Chairman: This must mean for the FRG government.

Klein: I don't know what that means and haven't been able to find out."

Chairman Church: I am asking, did Justice [department] write you a letter asking you to itemize your expenses and disclose your principals?

Klein: My contract with Mannesmann Co. I had that client for 10 years … I represented Schenley for many years and the income was more than this year $150,000 or $160,000.

On page 1909 of the hearings, the following heading appears:

LETTERS AND DRAFT RESOLUTION CONCERNING GERMAN REUNIFICATION

Letters on May 14, 1962 from Julius Klein to Hon. Thomas Dodd and Senator Scott. Letter from Julius Klein to Dodd "DRAFT OF PROPOSED RESOLUTION" Welcoming the statement of the Chairman of the Council of Ministers of the USSR before the Senate Foreign Relations Committee of September 16, 1959 "On March 5, 1960 the above chairman said in Moscow (the right of self-determination of all peoples) approving of the above chairman as expressed at the Geneva Summit July, 1955 that the four powers be charged with 'principles regarding German Re-unification.'" "Requesting a plebiscite in East Germany as to whether the East Germans want to be under the USSR, be independent, or join West Germany."

Chairman: Is this resolution made [drafted] in pursuance of your employment by a foreign principal?

Klein: No. It's only my point of view.

Chairman: Does that letter in any way indicate it is being submitted by a registered agent of a foreign principal? Was this letter introduced in the Senate by either Senator Dodd or Senator Scott?

Klein: I really do not know, Senator.

To-do list from Julius Klein Public Relations, which describes the upcoming agena of the P.R. firm:

1. Start a stream of cablegrams to German former Foreign Minister Heinrich von Brentano from Senators Hruska, Kefauver, Javits, Dodd and Bridges. Dirksen and Morton have declined for political reasons.

2. Work on a Cuban deal.

3. [deleted]

4. [deleted]

5. [deleted]

6. [deleted]

7. Work on Uberseebericht [Oversees Report] items.

8. We are working on getting a JFK appointee to the U.S. Advisory Commission on Information.

9. Office details.

10. Service Operations.

11. As you know, General Buchanan [Klein's assistant] is also busy with Hispano-Suiza, Mannesman, working on Rheinmetall and sometimes calls on us to assist him with Lionel.

12. We have made a $31,000 per year proposal to the Government of Pakistan.

Chairman: What was the "Cuban deal?"

Farkas [Farkas is the Julius Klein P. R. firm bookkeeper who was also a witness]: The deal in this memo was with Cuban refugees who approached us to help them against Castro.

Klein: I will say that at the same time, we were offered a contract…
for a P.R. job for the Dominican Republic but I turned it down because it
was headed by a dictator.

"Proposal for Group Protest of Cuban Confiscation of Property."

Chairman: Then it was not the refugees [in re Cuba] but the return
of [Cuban] property?

Klein: Both.

Chairman: Tell us, how did you assist the public relations for Mr. Nixon?

Klein: I gave advice to Nixon not to accept the TV debate because it
would give Kennedy (an unknown) free TV time. Also, JFK was imma-
ture and lacking the needed experience for the office of President.

Next in the record was a transcription of an interview with Julius
Klein in the Armed Forces Network, Europe, December 3, 1960 presented by correspondent Bill Marsh. In the interview, Klein relates that Under
Secretary of State for Political Affairs C. Douglas Dillon and Treasury Secretary Robert Anderson, both in the Eisenhower Administration, went to
Germany in an attempt to get $600 M in troop support [from West Ger-
many] only to be refused because people in Germany would think they
were paying for foreign occupation of their country.

In an inter-office memo of 12-21-61, it is stated "we are working on
pulling strings to get Julius Klein appointed to the U.S. Advisory Commission on Information."

Chairman: Were those who proposed you for this told of your status
as a foreign agent?

Klein: Yes, those who proposed me starting with Speaker of the House
John W. McCormack. I would have gotten the post, but it was filled by
Robert Kennedy's own public relations man.

At page 1941 appears a letter inviting German Ambassador Karl
Heinrich Knappstein and Dr. and Mrs. George A. Federer to a dinner "Salute to Senator Javits."

Chairman: Is making political contributions to Senators part of your
work for your foreign principals?

Klein: I paid from my personal money.

Senator Gore: How many tickets did you buy?

Klein: I bought a whole table.

Senator Gore: Would you say your are a rich man?

Klein: A well-to-do man, Senator. I was an editor for Mr. Hearst. I
was a story editor for Universal Studios and RKO studios. I used to make
$50,000 to $75,000 per year.

On pages 1951 to 1957 are miscellaneous auditing and expense items
regarding work done for Daimler-Benz AG, Mannesman.

Then follows this quote: "Send copies of this to branches marked
confidential. Now send Hoppe same letter re Medaris we wrote to oth-

ers, as he hopes that Medaris will visit Stuttgart and if you have already written Hitzinger on Medaris, then all you need to do is to send copies to Hoppe…also, they have been selling engines to the Army and Navy, especially the Navy and that would be something for Washington and strictly confidential; they also hope to make a deal with Boeing on missile program."

Memo from [General Kenneth] Buchanan to Klein in re Mannex. Mannex was a Julius Klein client which was seeking defense contracts. Mannex was a wholly-owned subsidiary of Mannesmann [a large German company].

RECEIPT OF FEES FROM THE FEDERAL REPUBLIC

Chairman: You mentioned earlier that you advised Chancellor Adenauer many times; you are a very good friend of his, did you not?

General Klein: I said I am a very good friend of his. I didn't say I advised him. I am a very good friend of his.

Chairman: You said you advised him.

General Klein: No; I would feel very flattered, and I hope he takes my suggestions, but I wouldn't say I advised him.

Chairman: Were you in any way reimbursed for this advice?

General Klein: I was not.

Chairman: And it is quite clear—I want the record to show that you testified that you have not received any funds any fees from the Government of West Germany?

General Klein: I didn't testify to this, Mr. Chairman.

Chairman: Well, let's make it clear, then.

General Klein: "…to the best of my knowledge, they do contribute, on the contrary."

Chairman: Oh, they do?

General Klein: But I have no evidence for it … they are contributing and subsidizing a lot of these funds like our own United States is doing in Europe, too. Our own Government has the largest group of foreign agents in foreign countries. They are doing the same thing.

Chairman: Do you have any evidence for that?

General Klein: I just happen to know it. You mentioned before the U.S. Trade Center yourself, Mr. Chairman. I tried to get the public relations for it. An Italian public relations man got it in Rome. The people in Germany don't know [that the U.S. Government funds certain groups]. I mean for Amerika House.

At page 1994: A letter to J.W. Fulbright from Frederick G. Dutton, Assistant Secretary of State, concerning the identity of German principals of Julius Klein. "Inquiries in Bonn and Dusseldorf indicate little or no awareness of the organization 'Foerderkreis Fur Deutsch-Amerikanische

Zusammenarbeit." [literally Society for Germany and America Working Together]. The board of directors:

1. Secretary-General' Dr. Gerhard Hempel.

2. Dr. Walter L. Leiske, Deputy Mayor of Frankfurt, 1948-1959.

3. Toby E. Rodes, former U.S. Embassy employee in Bonn; European executive of Knoll International, a U.S.-owned firm with an office in New York, a resident of Basel Switzerland.

4. Dr. Othmar Zeigler, an associate of Max Klein, brother of Julius Klein, Director of European Operations for Exchange National Bank of Chicago with offices in Frankfurt, a partner in Banking House of Hermann and Hauswedell, Hamburg, Germany 1953-1956 and executive manager Deutsche Transport Bank, Frankfurt, 1955-1957, born in Britain in 1896 and holds a British passport and is married and holds a U.S. Visa.

5. Udo Boeszoermeny, full partner in finance brokering from Deutsche Kredit Versicherung in Duesseldorf.

6. Dr. Paul Schroeder, director of a medical co-operative bank (Deutsche-Apotheker & Aerzt Bank).

It is clear from all the above information that when Senator Dodd's biographer James Boyd characterizes Klein as a buffoon and an incompetent con man, that Boyd is dissembling in a major way. General Julius Klein was deeply involved with the relationship between the U.S. and Germany and was operating in an out-of-control manner. It's no stretch to suggest that he was probably involved with bribing Senators and that he was also working directly for the faction in Germany graphically described by author T.H. Tetens in *The New Germany and the Old Nazi's*. These were former Nazis or pro-Nazis such as Ludwig Erhard, Gerhardt Schroeder, Hans Globke and Heinrich von Brentano. We will see the rest of this sordid arrangement unfold in the hearings before the Senate Ethics Committee on the matter of the Censure of Senator Thomas J. Dodd. It is the strong belief of this author that Klein and Dodd were involved in the procurement of the assassination of President John F. Kennedy with the aid and comfort of key persons in the Government of the FRG, West Germany.

Notes:

For the citation for the hearing on General Klein, see the following publication: Activities of Non-diplomatic Representatives of Foreign Principals in the U.S. : hearings before the United States Senate Committee on Foreign Relations, Eighty-Eighth Congress, first session. PT.1-13 by United States. Congress. Senate. Committee on Foreign Relations. Published 1963.

Der Spiegel, October 4, 1963, see: http://www.spiegel.de/spiegel/print/d-45143029.html [retrieved 09-25-2017 by author].

See the following unpublished Master's Degree thesis at the University of Wisconsin-Madison: *A History of the Foreign Agents Registration Act of 1938 and the Role of Public Relations Representatives Serving Foreign Clients* by Louis J. Haugh, University of Wisconsin--Madison, 1967.

Cited in text is: *The New Germany and the Old Nazis,* by T.H.Tetens, p. 100.

Chapter 37

GENERAL JULIUS KLEIN AND THE DODD CENSURE INVESTIGATION

Immediately prior to the 1964 Senatorial election, Dodd's own staff began to covertly investigate him for corrupt financial practices. By December, 1964, the staff had proven that Dodd had siphoned off $200,000 from the campaign for his personal use. Around the same time, Dodd's relationship with other Senators began to suffer.

In *Above The Law*, James Boyd involves the Senate Internal Security Subcommittee counsel Julian G. Sourwine in questionable activities. Boyd relates that Sourwine wrote a bad check in Las Vegas for $2500 and was able to ask Senator Dodd to cover the bad check as a loan. Boyd characterized the transaction as a shakedown of Dodd by Sourwine because the loan was never intended to be repaid. Boyd infers that Sourwine had something to hold over the head of Dodd. In light of the Dodd staff mutiny and the prior statements about Kennedy on the part of Senator Dodd, the most obvious theory would be that Sourwine knew something about Dodd and the JFK assassination. That act [the assassination] was in all likelihood at least in part, the dirty-work of SISS and would have involved more than any other two persons, cooperation between Dodd the chairman and Sourwine the chief counsel.

Senator Dodd encountered problems in his relations with the U.S. Senate. In 1967 Dodd became the first Senator censured since Joseph McCarthy in 1954. Dodd was one of only six people censured by the Senate in the 20th century. After Dodd's pursuit of gun restrictions, the outraged firearms industry, which Dodd represented, also, along with Dodd's staff, Drew Pearson and the Ethics Committee, investigated Dodd for misbehavior. The resulting censure was a condemnation of Dodd and a finding that he had converted campaign funds to his personal accounts and spent the money.

In fact, when one reads the testimony in the Dodd censure hearings, there is very little regarding his financial dealings. In fact, the only overt mention of any financial misdeed centered on a certain oriental rug which Dodd and his wife were given by a lobbyist. This lone rug would be a thin pretext for which to censure a Senator.

The testimony in the censure hearing in fact focused on Dodd's mysterious relationship with West German public relations representative Julius

Klein. The Senate Ethics Committee believed that Klein had some strong but invisible power over Dodd, almost describing Klein's power as suggesting blackmail of some kind. Klein was sometimes labeled, in effect, a lobbyist for the West German Government and German private interests.

Klein had enmeshed Dodd with German individuals living in Germany. Klein had insisted on Dodd making a trip to Germany just before November 22, 1963. At the time, there was some (possibly minor) tension between West Germany and the U.S. over the issue of NATO. Some evidence suggests that the West German connection with Dodd was made up of "bankers," other evidence points to "industrialists." Still others would emphasize relations with Adenauer and von Brentano, the German Secretary of State. Also, the case of Stashynsky, the Soviet defector, assassin and spy was involved. Dodd was to gather information over in Germany about Stashynsky. There was at least one accused former Nazi V.I.P. for whom Klein was advocating in the U.S. The true nature of Dodd's relationship with the diverse West German interests was explored but never explained or solved.

In hearings before the Senate Ethics Committee in November 1966, it came to light that Dodd employed over forty members of his various staffs. The Senate censure investigation focused mostly on Klein.

It is here that the facts regarding Julius Klein were obviously misrepresented by Dodd's biographer James Boyd. It is the opinion of this author that Boyd essentially admits that the mutiny of Dodd's employees was inspired by the knowledge that Dodd was involved in the Kennedy assassination. Dodd's staff staged their investigation of Dodd's finances out of a true motive of revenge against Dodd for his inexcusable complicity in a murder and a desire on their part to avoid suspicion of their own complicity in the JFK assassination.

The Boyd information involves a common strategy of authors writing about the JFK assassination. Let's take for example, *The Ordeal Of Otto Otepka*, by William J. Gill. It is the opinion of this author that Gill had inside knowledge of the true assassination conspirators in real time. Yet in his book about Otto Otepka there is only one reference to any theory which could be taken to explain the truth of what happened to JFK. That theory, per Gill, was that Kennedy had ordered the destruction of certain nuclear facilities in China, and that the Soviets had therefore ordered JFK killed. But author Gill then explains that even Otto Otepka didn't necessarily believe that story. In his book, Gill sets out the entire sequence of events regarding the assassination. But to protect himself, he leaves out the smoking-gun evidence. Hence, the reader has to bring to Boyd's book a background knowledge of the facts to complete the picture. This gets authors Boyd and Gill off the hook for possibly spilling sensitive national security information. Thus Boyd and Gill are protected from punishment for "spilling the beans."

Boyd pointedly mentions that Dodd essentially cheered the death of JFK. (Boyd in *ATL*, p. 106). Taking that fact as truth, there must have been a whole bunch of related background facts known to Boyd which he did not present in his biography of Dodd.

To explain away the role of Julius Klein in the Dodd story, Boyd tried to portray Klein as a buffoon.

Putting two plus two together, combining the information in the *Executive Intelligence Review* article cited above together with the information from the Dodd hearings on censure and Boyd's biography, the bottom line was that Julius Klein was primarily a "bag man." In other words, his main role was in bribery and laundering money. Permindex, with which Klein had been associated, was primarily a complex money-laundering appartus for Germany, ex-Nazis, Italian fascists, the CIA and similar interests. And Boyd recounts that Klein moved around carrying thousands of dollars in cash on his person and delivering envelopes full of cash to members of Congress. One of the Senators who used his Essex House suite had appointed him for a time to the staff of a Senate committee, so he could travel to Europe with official credentials.

Senator John Stennis, the chairman of the Senate Ethics Committee investigating Dodd asked the most important question. What kind of influence did Klein seem to have over Dodd, considering the abusive tone of Klein's letters to Dodd? (See Boyd, p. 209).

The incredible fact in regard to the above, was that Julius Klein was the only major witness in the Senate Ethics Committee probe of Senator Thomas J. Dodd. Circumstantially, the Senate Ethics procedure has the look of a "cover your tail" operation.

The censure hearings for Senator Thomas J. Dodd must unavoidably be considered as a non-explicit, furtive investigation of the activities of SISS, Dodd, Eastland, Dirksen and the whole cast of characters who apparently signed off on the JFK assassination. It was an investigation of the JFK assassination, but this fact was never mentioned and was never made explicit. This censure investigation was done, apparently, under pressure from investigative reporters Drew Pearson and Jack Anderson. A kinder interpretation could describe the Dodd investigation as a mere fact-finding mission regarding the assassination. Let you, the reader be the judge.

One thing is crystal clear to this author. If there were five Senators in the twentieth century who were censured and two of them were named McCarthy and Dodd, then this fact alone points to the hypothesis that the JFK assassination was part and parcel of the Red-baiting outrages of the 1950s and 1960s. These censures were like the ammunition exploding when the heat generated in a battle reached the breaking point. As has been explained many times in prior chapters, the strategy of the Red-baiters in the 1950s was to buy a mean dog, i.e. Joe McCarthy. When your mean dog bites the wrong person (as when McCarthy "bit" the U.S. Army), then put him down in public. And then go buy another mean dog (this time Senator Thomas J. Dodd). Dodd again "bit the wrong person," i.e. he plotted the murder of the President. (That was bad collateral damage).

Author Boyd explains that Julius Klein blatantly misrepresented himself as an international statesman and also an advisor to U.S. Presidents and European chancellors.

The Dodd censure hearings before the Senate Ethics Committee began on June 22, 1966. The official title of the committee was the U.S. Senate Select Committee on Standards and Conduct. Because of the complex nature of the charges, the Committee decided to limit the initial hearings to the relationship of Senator Dodd to General Julius Klein. The Chairman was Senator John Stennis who had also served on the Committee which censured Senator Joseph McCarthy.

James Boyd, Dodd's speechwriter and biographer was the first witness against Dodd.

General Julius Klein had written a letter where he stated that he and Dodd were both in Germany together when the Berlin Wall went up on August 13, 1961.

The evidence began immediately to include names of infamous Nazi's found in correspondence between Klein and Dodd. The first was Dr. Wolfgang Pohle, who had told General Klein confidentially that Franz von Papen had been speaking out against Klein in Germany. Of course von Papen's father had been the leader of the German spies in the U.S. during World War I and was expelled from the U.S. for that reason. He was later Chancellor of Germany in 1932 and served briefly as Vice-Chancellor to Hitler. Julius Klein was a name that was on the tongue of this man so well connected to German history.

Pohle began his career in an association of Ruhr mining interests. In 1940, he became General Counsel to Mannesmann AG. From 1954 to 1959, he was a member of the board of Mannesmann AG . In 1959 he was General Manager of Friedrich Flick KG and from 1965 to 1971 was a personally liable partner.

As a lawyer in 1946 to 1948, Pohle had defended German industrialists at the Nuremberg Trials. He also defended the Krupp, Flick and IG Farben industrialists when they were tried by the U.S. for war crimes after the war.

Another letter from Klein to Dodd instructed Dodd on what to do when he next traveled to Germany. Klein told him to meet with Chancellor Ludwig Erhard, former Chancellor Konrad Adenauer, former Foreign Minister Heinrich von Brentano and State Secretary Karl Karstens "who was a Yale graduate." But Dodd was told by Klein to first talk to Dr. Hans Globke to get a briefing on the situation in Germany now that LBJ and Ludwig Erhard were leading their respective countries.

In his landmark book, *The New Germany and the Old Nazi's*, author T.H. Tetens features Dr. Hans Globke as a major villain, possibly the *most important* villain in postwar West Germany. Under the Nazis, Globke was the top official in the Office for Jewish Affairs in the Interior Ministry. It was in this ministry that the Nuremberg Laws were written. The man who signed those laws, Dr. Wilhelm Flick, was hanged as a war criminal for that reason. But the man who drafted the Nuremberg Laws was Dr. Hans Globke, who went untouched.

Tetens states "it is possible that Dr. Globke has done more than anyone else to re-Nazify West Germany." Further, he writes "why Dr. Adenauer could not find another man capable of setting up a true democratic civil service has never been explained. Whatever lies behind this mystery, the fact is that Dr. Hans Globke, who faithfully served the Nazi hierarchy, became one of the most powerful men in the Federal Republic."

So this is not a pretty picture. You have Senator Dodd who was the second-in-command prosecutor at Nuremberg openly collaborating with the worst of the leftovers from Nazi Germany in order to help assassinate John F. Kennedy and to perpetrate who knows what other atrocities.

The sorry bit of information is a hard act to follow. What else can we reveal after this has been revealed? It can't get any worse. But we must go on and tell the rest of this sorry tale.

Klein further instructs Dodd, "I suggest, Tom, that you see each person (i.e. each ex-Nazi) alone, without anybody from the [German] Embassy or the Foreign Office."

In a letter from Julius Klein to Dodd, we read "when in Bonn, see him (Globke) first ... as a confidante of the Vatican, he did all that he could to save lives in Germany."

And further, "Mr. Abs is a leading German banker and a member of the board of directors of many of my German clients. The brunt of the attacks against me began when I started to fight for Abs." "If you go to Duesseldorf, be sure to see your old colleague, Dr. Wolfgang Pohle. Dr. Pohle is one of the executives of the Flick concern."

Quoting from *The Warburgs* by Ron Chernow, "As Goering tried to expel Jewish owners from industries of strategic importance, especially in mining and metals, he found an enthusiastic supporter in Friedrich Flick, later a convicted war criminal. With a crude steel empire that by 1932 rivaled that of Krupp, Flick had lavishly subsidized Heinrich Himmler and the SS. By 1937, he sat atop the largest privately owned iron and steel combine in Germany." (Chernow, p. 463).

Chairman: You [Klein], the late Senator Bridges, Senator Javits and Congressman Celler entertained him when he was in the U.S. Also, Speaker McCormack gave him a luncheon.

Klein: His company controls company controls Daimler-Benz. Pohle used to be chief counsel for Mannesmann AG, another account that I lost.

Pohle is an important voice in industrial circles. He told me that von Papen, Jr. is not too friendly to me.

In a memo about Heinrich von Brentano, "Brentano is strictly Adenauer. He supports Chancellor Erhard but opposes his appeasement [the policy of] certain people in the German Foreign Office.... Brentano is 100% against Soviet appeasement, hence his clash with Foreign Minister Schroeder and Mayor Willi Brandt. Brandt spends $300,000 annually in public relations man Roy Bernard [a business rival to Julius Klein's firm]."

In a memo dated October 21, 1962, for Senator Dodd from Charles J. Kersten, "I am leaving for Germany to participate in the trial of Stashynsky. Again, congratulations, Tom, as you are one of our most important patriots in today's world.

"Mr. Boyd did not know about the Stashynsky Affair until Dodd left for Germany in 1964." Boyd testifies: "My belief is that the Stashynsky case is a cover-up and nothing more." (Hearings, p. 89)

A long list of Senators wrote letters to Germany in support of Julius Klein in the week before the assassination: William (D. DE), Gore (D. TN), Morton (R. KY), Jackson (D. WA), Long (D. LA), Keating (R. NY), Javits, (R. NY), Hickenlooper (R. IA), Sparkman (D. AL), Symington (D. MO), Scott (R. PA), Ribicoff (D. CT), Mundt, (R. SD), Morse (IN. OR) [In a letter Morse said] "I have known J.K. for the 19 years I have been in the Senate," and Humphrey (D. MN).

Senator Eugene McCarthy inquires of witness James Boyd, (Dodd's speechwriter):

"Yours, Dodd's and Klein's views on foreign policy, were they all the same?"

Dodd: "Klein's views were not to my liking."

In an undated memo to file, presumably written by Julius Klein, the following statement was made, "Not a single U.S. Senator or Congressman criticized me after the Fulbright hearings. Somehow the people in Germany did not understand that this was not an attack against me but against the Federal Republic's strong stand on the Soviets by the appeasers."

One questioner asked Boyd, "Will you state as best you can when you first became concerned about Senator Dodd's relationship with General Klein.?"

Boyd: I questioned the propriety of accepting gratuities from a foreign agent ... but I did not think that that by itself was a matter for me to become concerned about until I began to think of it in terms of what I thought was a misappropriation of hundreds of thousands of dollars in campaign funds.

The most important statement in all of the hearings came when chief counsel Benjamin R. Fern was addressing questions to Marjorie Carpenter, a secretary to Senator Dodd.

Carpenter: He [Dave Martin, Dodd's staffer who dealt with foreign relations] said that Senator Dodd had mentioned General Klein's name to all the German officials they had visited while in Germany, and then he said "I wonder how much General Klein paid Senator Dodd to do that." And Mr. Zeiller [another Dodd staff worker] said 'Oh, I have known General Klein for a long time. I knew him when I worked for Senator Bridges [Sen. Styles Bridges, (R,NH)],' and he sort of laughed. And Mr. Martin said 'He must have paid at least $10,000,' and Mr. Zeiller said 'Oh, easily.'"

Against objection, acting Chairman Cooper ruled that this claim of a bribe would be left in the record until Martin and/or Zeiller could be called to either affirm it or deny that it had been said or whether there was any evidence to support it.

Per staffer Dave Martin, Senator Dodd's trip to German in 1964 was only for the purpose of interviewing Bogdan Stashynsky.

Miss Helen Batherson of Julius Klein Public Relations testified.

Counsel Fern: Who were Julius Klein's main clients?

Batherson: Society for German-American Co-operation, Mannesmann AG, Rheinmetall, Der Spiegel Magazine, Flick AG, the Travel Bureau of the State of Hesse and Bayer Aspirin and Pharmaceuticals.

Per a J.K.memo, "Adenauer has a picture of John Foster Dulles on his wall ... it is I who brought these two great statesmen together ... Adenauer will try to bring de Gaulle back to the hard line"

In Exhibit 48, a letter from Klein to Dodd, dated 8/15/64, the following appears: "To save you time, I am enclosing herewith a rough draft. Maybe you want to paraphrase it and add a little about the President's stand on Vietnam, especially since Westrick is a 100% believer in your strong policy. This also included the Congo. Both Westrick and Speaker McCormack have the same decoration from the Vatican. They are good friends. The Speaker too went out of his way with Westrick to give me a big boost." This letter contains the annotation by Julius Klein "Please destroy this letter. I made no copy."

Another witness was former Congressman Charles Kersten. In a letter dated February 19, 1963 Kersten wrote to Dodd about the Stashynsky case. As described in a previous chapter, Kersten was an attorney representing the family of the slain Ukrainian hero Stepan Bandera. He explained that he had been hired for that purpose by the Ukrainian Congress Committee in the U.S. In the mid-1950's, Kersten and Dodd had served together on the House Select Committee on Communist Aggression. Kersten made reference to Dr. Lev Dobriansky, the long-time Georgetown University professor and militant Catholic anti-Communist. Kersten offered to arrange for the Chief Justice of the West German Supreme Court to travel to the U.S. and appear before the Senate Internal Security Subcommittee about the Stashynsky Case.

The Kersten letter went on to rant as follows: "It is also the diabolical subversive tactics that the Communists employ all over the world, and in this case the potential of swift, silent and unattributable murder of even the highest officials in the United States who oppose the Soviets.

We have seen in the chapter on Kersten that he was considered an unreliable "loose cannon" by others in the Congress. Here he unleashes a thinly-veiled reference to the JFK assassination, trying to tie the Soviets to the murder of JFK, knowing that the connection was disingenuous in the extreme. This is another smoking-gun statement out of the mouth of Kersten.

What Kersten wanted from Dodd was for SISS to endorse the conclusions of the West German Supreme Court regarding Soviet overseas murders. *Life* magazine had published an article on September 9, 1962 on the subject of Stashynsky prior to his trial in Germany, so the Senators were questioning why Dodd would have to go to Germany to publicize the Stashynsky case.

Let the reader take careful note of this paragraph. In his statement, Kersten almost proves to the reader that the frameup of the Soviets for the JFK murder was part of a general strategy which involved Stashynsky-type provocation, i.e. German-Soviet game-playing. This type of idea was apparently on the drawing boards as early as 1959 or 1960. This paralleled in time the defection of Oswald and the false-defector program. This was apparently a stew brewed up primarily by the Germans and the U.S. right wing.

Kersten verified that there was a branch of the Ukrainian Congress Committee in Connecticut and a large Ukrainian community in Hartford. Kersten testified that he had approached Senator Dodd as early as 1960 with a concern about a Soviet murder agent. In August, 1961, with Stashynsky's preliminary confession, Kersten met with Dodd and Boyd and asked them to arrange for an East European expert to be hired by the SISS committee. Stashynsky defected to West Germany on August 12, 1961, the day before the Berlin wall went up.

In testimony by David Martin, the foreign policy specialist on Dodd's staff, Martin discussed his role in the Dodd-Stashynsky case. According to Martin, he drafted a letter from Dodd to Senator Eastland because Eastland was chairman of the Senate Subcommittee on German Security. [When searching the Internet for this subcommittee, there is no record of it ever having existed].

Senator Dodd wrote to Senator Eastland, "In light of JFK's assassination, we need a hearing on Stashynsky."[13]

Prior to Dodd's trip, Julius Klein had given him a folder which contained detailed instructions as to what Dodd should say to Chancellor Erhard and similar directives. Staffer Martin testified that he "exploded" when he saw this and considered it an affront and extremely presumptuous on the part of Klein.

Mr Martin submitted for the record a diary and notes of the trip to Germany with Senator Dodd. Some of the details from that exhibit are as follows:

1. Adenauer asked "what's wrong with Fulbright?"

2. Per Adenauer, de Gaulle's hold on power has been challenged by repeated conspiracies in the French Army.

3. Adenauer was never critical of the U.S. but he was critical of Britain.

4. Adenauer was very critical of American policy under Kennedy.

5. Arthur H. Stimson of the U.S. Embassy picked us up and drove us to Cologne to the German FBI. We met with the head, Mr. Hubert Schruebers and his assistant Dr. Richard Meier.

6. Mr. Ford of the Embassy took us to where the Auschwitz trial was being held.

7. Dodd interviewed Stashynsky.

8. They met with Yaroslav Stetzko [a Nazi collaborator and] President of the Anti-Bolshevik Bloc of Nations. [Kersten was involved with the ABN].

Senator Bennett: In this whole process, were the Senators on SISS consulted? How many Senators were on SISS?

Martin: Four Democrats and three Republicans.

Bennett: Was there any meeting of SISS called at which this report [which was titled Murder International, Inc.] was made?

Martin: No.

Bennett: This looks like a "one Senator/one staff" trip in which no other members of the committee were involved. When does an activity become a personal activity and when does it become an official Committee activity? This was apparently a personal trip by Senator Dodd.

Martin: A copy of the report was circulated and the Senators signed off on it with no hearings or anything. (Hearings, p. 420).

Senator Cooper: In the documents from Julius Klein to Senator Dodd asking him to go to Germany, why did Klein display such a demanding tone?

Dodd testifies: "General Klein was a good friend of the late Robert A. Taft. I believe he was with him when he died. He was also a friend of

Herbert Hoover and General MacArthur. [This is almost a who's-who of American pro-fascism].

Dodd: Regarding the possible appointment of General Klein to the U.S. Advisory Committee on Information, Klein was recommended by McCormack, Morse, Neuberger, Kefauver and Javits.

Chairman Stennis: Now 2 years had elapsed since the murder happened when you went over there and a year had passed before there were any hearings. It was Friday, March 26, 1965 when there was a hearing. Why the delay?

Dodd: There were some investigations going on, the Otepka case being one. Also, the Juvenile Delinquency Subcommittee was holding hearings.

Dodd: I was impressed here that former Congressman Kersten emphasized the need to get this out with some kind of official stamp or document of some kind to make it more impressive and authentic, and that he had urged me to go and was anxious for me to go. There is a wide variety of groups that are troubled by the Soviet apparatus. They are particularly people from the Eastern European countries. There is constant pressure of one sort or another.

Senator Bennett: This [lack of a hearing] leaves the other members of the subcommittee without the opportunity to share... the knowledge that I am sure you received... from the prisoner and with the judicial officers in Germany. Why did you want to get the information out to the American public and not to the members of SISS?

Senator Cooper: You [Dodd] were a member of the Senate Foreign Relations Committee when General Klein was before that committee. Did you attend the hearings?

Dodd: No.

Senator Cooper: [reading from a letter from Klein to Dodd] "I am ashamed of you [Klein is ashamed of Dodd]. What are you afraid of? You are the only one of my friends in the Senate who have remained silent."

Senator Cooper: Did Klein ever give you anything of value or contribute anything to your campaign?

Dodd: Only a rug, but he did contribute to my campaign.

Dodd: In exhibit 17, Dr. Carstens was the Under-Secretary of State for Germany. [under Foreign Minister Heinrich von Brentano] Carsten's office subsidized or contributed heavily to the Wiesbaden Group which engaged me at the recommendation of Dr. Adenauer.

General Julius Klein testifies:

Counsel Fern: [On the Society for German-American Relations]; Who controls the society?

Klein: I do not know.

Fern: Who elects the directors of the Society?

Klein: I do not know.

Fern: When did you meet Senator Dodd?

Klein: In the office of the Secretary of War Robert Patterson, during and after World War II, when Dodd was at Nuremberg.

Fern: How often did you see him in 1945-1946?

Klein: 20 to 100 times, including 2 to 10 times after he came back from Nuremburg. [This shows that Dodd was plotting nefarious activities even while a prosecutor at Nuremberg. No wonder he never once discussed events at Nuremberg].

Fern: Can you give me a rough estimate of how often you saw him from 1946 to 1953?

Klein: Quite often when he was a Congressman, between once a week to once a month.

Fern: And from 1953 to 1959?

Klein: About the same.

Chairman Stennis: How often did you write or phone Senator Dodd about going to Germany?

Klein: Less than 15. My staff did some, too.

Klein: [In re his instructions to Dodd on going to Europe] All members of the Senate Foreign Relations Committee who were going to Europe got a similar memorandum [i.e. biographies of German officials] from me.

Klein: In the Fulbright hearings, it was only Senator Fulbright who was critical of me and no one else. The "censure" or "hearings" about me [the 1963 Fulbright hearings] were being carried in the press behind the Iron Curtain. Radio Free Europe provided me with what was being said in Europe about this.

Fern: [Reading from an exhibit] "Globke was the liaison man with whom I worked closely while working with Adenauer and Brentano." [As described above, Globke was the main instigator of the ex-Nazi's who regained their power in post-war West Germany, per author T H Tetens].

Senator McCarthy: As I read it, you were in Germany when Senator Javits was in Germany. Is that correct? Did you want Senator Dodd to do whatever Senator Javits did?

Klein: Yes. Senator Javits took an interest in my case because I was portrayed as a Jew and a Nazi-lover. Senator Javits took an interest because he was a prominent Jew.

Fern: Why did you request Senator Dodd to see Hermann J. Abs?

Klein: He is head of Germany's largest bank. [Hermann Abs was involved with the Nazis and the Hitler regime in a gigantic way pre-World War II].

Chairman Stennis: Did you get the list of the people that Senator Dodd was supposed to see from the State Department or did Dodd give it to you?

Klein: The State Department.

Senator Cooper: General Klein, it is unclear from your testimony whether the list [of persons to see in Germany] was prepared by you, the State Department or Senator Dodd. Did you name the persons?

Klein: Yes. Dr Globke also served under Hitler. I told Senator Dodd that Globke worked on the Israeli restitution treaty and was also the right-hand man to Adenauer. We [Dodd and I] talked about NATO and the Test Ban Treaty.

Klein: He [Dodd] spoke to Chancellor Adenauer about me. Chancellor Adenauer brought up the subject of Senator Fulbright. He brings up the subject with everyone who sees him ... I saw Chancellor Adenauer only 10 days ago when I was in Germany.

Globke was to Adenauer what Sherman Adams [Ike's closest advisor] was to Ike. Globke retired the same day that Adenauer retired.

Klein: [On when he first met Dodd] I invited Senator Dodd to Chicago for the Chicago World's Fair in 1933 (he was in the FBI then). [This dates the FBI rabid anti-Communist clique back to 1933. This could have included Hoover, Dodd, Guy Banister, Rep. Charles Kersten, Rep. John W. McCormack and Father Joseph Cronin among others].

Senator Cooper: In your activities as the public relations representative of the Society, were you called upon to promote any political positions of the German Government?

Klein: No, but it is my personal position to advocate for the re-unification of Germany.

Cooper: What about a political interest of the Republic which is not in the interest of the United States?

Klein: My country comes first.

Senator Stennis: Mr. Klein, you had a self-adulatory statement that you asked the committee to allow into the record, but before the committee ruled, you released this statement to the press. A great part of the statement was on Drew Pearson and Jack Anderson. A great part of the rest of the statement was an attack on the witnesses who have appeared here at our committee. This statement calls people liars. It is not going to be part of this record and it is expressly rejected.

Exhibit 5 A Memorandum from David Martin to Senator Dodd dtd. 12-2-1963.

> As you know, we have had to put these hearings off several times because of the priority accorded the hearings on State Department Security [the Otepka hearings]. However, I had a long talk with Leo Dobriansky about this matter the other day, and we are both agreed that the Kennedy assassination would make hearings on the subject of the Soviet murder apparatus particularly appropriate at this time. It is not a matter of accusing the Soviet Union of

planning the assassination of the President or involvement in the assassination. But the basic point should be made that the Soviet Union does employ murder as an instrument of policy and that it does maintain a special apparatus for the purpose of implementing this aspect of its policy. From that point on, people draw their own conclusions or make their own assumptions.

So, here we see the bottom line in Dodd's activities. His expert in foreign affairs, David Martin suggests to Dodd that the two of them arrange hearings which will lead the American public to blame the Soviet Union for the assassination. From the legal perspective, participating in the cover-up of a murder before the murder occurs makes a person legally an accessory to murder.

Notes:

Dodd censure hearings are published by the U.S. Senate as: Investigation of Senator Thomas J. Dodd. : Hearings, Eighty-ninth Congress, second session ... pursuant to S. Res. 338, 88th Congress. PT. 1-2 by United States. Congress. Senate. Select Committee on Standards and Conduct. Published 1966, beginning at p. 11.

The New Germany and the Old Nazis (1961) by T.H. Tetens.

The Warburgs: The Twentieth-Century Odyssey of a Remarkable Jewish Family (1993) by Ron Chernow, p. 463.

Chapter 38

FORMER GERMAN NAZIS, WEST GERMAN OFFICIALS AND THE ASSASSINATION

This chapter is meant to be only a very brief summary of the significance of the role of certain Germans, mostly ex-Nazis, in the assassination of JFK. It is not intended to be an in-depth analysis, because their roles are discussed more specifically in other chapters.

Some background on the JFK-Nazi connection is in order. In a book edited by Avi Beker, in a chapter describing German assets still in Switzerland at the end of World War II, an alarming statement is made. "As the Second World War in Europe was ending, the Allies insisted that all German external assets be turned over to them. This action reflected the considerable evidence that the Nazis were going to use these assets, much of them hidden, to finance a Third World War."

Again in Beker's book, "At this stage, the Americans, worried about the Nazis' postwar plans, warned the Swiss that their collaboration with the Nazis to protect their loot would enable them [the Nazis] 'to preserve the power of the Nazi party and plan again for world domination.'" (Beker, p.142).

In the London *Daily Mail*, May 9, 2009, a bit of shocking news is revealed.

A document called the "Red House Report" gives a detailed account of a secret meeting in Strasbourg, Germany on August 10, 1944. The meeting was held at the Maison Rouge Hotel. In the secret meeting, top Nazi officials had gathered an elite group of German industrialists. They ordered these businessmen to begin planning a post-war economic recovery which would prepare the way for the Nazis' return to power. They demanded that they should work for a "strong German empire." In other words: the Fourth Reich. (See notes, dailymail website). There is overwhelming support for the theory that the EEU was planned as a European Fourth Reich for the Germans and as a vehicle for the Germans to dominate Europe. To the extent the Nazis succeeded in holding on to power in postwar Germany, the plan could have, at least in some sense, succeeded.

CHANCELLOR KONRAD ADENAUER

Dr. Konrad Adenauer was West Germany Chancellor from September 15, 1949 to October 16, 1963. Adenauer served as Mayor of Cologne, Germany from 1917 to 1933. He was considered a Catholic activist politician and was at that time affiliated with the Center Party. During the years of the Weimar Republic, he was president of the Prussian State Council from 1921–33, which was the representative of the provinces of Prussia in its legislation. Though located very near France and the Netherlands, Cologne was nevertheless part of Prussia. Ironically, Adenauer sometimes expressed his dislike of the Protestant influence in Germany due to the role of Prussia.

Adenauer was dismissed as Mayor of Cologne and jailed twice under the Hitler regime. He spent the Hitler years on the run from the Nazi bosses. His natural cunning undoubtedly helped him in avoiding the Nazi tentacles. He was even able to begin drawing his pension which he had earned from his years of public service.

Following World War II, the first election to the Bundestag of West Germany was held on August 15, 1949. Adenauer had founded the Christian Democratic Party, which won that first election and emerged as the strongest party in West Germany. Adenauer became the new Chancellor.

The Oder-Neisse boundary was never accepted by the Adenauer government as the eastern frontier of Germany. This refusal was mostly because of domestic political considerations. There were 10 million expellees in Germany who were demanding the right to return to their homes in the lost eastern provinces. Adenauer also considered this refusal as a way to avoid any negotiations with the Soviets or the Eastern Bloc. He knew the Soviets would never agree to change the Oder-Neisse line and so this rendered any attempt at negotiations moot. Privately, Adenauer considered these former provinces to be forever lost to Germany.

In October 1950, Adenauer received a memorandum from four former Wehrmacht generals that stated there would be no German rearmament without the release of German war criminals. They also wanted a statement from the WWII allies that the Wehrmacht had not committed any war crimes. To appease Adenauer and the Generals, the commander of NATO, Dwight Eisenhower, issued a statement saying that the majority of Wehrmacht soldiers had fought honorably.

Laws were passed in West Germany by 1951 which ended de-Nazification. Adenauer wanted to change the emphasis to reparations and compensation for victims. (These things never really happened, either). Former Nazis could now take jobs in the civil service except for certain cases which were ruled as egregious.

In 1952 Joseph Stalin proposed an initiative whereby Germany would be unified as a neutral state, similar to the status of Austrian and Finland.

This would lead away from the dangerous superpower confrontation in central Europe. This confrontation had caused several Berlin crises and led to the building of the Berlin Wall. Stalin's idea was probably unrealistic. Unlike Austria and Finland, Germany had traditionally been the second largest economy in the world next to the U.S. Any major German policy would not be a neutral policy. It would be a German policy which carried its own center of gravity. Adenauer rejected this overture by Stalin and so did all of his cabinet and even opposition parties.

Stalin came back with a second effort for his proposal. Many in the German public were open to Stalin's idea. In retrospect, Adenauer was foolish to refuse a deal for German unification when it was available on the grounds that he couldn't accept the eastern boundary, the Oder-Neisse line. When Germany was finally reunified in the 1980's, it was with the Oder-Neisse line as the boundary. So nothing was gained by almost 40 more years of a divided Germany.

In retrospect, the true reason for the opposition of Adenauer was his Catholic perspective. The big worry for the Catholic Church in Europe was the possible loss of France and Italy to Communism. A neutral Germany would, by definition, not be fighting Communism, which was a bottom line issue with the devout Adenauer.

The West Germans began the drive to compensate Jewish victims of the Nazi's by negotiating a treaty with Israel for this purpose. Germany agreed to pay compensation to Israel. Jewish claims were funded in something called the Jewish Claims Conference. This conference purported to represent the Jewish victims of Nazi Germany. Germany paid 450 million Marks to the claims conference and 3 billion Marks to Israel. Many radical groups in Israel opposed such an arrangement. This led to the assassination attempt by these Jewish groups against Adenauer. A package addressed to Adenauer exploded in the Munich police station on March 27, 1952. It was traced to Menachem Begin, a terrorist who would later become the Prime Minister of Israel.

The problem was, of course, that a treaty was not needed with Israel. Why should any of the former Nazi regimes pay money to Israel as a substitute for paying actual victims individually. This amounted to a public relations gimmick. We could expect to find General Julius Klein or similarly two-faced Jewish activists to be involved in this concept. Klein was instrumental in arranging the first sit-down conference between West Germany and Israel. This West German-Israeli Reparations Treaty merely allowed West Germany to avoid signing any treaty with France, the U.S., the U.K. and other countries which would return the looted property of the Jews to the owners living in the Western countries. It was an unbelievably cynical device.

But there were billions of dollars of sequestered assets in various countries which had been seized from Germany and Germans and were available to settle claims by Jews who had been the victims. Treaties were needed between the U.S., the U.K. and probably other countries.

A reparations treaty was finally signed between the U.S. and Austria in 2000. There was an accord between the U.S. and Switzerland in 1946, but Switzerland reneged on their promises. Meanwhile, Jews around the world were never even allowed to recover their lost bank accounts in the former German and German-occupied countries, and of course they got nothing from the Communist Eastern countries. In 1953, the German Restitution Laws were passed. These allowed some victims to claim restitution. The law were written to sharply limit the number of people entitled to collect compensation.

West Germany joined NATO in May, 1955. In November of that year the Bundeswehr was founded. In the 1956 Suez Crisis, Adenauer supported the Anglo-French-Israeli military action against Egypt. The Western Allies other than the United States considered President Nasser of Egypt to be basically a Communist. Adenauer feared that the U.S. response to Suez meant that the U.S. and the Soviets wanted to carve the world into two spheres of influence and that Europe would be the odd man out. In 1959, Chancellor Adenauer announced he would run for the Presidency of Germany, but pulled out because he feared that Ludwig Erhard would then become Chancellor. He reportedly thought little of Erhard.

The construction of the Berlin Wall in August 1961 weakened the image of the Adenauer government. In October 1962, there was a major scandal when five journalists working for *Der Spiegel* magazine were arrested for espionage because they published an article critical of the West German military. Adenauer defended the person responsible for the arrests. Defense Minister Franz Josef Strauss denounced the journalists for being involved in treason.

Being a Francophile, Adenauer put a great deal of faith and hope in a Franco-German partnership. He shared de Gaulle's view that Britain would disrupt the EEC if it became a member. Adenauer tried to block Ludwig Erhard from becoming his successor, which had been his longtime goal, but he failed and in October 1963 Ludwig Erhard became the new West German Chancellor. Adenauer died in 1967 at age 91. Although some saw Adenauer as one of the greatest Germans in history, his critics summarized the actions of Adenauer by saying that Adenauer was basically just a "mean old man."

Was Dr. Konrad Adenauer complicit in the JFK assassination? It is difficult to exclude him since he was the number one champion of General Julius Klein in Klein's role as the West German "shadow ambassador" and public relations man. Klein was definitely the "bag man" for assassination funds as well as the go-between with Senator Thomas Dodd and his West German ex-Nazi contacts.

Adenauer was not a totalitarian-type ruler like Stalin or Hitler. He would not necessarily know about everything that went on in his country, no more than JFK knew which people in his government were out to murder him. But Adenauer spent his career covering up for the ex-Nazis both in his country and in his government. Due to his close relationship to these co-workers who had murdered 12 million people in cold blood, there could be no real moral definition as to what Adenauer would countenance or what he would forbid when it came to murder.

Adenauer was a truly devout Catholic. His contemporary, Pope John XXIII, would have condemned the assassination of a fellow Catholic, just as JFK refused to approve the murder of the Diem brothers in Vietnam in part because they were fellow churchmen. But Adenauer was cunning and he had to suspect something was going on in his country. The murder plot for JFK was probably planned in large part by his own BND (West German Intelligence Agency). He must have given the plot at least tacit approval and turned a blind eye.

Hans Globke

Hans Josef Maria Globke, who was born on September 10, 1898 was a German lawyer, civil servant and politician who served as first Under-Secretary of State and then Chief of Staff to the German Chancellor October 28, 1953 to October 15, 1963. He was one of most influential officials in the government of Chancellor Konrad Adenauer. He was the Chancellor's closest confidant during his term as Adenauer's chief of staff.

Under the Nazi regime, Hans Globke served as the top official in the Office for Jewish Affairs in the Interior Ministry. (Tetens, p. 38). While the man who drafted the anti-Semitic Nuremberg laws was hanged as a war criminal, the man who signed them, Hans Globke, became the closest advisor to Chancellor Konrad Adenauer. Globke, but also wrote the "commentary" by which they were interpreted and enforced. So much for de-Nazification.

A major controversy broke out in 1950 when it became known that Hans Globke had played a major role in drafting the Nuremberg Laws. It was well known that it was by these laws that the Jews in Germany met their fate. Adenauer kept Globke on as Secretary of State because he had decided he had to re-integrate most of these Nazis into society and public service as a practicality.

Evidence which has since come to light shows that Globke was a major administrator in the extermination of the Jews. Globke's boss in the interior ministry under Hitler resigned rather than participate in the liquidation of the Jews. Globke eagerly stepped into his boss's vacated position.

No one has ever explained why Chancellor Konrad Adenauer couldn't have found someone else to set up his system of civil service. The Minister of the Interior under Hitler, Dr. Wilhelm Frick, once wrote a letter during the Third Reich, praising Globke as "the most capable and efficient official in my ministry."

The post-war German press called Globke the "power behind the throne" and referred to him as "The Spider." According to author T.H. Tetens, an expert on German affairs, "it is possible that Dr. Globke had done more than anyone else to re-Nazify West Germany. In October, 1951, a leader of the opposition Social Democrats charged Globke with packing the Foreign Ministry with ex-Nazis. The *Deutsche-Zeitung* reported that Globke was the head of a huge staff, a super-ministry led by thirty-six senior officials. The result of this was that every official ministry of the entire West German government was in reality run by dependable friends and servants of Dr. Globke.

Under Globke's control was the Office of the Protection of the Constitution (the West German FBI) and the BND, the West German Intelligence Agency run by General Reinhard Gehlen a former employee and long-time partner of U.S. CIA Director Allen Dulles. The above facts are more than enough to convince any reader that there was ample mechanism in place in West Germany for the ex-Nazi's such as Globke and the others to have the motive, means and opportunity to murder John F. Kennedy. There is really nothing more to be said about this terrible situation.

AMBASSADOR WILHELM GREWE

There is not a lot of information available about West German Ambassador to the United States, Dr. Wilhelm Grewe. A 1962 article provides some information. (See archive.org article in notes). The article states that Ambassador Grewe is alleged to be a former member of the Nazi Party. He did not respond to a telegram inquiring about his Nazi past. The article points out that if Grewe did not deny it, it could point to its accuracy.

Author T.H. Tetens in *The New Germany* quotes a newspaper called the *Bonn Chronicle,* which said that Adenauer was "surrounded by arrogant nationalists and defenders of the past, such as the Bundesministers [Gerhard] Schroder, [Theodore] Oberlander, [Waldemar] Kraft, and [Emanuel] Preusker, by men like [Hans] Globke, [Hermann] Abs and Professor [Wilhelm] Grewe, who all had served Hitler..." (Tetens, p. 70).

Tetens goes on to write that militarists in Hitler's Germany were assisted by diplomats and legal experts. The Ribbentrop-controlled Monatschefte feur Auswaertige Politik of September, 1941, proclaimed prematurely the dissolution of the Soviet Union "whereby all positive norms of international law have become void and inapplicable." The author of the article was Ribbentrop's legal expert, Dr. Wilhelm Grewe, a member of the Nazi party and later Bonn's ambassador to Washington.

As was reported in the previously cited article in *Der Spiegel* on October 4, 1963, President Kennedy had demanded that Adenauer recall Ambassador Wilhelm Grewe. The reason is cited as the arrogant and haughty manner of Wilhelm Grewe which rankled JFK. Although Grewe was not a major ex-Nazi, he was one of the Germans who interacted with JFK face to face. As Ambassador to Washington, his reports would be going to Bonn regarding American affairs. If JFK ran him out of town, that would not bode well for the opinions about Kennedy which Grewe would be reporting to Adenauer.

HEINRICH VON BRENTANO

Heinrich von Brentano was born on June 20, 1904 in Offenbach, Germany. Brentano was a founder and the party leader of the CDU, the Christian Democratic Union, which was the party of Konrad Adenauer. He was foreign minister of the Federal Republic of Germany from 1955 to 1961. Von Brentano was extremely anti-Communist and motivated in this by his strong Catholic affiliation.

After his first entry into politics in 1945, Brentano began his career by helping to found the Christian Democratic Union of Hesse. As a member of the provisional assembly, he helped draft the constitution of the new West German republic. He served in the first federal Bundestag 1949. From 1949 to 1955 he was parliamentary leader of the CDU. He served again in that capacity from 1961 to 1964. It was in this period that he was collaborating with Senator Thomas Dodd in Dodd's assassination-related trips back and forth to Germany in 1963 and 1964. Von Brentano worked tirelessly on the Schuman Plan in 1952 and 1953. This plan was the predecessor of the EEU. He also helped draft a constitution for the future Common Market. Von Brentano became foreign minister under Chancellor Konrad Adenauer in June 1955.

Brentano traveled to the Vatican to advocate for Germans who were having difficulties with post-war legal issues. Curiously, in 2016, there is at this moment a 1956 wire photo of Germany's Konrad Adenauer, Heinrich Von Brentano and Pope Pius XII for sale on a website. It was Von Brentano's adamant anti-Communism based on his Catholic affiliation and beliefs which brought him into his special relationship with Senator Thomas Dodd as Dodd got deeper and deeper into the assassination plot.

In a November 14, 1964 article in the *New York Times* announcing his death, the *Times* said that von Brentano was a spokesman for a pro-French as well as a strongly anti-Communist foreign policy.

"But finally he had become known as perhaps the most adamant anti-Communist among the major political personalities in Bonn" reported the *New York Times*.

Von Brentano died unexpectedly of cancer in November, 1964.

HERMANN ABS

It would be remiss to not mention Hermann Abs, since Abs was in the center of the "assassination shuttle" carried out by General Julius Klein and Senator Thomas Dodd in 1963. (Tetens, p. 70).

Abs was a young banker starting out in the 1920's when he became acquainted with the Warburgs who, owned the M.M. Warburg investment bank. Abs went on to be the most influential banker in Hitler's quest to conquer the rest of Europe. Abs worked diligently on behalf of Deutsche-Bank to develop the concepts of banking and the control of credit as Hitler took over country after country.

Abs had been an employee of a smaller bank, Delbruck Schickler & Co. From that smaller bank, Abs ascended to the managing board of the much larger Deutsche-Bank which, along with the Dresdner were the two largest banks in Germany during World War II.

Hermann Abs was possibly the most controversial man in Germany, all things included. In 1970, an author named Eberhard Czichon wrote a biography of Abs and Abs sued him in the courts for libel and slander. (See Czichon). Abs was the top banker in Hitler's war effort and continued on to lead the Deutsche-Bank until 1967. His family was also financially interested in coal-mining and mineral resource businesses. The unique fact about Abs was that he functioned only as a banker during Hitler's war effort. He was brought in to make Deutsche-Bank look more Aryan. In fact, since Abs was such a well-known Catholic, Deutsche-Bank under Abs went from technically being a bank partially controlled by Jewish interests to being considered a "Catholic" bank by some.

His biggest challenge was to exploit the Austrian bank BUB which was taken over by Germany when Hitler invaded Austria. Abs was not a Nazi Party member. Although Abs did not commit any war crimes as such, he was basically in charge of helping Hitler devour bank after bank in occupied Europe. Without Abs, the financing of Hitler's war machine might have been lessened. Abs' talents undoubtedly prolonged the war. But under the standards of the War Crimes regime, Abs was able to avoid any prosecution or jail.

GENERAL REINHARD GEHLEN

When considering the plot to kill JFK, one has to ask the question whether it was one man alone who had either invented and/or created the plot structure. The next question is, assuming the plot was created by multiple people, did one man have overall operational control?

If there were only one man who created the plot or one man in operational control, that man might well have been General Reinhard Gehlen, the head of the BND, the West German intelligence agency. In an excellent biography of Gehlen, author E. H. Cookridge paints a very vivid picture of the master spy.

Reinhard Gehlen was born to a Catholic family in Erfurt, Germany in 1902. He served at the head of the German Army intelligence department for the Eastern Front during World War II. He was given that assignment in 1942.

In addition to the Cookridge biography, Gehlen wrote a personal memoir called *The Service*. In his memoir, Gehlen claimed to be a part of the famous attempt by several Generals to assassinate Hitler on July 20, 1944. As might be expected from someone like Gehlen, although the other conspirators were shot, Gehlen escaped punishment and had only a minor role.

Gehlen also claimed to have been dismissed from his post by Hitler for the reason that he was providing pessimistic reports to Hitler. Gehlen was at his post from 1942 to 1945 and almost the entire time, the Germans were staging a desperate defense against unavoidable defeat. Gehlen was supposedly dismissed in April, 1945, which would have been within a week or two of Hitlers suicide and the German surrender. So, like reports offered by other intelligence professionals, Gehlen's story does not add up.

After the Battle of Stalingrad when German defeat became a certainty, Gehlen began hiding away the records of his intelligence agency, the FHO. He buried these in the Austrian Alps. On May 22, 1945, Gehlen surrendered to the American Counter-Intelligence Corps known as the CIC. He immediately bartered the hidden German intelligence records for freedom and privileges for his compatriots in American custody.

Typically, in their dealings with Gehlen and other Nazis, the U.S. Army did not do the obvious. Once they had custody of the records, they could have simply changed their mind and imprisoned Gehlen once again. But Gehlen was now dealing with the OSS representative Allen Dulles, a likely Nazi sympathizer and an egregious anti-Semite. So on September 20, 1945, Gehlen was flown to the Pentagon to begin working with the U.S.

On December 6, 1946, Gehlen was flown back to Germany. Working with former German intelligence officers, Gehlen set up an intelligence redoubt in the small town of Pullach, Bavaria in the mountains of southern Germany. In 1947, Gehlen's official association with American intelligence switched from U.S. Army Intelligence to the CIA. During much of the Cold War, Gehlen's organization was in charge of the only intelligence being carried out by the U.S. in the Soviet bloc. The Gehlen organization grew to employ 4000 people.

On April 1, 1956, the Gehlen Organization was officially transferred to the West German Government and became the Bundesnachrichtendienst or BND. The Federal Republic of Germany, the FRG a/k/a West Germany was created on May 23, 1949. So for seven years, the West German government had a parliament, a President, a Chancellor and armed forces, but was content to allow the CIA to run its intelligence agency. Since Europe was the major focus of the Cold War during this period, this would almost amount to a merger of German intelligence and the CIA.

In his memoir *The Service*, Gehlen states that transfer of his organization to West German control was resisted as early as 1953 because members of the Bundestag questioned whether the BND would be working in the interests of West Germany. But according to Gehlen, it was Adenauer and ex-Nazi Hans Globke who pushed to have the BND taken over by West Germany. Gehlen relates that Chancellor Konrad Adenauer asked him to have the BND spy on the opposition Social Democrats.

In another incident reported in *The Service*, the head of the German FBI, Otto John, defected to East Germany on July 20, 1954 and held a press conference. John claimed that the BND was spying on France and that West Germany was on the threshold of a new Nazi revival. When the BND became part of the West German government, it was "attached but not subordinate to" the office of the Chancellor.

In his memoir, Gehlen advocates the very common, yet bizarre theory that the state intelligence agency, in this case the BND, should be the first in line to recommend foreign policy, ahead of the West German (or American) State Department. Gehlen describes the British and Russian traditions of intelligence as "influencers," or working primarily to influence public opinion as opposed to gathering information or carrying out covert operations.

In *The Service*, Gehlen describes his theory regarding the organization of the intelligence function. He advocates the use of "cells" of no more than 10 persons into which the entire intelligence organization would be divided. According to Gehlen, after the BND was transferred to West Germany, the BND had spies in Eastern Europe, the Middle East, Vietnam, Korea, Chile, Cuba, but not in the United States. This last claim is very likely to be totally false.

When the Soviet Union and Communist China developed a rift in 1960, Gehlen felt that the U.S. should have exploited that rift. This would have implicitly involved exploiting the rift for the benefit of West Germany as well as the U.S. Gehlen criticizes JFK as being "a man of half-measures ... afraid to commit himself to the full to realize his aims."

Gehlen boasted that his agents at Pullach (BND headquarters) were proud of the role they played in the Cuban Missile Crisis. There is a generally accepted belief that U.S. intelligence could never penetrate Castro's intelligence agency. Gehlen seems to be boasting that he was a step ahead of the CIA in the Cuban Missile Crisis in gathering information inside Cuba. This, of course, implies that the BND had infiltrated the U.S. Cuban exile community as well as Cuba proper. In another startling revelation,

Gehlen claims that CIA director Allen Dulles requested that the BND supply former SS Officers to populate Egypt's secret service.

In his memoir, Gehlen lauds Chancellor Konrad Adenauer and the high ranking ex-Nazi Hans Globke who ran the BND as well as the German FBI. However, Gehlen states that the successor to Adenauer, Professor Ludwig Erhard disliked the very idea of having an intelligence service. Gehlen claims to have been influential in the U.S. decision to intervene in Vietnam. Gehlen retired on May 1, 1968. He died in 1979 at the age of 77.

Since we have seen that West Germany was, to a large extent, effectively under control of unrepentant Nazis, this further implicates CIA director Allen Dulles as being nothing more or less than a Nazi sympathizer and/or a co-conspirator with the Nazis in their control of West Germany. Although the recruitment of Reinhard Gehlen was one of the most significant acts of Allen Dulles as CIA director, Dulles makes no mention of it in his memoir called *The Craft of Intelligence*.

Since the BND reported directly to the Chancellor of West Germany and was charged only with operating outside of the borders of West Germany, it is no stretch to believe that Chancellor Konrad Adenauer could easily have employed Gehlen and the BND to plan, organize and carry out the JFK assassination.

Notes:

The Plunder of Jewish Property During The Holocaust, Edited by Avi Beker in Chapter 7, written by Sidney Jay Zabludoff, p.125.

Beker, ibid, Chapter 8, "Why Was Switzerland Singled Out? A Case Of Belated Justice," by Avi Beker, p. 142.

http://www.dailymail.co.uk/news/article-1179902/Revealed-The-secret-report-shows-Nazis-planned-Fourth-Reich--EU.html#ixzz4T22Cj4Mx

The New Germany and the Old Nazis, (1961) by T.H. Tetens , p.38.

As cited in text as archive.org, see: https://archive.org/stream/technocratwholen00unse_30/technocratwholen00unse_30_djvu.txt

As mentioned in text, see: *The Deutsche Bank and the Nazi Economic War against the Jews: The Expropriation of Jewish-Owned Property* (2001) by Harold James.

The allegedly slanderous book by Czichon is: *Der Banker und die Macht: Hermann Josef Abs in der deutschen Politik*, by Eberhard Czichon.

Gehlen: Spy of the Century by E. H Cookridge.

The Service: The Memoirs of General Reinhard Gehlen (1972) by Reinhard Gehlen (Author), David Irving (Translator).

Chapter 39

PROOF THAT OSWALD WORKED FOR SISS

Response to an article by Lisa Pease in *Probe*, March-April 1997 Issue (Vol.4 No.3) published on ctka.net as of April 1, 2016, retrieved by author on April 1, 2016. Ctka.net as of this writing is now called kennedysandking.com but the *Probe* article by Linda Pease dated April, 1997 is at https://kennedysandking.com/john-f-kennedy-articles/327

In regard to Otepka's investigation of Oswald, "a letter was sent out on October 25, 1960 from Hugh Cummings of State's Intelligence and Research Bureau to Richard Bissell at CIA, requesting information on defectors to the Soviet Union. Why did the State Department Intelligence Division want information about defectors? Author Jim Hougen explains that apparently the study of defectors was initiated by State because neither the CIA nor military would inform the State Department which defectors to the Soviet Union were double agents working for the United States. In the quote from Hougan, however, a use of the word "him" could also refer to Bissell of the CIA, Cummings or Otepka. In other words, the CIA could have initiated the informing of the State Department about the status of possible double agents. Either way, it is apparent that there was a double agent program not being run by the State Department. This request to the CIA was, essentially, buried or obscured by the CIA bureaucracy, bouncing around to various people.

This request reached the "bottom rung" in distribution, i.e. the desk of Margaret Stephens, who worked for Paul Gaynor, of CIA's Security Research Staff, SRS. Apparently, Gaynor gave instructions to his subordinate Margaret Stevens of SRS. When he passed the list on to her, he requested her to investigate *some* of the 18 defectors on the list, but not a particular seven persons on the list whom he excluded.

According to the *Probe* article, Otepka had a friend in the CIA Security Department who tried to exclude Lee Harvey Oswald's name from any further investigation by either State or the CIA.

So, at this point, there is some confusion:

1. William Gill in his biographical book on Otepka describes the incident, but doesn't mention any letter from Hugh Cummings

of the State Department Intelligence and Research Bureau to the CIA.

2. The *Probe* article mentions letter from Cummings to State, but does not say that Cummings asked Otepka to research the list. If Cummings (who worked for State Department intelligence) wrote the letter to State, why wouldn't he be depending on State to answer his questions about the defectors? Why would Cummings involve Otepka? Why would Cummings think that Otepka would be able to find out who among the list of defectors was a double agent? And if Otepka had the ability to find out, why would he, Cummings, bother to inquire of the CIA? Why wouldn't Cummings keep the matter open on his own desk until he heard from State, whether it was either before or after he passed it down to Otepka? It appears that a man in the CIA security department named Robert Bannerman was a friend of Otepkas. It appears that Otepka and Bannerman worked together to try and direct the investigation of LHO to the desk of Otepka and not by anyone else. There was a CIA personnel file (201 file) opened on Oswald only after State inquired about LHO. Apparently, Otepka tried to keep to himself an Oswald file which he intended to keep open indefinitely, until it was physically stolen from his office.

3. Author Joan Mellen wrote on maryferrell.org an article that states that Robert B. Elwood wrote a letter requesting information to State and it was not Hugh Cummings who did so.

4. Joan Mellen relates that [at some uncertain time], on the list of defectors [sent from State to CIA or the reverse] the words were written by the CIA "Lee Oswald, tourist" in quotes. When Hugh Cummings/Robert B. Elwood wrote the letter requesting info on the list of defectors, from where did they get the list? If the words "Lee Oswald, tourist" were written on that list, did Cummings/Elwood at State get the list from the CIA in the first place? If so, why the complaint that CIA never informed State about double agents? If the CIA did send such a list of defectors, CIA was apparently informing State about defectors, but not naming the defectors as a double-agents. *Why should they identify double agents to State?*

5. In *Farewell to Justice*, Joan Mellen states that, in the final interview with Otepka in 2006, she asked Otepka several times the key question: since Oswald was not an employee of State, why was he investigating him? The answer to Mellen was that Otepka had the duty to "correlate the existing files of people whose names were on that list of defectors..." Mellen apparently got a very clear answer to that question from Otepka. Quoting from Mellen, "Otepka's role was to correlate the existing files of people whose names were on that list of defectors." Taken literally, that would mean that

unless there were an existing file on Oswald, Otepka would know that there was no file on Oswald and he simply would have gone on to the next person on the list. Stated differently, Otepka was correlating existing files to names on the list of defectors. This implies that if there were no existing file on Oswald, then the task of correlation was finished. There was no correlation between the list of defectors which bore the name of Lee Harvey Oswald and existing files. Since Otepka proceeded to investigate Oswald, therefor there must have already been a State Department file on Oswald.

6. Otepka was in possession of a file on Oswald. Apparently Otepka kept his own, parallel, possibly redundant set of files on many different persons. This filing trove was apparently separate from the State department filing system. *In Ordeal of Otto Otepka*, p. 52 we read "McLeod's office instructed Otepka to keep a separate set of files on these 258 questionable cases..." And at page 225, "Digging into the files he kept in a special safe in his office..." At page 47 Scott McLeod found "There were more files outside the file room than inside the file room" Adding all this together, one comes up with the conclusions that 1) Otepka was handed a list [from some uncertain source] of defectors to and/or from the Soviet Union. 2) That one of Otepka's interests was as to *whether an individual was a double-agent* as was stated by Lisa Pease in *Probe*. March-April 1997.

7. Another interest of Otepka was whether these defectors already had a State Department Security file or [possibly] whether their name was mentioned in any existing SD files.

8. Otepka apparently kept files in his office on any subject or person whatever, where he thought in his own judgment, the information had any bearing on State Department Security in any way at all, at his own discretion.

9. That the quote in paragraph one, above, from Jim Hougan is ambiguous when it says the investigation of Oswald was initiated by "him." Him could refer to either Hugh Cummings of State or Otepka himself.

Adding together all of the above information, the conclusion that makes the most sense is that 1) State either created or received a list of defectors to the USSR, 2) current or possible double-agents would be on that list but not designated as such, 3) Otepka was given the list with a completely open-ended assignment of determining whether those on the list had any bearing of any kind on State Department security, 4) he kept an open file on those he suspected of being double-agents. This would be crucial because having a double-agent in the State Department without the knowledge of State would be the ultimate disaster for Otepka and many others. 5) Since Otepka thinks that he was harassed and fired because of his investigation of Oswald, then Oswald would most likely have been a double-agent.

Stated differently, since the whole issue surrounding the list of defectors was the issue of double-agency, why would anyone, Otepka or otherwise, keep an open file on Oswald unless he was a double-agent or a spy of some sort.

We should also ask the obvious question: if there were double-agents on the list of defectors, which department of the U.S. Government was running them? In World War II, double-agents were run by the FBI, not the OSS or the military. Since the CIA was legally prohibited from spying inside the U.S., then the CIA couldn't legally run double-agents such as Oswald who would have been living inside the U.S. and doing their double-agent side of work in the U.S. Richard Case Nagell, ostensibly the only double-agent reported in all the JFK assassination literature, was being run by the CIA and the KGB, but not even Nagell himself really knew who his supervisors were on either side. At the end, Nagell suspected he was being misled into believing he was a double-agent. He believed that both ends of the double-agency were actually being run only by a single agency. Nagell had no way to find out for sure.

One thing would be certain. Whichever agency was operating double-agents, that fact, and the identity of the agents would have to be the best kept secret in Washington. If Otepka were keeping his own filing system on persons he believed to be double-agents, then that would create a hideous risk to the lives of those agents. If Otepka betrayed the identity of a U.S. double agent being run by our government and that agent was killed as a result, that situation could easily have landed Otepka a life sentence at hard labor in Leavenworth.

Since unauthorized double-agents with the Soviets in the State Department would likely, if discovered, be covered up, then the Senate Internal Security Subcommittee would have it as a top priority to discover Soviet/U.S. double-agents in the State Department. Otepka was the SISS "informant" in the State Department for this and other purposes. Ergo, the impetus for Otepka's continuing "hot" investigation of Oswald was most likely being directed by SISS and battled against by Robert Kennedy.

Why would Robert Kennedy want to know about U.S./Soviet double-agents? 1) He would want to avoid embarrassment of the administration 2) he might have in mind using these agents directly out of the White House to get intelligence or to pick their brains, and 3) the joint relationship between the agents, the U.S. and the U.S.S.R. might be used as links which would further the policy of détente with the U.S.S.R.

In conclusion, all of the above information points to the involvement of Robert Kennedy with Oswald in some way long before the assassination. It also points to further involvement of the Senate Internal Security Subcommittee in the same way with Oswald. This ties in with the use that SISS was making of Otepka as their spy or informant inside the State Department. Oswald could have been a double agent. Since he was married to a girl whose father was high up in the Soviet NKVD, this might amount to the same thing, especially since Oswald had spent 2 ½ years in the Soviet Union.

The timing of the buildup of harassment of Otepka from December 1960 to October 1963 completely parallels the buildup of tension between the Kennedys, anti-Communists in the Congress, disgruntled officers in the military, certain foreign governments and segregationists. All of these forces came together to result in the assassination.

At the same time they were involved with the Otepka battle, the Senate Internal Security Committee was also involved, through Chairman Thomas Dodd, with Oswald's particular weapons vendors, Oswald's Fair Play for Cuba Committee (FPCC) and Oswald's Socialist Workers Party SWP.

In his book *General Walker*, author Dr. Jeffrey Caulfield conclusively shows that Lee Harvey Oswald was busy infiltrating as many as 5 allegedly Communist groups in New Orleans under the direction of SISS Chairman James O. Eastland. This was part of Eastland's plan to render the Civil Rights movement to be considered illegal due to alleged Communist activities.

Where there is such an overwhelming odor of smoke, there can be little doubt about the existence of the fire in the Oswald-SISS relationship. The marvel is that Oswald got around so much and wore so many intelligence-related hats. One could even argue that it was Lee Harvey Oswald, not German BND General Reinhard Gehlen, who was the real "Spy of the Century."

In many respects, solving the mysteries of the Otepka case could help lead to a solution for the case of the JFK assassination.

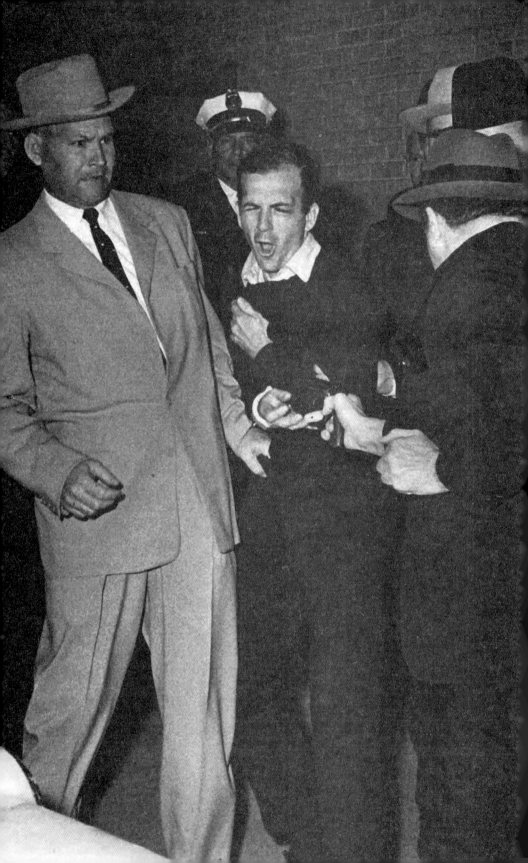

Chapter 40

THE MOTIVATION OF JACK RUBY

There has never been an adequate explanation for a situation described in *Assignment Oswald*, First Edition, by James P. Hosty or for the motives or actions of Jack Ruby in murdering Oswald.. In his book *Assignment Oswald*, FBI Agent Hosty reports that the SAC for Dallas Gordon Shanklin took a phone call with other agents standing by as witnesses. The phone call said that a committee would kill Lee Harvey Oswald and that they could not be stopped in doing that.

It is assumed that if there were a committee who murdered Oswald, that it would be the same committee who murdered JFK. But that is not necessarily so.

Jack Ruby was a devout, practicing member of the Jewish faith. On the weekend of the assassination, he went to the synagogue for spiritual support. When he saw a billboard attacking John F. Kennedy which was signed by Bernard Weissman, he had a strong reaction. Ruby sensed that billboards virtually never have signatures. If you see a political billboard, then there is normally a group, not just one individual, responsible for the message on the billboard and payment for it. When he saw a Jewish name associated with such a shocking billboard, he sensed that something bad was in the air.

Jack Ruby was born Jack Rubenstein in Chicago in 1911. In Chicago, Ruby had actually worked as a courier for Al Capone. Through a freak occurrence, a random researcher came across a memo in the FBI files that Richard Nixon had requested that a Jack Rubenstein be excused from testifying before a committee of Congress because Rubenstein was working as an informant for Nixon.

Ruby moved from Chicago to Dallas in 1947. Around that time, both he and his other family members changed their names from Rubenstein to Ruby. This was apparently due to their wish to assimilate more closely into their community. Ruby did not consider himself any less a Jew for doing this and he attended his synagogue as his chosen place of worship like any other member of his faith.

As most Americans know, Ruby was the owner of a strip club in Dallas called the Carousel Club in partnership with his sister. He also had an interest in a second club in Dallas of a similar nature. Ruby was allegedly involved with organized crime. He made frequent phone calls to known members of the "mafia" as loosely defined. He claimed that he only worked with these people because his girls who worked at his club were affiliated with a union which was controlled by the mafia.

As mentioned above, the billboard bearing the name of Bernard Weissman caused Ruby to become upset with the situation of the President's visit even before JFK's plane landed. It is likely that Ruby had contacts not just in mafia circles but in Jewish circles as well, whether in Dallas or elsewhere. Ruby's concern about the billboard bearing the name of Bernard Weissman was well placed. Bernard Weissman was a soldier who had come from Germany within months OF being stationed in Germany. He was accompanied by fellow enlisted men Larrie Schmidt and his brother Bob Schmidt. It is well-documented that General Edwin Walker and retired General Charles Willoughby had long wished for a program which would foster face-to-face relationships between U.S. soldiers stationed in Germany and ultra-right elements in Germany. Apparently, this effort (to some extent) had succeeded.

On Sunday, November 24, 1963, at around 11:20 A.M., Jack Ruby entered the parking garage of the Dallas Municipal Courts Building and shot Lee Oswald in the abdomen at point blank range. Oswald died soon after.

But Jack Ruby had been stalking Oswald for two days. On November 22, 1963, Ruby spent 8 hours on the upper floors of the police station where Oswald was being jailed and interrogated. At one point, Ruby tried to force his way into an office where Oswald was sitting and had to be restrained. At the famous "midnight press conference" on 11-22-63, Oswald was brought before the press in a press room on the same floor. Ruby corrected a statement made by District Attorney Henry Wade regarding Oswald's associations. Ruby shouted out that Oswald was in fact a member of the Fair Play for Cuba Committee, rather than the Cuban group mentioned by Wade.

In 1959, Jack Ruby had been involved in gun-running into the island of Cuba during the chaotic rise of Fidel Castro to power. He may have been running guns to opponents of Castro or to Castro and his forces. He could have been selling to both sides.

In between these stints at the Police Station, Ruby went from place to place in Dallas including the Cabana motel in Dallas. Some followers of the "lone gunman theory" use the frantic behavior of Ruby as proof that he killed Oswald acting on an irresistible impulse. This impulse was allegedly driven by a sense of patriotism and/or admiration for John F. Kennedy.

Most assassination researchers now believe that Ruby and Oswald were to some degree acquainted. But it is the nature of this acquaintance and the reason for it which has remained shrouded in secrecy. Ruby and Oswald were seen together at a table at Ruby's club, possibly more than once and this has been reported by numerous witnesses. Author Judyth Vary Baker, who was likely a girlfriend of Oswald in 1963, claims that Ruby came to New Orleans as a guest of New Orleans mafia boss Carlos Marcello, which places Ruby and Oswald in close proximity.

Most authors who blame the assassination on the mafia, use the role of Jack Ruby as their prime evidence. Since Ruby had mob connections, then he obviously murdered Oswald under orders from his mafia superiors. The problem is this: there has never been any evidence found of any mafia boss or operative being in contact with Ruby the weekend of the assassination for this purpose, despite Ruby's peripatetic behavior.

What was in Ruby's mind when he murdered Lee Harvey Oswald and with whom was Ruby in contact just prior to that infamous act? If not the mafia, then who?

One clue is the multitude of anguished statements made to the Warren Commission when he was interrogated about the murder of Oswald.

Ruby demanded that he be given a lie detector test regarding his statements to the Warren Commission. He was given one, but it was deliberately botched by the Warren Commission so the results were inconclusive. Ruby demanded to be taken to Washington, D.C. His reason for this: he was afraid of being murdered by "anti-Semites."

On Sunday night, November 24, 1963, there was a meeting in Jack Ruby's apartment in Dallas. Present at that meeting were five people. These included Ruby's roommate George Senator, Attorney Tom Howard, newsmen Bill Hunter of Long Beach California, Jim Koethe of the *Dallas Times Herald*, and a friend of Senator by the name of Jim Martin. A possible sixth person was there as well. Of those six people who were at the apartment, some researchers believe as many as three were murdered in order to obtain their silence. George Senator, the roommate of Ruby apparently knew something very disquieting about the actions of Jack Ruby.

Dorothy Kilgallen's name was a household word in 1963. She was a journalist and permanent guest on the TV show "What's My Line?" Kilgallen was an investigative journalist by trade. When Jack Ruby was convicted and sentenced to death for the murder of Oswald and was being held in the Dallas jail, Kilgallen was granted an interview in a private room with Ruby. After the interview, she boasted to a friend she had "broken the JFK case." Ms. Kilgallen did not live to see the sun go down on that fateful day. She was murdered and her notes stolen. Other notes which she had entrusted to a friend were also stolen.

So what was the secret that Jack Ruby knew? The answer is fairly simple. As usual with statements which were made by assassination figures which sounded crazy, they almost always turned out to be accurate. So when Ruby said he was afraid of being murdered by "anti-Semites," he wasn't blowing smoke. The anti-Semites to which he referred were in fact the most prominent ex-Nazis in the world who had survived and prospered after World War II. Probably, Ruby knew that the source of the JFK plot was a group of Nazis, or at least people whose agenda was driven by anti-Semitism.

Jack Ruby had been an informant for Richard Nixon (and implicitly HUAC) while still a young man. Ruby was not a babe in the woods. He had to know a thing or two about our government and about sinister secret activities.

There are names of the very top echelon of prominent U.S. and Canadian Jews which have been associated with some sort of inside role very close to the assassination plot. There was General Julius Klein, former President of the Jewish War Veterans of America. There was Major Louis Bloomfield, a Canadian who was very high up in British intelligence circles. Both of these men were members of the powerful Sonneborn Institute which sponsored the nuclear program for the State of Israel.

And there was the Israeli Mossad itself which doubtless had contacts inside the U.S. who knew about things that were unknown to the average American. And Stanley Marcus of Dallas was one of the most prominent Jews among those involved in international relief organizations for holocaust victims and similar causes. He was the owner of the exclusive Nieman-Marcus department store in Dallas.

It is very likely that the names of Bernard Weissman and Jack Ruby were deliberately associated falsely with the JFK assassination in the hope that Americans would somehow blame Jews for the murder of JFK. Since this was, apparently, the motive behind involving Bernard Weissman and Jack Ruby, this presents a prima facie case of the involvement of the Old World in the murder of JFK. To a former Nazi, it would be assumed that Americans would eagerly blame Jews for the death of JFK. But any American would know that this would never happen. To most Americans, the religion of the assassin or his associates would be irrelevant.

Ruby was indeed in a state of complete emotional upset when he went out to murder Lee Harvey Oswald. But his upset was due to his situation. He was caught between a despicable act of ex-Nazis and the fears of his co-religionists. Powerful American Jews would be in a state of terror (or at least uncertainty) as to what would happen to them in a confrontation between the U.S. government and the worldwide network of former Nazis.

Americans could scarcely think of Nazis without at the same time thinking of Jews. Would they think that JFK was murdered due to a vendetta between Nazis and Jews?

Jack Ruby knew he had to resolve this situation by murdering Oswald. The "committee" that, according to rumors, had decided to murder

Oswald could have been a committee of concerned Jews or their allies. We will probably never know the precise details of that.

But what we do know for sure, is that if ex-Nazis had murdered JFK and if Jack Ruby knew that to be the case, that could explain Ruby's willingness to face the electric chair for the murder of Oswald. That would explain the seemingly irrational actions of Ruby. In fact, once the blame for the murder of JFK is laid at the door of the Nazi's, then the actions of the Jewish Ruby are no longer a mystery.

Another footnote to the Ruby-Judaism theory just described is the behavior of film-shooter Abraham Zapruder. Zapruder was another Jewish citizen of Dallas. Zapruder famously mounted a concrete pedestal in Dallas to film the assassination. The pedestal was just a few feet away from the limo when JFK was killed. Mounting the pedestal had to require very strenuous effort for the businessman Zapruder. Could Zapruder, as a Jew, been part of a desperate plan by powerful Jewish interests to foil the plot by his actions in filming? Or could his filming have been intended as a way to strike back against Nazi conspirators by proving the extent of the conspiracy, and thus leading to their being exposed? This could be another of those "coincidences" where someone just happened to be in the right place at the right time.

			Tri-lateral Commission	Council on Foreign Relations	Bilderberg Group and SS Chmn Prince Bernard,Neth.	Chmn Chase Manhattan Bank David Rockefeller	CEO Dillon, Read Banker Clarence Dillon	European Intl Banker Mayer Rothschild							
						Chair Council on Foreign Rel. John McCloy		Chicago Mayor Richard J Daley	Speaker of House of Reps John McCormack	<-------------------	-------------------	-------------------	------------------->	Vatican ^ | v	
			Ex CIA Director Allen Dulles	Nat.Sec.Advis or McGeorge Bundy	Asst Secy of Def. Internat. Security Paul Nitze	Sec. of State Dean Rusk	SISS Chairman Senator James O Eastland	Acting SISS Chairman Senator Thomas J Dodd	----------------->	-----------------> German PR, U.S.Ret. General Kenneth Buchanan, of Julius Klein Inc.	West German "Shadow Ambassador" U.S.General Julius Klein (W. German PR rep)	Hans Globke, Former Nazi, National Security Advisor to Adenauer	West German Chancellor Konrad Adenauer	Ex-West German Foreign Minister Baron Heinrich von Brentano	<? | | | |
	[CIA Intel Scientist and Oswald Mistress Judyth Vary Baker]		Dir New Orleans Trade Mart CIA Agent Clay Shaw	Dep. Natl Sec Adv & Dir of Policy Plng Dept of State Walt Rostow		Secretary of the Treasury C. Douglas Dillon, Head of Secret Service, ATF	Counsel for Bureau of Alcohol, Firearms Thurmond Shaw	SISS---- Dirksen [Ervin] [Hruska] [Keating] [McClellan] [Scott] [Johnston]	Chief NASA Marshall-Redstone Missile Pgm German Baron Gen. Wernher von Braun	Ret Army Gen John B Medaris Former Cmdr Army Redstone Missile Program	Owner of Lionel Corporation and McCarthy Chief Counsel Roy Cohn	New York Mafia figure and Owner of Lionel Corporation Joseph Bonanno	NATO Commander and former Head of Joint Chiefs of Staff General Lyman Lemnitzer	Chief of West German BND Intel Service and former head of CIA Europe group, General Reinhard Gehlen	<? | | | | |
Majority whip for U.S.House of Reps. Hale Boggs of Louisiana	Influential member of Anti-Communist INCA in New Orleans, Dr Alton Ochsner	Executive Dir. Of Anti-Communist INCA New Orleans Ed Butler	CIA Operative David W Ferrie		Sec Svc Chief James J Rowley		Chief of Dallas ATF Frank Ellsworth	Dallas Mayor Earl Cabell	Chief of Weapons Dev. Bell Aircraft German Gen Walter Dornberger	West German Intel Agent Walter Becher	Fmr CIA Deputy Director Gen Charles Cabell	Ex-SISS Counsel Robert J Morris	German Baron US General Charles A Willoughby	German Nazi General, NATO Mil.Cmte.Chmn Adolf Heusinger	<? | | |
Cuban Exile leader Carlos Bringuier	Cuban Exile leader Sergio Arcacha Smith	FBI, CIA Intel-Coordinator in New Orleans, Guy Banister	Lee Harvey Oswald New Orleans		Dep Sec Svc Chief Paul J Paterni		Lee Harvey Oswald Dallas	Dallas Chief of Police Jesse Curry	Bell Aircraft Engineer Michael Payne		CEO Schlumberger Jean de Menil, aka John de Menil	Nazi involved Ex-CongressmanCharles Kersten	CIA/ex-German Nazi Mole Baron George de Mohrenshild	Retired General Edwin Walker	Retired British U.S.Branch Intel Chief Sir William Stephenson
					Sec Svc SAC Forrest Sorrels			Dallas Detective Will Fritz	Ruth Payne		Dallas right- wing activist/agent Paul Ragiorodsky	Dallas Mayor Earl Cabell	Lee Harvey Oswald Dallas	Owner Texas School Book Depository D Harold Byrd	
	Fake Secret Svc Shooter #1	Fake Secret Svc Shooter #2	Fake Secret Svc Shooter #3	SS Agent William Greer	SS Agent Roy Kellerman			Jack Ruby	Lee Harvey Oswald Dallas						

Chapter 41

THE ORGANIZATIONAL CHART OF THE KENNEDY ASSASSINATION

This is the organizational chart of the assassination. It traces the lines of authority which ran from the highest levels of influence on planet earth, right down to the lowly people on the street, the Lee Harvey Oswalds, the Jack Rubys and Officer J.D. Tipits.

When JFK was murdered, it was the first time that the most powerful person on earth had been assassinated since the assassination of Julius Ceasar on the Ides of March, 3/15/44 B.C. Something like this cannot happen with the act of a lone gunman when there followed four governmental investigations, hundreds, perhaps thousands of books written and the names of many of the most powerful in the world brought into question. If one puts all the cards on the table, the above chart is what results. All the other chapters herein describe the role of most, if not all of the persons on this chart. Out of approximately 350 names which are cited in the top 100 of more than one of the 30 best assassinations books, only the 65 names on the above chart had a functional role in the assassination. The test of whether to include a name in the chart is basically a legal one: it hinges on whether the individual did some act which furthered the plot or participated in the cover-up before the fact which includes the on-the-ground pre-planned cover-up in Dallas in the aftermath.

The roles of each of the persons on the chart are treated in the various other chapters. The chart, showing the lines of authority, speaks for itself.

Chapter 42

FACTOR ANALYSIS AND JFK ASSASSINATION RESEARCH

In order to use statistical methods to analyze the JFK assassination books and identify which theories they are following, it is necessary to reduce the information into quantitative form.

To do this, I used the data found in the indexes of various books. I attempted to identify the names which were roughly the top 100 names cited in each book. If the top 100 or so were cited three times each, then 3 citations was the cutoff. This method would obviously not yield exactly 100 names. The range of names cited nearest to the top 100 actually varied from about 80 to 120. In each book there were almost exactly 50% of the names which were duplicates with at least one other book. In assembling the names, a database was gradually developed consisting of approximately 1500 names. The statistical software which was used allowed a maximum of 1500 names as data and this limit was reached at around 30 books. The software package used was one of the simplified editions of SPSS, which is the gold standard for statistical software.

The statistical technique chosen to analyze the data is known as factor analysis. This sounds technical but it is actually fairly simple. Let's take the example where the 30 books were the variables. In factor analysis, the computer calculates the correlation of the frequency of citations of the names between books.

For example, the Warren Commission Report and *Rush To Judgment* by Mark Lane are highly correlated. The WC might cite Lee Harvey Oswald on 100 pages. Mark Lane might cite Oswald on 90 pages. The WC might cite James Hosty on 20 pages. Mark Lane might cite him on 35 pages, and so on. In this manner, the correlation between the frequency of citations for each book to each of the other 30 books is put, by the computer, into a matrix. It would be a 30 x 30 matrix. Then the rows in the matrix are moved around so that the books that are most highly correlated are in the first four or five rows and columns. Four books that have high correlations in the number of citations of names are *Rush To Judgment* by Lane, the WC Report, *Deep Politics* by Peter Dale Scott and *Accessories After The Fact* by Sylvia Meagher.

So these four books are grouped in the upper left hand corner of the matrix.

Next, a second group of books that are highly correlated are identified. For example, these four books are next highest in correlation: *A Farewell to Justice* by Joan Mellen, *Heritage of Stone* and *On The Trail of the Assassins* by Jim Garrison and *Me & Lee* by Judyth Vary Baker. This makes sense because all four books are dealing with suspects located in New Orleans and three of them actually deal specifically with the Garrison investigation. So these books form the next grouping on the matrix, just below and to the right of the books which correlate to the Warren Commission.

The process is repeated until all 30 books are thus grouped. Some books don't correlate to any other books. For instance, *The Last Investigation* by Gaeton Fonzi has virtually no correlation to any other book. That's because Fonzi focuses almost exclusively on the anti-Castro Cubans and suspects like Antonio Veciana. After these groupings are complete, one can easily see which books are similar and one can also easily see which books are the most diverse. *Farewell America* by James Hepburn correlates to four different groupings.

Next, the groupings have to be interpreted and identified. That can be done by simply examining the names most often cited in the four books in the grouping. If the names are mafia names, then that group is a mafia-oriented book. If the names include a lot of Warren Commission witnesses, then it is a Warren Commission-oriented book.

Six books were included which are not JFK assassination books. These books were written about groups like the Minutemen and the John Birch Society. This was done to make it easier to sort out the multitude of right-wing organizations often accused of complicity in the assassination. It is easy to identify Carlos Marcello as a mafia person. It is not so easy to place a name like Clarence Manion, who was one of the founders of the John Birch Society.

There is one technicality which might iinterest statistically-oriented readers. As we have seen, the books are grouped together. In one technique, once the books are grouped, they are eliminated from the matrix and the remaining books are then grouped without them. If they are totally eliminated after grouping, this is called "without rotation." If they are left in for the next grouping, this is called "with rotation." The option "without rotation" gives cleaner groupings. But using "with rotation" allows for the overlapping nature of factors. For example, LBJ might be in a grouping of "Texas cronies" or he might be in the grouping for "world leaders." So something might be gained by not totally eliminating him after the first grouping.

Note that we have also switched from grouping books to grouping individuals like LBJ, RFK, Lee Harvey Oswald and so on. The same technique that we used on grouping books can be used on the individuals cited.

To do this, the names of individuals appearing most frequently in the 14 most diverse assassination books were used. Then, for statistical reasons, persons cited frequently in only one book were eliminated. This narrowed the list of names from 1500 down to 191.

Since we did our procedure on 191 individuals, that gives a matrix 191 by 191, which is a very large matrix.

But the power of doing this should be readily apparent. In this situation, the computer could theoretically determine which individuals were working together by putting them in groups where the human mind might not recognize a relationship.

This produces some spectacular results. As mentioned later, when each of the factors are examined and the order of "loadings" for each factor are sorted by individual, the computer can put people together in an amazing way. When the group of 191 names was examined in this way, Allen Dulles and John Foster Dulles appeared next to each other on the list for factor two. They were, of course, brothers. But the Dulles brothers are normally not intentionally discussed together in any of the JFK assassination books.

FACTOR ANALYSIS USING THE *INDIVIDUALS* AS THE VARIABLE

The following is a listing of the seven factors which are obtained by treating the individuals, not the books, as the variable. Instead of 30 books as variables, we have 191 individuals which can be used as variables because they are cited in the top 100 citations in more than just one book.

In the listing of the factors below, 14 books were selected for the diversity of the theories and the correlation of the books between each other. Only individuals who were cited often in at least two of these books were considered.

The books selected were *Deep Politics* by Peter Dale Scott, *Brothers in Arms* by Guy Russo, *TMWKTM* by Dick Russell, *Bloody Treason* by Noel Twyman, *Farewell America* by James Hepburn, *Me & Lee* by Judyth Vary Baker, *On the Trail of the Assassins* and *Heritage of Stone* by Jim Garrison, *LBJ: Mastermind* by Philip Nelson, *Permindex* by Executive Intelligence Review (*EIR*), *The Torbitt File* by William Torbitt, *JFK: The CIA, Vietnam* by L. Fletcher Prouty, *General Walker* by Dr. Jeffrey Caulfield, and *Final Judgment* by Michael Collins Piper.

There were serious limitations on the software available for the analysis by individuals. The program used only allowed for 50 variables and there were actually 191 individuals to be analyzed. This problem was solved by breaking the 191 into four groups of less than 50. The first factor was extracted from each group. Then the four output matrices of the correlations to each factor were combined and sorted. This created one matrix of the seven most important factors.

Next, those individuals loaded for the first factor were removed from the list and the process was repeated for each of the next 7 factors. However, for factors 5, 6 and 7, the matrices were combined and the factors which were extracted for 5, 6 and 7 were used, without eliminating each list of individuals separately. This was done in the interest of saving time and the last three factors are obviously of less importance than the first four.

Factor 1 shows 15 out of the 33 suspects on our list of 191 names. These 191 represent names which are cited in approximately the top 100 most-often cited in the 14 most diverse assassination research books. Only the names which are cited in two or more books in the top 100 were considered. Note that Perry Russo has been classified as a suspect when he was merely present when Clay Shaw allegedly paid money to Lee Harvey Oswald. That is apparently why the computer has grouped him with others who are true suspects. Note the Vietnam connection of the world leaders on the list, especially Henry Cabot Lodge, the Kennedys and the Diems.

In some cases, individuals were highlighted as suspects when they are not actually on the organizational chart. An example is General Edward G. Lansdale.

One of the most amazing results was in regard to the Dulles brothers. When the list for factor 2 is sorted by loadings, rather than as printed here, Allen Dulles and John Foster Dulles appear next to each other. The two brothers are never discussed in the assassination books in relation to each other. But the computer seemed able to place them next to each other in the list of the 191 people sorted by factor and then by loading.

Also note that Reverend Billy James Hargis and Reverend Carl McIntyre appear next to each other as they were associated by the computer.

Note that most of the CIA agents are grouped by the computer as well as the Cubans. Both are grouped under the same factor because the CIA was working so closely with the Cubans.

Richard Case Nagell groups with three other CIA-involved individuals. Ambassador Thomas Mann was technically not a CIA employee, although he was the U.S. Ambassador in Mexico City where the CIA was very active. This is apparently why he correlates with the CIA agents.

Note that of the world leaders listed in factor 1, they were basically currently serving as world leaders. However, the world leaders in factor 2 were predominantly past world leaders such as Harry S. Truman and Winston Churchill. These past world leaders were nevertheless highly correlated as a group, falling into the second-highest factor.

Key: Suspects (1), World Leaders (2), Spies and Informants (3), Right-wing Persons (4), Cubans (5), Mafia (6), Authors (7), Others (8)	Suspects are always in italics at the top of the lists.			Totals: Suspects (33), World Leaders (37), Spies and Informants (17), Right-wing People (17), Cubans (10), Mafia (11), Authors (10), Others (32)		
Category				Category		
Factor 1				Factor 2		
Name	Short Name	Correl		Name	Short Name	Correl
1 Lemnitzer, Gen Lyman	LEMNI	0.894		1 Bundy, McGeorge	BUNDYMC	0.847
1 DeMenil, Jean	DEMENIL	0.877		1 Dulles, Allen	DULLESA	0.796
1 Bonanno, Joseph	BONANO	0.849		1 Oswald, Lee Harvey	OSWALLH	0.503
1 Dornberger, Gen Walter	DORNBERG	0.843		2 ChaingKaiShek	CHAIN	0.902
1 Kellerman, Agent Roy	KELLERMN	0.820		2 Dulles, John Foster	DULLEJF	0.875
1 Cohn, Roy	COHN	0.814		2 King, Martin Luther	KINGML	0.843
1 Lansdale, Gen Edward	LANSD	0.793		2 Stevenson, Adlai	STEVEAD	0.806
1 McCloy, John B	MCCLO	0.790		2 Truman, Harry S	TRUMA	0.784
1 Bloomfield, Louis	BLOOMFD	0.765		2 Meredith, James	MEREDITH	0.778
1 Raigorodsky, Paul	RAGIOROD	0.701		2 Goldwater, Barry	GOLDWATE	0.774
1 Willoughby, Gen Charles	WILLOUGH	0.698		2 Clifford, Clark	CLIFF	0.763
1 Walker, Gen Edwin	WALKE	0.695		2 Eisenhower, Dwight	EISENDW	0.738
1 Shaw, Clay	SHAWCLAY	0.691		2 Ford, Gerald	FORD	0.701
1 VonBraun, Wernher	VONBRAUN	0.518		2 Roosevelt, Franklin	ROOSEF	0.648
2 Lodge, Henry Cabot	LODGE	0.908		2 Ellsberg, Daniel	ELLSB	0.562
2 NgoDinhDiem	NGODIDM	0.900		2 Churchill, Winston	CHURC	0.485
2 McNamara, Robert S	MCNAM	0.881		4 Hargis, Rev Billy James	HARGI	0.894
2 NgoDinhNhu	NGODINU	0.856		4 McIntyre, Rev Carl	MCINT	0.837
2 Humphrey, Hubert	HUMPH	0.846		4 Gill, G Wray	GILL	0.799
2 Kennedy, Robert F	KENNERF	0.843		4 Wedemeyer, Gen Albert	WEDEM	0.724
2 Kennedy, Joseph P	KENNEJP	0.804		4 Martin, Jac,	MARTI	0.718
2 Galbraith, J Kenneth	GALBR	0.791		4 MacArthur, Gen Douglas	MACAR	0.712
2 Fulbright, J William	FULBRIGH	0.790		4 Hunt, Nelson Bunker	HUNTNB	0.698
2 Kennedy, Ethel	KENNEET	0.752		4 Pawley, William	PAWLEY	0.667
2 Kennedy, Edward M	KENNEED	0.716		4 McCarthy, Joseph	MCCARTHY	0.625
2 Nixon, Richard M	NIXON	0.693		4 Surrey, Robert	SURRE	0.571
2 Kennedy, Jacqueline	KENNEJQ	0.657		4 Murchison, Clint	MURCH	0.528
2 Johnson, Lyndon B	JOHNSLBJ	0.656		4 Hunt, HL	HUNTHL	0.504
2 DeGaulle, Gen Charles	DEGAU	0.650		3 Hall, Loren	HALLLORE	0.745
2 Warren, Earl	WARRE	0.614		3 Sturgis, Frank	STURG	0.682
2 Khruschev, Nikita	KRUSC	0.388		3 Morales, David	MORAL	0.496
3 Carroll, Gen Joseph	CARROLLJ	0.857		3 Sullivan, William	SULLIVAN	0.478
3 Sheridan, Walter	SHERI	0.739		6 Traficante, Santos	TRAFFICS	0.747
3 Bissell, Richard	BISSE	0.659		6 Roseli, Johnny	ROSEL	0.739
3 Phillips, David Atlee	PHILLIPD	0.603		7 Summers, Anthony	SUMME	0.634
3 Stephenson, William	STEPHENS	0.599		8 Odonnel, Kenneth	ODONN	0.611
3 Seymour, William	SEYMO	0.567		8 Ward, Hugh	WARD	0.542
3 McCone, John	MCCON	0.449		8 Forrestal, Michael	FORRE	0.478
3 Thornley, Kerry	THORNLEY	0.353		8 Zapruder, Abraham	ZAPRU	0.461
7 Lawrence, David	LAWRE	0.646				
7 Garrison, Jim	GARRI	0.542				
7 Russell, Dick	RUSSEDK	0.539				
8 Russo, Perry	RUSSO	0.794				
8 Challe, Maurice	CHALLEMA	0.740				
4 Rothermel, Paul	ROTHERML	0.636				
8 Lemay, Gen Curtis	LEMAY	0.602				
6 Marcello, Carlos	MARCE	0.485				
8 Sciambra, Andrew	SCIAM	0.399				

Category				Category			
Factor 3				Factor 4			
Name	Short Name	Correl		Name	Short Name	Correl	
1 Hidell, Alec	HIDEL	0.692		1 Medaris, Gen John B	MEDARISJ	0.739	
1 Banister, Guy	BANISTR	0.529		1 Ruby, Jack	RUBYJACK	0.558	
1 Paine, Ruth	PAINERUT	0.391		1 Rusk, Dean	RUSK	0.470	
3 Nagell, Richard Case	NAGELRC	0.842		5 Artime, Manuel	ARTIM	0.705	
3 Morrow, Robert	MORRO	0.828		5 Batista, Fulgencio	BATIS	0.662	
3 Fitzgerald, Desmond	FITZGDS	0.820		5 Cubela, Rolando	CUBEL	0.737	
3 Mann, Amb Thomas	MANN	0.785		5 Duran, Sylvia	DURAN	0.878	
3 Angleton, James	ANGLE	0.779		5 Escalante Fabian	ESCAL	0.898	
3 Barnes, Traccy	BARNSTR	0.752		5 Guevara, Che	GUEVA	0.725	
3 Fensterwald, Bernard	FENST	0.731		3 Harvey, William	HARVE	0.783	
3 Scott, Winston	SCOTTWI	0.723		3 Hoover, J Edgar	HOOVE	0.609	
3 Helms, Richard	HELMSRI	0.678		3 Novel, Gordon	NOVEL	0.883	
3 Brooks, Jerry Milton	BROOKS	0.538		3 Osborne, Albert	OSBOR	0.894	
3 Leopoldo	LEOPO	0.835		8 Korth, Fred	KORTH	0.778	
3 Masferrer, Rolano	MASFE	0.804		6 Levinson, Ed	LEVIN	0.795	
3 Castro, Fidel	CASTROF	0.773		6 McWillie, Lewis	MCWILLIE	0.890	
3 Veciana, Antonio	VECIA	0.737					
3 Angel	ANGEL	0.682					
8 Rankin, J Lee	RANKI	0.828					
8 Lee, V T	LEEVT	0.677					
8 Oswald, Marguerite	OSWALMG	0.623					
6 Murret, Charles	MURRECH	0.501					

Category				Category			
Factor 5				Factor 6			
Name	Short Name	Correl		Name	Short Name	Correl	
	factor 5				factor 6		
1 Eastland, James O	EASTL	0.729		1 Ferrie, David W	FERRI	0.527	
1 Boggs, Rep Hale	BOGGS	0.716		1 DeMohrenschildt, George	DEMOHG	0.431	
1 Fritz, Will	FRITZ	0.650		1 Tipitt, J D	TIPPI	0.427	
1 Sorrels, Forrest	SORRELS	0.639		1 Gehlen, Gen Reinhard	GEHLE	0.084	
2 Symington, Sen Stuart	SYMIN	0.931		4 Martin, Jack	MARTINJK	0.677	
2 Rayburn, Rep Sam	RAYBU	0.873		4 Milteer, Joseph	MILTE	0.509	
2 Connally, Gov John	CONALJHN	0.708		3 Hunt, E Howard	HUNTEH	0.730	
2 Russell, Sen Richard	RUSSESEN	0.681		3 Philbrick, Herbert	PHILB	0.570	
2 Baker, Bobby	BAKERB	0.567		6 Hoffa, James	HOFFA	0.647	
2 Mattei, Enrico	MATTEIEN	0.548		7 Lane, Mark	LANE	0.533	
2 Blough, Roger	BLOUGHRO	0.449		8 Alcock, James	ALCOC	0.761	
4 Manchester, William	MANCH	0.946		8 Finck, Pierre	FINCKPIE	0.632	
4 Schlesinger, Arthur Jr.	SCHLE	0.661		8 Haley, J Evetts	HALEY	0.627	
5 DelValle, Eladio	DELVA	0.721		8 Weisberg, Harold	WEISB	0.617	
8 Black, Fred	BLACKFR	0.628		8 Andrews, Dean	ANDRE	0.605	
8 Bradley, Edgar Eugene	BRADLEY	0.626		8 Estes, Billie Sol	ESTES	0.527	
8 Behn, Gerald	BEHN	0.579		8 Craig, Roger	CRAIG	0.494	
8 Lifton, David	LIFTO	0.445		8 Ivon, Louis	IVON	0.490	
8 Jenkins, Walter	JENKI	0.343		8 Mercer, Julia	MERCER	0.387	
8 Oswald, Marina	OSWALMA	0.271		8 Hilsman, Roger	HILSMANR	0.254	
8 Oswald, Julie	OSWALJU	0.157		8 Harkins, Paul	HARKINS	0.135	

For some reason the suspects who have fallen down to the level of the 5th factor are there because they are mostly suspects who were identified with the localities of New Orleans and Dallas. It could mean that the relationship between the suspects in factor 1 and factor 5 was somehow different. Note that Senator James O. Eastland and Representative Hale Boggs appear next to one another. They were the members of Congress most closely involved in the New Orleans area.

Category			
	Factor 7		
	Name	Short Name	Correl
1	*Cabell, Gen Charles*	*CABELLCH*	0.366
1	*Curry, Jesse*	*CURRYJES*	0.359
7	**Prouty, L Fletcher**	**PROUTY**	0.738
7	**Fonzi, Gaeton**	**FONZI**	0.686
7	**Stone, Oliver**	**STONE**	0.662
7	**Brown, Madeleine**	**BROWN**	0.606
7	**Blakey, G Robert**	**BLAKELY**	0.442
3	Hemmings, Gary Patrick	HEMMI	0.846
3	Hosty, Agent James	HOSTY	0.552
3	Kostikov, Valery	KOSTIKOV	0.511
3	Gatlin Maurice	GATLINMA	0.483
5	Arcacha-Smith, Sergio	ARCAC	0.436
5	Odio, Sylvia	ODIO	0.343
5	Bringuier, Carlos	BRING	0.299
6	Giancana, Sam	GIANC	0.796
6	Luciano, Charles	LUCIA	0.608
6	Lansky, Meyer	LANSK	0.580
6	Taylor, Gen Maxwell	TAYLO	0.651
8	Klein, Frank	KLEINFRA	0.345
8	Humes, Dr. James Humes	HUMES	0.158

Also significant is the fact that General Medaris and Jack Ruby are grouped next to the Cubans in factor 4. The mafia involvement of Jack Ruby is well documented and the Cubans were working with the Mafia in the attempt to assassinate Fidel Castro. In 1959, Jack Ruby was involved with running guns into Cuba.

Another surprise here is that the *very lowest correlation* out of the entire 191 names analyzed was that of General Reinhard Gehlen. Ironically, there is a remote possibility that Gehlen was the one individual who planned the entire JFk assassination. Perhaps we get our result because Gehlen was so good at keeping himself distanced from the other plotters.

Factor Analysis Using The Books As The Variable

The percentage of variance explained is listed across the top of the matrix. The captions at the top such as "Warren Commission Evidence" represent the best interpretation of the data for that factor. Note that the Warren Commission evidence accounts for 34% of the variance. Second is the Castro-Mafia factor. Third are the Jim Garrison (New Orleans) suspects. Fourth is the LBJ – J Edgar Hoover theory. The percentages fall off quickly after that.

The overriding discovery in the analysis is that roughly one-third of the information published about the assassination traces back to matters introduced by the Warren Commission. To the extent that this was intended as disinformation or that the Warren Commission excluded relevant information, one sees how influential and successful the Warren Commission was in biasing the universe of data.

Another interesting discovery is exactly how many factors a particular book might be correlated with. In other words, which books are more broad and not merely focused on one theory. In that respect, Peter Dale Scott, James Hepburn, Noel Twyman, William Torbitt, Judyth Vary Baker and Jim Garrison-Joan Mellen each have higher loadings on four factors. None are loaded on five.

So what can be concluded from the above? The books that have the most diverse loadings happen to be the books which are working from

Rotated Component Matrix

Component factor labels (by column):

1. Warren Commission Evidence
2. Castro-Mafia-Cubans
3. New Orleans Defendants
4. LBJ-Hoover
5. John Birch Society
6. British-Zionists
7. Military-Ind Complex
8. Anti-Castro Cubans
9. Walker-Right Wing
10. Southern Politicians
11. Zionists
12. Dallas Solidarists
13. White-Citz-Cncls
14. Rt-Wing Preacher
15. Minutemen

	1	2	3	4	5	6	7	8	9	10	11	12	13	14	15
	34%	7%	6%	6%	5%	4%	3%	3%	3%	3%	3%	2%	2%	2%	2%
RUSHJUD	0.88	0.06	0.02	0.10	0.01	0.05	0.00	0.01	0.11	0.04	0.10	0.02	0.06	0.02	0.01
MEAGHER	0.85	0.21	0.25	0.07	0.00	0.01	0.03	0.09	0.02	0.01	0.01	0.20	0.01	0.00	0.00
WARRENC	0.75	0.32	0.29	0.08	0.00	0.00	0.01	0.08	0.03	0.05	0.04	0.28	0.02	0.00	0.01
BLAKEY	0.64	0.41	0.18	0.28	0.00	0.08	0.04	0.09	0.15	0.10	0.31	0.04	0.06	0.03	0.00
PDSCOTT	0.55	0.35	0.17	0.46	0.02	0.17	0.06	0.11	0.15	0.16	0.23	0.01	0.10	0.04	0.01
KAISER	0.28	0.77	0.18	0.18	0.01	0.06	0.03	0.14	0.06	0.07	0.22	0.03	0.05	0.03	0.02
CASTRO	0.24	0.76	0.17	0.14	0.04	0.00	0.10	0.01	0.12	0.15	0.05	0.17	0.06	0.01	0.02
TMWKTM	0.17	0.63	0.19	0.16	0.02	0.07	0.02	0.16	0.27	0.07	0.10	0.23	0.01	0.02	0.02
BTREASON	0.36	0.51	0.32	0.48	0.02	0.07	0.13	0.24	0.12	0.00	0.14	0.06	0.02	0.01	0.01
DOUGLASS	0.38	0.50	0.39	0.16	0.06	0.04	0.28	0.25	0.05	0.07	0.00	0.08	0.07	0.05	0.02
HEPBURN	0.10	0.44	0.03	0.30	0.10	0.19	0.43	0.04	0.22	0.33	0.09	0.00	0.13	0.14	0.01
MELLEN	0.10	0.25	0.68	0.10	0.06	0.28	0.08	0.12	0.36	0.07	0.11	0.03	0.01	0.02	0.01
MENLEE	0.23	0.36	0.67	0.09	0.05	0.08	0.15	0.14	0.20	0.14	0.15	0.05	0.07	0.02	0.01
HERITAGE	0.57	0.27	0.59	0.15	0.00	0.05	0.09	0.22	0.03	0.05	0.07	0.15	0.05	0.03	0.01
TRAILASS	0.22	0.11	0.81	0.08	0.04	0.27	0.07	0.14	0.24	0.05	0.08	0.12	0.00	0.00	0.01
LBJMAST	0.03	0.16	0.08	0.88	0.02	0.00	0.14	0.05	0.01	0.16	0.06	0.04	0.06	0.00	0.00
HOOVER	0.33	0.23	0.09	0.81	0.03	0.14	0.06	0.03	0.09	0.03	0.11	0.01	0.02	0.01	0.02
EXTREMIS	0.00	0.02	0.00	0.05	0.94	0.01	0.01	0.01	0.09	0.05	0.02	0.00	0.03	0.04	0.02
JBSBIG	0.00	0.03	0.03	0.02	0.93	0.02	0.09	0.00	0.08	0.08	0.01	0.00	0.04	0.05	0.01
EIR	0.03	0.06	0.19	0.08	0.03	0.93	0.01	0.03	0.01	0.01	0.09	0.00	0.02	0.01	0.00
TORBITT	0.38	0.09	0.42	0.43	0.00	0.50	0.00	0.09	0.06	0.04	0.01	0.08	0.02	0.01	0.01
PROUTY	0.03	0.09	0.04	0.14	0.05	0.03	0.93	0.02	0.04	0.03	0.04	0.01	0.00	0.06	0.01
FONZI	0.15	0.19	0.13	0.05	0.01	0.01	0.03	0.91	0.04	0.03	0.10	0.05	0.03	0.01	0.00
WALKER	0.16	0.08	0.21	0.12	0.25	0.01	0.04	0.06	0.79	0.17	0.03	0.02	0.07	0.01	0.07
GOTHICPO	0.02	0.01	0.02	0.12	0.02	0.01	0.05	0.03	0.11	0.88	0.01	0.02	0.25	0.02	0.00
FINALJUD	0.19	0.19	0.19	0.18	0.01	0.11	0.06	0.11	0.04	0.03	0.87	0.07	0.02	0.01	0.00
RINELLA	0.23	0.20	0.11	0.04	0.00	0.02	0.01	0.05	0.02	0.02	0.06	0.90	0.01	0.01	0.00
CITZCNCL	0.02	0.00	0.01	0.03	0.01	0.02	0.02	0.03	0.05	0.22	0.01	0.01	0.94	0.01	0.01
CHFRIGHT	0.01	0.02	0.01	0.02	0.09	0.01	0.01	0.01	0.01	0.03	0.00	0.00	0.01	0.99	0.02
MINUTEMN	0.00	0.02	0.00	0.02	0.03	0.00	0.01	0.00	0.05	0.00	0.00	0.00	0.01	0.02	1.00

Extraction Method: Principal Component Analysis. Rotation Method: Varimax with Kaiser Normalization.

a   Rotation converged in 12 iterations.

original sources. Jim Garrison and Judyth Vary Baker had their own unique sources. Torbitt and Hepburn are pseudonyms and both appear to be information drawn from inside sources.

The Hepburn data has loadings on factors 2,4,7 and 10. The Torbitt data is loaded on factors 1,3,4 and 6. So if both of these anonymous writers were drawing on "inside" information, there was not much overlap between the names which they featured.

The books in the book matrix are listed in order as follows:

Rush to Judgment by Mark Lane, *Accessories After the Fact* by Sylvia Meagher, *The Warren Commission Report: Report of the President's Commission on the Assassination of President John F. Kennedy,* by President's Commission on The Assassination, *The Plot to Kill the President* by George Robert Blakey,*Deep Politics and the Death of JFK* by Peter Dale Scott, *The Road to Dallas: The Assassination of John F. Kennedy* by David Kaiser, *Brothers in Arms: The Kennedys, the Castros, and the Politics of Murder* by Gus Russo and Stephen Molton, *The Man Who Knew Too Much: Hired to Kill Oswald and Prevent the Assassination of JFK* by Dick Russell, *Bloody Treason: On Solving History's Greatest Murder Mystery : The Assassination of John F. Kennedy* by Noel Twyman, *JFK and the Unspeakable: Why He Died and Why It Matters* by James W. Douglass, *Farewell America: The Plot to Kill JFK* by James Hepburn and William Turner, *A Farewell to Justice: Jim Garrison, JFK's Assassination, And the Case That Should Have Changed History* by Joan Mellen, *Me & Lee: How I Came to Know, Love and Lose Lee Harvey Oswald* by Judyth Vary Baker, *A Heritage of Stone* by Jim Garrison, *On the Trail of the Assassins* by Jim Garrison, *LBJ: The Mastermind of the JFK Assassination* by Phillip F. Nelson, *Act of Treason: The Role of J. Edgar Hoover in the Assassination of President Kennedy* by Mark North, *The Strange Tactics of Extremism* by Harry A. Overstreet and Bonaro Wilkins Overstreet, *The John Birch Society: Anatomy of a Protest* by J. Allen Broyles, *Permindex: Britain's International Assassination Bureau,* by Jeffrey Steinberg and David Goldman, *NASA, Nazis & JFK* by William Torbitt and Kenn Thomas, *JFK: The CIA, Vietnam, and the Plot to Assassinate John F. Kennedy* by L. Fletcher Prouty, *The Last Investigation* by Gaeton Fonzi, *General Walker and the Murder of President Kennedy: The Extensive New Evidence of a Radical-Right Conspiracy* by Jeffrey H. Caulfield M.D., *Gothic Politics in the Deep South: Stars of the new Confederacy* by Robert Sherrill, *Final Judgment: The Missing Link in the JFK Assassination Conspiracy* by Michael Collins Piper, *Lee Harvey Oswald as I Knew Him* by George de Mohrenschildt (Author) and Michael A. Rinella (Editor), *Men of the Far Right* by Richard Dudman, *The Citizens' Council: Organized Resistance to the Second Reconstruction, 1954-64* by Neil R. McMillen, *The Christian Fright Peddlers* by Brooks R Walker and *The Minutemen* by J. Harry Jones.

The following is a breakdown of which names tend to be cited in the various types of books according to their factors. It is easy to see that the *Torbitt File*, the *Executive Intelligence Review* publication and *Farewell America* by James Hepburn contain the most accurate information, if one had to choose between books. Coincidentally, both Torbitt and Hepburn are pseudonyms and were published "on the sly." Both of these books clearly contain inside information. These two, along with the book by L. Fletcher Prouty probably contain the only inside information that fans of JFK assassination research will ever see in our lifetimes.

Factor 1			Factor 2	
Most frequent citations in books which are biased in the direction of Warren Commission evidence.			Most frequent names in books blaming Castro-Mafia and anti-Castro Cubans	
Oswald, Lee Harvey	112		Oswald, Lee Harvey	115
Ruby, Jack	80		Castro, Fidel	68
Oswald, Marina	43		Kennedy, Robert F	56
Hoover, J Edgar	31		Johnson, Lyndon B	44
Tippit, J D	23		Oswald, Marina	28
Kennedy, Robert F	21		Hoover, J Edgar	26
Connally, John	16		Nagell, Richard Case	24
Rankin, J Lee	15		Eisenhower, Dwight	24
Paine, Ruth	14		Khrushchev, Nikita	24
Curry, Jesse	14		Ruby, Jack	19
Fritz, Will	13		Hunt, H L	16
Warren, Earl	12		Dulles, Allen	16
Castro, Fidel	12		Walker, Edwin	15
Randle, Linnie	11		Marcello, Carlos	14
Walker, Edwin	10		Cubela, Rolando	13

Factor 3			Factor 4	
Most frequent citations in books loaded in the direction of Garrison-New Orleans suspects.			Most frequent citations in books which blame Lyndon Johnson and J. Edgar Hoover.	
Oswald, Lee Harvey	93		Johnson, Lyndon B	42
Ferrie, David	42		Hoover, J Edgar	31
Shaw, Clay	38		Baker, Bobby	27
Garrison, Jim	34		Oswald, Lee Harvey	22
Banister, Guy	21		Kennedy, Robert F	15
Vary, Judyth	17		Estes, Billie Sol	11
Ruby, Jack	15		Marcello, Carlos	11
Castro, Fidel	15		Ruby, Jack	11
Baker, Robert	14		Ferrie, David	5
Kennedy, Robert F	14		Levinson, Ed	5
Ochsner, Alton	10		Manchester, William	4

Martin, Jack	10		Harvey, William	4
Marcello, Carlos	9		Haley, J Evetts	4
Oswald, Marina	8		Carter, Cliff	4
Ivon, Louis	7		Oswald, Marina	3
Beckham, Thomas E	7		Hoffa, James	3

Factors 5,9,10,13,14,15			Factor 6	
Most frequent citations in books blaming the John Birch Society and related individuals.			Most frequent citations in the Torbitt File and the EIR, which blame the British and the Zionists.	
Welch, Robert	72		Oswald, Lee Harvey	26
DePugh, Robert	37		Bloomfield, Louis	24
McCarthy, Joseph	26		Hoover, J Edgar	23
Eisenhower, Dwight	25		Shaw, Clay	22
Barnett, Ross	25		Cohn, Roy	13
Eastland, James O	22		DeMenil, Jean De	13
Wallace, George	20		Stephenson, William	12
Perez, Leander	20		Garrison, Jim	11
Hargis, Billy James	20		Banister, Guy	10
Hall, Gus	20		Ruby, Jack	10
Simmons, William	19		Ferrie, David	10
Harris, Roy V	17		Bonanno, Joseph	9
Johnson, Lyndon B	17		Seymour, William	8
McIntire, Carl	16		VonBraun, Wernher	7
Thurmond, Strom	16		Nagy, Ferencz	7
Warren, Earl	16		DeGaulle, Charles	7
Most frequent citations in Torbitt and Hepburn combined.			Most frequently cited in the six most diverse assassination books which feature a New Orleans connection.	
Oswald, Lee Harvey	28		Oswald, Lee Harvey	106
Johnson, Lyndon B	18		Kennedy, Robert F	48
Kennedy, Robert F	17		Johnson, Lyndon B	37
Eisenhower, Dwight	16		Hoover, J Edgar	35
Hoover, J Edgar	16		Shaw, Clay	33
Roosevelt, Franklin	12		Garrison, Jim	30
Ruby, Jack	11		Ferrie, David	29
Shaw, Clay	11		Ruby, Jack	29
Hunt, H L	10		Castro, Fidel	27
Ferrie, David	8		Hunt, H L	21
Cohn, Roy	8		Eisenhower, Dwight	21
Connally, John	7		Khrushchev, Nikita	18
Nagy, Ferencz	7		Banister, Guy	18
DeGaulle, Charles	7		Walker, Edwin	16
DeMenil, Jean De	6		Roosevelt, Franklin	11
Banister, Guy	6		Dulles, Allen	10

Most frequently cited in all assassination books combined.		
Oswald, Lee Harvey	423	
Ruby, Jack	152	
Kennedy, Robert F	125	
Johnson, Lyndon B	122	
Hoover, J Edgar	122	
Castro, Fidel	111	
Oswald, Marina	98	
Ferrie, David	80	
Garrison, Jim	73	
Shaw, Clay	65	
Banister, Guy	53	
Marcello, Carlos	50	
DeMohrenschildt, George	49	
Dulles, Allen	41	
Eisenhower, Dwight	37	
Walker, Edwin	35	

Chapter 43

SUMMARY AND CONCLUSIONS

The evidence for German and/or Nazi sponsorship or co-sponsorship of the JFK assassination is overwhelming. The following is a list of the most important items of proof:

1. Clay Shaw was the only person prosecuted for the murder of JFK. During World War II, Shaw worked for Army Intelligence on German property claims. Papers on Shaw were found by a researcher in a file of papers relating to the IG Farben legal case, also known as the GAF case. Farben was the largest German multi-national corporation.

2. James O. Eastland was employing Lee Harvey Oswald as an informant in New Orleans in the summer of 1963. This matter has been proved by author and researcher Dr. Jeffrey Caulfield in his book *General Walker*. Eastland employed Oswald to infiltrate as many as five civil rights and other groups.

3. Senators James O. Eastland and Senator Thomas J. Dodd essentially shared the chairmanship of the Senate Internal Security Subcommittee.

4. Senator Dodd was closely involved with General Julius Klein. Klein was described by the German magazine *Der Spiegel* as the "shadow ambassador" for West Germany. Dodd and Klein worked closely together on Dodd's frequent visits to West Germany.

5. In an op-ed article in a major newspaper, General Klein was accused by Senator George Smathers of working for I G Farben.

6. In the summer of 1963, General Julius Klein was investigated by the Senate Foreign Relations Committee for improper activities on behalf of the Government of West Germany and on behalf of major German industrialists and bankers.

7. When Dodd visited Germany, which was quite often, he always met with Hans Globke.

8. Hans Globke was described by German expert T.H. Tetens as doing more than any other person to enable the re-entry of ex-Nazis to positions of power in the West German government.

9. Hans Globke was the Nazi who personally wrote the Nuremberg Laws which laid out the plan and provided the legal basis for the Holocaust.

10. At the time of the assassination, both Reinhard Gehlen who was head of West German Intelligence (BND) and the West German counterpart of the FBI reported to Hans Globke.

11. When Senator Dodd visited Germany, he also met quite often with Hermann Abs. General Julius Klein stated that he only got in trouble with the U.S. government when he began advocating for Hermann Abs. Abs was CEO of Deutsche-Bank and was involved in representing Germans in their battles in the U.S. relating to World War II property claims that had not been resolved as of 1963. Abs' own family had property claim issues in Czechoslovakia. Abs had also been one of the top three bankers involved in Hitler's occupation of his neighboring European countries from 1937 to 1945 and beyond.

12. Senator Thomas J. Dodd was brought before the Senate Ethics Committee in 1966 and questioned exclusively about his relationship with General Julius Klein.

13. There was testimony in the Dodd censure hearings that Dodd had likely been bribed by General Klein. There were several other key Senators also involved with General Klein. There were indications in the hearings that as many as 20 Senators were involved with General Klein. If Dodd was being bribed, the others might have been also.

14. Senator Dodd was censured by the Senate, allegedly for financial dealings although there were vitually no financial irregularities proven in the hearings.

15. Senator Dodd had been the assistant head prosecutor for the U.S. at the Nuremberg war crimes trials in Germany after World War II.

16. John J. McCloy was named to the Warren Commission. McCloy was said to have, more than any other member, managed the Warren Commission proceedings.

17. John J. McCloy had served as High Commissioner for the U.S. Sector in Germany from 1949 to 1952.

18. As High Commissioner, McCloy commuted the sentences of major ex-Nazis and German industrialists who had been imprisoned for war crimes.

19. McCloy was described by German expert T.H. Tetens as "pathologically pro-German."

20. John J. McCloy had worked his entire career on German issues. He had worked for 9 years in the legal case involving German sabotage in World War I. He had shared Adolph Hitler's box seats at the 1936 Berlin Olympics with Hermann Goering and Heinrich Himmler.

21. Allen Dulles was also a member of the Warren Commission. Next to McCloy, Dulles was most active and involved in the Warren Commission hearings.

22. Allen Dulles had worked in Switzerland during World War II. His job was to negotiate with Nazi generals and scientists when Germany started to lose the War. He recruited Wernher von Braun and General Walter Dornberger. Dulles also worked with Gen. Lyman Lemnitzer in the secret peace negotiations with General Karl Wolff.

23. Allen Dulles recruited Nazi General Reinhard Gehlen to head up all intelligence efforts for both the U.S. and West Germany in the Iron Curtain countries from 1945 through 1963. In his voluminous memoirs, Dulles apparently never mentioned his recruitment of Reinhard Gehlen.

24. General Reinhard Gehlen had been head of intelligence on the Eastern Front for Hitler and the Nazi war machine.

25. Senator John Sherman Cooper was another member of the Warren Commission. During and after World War II, Cooper worked on the management of occupied Germany for the U.S. Army. Cooper was responsible for placing Gerhard Schroeder in his first governmental job in Germany.

26. Gerhard Schroeder became German Chancellor just 4 weeks before the assassination and was invited that month to the LBJ ranch, the only such invitation to a world leader.

27. Senator John Sherman Cooper was named as the first U.S. Ambassador to East Germany.

28. In persuading his confidants by phone about the creation of the Warren Commission, LBJ stated that McCloy and Cooper could help with the "international" aspects of the assassination investigation. Their only international expertise was with Germany.

29. The General Aniline and Film Corp. had been seized by the U.S. Government during World War II under the Trading With The Enemy Act.

30. IG Farben was the real owner of GAF and had pressed the U.S. Government and maintained a major lawsuit to force the U.S. Government to sell or return GAF to private ownership from 1946 to 1963.

31. In the GAF case, along with the I G Farben company, there was also the involvement of influential major American corporations such as Standard Oil of New Jersey and DuPont chemicals.

32. Don Cook, president of American Electric Power became chairman of the committee which supervised the sale of GAF. LBJ and Cook spoke on the phone in the week following the assassination when Cook asked LBJ to meet with a group of unnamed men.

33. The sale of GAF was approved by LBJ just four weeks after the assassination after being tied up in court for almost 20 years.

34. General Edwin Walker was involved in the attempt to frame Lee Harvey Oswald for an alleged shooting incident at the Walker home.

35. Walker had been serving in Germany and was fired by JFK for handing out right-wing materials to his troops serving in Germany.

36. There were three soldiers who came directly from Germany in the months before the assassination. They were Larrie and Bob Schmidt and Bernard Weissman.

37. Bob Schmidt was employed as a chauffeur by General Edwin Walker.

38. The Schmidt brothers were responsible for purchasing threatening newspaper ads and billboards which appeared when JFK visited Dallas.

39. The Schmidt brothers insisted that the signature of Bernard Weissman appear on the hostile advertisements. This was done in the hope that Americans would blame the Jews for the assassination. Any American would know that the American public would not blame Jews based on this tactic. Only an Old World, Nazi mentality would cause someone to believe that Jews would be blamed because of this association.

40. On the weekend of the assassination, General Edwin Walker spoke by telephone with a neo-Nazi newspaper in Germany shortly after the assassination occurred.

41. The name Dan Burros appeared in the notebook of Lee Harvey Oswald.

42. Dan Burros was a member of the American Nazi Party and had a history of corresponding with an exiled Nazi leader in Egypt named Colonel Hans-Ulrich Rudel. Rudel had lived in Argentina. Rudel was involved witht the most conspiratorial of the post-WWII ex-Nazis. That included Otto Skorzeny and Wernher Naumann. Rudel also founded the Kameradenwerke group which financially supported convicted war criminals.

43. There were five persons with proven prior knowledge of the assassination. One of them was an NSA whistleblower named Eugene Barry Dinkin. He was stationed only 120 miles from Bonn, the capital of West Germany.

44. Dinkin must have learned about the JFK plot from spying activities. Due to his proximity to Bonn, he was most likely spying on people in Germany and possibly other nearby countries.

45. General Charles Willoughby has been accused by many assassination researchers as being involved in the assassination. Willoughby came over from Germany in World War I and was investigated soon after for involvement with a female German spy.

46. In a letter to CIA director Allen Dulles, General Willoughby claimed to have close connections to former friends of Kaiser Wilhelm II who was, around this time, exiled in the Netherlands following World War I.

47. George de Mohrenschildt befriended Lee Harvey Oswald when Oswald returned from Russia and moved to Dallas-Fort Worth, Texas. During World War II, de Mohrenschildt was determined to be a Nazi spy or active Nazi sympathizer by several Federal agencies including the FBI.

48. Shortly before World War II, George de Mohrenschildt was involved in the production of a propaganda film with Count Konstatin Maydell.

49. DeMohrenschildt claimed that Maydell was a cousin when he was not.

50. Count Maydell served time in a U.S. prison as a Nazi spy during World War II.

51. Following World War II, General Walter Dornberger was held in solitary confinement by the British government.

52. Dornberger was identified as the head of the informal network of German Nazi prisoners in Allied custody following the War.

53. British Intelligence wrote that Dornberger was a dangerous person and was capable of fomenting World War III.

54. In November, 1963, General Walter Dornberger was chief scientist for Bell Aerospace which had a facility in Dallas.

55. Michael Paine was a research engineer for Bell Aerospace and, in that capacity, was a subordinate of General Dornberger.

56. Dornberger was the best friend of Wernher von Braun. The United States was entirely dependent on the missile scientists who worked for von Braun at the Redstone Missile Facility in Alabama for U.S. national defense.

57. Von Braun had been a member of the SS during World War II when he was working closely with Dornberger on the development of the V-2 missile.

58. Lee Harvey Oswald slept the night before the morning of the assassination in the house normally occupied by Micheal Paine. Paine who had allegedly been estranged from his wife who lived there, moved back into the house four weeks after the assassination.

59. The Permindex organization had a common board of directors with Centro Mondo Commerciale in Italy and Switzerland. Permindex had former Nazis as members.

60. Clay Shaw who was prosecuted in the JFK murder case was CEO of Permindex and had ties to the GAF case.

61. "Centro" of Switzerland was identified by German expert T H Tetens as a welfare fund for jailed and exiled former Nazis.

62. The Russian Orthodox Church members befriended Lee Harvey Oswald before the assassination and cared for Oswald's widow Marina after the assassination including arranging for translators.

63. The head of the Russian Orthodox Church in the U.S. was Metropolitan Anastasy. He had been involved in issues of spying in East Germany in the case of the kidnapping of Dr. Walter Linse.

64. Walter Becher was a German politician who spent a great deal of time in the U.S. in lobbying members of Congress and similar duties.

65. Walter Becher died in Pullach, Bavaria at age 93. Pullach was very small community which housed the headquarters of the BND, which was the West German Intelligence service which was headed by General Reinhard Gehlen. Pullach was to West Germany what Langley, Virginia is to U.S. Intelligence. The BND had been part of the CIA during the early 1950's and had been founded by Warren Commission member Allen Dulles.

66. Jack Ruby testified before the Warren Commission. He stated he was afraid of that both he and his extended family might be murdered. When asked by whom they might be killed, he replied "anti-Semites." Although Ruby is often associated with the Mafia and a probable fear of the Mafia as his motivation in killing Oswald, his blaming of "anti-Semites" is more in line with accusing Nazis. Through contacts

from his Jewish co-religionists, Ruby's motivation was probably due to a desire to strike back against the Nazis due to their massacre of the millions in World War II as well as the murder of his President.

67. In 1963, NATO was controlled by Secretary-General Dirk Stekker. Stekker had run a business in the Netherlands during WWII and was a close personal friend of German Chancellor Konrad Adenauer.

68. In 1963, the top military authority in NATO was the Chairman of the Military Committee. That man was Adolf Heusinger who had been the top planner and worked side-by-side with Hitler on the Eastern front. As can readily be understood from the above list of items of circumstantial evidence, there was a close involvement of ex-Nazis and probably certain high-ranking member of the West German government in the assassination of President John F. Kennedy.

69. Some experts on the Jim Garrison investigation believe that Garrison's staff thought that the money for both the de Gaulle assassination and the JFK assassination had been laundered through NATO headquarters.

70. As Chairman of the NATO Military Committee, ex-Hitler right-hand man Alolf Heusinger had an office in the Pentagon and supervised a staff of around 400 there. His rank was equal to U.S. Service Commanders at the Pentagon.

71. Conserative activist William J. Gill was close to the Goldwater Campaign, the CIA-involved Buckley Brothers, the Eastland-Dodd SISS Committee and their counsel Jay Sourwine. Gill clearly had inside information about the assassination plot in order to write his biography of Otto Otepka. Gill's wife was a German Countess and a famous female spy for Hitler's Abwehr intelligence department. She had served as a Nazi spy in Spain in 1937 and in 1943. She was mentioned in almost all of the books about the attempt to assassinate Hitler 07-20-1944. She was mentioned in the memoirs of Allen Dulles who was also involved in that Hitler plot as well as negotiations with countless Nazis and ex-Nazis. She was living in Washington D.C. at the time of the assassination. The spy Countess Podewils, wife of William J. Gill, was apparently recruited by Allen Dulles as part of Operation Paperclip and brought to the U.S. The FBI kept a file on Countess Podewils.

The following are the final conclusions of the author based on the information which is set forth in *The Three Barons*.

1. The West German Government can be described as possibly involved in the assassination plot.

2. Certain former WWII Nazis were likely involved in the plot.

3. The Permindex organization was primarily a welfare fund for fugitive and other ex-Nazis.

4. James O. Eastland was likely using Lee Harvey Oswald as an agent in New Orleans in his Communist-busting role as official Chairman of the SISS committee.

5. Senator Thomas Dodd played a key role in the assassination plot.

6. The plot to kill JFK could likely have included the intention of killing LBJ as well.

7. The Civil Rights Act was the price that Civil Rights groups required in order to keep silent about the possible assassination conspiracy.

8. The Metropolitan Anastasy of the Russian Orthodox Church was likely directly involved in the plot or its promotion. Anastasy was to a large extent CIA-funded.

9. NATO and its SACEUR General Lyman Lemnitzer could have been at least tacitly involved in the plot along with NATO Secretary General Dirk Stikker and the highest NATO General Adolf Heusinger, the right-hand man for Hitler on the Russian front.

10. The plot could have been created by West German Intelligence Chief General Reinhard Gehlen and he was almost certainly involved in or very aware of the plot.

11. The British Intelligence retired agent Sir William Stephenson could likely have held a meeting of some kind regarding the plot near Montego Bay, Jamaica.

12. That Clarence Dillon, father of Treasury Secretary C. Douglas Dillon was likely involved in the plot and was likely high up in the command of the conspiracy. Dillon owned a resort home near Montego Bay, only a mile away from the compound which was a center for Sir William Stephenson.

13. The National Security Council through members Dean Rusk, McGeorge Bundy and former employee W.W. Rostow were likely at the center of the plot, at least to the extent that it required highly-placed individuals in the JFK administration. Certain officials of the CIA and/or military intelligence were likely loaned to the National Security Council as was done in the Iran/Contra plot to avoid Congressional oversight.

14. Lee Harvey Oswald was involved with American Nazi Dan Burros and likely involved with the famous Federal informant and/or agent Roy Frankhouser, through Burros.

15. Some of the same people who attempted to kill Charles de Gaulle were likely involved at least in helping foment the plot to kill JFK.

16. That it is likely that Catholic activists Judge Robert Morris, former Congressman Charles Kersten, West German official Heinrich von Brentano, Senator Thomas Dodd, Mayor Richard J. Daley and possibly Speaker of the House John W. McCormack were involved (though not proven) to be involved in the assassination plot. This is based on circumstantial evidence. However the Catholic Church as an entity was not in any way involved other than some specific individuals both in Europe and the U.S. 99.99% of Catholics were devastated. There is absolutely no hint of any involvement of the Vatican and no Pope would ever dream of being party to premeditated murder, nor would have any radio preacher like Rev. Carl McIntyre. The same cannot be said of the Russian Orthodox Church hierarchy, however.

17. Congressmen Hale Boggs and Edwin Willis of HUAC had some role in the assassination. At minimum, Boggs was involved in the cover-up before the fact and had advanced knowledge of the assassination. Willis has been implicated only by author Judyth Vary Baker in her memoir.

Many of the above conclusions are revealed for the first time in *The Three Barons*.

The basic fact is that the Nazi's were not completely defeated in World War II. German intelligence and German cartels apparently viewed the JFK assassination as a way to gravely wound their former enemy, the United States and move along with their hopes of fomenting World War III.

Epilogue

NAZI SPY COUNTESS PODEWILS AND HITLER'S PLANNER, GENERAL HEUSINGER OF NATO

Information in this chapter about Adolf Heusinger can be found in an excellent biography titled: *Heusinger of the Fourth Reich* (1963) by Charles R Allen

As the engine of national JFK assassination research rumbles down the road, it passes all recognizable landmarks and enters the wilderness of historical revision and astounding and fantastic conclusions. In this new and desolate landscape, the reader will encounter a high level of discouragement with our government and the narrative which was created during World War II and beyond. This is historical no-man's land. Yet we must push on.

The new information which is now available on the Internet continues to expand literally every day. That is why, when the above chapter on William J. Gill was written, some key information had not yet found its way to the public. We can now report shocking new information relating to William J. Gill.

As stated in the chapter on Gill, in order to write his biography of State Department employee Otto Otepka, Gill was obviously privy to some major inside information about the assassination. Gill was also co-author on a book about the Goldwater campaign in 1964. His co-author on that book was Goldwater's campaign manager, William S. White. Through reading the Otepka biography, one can conclude that Gill was close to the Senate Internal Security Subcommittee, chaired by both James O. Eastland and Senator Thomas J. Dodd.

The more recently available information on Gill indicates that probably he, (or someone with the same name) was chief of the Catholic War Veterans Association and was also active on the Committee for American-African relations. But most shocking of all was the background of Gill's wife.

In a story which is more astounding than fiction, Gill's wife, Countess Mechtild von Podewils had a background as a Nazi spy, working for the Nazi spy agency, the Abwehr, both before and during World War II.

Countess Podewils was the daughter of Hitler's Consul General in Calcutta and formerly the Minister in Columbia, Count Podewils.

According to sources on the Internet, she was both a spy for Hitler in Spain during the Spanish Civil War, working on the side of Franco and the fascist Falange, and then she was working in Spain for Hitler as of 1943, attempting to secure the cooperation of Franco and Hitler as of that date. While in Spain, she was associated by some with the death of famous British actor Leslie Howard, a likely British spy whose plane was shot down by the Nazis. This incident has inspired many investigations and stories since it happened in 1943.

Quoting from the memoir of Allen Dulles called *Secret Surrender*, we find:

> ... As he shook hands with [Nazi General Karl] Wolff, Gaevernitz, in order to relieve the tension, told him that they had a friend in common, the beautiful Countess Mechtilde Podewils, Gaevernitz hinted to Wolff that he knew the Countess had come to Wolff in Berlin some years before to ask his help...

Intriguingly, her name appears in at least four books on the subject of the attempted assassination of Hitler as well as in the biography of Nazi General Wolff and the Dulles memoir. There is a record of Countess Podewils traveling to the U.S. in 1960. It has not yet been possible to determine when, how and why she married William J. Gill. But it is fairly certain that she was married to him at least as of 1960 and during 1963 and until her death.

Countess Podewils had, apparently, the following: (1) experience in helping plan the assassination of Hitler, (2) a relationship not only with Allen Dulles of at least 20 years, but also with top Nazi Generals like General Karl Wolff and the head of the Abwehr, Admiral Wilhelm Canaris as well as possibly many still living in Argentina and elsewhere (3) She apparently also had an association with Spain's General Franco where many ex-Nazis had sought refuge post-World War II and who was still in iron-clad control of Spain from 1936 to 1975 (4) a strong connection to the Catholic Church since her husband had apparently served as chief of the Catholic War Veteran's Association and also through Vatican main-stay General Franco.

During or following the period of the assassination and extending from the 1980's, through the 1990's, Mr. and Mrs. Gill ran a bookstore in Washington D.C. William J. Gill died in 2003 and she died in 2010. Knowing the above, it would be difficult to name anyone who had more of a motive, means and opportunity to be a ringleader in the JFK assassination than Countess Podewils. It may sound unfair to jump to that conclusion, but—if you don't want to be posthumously and unjustly suspected of assassination—then don't work as a spy for Hitler!!!

As we have discussed in an earlier chapter, some in the Jim Garrison investigation in New Orleans believed that the same interests who attempted several times to assassinate President Charles de Gaulle of France were also the murderers of JFK. There is also a story out there in the research community that French Intelligence traced the source of funds which paid for the de Gaulle attempts into and out of one of the various NATO headquarters. There were several of these in Washington, Paris and Belgium and possibly could include regional headquarters elsewhere.

The bald fact which has been largely concealed about NATO in the early 1960's was that NATO was almost totally controlled by West Germany (and Konrad Adenauer) at that time. Of course, NATO had a SACEUR. That stood for Supreme Allied Commander, Europe. And the story went that the SACEUR was, by agreement, always to be an American. Further, the SACEUR wore "two hats," that is, he reported both to NATO and to his US military superiors in Washington. That gave Americans comfort that their national interests were being attended to by NATO.

Apparently, this was not exactly the truth. NATO was run by The North Atlantic Council. Below that council in the organization was the Defense Committee, made up of the Defense Ministers of the member countries. And below the Defense Committee was the Military Committee which was made up of the Chief Military Commanders or Military Representatives from the members. That Military Committee was the highest military authority in NATO and it directed the SACEUR.

Beginning at least in 1950, there had been calls for West German troops to play some kind of role in the defense of Europe against the Soviets. But in the beginning, it was proposed that this could happen without actually restarting a German Army on an equal basis with the other Allies. At the time, Germany was still under Allied occupation and national sovereignty had not yet been restored.

The World War II German Wehrmacht (the name of the German Army at the time) was run by the German General Staff. This General Staff had been in continuous control of the German military dating back to 1806 basically without interruption. It had played a very large role in German government after World War I with Field Marshal Paul von Hindendburg serving as German President in 1925 under the Weimar Republic. General Dwight Eisenhower famously stated in 1945 "The German General Staff itself must be utterly destroyed."

The German Wehrmacht was proved to be a very active participant in the war crimes of World War II, including the massacre of millions of Jews. But they also committed atrocities against a variety of other groups including Slavic people, partisans, Russians in various categories, and many other people.

There was one single, most valuable military strategist on the German General Staff during World War II and that was General Adolf Heusinger. Heusinger was in charge of planning Operation Barbarossa, the invasion of the Soviet Union in June of 1941. He was Deputy Chief of Staff for planning (and for a while served as Chief of the General Staff). In his role, Heusinger worked daily with Adolf Hitler (often one-on-one) during the entire course of the campaign against the Soviet Union. On July 20, 1944, a large number of Wehrmacht officers conspired to plant a large bomb at Hitler's "Wolf's Lair" headquarters in East Prussia. When the bomb went off, Heusinger was standing next to Hitler and he took much of the force of the blast, in effect shielding Hitler from death. As a result, Heusinger was hospitalized for 10 weeks following this famous incident.

Following the German surrender, Heusinger was taken prisoner along with the other top Generals. Heusinger had never actually joined the Nazi Party. Many top German officers had also chosen not to join the Nazi Party, either for religious reasons or because they thought it not to be professional. An even stronger reason was they knew it would look bad after an inevitable German defeat.

Heusinger was a member of the army department known as OKH which along with OKW made up the German General Staff. The Allies named the OKH as a criminal group along with the likes of the SS, the Gestapo and the other such infamous suspects. According to journalist Heinz Pol, "... Heusinger's name was [listed] on the first Allied list of war criminals in 1945." Quoting the top American prosecutor at Nuremberg, General Telford Taylor, Heusinger was never "cleared" nor was he a "consultant." Although Heusinger got some sort of immunity at Nuremberg, he was never a witness. All that it known is that he wrote an affidavit which was entered into evidence before the judges of the Allied Military Tribunal. For this apparent reason, the clemency for Heusinger was arranged. During his captivity, Heusinger lived in a "country club" style of imprisonment and was assigned the job of writing summaries and memoirs suggested by his captors during his captivity.

In a previous chapter, the life and career of Senator Thomas J. Dodd has been discussed in detail. Thus, we know that Dodd was the second-in-command among American prosecutors at Nuremberg. And we know that Dodd refused ever to discuss the topic of Nuremberg for the rest of his life. It seems likely that Dodd would have known and worked with Heusinger. Dodd could have been the person who saved Heusinger from a prison term or the gallows.

The next important period involving Heusinger was the post World War II era and the need for plans regarding West German military security. West Germany was basically unified and functioning as a country following the war. Though occupied by the Allies, West Germans obviously had to continue to survive and clean up from the utter destruction that they had experienced. The planning for restoration of security to West Germany was immediately begun by Chancellor Adenauer, ex-Nazi Intelligence leader Reinhard Gehlen and two former Wehrmacht Generals, Adolf Heusinger and Hans Speidel. Another General, Gerhard Schwerin played a role, but Heusinger and Speidel had the inside track with Adenauer when it came to military planning from 1945 to 1963 and after.

NATO was formed in 1949 by the signing of the North Atlantic Treaty. It soon had 15 members. These included both the major and minor countries of Western Europe who found themselves in a postwar confrontation against the massive Soviet bloc of nations which threatened them. From the beginning, planners began looking for a way to get German troops of some kind engaged in defending postwar Western Europe. The rough estimates always considered that 50% of the defenders of Western Europe would sooner or later have to be German. This was due to both financial and economic reasons, and also because of the geography and the relative populations of the Western countries.

Though at first organized piecemeal, the German Army was officially reconstituted in the mid-1950's and by 1958, West German troops were part of NATO under the name Bundeswehr. The new army disclaimed any tradition or succession based on Hitler's Wehrmacht. But, as of 1956, the newspaper *Die Welt* stated that a large share of officers in the new Bundeswehr were formerly of Hitler's Wehrmacht: 31 of 38 generals, 100 of 257 colonels and 84 out of 225 lieutenant colonels had served in the Wehrmacht.

When in 1958, the Bundeswehr became a unified, official part of the NATO forces (under the first exclusively German command) certain problems began immediately. Comprising over half of the NATO troop strength, the Germans naturally wanted at least half of the control of NATO. During this same period from 1958 to 1963, there also arose problems of possible neo-Nazi proclivities appearing among U.S. troops who were in close contact with a variety of Germans in Germany, including the Bundeswehr. In the JFK assassination research, the case of General Edwin Walker is well known. He was fired in 1961 by JFK for attempting to indoctrinate his troops with extreme right-wing political propaganda in Germany.

Getting back to the NATO organization, in the period 1960 to 1963, most of the top positions in NATO were held by West Germans. As mentioned above, the NATO Military Committee controlled all military issues within NATO. In the 1950's, the Military Committee featured a "standing" executive committee with three members: one from the US, one from the UK and one from France. This was called the Standing Group and it was a subset of the Military Committee.

In addition to the above-mentioned NATO officials, there was a Secretary-General of NATO who supposedly handled diplomatic and political issues between the member countries. His office was in Belgium. In April, 1961, a man named Dirk Stikker was named Secretary-General of NATO. Although he was Dutch, Stikker was a close personal friend of Chancellor Konrad Adenauer and the two often spent weekends and vacations at adjoining villas on Lake Como in Italy. Stikker had remained in the occupied Netherlands and operated a business there during World War II.

In the 1950's, while Dirk Stikker was Foreign Minister of the Netherlands, he apparently traveled to the U.S. possibly multiple times in the company of the Prince of the Netherlands. The Prince of the Netherlands was a German named Bernhard, Prince of Lippe-Biesterfeld. Bernhard was also a one-time member of the SS, a friend of the Nazi affiliated General Juan Peron of Argentina and most importantly, the permanent nominal host of the mysterious Bilderberg Group, which some people believe secretly ruled, (and still rules), the Western World.

As described in the discussion about General Lyman Lemnitzer elsewhere in our study, we know that Lemnitzer was fired by JFK in 1962 following the ill-fated Bay of Pigs invasion. (Lemnitzer had approved of it). Lemnitzer was also involved in planning the essentially criminal Operation Northwoods which planned phony terror attacks within the U.S. in order to blame Castro. Lemnitzer also had testified to the Senate concerning the right-wing activities of General Edwin Walker over in Germany.

The Joint Chiefs of Staff, (while Lemnitzer was the Chairman) was also planning a "first strike" preemptive nuclear attack on the USSR. This would, of course, invite the partial destruction of the U.S. (which would soon follow from a Soviet counter-attack). JFK considered these plans and ideas as fundamentally insane. After being fired by JFK, Lemnitzer was "kicked upstairs" by being named Supreme Allied Commander of NATO beginning in 1963. He was appointed by JFK after the intervention on his behalf of Chancellor Konrad Adenauer and the British Prime Minister Harold MacMillan. So we had both the Supreme Allied Commander as well as the NATO Secretary General "in the pocket" of Chancellor Konrad Adenauer. By far the biggest scandal revolving around the JFK-NATO question, however, was the nomination in November, 1960 of General Adolf Heusinger as chairman of the Military Committee of NATO.

But first, another General must be mentioned. Beginning in 1956, the Supreme Allied Commander of NATO (always an American) was Air Force General Lauris Norstad. Norstad had planned the details of the atomic bombing of Hiroshima and Nagasaki in 1945 despite some opposition against that decision to use the atomic bomb in that setting. Norstad was considered mostly a planner and technician, but he also dabbled in Washington DC-style social, dinner-party politics. When JFK became President in 1961, he and his Secretary of Defense Robert S. McNamara soon found themselves at cross-purposes with Norstad. Norstad had become the champion of transforming NATO itself into becoming the "fourth nuclear power." Norstad had managed to get control (for NATO) of some squadrons of intermediate range missiles in Italy and Turkey which were aimed at the USSR.

In conferences with Norstad, JFK and McNamara opened criticized, indeed almost ridiculed the lack of loyalty to the U.S. over NATO which they perceived as coming from Norstad. Famously, at the height of the Cuban Missile Crisis, in his high-tension conferences involving Khrushchev, JFK bargained away these NATO missiles. Since at this time, West Germany (and Konrad Adenauer) had virtual control over NATO, JFK was effectively taking these nuclear missiles off the NATO plate and out of the control of the Germans.

So in 1960, the U.S. and the Germans acting in concert had arranged the approval of General Adolf Heusinger as chairman of the Military Committee of NATO. At some point in the 1950's, the chairman of the Military Committee of NATO became a permanent job with a fixed term of three years. The Chairman had substantial independence. He may have even been able to act on his own in important respects, without a vote or even consultation with either the Standing Group (U.S.,U.K. France) or any other member countries of the Committee. Shockingly, this chairman had an office in the Pentagon and was on a level equal to other top Generals who worked beside him in the Pentagon. Writing over a decade after 1963, one author stated that the Military Committee employed a staff of over 400 persons. It is likely that in 1963, the Committee employed staff numbering in the several hundreds (maybe 400+) all working in the Pentagon.

Again, shockingly, it was the U.S. and the West Germans who insisted on the appointment of Heusinger to this position. Heusinger had been Adolf Hitler's "boy" if you will. Following the infamous July 20, 1944 assassination attempt on himself, Hitler had given a special medal to Heusinger (and a few others) commemorating their mutual survival of the assassination attempt.

There were, in fact, protests around the world about the appointment of this (Hitlerite) general to this powerful position, perhaps the most powerful military position in the world. In reaction to Heusinger, the Soviet Union immediately requested the extradition of Heusinger for WWII war crimes.

In mid-1963, author Charles R. Allen published a book called *Heusinger of the Fourth Reich*. The book warned of the dire consequences which could follow the appointment of Heusinger. The most vocal critic of this nomination in the Senate was maverick Oregon Senator Wayne Morse. As we have mentioned in another chapter, Senator Morse was possibly the Senator who was most closely monitoring the activities of the alleged JFK assassination conspirator General Julius Klein. Morse was a high-ranking member of the Senate Foreign Relations Committee. We have seen the circumstantial evidence that this Committee could have had concrete suspicions about a possible assassination attempt or similar plotting prior to 11-22-63.

The location in the Pentagon of such a virulent pro-Nazi figure along with hundreds of staff persons could provide an answer as to why a certain faction there, at least, seemed to be loosely involved with the JFK assassination plot. Colonel Fletcher Prouty, the well-known JFK assassination writer, was serving at the Pentagon on 11-22-63. Yet all Prouty essentially knew was (1) he had been sent to Antarctica when JFK was shot and (2) the security protection for JFK in Dallas which should have come from Military Intelligence, was compromised. We also know that the JFK autopsy had apparently been planned well in advance by the military, (probably by figures who might have been in the autopsy room).

The harsh, unspeakable reality from all of the facts recited above is that following 1 P.M., 11-22-63, the West German Government was possibly in control of Washington DC, the U.S. Government and thus in control of the United States for an unknown period of time: this situation possibly lasted for a very short time, or possibly longer. Vladimir Lenin once wrote, "he who controls Berlin, controls Germany: and he who controls Germany, controls Europe: and Europe controls the world." We know that very soon, Chancellor Ludwig Erhard (alone among world leaders) traveled to Texas to visit the LBJ ranch. We know that at the JFK funeral, General Charles de Gaulle insisted on walking with the JFK casket down Pennsylvania Avenue in DC along with other leaders, to show he was not afraid. By 1966, de Gaulle ordered all NATO troops and officials *totally off of French territory!* (That happened in 1966). To this day, both the French and Spanish armies refuse to have their militaries "merged" with NATO in Europe. They are only "partners," not integrated. This is out of apparent fear of the kind of thing that happened to JFK.

Author Charles Allen in *Heusinger of the Fourth Reich*, presents a lengthy list of military allies of Heusinger (with Nazi Wehrmacht experience) within the Bundeswehr and at the same time serving NATO:

(1)   General Hans Speidel

(1)   General Count Johann Adolf von Kielmannsegg

(2)   General Friedrich Foerstch

(3)   Admiral Karl-Adolf Zenker

(4)   Colonel Willi Mantey

(6)   Lieutenant General Max Pemsel

(7)   Admiral Gerhard Wagner

(8)   General Ernst Kusserow

(9)   General Joseph Kammhuber (one of Goering's closest associates).

Others with similar backgrounds who were serving in the Bundeswehr but not NATO were:

(1)   General Hans Roettiger

(2)   Col. T. Fett, former deputy to Hitler

(3)   Admiral Oskar Ruge

(4)   General Walter Wenck (connected to Einsatzgruppen atrocities).

(5)   General Ludwig Cruewell

(6)   Lt. Gen. Count Gerhard Schwerin

(7)   General Maximilian Freiherr (Baron) von Edelsheim

(8)   Major General Rudolf Christoph Freiherr (Baron) von Gersdorf

(9)   General Wend von Wieteresheim

(10)   Major General Freiherr (Baron) Smilo von Luettwitz

So there are three barons just on the above list alone. (So much for the idea that German militarism was ended with the defeat of Germany in April, 1945).

There remain several questions which we have not specifically answered. First, if these German, ex-Hitlerite military figures helped plot and carry out the JFK assassination, what was their motivation? The apparent answer was that the elite of the ex-Nazis worldwide had been plotting such a strike-back against the U.S. ever since the Battle of Stalingrad had made German military defeat inevitable. This would merely be reflecting the desire of military people to win battles, any battles! In effect, the motive was revenge.

Second, there were some of their ex-Nazi compatriots who were still being hunted for their crimes. Perhaps (behind the scenes) JFK had been a little too aggressive and sympathetic to the Nazi hunters. We know that Adolf Eichmann was tried in Israel in 1961. Also, as late as 1979, one of the heroes of the U.S. Space Program, ex-Nazi scientist Arthur Rudolf was stripped of his U.S. residency and deported back to Germany, thus avoiding imprisonment. So they may have been operating out of fear, seeking a display of power and influence against their pursuers.

Third, these alleged plotters could have been unhappy with the military strategy of JFK and McNamara which emphasized conventional forces. They might have hoped for a better deal vis-a-vis nuclear weapons from LBJ or Speaker John W. McCormack as successors to JFK.

Fourth, they may have been mere accomplices who were working with their natural right-wing allies, the Southern Segregationists, right-wing Republicans and alleged fascist sympathizers such as banker Clarence Dillon, former President Herbert Hoover and retired General Douglas MacArthur.

Author Charles Allen believed that the US government supported the rabid ex-Hitlerites from Germany over other, more moderate Germans, because these ex-Nazi types were the toughest available people on the issue of opposing Communism. They were experienced killers, they had murdered Communists by the thousands on the Eastern Front and they would gladly do the same in Eastern Europe in 1963 should they have to. If fact, the U.S. intelligence services had allied themselves in Germany with people who thought that those who tried to kill Hitler on July 20, 1944 were actually traitors to Germany and should be shunned. This shows the cynicism of the U.S. National Security State (which is still with us at this writing).

But the most relevant quote regarding Heusinger, taken from *Heusinger of the Fourth Reich* by author Allen is this quote from Mr. I. R. Starr, a leader in B'nai Brith (a Jewish group):

"The placing of Adolf Heusinger in the position of trust and honor as the guest of our government, with headquarters in Washington, DC, would be a great aid to those forces which seek to resurrect Nazism. The presence of a Heusinger in Washington would be a great comfort and stimulant to George Lincoln Rockwell, head of the American Nazi Party, all anti-Semites, all reactionaries."

Notes:

This chapter is largely, though not entirely, based on information available on Heusinger in an excellent biography titled: *Heusinger of the Fourth Reich* (1963) by Charles R Allen. Further information can be found in the book *HRH Bernhard, Prince of the Netherlands: An Authorized Biography* by Alden Hatch and *Men of Responsibility*, by Dirk Stikker.

Index

Eden, Anthony 202

Eisenhower, Dwight D. viii, ix, 84-85, 88, 102, 110, 117, 119, 125-129, 137, 142, 146-148, 151, 156, 160, 165-168, 172, , 181, 184-185, 194-195, 201, 203-204, 206, 222, 229, 259-260, 284-287, 296, 307, 312, 324, 350, 353-354, 358-359, 361, 365-366, 368, 370-373, 377, 389, 403, 406-409, 412-413, 416, 444, 455-456, 463,478, 481, 527

Ellsworth, Frank 44-45, 203, 267

Embick, Stanley 164-165, 167

Erhard, Ludwig 72, 228, 240, 280-281, 286, 411, 455, 460-461, 465, 470, 472, 474, 483, 490, 532

Ervin, Samuel 130, 251, 319, 368, 394

Executive Intelligence Review viii, 124, 181, 186-187, 189, 192, 194, 457-458, 469, 506, 513

F

Farenthold, George Edward 59

Farewell, America 39

Farewell to Justice 28, 31, 195, 232, 241, 492, 505, 512

Farrand, John 122, 123

Faux Baron 54, 66, 211

Federal Bureau of Investigation (FBI) 2-4, 7, 10, 15-16, 19, 21, 30, 33, 37, 44-46, 50, 52, 56-57, 59-60, 62, 64, 66, 83, 93, 95, 97-99, 107, 114-115, 120, 123, 125-126, 136, 141, 177-179, 183-184, 186, 188-189, 213, 217, 221, 226, 232, 236-240, 248, 266-267, 287, 303, 314, 316, 319, 322, 328, 330-331, 352, 356, 359, 362, 371, 373, 378, 380, 382, 388, 391, 394, 397, 415-416, 419, 451, 457-458, 475, 478, 485, 489, 490, 494, 497, 517, 520, 522

Fellers, Bonner 74

Fensterwald, Bernard "Bud" 92, 99

Ferdinand, Franz viii, 35, 140, 161, 198, 200, 205, 208

Ferguson, Homer 119, 255

Fermi, Enrico 204

Ferrie, David viii, 65, 185, 215, 224, 231-232, 234-236, 238, 266-267, 342

Final Judgment 139, 171, 344, 345, 348, 506, 512

Fisher, N. T. 43, 191

Fleming, Ian 202

Ford, Gerald viii, 35, 222, 230, 321, 323

Ford, Henry II 156

Foreign Affairs 149

Forrestal, James 107, 161, 167, 198, 200-202, 205, 208, 369

Franco, Francisco 56-57, 69-71, 74, 79, 106, 108, 244, 254, 411, 483, 526

Frankhouser, Roy viii, 64, 139, 173-180, 183, 187-189, 191, 447, 523-524

Frawley, Patrick J. 135

Freyss, Pierre 60

Fritz, Will 15, 51, 52, 73, 198, 416-417

Fruge, Francis 13-15, 23

Fuhrman, Mark 38

Fulbright, J. William x, 92, 230, 252, 284, 407, 409, 419, 423, 459-460, 464, 472, 475, 477-478

G

Gale, William P. 2, 16

Garrison, Jim viii, 12, 23, 28, 30-32, 42, 53, 66, 95, 159, 182-183, 185, 213, 221, 224, 231-232, 234-238, 241, 279, 306, 335, 339-340, 361, 399 400, 458, 505-506, 510, 512, 522, 527

Gavin, James 148, 168

Gehlen, Reinhard x, 57, 59, 64, 66, 70, 72-73, 75, 78-79, 191, 234, 337, 413, 418, 430, 437, 443-444, 485, 487-490, 495, 510, 517-518, 521, 523, 529

Gelber, Judge 17

General Walker and the Murder of President Kennedy vi, 16, 21, 27, 29, 39, 73, 75, 78, 90, 134-135, 138, 174-175, 179, 224, 236, 263-264, 315-317, 324, 326, 338, 341-343, 415, 495, 506, 512, 516

Geneva Diplomat 9

Gibson, Charles Dana 199

Gillespie, Nora A. 81

149-152, 154-155, 158-160, 168-169, 193, 196, 204, 206, 222, 228, 230, 241, 267, 271-275, 278-288 306-307, 314, 319-320, 330, 394-398, 406, 411, 419, 422-423, 470-471, 505-506, 510, 512, 518-519, 523, 532, 534

Johnson, Marion 96
Johnspn, Olin 251, 377
Johnson, Skip 100
Jones, Clifton 182
Jones, Harry 512
Jones, Penn 183
Jones, Robert 46
Jones, Roger 364, 373, 376, 398
Jordan, Alex 123
Judd, Walter E. 76, 80

K

Kaiser, David 3, 55, 71, 512, 520
Katzenbach, Nicholas 150, 221, 385, 398, 404
Keefe, Frank 82
Kellerman, Roy 44
Kennan, George F. 149, 167
Kennedy (book) 146
Kennedy, Edward M. 26, 81, 90, 256, 269, 313, 322, 324, 386, 399
Kennedy, Jackie 42, 51, 57, 147, 158, 193, 282, 284, 285, 404, 406, 452
Kennedy, John F. x, 1, 5-13, 16, 26-29, 32, 36, 42, 44-45, 50-51, 53, 55, 82, 86, 90, 93, 96, 99, 101, 102, 103, 112, 116, 124, 126, 138, 141, 144, 146, 151, 153-156, 158, 160, 171, 172, , 175, 179, 194, 206, 221, 224, 225, 229, 250, 260, 263, 270, 306, 318, 320, 324, 343, 349, 360-361, 364, 372, 384-387, 393-394, 403-405, 413, 414, 421, 423, 428, 431, 438, 457, 465, 471, 485-486, 497, 498, 512, 522
Kennedy, Joseph P. 107-108, 116, 118, 124-125, 140, 147-148, 197, 246, 259-260, 271, 324, 375, 403, 405-406

Kennedy, Robert F. x, 6, 9,11, 22, 26, 35, 92, 99, 101-104, 108, 110, 112, 116, 125-126, 128-129, 156, 237-238, 246, 259-261, 272, 324, 336, 337,349, 361, 363, 366, 367, 370, 373-376, 379, 387-390, 394-398, 404-405, 419, 447, 452, 463, 494

Kerr, Jean 128
Kerr, Philip 105, 199
Kersten, Charles vii, 21, 25-26, 28-29, 62, 78, 81-88, 90-91, 102, 133, 146, 155, 277-278, 428, 438-439, 443-444, 472-476, 478, 524
Kersten, Charles Herman 81
Khrushchev, Nikita 17, 218, 389, 410, 432
Kilgallen, Dorothy 40, 499
Kilpatrick, Lyman 88
King, Dennis 174, 180, 190-192
King, John 124
King,ML Jr. 17, 18, 330, 336-337
Kirk, Alan 145
Klein, Julius x, 124, 181, 183, 195, 267, 337, 380, 401, 411, 413-414, 423-424, 446-447, 454-465, 467-478, 482-483, 487, 500, 516-517, 532
Klopfer, Susan 20, 24, 258, 270, 315-319, 323-325
Knowland, William 130
Kohlberg, Alfred 125, 133-134, 254
Ku Klux Klan (KKK) 173-174, 176-179

L

Lane, Mark 37-38, 95, 504, 512
Larin, Lilia 59
Lattimore, Owen 115, 133, 137, 367-368
Laval, Pierre 200, 207
LBJ: The Mastermind of the JFK Assassination 1,3, 23, 274, 279, 506, 512
Lebedev, Mikhail 70
LeMay, Curtis 156, 158, 389
Lemnitzer, Lyman viii, 33, 135, 161-171, 518, 523, 530
Lenin, Vladimir 72, 109, 119, 360, 374, 532
Life and Times of Joe McCarthy: A Biography, The 113, 117, 131

Morse, Wayne 168, 472, 476, 532
Mullins, J.P. 97- 98, 100
Mundt, Karl 125, 127-128, 376, 472
Murchison, Clint 62, 115, 129, 182
Mussolini, Benito 56, 69, 118, 244

N

Nagell, Richard Case vii, 1-4, 70, 494, 507
National Security Agency (NSA) 4, 6-7, 140, 200, 205, 362, 520
National Security Council (NSC) viii, 64, 79, 139-147, 150, 152, 153, 155-156, 158-159, 161, 167-169, 171, 173, 176-178, 183, 189, 200, 205, 408, 444, 447, 523
National Zeitung 29
NATO x, 4, 33, 74, 148, 154, 162-165, 167-171, 228, 387, 407, 409-410, 468, 478, 481, 483, 522-523, 525, 527, 529-533
Nelson, Phillip F. 1, 23, 274, 512
Neustadt, Richard 147-149
New Germany and the Old Nazis, The 28, 39, 76, 80, 240, 460, 466, 479, 490
Newsweek 9
New York Journal 67
New York Times 87, 173, 176-177, 228, 265, 321-322, 324-325, 365, 393, 399, 404, 486
Ngo Dinh Diem 73, 354
Nieburg, H.H. 157
Nimitz, Chester 121
Nitze, Paul 146-148, 161, 167-168, 198-201, 409-410
Nixon, Richard M. vii, 70, 75, 82-84, 90, 111, 116, 126-128, 137, 143, 146, 152, 160, 183, 189, 206, 231, 248, 259, 261, 271, 286, 321, 324, 350, 369, 371, 382, 394, 398, 406, 409, 413, 463, 497, 500
Norden, Eric 27, 173-174, 189, 440, 443, 445
Norstad, Lauris 33, 165, 168-169, 171, 285, 286, 530, 531
North, Mark 265, 270, 272, 512
North, Oliver 139

O

Ochsner, Alton 65, 235-236, 260, 266, 269, 333
O'Connor, Herbert 100, 119, 255
Odio, Silvia 3
O'Donnell, Kenny 44
Office of Strategic Services (OSS) 60, 68-69, 150, 191, 233, 372, 488, 494
On Active Service 145
One More Victim 174, 179
On The Trail Of The Assassins 28, 182, 306
Operation Mongoose 22, 376
Operations Northwoods 169
Oppenheimer, Robert 204, 284, 288, 367, 412
Ordeal of Otto Otepka, The 39-40, 131, 136-137, 195, 345-346, 359, 366, 385, 415, 493
Organization of American States (OAS) 12, 32-34, 170, 182, 185, 232, 308, 412
Orlov, Lawrence viii, 62-63, 209-215, 220
Oswald, Lee Harvey vii, ix, x, 1-4, 13-16, 23, 27, 29, 35, 37, 44-45, 47-53, 63-66, 70, 92-96, 123, 97, 99, 100, 122-124, 136-137, 173-177, 185-186, 188-189, 195, 209, 212-218, 222, 224-225, 232, 234-236, 270, 261, 264-270, 273, 278, 281, 283, 286-287, 289, 304, 308, 317-319, 33-336, 338-342, 362, 375-376, 381, 383, 393-395, 406, 425-426, 428, 431, 438-439, 441, 446-452, 474, 491-495, 497-501, 504-505, 507, 512, 516, 519-521, 523
Oswald, Marina 45, 209, 214-215, 217-218, 521
Otepka, Otto ix, x, 39-40, 113, 115, 126, 131-132, 136-137, 150, 195, 248-249, 261, 264, 344-347, 349-354, 357-361, 363-364, 366, 368, 370, 372-375, 377, 379, 384, 385, 388, 393-396, 398-399, 415, 468, 493, 525
Overseas Weekly 73
Oxnam, G. Bromley 127

S

Salan, Raoul 32, 34
Sallet, Richard 78, 80
Saud, Ibn 167
Savage, William Charles "Ted" 61
Schacht, Hjalmar Horace Greeley 71
Schine, G. David 126, 129
Schlesinger, Arthur Jr. 85, 147-148, 171, 324, 379
Schmidt, Bob 136, 498, 519
Schmidt, Larrie 135, 136, 498, 519
Scott, Hugh 252, 313, 368, 373, 377, 461-462, 472
Scott, Paul 428
Scott, Peter Dale 44, 50, 96, 444, 447, 504, 506, 510, 512
Scott, Win 2
Scoville, Herbert 149
Secret War Against the United States in 1915, The 68, 401
Self-Destruct: Dismantling America's Internal Security 41, 135-138
Service, John Stewart ix, 113, 115, 121, 123, 355-357, 368, 399
Sharp, Frederick D. 76
Shaw, Clay viii, 28, 65, 183-185, 231-235, 237-238, 241, 446, 450, 458, 507, 516, 521
Sheen, Fulton J. 73
Shoup, David M. 163
Simple Act of Murder: November 22, 1963, A 38
Simpson, Christopher 293, 297, 299, 304, 308
Simpson, O.J. 31, 38
Singlaub, John K. 135
Skolnick, Sherman 95-96
Skorzeny, Otto 70-71, 175, 519
Slatter, Michael 175
Smith, Ben S. 338
Smith, Earl 365
Smith, Gerald L.K. 62
Smith, Howard K. 346, 419
Smith, John Chabot 270
Smith, Ralph C. 74
Smith, Steven S. 250-251
Smith, Truman 74

Smith, Walter Bedell 86
Smith, Willis 119, 255
Smoot, Dan 17
Snowden, Eric 6
Sokolsky, George 126
Somersett, Willie 16-20, 23, 99
Sommerfeld, Felix 68
Sonnett, Mr. 25-26
Sorensen, Theodore 146-147, 154, 156, 172, 281 367
Soustelle, Jacque 12, 170, 182, 412, 413
Speidel, Hans 74, 529, 532
Spellman, Francis 62, 127, 130-131, 184, 186, 220, 271
Stages of Economic Growth: A Non-Communist Manifesto, The 150, 151
Stalin, Josef 62, 76-77, 84-85, 102, 106, 108-109, 118, 126-127, 140, 166, 219, 245, 248, 254, 352, 360, 374, 416, 432, 481- 482, 484
Stallforth, Frederico 68
Stamphi, Emile 123
Stars and Stripes 8
Stashynsky, Bogdan x, 5, 26-27, 36, 88, 91, 426-428, 431-445, 468, 472-475
Steinberg, Jeffrey 39, 181, 184, 186, 190, 192, 457, 458, 512
Stennis, John C. 130, 229-230, 276, 310, 323, 337, 389, 456, 469-470, 476-478
Stephan, John J. 63, 66
Stephenson, William 58, 110, 191, 202, 457, 523
Stern, Sheldon 153
Stevenson, Adlai 85, 146-147, 251, 382, 385, 387, 391
Stikker, Dirk 33, 523, 530, 534
Stimson, Henry L. 144-145, 475
Stone, Oliver 30, 221, 231
Stratemeyer, George E. 74
Strauss, Lewis 137, 140, 203-204, 206, 284, 367, 389, 413, 483
Summers, Anthony 22, 24
Surine, Don 114-115, 120, 122-123, 126, 130, 134
Symington, W. Stewart 125, 147, 472
Syngman Rhee 73

T

Tampa Tribune 97, 100

Target de Gaulle: The True Story Of The 31 Attempts On The Life Of The French President 12, 31, 32, 36

Taylor, Maxwell D. 76, 128, 162-163, 167-169, 422, 528

Tetens, T. H. 28-29, 31, 39, 74-78, 80, 222-223, 228, 234, 240, 443, 460, 465-466, 471, 477, 479, 484-485, 487, 490, 516-517, 521

Texas In The Morning 129

Thomas, J. Parnell 113, 155, 328

Thomas, Kenn 96, 181, 186, 512

Thomas, R. 10

Thornton, Charles "Tex" 156

Thurmond, Strom 16, 78, 128, 229, 252, 256, 272-273, 310, 319, 337, 385, 389, 396-397, 424, 446, 450

Thyssen, Fritz 198

Time 9, 96, 270, 287, 382

Tippit, J.D. 48, 50, 268

Tolstoy, Alexandra 60, 218- 219, 429, 431

Torbitt File, The viii, 181-186, 194, 202, 216, 237, 304, 306, 457, 506, 512-513

Torbitt, William 181, 202, 506, 510, 512

Toshisuke, Ayukawa 201

Tower, John G. 135, 424

Trafficante, Santos vii, 22

Truly, Roy 48-49

Truman, Harry S. 70, 83, 85-86, 91, 107, 110, 113-115, 118-121, 124, 140, 146, 148, 200-201, 208, 272, 296, 324, 358-359, 366-367, 369-370, 381, 388, 392, 395, 398, 400, 406, 412, 418, 455, 507

Tscheppe-Weidenbach, T. vii, 67, 68, 71, 140

Tydings Committee 114, 115, 133, 423, 424

Tyler, S.R. 122, 210

U

Ultimate Sacrifice, John and Robert Kennedy, the Plan for a Coup in Cuba, and the Murder of JFK 92, 99, 100

V

Vallee, Thomas Arthur 93,-96, 98-99

Vandenberg, Arthur 73, 106

Venable, James 92, 99

Vincent, John Carter 38, 123-125

von Braun, Wernher ix, 55, 64, 69, 71-72, 78, 140, 167, 184-185, 191, 194-195, 234, 237, 289-302, 305-308, 518, 521

von Feilitzsch, Heribert 68, 79, 401, 414

Vorys, John 87

W

Waehauf, Franz 2

Waldron, Lamar 92, 94, 97-100

Walker, Edwin vi, ix, 16, 20-21, 27, 29, 39, 64, 73, 75, 78, 90, 133-136, 138, 174-176, 179, 224, 236, 263-264, 315-318, 320, 324, 326, 338, 341-343, 415, 446, 495, 498, 506, 512, 516, 519, 529-530

Wallace, George 35, 336-338

Walter, Francis E. 76

Warburg Family viii, 204-205, 207-208, 223, 241, 487

Warburg, Eddie 204

Warburg, Eric 223

Warburg, Jimmie 204

Warburg, Max 204

Warburg, Paul 203

Warburg, Siegmund 205

Warburgs, The (book) 203-204, 241, 471, 479

Washington, George 431

Washington Through a Purple Veil 40, 240

Watkins, Arthur 119, 130-131, 255

Wayne, David 15, 23, 41, 186

Weber, Eugen 34

Weber, Ted 95

Wedemeyer, Albert 73-74, 77, 170, 357, 369

Weeks, Stephen 38

Weiford, Nancy Wertz 53-54, 56-57, 59, 60, 62, 66, 211, 214

Weisberg, Harold 17, 23, 270